CW01306463

O HUMANKIND
SURAH YA-SIN

O HUMANKIND
Surah Ya-Sin
CEMALNUR SARGUT

ISBN: 978-605-9901-80-2

Original Name: Ey İnsan
© Cemalnur Sargut

Copyrights of the Translated Edition (English):
© Nefes Yayıncılık A.Ş.
© Fons Vitae
© Victoria Rowe Holbrook

All rights reserved. No parts of this publication may be reproduced in any form or by any means, electronic, mechanical, photocopying, recording or otherwise, without the prior permission of the publisher.

EDITOR: Nazlı Kayahan, Neşe Taş
TRANSLATOR: Victoria Rowe Holbrook
COVER PAGE DESIGN: Gül Türkmen
PAGE LAYOUT: Melik Uyar

NEFES YAYINCILIK
Bağdat Cad. No:167/2 Çatırlı Apt. B Blok D:4
Göztepe/Kadıköy/İstanbul
Tel: (216) 359 10 20   Faks: (216) 359 40 92
www.nefesyayinevi.com
✉ irtibat@nefesyayinevi.com
f /nefesyayinevicom
🐦 /nefesyayinevi
📷 /nefesyayinevi
CERTIFICATE NO: 15747

O HUMANKIND
SURAH YA-SIN

compiled by
Cemalnur Sargut

translated by
Victoria Rowe Holbrook

NEFES

FONS VITAE

Contents

YaSin: Love, The Prophet, and Humanity at the Heart of the Qur'an
Foreword by Omid Safi 17

Acknowledgement 27

Translator's Note 29

Author's Preface 35

Chapter Ya-Sin 37

1. Ya-Sin 39

2. By the wise Quran / *Wa'l-Qurʾāni'l-ḥakīm* 63

3. You are indeed among the messengers of God / *ʾInnaka la mina'l-mursalīn* 79

4. On a straight path / *ʿAlā ṣirāṭin mustaqīm* 85

5. It is a revelation sent down by the Exalted, the Compassionate / *Tanzīla'l-ʿazīzi'r-raḥīm* 93

6. That you may warn a people whose fathers were not warned, so they are heedless / *Li tundhira qawman mā'undhira 'ābā'uhum fahum ghāfilūn* 99

7. Indeed the word is proven true on most of them, for they do not believe / *Laqad ḥaqqa'l-qawlu 'alā 'aktharihim fahum lā yu'minūn*........ 99

8. Truly We put fetters around their necks that press against their chins, so that their heads are fixed in a gesture of refusal. Truly We have put fetters around their necks that press against their chins, so that their heads are fixed in a gesture of refusal / *'Innā ja'alnā fī 'a'nāqihim 'aghlālan fahiya 'ilā'l-'adhqāni fahum muqmaḥūn* 109

9. And We put a barrier in front of them and a barrier behind them, and We covered them so that they do not see / *Wa ja'alnā min bayni 'aydīhim saddan wa min khalfihim saddan fa'aghshaynāhum fa hum lā yubṣirūn*.. 109

10. It is the same to them if you warn them or do not warn them; they will not believe / *Wa sawā'un 'alayhim 'a 'andhartahum 'am lam tundhirhum lā yu'minūn* 119

11. You warn only whoever follows the remembrance *(the Quran)* and fears the Merciful in the Unseen. Give such a one glad tidings of forgiveness and a generous reward / *'Innamā tundhiru mani't-taba'a'dh-dhikra wa khashiya 'ar-raḥmāna bi'l-ghaybi fabashshirhu bimaghfiratin wa 'ajrin karīm*... 123

12. Truly it is We who bring the dead to life, and We write down what they send before them and what they leave behind, and We have taken account of all things in a discriminating book / *'Innā naḥnu nuḥyi'l-mawtā wa naktubu mā qaddamū wa 'athārahum wa kulla shay'in 'aḥṣaynāhu fī 'imāmin mubīn*... 139

13. And set forth to them as a parable of the Companions of the City when the messengers came / *Wa'ḍrib lahum mathalan 'aṣḥāba'l-qaryati 'idh jā'ahā'l-mursalūn* 147

14. We sent them two messengers, but they rejected them. But We strengthened them with a third. They said, "Truly we have been

sent to you as messengers." / *'Idh 'arsalnā ' ilayhimu'thnayni fakadh-dhabūhumā fa'azzaznā bithālithin fa qālū innā 'ilaykum mursalūn*.........147

15. They said, "You are only mortal creatures like ourselves and the Merciful sent no such revelation; you do nothing but lie." / *Qālū mā 'antum 'illā basharun mithlunā wa mā 'anzala'r-raḥmānu min shay'in 'in 'antum 'illā takdhibūn* 155

16. They said, "Our Lord knows, truly we have been sent as messengers to you / *Qalū rabbunā ya'lamu 'innā 'ilaykum la mursalūn*...........165

17. And our duty is only clear deliverance of the message." / *Wa mā 'alaynā 'llā'l-balāghu'l-mubīn*...165

18. "Truly we find in you an evil omen, and if you do not desist, we will certainly stone you, and grievous harm will surely be inflicted on you by us / *Qālū 'innā taṭayyarnā bi kum la 'in lam tantahū lanarjumannakum wa layamassannakum minnā 'adhābun 'alīm* 171

19. They said, Your evil omens are with yourselves, although you have been admonished. On the contrary, you are a people transgressing all bounds." / *Qālū ṭā'irukum ma'akum 'a 'in dhukkirtum bal 'antum qawmun musrifūn*...171

20. And a man came running from the outskirts of the city, saying, "O my People, follow the messengers / *Wa jā'a min 'aqṣā'l-madīnati rajulun yas'ā qāla yā qawmi 'ttabi'ū'l-mursalīn* 177

21. "Follow those who ask no reward of you, and who have been guided / *'Ittabi'ū man lā yas'alukum 'ajran wahum muhtadūn* 183

22. "What do I have that I should not worship the one who created me, and to whom you will be returned? / *Wa māliya lā 'a'budu'lladhi faṭaranī wa 'ilayhi turja'ūn* 189

23. "Shall I take gods other than He? If the Merciful should intend adversity, their intercession will be of no use to me at all, nor would they save me / *'A 'attakhidhu min dūnihi 'alihatan 'in yuridni'r-rahmānu biḍurrin lā tughni 'annī shafa'attuhum shay'an wa lā yunqidhūn* 193

24. "I would then truly be in manifest error / *'Innī 'idhan lafī ḍalalin mubīn* 193

25. "Truly I have faith in your Lord, so listen to me." / *'Innī 'amantu birabbikum fa'sma'ūn* 201

26. It was said to him, "Enter the garden." He said, "Alas! If only my people knew / *Qīla 'dkhuli 'l-jannata qāla yā layta qawmī ya'lamūn*... 205

27. "How my Lord forgave me and placed me among those to whom He is generous!" / *Bimā ghafara lī rabbi wa ja'alnī mina'l-mukramīn* 209

28. We did not send down upon his people after him any army from the skies, nor were We going to / *Wa mā 'anzalnā 'alā qawmihi min ba'dihi min jundin mina's-samā'i wa mā kunnā munzilīn* 213

29. It was no more than a single cry, and then they were extinguished / *'In kānat 'illā ṣayḥatan wāḥidatan fa 'idhā hum khāmidūn* 213

30. Alas for the servants! There comes to them no messenger but they mock him / *Yā ḥasratan 'alā'l-'ibādi mā ya'tīhim min rasūlin 'illā kānū bihi yastahzi'ūn* 213

31. Do they not see how many generations We destroyed before them, that will not return to them? / *'Alam yaraw kam 'ahlaknā qablahum mina'l-qurūni 'annahum 'ilayhim lā yarji'ūn* 223

32. But each of them—all—will be brought before Us / *Wa 'in kullun lammā jamī'un ladaynā muḥḍarūn* 229

33. A sign for them is the dead earth; We give it life and produce seed from it that they may eat of it / *Wa 'āyatun lahumu'l-'arḍu'l-maytatu 'aḥyaynāhā wa 'akhrajnā minhā ḥabban faminhu ya'kulūn* 233

34. And we put there gardens of date palm trees and grapevines, and made springs gush forth in them / *Wa ja'alnā fīhā jannātin min nakhīlin wa 'a'nābin wa fajjarnā fīhā mina'l-'uyūn* 241

35. That they may eat of its fruits and of what their hands produce from it. Will they not then give thanks? / *Liyā'kulū min thamrihi wa mā 'amilathu 'aydīhim 'afalā yashkurūn* 253

36. Glory to the One who created all things in pairs from what the earth produces, and from their souls, and from things they do not know / *Subḥāna'lladhī khalaqa'l-'azwāja kullahā mimmā tunbitu'l-'arḍu wa min 'anfusihim wa mimmā lā ya'lamūn* 259

37. And a sign for them is the night; We draw from it the day, and then they are in darkness / *Wa 'āyatun lahumu'l-laylu naslakhu minhu'n-nahara fa 'idhāhum muẓlimūn* 277

38. And the sun runs in the place appointed for her; that is the measuring out of the Exalted, the All-Knowing / *Wa'sh-shamsu tajrī li-mustaqarrin lahā dhālika taqdīru'l-'azīzi'l-'alīm* 293

39. And for the moon We have measured out mansions until he returns like the curved date-stalk / *Wa'l-qamara qaddarnāhu manāzila ḥattā 'āda ka'l-'urjūni'l-qadīm* 301

40. It does not befit the sun to catch up with the moon, nor the night to outstrip the day; each swims round a sphere of the sky / *Lā'sh-shamsu yanbaghī lahā 'an tudrika'l-qamara wa lā 'l-laylu sābiqu'n-nahāri wa kullun fī falakin yasbaḥūn* 313

41. And a sign for them is that We carried their progeny in a loaded ship / *Wa 'āyatun lahum 'annā ḥamalnā dhurriyyatahum fī'l-fulki'l-mashḥūn* 319

42. And We created for them its like upon which they ride / *Wa khalaqnā lahum min mithlihi mā yarkabūn* 325

43. And if We will it, We drown them; then there would be none to help them, nor would they be saved / *Wa 'in nasha' nughriqhum falā ṣarīkha lahum wa lā hum yunqadhūn* 333

44. Except by a mercy from Us and provision for a time / *'Illā raḥmatan minnā wa matā'an 'ilā ḥīnin* 341

45. When they are told, "Fear what is before you and what is behind you, that you may receive mercy." / *Wa 'idhā qīla lahum'uttaqū mā bayna 'aydikum wa mā khalfakum la'allakum turḥamūn* 345

46. No sign came to them from the signs of their Lord but they turned away from it / *Wa mā ta'tīhim min 'āyatin min 'āyātin rabbihim 'illā kānū 'anhā mu'riḍīn* 353

47. And when they are told, "Spend of that which God has provided for you," those who disbelieve say to those who have faith: "Shall we feed those whom God would have fed if He wished? You are in manifest error, nothing more." / *Wa 'idha qīla lahum 'anfiqū mimmā razaqakumu'llahu qāla'lladhīna kafarū lilladhīna 'āmanū 'anuṭ'imu man law yashā'u'llahu 'aṭ'amahu 'in 'antum 'illā fī ḍalālin mubīn* 359

48. And they say, "When will this promise come to pass, if you be truthful?" / *Wa yaqūlūna matā hādhā'l wa'du 'in kuntum ṣādiqīn* 365

49. They wait for nothing but a single cry; it will take them while they argue amongst themselves / *Mā yanẓurūna 'illā ṣayḥatan wāḥidatan ta'khudhuhum wa hum yakhiṣṣimūn* 369

50. And then they will be able to make no bequest, and they will not return to their people / *Falā yastaṭi'ūna tawṣiyatan wa lā 'ilā 'ahlihim yarji'ūn* 373

51. And the trumpet will be blown and then, behold, they will rush from the graves to their Lord / *Wa nufikha fī'ṣṣūri fa'idhā hum min al-'ajdāthi 'ilā rabbihim yansilūn* 373

52. They will say, "Ah, woe to us, who has raised us from our beds of repose? This is what the Merciful promised, and the messengers spoke the truth." / *Qālū yāwaylanā man ba'athanā min marqadinā hādhā mā wa'ada'rrahmānu wa ṣadaqa'l-mursalūn* 389

53. It was but a single cry and then all of them were immediately brought before Us / *'In kānat 'illā ṣayḥatan wāḥidatan fa'idhā hum jamī'un ladaynā muḥḍarūn* 389

54. On that day no soul will be wronged in the least, and you will suffer only the requital for what you have done / *Fa'l-yawma lā tuẓlamu nafsun shay'an wa lā tujzawna 'illā mā kuntum ta'malūn* 393

55. Surely the people of Paradise that day have joy in what occupies them / *'Inna 'aṣḥāba'l-jannati'l-yawma fī shughulin fākihūn* 399

56. They and their spouses are reclining on couches in the shade / *Hum wa 'azwājuhum fī ẓilālin 'alā'l-'arā'iki muttaki'ūn* 399

57. There is a fruit therein for them, and whatever they ask for / *Lahum fīhā fākihatun wa lahum mā yadda'ūn* 399

58. A word of greeting from a Merciful Lord / *Salāmun qawlan min rabbin raḥīm* 413

59. And, O you sinners, depart today! / *Wa'mtāzū'l-yawma 'ayyuhā'l-mujrimūn* 423

60. Did I not enjoin you, O children of Adam, that you should not worship Satan? Surely he is an evident enemy to you / *'Alam 'a'had 'ilaykum yābanī 'adama 'an lā ta'budū'sh-shayṭāna 'innahu lakum 'aduwun mubīn* 431

61. And that you should worship Me. That is the straight path / *Wa 'ani''budūnī hādhā ṣirāṭun mustaqīm* 431

62. And he did lead a great multitude of you astray. Then did you not use intellect? / *Wa laqad 'aḍalla minkum jibillan kathīran 'a fa lam takūnū ta'qilūn* 463

63. This is the Hell that you were promised / *Hādhihi jahannamu'l-latī kuntum tū'adūn* 471

64. Burn there today, since you disbelieved / *'Iṣlawhā'l-yawma bimā kuntum takfurūn* 471

65. That day We will set a seal upon their mouths, but their hands will speak to Us, and their feet bear witness to what they have earned / *'Al-yawma nakhtimu 'alā 'afwāhihim wa tukallimunā 'aydīhim wa tashhadu 'arjuluhum bimā kānū yaksibūn* 495

66. And if We wished, we would have obliterated their eyes. They would race toward the path, but how would they see? / *Wa law nashā'u laṭamasnā 'alā 'a'yunihim fa'stabaqū'ṣ-ṣirāṭa fa'annā yubṣirūn* 503

67. And if We wished, we would have transformed them where they stood, and they would not have been able to move forward or go back / *Wa law nashā'u lamasakhnāhum ʿalā makānatihim famā'staṭāʿū muḍiyyān wa lā yarjiʿūn* 507

68. He whose life We extend, We reverse him in creation. Then will they not think? / *Wa man nuʿammirhu nunakkishu fī'l-khalqi ʾa fa lā yaʿqilūn* 515

69. We have not taught him poetry, nor would it be suitable for him. This is but a reminder and clear recitation [Quran] / *Wa mā ʿallamnāhu'sh-shiʿra wa mā yanbaghī lahu ʾin huwa ʾillā dhikrun wa qurʾānun mubīn* 523

70. That those who are living should be warned, and the word be proved for those who disbelieve / *Liyundhira man kāna ḥayyan wa yaḥiqqa'l-qawlu ʿalā'l-kāfirūn* 531

71. Do they not see that among what Our hands have fashioned We created for them gentle animals that are under their dominion? / *ʾAwalam yaraw ʾannā khalaqnā lahum mimmā ʿamilat ʾaydīnā ʾanʿāman fahum lahā mālikūn* 537

72. And that We have subjected them to their use, so that some they ride and some they eat? / *Wa dhallalnāhā lahum faminhā rakūbuhum wa minhā yaʾkulūn* 537

73. And in them they have benefits, and drink. Will they not then give thanks? / *Wa lahum fīhā manāfiʿu wa mashāribu ʾa fa lā yashkurūn* 537

74. Yet they take gods other than God, as if they would be helped / *Wa't-takhadhū min dūni'l-lāhi ʾālihatan laʿallahum yunṣarūn* 547

75. They are not able to help them, though they be an army ready for them / *Lā yastaṭīʿūna naṣrahum wa hum lahum jundun muḥḍarūn* 547

76. So let what they say not grieve you. Surely We know what they conceal and what they disclose / *Falā yaḥzunka qawluhum ʾinnā naʿlamu mā yusirrūna wa mā yuʿlinūn* 551

77. Does man not see that We created him from sperm, yet he has become an open adversary? / *'A wa lamyara'l-'insānu 'annā khalaqnāhu min nuṭfatin fa 'idhā huwa khaṣīmun mubīn* 555

78. He strikes a likeness for Us, and forgetting his own creation, says, "Who gives life to bones that are decomposed?" / *Wa ḍaraba lanā mathalan wa nasiya khalqahu qāla man yuḥyi'l-'iẓāma wa hiya ramīmun* 555

79. Say, "He who made them for the first time will raise them to life, and He knows every kind of creation / *Qul yuḥyīhā'l-ladhi 'ansha'ahā 'awwala marratin wa huwa bikulli khalqin 'alīm* 555

80. He who produces fire out of the green tree for you and you kindle fires with it / *Alladhī ja'ala lakum mina'sh-shajari'l-'akhḍari nāran fa'idhā 'antum minhu tūqidūn* 563

81. Is not He who created the heavens and earth able to create the like? Yes indeed, He is the Creator, the All-Knowing / *'A wa laysa'l-ladhī khalaqa's-samāwāti wa'l-'arḍa biqādirin 'alā 'an yakhluqa mithlahum balā wa huwa'l-khallāqu'l-'alīm* 571

82. Truly His command when He wills a thing is "Be!" and it is / *'Innamā 'amruhu 'idha 'arāda shay'an yaqūla lahu kun fayakūn* 575

83. So glory be to Him in whose hand is the sovereignty of each thing, and to Him you will be returned / *Fasubḥāna'l-ladhī biyadihi malakūtu kulli shay'in wa 'ilayhi turja'ūn* 589

Index 601

YaSin: Love, The Prophet, and Humanity at the Heart of the Qur'an

Cemalnur Sargut, the luminous Turkish female Sufi saint, is a reminder and a confirmation that the gates of heaven are still open to Earth.

We so often speak of the word "tradition" as something in the past. When we speak of something being "traditional", there is the implication that it is old, old-fashioned, and perhaps conservative. Yet *tradition* is always a tradition-in-process, a teaching in transmission. A tradition is always evolving and overflowing, just as a river is always flowing, and the breeze the poets wrote about (*saba*) is always carrying the scent of flowers from the garden of the Beloved. The word tradition is etymologically linked to the notion of "transmission", and there is something about the process of passing on, internalizing, making indigenous, transmuting, and re-offering that is part of how the leaven of the ancients gives rise to the new bread. This "rising" of the bread of life is itself a powerful metaphor for the transmission.

In Cemalnur's teachings about the Qur'an, we see this bread of life, this ancient leaven rising. This rising is a reminder that the spiritual realm is also here and now, mingling, inspiring, and giving rise to the wave. The wave is part of the sea, and when it rises we call it a wave. Likewise the teachings of a sage like Cemalnur are both a part of this ancient tradition and a rising up that reaches the shores of our own existence.

■ ■ ■

The great Muslim sage Mawlana Jalal al-Din Rumi, of whose teachings Cemalnur possesses an intimate mastery, says that one reason so many people have a hard time accessing the beauty of the Qur'an is that the Qur'an acts like a shy bride, hiding her beauty from the casual reader. Many people take a peek inside the first few pages of the Qur'an, find a harshness in the language of Divine majesty (*jalal*), and rush off. Many never return. That is part of the coquetry of the Qur'an, the appearing-to-be-disinterested-and-hard-to-get quality of the playful beloved who is looking to see who is truly in love and who merely there to be tantalized. According to Rumi, it is only to the patient lover that the Qur'an reveals her beauty in an erotically spiritual process of unveiling (*kashf*). To sit at Cemalnur's feet as she takes us through the Qur'an is to be reminder that the whole of the Qur'an is a love letter from the Divine Beloved. It is an unveiling of the beauty of the Qur'an for the initiated, the sincere, and the seeking. Her reading is consistent with the loftiest aspect of the distinctly Turkish Sufi tradition that is shaped in equal parts through Mawlana Rumi and Ibn 'Arabi.

■ ■ ■

Within the early Islamic tradition, we are blessed with a series of complementary teachings about how to dive into the ocean of meanings found in the Qur'an. To begin with, and ultimately above all else, it is God's own Being who takes on the task of transmitting the inner meanings of the Qur'an:

Al-Rahman

The Ever-Merciful God
Taught the Qur'an

Created humanity.
[Qur'an 55:1-3]

That God's teaching of the Qur'an is mentioned before the creation of humanity is one indication of the pre-temporal Divine origin of wisdom about the Qur'an. Ultimately, insight about the Qur'an has to be generated in the Divine realm and not restricted to mere human speculation. It is God who teaches the Qur'an and opens up the sacred text, and in the process opens up the heart. In this sense, the *Ya Fattah* ("God who opens, over and over again") who begins the *Fatiha* (the

YaSin: Love, The Prophet, and Humanity at the Heart of the Qur'an

opening chapter of the Qur'an), which leads to the *Fath*, opening and illumination of the heart (as in the *Futuhat al-Makiyya* of Ibn 'Arabi).

In another powerful verse of the Qur'an, God mentions having sent down the "Scripture and the Light." Whereas the Scripture (*Kitab*) is readily identified with the Qur'an, the Light is often identified in the Sufi tradition as the *Nur Muhammad*, the Light of Muhammad, that pre-eternal effusing of Divine light that overflows in all the prophets, and after them through the saintly beings. To see Cemalnur's extraction of meaning from the oceans of mercy in the Qur'an is to benefit from both the Scripture and the Light.

The reality that the Qur'an is not restricted to that which is "between the two covers" continues through the person of those who have become the embodiment of this light. The Prophet Muhammad himself was called "the walking Qur'an", and in another version his wife 'Aisha said that his whole nature was the Qur'an. This has been the mark of a tradition that has never been "Protestant" in the nature of rendering the ultimate authority merely to texts, but also to people whose whole being has becoming the living embodiment on the texts and the first commentary on those authoritative texts.

This Muhammadan Light keeps flowing over and over again, from God to the Prophet, from Prophet to Imam Ali, and from Ali to the whole community of saints. The heart knowledge of the Qur'an is perhaps most clearly seen through the traditions attributed to Imam Ali, who received the esoteric interpretation of the Qur'an directly from the Prophet. Let us explore a bit of how Imam Ali, who is at once the first Imam of the Shi'a and the gate to Prophetic knowledge in the whole of the Sufi tradition, invites us to explore this opening up of the Qur'an.

At one point, Ali said: "All of the books of God are in the Qur'an, all of the Qur'an is in the Fatiha, all of the Fatiha is in the Basmala, and all of the Basmala is in the nuqta of the bā. I am the nuqta."

In Cemalnur's retelling this notion of Imam Ali being the speaking Qur'an is traced back to the Ibn 'Arabi's heir in the Akbarian school, al-Jili:

When enemy soldiers stuck pages from the Gracious Quran on the ends of their spears, Hazret Ali (*may God ennoble his countenance*) said; "Anā'l-qur'ānu'n-nātiq (I am the talking Qur'an)."

Ali is the talking Qur'an. Without Ali, and those who embody Ali's qualities, the Qur'an would be silent. Scripture has to be spoken, lived, breathed, and walked. There had to be a walking Qur'an in Muhammad, and a talking Qur'an in Ali. In tracing this line from Muhammad to Ali to today, Cemalnur is consistent with much of the Sufi tradition which seeks the heart wisdom of the Prophet overflowing to Imam Ali, and from Imam Ali to all the friends of God (awliya') down to our own age.

At another point, Imam Ali said:

"*All of the knowledge of previous scriptures are contained within the Qur'an. And the whole of the Qur'an is contained within the Surah Al-Fathiha, and the whole of the Al-Fathiha is contained in the opening line, 'In the Name of God, the most Gracious and the Most Merciful', and the essence of everything is contained within the beginning of the beginning, the first letter, the 'ب', which contains within it the secret of 'Whatever became, became through Me, and whatever will become will become through Me'. And the essence of all essences is in the dot under the letter 'ب'.*"

From time to time, we hear accounts in the Sufi tradition that seem implausible to any mere mortal understanding of limitations of time and space: Ibn 'Arabi is said to have written over 700 books, with the massive *Futuhat al-Makiyya* being one of them. Rumi is said to have tens of thousands of line of poetry, each of them magnificently capable of opening up a heart. And this ability to transcend mere human creativity is also witnessed in the realm of Qur'anic interpretation. In another tradition, Imam Ali states:

"*If I had wished, I could have loaded eighty camels with books explaining the sciences concerning the dot beneath the Arabic letter bā' [in the Basmala].*"

These kinds of statements, both intended to saturate and overwhelm the rational faculty of the intellect to the point of bewilderment (*hayra*) are not merely pious exaggerations. To see Cemalnur channel the Qur'an is to get a sense of how something like this operates through beings whose whole heart has become a polished mirror for the divine. I once held in my hands a book that numbered in the hundreds of pages, dealing with Qur'anic interpretation that Cemalnur had composed on the first 10 verses of one single Qur'anic chapter. It reminds one that Imam Ali's statement is no mere boast.

The companion of the Prophet Ibn 'Abbas says one night he stayed awake from dusk to dawn, sitting at the feet of Imam Ali, and he experienced himself as a vase before a vast ocean. This is what it feels like to sit at the feet of Cemalnur, who has emptied herself to the point that oceans of meaning pour not from her but rather through her.

■ ■ ■

Cemalnur's *Ya Sin*, rendered here as "O Humankind" through the exquisite translation of Victoria Holbook is a most worthy project, and Fons Vitae is to be heartily translated. The translation is among the significant and ambitious projects on the Qur'an to appear in the last few decades. It is of interest to students of the Qur'an, to all those searching for Sufi engagements with the Qur'an, for those yearning to hear more directly the religious insights of Muslim women, as well as those seeking to hear more contemporary interpretations of the Qur'an. All of these communities are indebted to Victoria Holbrook and Fons Vitae.

This is particularly the case given the reality that Cemalnur speaks (mostly) Turkish, and occasionally English. There is still a limitation that far too many scholars of Islamic studies have, that their language training is largely restricted to Arabic. (It remains one of the archaic traits of graduate training in Islamic studies, and a fossilized rule dating back to the Biblical training of older Orientalist training that most graduate programs require French or German—essential language for Biblical studies—rather than encouraging students of Islamic studies to truly master a second Islamic language like Persian, Turkish, or Urdu.) Cemalnur's popularity in Turkey easily ranks her as the most prominent female religious figure in contemporary Turkey, one that is frequently and accurately compared with that of Oprah in the recent American landscape. She is increasingly being featured on the global scene of leading Sufi teachers. There is little doubt that if her writings had been in Arabic (or English!) rather than Turkish, we would have already had many dissertations on her. All of us are indebted to Fons Vitae for sharing the luminous insights of this powerful and original transmission. And thanks to Victoria Holbrook who has done the almost impossible of weaving together the often ornate expression of texts from the thousand years' network of the modern and Ottoman Turkish, Persian and Arabic Islamic tradition. Her translation is another masterpiece.

Let us go over a few of the highly original and authentic interpretations that Cemalnur offers. Even for readers well-verses in the study of the Sufi tradition, these are beautiful interpretations that can each open up the heart. I have taken the liberty of picking out a few of the themes that come out through Cemalnur's commentary on the YaSin.

Divine Qualities to Prophetic Qualities:
In classical Sufi texts, one often hears the advice to "adorn oneself with the qualities of God." In Cemalnur's interpretation, that meaning is directly connected to following the Prophetic qualities. In other words, the Prophet has become such an embodiment of Divine qualities that to follow the Prophet is to adorn oneself with the akhlaq allah. "*O my brothers, assume the character traits of God*. The meaning of this hadith is that one should embrace the sunna of the Messenger (s.a.s.)"

Cloak Yourself with the qualities of the Prophet:
The name of the Prophet Mudaththir is usually described as the one who was covered (with a cloak). In Cemalnur's reading, it is one who is cloaked with the qualities of the Prophet. This adornment is not restricted to the external qualities that are the domain of *shari'a*, but carried over to the inner and the heart level concerns of *tariqa, haqiqa,* and *ma'rifa*.

Muhammad a Prophet between water and clay:
In Cemalnur's reading, when the Prophet indicates that he was a messenger already when Adam was between water and clay, it does not mean that the Prophet existed in a human form, but that he was already a messenger. In other words, it is another sign of the qualities of a messenger pre-figuring creation.

God's form:
Contrary to the modern traditions which see the "human" as a fallen creature, or a "talking/rational animal", in Cemalnur's sacred anthropology, the human being is "God's form, and the world is the mirror that this form reflects in itself. And God is the essence of the

human form." Humanity is God's secret, and God is humanity's secret. Echoing her grand-teacher Kenan Rifa'i, Cemalnur states that with God's Self-manifestation in the human being, Earth became a more sacred place than Heaven.

Ya-Sin, Humanity, and the Prophet:
The Ya-Sin is both the perfect human being and the very being of the Prophet Muhammad. As such, the human being combines in herself the beings of the various realms: Nasut, Malakut, Jabarut, and Lahut.

The Scripture and the Wisdom:
The Qur'an talks about a prophet who will be "raised up among yourselves" and teach you the *Kitab* and the *Hikma*, the Scripture and the Wisdom [Qur'an 2:151]. According to Cemalnur, the *Kitab* (Scripture) refers to the outwards dimensions of the religion, and the *Hikmat* (Wisdom) to the inward dimensions. Both of these realms are connected to the Prophetic dispensation.

Muhammad as Divine Theophany:
In distinction to many contemporary interpretations of the Prophet which reduce him to a "mere man" and almost a delivery man of the Qur'anic revelation alone, in Cemalnur's Ibn 'Arabi-inflected interpretation the very being of the Prophet is a site of Divine manifestation: *"When Hazret Muhammed's (s.a.s.) body came into existence with all the divine realities, it became the site of self-disclosure of the name One* (Wāḥid). *The Messenger's interior was unity* (aḥadiyya) *and his exterior was oneness* (waḥdāniyya)." Due to this essential emobidment of Divine qualitis, Cemalnur sees the Prophet as having received the totality of the Qur'an as *"a single sentence."*

Ya-Sin and the Prophet:
The phrase Ya Sin, said to be the heart of the Qur'an, which also graces the title of this book in the Turkish original, refers to "O protective guide to peace and well-bring." While Ya Sin does refer to the humanity, it refers above all to the epitome of humanity, which is to say, the being of the Prophet. It is the Prophet's quality of the *Insan al-kamil*, the completely realized and mature human being, who embodies the qualities of the YaSin.

The Straight Path is through the Insan al-Kamil:
In both the opening chapter of the Qur'an and the Surah of Ya-Sin, the Qur'an talks about the "straight path." There is at times a tendency among some Muslims to define the "straight" path as the straight and narrow, but that is a far cry from Cemalnur's take. In her reading, the straight path is nothing other than the shortest distance to behold the One (Ahad), which is to enter the heart of a realized human being, epitomized in the Prophet.

The Heavenly Ascension:
In Cemalnur's interpretation of the *Mi'raj* (Prophet's heavenly ascension), there is a profound outpouring of Divine mercy that takes place due to prophetic intercession. She records God as having revealed to Muhammad:

"Whatever you wish is accepted by Me. Your community will always have three groups: Those who rebel, those who obey, and those who long for their God as people thirsty in the desert long for water. I will send my mercy and forgiveness to your rebellious bondsmen. I will give My paradises to those who obey. As for the felicity of beholding My infinite beauty, I will offer it to the thirsty."

This is the face of mercy, forgiveness, love, and beauty. Those who have disobeyed God's call, rather than being met with the punishment they would have deserved are greeted with Mercy and Forgiveness. Those who have been obedient receive paradise. But there are those select few who thirst for God, for whom Beholding the Face of God is sougth like a thirsty soul seeks the water of life in a desert. To these it is the Infinite Beauty that is offered. This is the same *Jamal-e Baqi* that Hazrat Rabi'a prayed for in her famous prayer, and the same face of love and beauty that is characterized in the being of the Prophet as the mercy to all the worlds (Qur'an 21:107).

Be greeted in peace by every stone, every tree:
Part of the YaSin interpretation is to enjoin on the reader to move from a state of limited rationalistic view (which she identifies with that of "philosophers") to being rooted in a more beatific vision of spirit and love. This is not philosophy in the real sense of love of sacred wisdom, but that which passes as philosophy, a more abstract

YaSin: Love, The Prophet, and Humanity at the Heart of the Qur'an

knowledge without presence, without tasting, and without becoming. Cemalnur contrasts that with the kind of tasted knowledge that the sages of Islam possess and strive for, such as that of Imam Ali and Hazrat Muhammad. In one passage, she quotes this knowledge-by-presence that Imam Ali experience as: "O Messenger of God, when I go out to the desert from Mecca, I do not see one stone or tree that does not greet me."

There is more, much more than the brief highlight I have pointed out here, but let this suffice. There is an ocean that awaits you, and let us have faith that there is a whole ocean contained in every drop.

■ ■ ■

Let us come back to Cemalnur. Her Qur'anic commentary is so extraordinarily voluminous and ever-flowing that it is a reminder of how this is not a work of authorship in the mere human sense, but an opening up of the heart, emptying the ego, and standing back as the *al-Qahhar* overwhelms and opens up the floodgates. Her commentary is so powerful that it is bound to be of interest to all students of the Qur'an, of women's spirituality, of contemporary Islamic thought, and of Sufism.

Within the Sufi tradition, names are a bridge to the inner reality. Rarely has a Sufi master been more properly named that Cemalnur: *Jamal-Nur*. Beauty and Light.

Read this book, and take in the Beauty of the one Divine Beloved who is the Source of All beauty, and who loves Beauty; the One who is the Source of Light, and is above all the Light of the Heavens and the Earth.

Ya-Sin.

May the Protection of the One guide us all towards Salamat, well-being, well-doing, and an illuminated heart by walking in the path of the friends of God, all those bathed in the Nur Muhammad...

Omid Safi
Director of Islamic Studies Center
Duke University

Acknowledgement

I wish to express my deepest gratitude to my mother and my guide Cemalnur Sargut for this beautiful commentary on the chapter Ya-Sin, known as "the heart of the Quran." I also would like to express my special thanks to Nazlı Kayahan, the right-hand assisting her in selections from a vast literature of Quranic commentaries produced by saints and sages over ten centuries. And I am grateful to Victoria Rowe Holbrook, one of the most hardworking people I ever met in my life, for making this work available in English. Thanks to Layla Cadavid, editor of the English version, for putting her heart into this book. And Gray Henry, my co-publisher and my "dost," for being with us throughout the process. And, thanks to Omid Safi for writing the most beautiful foreword ever.

Hasan Kerim Güç
Executive Editor, Nefes Publishing

Translator's Note

This book is a compilation of mostly late Ottoman and early modern Turkish writing about Ya-Sin, chapter thirty-six of the Quran, and translations of medieval Arabic and Persian classics commenting upon it. Thus the compiler Cemalnur Sargut offers a commentary derived from the Ottoman Turkish intellectual tradition and more modern translation practices. That tradition was so thoroughly infused with the special terminology of Ibn Arabi's thought that there are few discussions in this book that do not contain his characteristic terminology and thought.

All of this presents special challenges for English translation. In order to maintain consistency in translation of special terms, I have in almost all cases followed William Chittick's English practice in his *The Self-Disclosure of God: Principles of Ibn al-'Arabi's Cosmology* and his earlier *The Sufi Path of Knowledge: Ibn 'Arabi's Metaphysics of Imagination*, some of whose usage he revised in *The Self-Disclosure*. I find Chittick's the most accurate and systematic English translation of Ibn Arabi's terminology. By recommending a contemporary American scholar's translation of Ibn Arabi's thirteenth-century terminology as a key to understanding Ottoman thought, I am not implying that alteration in the meaning of terms did not occur throughout the centuries of their use in Ottoman, not to mention modern Turkish, discourse. Of course the usage of terms and understanding of concepts changes over time, and the Arabic loan words in Turkish aquired nuances special to the Turkish milieu. There is no study of this matter, however, and I have had to rely on my feel for the material.

One important point. There is in this discourse a distinction between the soul/self (Ar. *nafs*, Tr. *nefis*) and the spirit (*ruh*), on the rule that the soul is what arises when the spirit enters the body; and it is the spirit that survives after death.

I have used the United States Library of Congress Romanization for verses and terms from the Quran. Names are usually spelled as in the original text. For well-known Arabic and Persian names I have tried to give the spellings most often used today, without special transliteration characters—spellings the reader can easily use to find out more about the individuals by searching the internet. On first usage of many special terms I usually give the Turkish italicized in parentheses;[1] if it is an Arabic loan word, in certain special cases I give Arabic transliteration. One might argue that I should have always given Arabic transliteration for Arabic loan words. This would have made it easier for scholars of Arabic to recognize them; but this book is intended for a much broader audience, and here I am concerned with Turkish usage. Italic translated material in parentheses indicates Sargut's clarifications; brackets indicate my few explanatory interpolations.

Several of the Turkish translations of Arabic and Persian material upon which Sargut draws are idiosyncratic, by which I mean they are not standard, and almost none include scholarly apparatus that would make it possible to check them against the originals. I translated from the Persian the many quotations from Mevlana Rumi's *Spiritual Couplets*,[2] but for the most part I had no choice but to translate from the Turkish translations. The perils of doing this are well known. However, the Turkish translations are usually rewritings aimed at new audiences, using vocabulary familiar to those new audiences. The text includes Ottoman rewritings of Arabic and Persian material aimed at Ottoman audiences, and modern Turkish rewritings of Ottoman and Arabic and Persian material aimed at contemporary audiences. It is worth mentioning that Ottoman translation of Arabic and Persian texts was rare. Literate Ottomans read those languages and thus translation only began to be practiced late, as that knowledge was gradually lost, and it has the idiosyncrasy of a translation practice that is new. I believe it is important to convey

---

1. I often omit the Turkish "şapka," ^, a vowel-lengthening sign used in the text, because it is rarely used elsewhere today and would make it difficult for readers to search for the term.

2. I located the couplets in Nicholson's edition and cited its verse numbers in brackets at the end of the Turkish footnote when they were not given there; Jalal al-Din Rumi, ed. and trans. Reynold A. Nicholson, *The Mathnawi of Jalal al-Din Rumi*, E.J.W. Gibb Memorial Series, N.S: (Leiden: 1925-1940).

Translator's Note

these characteristics, in order to give my readers insight into the Turkish mileux.

The text makes use of hadiths, which are reports on sayings and doings of the Prophet Muhammed, or, in the case of "noble hadiths," direct quotations from him. In "sacred hadiths" the speech of God is quoted by Muhammed. The text sometimes uses the hadith science categories *sahih* and *hasan*. A *sahih* hadith, the most trustworthy of all, is one transmitted through an unbroken chain of narrators all of whom were judged by hadith authorities to have good character and strong memory. The second degree, *hasan*, designates a hadith not contradicted by a *sahih* hadith and transmitted through an unbroken chain of narrators all of whom were judged to have good character but weak memory.

For the Quran and hadith I have drawn upon several translations as well as my own knowledge. In many cases I found it necessary to follow the Turkish translation given, even though I might have translated the Arabic differently, because the Turkish translation is integral to the commentary. Quotations from Quran and hadith are given in italics and, in the case of the Quran, followed by the chapter and verse numbers in parentheses where the text gives them.

In Turkish it is very common to paraphrase a quotation and put the paraphrase in quotation marks, even if the text quoted is Quran or hadith; quotation marks do not necessarily indicate an exact quote. Authors quoted in this book often employ such paraphrase, and my task is to faithfully translate what they wrote, so that readers may observe how they understood the texts they referenced.

Ken'an Rifai's *Şerhli Mesnevî-i Şerif*, published in my English translation as *Listen: Commentary on the Spiritual Couplets of Mevlana Rumi*, is often quoted herein in paraphrased form, and I have modified my translation of that text accordingly; I have also sometimes revised terms in my published translation of that text to conform to usages I established for this book.

In Turkish God is most often referred to as "Hak," and sometimes as "Cenab-ı Hak," interchangeably. I render both as "God the Truth," or when repitition makes that unwieldly, simply as "God."

The title "Hazret" here is a title of exaltation indicating a specific personage. If one says "Hazret Muhammed," for example, it is understood that one is speaking of the Prophet Muhammed and not another man named Muhammed.

The Prophet Muhammed is usually referred to in the text as "the Messenger" (*peygamber, resul*), "the Messenger of God" (*resullullah*), and "our Efendi." The letters "s.a.s" in parentheses after mention of his name are an abbreviation of *ṣalla'llāhu ʿalayhi wa sallam*, meaning, "May the blessings and peace of God be upon him." Less often for him, but for other prophets and certain personages the phrase is *ʿalayhi's-salām*, meaning, "May the peace of God be upon him," abbreviated "a.s." For Imam Ali, *karrama'llahu wajhahu* is used, meaning, "May God honor his face," abbreviated "k.w." For saintly persons the phrase is *qudissa sirruhu*, meaning, "May God sanctify his secret heart," abbreviated "q.s." Occasionally God's name is followed by *jalla jalāluhu*, meaning, "May His majesty be glorified," abbreviated "j.j." Sometimes mention of a deceased person is followed by *raḥmat'ullāh ʿalayhi*, meaning, "May the mercy of God be upon him," abbreviated "r.a." These abbreviations appear in italics because that is how they were printed in the text, indicating that Sargut added them to the material she quoted.

The Prophet Muhammed is also referred to as Mustafa and Ahmed.

"Servant" (Arabic *ʿabd*, Turkish *kul*) refers to all of God's creatures. In other words, we are all termed God's servants.

Victoria Rowe Holbrook, Istanbul 2019

O my brothers, assume the character traits of God. The meaning of this hadith is that one should embrace the sunna of the Messenger (s.a.s.) and acquire his character traits. His character is the Quran. The Quran is the speech of God, in which there is nothing in vain. It existed before the creation of the world and will exist forever. It was transcribed and collated by the Messenger's companions. The Quran, as God declared in the verse, *"We sent it down and We will preserve it,"* is beyond any and all falsification, corruption or alteration.[3]

---

3. Ahmed er-Rifâî, trans. Dr. Ali Can Tatlı, *Sohbet Meclisleri* (Istanbul: Erkam Yayınları 1996), p. 7.

Author's Preface

Dear Friends,

For five years we have been working to reflect upon the divine gift of chapter Ya-Sin through the commentaries of perfect human beings who are without doubt heirs to the Messenger and through the interpretations of scholars who devoted their lives to understanding the Gracious Quran.

This effort, which opened incredibly vast horizons in our hearts and minds, drawing our study group from the realm of density to the realm of subtlety and conveying us from the unseen world to the here and now, moved us to share our work with you, beyond our capacity though it may be.

We worked with the hope that, in Hazret Mevlana's phrase, the Mighty Quran would *raise its veil for us like a bride if we paid the price for that vision out of our own selves.* I want to say that we experienced the most vibrant time of our lives during these happy years when we struggled to transform what we learned into a spiritual state. The concept of time that consists of the present moment, the concept of time that is *"Kun fayakūn,"* became comprehensible only by tasting the pleasure of the Quran.

It brought understanding of unification (*tevhid*), which is the straight path to the sublime Essence of God, to become a thing lived, even if in stages. Let there be thanks thousandfold.

It is our wish that this work will steer readers toward the vast depths and pleasures of the Quran and encourage them to reflect upon the verses we have studied. For we believe and we comprehend that each and every word of the Gracious Quran is a miracle and has the power to draw a person to the deep horizons of spirituality. In the course of our work we saw that each of the unveilings and interpretations offered by the perfect human beings were appropriate for several verses. This is because the verses contain meanings so limitless as to comprehend the infinity of God.

In sum, we who on the last day of our first umrah journey heard the call, "O humankind!" while reciting chapter Ya-Sin in prostration before the prayer-niche of love, and try, if it please God, to rise from the level of the creature to the level of the human, present for your attention this work that intoxicated us as we prepared it for publication.

Flaws and errors are always our own. May God be the helper of us all. Amen.

Cemalnur Sargut

Chapter Ya-Sin

Chapter Ya-Sin was revealed in the Meccan period. It has also been known as 'Azīma, Mu'imma, Mudāfi'a-i Kādiya, and Qalb-i Qur'ān.

Alusi related: "Abu Nasr Sajzi in his *Ibāna* reported on the authority of Hazret Aisha, categorizing the report as *hasan*: Hazret Aisha has said that the Messenger of God said: 'There is a chapter of the Quran known to God as ''Azīma'. He who possesses it is known to God as "noble" (*şerif*), and on Resurrection Day will intercede for more people than are found in Rabia and Mudar.'"

Said ibn Mansur and Bayhaqi related from Hassan ibn Atiyya that the Messenger of God said: "Ya-Sin is called Mu'imma in the Torah. It generalizes the good of this world and the Hereafter for him who possesses it, offers resistance against his worldly and otherworldly troubles, and removes his worldly and otherworldly fears. It is also called Mudāfi'a-i Kādiya. It forbids all evil for him who possesses it, and meets all his salutary needs."

By way of Tirmidhi, Qutayba and Sufyan ibn Waki', Qatadah relates from Anas that the Messenger (s.a.s) said: "Every thing has a heart, and the heart of the Quran is Ya-Sin."[4]

Chapter Ya-Sin signifies attainment of the level of the Preserved Tablet, because Ya-Sin corresponds to the Preserved Tablet. It is called the Heart of the Quran on that basis.

O my Lord! I am your servant, fleeing from the evil of my soul and Satan to take refuge in You. I cry for help against their evil and take refuge in Your mercy. In reality there is no place where one can take refuge.

---

4. Elmalılı M. Hamdi Yazır, *Hak Dini Kur'an Dili* (Istanbul: Feza Gazetecilik 1992), vol. 6, pp. 394-395.

O Humankind

O my Lord! I begin this work with Your name. My God, who self-discloses with all His divine names in the Beloved (*habib*) [Muhammed] and who has opened the straight path to everyone by sending him as Messenger to all His servants! I begin with Your name.[5]

---

5. Şemseddin Yeşil, *Füyûzat* (Istanbul: Ş. Yeşil Yayınları 1984), vol. 6, pp. 227-229.

1. Ya-Sin

- Scholars have interpreted the letters that make up the first verse of the chapter in the following ways:

   a. They are the name of the chapter.
   b. They are an oath.
   c. They are a key to terms provided by God the Exalted (*Allah Teâlâ*).
   d. They mean, "O Humankind!" (*reported from Ibn Abbas by way of 'Ikrima*).
   e. Sulami, author of the commentary *Haqāyiq*, related from Wasiti and Jafar ibn Muhammed that Ya-Sin means "O Master" (*ya seyyid*).
   f. They spell a name of the Messenger.

   Naqqash related from the Messenger: "I have seven names in the Quran: Muhammed, Ahmed, Ta-Ha, Ya-Sin, Muddaththir, Muzammil, and Abdullah."[6]

- Ya-Sin is the other name for our Efendi after he passed the furthest Lote Tree (*a station in the seventh heaven that Hazret Muhammed [s.a.s.] reached with Gabriel on the night of the Miraj; in tasavvuf, the ultimate station in knowledge of God the Truth attainable by human intellect and the knowledge acquired through intellect*).[7] On this side of the Lote Tree, Muhammed is Mustafa (s.a.s.).[8]

---

6. Elmalılı M. Hamdi Yazır, *Hak Dini Kur'an Dili* (Istanbul: Feza Gazetecilik 1992), vol. 6, p. 398.

7. İlhan Ayverdi, *Kubbealtı Lugati: Misalli Büyük Türkçe Sözlük* (Istanbul: Kubbealtı Yayınevi 2005), vol. 3.

8. Halûk Nurbaki, *Yâ-Sîn Sûresi Yorumu* (Istanbul: Damla Yayınevi 1999), p. 8.

- Sin indicates God's secret heart (*sır*). Know that the human being, who is made of God's secret heart, signifies Hazret Muhammed Mustafa (s.a.s.), chief of the two worlds. Ya-Sin means "O humankind!" and its interlocutor is the Messenger of Greatness. That is to say, "O humankind, identical to My essence and the Wise Quran." In other words: "O human being, essence with My Essence, the Gracious Quran is identical to you."

When enemy soldiers stuck pages from the Gracious Quran on the ends of their spears, Hazret Ali (k.w.) said, *'Anā'l-qur'ānu'n-nātiq*, "I am the talking Quran."[9]

- The written word "Muhammed" has been stretched and spread across the pages of creation from eternity without beginning to eternity without end. ... The letter "m" [*mim* م], the first letter of "Muhammed," is tied by the length of its tail to the Realm of Sovereignty (*melekut*). And its face [the round part of the letter] has been lowered onto the Realm of Kingdom (*mülk*). The length of the letter *mim* has encircled the worlds entirely. It contained the fixed entities while the worlds were coming into being. The diacritical mark above the letter *mim* indicating the "u" vowel in the name "Muhammed" is a sign of his rise to the stations of "very sublime prophethood" (*nübüvvet-i uzma*), "the greatest messengerhood" (*risalet-i kübra*), and the most sublime honor of the station of holiness (*kuds*). It is such a sublime honor that its final limit cannot even be comprehended by any of the truthful (*sadık*) or intimates (*those angels nearest to God*) except the masters of determination (*ulu'l-azm*; *those Messengers who despite the great difficulties they encountered carried out their offices of messengerhood to perfection with superior determination and decisiveness; Hazret Noah, Hazret Abraham, Hazret Moses, Hazret Jesus, and Hazret Muhammed (s.a.s.)*).

The letter "h" (*ḥ*) in Muhammed shows the highest limit of the Messenger's stations, which are due to the sublimity of his spiritual value and situation. His spiritual level is between a station of love mixed with fear and one of spiritual ascension. The real source of his love, sprung of fear, is his move toward servanthood (*kulluk*) with

---

9. Abdü'l-Kerīm ibn Ibrahim al-Jīlī, trans. Seyyid Hüseyin Fevzi Paşa, *Besmele'ni Şerhi* (Istanbul: Kitsan Yayınları), p. 59.

1st Verse

the wariness (*haşyet*) he felt while speaking with God the Truth at the furthest Lote Tree.

The "a" vowel mark above the "h" shows his conveyance with the guarantors of intimacy from the talismanic Mount Sinai, from eternity without beginning to eternity without end. This spiritual conveyance is happening continuously, and was continuous before him. To understand this completely is true comprehension.

The central letter *mim* is the point in understanding Hazret Messenger where people comprehend the boons granted them and know that those boons are beyond the comprehension of all existents. Because he became manifest when the property of the Realm of Command arrived at manifestation from secrecy. And this manifestation was by way of illiteracy.

The diacritical mark above the letter *mim*, indicating doubling, gives Hazret Messenger two titles of illiteracy. The first is the illiteracy regarding his not knowing how to read or write, and the second is the illliteracy (*ümmilik*) showing his community's (*ümmetinin*) affiliation to him.[10]

The letter "d" (*dal*) at the end of his name is his eternal rule, which means that as long as creation keeps turning, the earth will be dedicated to him and those who take his path. He is the best of those to whom command over the earth has been given.

That the "d" in Muhammed has no vowel signifies the stability in his station of sultanhood, his turning toward the zodiacal signs of eternal felicity, and his ascension from one boon to another and one proof to another. All judgment and wisdom are special to him. He is Muhammed (s.a.s.). He is the stairway to the Realm of Domination (*ceberut*). He is the owner of command and negation till Resurrection Day.[11]

- There is no limit to either the manifest or the spiritual greatness of Muhammed. In order to show both of his aspects, Frithjof Schuon used his worldly and heavenly names Muhammed and Ahmed in one model:

---

10. [The connection here is that the words "illiteracy" and "community" share the same Arabic root.]

11. Ahmed er-Rifâî, trans. Dr. Ali Can Tatlı, *Sohbet Meclisleri* (Istanbul: Erkam Yayınları 1996), pp. 61-63.

Muhammed is the praised, the manifest divine self-disclosure, the silver of the last two bricks; the meaning of the Quran descends upon him. Ahmed is the praised, the inward (*batini*) divine self-disclosure, the golden of the last two bricks, and the interior of Hazret Muhammed (s.a.s.) that comprehends the Miraj.[12]

• The name Muhammed is connected with the Night of Power when the Quran was first revealed. It is the self-disclosure of God's aspect of Majesty and represents the Messenger's role as a servant (*abd*); it is the active role of prophet and messenger.

Ahmed is connected with the night of the Miraj; here he is given the interpretation of "beloved," and for that reason represents God's aspect of Beauty; he is illiterate, in other words he is the recipient of revelation.[13]

• The Night of Power is a specified night during the last third of the month of Ramazan. If we think of Ramazan as patience, difficulty and night, a human being's comprehension of the Quran, which is the self-disclosure of the spiritual meaning of Power, that is, God, is only revealed to those who bear with this difficulty.

Here one thinks of the following hadith: In the last third of the night, God the Truth descends from the sky, saying, "Is there no one who wants anything?"

If the servant is a believer who gives thanks in the extremity of difficulty (*the final third*), he forms a connection with God and becomes the site of manifestation for "the moment." This spiritual state is the manifestation of Muhammed. The Miraj is the spiritual meaning to which the Messenger ascended with his own reality. And this is the manifestation of Ahmed.

---

12. The Messenger's saying, "I am the last brick of the house of character," is "I am the last two bricks" in Muhyiddin Ibn Arabi's *Fusûs*. These two bricks represent one brick. The golden brick is connected with his being the Seal of the Saints, and the silver brick with his being the Seal of the Prophets. That is, the golden brick describes his station of friend of God, his interiority, and the silver brick his station of prophethood, his exteriority. [The Miraj is the "night journey," during which the Prophet ascended the heavens to meet God.]

13. Annemarie Schimmel, trans. Ekrem Demirli, *Tanrı'nın Yeryüzündeki İşaretleri* (Istanbul: Kabalcı Yayınevi 2004), p. 245.

1st Verse

The letter *mim* is shared by both Muhammed and Ahmed. If the *mim* in Ahmed is removed, it becomes *ahad* [one]. And this is the self-disclosure of the Lord in the servanthood of the Messenger.

So Muhammed is the site of manifestation of revelation. And because Ahmed is the name of the Messenger's reality, the self-disclosure of God's essence in the Messenger, it is divine beauty, love, and the meaning of the Miraj.

He is that Hazret who in being an example has been distinguished from all other creatures and risen to the station of incomparability. He is the source of Lordly Instruction (*maarif*). He is the kindliness of divine mysteries. He is the endpoint of the aims of the desirous. He is the proof for those amazed on the path of God the Truth. He is Muhammed, and in his quality and essence he is Mahmud. He is the Ahmed of what is past and what is to come. Ahmed is the noble name of the Messenger's (s.a.s.) ancient axis. For that reason Hazret Moses (a.s.) said, "My God, make me part of Ahmed's community," and Jesus (a.s.) gave the good news, *"O children of Israel! I am God's messenger to you, confirming the Torah that came before me and giving glad tidings of a messenger who will come after me named Ahmed"* (61:6).

The name Ahmed has the meanings of exceedingly praising (*hamid*) and exceedingly praised (*mahmud*). And some of the great have said he was named Muhammed because of his repetition of praise, and Ahmed with respect to his bearing the flag of praise.[14]

- Hazret Ahmed requested help and strength from God the Truth, and He said: "O Ahmed, what stature can worldly strength and power have? Look at the moon in the sky of the heavens and split its brow, O my beloved! For the people on the face of the earth to obey you is not a difficult thing. I have made the things in the heavens (*orbit and measuring out*) and the skies obey you. That is, in the hand of power I made the angels, the heavens, the moon and the sun powerless and obedient to you. See the moon circling in this orbit and if you wish, split it in two, for I have granted you that level of power and strength and helped you."

And truly he did split the moon with a signal; his quality and effect became manifest in the body of the moon and thus it was ap-

---

14. İsmail Hakkı Bursevî, *Mesnevî Şerhi*, (İnsan Yayınları), p. 434.

propriate to call that age the Age of Ahmed. The sun of self-disclosure of essence and attribute became manifest in that age.[15]

The Messenger, with his essence, separated the material (soul) and meaning (spirit and secret heart) of those who were bound (bağlanan) to him. Thus Lord and servanthood were separated. He made it possible for people to see within themselves the meaning of "He who knows his self knows his Lord." The names of our Messenger Hazret Muhammed in the Quran are the following:[16]

- **Mudaththir:**

The base word is *mutadaththir* and means "one who covers himself."

According to 'Ikrima ibn Abdullah al-Barbari, it means "one who covers himself with messengerhood and maturity of soul": Muhammed who tries to hide the truths given to him from the regard and opinions of the people.[17]

- **Ta-Ha:**

The letter ṭ indicates the name Tahir (*clean*), and the letter h indicates the name Hâdî (*one who guides, who shows the way*).

- **Muzzammil:**

The base word is *mutazzammil*, which means "he who is covered." He may have covered himself or been covered by another.

It has also been said that it means "to take on a burden," from the root *za-mim-lam*. It is said in the fifth verse of the seventy-third chapter of the Quran, "Muzzammil": "We will send down to you a weighty speech."[18]

---

15. Ken'an Rifâî, ed. Kâzım Büyükaksoy, *Mesnevî Hatıraları* (Istanbul: İnkilap Kitapevi 1968), p. 191.

16. Compiler's comment.

17. Elmalılı M. Hamdi Yazır, Hak Dini Kur'an Dili (Istanbul: Feza Gazetecilik 1992), vol. 8, p. 416.

18. Elmalılı M. Hamdi Yazır, Hak Dini Kur'an Dili (Istanbul: Feza Gazetecilik 1992), vol. 8, p. 392-393.

1st Verse

- **Abdullah:**

Servant of God. The word *abd* is made from the verbal noun *ibadet* [worship]. *Ubudiyet* means servanthood.[19]

- The absolute servant worships God for Himself alone and does not have the quality of mastery over any creature. Such a person sees himself as being in need of every thing in the world. This neediness is with respect to his being the same as God the Truth behind one of the name-veils of the world.[20]

- **Mahmud:**

Praised, eulogized.

The Station of Mahmud:

Hazret Muhammed's (s.a.s.) greatest station of intercession, Paradise.

Whatever we take it to mean, it draws attention to the true human being.

"Ya" indicates the name Protector (*Vaki*) and "Sin" indicates the name Peace (*Selam*). That is to say, because I have since eternity without beginning kept you safe (*salim*) from lacks and flaws, I have protected you from the veils of joy and custom (from being ensnared by the customs of human beings). For that reason you have the name Protector. Your innate disposition is peace (*sin*) and your meaning is "one who brings to safety (*selamet*)." Your perfection, born of being, covers all creatures and is the meaning of the Quran, which contains all wisdom. With the Wise Quran and Ya and Sin you are on the path of unification (*tevhid*). Your innate disposition, the perfection of your manifestation, gave safety to all hearts. The entire meaning of God came to occur with Hazret Messenger. The perfection of your preparedness is hidden in the Quran. It is explained in the Quran.[21]

---

19. Elmalılı M. Hamdi Yazır, *Hak Dini Kur'an Dili* (Istanbul: Feza Gazetecilik 1992), vol. 1, p. 102.

20. Suad el-Hakîm, trans. Ekrem Demirli, *İbü'l-Arabî Sözlüğü* (Istanbul: Kabalcı Yayınevi 2005), p. 481.

21. Kemâlüddin Abdürrezzak Kâşâniyyüs Semerkandî, trans. Ali Rıza Doksanyedi, ed. M. Vehbi Güloğlu, *Te'vilât-ı Kâşâniyye* (Ankara Kadıoğlu Matbaası 1988), vol. 3, p. 10.

- You should know, God help you, that by means of the existence of the movement of the heavens God created spirits as directors of bodies limited by time so that chapters of the Quran known to Him might become determinate. When time was first created with the movement of the heavens, God created the spirit of Hazret Muhammed (s.a.s.) as the first governing spirit. Then the rest of the spirits came to be by means of the movement of the heavens. Thus the spirit of Hazret Messenger existed in the Realm of the Unseen before it existed in the Realm of Witness. God announced his messengerhood to him, giving him the good news when Adam was still, as Hazret Messenger said, "*between water and earth.*" Time reached the becoming of a body for Hazret Muhammed (s.a.s.) and spirit's forming of a connection with it through the name al-Batın (non-manifest). (*When his body became existent and spirit joined with it*). At that point the property of time flowed into the name al-Zahir (manifest). Thus Hazret Muhammed (s.a.s.) came into being with his essence as body and spirit. While the authority of all divine law that came into existence by means of messengers belonged to him inwardly at first, now it was his outwardly (*zahirde*) also. Thus although the Lawgiver is one and He is the owner of divine law, in order to explain the difference between the authority of the two names all the divine law put forth by the name Non-Manifest was invalidated by authority of the name Manifest.

Hazret Messenger said, "*When I was a messenger.*" He did not say, "When I was a human being," or, "When I existed." Messengerhood can only be realized through law set down by God. Thus Hazret Messenger, as we have asserted in other sections of our book, was a messenger before the existence of the messengers who have the position of his deputies in this world.

So the cycle of time consists in the Age of Hazret Messenger, which ended with the name the Non-Manifest, and another age that began with the name the Manifest. In this regard Hazret Muhammed says: "*Time has returned to the state of the day God created it.*" This means that while authority belonged to Hazret Muhammed (s.a.s.) inwardly during the first age, in this age it belongs to him outwardly. Authority in the first age belonged outwardly to the those who brought divine law, such as Hazrets Abraham, Moses, Jesus and all the other prophets and messengers.

1st Verse

There are four prohibited months that correspond to the messengers Hud, Salih, Shuayb and Muhammed. These months are Dhu'l-Qa'da, Dhu'l-Hijja, Muharram and Rajab. Because the Arabs follow a lunar calendar, prohibited months become permitted months, and permitted months, prohibited months. When Hazret Messenger came, he returned time to the basis upon which God had created it. Thus the prohibited months were determined in the manner God created them and because of that, Hazret Messenger said in outward speech: *"Surely time has returned to the state of the day God created it."*

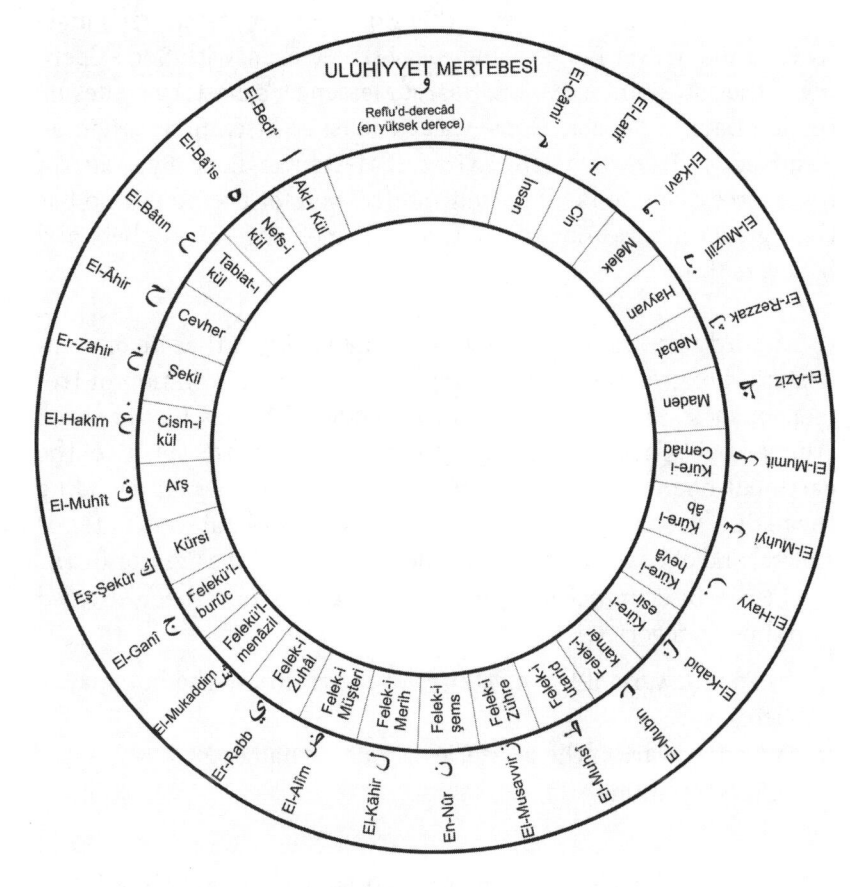

Figure 1. Caption: Figure 1: Niyâzî-I Mısrî,
trans. Süleyman Ateş, İrfan Sofraları
(Istanbul: Yeni Ufuklar Neşriyat n.d.), p. 62.

Thus is the turning of time. God manifested Hazret Muhammed (s.a.s.) as body and spirit with the name Manifest, and he invalidated what God wanted invalidated from the previous divine law, leaving what He wanted left. This is not with regard to the essence but the properties.

Without doubt, just as Hazret Messenger's mastery of knowledge is fixed in the world, so is his mastery of judgment. As he said, "If Moses had gone on living, there would have been nothing he could do but follow me." Hazret Messenger explains the same thing by the descent of Hazret Jesus and his giving of judgments according to the Quran among Muslims. Thus in this world Hazret Messenger's mastery is valid in every regard and every sense. Then, with God's opening of the gate of intercession, Hazret Messenger's mastery on Resurrection Day over other people was established also. Intercession on Resurrection Day will belong to Hazret Messenger alone. By means of his intercession, God will permit intercession for everyone who has the right of intercession, such as angels, messengers, prophets and believers.[22]

- According to tasavvuf, only the human being is the site of manifestation of greatness while being the site of manifestation of tremendousness and the sum of all engendered things (*mükevvenat*). "Human being" means not only a creature living on the sphere of the earth but one possessed of a conscience capable of comprehending the realities of things in the Realm of Eternity, in whatever center or sphere, and of bearing witness to the unity of God the Creator (*bari*).

In the Discriminating Quran the creatures have been divided into three categories.

    a. Those aware of the mysteries of the reality of the human being
    b. Those aware of the mysteries of Adam's names
    c. Talking animals[23]

---

22. Muhyiddîn İbnü'l-Arabî, trans. Ekrem Demirli, *Fütuhât-ı Mekkiyye* (Istanbul: Litera Yayıncılık 2006), vol. 1, pp. 415-418.

23. Şemseddin Yeşil, *Kitab'üt-Tasavvuf; Mesnevi'den Hikmetler* (Istanbul: Ş. Yeşil Kitabevi 1986), pp. 91-92.

1st Verse

Humans have been created by God in the **most beautiful of statures** envied even by the angels, that is, in the most superior form and composition with the most beautiful proportions upon a divine character.[24] "*We created the human being in the most beautiful stature*" (95:4).

When the divine will made necessary the manifestation of the world, or a mirror in which God the Truth would see Himself as Being, this mirror had to be silvered in order for the meaning of seeing to be completely realized. Thus Adam (*the human being*) became this silvering itself, because if not for Adam, the mirror of being would have been dark and blind, and the divine perfection would not have been reflected on a surface in which it could be seen and known. The aim of creation, as we have said, is for God to be known, for his word and perfections to be comprehended. For the mirror to be silvered is for being and its mysteries to be unveiled by the intellect and the light of the heart. And this is possible only for the human being. Thus the human being facing God is the eye's pupil; and facing being, humans are in the position of the beating heart of being and the intellect comprehending the realities of being. ... For that reason they are named "human beings." With them, God the Truth looks upon what He has created and has mercy upon them.

God created the world in order to be known, and only the human being is able to know God with the perfect knowledge worthy of Him. ...

Thus "the human being" is the beginningless newly arrived human being. What is eternal is the continuous joy (*neş'e-i daim*). What gathers together is the separating word. Thus the world is completed with his being. And so the human being is like the "bezel" of the ring on the world's ring. The bezel is the seal and sign that seals the Shah's treasury.

The human being has two aspects. The first is the newly arrived aspect; this is the aspect that has to do with his elemental, bodily form. The other is his eternal and beginningless aspect; this is the aspect that has to do with the human being's divine rank. Thus the human being is both God the Truth (*hak*) and created (*halk*), both beginningless and now coming into being; he has opposing attributes,

---

24. Ken'an Rifâî, *Şerhli Mesnevî-i Şerif* (Istanbul: Kubbealtı Neşriyatı 2000), p. 81.

such as eternal and mortal. Without doubt, because the human being, and indeed all things that exist, have two aspects, they encompass these opposing attributes. These two aspects are "divinity" and "humanity."

The reason why the word "human" both separates and gathers together is that the human being stands as a dividing line between God and the world. For the human being is God's form, and the world is the mirror that this form reflects in itself. And God is the essence of the human form. For that reason the human being is an intermediate realm (*barzakh*).[25] The reason why "human" is "a word that gathers together" is that it brings together all of the divine names in itself as a site of divine self-disclosure.

As long as the human being is in the world, the world is preserved. The perfect human being is the protector of being and the reason for its continuance. The human being is the aim of the creation of the world and when he leaves it the world must cease to exist, that is, the forms of creation must dissolve and return to the divine essence that is their origin. When the cause of manifestation in God the Truth's forms of being is gone, the world that is the sum of these forms will also be removed. The divine essence will abide alone without being manifested in any thing and without being known by anyone.[26]

The human being is a piece of God (*Tanrı parçası*) sent to earth in order to rise to the skies. The human is the self-disclosure and manifestation of divine light on the face of the earth.[27]

- It was with the self-disclosure of God Himself in the human that, spiritually, earth became more luminous than heaven.[28]

- The human comes into bodily existence at the point where the divine substance (*cevher*), having set out from God on the arc of descent and passed through the levels of fire, air, water, earth, vegeta-

---

25. [A *barzakh* stands between and separates two things, while combining the attributes of both.]

26. Ebu'L-Alâ Afîfî, *Fusûsu'l-Hikem Okumaları İçin Anahtar* (Istanbul: İz Yayıncılık), pp. 78-82.

27. Ken'an Rifâî, *Şerhli Mesnevî-i Şerif* (Istanbul: Kubbealtı Neşriyatı 2000), p. 82.

28. Ken'an Rifâî, *Şerhli Mesnevî-i Şerif* (Istanbul: Kubbealtı Neşriyatı 2000), p. 421.

ble and animal, takes its first step on the arc of ascent. The human is the manifestation of the divine substance at that point.

After reaching that point, a person is able to return to his origin, that is, to reach God, in two ways: If he passes away with death, having completed the flow of his lifetime, he will not gain much from this, will not have covered much ground. If he never knew what he was in this realm, his condition in the next world is one of ignorance also.

But if a person meets a perfect human in this world, that is, if a murshid, a spiritual guide, awakens him and he comes to recognize his own substance, he will understand what the object of the profound longing he feels is. He finds God first in the external world and then in himself. The state in which God's being comes to be sensible within a person is called "self-disclosure" (*tecelli*). A person who attains to self-disclosure has attained the secret (*sır*) of looking at creation with God's point of view and seeing God wherever he looks. The divine substance separated from God completes the arc of descent, and in order to do so passes through the states of fire, air, water, earth, vegetable, and animal; at the point where it takes its first step on the arc of ascent the human being aquires existence. The human being is the appearance of the divine substance at that point.[29]

- The true home of God is the human conscience (*vicdan*), the human heart.[30]

The human being is the monument of creation, the masterpiece of creation. Whatever exists in the world exists in the human being. The human being is the Discriminating Book, in which all mysteries are hidden. Only the heart understood the Trust that God charged humankind to uphold; the heart encompassed it. Love was offered to the inanimate things, yet no existent but the human being could bear it.[31]

---

29. Ken'an Rifâî, *Şerhli Mesnevî-i Şerif* (Istanbul: Kubbealtı Neşriyatı 2000), pp. 3-4.
30. Ken'an Rifâî, *Şerhli Mesnevî-i Şerif* (Istanbul: Kubbealtı Neşriyatı 2000), p. 67.
31. Meşkûre Sargut, *Ârifler Bahçesinden* (Istanbul: Seyran İktisâdî İşletmesi 1993), p. 38.

- O heart! Since you are the Sultan of such a clime, know the value of your domain! Be a righteous judge in your country as Solomon was! ... You know that the human body is a symbol of the divine image and God's site of self-disclosure. You should also know the value of having and ruling such a body. Be a Sultan who rules justly over the domain you possess. If you do not, if you allow Satan to steal the ring on your hand, if you enslave that mighty talisman to the soul, your entire sultanate, your good fortune, and your prosperity will be wiped out.

  So, you who lose the greatest of all pleasures, felicities and bounties to the devil of the soul and the pleasures it promises, what you are doing means that your heart will continue to be stabbed full of holes with the dagger of sighs until the Day of Resurrection. If you wish proof of this, then read chapter Ya-Sin of the Gracious Quran. There you will find made plain the disappointments and sighs of those who take the wrong path.

  And if you take an even worse path and say that you are on the right road, that you are not misbelieving and denying, and even though you are, delude yourself, you will be even worse off than they.

  For the scales that you have not employed in the path of God and goodness will weigh your state one day.[32]

- Pour dust on your head, mourn me before I die
Bear in patience and don't mourn me when I die

  At the time when Satan lay in wait unseen
  That was when you should have recited Ya-Sin

  Once your life's taken by Satan's mean assault
  "I take refuge" and the Fatiha lack salt[33]

- **The Five Presences:**
  1. The Realm of Divinity (*Lahut*) (The Realm of the Unbounded Unseen) (*Mutlak Gayb Alemi*): The level of Non-Entification (La

---

32. Ken'an Rifâî, *Şerhli Mesnevî-i Şerif* (Istanbul: Kubbealtı Neşriyatı 2000), p. 526.

33. Mevlânâ Celâleddin Rûmî, trans. Veled İzbudak, ed. Abdülbaki Gölpınarlı, *Mesnevî* (Istanbul: Milli Eğitim Basımevi 1991), vol. 6, vs. 538, 540, 552.

Taayyün). Because this is the station of infinite Oneness (Ahadiyyet), it cannot be understood or perceived.

2. The Realm of Domination (*Ceberut*): The First Entification is the level of the Muhammeden Reality. This is a sacred realm that can be understood by entering into the divine order, experiencing and sharing in it. Abu Talip Makki calls the Realm of Domination the realm of infinity. According to Jurjani, this is the realm of God's names and attributes. According to Ghazali, it is an intermediate realm between the Realm of Kingdom and the Realm of Sovereignty.

3. The Realm of Sovereignty (*Melekut*): The level of the Imaginal (*misal*) Realm, the Realm of Spirits, and the second entification. Ibn Arabi defines it as the Realm of the Unseen. According to Frithjof Schuon, the Realm of Domination is the sky as macrocosm. The microcosm is the created intellect belonging to human beings. The Realm of Sovereignty is the realm directly dominating the physical world. According to Aziz al-Din Nasafi, the Realm of Kingdom has a sensory level, the Realm of Sovereignty an intellectual level, and the Realm of Domination a reality level. In other words, the senses bring a person to the Realm of Kingdom, the intellect to the Realm of Sovereignty, and love to the Realm of Domination. The Realm of Domination is the realm of quiddity, the "whatness" of things. Kingdom and Sovereignty are sites of manifestation for Domination's attributes. Everything that is hidden and essential in the Realm of Domination is manifested in detail in Kingdom and Sovereignty. Kingdom is the realm of opposites, Sovereignty the realm of compatible levels, and Domination the realm of unity. Abd al-Qadir Gaylani writes in his *Risālat-i Ghawthiyya*:[34] Every level between the Realm of Kingdom and the Realm of Sovereignty is divine law (*şeriat*), every level between Sovereignty and Domination is the path (*tarikat*), and every level between Domination and Divinity is reality (*hakikat*). That which can be apperceived with love and the spiritual faculties is the unseen, spiritual, angelic realm.

4. The Realm of Kingdom (*Nasut*) (The Realm of Witnessing/ Kingdom) (*Şehadet-Mulk Alemi*): This world of matter, the realm perceivable by the physical senses.

---

34. A ghawth *is a person from the Realm of the Unseen and a friend of God with whom one takes refuge in time of need.*

5. The Perfect Human Being: The realm that collects within itself all the previous levels.

Ibn Arabi used the word "presence" to mean "the general levels of being and divine and engendered existential realities together with all their self-disclosures in the world."

According to the Sufis who employ manifestation (*sudur*) and self-disclosure theory to explain how the world came to be, beings appear through manifestation from God by becoming more distant and descending from Him in levels. This is termed "descents" (*tenezzülat*). A traveler on the path who wishes to reach God (*who turns toward his own reality*) must go upwards, transcending these descents step by step. The stations on this upward progress are called "presences." The number of presences a traveler can surmount determines his spiritual level and sanctity.

- **Unification (*tevhid*)** [35]:

Unification[36] is to have faith in God's unity. When Junayd-i Baghdadi was asked, "What is unification?" he said: "Unification is for you to know the movement and rest of creatures to be God's action." The Sufis say that unification can only be reached through lived experience, sense and inspiration, not by way of intellect.

1. Unification of Will (*kusudi tevhid*) (disciple's unification, the sincere will that moves the traveler on the path to action, pure intent, resolution) (*vahdet-i kusud*): The binding of servants' wills to God's will; their seeing God's will in every thing. In other words, for God's will and wish to be one and the same as the thing servants will and wish. Here the servants have arrived at a result by bringing their own will to be compatible with God's will. This station is expressed by the formula, "There is no goal, nothing wished, and no desire other than God" (*lā maqṣūda wa lā maṭlūba wa lā murāda illā'llah*).

---

35. [In the following discussion the author equates the term *tevhid* with the term *vahdet*, in the meaning of an action, thus I have translated them both as "unification."]

36. According to Ken'an er-Rifāī, unification means to not ascribe partners to God the Truth. Furthermore, he says, "The unification of exalted and mature persons is to see nothing in creation but God and have transactions only with Him." (Compiler's comment.)

2. Unification of Witness (*şuhudi tevhid*) (the unification special to those mid-way along the path) (*vahdet-i şuhud*): The psychological state in which the servant sees every thing that exists in the world as God's self-disclosure, and sees no one but Him. It shows itself in ecstatic states known as drowning, drukenness, unconsciousness, and victory. When it passes, the traveler sees God the Truth and creation as separate. He repents of the things he said while in that state. In both of these types of unification there is a God-world duality.

3. Unification of being (*vücudi tevhid*) (the unification of the traveler who has reached perfection) (*vahdet-i vücud*): In this phase, and as in that of Will and Witness, unity is accepted with regard to being as well, and the principle that none other but God has true being is adopted. At this highest level of unification the elite servant is an image (*hayal*) before God. There is no third thing between him and God. The person who arrives at the reality of nearness to God, His true oneness, does only what God wants him to.

In unification of witness the traveler temporarily sees everything as one; unification is not in knowledge. But in the unification of being, unification is in knowledge. That is to say, the traveller knows that there is one real being, that it consists in God the Truth's being, and that nothing has real being but God the Truth and His self-disclosures. Unification of witness can be summarized as "There is no witness but God," and unification of being as "There is no being but God." According to those who accept the unification of being, because the level of nearness to God in unification of being is higher than that in unification of witness, a state is produced in the servants such that they know everything but God, even themselves, to be naught. (...)

Just as on a starry night the trembling light of millions of bright stars makes sensitive hearts shiver, and the constellations run to the valley of annihilation when the sun tosses off its purple covering and emerges from its sleeping chamber, so do the caravans of things that once seemed to be flee to the desert of not-being when the real sun rises from the horizon of the heart. In the same way everything but God the Truth becomes naught for the gnostic who has lost himself in His love and witnessing. (...)

According to the Sufis who accept the unity of being and especially to Ibn Arabi, being is one and that being is God the Truth's being.

Things have no other being. Things consist of the forms exterior to them. God is not the things themselves. But with respect to being, He is the entity (*ayn*) of all existents and of everything in a state of manifestation. God is God and the things are the things. The unbounded essence has manifested itself in the form of the things and the world. Things and engendered existents are God's exteriority, and God is in the position of the interiority and spirit of the things and the engendered existents, and no being outside of His being can be imagined.

So being is of two kinds: One is real being, and the other is relative being. It is not possible to comprehend real being. Relative being consists of the determination of real being by its names and attributes without limitation. This is the being that can be comprehended, as can the being of the world and the things in it. Being is the being a person discerns after having passed from the dimension of experiential comprehension to the dimension of comprehension beyond experience.

In unification of being unity is accepted with regard to imagination, will and existence. Each of God's attributes self-discloses in an existent. God, who is single and unbounded being, is the origin of all existents. With the coming to be of each of His attributes, one of the things or events also comes to be. According to the unification of being, the quiddity of the world cannot be included in the quiddity of God. O the contrary, the being of the world depends on God's being. The world possesses being as a gift from God.

> *Although the self-disclosures of the levels of being can be analyzed in several different categories, the general opinion is to accept five or seven. The seven levels are defined thus:*[37]

Regarded from the point of view of the world, "the divine principle" (*ilahi ilke*) is hidden behind veils. The first of these veils is matter. Matter appears as a layer, cover or shell on the outside of the invisible divine world:

1. The level of Non-Entification (*La taayyün*) (*ahadiyyet*): At this level being is incomparable, beyond the ties of attribute and quality and all limitation. This level has been named "the level of oneness" (*ahadiyyet*). This level is God's essence (*kunh*) and reality. There is no

---

37. Compiler's comment.

level higher than this. According to a noble hadith, Abu Razin al-Uqayli asked, "Where was God before He created the world?" Hazret Messenger replied, "In a mist with no air above or below it" (*A realm where nothing has been created and being has not emerged*).

2. The level of the First Entification: This level expresses the first action of the divine essence with respect to its descent into the field of being. At this level God knows His essence, His attributes, His names and all the existent things as a whole, without differentiation between them. Here it is a matter of the first beginning of becoming. Among the names given to this level are "unity" (*vahdet*), the "Reality of Muhammed," and unbounded knowledge. It is accepted that at this level the concept "God" is an all-comprehensive name that brings together within itself all the divine attributes and names, and thus this level is also called the level of divinity (*uluhiyya*).

3. The level of the Second Entification: Because the knowledge-forms are differentiated from one another at this level, they are called unity (*vahidiyyet*), the fixed entities (*ayan-i sabite*) and the human reality (*hakikat-i insaniyye*). The level of the first entification is the interiority of this level, and this level is the exteriority of that one. At this level all of the divine names and attributes are differentiated. It has also been called the level of lordliness. Each knowledge-form entified at this level is the reality of an externally manifest thing, and is its specific lord (*rabb-i hass*) who educates it. For each of God's names there is a servant, and that name is that servant's specific lord. The servant is that name's site of manifestation. The Sufis define the fixed entities as the realities of the possible things fixed in divine knowledge, and they say that these realities have not caught the scent of being. While the Sufis accept the being of the fixed entities in divine knowledge as "the holier effusion" (*feyz-i akdes*), they say that the external manifestation of the possible things, which are the forms of the entities, is the result of "the holy effusion" (*feyz-i mukaddes*). "The holier effusion" means the sensory self-disclosure belonging to the essence that causes the being, or more precisely the fixedness, of the things and the preparedness in things, firstly in divine knowledge and secondly in the moment of determination. "The holy effusion" means the self-disclosure of the names that make necessary the outward manifestation of whatever the preparedness in the entities requires. So the holier effusion is the name given to the fixedness of the fixed entities and their root preparedness in divine knowledge, and the holy effusion is the name given to the outward manifestation of what the fixed entities require and elements connected to them. In other words, in the sense that the fixed entities are the forms of the divine names and attributes, they are divine realities.

4. The level of the Realm of Spirits (*Ervah alemi*): Being descends to the level of spirits after the first and second levels of entification. At this level each of the knowledge-forms manifests as a simple substance. These simple substances have no form or color, nor are they qualified by time or place. For time and space come into being in bodies. These are not bodies. It is not possible for us to comprehend or point to this realm with our sensory organs. At this level each spirit comprehends God the Truth as its self, its own likeness, and its own beginning. The feast of Alast[38] mentioned in the Gracious Quran points to this. Among the names given to this realm are "the Realm of spirit," "the key of being," and "the Realm of Command."

5. The level of the Imaginal Realm (*Misal alemi*): This level is the outward manifestation of the essence in many forms. It is called the Imaginal Realm because every single thing coming from the Realm of Spirits appears in this realm in a non-corporeal form resembling the corporeal form it will take on in the world of bodies. The Jinn are also from this realm. It is a non-elemental realm where meanings are represented by substances (*maddeler*) special to them, and things are realized there before they acquire being on earth. In the Quran it is said: "We sent to her [Mary] Our spirit and it imaginalized to her as a fully created man" (19:17). The connection between the Imaginal Realm and the faculty of imagination is most pertinent and strong. Because imagination is the basis, spirit and life of being. The essence found there is the perfection of the manifestation of the worshipped. One sees that our faith in God consists of the names and attributes belonging to Him. The thoughts we have about God belong to the Imaginal Realm. Imagination is the root of all realms, because God, whom we know through imagination, is the root of all created

---

38. [The feast or pact of Alast is a gathering before the creation of the world at which God asked the spirits of all human beings, "Am I not your Lord?" (*Alastu bi rabbikum*).]

things. Imagination expresses the conceived condition of beings before they come into the state in which our senses can discern them. Other names given to this realm are "the intermediate realm" (*alem-i berzah*), "the presentation of reality" (*arz-i hakikat*), and "the Realm of Sovereignty."

6. The level of the Realm of Witness (*Şahadet alemi*): This level is the self-disclosure of the essence in outwardly visible corporeal forms. Unlike the forms of the Imaginal Realm, these are qualified by division, partition, flammability and vulnerability. It is called the Realm of Witness because it can be seen and sensed with all five senses. Forms in the Imaginal Realm cannot be grasped with the hand and shown to others, but those in the Realm of Witness can be. Ibn Arabi defines Kingdom (*mulk*) as the realm of manifested beings and the Realm of Witness, and defines the Realm of Sovereignty as the Realm of the Unseen. It is said in the Gracious Quran: *"We showed Abraham the sovereignty of the heavens and earth so that he should be among those who attain certain knowledge"* (6:75). Kingdom and Sovereignty are the exteriority and interiority of the same being; the form and the essence. Kingdom is the outward manifestation of creation, and Sovereignty its non-manifest inwardness. In the Gracious Quran it is said, *"He is the Glorious, in whose hand is the sovereignty of each thing..."* (36:83), stating clearly that each thing has a sovereignty. And it is said in the Gospel: *"If a man be not born again, he cannot enter the sovereignty of the heavens."* A person's physicality makes up his kingdom, and his inner faculties and meaning, his sovereignty. In order to see the Realm of Sovereignty one must have the eye of the heart, that is to say, insight (*basiret*). God's friends speak of two births. With the first, a person is born into the Realm of Kingdom. One must be born again in order to enter the Realm of Sovereignty. Other names given to this realm are "the realm of forms," "the realm of generation and corruption," and "the realm of bodies."

7. The level of all-comprehensiveness (*camia*) (The human level) (*mertebe-i insan*): The level at which all of the levels listed thus far are brought together. This level is the human Realm. The human being brings together all levels, whether of light or matter, in himself. But what is meant here is the perfect human being, in the sense understood by the Sufis. Just as the all-comprehensive name has gathered all of God's names within itself, the perfect human being has gathered all of the realms within himself. With the perfect human being, God's names and attributes have been perfectly manifested and the divine will has been realized. Just as all creation is the sum of God's names and attributes, the human being as an exemplar of creation is the sum of God's names and attributes. That is why our Messenger said: *"God created Adam in His own form."* Because all the divine names would be manifested in the human being, he was seen worthy of vicegerency [for God].

The human is a being existing in eternity without beginning (*ezel*) from the point of its existence in God's knowledge. We call this the second entification or the human reality. And there is its appearance at the last level of being, which we call the level of humanity. The human being is the last in manifestation, but the most sublime being. That is to say, the human being existed before anything else in beginningless knowledge as the goal of being. But because the human is the goal of being, its manifestation occurred at the end. The human being has a beginningless essence. Its aspect as the last is the aspect that bears that essence. When it is said that being develops to arrive at the human, it is this aspect of bearing that essence that is meant.

The aspect of being that is turned toward God is determined through the realm of command. The first step of this realm is the heart. Those occupied with the intellect cannot discern or comprehend realities of the realms of command, which are discerned by the heart. All reality and truth is in the Unseen.

The unification of being is a state that is experienced. It cannot be explained as an idea. It is a mystery unveiled only in the worlds a person reaches through love. The intellect has doubts; love has no doubt.

The faith in unification of being attained by the Sufis is not just a lot of talk or something like a fantasy; it is based on an important foundation. And that is the goal of realizing servanthood, in the perfect meaning of the word, by attributing being entirely to God, giving metaphorical beings only the value of which they are worthy and turning with all one's being to the one true being.

What is presented to us by the Sufis when they explicate "the dimensions of becoming" is experiential knowledge acquired by un-

1st Verse

veiling and arrived at by witnessing as a result of the natural capacity and inner experience bestowed upon them by God as a result of the worship they have performed.[39]

---

39. İsa Çelik, "Tasavvuf," *İlmi ve Akademik Araştırma Dergisi*, n. 10 (2003), pp. 159-184.

2. By the wise Quran

Wa'l-Qur 'āni'l-ḥakīm.

- Wise: Possessed of wisdom, imparting wisdom, or very firm, sound.[40]

- God is the one who teaches understanding. The Messenger is the one who teaches judgment and wisdom. In addition, because our Messenger knows the pathways of comprehension, he guides and motivates people to acquire knowledge.[41] What is meant by wisdom is reality. Supposition (*vehim*) and fantasy veil wisdom and reality.[42]

- Because the Quran is the self-disclosure of God's Essence, the Essence's knowledge is wisdom. Supposition and fantasy are reflection (*tefekkür*) about things seen with the eyes. Wisdom is the true faith brought by the things witnessed with the eye of the heart.

- Wisdom is to know the realities of things and to act in accord with the requirements of those realities. ... The Sufis, relying upon the Quranic verse, *"We have sent among you a messenger who is one of you. He recites Our signs to you and purifies you and instructs you in the book and in wisdom..."* (2:151), made a comparison between "wisdom" and "book." They assert that what is meant here by "book" is the teachings of law and judgments belonging to religion, or what they call in general "outward knowledge (*zahir ilim*) and what is meant by

---

40. Elmalılı M. Hamdi Yazır, *Hak Dini Kur'an Dili* (Istanbul: Feza Gazetecilik 1992), vol. 6, p. 399.
41. Ahmed er-Rifâî, ed. Dr. H. Kâmil Yılmaz, *Marifet Yolu* (Istanbul: Erkam Yayıncılık 1995), p. 167.
42. Ken'an Rifâî, *Sohbetler* (Istanbul: Kubbealtı Neşriyatı 2000), p. 623.

"wisdom" is the "inward teachings" of Hazret Messenger, which he bequeathed to his inheritors after him. They call this "inward knowledge." According to them, inward knowledge is none other than the knowledge of the Sufi path and the realities of things and meanings of the Unseen that are known to the Sufis.

According to Ibn Arabi, wisdom is the inward inheritance that all the messengers and friends of God have received from the "Reality of Muhammed," or the knowledge they received from Hazret Messenger's "lamp niche" (*mişkat*).

One of the characteristics of the wisdom we have indicated is that it descends upon the heart, not the intellect. According to the Sufis, the heart is the place of unveiling, the instrument of gnosis, a mirror upon which the meanings of the Unseen are reflected.[43]

The wisdom that descends from the heavens does not settle in the hearts of persons who have these four traits:

1. Those turned toward the world and concerned for tomorrow.
2. Those who love men of state and desire to be near them.
3. Those who love men of the world and wish to be like them.
4. Those who envy the Sufis.[44]

The eighth of the eight gardens in the heart of a man possessed of intellect is wisdom, which is to be honest in word, act, and demand. That is to say, to speak of God, to act for God, and to have desire for none other than God.[45]

• What is meant by the macrocosm (*alem-i ekber*) is intellect. And that is in you. Your body, which you see as smaller than the realm that is rolled up within you, is manifest. If your body had not been considered worthy of the honor of being able to encompass a macrocosm, there would have been no place and no position for it. So try to acquire a great zeal capable of encompassing such a vast realm, the frame of corporeality (*heykel-i cismaniyet*), for the rays and the won-

---

43. Ebu'L-Alâ Afîfî, *Fusûsu'l-Hikem Okumaları İçin Anahtar* (Istanbul: İz Yayıncılık), pp. 69-71.

44. Ahmed er-Rifâî, trans. Dr. Ali Can Tatlı, *Sohbet Meclisleri* (Istanbul: Erkam Yayınları 1996), p. 89.

45. Ken'an Rifâî, *Sohbetler* (Istanbul: Kubbealtı Neşriyatı 2000), p. 451.

ders of the macrocosm rolled up within you are capable of rising to every station and reaching to every presence. All of the transactions of God the Exalted are with the intellect, that is the macrocosm. He gives according to it, forbids and cuts off according to it, and applies loss, union, gathering, positioning, removing and whatever there is, all of it according to the intellect. The performance of all creation also turns on the intellect. The intellect is considered to be one of Hazret Adam's great substances and the first of the creatures to be created. And just so, the Messenger (s.a.s.) informed us of this truth: *"The first thing God created was intellect."*[46]

- Wisdom means to do right in word, deed and desire. If you ask how, it is to speak with God the Truth, to see with God the Truth, and whatever you do, to do it for God the Truth and to desire nothing but God the Truth.[47]

  Wisdom is for servants to speak with God the Truth, to work for God, and to have God as their desire, for their words to be God's speech, that is, the speech God loves, and for the things they do to be the actions God loves and their request to be neither for this world or the Hereafter but only for God the Truth. It means that whatever they say, whatever they do, whatever they want, underneath it all they secretly speak and act seeking God's acceptance and desire only God's beauty.[48]

- This world is the home of wisdom for those who seek examples of what to avoid, and the home of safety for those who comprehend the meaning of wisdom.[49]

- The language of every event relates wisdom to a human being.[50]

- It is the work of the gnostic to see wisdom hidden in every thing.[51]

---

46. Ahmed er-Rifâî, *El-Burhânü'l-Müeyyed* (Istanbul: Erkam Yayınları 1995), p. 53.
47. Ken'an Rifâî, *Sohbetler* (Istanbul: Kubbealtı Neşriyatı 2000), p. 449.
48. Ken'an Rifâî, *Sohbetler* (Istanbul: Kubbealtı Neşriyatı 2000), p. 453.
49. Ken'an Rifâî, *Sohbetler* (Istanbul: Kubbealtı Neşriyatı 2000), p. 435.
50. Ken'an Rifâî, *Sohbetler* (Istanbul: Kubbealtı Neşriyatı 2000), p. 407.
51. Ken'an Rifâî, *Sohbetler* (Istanbul: Kubbealtı Neşriyatı 2000), p. 525.

- Coincidence (*tesadüf*) is the hidden wisdom of life, in which are concealed the requital or recompense for our deeds and actions.[52]

- Religion is wisdom, humanity and character.[53]

- "Changing eyes" means that the eyes of travelers on the path before they were dervishes change after they become disciples and begin the forty days of ascetic practices under the guidance of their murshid, so that their eyes see with the light of wisdom bestowed upon their hearts. Certainly there is a great difference between this eye and the earlier eye. It is this eye they call the eye of insight. Our Master the Messenger of God says: *"If a person practices sincerity for forty days, works of wisdom will manifest from that person's tongue."* Without doubt, the light of a warning example manifests from the eyes of these persons and wisdom flows from their tongues.[54]

- Sustenance is of two kinds, material and spiritual. Material sustenance is riches and every kind of wealth, while spiritual sustenance is knowledge, gnosis and wisdom.[55]

- If one who reads the Gracious Quran reads it thinking he is talking to God, that is reverence for God. With reverence for the people of God and the Sufis, your supposition is removed and your wisdom increased.[56]

Speaking of the difference between someone possessed of knowledge and someone possessed of wisdom:

"While Moses was a great messenger, he had need of Hizir (a.s.). But Hizir did not need him. The wise man does not need the scholar, but the scholar needs the wise man. Hizir imparted more wisdom to Moses than the intellect can comprehend.[57]

---

52. Ken'an Rifâî, *Sohbetler* (Istanbul: Kubbealtı Neşriyatı 2000), p. 479.
53. Ken'an Rifâî, *Sohbetler* (Istanbul: Kubbealtı Neşriyatı 2000), p. 486.
54. Ken'an Rifâî, *Sohbetler* (Istanbul: Kubbealtı Neşriyatı 2000), p. 545.
55. Ken'an Rifâî, *Sohbetler* (Istanbul: Kubbealtı Neşriyatı 2000), p. 591-592.
56. Ken'an Rifâî, *Sohbetler* (Istanbul: Kubbealtı Neşriyatı 2000), p. 646.
57. Ken'an Rifâî, *Sohbetler* (Istanbul: Kubbealtı Neşriyatı 2000), p. 460.

- Our Master the Messenger of God says: *"Do not give wisdom and knowledge to those who are not its people. And if you deny it to those who are, you will oppress the people of that wisdom, the people worthy of it."*[58]

- Our Master the Messenger of God says: "Wisdom is the believer's loss." That is why those who were sites of manifestation of God's beauty in eternity without beginning have wisdom, and even if when they come into the world they become distracted by worldly necessities and forget that wisdom, once they meet a murshid they remember it and awaken. Whatever his religion or school, he who has been the site of manifestation of wisdom, finds it. But he who does not find it, be he turbaned professor or shaykh, will not find it no matter what he does.[59]

- O brother! God's wisdom is flowing over your spirit and your understanding. But this wisdom flowing over you flows from the light of the being of God's Substitutes, that is, from perfect humans, it flows from their riverbeds.[60]

- When human beings come here from the realm of Alast, they lose that Joseph of wisdom[61] and wander the world in search of it. If you try hard and find the Joseph you lost at Alast, you will reach Canaan (*the spiritual realm*).[62]

- *If a gnostic is prepared to understand revelation*
  Each dust-mote's like Gabriel bringing him the command of God[63]

- **Jili says of the Quran that is the mother of attributes:**
  "The essence of the Mother of the Book is one dot where the attributes appear in the divine essence.

---

58. Ken'an Rifâî, *Sohbetler* (Istanbul: Kubbealtı Neşriyatı 2000), p. 473.
59. Ken'an Rifâî, *Sohbetler* (Istanbul: Kubbealtı Neşriyatı 2000), p. 412.
60. Ken'an Rifâî, *Şerhli Mesnevî-i Şerif* (Istanbul: Kubbealtı Neşriyatı 2000), p. 477.
61. [The idea here is that wisdom is as beautiful and beloved as the proverbially beautiful Joseph, beloved of his father Jacob.]
62. Ken'an Rifâî, *Sohbetler* (Istanbul: Kubbealtı Neşriyatı 2000), p. 643.
63. Ken'an Rifâî, *Sohbetler* (Istanbul: Kubbealtı Neşriyatı 2000), p. 31.

"It is like the ink in an inkwell. Letters appear from that ink in the designated order.

"The undotted [Arabic] letters connect the essence with the eternal.

"The dotted letters consist of newly arrived things [*ḥādith*; as opposed to *qadīm*, eternal]. And the things occur on those dots.

"Whenever letters are compounded, words are the result. Those words are the same as created things."

The Mother of the Book consists of the quiddity of the essence's essence. ... The quiddity of the essence's essence is the location of the things and the place where being come to exist. Being exists in the quiddity as the date palm tree exists in the date stone.

"The Book" means unbounded being, of which not-being cannot be imagined.

The Book is made up of chapters, verses, words and letters.

"Chapters" means the essential forms (*zati suretler*) made up of the self-disclosures belonging to perfection. In every chapter there must be meanings special to it that separate it from the others and make it recognizable. An essential task (*sha'n; action and free disposal*) is necessary to every divine form belonging to perfection, and that form is separated from others by that essential task.

Verses consist of the realities of gathering-together (*cem'*). Each verse indicates the divine gathering-together with respect to its special meaning. And that divine gathering-together is understood from the meaning of those verses when they are read.

Every gathering-together requires there to be a name of Beauty and a name of Majesty. The divine self-disclosure in that gathering-together comes into being with respect to that name.

A verse is a single statement made up of words. Gathering-together is witnessing various things with the divine one entity belonging to God the Truth.

(*Divine*) words consist of the realities of created entities. That is to say, they are created things that come into being in the Realm of Witness.

As for letters, they are of two kinds, dotted and undotted:

The dotted letters consist of the fixed entities in divine knowledge.

2ND VERSE

The undotted letters are of two kinds: The first kind does not connect with other letters, although other letters can connect with them.

There are five of these:

1. *alif.* 2. *dal.* 3. *ra.* 4. *waw.* 5. *lam-alif.* These letters are signs of the requirements of perfection.

There are five requirements of perfection:

1. Essence. 2. Life. 3. Knowledge. 4. Power. 5. Will. Just as it would be impossible for four of these to exist without essence, the perfection of the essence would be impossible without these four.

The second type of undotted letter does connect to other letters, and other letters connect to them. In other words, they connect on both sides. There are nine of them:

1. *ḥa.* 2. *sin.* 3. *ḍad.* 4. *ṭa.* 5. *ʿayn.* 6. *kaf.* 7. *lam.* 8. *mim.* 9. *ha.* These nine letters indicate the perfect human being. For just as perfect human beings encompass the five divine presences, they also encompasses the things made of the four elements that belong to being. That is to say, the five qualities that are divine and the brain of the four qualities belonging to the creatures are united in the quality of perfection. The reason why the letters of the perfect human being are undotted is that God the Truth created them in His own form. But, the non-delimited divine realities are separated from the delimited realities belonging to the human being. Because the human being is supported by the Giver of Existence who brings him into being. For that reason the undotted letters (*belonging to the human being*) connect with other letters and other letters are connected to them.

All the letters originate from *alif*, and *alif* originates from the dot [*used above and below letters*].

The necessary being is self-existent and all beings are in need of it, while it has no need of any other. The letters put in the divine book in order to indicate this are the undotted letters. For while the other letters need to connect to *alif, dal, ra, waw* and *lam-alif*, they do not need to connect to the others.

Letters are not words. Because the fixed entities are not under the compass of the word "be."

The fixed entities only come under the compass of the word "be" at the time the entities are given existence. But at their exalted apogee and entification in knowledge engendering does not include them. In this sense the fixed entities are God the Truth, not His creation.

For created things consist of things that come under the word "be." But the fixed entities in divine knowledge are not newly arrived things having this quality. On the contrary, it is through the property of connectedness that they have become included among newly arrived things. The reason for this is that the fixed entities, in their own essences, are the need of newly arrived things for the eternal. The existent entities called letters are included in the divine realm in the realm of divine knowledge, and in the divine realm they are included in God the Truth. In this respect the fixed entities are eternal.

The Quran that is unification, according to Jili:

To read the Quran with its sweet taste, with the delicacy it has that consists entirely of praise, is the Quran's external ornament. But from the point of view of the essence, the Quran has neither totality nor partiality. The taste of the Quran's essence is due to its (*spiritual*) pleasure; it does not have the meaning of tasting a material thing. The Quran is to be able to understand that taste. The entire reading is that taste. The Quran means the self-disclosure named by the unity that consists of the essence in which all qualities are naught. When God the Truth sent down the Quran in this sense to his messenger Hazret Muhammed (s.a.s.), the witnessing of Him in the created things became unity. The meaning of this sending down is that the realities of sublime, exalted "Oneness" in all its perfection became manifest in Muhammed's (s.a.s.) material body. Although descending and ascending was impossible in the realities belonging to "Oneness," descent to Muhammed (s.a.s.) occurred (*in that sublime reality*).

> *When Hazret Muhammed's (s.a.s.) body came into existence with all the divine realities, it became the site of self-disclosure of the name One (Vâhid). The Messenger's interior was unity (ahadiyet) and his exterior was oneness (vahdaniyet). It was termed "descent" because his reality entered a being. His interior is the first creation, of which God said, "I wanted to be known," or only "I was, and there was nothing with Me." It is the reality of Muhammed, that is to say, the essence. His exterior is the gathering of the names and attributes*

> *in one, as in a pomegranate, that is to say, oneness. This self-disclosure ensures his respect for the names and attributes in the created things, because each one of them is in him. But the totality and oneness in him is the expression of the words, "I created you upon the most beautiful character."*[64]

Hazret Muhammed (s.a.s.) became the site of self-disclosure of the divine realities with his body and the polish of unity with his essence. Furthermore, with his essence he is the same as the divine essence. It is because of this that Hazret Muhammed (s.a.s.) said: "*The Quran was revealed to me as a single sentence.*" This tells us that Hazret Messenger is bodily, totally and essentially the site of manifestation of the above-mentioned reality. The expression "Gracious Quran" indicates his being the site of manifestation of that one sentence. This gift is perfect divine generosity and grace. Because God the Truth withheld nothing and transferred all of His munificence onto Hazret Muhammed, as the generosity of the divine essence. But if the Wise Quran means the descent of divine realities, servants must, according to the requirement of divine wisdom, ascend in their essence by levels with divine realities to become sites of manifestation. Because thus is the requirement of divine wisdom in the matter of being in essence a site of manifestation to reality. That is to say, reaching truth must be done slowly. There is no other way to reach that effusion. Because it is not possible for all of the divine realities to appear at once in a human being's body at the beginning of their creation.

However, those who are created for the self-disclosure of sublimity and its root in their innate disposition begin to ascend by the gradual discovery of realities according to the divine order. God the Truth indicated this truth in the Gracious Quran with the verse: "*We have divided it into parts*" (17:106). This property of advancing and ascending by stages never stops and thus the servant continues to progress and God the Truth continues in self-disclosure. Because it is not possible to encompass an infinite thing all at once. For as everyone knows, God the Truth is infinite in Himself.

If one asks the meaning and benefit of the noble hadith, "*The Quran was made to descend to me as a single sentence,*" we can answer in two ways:

---

64. Compiler's comment.

The first answer is from the point of view of command. Because God the Truth commands that the one who self-disclosed its essence to the perfect servant was an infinite essence and descended without separation from the power of the sublime tremendousness in its root.

The second answer is from the point of view of encompassing the complete not-being of creaturely remnants and forms. Because when the divine realities with their traces (*eserleri*) become manifest in all the limbs of the body, it is obligatory for the forms pertaining to creation to become naught.

Thus the condition of the "single sentence" of the hadith is tied to the condition of "to me." According to this, the meaning of the second answer is that with the appearance of the divine realities all of the flaws pertaining to creation cease to be. Another prophetic hadith affirming this states: "*The Quran was made to descend to the sky of earth once. Then God the Truth made it descend to me in parts as verses.*" This second noble hadith can be considered to be the meaning of the first.

Thus the descent of the Quran to the sky of the world once is a sign of the self-disclosure of the reality belonging to the essence. And the descent of the verses in parts indicates, along with the gradual ascent of the servant in the essence, the manifestation of the traces of the names and attributes.

The Quran as referred to in the gracious verse, "*Without doubt it is your Lord who is the Perfect Creator and All-Knowing*" (15:86), consists in the totality of the essence without regard for essential tremendousness and descent. That is to say, it is the unbounded essential unity as the unbounded he-ness that contains the stages, attributes, tasks and their inward significance (*itibar*).

And the unbounded unity mentioned has been termed sheer (*sırf*) essence with all perfections.

It is for this reason that because of this tremendousness the Quran was mentioned with the term "The Tremendous" (*el-Azim*): "*Let it be sworn that We gave you the Seven Repeated Verses and the Tremendous Quran* (58:87). "The Seven Repeated Verses" (*Fatiha*) means the effusion that appears in the servant with the realization of the "Essential Seven Attributes" in the existence belonging to the body.

The gracious verse, "*The Merciful taught the Quran*" (55:1-2), indicates the taste of the Merciful that the servant finds in himself because of the Merciful's self-disclosure to the servant. That taste wins the servant the knowledge of the essence, and then the servant realizes the realities of the attributes. Furthermore, only the Merciful teaches the Quran to the servant. It is impossible to reach the essence without the self-disclosure of the Merciful, which consists of all the names and attributes. Because God the Truth can be known only by way of His names and attributes.

According to Jili, the following can be said of the Quran that expounds separation (fark):

"The Quran is God's essence, and His attributes are the Furqān [discrimination].

"The separation of gathering-together is realization (tahkik).

"The gathering-together of separation is conscience (vicdan).

"The separating (tefrika) and contradiction in the attributes is two gathering-togethers.

"The property of the essence in the unity of unification is the Furqān.

"Because quality is a "Task" inseparable from the divine essence..."

The Furqān consists in the realities of the names and attributes together with varied differentiation. That is, it means that separation appears in God the Truth Himself from the point of view of "the most beautiful names" and "the sublime attributes," because each attribute and name is separated from the others through those differentiations. Because "Compassionate" is different from "Violent," just as "Giver of Boons" is different from "Avenger." The attribute of "good pleasure" is different from the attribute of "wrath" (gazap). There is an indication of this in the sacred hadith, "My mercy preceeds My wrath." The precedent is superior to the antecedent.

The names belonging to the levels are also like that. For example, the level of "Mercifulness" is superior to the level of "Lordliness." The level of "Divinity" is more sublime than all the others.

Thus in this way some of the names are different from some of the others and separation among them becomes manifest.

The level of the divine name "High" (A'lâ) has greater virtue (fazilet) than the names that come after it.

Thus the name "God" has greater virtue than the name "Merciful," and "Merciful" greater virtue than "Lord," and "Lord" greater virtue than "King." And so on with the other names and attributes. The superiority of names and attributes is fixed in their entities. But this does not mean that in anything belonging to them there is an aspect of lack or inferiority.

This matter of superiority rules the other names and attributes required by the entities of the names and attributes. That is why the noble hadith states, "*I take refuge from Your requital in Your forgiveness, and from Your wrath in Your good pleasure. I take refuge from You in You; I cannot praise You as is right.*" As is understood from this hadith, there exists separation in the essence itself. The act of forgiving is superior to the act of punishing. That is why the Messenger of God took refuge from requital in forgiveness, and from wrath in good pleasure. Again, in the hadith the Messenger of God takes refuge from God's essence in His essence. Thus, just as "separation" is manifest in the acts and attributes, it is manifest in the oneness of God the Truth's essence. However much it is the case that there must be no separation in the oneness of the essence, the unification of two antonyms such as "impossible" and "necessary" is due to the strangeness of His tasks (*free disposal and action*). Because in the intellect there exists the expression for and permission to transmit every impossible thing.

You witness every thing in God that is impossible and impermissible to express as among necessary properties with regard to its existence in the essence.

It is due to this subtlety that Imam Abu Said al-Kharrāz (*q.s.*) said: "I knew God by gathering together two contraries."

Do not suppose that God encompasses only the outward and the inward, and the first and the last. On the contrary, just as God encompasses these, He also encompasses the Truth and the creation, the superior and the inferior, the impossible and the necessary, the non-existent and the existent, the limited and however many flawed contraries may exist, all of them to infinity. God the Truth is the one who gathers these together with the essence of His task. His he-ness consists in this.[65]

---

65. Abdü'l-kerîm b. İbrahim el-Cîlî, trans. Seyyid Hüseyin Fevzî Paşa, *İnsan-ı Kâmil* (Istanbul: Kitsan Yayınları), pp. 345-362.

2nd Verse

- According to Hazret Mevlana [Rumi], the best commentary on the Quran is the Quran itself, and the true Muslim is he who is in love with it.[66]

- Ask the meaning of Quran from the Quran
And from one who has set fire to idle want

Who bows low and for the Quran gives his life
So the Quran is the essence of his life

If the rose oil gives its life up for the rose
You can sniff the oil if you wish, or the rose[67]

- They have written many commentaries on the Quran. But few have been able to explicate the goal of the Quran. Everyone has explicated the meaning of "those who have faith" by their own faith. But Hazret Muhammed's faith and its goal are hidden. Everyone has explicated "those who do good works" by their own works. But who has explicated the Messenger's works?[68]

- Muhammed's heart is a book, like the books scribes write on their boards, inside of which God wrote the Quran. Judging from appearances, writing depends on knowledge and a board to write on. But because the Quran was written in Muhammed's heart through Gabriel, Gabriel has the property of a pen. The thing written is eternal, because it is beginningless speech. Both the writer (*Gabriel*) and the written (*Muhammed*), peace be upon him, are creatures, like the Pen and Tablet. Although they are created, the Quran is eternal (*has no beginning*), because it is beginningless speech.[69]

---

66. Hüseyin Güllüce, *Ku'ran Tefsîri Açısından Mesnevî* (Istanbul: Ötüken Neşriyat 1999), p. 111.
67. Mevlânâ Celâleddin Rûmî, trans. Veled İzbudak, ed. Abdülbaki Gölpınarlı, *Mesnevî* (Istanbul: Milli Eğitim Basımevi 1991), vol. 5, p. 256, vs. 3128-3130.
68. Hüseyin Güllüce, *Ku'ran Tefsîri Açısından Mesnevî* (Istanbul: Ötüken Neşriyat 1999), p. 112.
69. Ahmed er-Rifâî, ed. Dr. H. Kâmil Yılmaz, *Marifet Yolu* (Istanbul: Erkam Yayıncılık 1995), p. 169.

- A certain hafiz recites the Quran correctly. Yes! He recites the form of the Quran (*its letters*) correctly. But he has no understanding of its meaning. Actually, if its true meaning were explained to him, he would not accept it and would go on reciting it heedlessly. This is like when a man has a groundhog in hand, and when they bring him a better one he does not want it; it then becomes clear that he does not know what a groundhog is. Someone has told him it is a groundhog, and he has taken it blindly. For example, if you try to give the nut or oil of a walnut to children who are playing with walnut shells, they will not take it. Because they believe that when you take walnuts in hand they make a rattling sound, but the nut and the oil of a walnut does not make any sound. The treasuries and sciences of God are many. If a hafiz recites the Quran knowing it, why would he not take another of God's books in exchange? I explained to someone who was reciting the Quran that the Quran says, *"If the ocean were ink for the words of my Lord, the ocean would run out before the words of my Lord, even if we added another like it to help"* (18:109). The Quran can be written with fifty dirhems of ink. This is a sign of God's knowledge, a part of it, not all of His knowledge. If an apothecary wrapped up some medicine in a piece of paper and you asked him if his whole shop is inside it, that would be stupidity. The Quran existed in the time of Moses, the time of Jesus, and in other times too; the speech of God existed then. But it was not in Arabic. This is what I could not explain. I saw it had no effect on the hafiz and I left him alone. They say that in the time of the Messenger, whoever among his companions memorized a chapter, or half a chapter, would be called a great man and people would point him out, saying he knows a chapter or half a chapter. Because it was as if they consumed the Quran (*they digested it well*). It is truly a difficult thing to eat a half or whole *batman* [30 lbs.] of bread. But if they chew and chew, eventually they can eat a hundred thousand donkey-loads of bread. Did not the Messenger say, "How many read the Quran and the Quran curses them?" This was said of those who recite the Quran without understanding its meaning. But even that is a good thing.[70]

---

70. Mevlânâ Celâleddin Rûmî, trans. Melika Ülker Anbarcıoğlu, *Fîhi mâ Fîh* (Istanbul: Milli Eğitim Basımevi 1985), pp. 128-129.

2ND VERSE

- Hazret Mevlana separates analogy, metaphor and truth, wanting us to understand what is being communicated.

- The Quran informs us about the spiritual states of the great messengers. It shows a person how to acquire their states. The messengers are the ones who know the secrets of the sea of divine truth. The Quran brought by the greatest of the messengers is the book that brings to light all the secrets beyond the dome of the sky.[71]

- Abraham (a.s.), known as the Sincere Friend of God, said, "I do not love those that set" (*stars, moon and sun*; 6:74-82). When swearing an oath by God the Truth, how could he intend to swear by something that dies?[72]

  The Quran was sent down to Muhammed (s.a.s.) as spirit.[73]

---

71. Ken'an Rifâî, *Şerhli Mesnevî-i Şerif* (Istanbul: Kubbealtı Neşriyatı 2000), p. 214.
72. Hüseyin Güllüce, *Ku'ran Tefsîri Açısından Mesnevî* (Istanbul: Ötüken Neşriyat 1999), p. 95.
73. Ahmed er-Rifâî, ed. Dr. H. Kâmil Yılmaz, *Marifet Yolu* (Istanbul: Erkam Yayıncılık 1995), p. 163.

3. You are indeed among the messengers of God.
'Innaka la mina'l-mursalīn.

- **Messenger (resul):** A person inspired with revelation (*vahy olunan*) and responsible for communicating that revelation (*vahy*) to others.[74]

- **Messengerhood:** The name given to the face[75] between the servant and other creatures. God created only Muhammed as the messenger to black and red, distant and near, so he was sent as messenger to the other creatures as well. Mercy to the worlds depends on this wisdom. Every messenger is a messenger of divine law. Every prophet (*nebi*) with a divine law is a messenger of sanctity (*the turning of the servant who is God the Truth toward creation*).

   Sanctity (vilayet): The name given to a specific face between his Lord and His servant.

   The prophethood of sanctity: The name given to the face of the friend of God (*veli*) that is shared between God the Truth and creation.

   The prophethood of divine law: The name given to the face of possessing independence in worship performed with his soul without need of anyone.[76]

- A friend of God (*veli*) is a person having perfection, wisdom and graciousness who acts with God's book and the sunna of the Mes-

---

74. Elmalılı M. Hamdi Yazır, *Hak Dini Kur'an Dili* (Istanbul: Feza Gazetecilik 1992), vol. 6, p. 496.

75. [Here and immediately below, the term "face" (*wajh*; *yüz* in Turkish) almost has the meaning of "interface," though not literally; a "face" is the side or aspect of something that faces something else, interrelating the two.]

76. Abdü'l-kerîm b. İbrahim el-Cîlî, trans. Seyyid Hüseyin Fevzî Paşa, *İnsan-ı Kâmil* (Istanbul: Kitsan Yayınları), vol. 2, p. 415.

senger of God. The highest level of sanctity is to do the things that Hazret Messenger (s.a.s.) did, transmit the things he said, and acquire his spiritual states.[77]

- That which was imparted to Hazret Muhammed (s.a.s.) came about through the instruction and communication of Gabriel (a.s.), whose knowledge has beginningless source. Gabriel's instruction means divine instruction. Because God the Truth teaches the angels without intermediary, they serve as intermediaries between God and His messengers. The messengers are intermediaries between the angels and us. Our Messenger did not impart the Quran in person; he is but the site of its reception. His duty is to receive the speech that God the Truth imparts.[78]

The prophets invite and lead. The friends of God follow them in a beautiful way. It is impossible for the follower to be superior to the followed, or the led to be superior to the leader.[79]

- He is God's sharp sword, the translator who gives voice to God the Truth's realities, the beloved of God who is the only one to lay down commands. ... He is such a master that God Most High has loaded Hazret Messenger with the messengerhood burden He sent to slaves and free men, black and white, Arab and Persian, even the Jinn. Hazret Messenger was burdened with this burden alone in that hard and unyielding society, without any helper. First he removed the intemperance in people's hearts and imparted faith and security to them. Then he put forth the principles by which they could reach the path of reality and ensured that these were firmly ingrained in their hearts.[80]

The Messenger of God is a greatest of the great human beings who united both the levels of prophethood and sanctity in himself and

---

77. Ahmed er-Rifâî, trans. Dr. Ali Can Tatlı, *Sohbet Meclisleri* (Istanbul: Erkam Yayınları 1996), pp. 64-65.
78. Ahmed er-Rifâî, ed. Dr. H. Kâmil Yılmaz, *Marifet Yolu* (Istanbul: Erkam Yayıncılık 1995), pp. 168-169.
79. Hucvirî, ed. Süleyman Uludağ, *Keşf'ul-Mahcûb Hakikat Bilgisi* (Istanbul: Dergah Yayınları 1996), p. 397.
80. Ahmed er-Rifâî, trans. Dr. Ali Can Tatlı, *Sohbet Meclisleri* (Istanbul: Erkam Yayınları 1996), p. 65.

became so annihilated in God that every state and action issuing from his hands, his tongue, and his eyes can be considered to be in reality God's states and actions.[81]

- A friend of God is a person who frees himself of all duality by making himself The Truth with The Truth, uniting with God in sensing, thinking and behavior. A prophet (*nebi*) is a perfect human who has been given the duty of calling people to God the Truth, showing the way and drawing them away from infidelity (*küfür*) and defiance.[82]

- The prophet has received a command to reveal his sanctity to people and warn them.

- The messenger became an envoy in order to bring his people to God the Truth. He was made an envoy to save those servants whose hearts are in the darkness of denial and ignorance from separation and the limitations of partial names, calling them to unification and the light of faith and the love of God and the essence of God the Truth, who owns the total names and attributes, and guiding them to discriminate between truth and falsehood.[83]

- He does all of these things by bringing the divine law. The inwardness of messengerhood is sanctity. Messengerhood is specific and sanctity is general. A person who has the quality of messengerhood also has the quality of sanctity. The messenger is turned toward creation, and sanctity toward the Creator. Messengerhood means to inform, and sanctity means intimacy.[84]

- Our Messenger's attribute was servanthood. When the attribute of lordliness became a helper to servanthood, its name became "self-subsisting" and its meaning "eternal." The divine decree was

---

81. Compiler's comment.
82. Ken'an Rifâî, *Şerhli Mesnevî-i Şerif* (Istanbul: Kubbealtı Neşriyatı 2000), p. 48.
83. Ken'an Rifâî, ed. Kâzım Büyükaksoy, *Mesnevî Hatıraları* (Istanbul: İnkilap Kitapevi 1968), pp. 159-160.
84. Azîz Nesifî, trans. M. Murat Tamer, *Hakikatlerin Özü* (Istanbul: İnsan Yayınları 1997), p. 25.

self-disclosed: *"And God will defend you from men"* (Quran 5:67). You see that the dynasties of many kings have ceased to exist and their rule changed hands while their followers went on. The attribute of lordliness eradicates the attribute of kingship and it ceases to be in them, and they go away.[85]

- True servanthood is such an attribute that its reality (*hak*) is to be cut off from everything but its master. Servanthood is to abandon everything, whole and part, less and more. Servanthood maintains the limit in the nature of Adamhood. As long as the servant does not reach the level of freedom, he cannot be a perfect servant. True freedom is to be completely free of all that is other than God.[86]

- Messengerhood is a great realm that gathers all realms within itself. The messengers are in reality the vicegerents of God on earth and they have sublime aspiration, heavenly hearts and divine mysteries. They have completely divested themselves of all that is other than God. They are commanders leading creation to God the Truth.[87]

- Someone came to Hazret Mustafa and said to him, "I love you." The Messenger said, "Gather your wits! Do you know what you are saying?" The man then repeated, "I love you." Hazret Mustafa said, "Gather your wits! Do you know what you are saying?" and the man replied, "I love you." Then Hazret Mustafa said, "Then be steadfast in that, for now I am going to kill you with my own hands. Woe to you!"

In the time of Mustafa (s.a.s.) a man said, "I don't want your religion. Take this religion back. I haven't had a day's peace since I entered your religion. I lost my property, lost my wife. My child died. There is no one left who respects me. My power and sexual desire are exhausted." The Messenger said, "God forbid! Wherever our religion has spread, it does not return without wrenching a man from his roots and destroying everything he has. *"None will touch it but those*

---

[85]. Ahmed er-Rifâî, ed. Dr. H. Kâmil Yılmaz, *Marifet Yolu* (Istanbul: Erkam Yayıncılık 1995), p. 89.

[86]. Ahmed er-Rifâî, ed. Dr. H. Kâmil Yılmaz, *Marifet Yolu* (Istanbul: Erkam Yayıncılık 1995), p. 80.

[87]. Ahmed er-Rifâî, ed. Dr. H. Kâmil Yılmaz, *Marifet Yolu* (Istanbul: Erkam Yayıncılık 1995), p. 141.

who are clean" (56:79). It is such a beloved that if there is so much as a hair left of your love for yourself, it will not show you its face nor will it allow you near it. In order for your friend to show you its face, you must be weary of yourself and the world and be an enemy to yourself. Our religion does not let go of a heart where it has taken up residence until it brings that heart to God the Truth and separates it from everything that is not of use to our religion."[88]

---

88. Mevlânâ Celâleddin Rûmî, trans. Melika Ülker Anbarcioğlu, *Fîhi mâ Fîh* (Istanbul: Milli Eğitim Basımevi 1985), pp. 179-180.

4. On a straight path.
'Alā ṣirāṭin mustaqīm.

- "Ya" indicates the name Protector (Vaki) and "Sin" indicates the name Peace (Selam). Because I have since eternity without beginning kept you safe (*salim*) from lacks and flaws, I have protected you from being ensnared by the customs of human beings. For that reason you have the name Protector. Your innate disposition is peace (Sin) and your meaning is "one who brings to safety (*selamet*)." Your perfection, born of being, covers all creatures and is the meaning of the Quran, which contains all wisdom.

  Wise Quran, because of Ya and Sin you are on the path of unification (*tevhid*). The entire meaning of God came to occur with Hazret Messenger. The completion of your manifestation has given safety to all hearts. The perfection of your preparedness is hidden in the Quran and has been explained there.

  Because God is Exalted (*aziz*) and Compassionate He sent down your meaning, which is gathered together in you, in a differentiated form in the Quran, so that it can be discerned. That is why the Quran is wise; it is the totality of wisdoms.[89]

- The straight path is the way of witnessing that belongs to the One (*ahad*) that consists of God the Truth's self-disclosure with His essence to His essence.[90]

---

[89]. Kemâlüddin Abdürrezzak Kâşâniyyüs Semerkandî, trans. Ali Rıza Doksanyedi, ed. M. Vehbi Güloğlu, *Te'vilât-ı Kâşâniyye* (Ankara Kadıoğlu Matbaası 1988), vol. 3, p. 10.

[90]. Abdü'l-kerîm b. İbrahim el-Cîlî, trans. Seyyid Hüseyin Fevzî Paşa, *İnsan-ı Kâmil* (Istanbul: Kitsan Yayınları), vol. 1, p. 425.

- Everything seeks a way to enter the heart of a perfect human being and longs to reach its root by way of the straight path.[91]

- The shortest path is to say constantly, "God is my Lord," and to know everything as coming from God and to see God the Truth everywhere.[92]

- A path is a line born of the connection of dots. It is a straight (*doğru*) line. But this straightness does not mean it is a geometrical line. It is a straightness we obtain by connecting the dots of the most correct (*doğru*) things in every event.[93]

- One day Anas said: "O Messenger of God! We have believed in the Quran you brought, we have believed in you. Do you fear God too?" Our Master the Messenger said, "Yes, I also fear God." Anas asked, "Why, O Messenger of God?" He said, "*Because our hearts are between God's two fingers of power. He turns them every which way He wishes, and guides those He wishes to the straight path, that is why.*"[94]

    It is for this reason that our Master always said: "*O my Lord, fix my heart upon the straight path!*" And, "*O my God, who turns our hearts and eyes in the direction He wishes, fix my heart upon the straight path!*"

- The shortest path is to choose the heart of a perfect human being. Because everything reaches God from the heart of a perfect one. Everything, everything, finds reunion with God by entering his heart. Vegetal, animal, human, all reach God by the same path.[95]

- All of the names, all of the servants, are gathered together only in the one center of the name "Allah," that has gathered all the names and attributes in itself. The straight path of each creature, each dust-mote, is to be drawn to its Lord. But the straightest path is the straight path of the Muhammeden site of manifestation in "Show

---

91. Ken'an Rifâî, *Sohbetler* (Istanbul: Kubbealtı Neşriyatı 2000), p. 183.
92. Ken'an Rifâî, *Sohbetler* (Istanbul: Kubbealtı Neşriyatı 2000), p. 617.
93. Haluk Nurbaki, *Yâ-Sîn Sûresi Yorumu* (Istanbul: Damla Yayınevi 1999), p. 12.
94. Ken'an Rifâî, *Sohbetler* (Istanbul: Kubbealtı Neşriyatı 2000), p. 66.
95. Ken'an Rifâî, *Sohbetler* (Istanbul: Kubbealtı Neşriyatı 2000), p. 616.

4TH VERSE

us the straight path" (*'ihdina'ṣ-ṣirā'ṭul-mustaqīm*; Quran 1:6), that is to say, unification.[96]

• A person who finds the light of guidance, cleanses his heart of the dirt of nature and humanity and frees himself of all other than God and relations with the world is said to possess straight direction.[97]

• *"Without doubt God loves those who do battle in his path in ranks, like buildings bound together with lead"* (61:4). That is, no crack can appear in those ranks, because leaving a chink means to let devils in, but the path is one and that is God's path.

Whoever does not form ranks and do battle in this way on this outward path of God's cannot be among the people of God. In the same way, the rows of those praying in congregation (*in tight formation with people standing right next to one another*) are ranks formed in the way of God. Only then is the path of God in the true sense clearly visible. Whoever does not pray this way and leaves gaps in the row, he has tried to cut off God's path and has destroyed the true being of God's path and has cut it off. That is why God wants His servants to behave in the way He has specified. He wants this in order to add them to the group of those who create and do. In this regard God has said: *"God is the most beautiful of creators"* (23:14). God's path can only be this way, as in the lines made up of dots so that there is no gap among those dots that could allow that line to be cut. Then the shape of the line appears perfect. The rows formed in prayer are the same way. For God's path to be apparent there, those praying in a congregation must line up right next to one another tightly in a single row. To be sure, this requires a number of people to be present. And that means God's blessed and sublime "beautiful names" holding tightly on to one another. When the names hold on to one another in this way they manifest the path of creativity. Thus the attribute of Alive (Hayy) is interlocked with the attribute All-Knowing (Alim). There is no room between them for another name, there is no gap. The attribute Desiring (Mürid) is next to All-Knowing, then comes Nurturer (Mukit), then Justly Distributing (Muksit), then Governing (Müdebbir), then

---

96. Ken'an Rifâî, *Sohbetler* (Istanbul: Kubbealtı Neşriyatı 2000), pp. 122-123.
97. Ken'an Rifâî, *Sohbetler* (Istanbul: Kubbealtı Neşriyatı 2000), p. 91.

Differentiating (Mufassil), All-Provider (Rezzak), then Bringer to Life (Muhyi). This is how the divine names make a row so that the "path of creativity" made of the attributes lined up side by side may come to be. Once this path is made, there is no need to add anything else to the line of names. Thus the work of creating is determined with these divine names, or rather with their being lined up next to one another. This is how they must be for creation to be realized. In the work of creation the divine names are continuously in force; it is only in this way that they can be comprehended.

In the tarikat this is called "assuming the traits of God with the names." These divine names are manifested in the servant and become evident, just as in their manifestation when they come together continuously side by side to form the Straight Path. If there is a space between them in the act of creation, God's Path is lost.

Human beings taken in themselves also form a line in everything that puts them in motion. Therefore they perform all of their actions for God's sake; they give no place in their actions to anything but God, and thus no one can dissuade them from those actions, no one can turn them away from their path. For that reason the eyes of enemies are always turned upon them. They continuously watch all that they do, hoping to find a gap through which they can enter.

Every action that is performed is a "line," because that action is the sum of the divine names, the glorified attributes, and many actions. Thus the matter intensifies, grows bigger, and complex forms appear in the world. Two lines form a plane, and two planes form a body. And each body, in order to represent a perfect form consisting of one essence and seven attributes, has eight elements. Whoever forms his own "row" in this continuity, his own line, will become one of the creators.[98]

- The Arabic word ṣirāṭ means "path." The letters *qaf, waw* and *mim* are two roots: The first means "a society of humans" and the second, "tremendous" and "to stand erect" or "to be erected." From the first comes the word *qawm*, meaning tribe, race nation. From the other comes the verb form *qāma*, meaning, "he stood up." *Qawma* means "to

---

98. Muhyiddin İbnül'l-Arabî, trans. Mahmut Kanık, *İlahi Aşk* (Istanbul: Insan Yayınları 1998), pp. 107-109.

be set up once" as in *qawwamtu al-shay'a*, meaning, "I erected something and raised it up."

In the Quran the word *ṣirāṭ* means "path" and it acquires connotations from adjectives that qualify it: *"We chose them and We guided them to a straight path"* (6:87). *"Bring up the wrongdoers and their wives, and the things they worshipped other than God, and lead them to the path to Hell"* (37:22-23).

The word is also specifically used unqualified, in which case it indicates the straight path: *"Those who do not believe in the Hereafter turn away from the path"* (23:74).

The "straight path" means a road thinner than a hair and sharper than a blade. On the Day of Judgment this road goes from the Resurrection across Hell to reach Paradise. The believer crosses this bridge by means of the light in front of him. *"And if We wished, we could have blotted out their eyes. They would have groped for the path, but how could they have seen?"* (36:66)

The *ṣirāṭ ul-mustaqīm* means "path." This path is associated with attributes according to the divine level; in relation to humankind it is a spiritual, dynamic path to God. *"There is no living creature whom He does not have by the forelock. Without doubt my Lord is on a straight path"* (11:56). *"So follow me; I will guide you to a path that is level"* (19:43).

The path that you cross over and that God the Truth fixes your feet upon until you reach Paradise is the path of God (*ṣirāṭ al-hudā*). You yourself have built that path by means of your outward and inward wholesome actions during your worldly life. On Resurrection Day it begins at the Gathering (*haşır*) and stretches over Hell as a bridge perceptible to the senses that reaches to Gate of Paradise. When you see it, you understand that it is the product of your actions. You also understand that during your worldly life that bridge was a bridge suspended over the hell of your nature.

What emerges from the text is this: Human beings will be gathered together at the Gathering and will separate themselves between Paradise and Hell. A bridge will definitely be necessary in order to get to Paradise. That bridge is people's actions during worldly life. So when their good actions are many, the bridge grows wider and it is easy and comfortable to get across. According to Ibn Arabi, the straight path means "God's path" (*ṣirāṭ al-lah*), in other words, the path leading to God. In this theory unity is fundamental and the basic characteristics the word "path" loses by being associated with God are obvious. Here all roads or paths are straight for those who walk them and all paths lead to God. And for that reason the number of paths increases according to the number of creatures. The path of God is the straight path. It is the general path where all things take place and which leads the servants, wretched and felicitous, to God; because it has been attributed to the name God, which gathers within itself all the divine names, contradictory and not contradictory.

God's path is the path upon which all things take place and are led to God. For that reason all judgments laid down by divine law and by intellect enter in here. This path leads to God and includes good and bad people. This path is the path of which the folk of God say: "The paths leading to God are as many as the souls of creatures." Because God gathers within Himself all the names, contradictory and not contradictory.

The Arabic phrase *ṣirāṭ al-rab* means the Lord's path, but from the point of view of the names. The Lord's path seeks the one whose Lord it is in order to make that one straight in the light of divine law.

Your Lord's path is indicated in the verse: *"Those whom God wills guided, he opens their breast to Islam; those whom He wills straying, He makes their breasts closed and constricted, as if they would climb to the skies"* (6:125). This means that they would leave their own nature, and no thing can leave its truth. This path is named the Lord's path because it requires one whose Lord it is, and it makes that one straight. He who leaves that path has strayed and lost direction. The Lord's path depends upon divine law. When the prescriptive command is removed, it no longer has any true existence, and so this arrival will be arrival at divine mercy.

The path of exaltation (*ṣirāṭ al-ʿazīz, ṣirāṭ al-ʿizza, ṣirāṭ al-tanzīh*) is the path indicated in the verse: *"The way of the Exalted, the Praised"* (14:1). Only those who have, through tasting, removed their souls in one or in every sense from lordliness and mastership can reach it. Such a person is possessed of exaltation in the sense of being, behind the name-veil, the same as God the Truth. And this is the path of the Exalted, in which no creature has any possibility of knowing him or herself. Because this is the path of God which God brings down upon

His creatures. On this path God is with us wherever we may be. This path is a path of descent; no creature can rise up to it. If a creature could reach it, it would not be Exalted. God the Truth has descended to us with ourselves, and so the characteristic is not for Him, it belongs to us. In that case we are the path itself. Since the perfect human being is the path of the exalted, God the Truth descends specifically to him or her. In reality gnostics travel only in God. So God is their path, and this is their divine law. I am bound to that path, and He is bound to us: He is my path, and I am His path. God is on the path of the Exalted; because He is the Creator, and so no creature can reach Him.

With the word "Creator" it is understood that the path of the Exalted is a path no creature can reach. This is the path of creating. Thus in manifestation and self-disclosure the creatures are God the Truth's path. Since human beings are the most capable site of manifestation and self-disclosure, and the goal of the world's coming to be, they are the path of the Exalted. The specific path (*ṣirāṭ-i khass*) or Path of Muhammed is the law of Muhammed (s.a.s.), and that is the Gracious Quran.

The specific path is the Messenger's path and is dedicated only to him. This path is the Gracious Quran, God's firm rope, the comprehensive divine law. *"This is My straight path; follow it, and do not follow ways that will scatter you from His way"* (6:153). What is meant here is the path belonging to the Messenger.[99]

---

99. Suad el-Hakîm, trans. Ekrem Demirli, *İbü'l-Arabî Sözlüğü* (Istanbul: Kabalcı Yayınevi 2005), pp. 563-566.

5. It is a revelation sent down by the Exalted, the Compassionate.

Tanzīla'l-'azīzi'r-raḥīm

- The word *tanzīla* in the verse means "to appear in a mirror," "to penetrate and spread throughout existence," "effect" (*etki*), "free disposal" and other "likening," "representation," etc.

God the Truth has real being, and this being belongs to Him in His essence. God also has dependent being, which is the being in the entities of the possible things (*mumkinat*). Compared with God the Truth, this being is like a shadow that spreads throughout the other beings and with God's name, the Manifest, gives them their existences. In its outward aspect the world is like a shadow; its inward aspect and the substance that keeps it in place is "the Breath of the Merciful," which with its sublime and inferior parts opens out in the forms of being.

But the creation, that is to say the outward realm, is in a continuous process of changing and becoming other, or being re-created. God the Truth is in the state He has always been since eternity without beginning. When Ibn Arabi speaks of the creation of the world he does not mean creation from nothing or creation of the world at a specific time. According to him, creation is the continuous divine self-disclosure. God the Truth is manifesting in countless forms. Despite the multitude of manifestations, He never repeats Himself. Because the relationship of the divine essence to each one of the forms of being is different from its relationship to the other forms.[100]

- As Hazret Muhyiddin Arabi said, "We were huge letters. That is to say, we were we. We broke off from one another and separated. Then

---

100. Ebu'L-Alâ Afîfî, *Fusûsu'l-Hikem Okumaları İçin Anahtar* (Istanbul: İz Yayıncılık), p. 50.

we united again. And now it is as it was (*kamā kān*), we are we." The snow, rain or hail that falls from the sky, or the streams and rivers, all flow into the sea. But sometimes they cannot; they evaporate before they reach the sea and then become drops and fall as rain again. That is to say, they do not succeed in completing the arc of ascent after the arc of descent. If they reach the sea, then there remains no stream-ness, no river-ness, no ice-ness...[101]

- " (Muhammed) *is Messenger with the name Exalted; it grieves him that you should suffer. He is very fond of you; he is clement and compassionate to the believers*" (9:28) [sic]. Because the sorrow of requital has not been mixed into Hazret Messenger's mercy... Thus he became a mercy to all the worlds.[102]

- The word "exalted" (*'azīz*) in the verse means "valuable," "honored," and "always superior." It comes from the root *'izz*, meaning "to be so valuable and honored as to have no equal or like," "to be powerful and undefeatable." "Exalted" is the antonym of "contemptible" (*zelil*), meaning weak and powerless, and it means that God's power and strength is beginningless and does not change, unlike that of created things. Love of Him is also most sublime; but this sublime love of the endless beauty of the divine splendor also entails the greatest dependence.

  God has many servants who are exalted, beloved and loveable, and He pursues them. He does for them everything expected of a lover. Just as a lover says, "God willing, we will attain our desire," God most High says, "If my beloved wills it so."[103]

- The word "compassionate" (*rahim*) in the verse is an adjective indicating a mercy that distinguishes between beings. In other words, here God the Truth has expressed the more specific mercy He will show to those who believe in Him. This is an order of creation. Because to show

---

101. Ken'an Rifâî, *Sohbetler* (Istanbul: Kubbealtı Neşriyatı 2000), p. 31.

102. Abdü'l-Kerīm ibn Ibrahim al-Jīlī, trans. Seyyid Hüseyin Fevzi Paşa, *Besmele'ni Şerhi* (Istanbul: Kitsan Yayınları), vol. 1, p. 421.

103. Mevlânâ Celâleddîn Rumî, trans. Meliha Ülker Anbarcıoğlu, *Fîhi Mâ Fîh* (Istanbul: Milli Eğitim Basımevi 1985), p. 157.

5th Verse

a special mode of mercy to those who believe and thus observe goodness and beauty will be to show the differences between good and evil, it is definitely expected from a power that educates and develops the worlds. If not, there would have to be no difference in being between good and evil, light and dark, Moses and Pharaoh, and such a thing is the mystery of being and life and the reality of perfection.[104]

- "Compassionate" is more specific than "Merciful," and "Merciful" is more general than "Compassionate." The mercy that comprehends and includes all things is the effusion of the name Compassionate. The mercy specific to those who are wary of God and pay the zakat tax issues from the effusion of the name Compassionate.

In sum, the name Merciful comprises every kind of mercy, wherever it may be, in whatever condition and with or without requital attached to it. But the name Compassionate is not like that, because it is specific to the mercy that does not have requital in it. For that reason it is more likely for the name Compassionate to emerge in the Hereafter. Because it is impossible that the sorrow of requital should mix with the boons of Paradise. It is this effusion that is exclusively the self-disclosure of the name Compassionate.

In his noble hadith,"*The health of my community is in one of three things. In a verse of the Quran, or in licking honey, or in cauterizing with fire. But I do not wish for my community to be cauterized with fire,*" Hazret Messenger said he did not wish his community to be cauterized with fire, and because of that God the Truth gave him the name "Compassionate" in the Quranic verse, " (*Muhammed) is Messenger with the name Exalted; it grieves him that you should suffer. He is very fond of you; he is clement and compassionate to the believers*" (9:28).[105]

- "Compassionate" means one who himself teaches repentance and then forgives, without revenge, without reproach, without shaming.

When "compassionate" is mentioned together with "exalted" as the Compassionate Exalted, the meaning becomes clearer. The

---

104. Yaşar Nuri Öztürk, *Kur'an'ın Temel Kavramları* (Istanbul: Yeni Boyut 1994), p. 417.

105. Abdü'l-kerîm b. İbrahim el-Cîlî, trans. Seyyid Hüseyin Fevzî Paşa, *İnsan-ı Kâmil* (Istanbul: Kitsan Yayınları), vol. 1, pp. 420-421.

self-disclosure of God's infinite love and mercy manifests to one who loves that Beloved with the joy of faith and takes refuge in His sovereignty with great respect.[106]

> To meet difficulties well is the self-disclosure of the name Compassionate. To be able to see Beauty in Majesty, and for Majesty to not even seem to be Majesty, originates in the self-disclosure of the name Compassionate. When people are under special protection the ugliness of things is not visible to them.[107]

Ta-Ha.

O Muhammed! We did not send down the Quran to distress you, but as an admonition to those who fear God,
A revelation from Him who created the earth and the heavens on high.
The Merciful rules upon the Throne (20:1-5).

It is a descent from the Compassionate Essence which, to prevent you from hindering the Quran hidden within your secret heart from discriminating and manifesting clearly upon your heart's site of manifestation, dominates the attribute of your selfhood and your soul's configuration and subjugates them with its power, and makes the Quran clear to you with the self-disclosure of the perfection of all the attributes. The Muhammeden Reality (secret heart of the Compassionate Exalted) is the reality of God's self-disclosure in human beings.[108]

- "Merciful" is a proper name with a generally comprehensive meaning, while "Compassionate" is a common noun with a specific meaning. The Merciful is one who nurtures everyone. The Compassionate is one who causes believers to have an inner life of peace and success. The Merciful brings one to a state of comfort through acts of goodness; the Compassionate illuminates one with spiritual lights and brings one to peace. The attribute "merciful" shows itself through self-disclosures, and the attribute "compassionate" through the kindness of paying attention to someone. The attribute "merci-

---

106. Haluk Nurbaki, *Yâ-Sîn Sûresi Yorumu* (Istanbul: Damla Yayınevi 1999), p. 12.
107. Compiler's comment.
108. Kemâlüddin Abdürrezzak Kâşâniyyüs Semerkandî, trans. Ali Rıza Doksanyedi, ed. M. Vehbi Güloğlu, *Te'vilât-ı Kâşâniyye* (Ankara Kadıoğlu Matbaası 1988), vol. 3, p. 10.

ful" self-discloses with that which brings one to faith, and "compassionate" with that which makes one achieve gnosis (*the power to know the mysteries of the universe by way of a divine effusion of grace*). The attribute "merciful" appears with that which gnosis bestows, and "compassionate" with that which forgiveness bestows. The attribute "merciful" self-discloses with that which forgiveness bestows, and "compassionate" with that which contentment bestows. The attribute "merciful" self-discloses with that which is hidden, and "compassionate" with that which is shown in a vision.The attribute "merciful" shows itself by causing the Folk of Aspiration, who divest themselves of everything and turn toward Him, to succeed in transactions, and the attribute "compassionate" shows itself by causing the Folk of Union to reach the truth on the path of union. The attribute "merciful" shows itself by making the things beneficial to God's servants in the most beautiful way and protecting them, and "compassionate" by driving away the things that harm them and by taking pains with them.[109]

• Because God taught the angels without mediator, they serve as mediators between God and His messengers. The messengers are mediators between us and the angels. Our messenger did not personally deliver the Quran, he is only its site of reception. His function is to receive the speech God the Truth delivers. The Messenger guides through mediation, not by way of anagogic interpretation (*te'vil*).[110]

• Hazret Messenger is a trustworthy, sound, truthful Most Gracious Friend to whom the mysteries of the Quranic verse, "*By the letter nun, the pen, and what they have written*" (68:1) have been granted. His hand of mercy is a sublime hand extended at once to every single individual in the progeny of Adam.

Beautiful character and sublime behavior are found in all of the messengers. But there is nothing in this beautiful character and behavior that is not crowned by the sublime character of Hazret Mes-

---

109. Ali Akpınar, "İşari Tefsir ve Küşeyrî'nin Besmele Tefsiri," *Tasavvuf: İlmî ve Araştırma Dergisi*, vol. 3, no. 9, 2002, p. 79.

110. Ahmed er-Rifâî, ed. Dr. H. Kâmil Yılmaz, *Marifet Yolu* (Istanbul: Erkam Yayıncılık 1995), pp. 167-169.

senger. The aspects of his perfection and superiority are beyond count or expression.[111]

Hazret Muhammed (s.a.s.) drew his light, his inspiration and his strength from God and had no need of anyone's counsel. Still, it was said in 3:159 of the Quran: *"It is due to the mercy of God (O Muhammed) that you are gentle with them. If you were severe and hard-hearted, they would have scattered away from you. Forgive them, ask forgiveness for them, and seek their counsel in affairs. But when you have reached a decision, put your trust in God, for God loves those who put their trust in Him."*

If all of people's sins, all their shame, were thrown into their faces by their betters, life would be much more difficult. Of course that lion of the path knows yours thoughts and feelings. But far from telling you your secrets, he finds it right to pretend not to know, not to sense them, and he smiles at you, wishing those shameful thoughts to be veiled by a smile and shed by the sinner and become naught.[112]

- On the night of the Miraj, when Hazret Muhammed asked God for mercy and forgiveness for his community, great God said, "Whatever you wish is accepted by Me. Your community will always have three groups: Those who rebel, those who obey, and those who long for their God as people thirsty in the desert long for water. I will send my mercy and forgiveness to your rebellious bondsmen. I will give My paradises to those who obey. As for the felicity of beholding My infinite beauty, I will offer it to the thirsty."

"Whatever the tribes of Moses and Jesus wished for according to their preparedness, they saw it. But your community is made up of those who wish for My spiritual realm, the divine power I bestow upon spirits, in a word, the path leading to Me. I will give them My friends as examples so that they may go straight on the path they wish for."[113]

---

111. Ahmed er-Rifâî, trans. Dr. Ali Can Tatlı, *Sohbet Meclisleri* (Istanbul: Erkam Yayınları 1996), p. 39.

112. Ken'an Rifâî, *Şerhli Mesnevî-i Şerif* (Istanbul: Kubbealtı Neşriyatı 2000), p. 442.

113. Ken'an Rifâî, *Şerhli Mesnevî-i Şerif* (Istanbul: Kubbealtı Neşriyatı 2000), p. 552.

6. That you may warn a people whose fathers were not warned, so they are heedless.

Li tundhira qawman mā'undhira 'ābā'uhum fahum ghāfilūn.

7. Indeed the word is proven true on most of them, for they do not believe.

Laqad ḥaqqa'l-qawlu 'alā 'aktharihim fahum lā yu'minūn.

- The meaning of the verb "warn" (*tundhira, 'undhira*) in the verse is the mystery of the transference of a truth into one's heart.[114]

- It has been sent down to warn of torment and punishment a tribe who, when their preparedness was completed, reached a level not reached by their fathers, who were not warned. They reached a limit the preparedness of no community before them could, and remained unaware of the preparedness given to them.

In the time of the former decree (*kaza-yi sabıkta*) the property of being wretched was fixed upon most of them (*fahum lā yu'minūn—for they do not believe*). Those for whom being wretched is a property and decree can never believe. For in your time, when degrees of preparedness were strong, just as those felicitous in goodness were strong, so were those wretched in evil.[115]

---

114. Haluk Nurbaki, *Yâ-Sîn Sûresi Yorumu* (Istanbul: Damla Yayınevi 1999), p. 14.

115. Kemâlüddin Abdürrezzak Kâşâniyyüs Semerkandî, trans. Ali Rıza Doksanyedi, ed. M. Vehbi Güloğlu, *Te'vilât-ı Kâşâniyye* (Ankara Kadıoğlu Matbaası 1988), vol. 3, p. 11.

- "*Whoever denies God, His angels, books, messengers, and the Last Day has surely gone profoundly astray.*" "*It is they whom God has cursed, struck dumb and blinded their vision. Do they not consider the Quran? Or are their hearts locked?*" (4:136,47:23-24).

The meaning of the word "heedless" in the former verse is that they were dumb and blind and unable to know the truth. How should someone who does not understand the reality of the Quran consider His wisdom? How should he comprehend the descent of the Quran? How should he reflect upon Him who sent down the Quran? How should he understand the person in whom the Quran was brought down?

The basis of the matter is the properties of the Preserved Tablet that were decided in eternity without beginning: "The felicitous is felicitous in his mother's womb, and the wretched likewise." Thus are the unchanging rulings of the divine measuring out (*kader*).

Those for whom being wretched was ruled and decreed never have faith. When the realities became evident with the manifestation of our Master the Messenger, the manifestation of the felicitous and the wretched became stronger.

If the sun strikes a rose, its scent becomes evident, and if it strikes a garbage heap filthy odors become evident.

God gives to those He creates only what their preparedness requires, what it desires. Whichever name was appropriate for them in their measuring out (*kader*), He determines (*takdir*) it. The body and spirit, preparedness and behavior of persons are all inscribed in their sperm and they are compelled to become their own body and spirit. They are compelled to become their own preparedness. Only in their behavior are they free.[116]

- Pharaoh asked Moses: "*Who is your Lord, O Moses?*" Moses answered, "*Our Lord is such a God that He gave to every creature what was required by its own nature, then doing that work became that creature's straight path and He ordered this thing for that creature and guided it.*"

To say that every thing became a site of manifestation for a name means that it fulfilled the duty of the site of manifestation for that name.[117]

---

116. Azîzüddin Nesefî, trans. Mehmet Kanar, *Tasavvufta İnsan Meselesi* (Istanbul: Dergâh Yayınları 1990), p. 98.

117. Ken'an Rifâî, *Sohbetler* (Istanbul: Kubbealtı Neşriyatı 2000), p. 136.

6TH-7TH VERSE

A person performs the action that is appropriate to his own task (sha'n). This means that every human being has a name inscribed on the Preserved Tablet. In reality what self-discloses is whatever has been written on this spiritual tablet, where the writing on the brow of every human being was inscribed in eternity without beginning. If a person's name on that Tablet is a good name, in this world he does what that name requires. If the name has been written there as a bad name, a person's behavior in this world will be bad also.[118]

In sum, whatever of wrath or beauty that name indicates, its owner will wander round and round and come to rest there.[119]

While the Arabs approved of Hazret Muhammed (s.a.s.), they did not accept the message he brought. The Jews accepted the message, but they thought he was the wrong man.[120]

- The meaning of *ḥaqqa* in the verse is "to strengthen a thing" and "for that thing to be sound"; *ḥaqq* [truth/true/reality/real/right] is the opposite of "false/unreal" (*bāṭil*).

  "Truth" (*ḥaqq*) is God.[121] The proof of this is: *"God is the truth, and what they worship other than Him is the false"* (22:62).[122]

- "Truth" means the divine law or judgment brought by the messengers. This law or judgment presents human beings with a living method in their relationships with themselves and each other.

---

118. Compiler's comment.
119. Compiler's comment.
120. Martin Lings, trans. Nazife Şişman, *Hazret Muhammad'in Hayatı* (Istanbul: İnsan Yayınları 1990), p. 85.
121. [The Arabic term *ḥaqq* under discussion here, from the same root that produces verb forms such as the one used in the latter Quranic verse, "prove true," is used in the following discussion sometimes as adjective and sometimes as noun; so it means not only "true/real/right"—"right" in the sense of "correct" and "right" in the sense of a natural, customary or legal right —but also "truth/reality. It is also a term used for God. I translate according to what I believe the author intends in the given instance, and capitalize when the author does.]
122. Suad el-Hakîm, trans. Ekrem Demirli, *İbü'l-Arabî Sözlüğü* (Istanbul: Kabalcı Yayınevi 2005), p. 219.

"We sent you with truth as a bearer of good news and a warner" (2:119). *"Do not clothe the truth in falsehood"* (2:42).[123]

- In Ibn Arabi, the Truth is God not with respect to His essence, abstracted of all characteristics and relationship, but with respect to His being the god (*ilah*) of the universe. The Truth self-discloses in the forms of all things. Because the things manifested with the Truth. That is why gnostics know that everything they see is the Truth.

The Truth is God while it self-discloses in the forms of things and is witnessed in the essences of the creatures. Unlike unreality (*batıl*) it is being and goodness (*not-being=evil*).

God did not bring forth the world from not-being, which consists of evil, only so that goodness should exist. God the Truth's goal is simply being. Because insofar as one face of the worldly realm is existence, it looks toward the Truth; its other face looks toward what is other than Truth, insofar as the things in it do not exist and are separate from the Truth.

Unreality definitely does not exist. Being is wholly the Truth. Unreality indicates not-being.

Unreality is not-being, it has no reality in being. If it had being, it too would be real.

The reality (*hakikat*) of being is single in its essence, while insofar as it has two faces it has two aspects. Ibn Arabi often describes the two faces with such paired terms as Truth and creation, Lord and servant, one and many, beginningless and newly arrived (*hadis*). While here Truth is the face that gathers within itself all the beginningless characteristics of reality, creation is reality's other face and gathers within itself all the characteristics of having come into existence later. Creation is in reality a site of manifestation and self-disclosure of Truth. In that sense it is the root and reality of Truth's being.

Truth directs the world, and the world directs Truth. Do you not see that God the Truth said in the Quran: *"I accept the prayer of the one who prays when he prays"* (2:186). Is it not giving direction to respond to prayer?

---

123. Suad el-Hakîm, trans. Ekrem Demirli, *İbü'l-Arabî Sözlüğü* (Istanbul: Kabalcı Yayınevi 2005), p. 219.

All of becoming is body and spirit, and the structure of being stands with these two. The world in relation to God the Truth is like body in relation to spirit.

The He-ness of God is the servants' hearing, sight and all their faculties. As for the servants, they exist by their own faculties. Thus the servants exist by virtue of God. The servants' exterior is the form of createdness, while their interior and their reality are all God the Truth's He-ness.

Although the worlds are many, they return to a single reality:

Every thing in being is truth; every visible thing is creation.

Truth manifests and appears in every created thing. Thus God the Truth is what is known in every act of understanding and what remains hidden from it. The one and only exception to this is the understanding of him who says, "The world is God the Truth's form and He-ness": In this case, God the Truth is the Manifest. At the same time, God the Truth is the spirit of every thing that manifests; in this case God the Truth is the Non-Manifest.

"Truth" means justice and equitable balance (*insaf*). These are the characteristics of the Perfect Human Being. Perfect humans give everything that has a right its right; *"Our Lord is He who gave to every thing its creation"* (20:50). The work special to God the Truth is creation, and the aspect of Perfect Humans that separates them from the world is truth. By virtue of this, the Perfect Human knows the right of everything and gives it its right. This is the characteristic termed "equitable balance."

"Truth" means the obligatory divine law as a method a person will follow in consideration of his nature (*doğası*).

Truth belongs to the world, and nature to the Hereafter. Because nature considers things neither permittednor forbidden (*mubaḥ*), while truth forbids.

"Truth" (*ḥaqq*) means absolutely right (*doğru*):

To speak behind someone's back is not truth, but it is right (*doğru*). Speaking ill of someone behind their back, gossiping, etc. are right but they are not truth; because something that is truth is obligatory. Something that is right is determined by the condition it is in. This can sometimes be necessary, and in that case it is truth; sometimes it is unnecessary, and in that case it is not truth, but it is right.[124]

---

124. Suad el-Hakîm, trans. Ekrem Demirli, *İbü'l-Arabî Sözlüğü* (Istanbul: Kabalcı Yayınevi 2005), pp. 220-221.

- *Say: If your fathers and your sons and your brothers and your spouses and your kin and the property you have acquired, and the commerce you fear will decline, and the houses in which you delight, are dearer to you than God and His messenger and striving in his cause, then await the decision of God; and God does not guide those who stray* (9:24).

On the Day of Judgment, what is within such people will come out. God most high said: There are among men those who worship God as if on a precipice. If good befalls them, they are content with it, and if trial befalls them, they turn on their faces. They lose both this world and the Hereafter. *That is evident loss* (22:11). But a person who is rooted does not stray. Adam's love for the beloved was rooted, but that of Iblis was insincere. What each had within him came out in a time of trial. Adam wept for two hundred years and his torment was not abated until his beloved accepted his repentance. But as soon as Iblis was cast out, he immediately went before humankind, behind them, beside them, to the right and to the left of them, content to lead them astray. He never wept after being cast out. This then shows what was hidden behind his earlier worship. And that Adam wept continuously until his beloved forgave him and was content with him shows how bound his heart was to his beloved. The like of Adam is found in these words of God: *The earth, for all its spaciousness, seems constrained to them, and their very souls straitened to them, and they understood there is no fleeing from God except to Him. Then He turned to them, that they might repent. Truly God is merciful and oft-returning* (9:118). The like of Iblis is found in this verse: "*In opposition to God's Messenger, those who were left behind rejoiced in remaining where they were. They hated to strive with their possessions and souls in the way of God, and they said, 'Do not go to war in the heat.' Say: 'The heat of Hell's fire is fiercer.' If they only knew* (9:81).

Thus is always the way with these two groups. Even among the disciples of a shaykh there are those for whom *the earth, for all its spaciousness, seems constrained*. Their torment does not cease until the shaykh is pleased with them. And there are those who "rejoice in being left out of the struggle with one's soul." They say, "The way of struggle is difficult," and encourage others to sit still and not work. They even try to chill lovers' ardor for the path, so they will become like them. The first type's service to his shaykh is like Adam's love.

6TH-7TH VERSE

That of the second is like Iblis's contrived worship and his state of mind when confronted with God's prescriptive commands. Among every people this balance obtains until Resurrection Day. A building cannot stand without a foundation. Make the foundation strong, so that the building will be strong. Verse:

If the arrow does not kill, the cure is easy
A bow's curve is not a flaw but a bow in prayer[125]

- Just as "What amazes me is how these Quran-memorizers do not understand the states of the gnostics," is the interpretation of *the despicable man, ready with oaths* (68:10), he is himself the slanderer: He says, "Don't listen to so-and-so, whatever he says, he is such-and-such a way with you." *A fault-finder going about with calumnies, hindering good, transgressing all bounds, deep in sin* (68: 11-12). He even says, "What a weird, envious sorcerer is the Quran." He so binds people to himself that he whispers openly into the enemy's ear. But the enemy has no understanding of that, or he hangs back and steals away. As in: *God has set a seal upon their hearts* (2:7), how well he recites, all the way from beginning to end, yet he does not understand! He speaks of it, but still does not grasp it: God is the Subtle, and His subjugation and His key are subtle as well. But His opening (*fetih*) key is so subtle, so subtle that it cannot be explained. If my parts were to be completely resolved and opened, that would be due to His infinite subtlety and capacity for opening, his matchless power of accessing. Never blame death or illness on my account. For they are there to cover up the truth of the matter. But what really slays me is His matchless subtlety. The drawn knife or sword is for distancing and covering the reality of the slaying of strangers' eyes, those ill-omened eyes, so that they will not see it.[126]

- The Christian surgeon related: A group of Shaykh Sadreddin's companions came to us, drank in our presence and said to me: "Is Jesus God, as you suppose he is?" I said: "We know that there is one

---

125. Niyâzî Mısrî, trans. Süleyman Ateş, *İrfan Sofraları* (Istanbul: Yeni Ufuklar Neşriyatı n.d), pp. 107-109.

126. Mevlânâ Celâleddîn Rumî, trans. Meliha Ülker Anbarcıoğlu, *Fîhi Mâ Fîh* (Istanbul: Milli Eğitim Basımevi 1990), pp. 213-214.

God. But in order to protect our religion, we especially hide this point and deny it." When Mevlana Rumi heard this he said: "Never! God's enemy lies. This cannot be. These are the words of one who has lost his way drunk on Satan's wine and been driven from God's door. How should a man weak and shorter than two *arsh*, who fled the wiles, tricks and lies of the Jews, be the protector of this firmament's seven heavens? When each of those heavens, if one were to traverse them, is so wide it would take five hundred years to cross it, and five hundred years to cross the spaces between them also. The free disposal of each of these 500-years' wide heavens and the seas numbering five times that in between each one, is in His hand. How could this weak man be their ruler, and how could you consider it? Furthermore, before Jesus, who was the creator of heaven and earth? God is incomparable with anything the wrong-doers say." They told him that and the Christian then said: "The part of Jesus that was dust went to the dust, and the part of him that was pure went to the pure." Mevlana's answer to that was: "If Jesus's spirit is God, where could that spirit have gone? Spirit goes only to its root, to its Creator. If Jesus is the Root and the Creator, where is the place he will go?" The Christian also said: "We received this faith from our fathers and made it our religion." My response to that was: "If your father leaves you counterfeit money and false gold, won't you exchange it for unalloyed gold? Or will you prefer counterfeit? If your father leaves you a maimed hand, and you find a doctor who can cure it, won't you accept his help? Will you say, 'The hand left to me by my father is maimed and I don't want to change it'? If the water in the country where your father lived and died is brackish, and later you find a country where the water is pure, the earth fertile and the people healthy, wouldn't you want to move there from that bad place, drink pure water and be free of all disease? Or would you remain there, saying, 'This water that makes people ill was here in this country when we found it, and we will stay here'? No one with intelligence and perception would ever say that. God gave you an intelligence different from your father's, a view of things and a power to discern between good and evil different from your father's. You should use these, and follow advice that leads you not to annihilation but to the right path...

Yorash's father sold used furnishings. Later he swore fealty to the Sultan. The Sultan taught him how to serve rulers with proper

6th–7th Verse

etiquette and to use arms. He raised him to high position. Yorash's father did not say, "We were born into our father's trade of selling used furnishings and that is how we want to remain. We do not want these high positions. Open a shop for us in the bazaar, and we will sell used furnishings there." A dog for example, inferior as it is, learns to hunt. It becomes the Sultan's hunter and forgets the passion it learned from its father and mother for sleeping on straw and rubble and eating dead carcasses. It follows after the Sultan's retinue. It chases after prey. The falcon does also. After the Sultan trains it, it does not say, "We learned from our father to live in isolated spots on mountaintops and eat carcasses. We won't now hold in esteem the sound of the Sultan's drum and his prey." When an animal finds better than what was left to it by its father and mother, it embraces that. When that is the case, it is a terrible thing for the human being, who is superior to all other creatures in intelligence and discernment, to be inferior to the animals in this regard. We take refuge in God from this. To be sure, it is right if they say, "The God of Jesus honored him and brought him near to Himself. Whoever serves Jesus, serves God, and whoever obeys Jesus, is counted as obeying God. If God has sent a messenger superior to Jesus, He has shown through him the same that he showed through Jesus and more. This, obedience to a messenger, is obedience to God, not obedience to him; worship of him is worship of God. To love him is to love God. The love of others than God is still for God. This goes all the way to your God. Everything reaches Him in the end."[127]

- The special faculty of the intellect is to see the ends of things. The intellect that does not see the end is the lower part of the soul. The intellect that is conquered by the soul has become soul.[128]

- Divine inspiration and Lordly aid is toward the soul alone.[129]

---

127. Mevlânâ Celâleddîn Rumî, trans. Meliha Ülker Anbarcıoğlu, *Fîhi Mâ Fîh* (Istanbul: Milli Eğitim Basımevi 1990), pp. 193-197.

128. Mevlânâ Celâleddin Rûmî, trans. Veled İzbudak, ed. Abdülbaki Gölpınarlı, *Mesnevî* (Istanbul: Milli Eğitim Basımevi 1991), vol. 2, p. 118 vs. 1548-1549.

129. Muhyiddîn İbnü'l-Arabî, trans. Vahdettin İnce, *Ris'aleler* (Istanbul: Kitsan Yayınları), vol. 3, p. 292.

- The servant needs divine knowledge because the servant can only learn the things worthy of his Lord and required of servanthood through the knowledge that comes from his Lord. Thus when a person learns his Lord's commands and proscriptions, when what is due God is performed and the duties of servanthood are fulfilled, then he knows his self. Once a person knows his self, he knows his Lord also. And a person who knows his Lord performs servanthood toward his Lord as his Lord has commanded.[130]

---

130. Muhyiddin İbnül'l-Arabî, trans. Mahmut Kanık, *Marifet ve Hikmet* (Istanbul: İz Yayıncılık 1995), p. 131.

8. Truly We put fetters around their necks that press against their chins, so that their heads are fixed in a gesture of refusal. Truly We have put fetters around their necks that press against their chins, so that their heads are fixed in a gesture of refusal.

'Innā ja'alnā fī 'a'nāqihim 'aghlālan fahiya 'ilā'l-'adhqāni fahum muqmaḥūn.

9. And We put a barrier in front of them and a barrier behind them, and We covered them so that they do not see.

Wa ja'alnā min bayni 'aydīhim saddan wa min khalfihim saddan fa'aghshaynāhum fa hum lā yubṣirūn.

- On their necks We have put the fetters of bodily nature and the chains of love for servile work. The chains come up to their chins.

  Hazret Pir[131] says, "Do not go to sleep without thinking of how everyone and everything is superior to you." Acceptance will bring you to free action in the house of the body. Inclination to bow the head, to bend and prostrate the body in annihilation of self, and sorrow due to these, does not remain. There is no fear of God.

  Perfections are produced only by annihilation, not-being, by being contemptible. It is because they are not inclined this way and do not bow their heads that they have been forbidden to accept the human perfections.[132]

---

131. [The title *pir* here refers to Ibn Arabi.]
132. Kemâlüddin Abdürrezzak Kâşâniyyüs Semerkandî, trans. Ali Rıza Doksanyedi, ed. M. Vehbi Güloğlu, *Te'vilât-ı Kâşâniyye* (Ankara Kadıoğlu Matbaası 1988), vol. 3, p. 11.

- And before them we have set a barrier from the divine direction, produced from the covering of the soul's manifestation and the attributes that occupy and capture the heart. That barrier forbids them to look up at the time when the bright and illuminated beauty of God is visible, so that they may long for God the Truth's face.

And behind them, that is to say from the direction of the body, we have put a barrier produced from the covering of the delights of nature pertaining to the body, that prevents them from acting according to proscriptions and commands. That barrier bars them from wholesome actions that prepare them to accept the attributes and benefits of divine majesty. For this reason the path of knowledge and works is closed to them. They remain with their idols, confused for eternity. We wrapped them in coverings because they were veiled with materiality, suffocating in the garment of flesh.

Because of the thick coverings from all directions in which they are wrapped, they cannot see anything; when they cannot see, and are not sorrowful, it is one whether you warn them or not.[133]

- *Truly We have placed the rope upon their necks*
We made the rope out of their charicteristics

There is no one, may they be pure or unclean
Who does not wear on their neck their augury

Your passion in doing evil is like fire
Coals are rosy from the rosy hue of fire

The coal's blackness is concealed inside the flame
When the fire is out, the blackness is the same

Your passion makes the dead black coal seem alive
What remains is charred coal when the passion dies

At the time that coal appeared to be alive
That was not beauty of deed but passion's fire

---

133. Kemâlüddin Abdürrezzak Kâşâniyyüs Semerkandî, trans. Ali Rıza Doksanyedi, ed. M. Vehbi Güloğlu, *Te'vilât-ı Kâşâniyye* (Ankara Kadıoğlu Matbaası 1988), vol. 3, p. 11.

8TH-9TH VERSE

Passion was the attraction of your action
Passion went, leaving the gloom of your action[134]

- God made reputation iron in ton weight
O how many there are by unseen bond chained

Arrogance and disbelief have blocked that road
In such a way that he cannot sigh out loud

God said, "fetters," and "they have their heads forced up"
The fetters on us do not come from without

"A barrier behind them," "We've covered them"
He does not see the walls fore and behind him

The raised wall appears to be open country
He does not know it's the rampart of decree

Your beloved keeps the Beloved's face hid
Your murshid keeps the words of the Murshid hid

Many disbelievers long for religion
Fetters are this and that, pride, reputation

The fetter is hidden, but worse than iron
The axe breaks in two the fetter of iron

It is possible to break an iron chain
No one knows the recourse for an unseen chain[135]

- Although people may repent in solitude as much as they like, if they continue to behave outwardly in pride and Pharaoh-like stubbornness, their repentance has no effect. At most they will deceive themselves and be inwardly confused. For arrogance and pride so block people's path that even if disbelievers find in their hearts a sigh and a longing for the light, it will not be projected outwards.

---

134. Şefik Can, *Konularına göre açıklamalı Mesnevi Tercümesi* (Istanbul: Ötüken Neşriyat 1997), vol. 4, vs. 1120-1126.

135. Şefik Can, *Konularına göre açıklamalı Mesnevi Tercümesi* (Istanbul: Ötüken Neşriyat 1997), vol. 1-2, p. 30 [Nicholson vol. 1, vs. 3240-3248].

And in the thirty-sixth chapter of the Gracious Quran, God the Truth said of such people: *"We have put iron rings on their necks reaching up to their chins. For that reason their heads (always) remain turned up."* But don't object, saying you do not see such shackles around the necks of disbelievers! Those shackles are not outwardly fastened upon their necks.

In the same chapter, God said: *"We have raised a barrier in front of them and a barrier behind them. And because We have covered their eyes, they can no longer see"* (36:9). What they cannot see is the divine oneness and beauty, the light of God.

The obstacles set up on the paths of such people are as wide as deserts. They think this broadness is wealth, plenty and ease. They cannot tell that such deserts of position, fortune, wealth and lust are actually insurmountable walls of steel, and that all these obstacles have been set up according to the requirements of the measuring out and decree.

The human bodily eye cannot see these obstacles and imperfections pertaining to the soul, each of which is a trap. These are the dangerous blocks that can only be detected by seeking the aid of a friend of God and learning from him the visible and invisible barriers that block one's way on the path to God. As long as a person does not do so, his life on earth is lived in vain.

As long as you fall in love with the beauty that is beloved of your soul and stay in love, you cannot see the light of the spiritual beloved. As long as you plunge into the pleasure of worldly delights and worldly bounties, and give your ear and heart to the voice of the guide belonging to your soul, you cannot hear the voice of the true murshid who shows you the ways to reach God.

There are disbelievers who burn with a longing for faith. But since they stubbornly suppose themselves to possess honor and reputation, pride and similar feelings prevent them from taking a spiritual path. Worldly ties rise up before them like an insurmountable wall.

To be sure, these walls are invisible. But they are stronger than steel. For an ax, or any tool, may undo iron chains. But who can break apart these invisible ties, and how?

If a bee stings a person, the body mobilizes all its powers to get rid of the pain, poison and evils that result from the sting. Pain and

8th-9th Verse

swelling is ameliorated by salve applied externally. But if the bee that stings your body does not come from outside, but is produced within you, in your constitution, you do not have the power to get rid of it, to get rid of the hidden wound it has opened inside your body. You feel burning pains within you, but you neither know what is wrong nor how to cure it.

I feel the desire within me to explicate this further. I want to further illuminate this truth. But I am concerned that what I say may plunge you into despair.

But while there is God, one cannot despair. Know that God definitely answers every call, rushes to help all who ask for help, and He is the Merciful and the Compassionate, and do not fail to ask from Him everything that is appropriate. He is the Creator who, if He wishes, will in an instant bring you from darkness to light, from infidelity to faith, from mourning to peace of mind and the greatest of all hopes.

O brother! Beware, do not be one of those who sees themselves everywhere. Do not let your view of yourself raise the dust of plurality and duality in you. O brother! God's wisdom is flowing over your spirit and your understanding. But this wisdom flowing over you flows from the light of the being of God's Substitutes, that is, from Perfect Humans, it flows from their riverbeds. The arrived of God have destroyed their own materiality and come near to the divine realm; they are spirits who have been freed from the darkness of body and reached the light of unity.

If you see a light reflected from them in yourself, do not mistakenly suppose that the light comes from you! To be sure, you are tasting the delight of finding illumination in the house of the heart. But do not forget that the illumination overflows from a neighbor's house, which spreads light everywhere around.

If a ray from that light falls into your house, be thankful! But do not be proud of it. For the first step toward error and denial is pride and arrogance.

Pity the person who becomes the site of manifestation of divine grace and supposes that the light of God reflected in him, the illumination of a prophet or friend, comes from within himself, and becomes proud; he makes claim to selfhood, or like the scribe of revelation Abdullah turns off into darkness again, just as this state of the soul has distanced many a community from the felicity of being the community of a messenger.

Real gnosis is that a person should find the ways to die to his own self before dying, and thus be born to that day of accounts as one of the arrived of God.

If you ask the philosopher, he will accept neither the signs of Resurrection Day nor the death before death. He does not believe that stones and trees will speak. Tell him to go and bash his head against those stones he believes will never speak, so that he may gather his wits! Tell him: Only men of heart understand the language of water, earth, roses and plants. When after years and years of ascending through the joy of naughting themselves they reach the level of being able to comprehend all truths, they see how mineral and vegetable, birds and all animals speak in remembrance of God. Others do not see and hear what the prophets and friends see and hear because they are still blind and deaf under the command of self and matter inside the body.

Can the philosopher understand what that date palm felt, how it trembled in awe and moaned deeply? Certainly he is unaware of the reality of the mysteries and meanings that the prophets and friends have seen up close and know. Because he is unaware, he tries to resolve these mysteries and meanings according to his own intellect.

The philosopher says that people affected by feelings of love create all sorts of conjectures and fantasies. The rays of creaturely love prepare the imagination of people so that such feelings, thoughts and beliefs arise. To suppose that wolves, birds, stones and trees are beings that can feel and think, believe and speak—such delusions are the result of these fantasies.

One day Hazret Ali said to Hazret Muhammed: "O Messenger of God, when I go out to the desert from Mecca, I do not see one stone or tree that does not greet me." To be sure, the philosopher does not understand the truth of that. In fact the reflections of his states of mind far from faith, his corruption and infidelity, lead him into such doubts and conjectures. He concludes that things he sees and imagines are illusory, and supposes that the friends and prophets have the same corrupt fantasies.He supposes that the friends and prophets of God have the same depraved fantasies that he does, that

8TH-9TH VERSE

just as he sees and imagines things and concludes that they are illusory, so do they.

The philosopher rejects the existence of jinn, satans and devils. He thinks these are all fantasies created by conjecture, and does not know that he is in the hand of the Satan he rejects even while he rejects him. He has become Satan's toy, his fool.

If you, O philosopher, cannot see Satan, look at yourself in a mirror. Observe the bruise on your forehead. This bruise occurs on the faces of those who bash themselves on stone after stone, rushing off day and night after pleasure and crazy behavior.

Look and see that color on your face, and since you are a philosopher, that is, since you are able to think, at least think about the mystery and the reason for this.

Even if people who have such doubts and darkness in their hearts hide themselves and pretend to be Muslims, the philosophy of denial is coiled in their hearts.

O believers! Don't be like the philosophers, like those who have lost their way! For there's a philosopher's vein in almost everyone. Almost everyone has moments of doubt. Within you too there are so many limitless realms you do not know of yet.

If you abandon the way of the friends and prophets and dip into the branches of philosophy, into the philosophers' paths all contrary to one another, at the end of the road you will meet only disappointment.

Every heart in which there is doubt and belief in error instead of perfect faith will tremble like a leaf in autumn on the Day of Resurrection.

Because you suppose yourself to be a good person and think that "superior people are distinguished by their rejection of the invisible"—that is, rejection of what you cannot see, you laugh at satans, devils and jinn. But to suppose that what you do not know and cannot see does not in fact exist is the clearest expression of ignorance and error.

If one day the spirit turns the sheepskin it wears inside-out, turns you inside-out, and the truths you have not seen dazzle your eyes like the sun while the invisible devils within you are spread out under the light of that sun, then look and see what groans will be heard coming from so many of the religious people, including yourself, who supposed themselves good men while in the world. Those groans arising when those who suppose themselves good people see the wretchedness of their inner selves are certainly heart-rending.

But as Hazret Muhammed (s.a.s.) said: "In whatever state a servant dies, whatever quality is dominant in him while he dies, when he is raised up again he will be raised up in that quality."

All the gilded things in the shop of the world are joyful and laughing with the pleasure of seeming to be gold. Those who sell them are bold because they can sell copper as gold to all who come along. The reason for this is that there is no touchstone around, or rather that the touchstone is hidden where eyes cannot see it.

So it is with people's behavior and beliefs, they are either of copper or gold. If the spirit and touchstone of gnosis that distinguishes the false from the pure gold of such belief and behavior is hidden behind a curtain and unable to function, people can be so mistaken as to think their own copper is gold.

However much false gold may swagger in the darkness of night, in the same shop side-by-side with pure gold and shiny as pure gold, pure gold does not mind. It laughs at the boasts false gold can make only in the darkness of night, and waits in dignified patience for the light of day, and speaks thus to the false metal beside it in its own language: "O pitiful liar! Do you think night lasts till Resurrection Day? Morning will come tomorrow anyway. Then you will see for yourself how you are bright red and I have the yellowness of gold."

Do you not know that the angels bowed down for hundred of thousands of years to Satan, whom God cursed. Satan, proud of being created of fire, had been for ages the teacher and commander of the angels.

But out of that same pride, disdain and arrogance, one day he engaged in contest with Adam, who was created of earth. He was so bold as to say to God, "I am better than he."

Later when he lost the contest he engaged in with Hazret Adam in the presence of the angels, the filth within him was exposed, in the way that the odors of dirty, filthy things are brought out when the light and heat of the sun strikes them.[136]

---

136. Ken'an Rifâî, *Şerhli Mesnevî-i Şerif* (Istanbul: Kubbealtı Neşriyatı 2000), pp. 476-482.

8th–9th Verse

- According to a report, God the Truth said to Moses (a.s.): "O Moses! You must come and seek closeness with me by bringing things I do not have in My treasuries. Moses (a.s.) said: "O my Lord, You are the Lord of all the worlds, how can there be anything lacking in Your treasuries?" God the Truth gave this reply: "O Moses, you should know well that My treasuries are filled with Greatness, Exaltation and Majesty. Come to Me with contemptibility, heartbreak and nothingness! Because I am with those who break their hearts for My sake. O Moses, I should not be approached with anything greater than these.[137]

- Abu Jahl was formerly known as Abu'l-Hakim, meaning, "One possessed of wisdom, honored." He is "Abu Jahl" (Father of Ignorance) because he did not recognize God. It is he who gave our Messenger the nickname "Emin" (Trustworthy). When our Messenger was an adolescent, Abu'l-Hakim would say, "Muhammed is trustworthy." He knew how to assess people but he was stubborn, his heart was sealed and his pride was an obstacle. When a Muslim slave bent over him to slit his throat at the Battle of Badr, he said, "Aren't you a bit above yourself?" That was the sort of pride Abu Jahl was afflicted with.[138]

- Do you think highly of yourself because you are descended from Adam? Most of his children are disbelievers. Many messengers have like him had children and descendants... Or is it your knowledge that makes you proud? As is well known, Iblis solved many conundrums and studied the pages of the existents to perfection... Or is it your wealth you are proud of? Think of Korah. He was destroyed because of the trial of wealth... Could Pharaoh's kingship and power save him from the wrath of God the Truth?[139]

- I warn you of your bad qualities, do not be qualified by them. For those qualities are a mortal poison.

To envy others is to wish for them to lose the bounty given to them.

---

137. Ahmed er-Rifâî, ed. Naim Erdoğan, *Vaazlar* (Istanbul: Pamuk Yayınları), p. 76.

138. Ömer Turğrul İnançer, *Sohbetler* (Istanbul: Keşkül Yayınları 2005), p. 15.

139. Ahmed er-Rifâî, ed. Naim Erdoğan, *Vaazlar* (Istanbul: Pamuk Yayınları), p. 94.

Arrogance is to believe you are superior to others.

To lie is to say things that are not true; it is to say ugly things that have no value.

Backbiting is to reveal the shame of others behind their backs.

Greed is to never be satisfied with worldly things.

Wrath is for the blood to rush to the brain in the desire for revenge.

Hypocrisy is to be pleased that others see your good sides and to show off just so that they will be pleased...

Oppression is to do what your soul wishes...[140]

---

140. Ahmed er-Rifâî, ed. Naim Erdoğan, *Vaazlar* (Istanbul: Pamuk Yayınları), p. 99.

10. It is the same to them if you warn them or do not warn them; they will not believe.

Wa sawā'un 'alayhim 'a 'andhartahum 'am lam tundhirhum lā yu'minūn.

• The great Mevlana Rumi says: "The root things (*asıl işler*) are judgments made in eternity without beginningand written on the Preserved Tablet. All things that come into this world are requirements of the market of eternity without beginning—farewell."

As our Master the Messenger said: "The wretched are wretched in their mother's womb, and the felicitous are felicitous in their mother's womb." He explained that the wicked are wicked in their mother's womb and the friends of God are His friends in their mother's womb. These are properties of unalterable measuring out. As the Quran says, you can do nothing for them:*God has set a seal on their hearts and on their hearing* (2:7). It is clear that the matter of whether the eye of a person's heart is open or covered depends on a beginningless claim.

In eternity without beginning, God the Truth addressed the spirits and asked: *Am I not your Lord?* When the spirits answered: *Yes, we testify* (7:172), they were sent to this realm to prove their claim, according to the rule that the claim of the tongue requires proof by the hand.

In fact the nature of those who came here to show if they were people of their word or not was known to God. But we have come to this world of mortality in order to teach our own selves to ourselves, to make ourselves known, and earn the right to the stamp of humanity.

Whether we are human or devil is our share from eternity without beginning. For a person to be a haram-eater, that is, for him to violate the rights of another out of a claim to selfhood, and be swept up in the passion for stinging another soul like a snake or a scorpion, hurting him and humiliating him, is a repetition in this realm of the soul-satan's words in eternity without beginning: "I am better than he."[141]

Those who are wretched in eternity without beginning are like rotten seeds; either they smother in the earth or are born and develop as cripples, and cannot attain perfection. Whatever you say, you cannot convince them, you cannot bring them to believe.[142]

- Those who follow their lower souls have become captive to their lustful desires and caprice and obedient to their commands. God has forbidden anything beneficial to occur in the hearts of such people. Even if they never stop repeating God's words, they take no pleasure in them. Because God the Exalted says: *I will turn away from My signs those who behave arrogantly on the earth in defiance of right* (7:146).[143]

- It is Satan and the lower soul that keep a person away from divine gnosis and faith in the angels, the scriptures, and the Day of Judgment.

  Whoever denies God, His angels, His books, His messengers, and the Day of Judgment, has gone far, far astray. They it is whom God has cursed and made deaf and blind. Do they not consider the Quran? Or are there locks upon their hearts? (4:136, 47:23-24)

  They have become dumb and blind and could not recognize the truth. How should they who cannot understand the reality of the Quran consider His wisdom? How should they comprehend the revelation of the Quran? How should they contemplate the One who sent it down? How should they understand the one upon whom it was sent down?[144]

- Surrounded on all sides by a cyclone of ignorance, taking up nonsense and lies... Lies, made-up stories being told...

---

141. Meşkûre Sargut, *Gönülden Gönüle* (Istanbul: Kubbealtı Neşriyat 1994), p. 120.

142. Compiler's note.

143. Ahmed er-Rifâî, trans. Dr. Ali Can Tatlı, *Sohbet Meclisleri* (Istanbul: Erkam Yayınları 1996), p. 87.

144. Ahmed er-Rifâî, ed. Dr. H. Kâmil Yılmaz, *Marifet Yolu* (Istanbul: Erkam Yayıncılık 1995), p. 165.

10th Verse

Everyone has chosen such a path and continues upon it; whom should we blame? We try to deal with people, yet we cannot please anyone because they pay no heed to our good behavior and fall into arrogance.

Clearly, what else can we do but practice verse 15:94 of the Quran: *Proclaim what you have been commanded and turn away from those who worship false gods.*[145]

Regarding the wretched we have been given the good news: *It is the same to them if you warn them or do not warn them; they will not believe* (36:10); and regarding the felicitous: *One who fears the Merciful in the Unseen* (36:11).

Does anyone born blind or hunchback call the doctor and demand to be healed? Even if they did, the doctors would say they were powerless to do so. For the doctor's function is to cure diseases that are transitory. The first verse applies to those who were blind, hunchback or lame in eternity without beginning, and so the messengers and murshids can do nothing for them. The second applies to those afflicted by transitory illnesses; guidance, sermons and advice are for them.[146]

- One day Abu Jahl wanted to test Hazret Muhammed. He picked up some small stones, went to Muhammed and said, "You say you are the messenger of God, so you must know something. Tell me, O Muhammed, what have I got in the palm of my hand? Tell me, be quick."

"If you really are the messenger of God, if you really know the mysteries behind the veil of the sky, then you should be able to guess something so nearby right away. Come now, tell me," he insisted.

Hazret Muhammed said to Abu Jahl: "Shall I say what you have in your hand, or shall the things in your hand speak and bear witness to my being the messenger of God?"

Abu Jahl was about to say, "The second thing is not possible; you guess and tell me," but Hazret Muhammed (s.a.s.) said, "No, the power of God is far beyond making the things in your hand speak. If He wishes, all inanimate things can become animate, and all of them

---

145. Ahmed er-Rifâî, ed. Naim Erdoğan, *Vaazlar* (Istanbul: Pamuk Yayınları), p. 67.

146. Ken'an Rifâî, *Sohbetler* (Istanbul: Kubbealtı Neşriyatı 2000), p. 494.

can speak like human beings do. In fact they are uttering many, many mysteries regarding the existence and unity of God, but of course you cannot understand their language."

While Hazret Muhammad was saying this, the stones in Abu Jahl's hand began speaking one by one. Each of them recited the profession of faith in a manner more eloquent and moving than many an eloquent human being.

When Abu Jahl heard the stones speaking, he became afraid and angry and threw them on the ground, saying:

"Lies! Lies!" he cried. "This is no miracle, it is sorcery, and you are a master sorcerer, no sorcerer in the world can rival you!"

And because he said that, he became the most accursed of all disbelievers. He was given the worst punishment of all—to be distanced from God's mercy for all eternity.

Just as when Satan looked at Adam, he saw a pile of earth in the form of a man instead of a human being created from earth, and because he saw Adam as dust, did not bow down to him and rebelled against God and was driven out of the heavens and earth, so was Abu Jahl incapable of seeing the divine self-disclosure in Hazret Muhammed (s.a.s.). His eyes were covered by a thick curtain of heedlessness, rage and disbelief, and thus he remained.[147]

---

147. Ken'an Rifâî, *Şerhli Mesnevî-i Şerif* (Istanbul: Kubbealtı Neşriyatı 2000), p. 312-313.

11. You warn only whoever follows the remembrance (*the Quran*) and fears the Merciful in the Unseen. Give such a one glad tidings of forgiveness and a generous reward.

'Innamā tundhiru mani't-taba'a'dh-dhikra wa khashiya 'ar-raḥmāna bi'l-ghaybi fabashshirhu bimaghfiratin wa 'ajrin karīm.

- Warning can only move those whose preparedness is luminous and pure and who conform to the remembrance (*zikir*),[148] and warning saddens such people, and because of the gnosis rooted in their preparedness and the tendency to unity rooted in their innate disposition, they accept guidance and take advice.

 And while they are absent from divine self-disclosure, by imagining His tremendousness they are wary of the Merciful and in order to bring what is absent to them into presence and see what its rays illuminate, they enter the path and follow the Merciful. Announce to them the good news of the amulet of forgiveness and concealment of sins by the veils of the acts, the attributes and the essence, and God the Truth's gracious recompense of the paradises of the acts, attributes and essence.[149]

- Hazret Riza, son of Musa Kazim, said: "Human beings need the people of remembrance. Remembrance is the Messenger of God, and we are the people of remembrance."

---

148. [Here "remembrance" (Ar. *dhikr*, Tr. *zikir*) refers to the Quran; more generally it refers to a program of recitation, of God's names for example, as a spiritual practice.]

149. Kemâlüddin Abdürrezzak Kâşâniyyüs Semerkandî, trans. Ali Rıza Doksanyedi, ed. M. Vehbi Güloğlu, *Te'vilât-ı Kâşâniyye* (Ankara Kadıoğlu Matbaası 1988), vol. 3, p. 12.

Hazret Ja'far al-Sadiq said: "Remembrance has two meanings in the Gracious Quran. One is the Quran, and the other is Muhammed (s.a.s.) and the People of the House, who are the Talking Quran. Human beings are responsible for the rights of both."[150]

Hazret Ali asked the Messenger: "O Messenger of God! Would you teach me the shortest path to God, the easiest one for human beings and the one most acceptable to God the Truth?"

The Messenger said: *The most beneficial remembrance that I and the messengers before me have taught is the profession of unity, "There is no god but God." If the seven heavens and seven earths were put on one side of the scales and the profession of unity on the other, it would outweigh them.* The Messenger of God added: *As long as there is someone on the face of the earth saying "God, God," the Day of Resurrection will not arrive.*[151]

God the Truth said to Hazret Moses: *Go to Pharaoh, because he has transgressed all bounds.* And Moses said to God the Truth: *O my Lord, in that case, rend my breast (here "to rend" means "to lift the darkness and bring forth light) and ease my task, remove the stutter from my tongue so that they may understand me well and hear well what I say; and give me a vizier from among my people, my brother Aaron, and strengthen me through him and make him a partner in my task so that we may utter much glorification and remembrance of you...* God the Truth said: *I have given you what you asked for, O Moses!* (20:24-36).

The inward meaning of these gracious verses is: "You command me to struggle with my own soul. So rend my breast, make intellect my vizier, and take away from me my tongue, which stutters doing the work of the subsistence intellect (*maaş aklı*), and make intellect my vizier in this regard, so that I may utter remembrance and glorification worthy of You, O my Lord."[152]

- According to Ibn Arabi, remembrance is the presence (*huzur*) that ensures witnessing and unveiling. Remembrance is the Gracious Quran.

---

150. Süleyman İbrahim, *Meveddet Pınarları* (Istanbul: Yeşil Yayınları 2000), p. 35.

151. Ahmed er-Rifâî, ed. Dr. H. Kâmil Yılmaz, *Marifet Yolu* (Istanbul: Erkam Yayıncılık 1995), p. 62.

152. Ken'an Rifâî, *Sohbetler* (Istanbul: Kubbealtı Neşriyatı 2000), p. 577.

11th Verse

Remembrance is the presence whose opposite is heedlessness. God sits with those who practice remembrance of Him. He who is sitting is visible in the one who utters remembrance. If the one uttering remembrance does not see God the Truth sitting with him, he is not truly practicing remembrance. Because remembrance of God spreads everywhere within the servant, but no such result comes of remembrance a person utters only with his tongue.

The heart found excitement and happiness with remembrance of God. The illumination of guidance shone on the servant and cast light on him. God lit a lamp in the servant's heart from the lights and gnosis of wisdom. Thus did the gates of mercy open. Upon those He created; and they were not locked.

Remembrance is the Gracious Quran. It is the greatest of remembrances. *We have, without doubt, sent down the remembrance* (15:9). Here "remembrance" means the Gracious Quran.

In that respect everything utters remembrance of God the Truth, because we can reach God the Truth through every thing in existence. Every existent thing is a site of self-disclosure for God the Truth, in which He self-discloses. Thus every thing God the Truth has put into existence practices remembrance.

Hazret Aisha reports that the Messenger uttered remembrance of God continuously every moment. At the same time he mingled with the young and old. All of them utter remembrance of God in the world; because everything practices remembrance of God. Thus anyone who sees something that is not uttering remembrance of God has not really seen that thing. Because God put every thing into existence to practice remembrance.

The true agent and actor in every thing is God the Truth. The creatures are acted upon and passive in every condition. Thus remembrance in a location—and the location is the servant—is an act belonging to God to Truth. What the servant does is limited to preparing the location by abstracting it, in the precise sense of the word, from every effect (*etki*). Thus the one uttering remembrance is God the Truth and the servant is the one remembered.[153]

---

153. Suad el-Hakîm, trans. Ekrem Demirli, *İbü'l-Arabî Sözlüğü* (Istanbul: Kabalcı Yayınevi 2005), p. 727-728.

- God is pleased with those who continuously practice remembrance of Him. One who pleases God has been re-united with Him. Remembrance can be established in the heart through the blessing (*bereket*) of fellowship. For one is on the path of the friend. I recommend that you come to us. Our fellowship is a tested cure, it is medicine. And to be distant from us is poison. You poor thing, distant from us! Do you leave us because you suppose that knowledge is enough for you? What good is knowledge without action? What good is action without sincerity? Even sincerity is by the side of the path of danger. Do you know who it is that will move you to action with sincerity, cure you of the illness of hypocrisy and show you the path of security? The All-Knowing and Informed Lord says: *Ask the people of remembrance, if you do not know* (16:43). Do you suppose you are one of them? If you were, you would not stay away from them. If you were one of them, you would not be deprived of the fruit of reflection. Your knowledge has become a veil for you, an obstacle to action. Just so, our Master, upon him be blessings and peace, said: *I take refuge from knowledge that has no benefit*. O you who seek to escape us! Embrace our gate, do not leave our threshold. Because every instant you spend at our threshold and every step you take is a means to reach a spiritual station and divine intimacy. For our returning to Hazret God the Sublime is true. God the Sublime says: *Follow the way of those who turn to Me* (31:15) [154]

- Remembrance means to mention. Only mention of God is remembrance. There are three types of remembrance: Mention with the tongue; for example, to repeat a certain number of times the names of God, "Alive" or "Merciful." It is for the heart to view and intuit (*sezmek*) divine wisdom continuously. To practice remembrance in action is to conform to the Quran; considering that in the Quranic verse it says, "those who conform to remembrance," not "those who practice remembrance," what is intended is the act of remembrance. To worship in the way commanded by the Quran, to avoid what is forbidden, to be compassionate, to be patient, are all acts of applied remembrance as intended in this verse. Considering that to follow the Quran

---

154. Ahmed er-Rifâî, ed. Dr. H. Kâmil Yılmaz, *Marifet Yolu* (Istanbul: Erkam Yayıncılık 1995), p. 46.

and conform to it is remembrance, another important definition of remembrance is conformity with the Muhammeden Character.[155]

- Know that God who is remembered is one, but remembrances are various. And the heart-levels of those who practice remembrance differ. The root of remembrance is to conform to God the Truth's commands. Because Hazret Messenger said: "Whoever obeys God practices remembrance of Him, though he may perform little ritual prayer, fasting and recitation of the Quran.[156]

Those who practice remembrance are those who avoid turning to other things. Because they remember God, they never want anyone else.

What those who practice remembrance of God need is to do so with the utmost respect and honor, not heedlessly or out of habit. It is because they abandon remembering God with respect and honor that they become veiled from God.

There are no believers upon whose hearts a devil does not stand, retreating when they practice remembrance of God and whispering when they forget God.

Know that true intimacy is to forget all others because one is engaged in remembering God and mentioning Him, and to leave off remembrance of everything other than God.[157]

- Remembrance is of two types. From one comes fear and wariness, and from the other, joy and love. The remembrance that brings forth fear and wariness is the one practiced by those who remember God with their soul and accept that the reason they remember God is that God remembers them; and there is the remembrance of those who do not know that when they remember God, God will remember them.

The other remembrance is that practiced by those who comprehend that before they came into existence, God was remembering

---

155. Haluk Nurbaki, *Yâ-Sîn Sûresi Yorumu* (Istanbul: Damla Yayınevi 1999), p. 18.

156. Ahmed er-Rifâî, trans. Dr. Ali Can Tatlı, *Sohbet Meclisleri* (Istanbul: Erkam Yayınları 1996), p. 96.

157. Ahmed er-Rifâî, trans. Dr. Ali Can Tatlı, *Sohbet Meclisleri* (Istanbul: Erkam Yayınları 1996), p. 131-133.

them in eternity without beginning and will remember them until they die. Thus they know that God's remembrance of them is beginningless and eternal, and that their own remembrance of God is heedless and clouded by lust. How different are those who remember God while seeing that He remembers them, and those who remember God while seeing His bounties and gifts. Compared to God's remembering the servant, the servant's remembering God is like dust under rain.[158]

• When a person prefers the Hereafter, the world is lost in the Hereafter. When remembrance of God comes to the fore, both the world and the Hereafter pass away, lost in this remembrance. When remembrance in the true sense is performed, both "servant" and "remembrance" cease to exist. All that is left is God the Truth and His attributes.[159]

• Right conduct in remembrance is to shed the ties of the world and what is other than God with perfect resolution and humility, and take refuge behind the shield of the name of Majesty, aware of a stable consciousness of sincerity and servitude.[160]

Remember Me with joy and love, that I may remember you by reuniting you with your desire and giving you intimacy...

Remember Me with My sublimity and superiority, that I may remember you with recompense of gratuitous bounties...

Remember Me with repentance, that I may remember you with forgiveness of sin...

Remember Me with a request, that I may remember you by granting your request...

Remember Me with regret for the errors you have committed, that I may remember you with generosity...

Remember Me with repentance, that I may remember you with forgiveness...

---

158. Ahmed er-Rifâî, trans. Dr. Ali Can Tatlı, *Sohbet Meclisleri* (Istanbul: Erkam Yayınları 1996), p. 134.

159. Ahmed er-Rifâî, trans. Dr. Ali Can Tatlı, *Sohbet Meclisleri* (Istanbul: Erkam Yayınları 1996), p. 91-92.

160. Ahmed er-Rifâî, ed. Dr. H. Kâmil Yılmaz, *Marifet Yolu* (Istanbul: Erkam Yayıncılık 1995), p. 68.

11th Verse

Remember Me with perfect will, that I may remember you with what benefits you...

Remember Me by leaving off evil things, that I may remember you by doing more and more good for you...

Remember Me with sincerity, that I may remember you by rescuing you from evil...

Remember Me with your hearts, that I may remember you by taking you out of troubling circumstances...

Remember Me by telling Me of your destitute circumstances, that I may give you strength...

Remember Me by repenting and asking that your sins be forgive, that I may remember you with mercy and forgiveness...

Remember me with faith, that I may remember you by giving you Paradise...

Remember Me by entering the path of Islam, that I may remember you with gifts...

Practice remembrance of Me with your heart, that I may remember you by opening the veils of spiritual meaning...

Remember Me knowing that you are mortal, that I may remember you with continuous remembrance...

Remember Me begging with your soul, that I may remember you by making you virtuous...

Remember Me by telling Me of your contemptible states, that I may remember you by forgiving your mistakes...

Remember Me by confessing what you have done, that I may remember you by erasing the sins committed...

Remember Me with purity of heart, that I may remember you with pure goodness...

Remember Me with fidelity, that I may remember you with indulgence and gentleness...

Remember Me with purity, that I may remember you with forgiveness...

Remember Me by exalting Me, that I may remember you by making you generous...

Remember Me by saying, "God is greatest," that I may remember you by saving you from my hell named Saʿīr.

Remember Me by abandoning cruelty, that I may remember you by keeping the promises made you...

Remember Me by abandoning error, that I may remember you with varied gifts.

Remember Me by working hard to serve, that I may remember you by giving you all of the bounty...

Remember Me by thinking what you are, that I may remember you with My own being...[161]

Remembrance has five main characteristics, and these five characteristics increase a person's value to God the Truth. They are:

In remembrance there is God's good-pleasure.

In remembrance there is safety from Satan.

Remembrance softens the heart.

It increases one's passion for worship.

It keeps the believer away from rebelliousness.[162]

- There is no servant who does not forget everything other than God when remembering God as He should be remembered. For them, God is the recompense for everything. Usually when gnostics wish to remember God, waves of magnification and awe break within their secret heart. In this way God becomes their tongue's trustee.[163]

- Ibn Abbas (r.a.) said: "There is a devil in the heart of every believer. But when the believer is engaged in remembrance of God, that devil becomes small.[164]

- Those who practice remembrance are those remembered by God the Truth.[165]

---

161. Abdülkadir Geylânî, trans. Abdülkadir Akçiçek, *Gunyetü't-Tâlibîn* (Istanbul: Sağlam Yayınevi 1991), pp. 714-716.

162. Es Seyyid Şeyh Muhammed Ebu-l Hüda Es Sayyâdî Er-Rifâî El Halebî, trans. Mahmud Nedim Aksoy, *Tarikat-ı Er-Rifâîyye ve er-Rifâî Yolunun Esasları* (Istanbul: Sultan Yayınevi), p. 54.

163. Ahmed er-Rifâî, trans. Dr. Ali Can Tatlı, *Sohbet Meclisleri* (Istanbul: Erkam Yayınları 1996), p. 132.

164. Ahmed er-Rifâî, ed. Dr. H. Kâmil Yılmaz, *Marifet Yolu* (Istanbul: Erkam Yayıncılık 1995), p. 51.

165. Ahmed er-Rifâî, ed. Dr. H. Kâmil Yılmaz, *Marifet Yolu* (Istanbul: Erkam Yayıncılık 1995), p. 67.

11th Verse

- God says: "I remember within myself him who remembers Me within himself. I remember within a group him who practices remembrance of Me within a group. I remember of Myself him who remembers Me of himself, and I give him wages accordingly."

Continue with remembrance of God, because remembrance is a magnet for union with God, a sound rope for intimacy with God. God is pleased with those who continue with remembrance of God. He who pleases God has reunited with Him. The blessing of fellowship makes it possible for remembrance to become settled in the heart.

The friends of God the Truth have said: "The person who remembers God is upon a light given by God. His heart has reached contentment, he has reached safety from the foe. Remembrance is the food of the spirit and the spiritual wine that has attained God the Truth's praise. And there can be no pleasure or delight as valuable as being engaged in remembrance of God the Truth.[166]

- The world is a veil and the states of the world are hidden by means of this veil. God gives good recompense, robes of honor and Paradise to those who believe in the Unseen, perform all kinds of worship, and believe in God without seeing Him and in what He does without seeing it. Because when God is seen without a veil there is no recompense for anyone's worship. Nor is such repentance acceptable. God is seen without a veil on the Day of Resurrection. *The day that secrets are tested* (86:9). Then there will be no use in repenting, weeping and moaning. God performs works in the world behind a veil and shows His servants friendship and succor behind a veil also. If He does these things without a veil, Resurrection Day will come. Resurrection will follow the extinguishing of the world. Resurrection is impossible in this world. And so He helps His servants behind the veil of causes, so that his servants may look to the causes and be heedless of God. For example, if a person throws himself off a minaret trusting in God, he will be ripped to pieces. If he cuts his belly or throat with a knife or a sword out of the same trust, he will immediately die or cease to exist. If people do these things with God's help and in His name and are not destroyed, it means they have seen God without a veil. It is not God's

---

166. Ahmed er-Rifâî, ed. Dr. H. Kâmil Yılmaz, *Marifet Yolu* (Istanbul: Erkam Yayıncılık 1995), p. 46-51.

custom to show Himself openly in this realm. If it were, the verse *"Who believe in the Unseen"* (2:3) would not be correct. A servant who is awakened and vigilant sees God behind the veil of causes and knows that his salvation is from God, not the causes. For some have tested it personally and seen that there is no benefit in causes. If health, salvation and wishes were fulfilled by causes, they would never be contradictory. And wishes would never exist independently of causes. That is why it is absolutely clear that as long as God does not wish it and does not help that believer and clever servant from behind the veil of causes, no result will be produced or effected. Believers know causes to be excuses and a veil. They see that felicity and wretchedness are from God. That is why the messengers avoid unbelievers.

Paradise is for those who believe and obey. Because they obey behind the veil and fear God, and they know all causes to be from Him. They acknowledge no other who does every thing and rules over all. They do not lose their way in this world and do not give up on their faith in God because the face of causes is covered. God created Paradise in recompense for their faith and righteousness, and because they abandon the delight and beauties of the present for the delights of the future, and created Hell for those who resist, deny, and acknowledge causes as their own God and run after them and take refuge in them and prefer the delights of this world.[167]

- Faith is in the Unseen (*the spiritual world not visible to the eye*).

Faith is the feeling of wariness experienced in the heart; in it there is a pleasure of love mixed with shivering.

Faith is an obligatory fire that the names of the Merciful have created in the heart. Those whose hearts are pure immediately find life with this current that is the warning of our Efendi [Muhammed], who is the most sublime of the universes; they have faith.

If the Quran, which is the wisdom of the Exalted, the Merciful, does not inspire awe in hearts, then those hearts are sick. They are crippled with pride and cannot find life.[168]

---

167. Sultan Veled, trans. Meliha Anbarcıoğlu, *Maarif* (Konya: Altunarı Ofset 2002), pp. 79-80.

168. Halûk Nurbaki, *Yâ-Sîn Sûresi Yorumu* (Istanbul: Damla Yayınevi 1999), p. 21.

11th Verse

- It is not without reason that God the Truth chose to remain in his own unseen realm until the Day of Resurrection.

By staying behind the veil of the Unseen God the Truth wants His servants to pursue hopes and goals and worship Him with hope. The servant's hope is either the Hereafter or the world. The gates of prayer are open to those who hope for either one. The wishes of those who want the Hereafter, that is to say spiritual delights and pleasures, and the hopes and goals of those who pursue worldly pleasures and desires, mean there is a bond between them and God the Truth. Every servant, knowingly or unknowingly, is tied to God by hope and anxiety.

Hope and anxiety are the veils of the unseen realm. Those who seek mercy from God behind the veil, whether through fear or hope, one day when the veil is rent see that realm in all its glory.

Because everything will be plain to see when the veil is rent, neither fear nor hope will remain. At that moment people will either see that their well-intentioned actions and wishes to reach God have been accepted, and either attain the recompense God has promised with the word "Paradise," or experience what they feared. If this were not the case, and every servant knew in this world what would happen at Resurrection, the people of the world and the wretched would grieve while the believers would always be happy. But the divine wisdom would not have found its effect. Because God wants not only believers but also the wretched and even disbelievers to have hope. And who knows, maybe one day if they awake from their heedlessness and ask God for help and goodness while still in the realm of body and the world, have no doubt that God is great enough to hesitate not for one moment to forgive them and count them among His good servants.

Groundless fears and anxieties grip a person when that which is sought remains hidden, invisible or incomprehensible. When what is sought comes into view, fears and anxieties cease and the spirit is face to face with the reality. When the truth self-discloses, the spirit that wants to see the beauty of God reaches its goal. As for those who bow to their own souls and fall into error, they suffer the punishment of fear and supposition.

People are close to God to the extent that they believe that the Unseen, from which they await mercy from the sky and greenery from the earth, will one day fulfill these expectations.

O Humankind

Faith is beautiful when realities are secret, invisible, when they are reached by way of thought, insight and comprehension. This is the wisdom in God the Truth's closing the window opening onto the Unseen in this transitory world.

God has done this for the good of humankind, so that people may attain the human level of finding the truth for themselves and in the end attain the felicity of reaching and experiencing such a level of humanity.

Worship of God and faith in Him, like the fidelity of the heroes of the limit, is worthy only prior to the day of death.

The faithless will see God near them on the day of death, comprehending His sublimity at the Resurrection, but the faith they have at that moment will surely not be pleasing to God.

God is pleased with those who love and find Him while He is in the Unseen, before they see Him.[169]

- *God has nor upon the earth nor heaven's span*
Anything more hid than the spirit of man

God has unfurled the scroll of the dry and wet
But made "of my Lord's command" seal of spirit

Once that tremendous eye has seen the spirit
Then for him there can be nothing else secret

Only the art of that man of fine insight
Whose eye recognized the Sultan in the night

The others were ghouls that lead men to despair
But the eye that saw the Shah and was aware

On the day of audience the Shah was shamed
Before him who had at night gazed on his face[170]

- To fear God is a virtue. God the Truth personally gives peace of heart to those who feel fear of God. He relieves and cheers them with

---

169. Ken'an Rifâî, *Şerhli Mesnevî-i Şerif* (Istanbul: Kubbealtı Neşriyatı 2000), pp. 532-533.

170. Mevlânâ Celâleddin Rûmî, trans. Veled İzbudak, ed. Abdülbaki Gölpınarlı, *Mesnevî* (Istanbul: Milli Eğitim Basımevi 1991), vol. 6, vs. 2877-2879, 2913-2915.

11th Verse

the good news that they should not fear, not grieve. As for the faithless who do not feel fear of God, He pities them and desires that they should know His servants' great truth. A true fear of God is in reality a great love of God. That fear is anxiety that one's love of the so loved God is not worthy, that knowing His limitless greatness intimately, one is not able to be a worthy servant to Him.

Surely God the Truth will be Merciful and Solicitous to those in whose hearts such anxiety burns. Surely He will make their hearts feel the pleasure of security.[171]

- God the Truth has bestowed the seed of that preparedness upon everyone. Everyone is born Muslim. Later their parents make them Christian, Zoroastrian, this or that.

So that preparedness is in everyone by birth. But various causes intervene to keep them from reaching their true homeland, their true beloved. Otherwise every seed that can be cultivated will grow and flourish. And if it does not run into an obstruction, it will reach perfection. What we have said here applies to those who are felicitous in eternity without beginning, that is to say, in the Mother of the Book. The eleventh verse of chapter Yā Sīn gives the good news: *One who fears the Merciful in the Unseen.*[172]

- Fear has three meanings: One is fear, one is wariness, and the other is awe (*hayba*).

The fear we are familiar with is a condition of faith. Wariness is a condition of works. Awe is a condition of gnosis.

To fear all kinds of punishment is the station of the soul. To fear God's wiles and trickery is the station of the heart and of peace.

Bur in the fear belonging to the station of the secret heart and witnessing there is awe and exaltation, which is the station of right conduct. As our Master the Messenger of God has said, "*I know God more than anyone, and I am more afraid than anyone.*" He who fears God is he who knows God.[173] Fear increases according to knowledge, it becomes greater the more one knows God.[174]

---

171. Ken'an Rifâî, *Şerhli Mesnevî-i Şerif* (Istanbul: Kubbealtı Neşriyatı 2000), p. 196
172. Ken'an Rifâî, *Sohbetler* (Istanbul: Kubbealtı Neşriyatı 2000), p. 494.
173. Ken'an Rifâî, *Sohbetler* (Istanbul: Kubbealtı Neşriyatı 2000), p. 319.
174. Ken'an Rifâî, *Sohbetler* (Istanbul: Kubbealtı Neşriyatı 2000), p. 48.

- "The Merciful" means the One who gives being and formal perfection to every thing according to the capacities of the entities (*realities*) in the way wisdom requires. The Merciful is specific to those in need. He has been named with a name in the intensive form, because of the universality of effects (*eserler*), how widespread they are, and the breadth of their field of disposal.[175]

- If darkness comes at nighttime and every friend remains alone with his own friend, My beloveds stand in prayer for Me, bowing their heads and praying with humble supplication. They take the path of My good-pleasure, asking nothing of Me but My love. Out of the perfection of My love I give them three things: The first is a light which I inspire in their hearts, and if they utter prayer continuously they give news of Me with it. The second: I turn toward them with My essence and attributes and make them attain many successes; many are the gifts I give to My friend to whom I turn. The third is a gift that only I know, and My servant knows, and all the things in the world and in heaven are little compared to it.

  O David, inform the servants who are My friends and seek My love that I have lifted the veils between us. They see with the eye of insight, and for that reason no harm comes to them if they are hidden from people, and although kindness and expansion reaches them from Me, the envy and wrath people feel toward them does not affect them and never makes them sorrowful.[176]

- *Remember your Lord when you forget yourself...* (18:24). In other words, practice remembrance of God in such a way that nothing but God remains, including your own self. Because true remembrance means that the rememberer, the remembered, and the remembrance are one. In the heart of one who practices that kind of remembrance there remains no duality and no selfhood. The true beloved gazes into that person's heart and sees His own beauty in that person's heart. Then he announces: "In this heart, in this domain, there is none but the beloved.[177]

---

175. Sadreddin Konevî, trans. Ekrem Demirli, *Esmâ-i Hüsnâ Şerhi* (Istanbul: İz Yayıncılık 2004), p. 39.
176. Noble hadiths from Ken'an Rifâî's notes.
177. Ken'an Rifâî, *Sohbetler* (Istanbul: Kubbealtı Neşriyatı 2000), p. 317.

11th Verse

- God the Truth taught Adam the divine names, and then asked him his own name. Adam said, "I have been made to forget, I don't know, my Lord!" God the Truth decreed: "In that case I have appointed you vicegerent (*nā'ib*) of God on earth. If someone forgets himself when he remembers the name of God the Truth, it is God Himself who does that remembering.[178]

---

178. Şemsettin Yeşil, *Şeyh-i Ekber Muhyiddin-i Arabî Hakikati Nasıl Anlatıyor* (Istanbul: Yaylacık Matbaacılık 1997). p. 42.

12. Truly it is We who bring the dead to life, and We write down what they send before them and what they leave behind, and We have taken account of all things in a discriminating book.

'Innā naḥnu nuḥyi'l-mawtā wa naktubu mā qaddamū wa 'athārahum wa kulla shay'in 'aḥsaynāhu fī 'imamin mubîn.

- If the oneness essence (*zat-ı ahadiyet*) did not give birth to the level of unity, the divine levels would not come to be. Expressions in the Quran such as "I created" and "I set up" refer to the unity essence (*zat-ı vahidiyet*). The state of gathering corresponds to the unity essence in which essence and attributes are together, as in "We created," "We set up."

    This does not mean that the essence is plural. Only the attributes must be plural, and this plurality does not negate the unity of the essence.[179]

- Ibn Arabi used the term *vahid* (*one*) to indicate the Axis, the One of the Age (*this "one" is not the same as the "one" of ahadiyet. Ahadiyet is infinite singleness. Vahid is the arrival of plurality at unity; it describes God the truth self-disclosed in the human being, therefore unity*).

    As indicated in the Quranic verse, "*He is with you wherever you may be*" (57:4), *One* accompanies all of the numerals. That is to say, you have no specific existence outside of One. The existences of the numerals occur by means of One. By whatever numeral One is multiplied, that numeral never increases nor multiplies. Because the numeral used to multiply One multiplies it in the unity of plurality, no increase in plu-

---

[179]. İsmail Hakkı Bursevî, trans. Abdülkâdir Akçiçek, *Kenz-i Mahfi-Gizli Hazine* (Istanbul: Bahar Yayınları 2000), p. 30.

rality results. There can be no question of One increasing, neither in itself nor in the thing by which it is multiplied. One is beyond residing in anything or being resided in by anything. One leaves the realities in the states in which they are found without changing them. Because if the realities were to change, One would also. It is not possible for the realities to change. The letter Alif spreads to the outlets of all the letters. This is the spread of One into the levels of the numerals.[180]

• The perfect human being is an abbreviated book and a superior exemplar of the mother of the book; "the Unity Level" is a level that gathers within itself all the obligatory active names; it harbors within itself all the Lordly attributes. Thus perfect humans are exemplars that contain the meanings and realities of the Realm of Domination as much as they do the wonders of the Realm of Sovereignty. They are books containing divine beauties and astounding arts; an amazing city comprising the sum of the spiritual and bodily, celestial and earthly, wordly and afterworldly realms. Thus, because the perfect human is a summary book that embraces the divine level, *God the Exalted created Adam upon the form of the Merciful* (hadith); *God the Exalted created Adam upon His own form* (hadith). By God's "form" is meant His names and attributes. Just as the names and attributes are called "forms" because they are manifest with the human form, it is also because God the Truth is manifest with the names and attributes.[181]

• Ibn Arabi's statements regarding the discriminating book present certain difficulties. He shares the opinion of the Quranic commentaries that the discriminating book is the Preserved Tablet. At the same time, sometimes he clearly says that it is the First Intellect or the Sublime Pen.

God has said in the Quran: "*He encompasses what is in their hands, and accounts by number for every thing*" (72:28). And of the book: "*It leaves out nothing small or great but takes account of it*" (48:49). This is the station of the scribe who has a *divan* and is the scribe of that divine

---

180. Suad el-Hakîm, trans. Ekrem Demirli, *İbü'l-Arabî Sözlüğü* (Istanbul: Kabalcı Yayınevi 2005), pp. 353-354.

181. İsmâil Rusûhî Ankaravî, ed. İlhan Kutluer, *Nakşel-FüsusŞerhi* (Istanbul: Ribat Yayınları n.d.), pp.15-16.

12th Verse

level. God said: *"We have taken account of all things in a discriminating book"* (36:12). The book of the book (*imâmın imâmı*) is The Book (*kitap*). And that is the Preserved Tablet, which includes erasure and abrogation. Thus all things are in it.[182]

- God is Alive, Knowing, Powerful, Willing, Hearing, Seeing, Speaking.

Human beings are the same. They too are Alive, Knowing, Powerful, Willing, Hearing, Seeing, Speaking.

Human beings are, with their realities that are bound (*bağlı*) to the Essence, the counterparts of God the Truth.

The perfect human being has a right to the names and divine attributes that are bound to the Essence.

The likeness of the perfect human with regard to God the Truth is that of a mirror. When one looks in a mirror, one sees there only one's form; is not possible to see one's form otherwise. God made the perfect human obligatory (*vacip*) to His essence so that His names and attributes should be seen only there.

All of this explained here is the meaning of this gracious Quranic verse:

Truly We offered the Trust to the heavens and the earth and the mountains, but they refused to bear it and feared it, but man bore it. Truly he is unjust and ignorant (33:72).[183]

- In this gracious verse we have said that God's manifest and non-manifest free disposal procedes forth from human beings and is not something they possess; they are only the instruments of God's free disposal, and human beings are unjust and ignorant because they do not know that this free disposal manifesting in them belongs to God.

We wish to say that in the esoteric commentary of the gracious verse, *"We are closer to our servant than his jugular vein,"* "We" means all existing things. In other words, Our actions, names, attributes and

---

182. Suad el-Hakîm, trans. Ekrem Demirli, *İbnü'l-Arabî Sözlüğü* (Istanbul: KabalcıYayınevi 2005), pp. 353-354.

183. Abdü'l-kerîm b. İbrahim el-Cîlî, trans. Seyyid Hüseyin Fevzî Paşa, *İnsan-ı Kâmil* (Istanbul: Kitsan Yayınları n.d.), p.259.

essence manifest in these existents you see around you. Therefore the verse means "We are close to you," that is, "you individual," with Our self-disclosure manifest in all things.[184]

- The reason why the human being is vicegerent on earth, and not in the sky or in Paradise or in Hell, is that the face of the earth is the place of gathering, combination and interaction. The earth is a place that gathers within itself different types of beings, compatible and incompatible. In other words, the earth is a place that includes gathered within itself realms of compassion and rage, subjugation and forgiveness, debasement and exaltation, poverty and richness, God the Truth and creature, creation and command, jinns and devils. Thus the earth is a gathering-realm (*toplayıcı bir alem*) and a place that encompasses all the names and all the things. A deputy must come forth in the form of the person whose deputy they are. Thus Hazret Messger said: *God created Adam upon His form*. While creating Adam, God used both of His hands (His attributes of Grandeur and Beauty) at once. The goal was to ensure that he should be powerful, because of the way he was created. Then the human being acquired knowledge of the names by means of his own reality. Thus the office of deputy on earth came forth for the human being alone. Thus the perfect human being is God the Truth's deputy on earth and God the Truth's trustee among creatures. The perfect human carries out on earth the judgments of the divine names according to the preparedness of the reality of the thing regarding which judgment has been given. Thus the perfect human appears on earth in various forms.

Perfect human beings are sometimes in the form of a powerful ruler. Sometimes they appear in the form of mercy, or of violence and power, vengeance and compulsion; sometimes in veiled form and sometimes as grace, sometimes happiness, or surprise, and sometimes with a smiling face. What is meant by "the perfect human being" is the level that encompasses all the divine names. And so perfect humans also gather within themselves the realities of all beings. In this respect, they know the principles of their becoming and the paths of their arriving (at being), their movement and stillness, their souls and everything belonging to them and issuing from

---

184. Ken'an Rifâî, *Sohbetler* (Istanbul: Kubbealtı Neşriyatı 2000), p.329.

them. Just as these things are the perfect human, so are they them. Perfect humans at the same time gather within themselves all the divine names. In this regard perfect humans possess command and free disposal over them; and they all surrender to and gravitate toward the perfect human being.[185]

• Jesus (a.s.) raised the dead with a mere breath because he was a "Spirit," as God named him, and God brought him to be in a fixed human form. Then God the Exalted confirmed him with the Holy Spirit; thus he is a Spirit purified of the filth and dirt of beings and confirmed with a pure Spirit. The fundamental principle in all of this is "the Beginningless Living," which is identical to "Eternal Life." The two sides, Beginningless and Eternal without End, were distinguished from God the Living with the existence of the world and its ontologically subsequent becoming.[186]

• The Hanging Tablet (*lawḥ-i muʿallaq; alterable destiny*) is the line of measuring out we ourselves draw using, to our favor or detriment, the partial will given to us so that we should acquire the courtesy proper to human beings. On this tablet God the Truth removes tribulation, requiting goodness with goodness according to given conditions.

In eternity without beginning God the Truth addressed the spirits and asked, *Am I not your Lord?* And when the spirits answered, *Yes, we testify* (7:172), they were sent to this realm to prove their claim according to the principle that the hand must offer proof for claims made by the tongue. And thus did the world become a way-station of gain or loss.

Whether we are devils or human beings, wretched or felicitous, is our share from eternity without beginning. But just as a jewel is cleaned and cut and made into a jewel through skill, a person of clean substance and superior ability must be handled by a guide in order to become capable of serving society.[187]

---

185. Muhyiddin Arabî, trans. Ekrem Demirli, *Allah Kimleri Sever?* (Istanbul: Hayy Kitap),pp. 19-20.
186. Muhyiddîn İbnü'l-Arabî, trans. Mahmut Kanık, *Marifet ve Hikmet* (Istanbul: İz Yayıncılık 1995), p.201.
187. Meşkûre Sargut, *Gönülden Gönüle* (Istanbul: Kubbealtı Neşriyat 1994), p.122.

- The springtime of the Unseen Realm sends to our world its spring breezes blowing with power. In our world the hearts of those who have arrived (*ermiş insan*) sense this springtime fragrance coming from the spiritual realm. At the same time every evil, arrogance, envy, greed or lust that defeats the human soul in the world lets loose an Autumn storm from the Unseen Realm that brings to the spirit profound damage, great torment and death.

- For those whose heart's eye is open, the birth, death, presences and absences of this world are all a likeness of Resurrection. This thought should wake us up. Like the dawning again of the sun whose light cannot be seen, like the greening and flowering again of skeleton-like trees denuded of their leaves, the coming of the Day of Resurrection that will raise up all human beings dead for centuries again is a reality of which we are informed by the Gracious Quran.[188]

- What is sought in moral beauty is righteousness of intention and works (*amal*). For surely there is a limit and consequence to the works of the bodily limbs. Good deeds also have limits. But there is no limit to intent. That is why our Master the Messenger of God said: "Practice is hidden within intention," and "People will be resurrected according to their intentions," and "God the Truth does not look at your works, he looks at your intentions and your hearts.[189]

- The fundamental goal is in the intention and works of the heart called wholesome works.[190]

- If love of God consisted only of meaning, actions involving the body in worship, such as ritual prayers and fasting, would not have been performed.
  The gifts given by those who love one another are not just love and respect. This love and concern leads people to give material gifts to one another also.

---

188. Ken'an Rifâî, *Şerhli Mesnevî-i Şerif* (Istanbul: Kubbealtı Neşriyatı 2000) pp.292-293.
189. Ken'an Rifâî, *Sohbetler* (Istanbul: Kubbealtı Neşriyatı 2000), p.424.
190. Ken'an Rifâî, *Sohbetler* (Istanbul: Kubbealtı Neşriyatı, 2000), p.98.

12th Verse

When the love between two hearts proceeds in this way, what is more natural than for a servant whose heart bears the love for the greatest beloved to give his God gifts of many different forms? Just as one gives material gifts to God by making works of art out of the various materials God has sent into the world, building mosques, minarets, prayer niches and setting up houses, writing beautiful, illuminated works, easing the way for God's servants by building roads and bridges, in the same way one gives gifts of the heart by encouraging the human body to draw the forms of prayer, fasting, pilgrimage and paying the zakat tax. It is enough that a perfect love and sincerity, appropriate to love of God, be founded in the heart. The love in the heart should take on form in the external world and become actions and works that prove love.

Form is witness to meaning, but there is in the world also pure and false worship belonging to form. Actions performed for the sake of hunting material and spiritual gain done in order to appear pious for the purpose of show, apparent worship, even if in the form of good deeds, taxes and donations, are no different than false witness.

Neither does the rosary in their hands count the names of God, nor are the dervish cloaks on their backs true dervish cloaks. The artificiality in the actions of such as these surely does not escape the eyes of those who know.

The sole nourishment for love of God the Truth and worship is purity of heart and heartfelt attachment to God.[191]

- To be sure, the outward motions of worship are all the same. Those who observe see the true Muslims side by side in the same row with those who imitate worship. But in reality they are as far apart as can be.

Only those who come to prayer for prayer's sake are in the presence of God, not those who come for the sake of imitation.

In the end everyone acts according to his or her own task (*şan*). This means that every human being has a name inscribed on the Preserved Tablet. In reality what self-discloses is whatever has been written on this spiritual tablet, where the writing on the brow [de-

---

191. Ken'an Rifâî, *Şerhli Mesnevî-i Şerif* (Istanbul: Kubbealtı Neşriyatı 2000), pp.382-383.

cree] of every human being was inscribed in eternity without beginning. If a person's name on that Tablet is a good name, in this world they do what that name requires. If the name has been written there as a bad name, a person's behavior in this world will be bad also.

In sum, whatever of subjugation or beauty this name leads to, its owner will wander far and wide and end up there. That is why Hazret Ali said, "Everyone fears their end, while I fear my beginning."[192]

---

192. Ken'an Rifâî, *Şerhli Mesnevî-i Şerif* (Istanbul: Kubbealtı Neşriyatı 2000), p.49.

13. And set forth to them as a parable of the Companions of the City when the messengers came.

Waḍrib lahum mathalan 'aṣḥāba'l-qaryati 'idh jā'ahā'l-mursalūn.

14. We sent them two messengers, but they rejected them. But We strengthened them with a third. They said, "Truly we have been sent to you as messengers."

'Idh 'arsalnā ' ilayhimu'thnayni fakadhdhabūhumā fa'azzaznā bithālithin fa qālū innā 'ilaykum mursalūn.

- Hazret Jesus sent two messengers to invite the people of Antioch to religion. The two messengers ran into a certain Habib-i Najjar on the road and said, "We are messengers." He said, "What is it that establishes your message?" They said, "We heal the blind, the scabious, and the slothful." Habib-i Najjar said, "I have a child afflicted by sloth, make him well." And he brought the child to them. They healed him, and thus Habib-i Najjar declared his faith. After that they arrived at Antioch. But the ruler had them thrown in jail because they did not submit.

    Hazret Jesus then sent Shamun. Shamun at first pretended to be one of them. He went into their houses of worship and prayed to the idols, and at the same time began healing the sick. In the end the ruler chose Shamun as his vizier and said, "You too heal the sick. There were two others from another religion who came here and they made the same claim." Shamun asked for them to be brought before the ruler. The messengers were brought. Shamun said to them: "Do you heal the blind?" They answered yes. Shamun said he also healed the blind, and he asked several more questions. When he received positive answers to all of them, he said, "Mercy, my ruler, these men have something." The ruler ordered that one of his relatives who had died seven days prior be brought. They brought the dead man and the messengers raised him to life again, asking what he had witnessed in the afterworld. The dead man said he had suffered much torment for seven days and finally on the seventh day was told to look at the sky, and when he looked, he saw these two messengers. Then Shamun said to the ruler, "Mercy, my ruler, let us tell our idols, so that they will raise the dead also!" The ruler said, "Do you not know that our idols neither see nor hear?" Shamun said, "In that case, I believe in these messengers," and the ruler declared his faith also.

At this point Habib-i Najjar arrived and said, "O tribe, follow these messengers!" But when the people heard this, they became enraged. They rushed forward to kill Habib-i Najjar. Habib-i Najjar saw the paradisical gardens prepared for him and saying, "O my Lord, if only they would see these blessings and have faith," wished the goodness shown to him for those who did evil to him.[193]

• According to the information given in the Quranic commentaries, while the messengers were in Antioch the people attributed the lack of rainfall and other misfortunes they were suffering to them, and for that reason considered them inauspicious and threatened to stone them to death if they did not desist. Hazret Mevlana Rumi explains that the verse telling how the people of Antioch considered the messengers inauspicious because of the material misfortunes they suffered, and their saying what they did, was because they were struck by the effects of the beautiful spiritual scent of the message brought by the messengers and lost control of themselves.

"The unbelievers were struck by the beautiful scent of the revelation that came with the messengers and lost control of themselves, crying, "You have brought us bad luck."[194]

• In this verse "the people of the city" and the three messengers may be anagogically interpreted as *the city of the body, spirit, heart*

---

193. Ken'an Rifâî, *Sohbetler* (Istanbul: Kubbealtı Neşriyatı, 2000), p.78.
194. Hüseyin Güllüce, *Kur'ân Tefsîri Açısından Mesnevî* (Istanbul: Ötüken Neşriyat1999), pp. 209-210.

13TH-14TH VERSE

and *intellect*. First the two messengers were sent to them. In light and darkness there was no connection between the messengers and the people of the city. Because the people of the city opposed these two messengers, they were strengthened and confirmed with the messenger of intellect (the First Intellect; divine knowledge, unity, and resembling the sun. As for the likeness of the Universal Intellect, it is the light of the sun falling on water. The Subsistence Intellect [*akl-i maaş*] is light reflected from water.[195] The station of unity and level of divinity is a hidden treasure. The thoughts that come into everyone's heart and mind, intellectual and sensory designs and forms, are all gleams and reflections of that treasure. These gleams are the effects of the bright reflections of the divine attributes, which have the nature of the gold of the treasure. But these gleams and reflections illuminate each person according to his or her preparedness[196]), who in desire and action was appropriate to the soul and invited the soul and the people to what heart and spirit had called them to and who succeeded with them. The people of the city saw the messengers as evil because the messengers tried to forbid them delight and repose and motivate them toward asceticism.

Their stoning of the messengers means that they were full of bodily desires and impulses.

That they denied what the messengers said means that animal lusts and desires occupied and dominated their bodies.

The man who came from the farthest corner of civilization, that is to say from the farthest corner of the city, is love, which has the highest and most sublime station in the body that invites verification of the prior beloved, the messenger who puts forth the religion of unification with the guidance and vision of the light of intellect.[197]

- Every human being, even if apparently small in body, is spiritually big. The seven heavens and seven earths and the things in them, the Throne, the Footstool, the Pen, Paradise and Hell, several times

---

195. Abdü'l-kerîm b. İbrahim el-Cîlî, trans. Seyyid Hüseyin FevzîPaşa, *İnsan-ı Kâmil*, vol. 2 (Istanbul: Kitsan Yayınları), p.97.

196. Ken'an Rifâî, *Sohbetler* (Istanbul: Kubbealtı Neşriyatı, 2000), p.265.

197. Kemâlüddin Abdürrezzâk Kâşânîyyü's-Semerkandî, trans. AliRıza Doksanyedi, ed. M. Vehbi Güloğlu, *Te'vilât-ı-Kâşâniyye* (Ankara: Kadıoğlu Matbaası 1988), pp.12-13.

a day enter into that city of the body, move around in it, and leave from the other side. But very few people can sense this. The human being is like a big city. In the center of it there is a great sultan sitting on a great throne. The sultan there is God's judgment. The spirit is his land, the heart his treasury, the intellect his measurers and weighers, and the comprehension is his measure and scale. This city has four Gates. The eyes, the ears, the tongue and the hands. All creatures enter by one side and exit from the other. Those who come into the city cannot leave without passing before the intellect. The comprehension chooses the good and the bad according to value, measure and weight, detaining those it likes and releasing those it does not. Of those in this caravan, some enter through the gate of the eye and leave through the gate of the hand. That is, they go in being seen, and come out as action, works and craft. Some enter through the gate of the ear and come out through the gate of the tongue. That is, they come in by being heard, and come out as speech. The intellect takes pictures of those who pass before it and gives them to the imagination. The imagination owns the intellect's notebooks. The intellect keeps the pictures it likes and releases the rest.

If you know that, know this: When the caravans enter the city of the body by way of seeing and hearing, there is no difference between believer and hypocrite. But there are many differences in how those who enter make use through action and speech of the capital they take. Among those who come in by way of ear and eye believers take the ones God finds good, and they do good and speak good. They turn one good into a thousand, and even more. That believer is like *a grain of corn that grows seven ears, and each ear has a hundred grains. God gives manifold increase to those He pleases* (2:261).

Of the caravans that enter by way of the ear and eye, hypocrites take in those God finds evil, and they do evil, and speak evil. Unlike the believer, they make of one evil a thousand and more. They are like a bad grain that yields many branches and upon each branch are many thorns.

The believer seeks out none but those who strengthen their faith, increase their knowledge and gnosis, perform their works purely and correct their character. The hypocrite seeks out none but those who strengthen their divisiveness, increase their satanity, disperse the all-comprehensiveness of their hearts and collect evil whispers. What is important is not seeing, but taking what you see and performing works with it. Character and speech are esteemed, not hearing. There is no honor in listening to what is beautiful; what is esteemed is the appearance of the beautiful fruit that comes of taking it in. What is important is not to look at the good but for that good to transform your practice into good works.

A human being is like a mirror before which everything passes. In some mirrors, forms are reflected correctly and appear beautiful, and in some they appear twisted. Or as God the Truth has said, human beings are like good or arid earth: *From land that is good comes forth greenery, by permission of its Lord, and from that which is bad nothing comes forth but stunted crop* (7:58).

Good earth improves bad seed. In the course of two or three seasons, it turns bad seed into good. Bad earth ruins good seed in two or three seasons. The human heart is like that too, when listening to true speech. Just as God the Sublime has said: If God had found any good in them, surely He would have made them hear. Had He made them hear, they would have turned back (8:23).

But in all of this the judgment is God the Exalted's judgment. All human beings may be counted as lords (*mevla*), because they perform actions according to God's decree.[198]

- Plato recognized three faculties in the spirit: One is the *nous* or intellect, in the head; the second is *thymoeides*, courage, located in the heart; and the third is *epithymetikon*, lust, located in the abdomen.

Plato likened the spirit to a racing chariot, in which the charioteer is intellect and the two horses pulling the chariot are courage and lust.

Courage is an extraordinarily noble and beautiful animal. The other horse is surly and continually inclined to go off the track. As long as intellect drives the chariot, it preserves the order of the race.

Plato also says: There is no voluntary evil in human beings. However evil, they arebound to the root of virtue. If evil comes before persons who are something of good, it will not be able to resist their

---

198. Niyâzî-yi Mısrî, trans. Süleyman Ateş, *İrfan Sofraları* (Istanbul: Yeni UfuklarNeşriyatı n.d.), p. 77-78.

shattering love. For they are that beautiful. Therefore, because virtue is to know the good and to resemble God, it means life within the circle of harmony and order.

Thus this virtue is divided into four powers. The first is the virtue of the intellect, which is prudence. The second is the virtue of the heart, which is courage. The third is the virtue of appetite, which is moderation. And there is a virtue born of these three, which is justice.

Thus a person is called just who lives a life appropriate to and harmonious with their self, their like, and the whole world.[199]

- There are three powers in human beings. One is nature, from which appetite derives. One is the soul, from which proceeds desire, and one is the heart, from which love proceeds.[200]

- From the Gospel: "Blessed are the peacemakers, for they will see God" [sic].[201]

- *What prevents you from prostrating yourself to what I created with My two hands?* (38:75)
The threes:
The vicegerent of God the Truth
The deputy of Hazret Messenger (*exoteric sciences*)
The deputy of our Master Hazret Ali (*esoteric sciences*) (*sciences concerning the secret heart and truth*).[202]

- There is no one stronger or more powerful than the Axis. But from the point of view of the attribute of servanthood, there is no one more powerless and weak. The Axis is the inwardness of prophethood, the inner aspect of messengerhood. The externality of the Axis is called prophethood, and interiority, friendship with God (*vilayet*).

With God (*Allah indinde*) the Axis's name is Abdullah; he directs everything at the center of the world, great and small. At the same

---

199. Ken'an Rifâî, *Sohbetler* (Istanbul: Kubbealtı Neşriyatı 2000), p.365.
200. Ken'an Rifâî, *Sohbetler* (Istanbul: Kubbealtı Neşriyatı 2000), p.582.
201. Ken'an Rifâî, *Sohbetler* (Istanbul: Kubbealtı Neşriyatı 2000), p. 265.
202. Ken'an Rifâî, *Sohbetler* (Istanbul: Kubbealtı Neşriyatı 2000), p. 555.

13th-14th Verse

time his name is Abduljami; this name indicates that he comprehends all of the divine names.

The Axes are deputies (*naip*) of Hazret Enoch.[203] The Axis is the heart of the world who gives the spirit of life to everyone and everything, from the highest to the lowest.[204]

- The name of the Imam of the Right is Abdürrab; he takes care of protecting the Realm of Sovereignty.

The name of the Imam of the Left is Abdülmelik; he is in charge of the affairs of the Realm of Kingdom.[205]

---

203. Mûsâ b. Şeyh Tahir Tokadî, İsmâil Hakkı Bursevî, Hacı Bektaş-ı Velî, Muhammed Nurü'l-Arabî, ed. Tahir Hafızalioğlu, *Gayb Bahçelerinden Seslenişler* (Istanbul: İnsan Yayınları 2003), p.103.

204. Mûsâ b. Şeyh Tahir Tokadî, İsmâil Hakkı Bursevî, Hacı Bektaş-ı Velî, Muhammed Nurü'l-Arabî, ed. Tahir Hafızalioğlu, *Gayb Bahçelerinden Seslenişler* (Istanbul: İnsan Yayınları 2003), p.106.

205. Mûsâ b. Şeyh Tahir Tokadî, İsmâil Hakkı Bursevî, Hacı Bektaş-ı Velî, Muhammed Nurü'l-Arabî, ed. Tahir Hafızalioğlu, *Gayb Bahçelerinden Seslenişler* (Istanbul: İnsan Yayınları 2003), p.110.

15. They said, "You are only mortal creatures like ourselves and the Merciful sent no such revelation; you do nothing but lie."

Qālū mā 'antum 'illā basharun mithlunā wa mā 'anzala'r-raḥmānu min shay'in 'in 'antum 'illā takdhibūn.

- God named Adam "mortal creature" (*beşer*) because when God created him with His two hands He touched him in a way appropriate to his rank with the two hands attributed to Him.

  The value of the mortal creature can be appreciated by those who know the meanings of the verse,"*What prevents you from prostrating yourself to what I created with My two hands?*"

  The reason he was named "mortal creature" is that the two hands touched him while he was being created.[206]

- Because he was a messenger and friend of God, people thought he had a different nature. They said: "Like us he eats, drinks, and walks the streets, he is a person like we are." As the Gracious Quran states, messengers cannot perform every miracle and wonder they wish. People suppose that a messenger should not eat or drink or walk the streets and should not be a mortal like themselves and should be able to perform any miracle they ask. When they see that he is not as they suppose, they say, "Messengers should be this way and that way, but he is not like that." They repudiate him. They do not know that the messengers of former times were that way also. If those who repudiate him had lived in the time of those earlier messengers, like the people of those times they too, with these corrupt suppositions of theirs, they would have repudiated them. As the time of each perfect

---

[206]. Suad el-Hakîm, trans. Ekrem Demirli, *İbnü'l-Arabî Sözlüğü* (Istanbul: KabalcıYayınevi 2005), p. 118.

human being of later ages arrives and passes, the deficient suppose them to be vested with the perfections they concoct but which are actually impossible, and they believe in them for that reason and so repudiate those of the present.

What necessitates friendship is being of the same genus, and of course, contact. A person who has in their nature a bit of the perfections found in the nature of messengers and angels immediately inclines toward them when they see and hear them. The perfections actively existing in the messengers attract the potential perfection in them. For this perfection to overtake them is like the situation of lover and beloved. When someone who does not have anything of this perfection in their constitution sees them, they flee them like a bat fleeing the sun.

There is a parable that takes place in a well: Joseph (a.s.) was thrown into a well and only got out by clinging to the bucket let down into the well. Now, the messengers and friends of God are caravans and convoys that come from God and return to God. Joseph, who possessed Lordly knowledge and actual divine human perfections, was imprisoned in the jail of nature. The world is one of the way-stations of the afterworld. The bucket is the book of God that comes down to human beings. The caravan-leaders (that is to say, the messengers') letting down the bucket is their inviting people to God's book. Clinging to the bucket is believing in those who bring the book and accepting them. But if the one inside the well is a frog, centipede, snake or one of the insects that live in wells and does not want to hang on to the rope that is let down, does not want to cling to it and get out of the well, who can do anything about it? Because the spirits of some people are beautiful and of superior nature. They do not feel friendship for base individuals. They seek a faithful friend to help them go to the sublime homeland. The spirits of some people are vicious, their nature is base. They feel friendship only for those who have their nature. They choose a homeland in the realm of nature. They do not love the travellers who ascend to the Sublime Realm. They accept no invitation. God the Exalted has said: *We have surely created the human being in the best stature. Then we bring him down to the lowest of the low* (95:4-6).[207]

---

207. Niyâzî-yi Mısrî, trans. Süleyman Ateş, *İrfan Sofraları* (Istanbul: Yeni UfuklarNeşriyatı n.d.), p. 72-74.

15th Verse

- Hazret Muhammed, who was the greatest of the messengers, for a long time bore from the divine source to the human realm the commands of religion and the duties that people should perform in the way of goodness, beauty, and eternity.

  He performed his office with that greatness of spirit he had, so that one day when he was as if not a body but a spirit, although he was still living, he was carried by a Buraq and ascended to the presence of God the Truth.

  For years decrees were sent to him by God the Truth. In the end he also became a giver of decrees.

  He performed his office as God's ambassador in such a limitless breadth that it was not to a tribe but to all humankind and jinn.

  Until he became a messenger he tread the path of the star that held out light to him. Up until that time he lived according to the writing on his own brow, but when his office of ambassador arrived and he became a messenger living among the people according to the truth, he was no longer judge and commander of his own star and own measuring out but of all stars. Because he now derived his power not from nature, not from food and drink, but directly from God.[208]

- It is easier to recognize and know God than to know His secrets. In the same way, if you want to see and recognize someone you can accomplish this with very little effort; but no matter how hard you try, you cannot know and understand the secrets hidden in that person's heart.

  Thus to know a person by how they appear is much easier than to know their hidden secrets. Someone may obtain a learned person's permission to visit by making a bit of an effort. But to acquire that person's learning requires a spirit willing to endure years of toil and suffer many difficulties in order to acquire something of that person's treasure of knowledge.

  In any city there are hundreds of thousands of people who worship God and seek their needs from God. They know God to be the one who can do all things, the one who provides sustenance to all, who disciplines, who shows the way, forgives all sins and at the same

---

208. Ken'an Rifâî, *Şerhli Mesnevî-i Şerif* (Istanbul: Kubbealtı Neşriyatı 2000), p.148.

time destroys all. They obey and worship him heart and soul. So do all generally. Some of them have a strong practice in knowing God, some little, some much. But among those hundreds of thousands of people very few have turned toward a Shaykh and a true friend of God. And of those, only one or two have been able to know that friend of God well. Thus it is known that to worship God and know of Him is universal. Everyone has a place and a way here. Even unbelievers worship God.

All beings and newly arrived things are veils obstructing people from worshipping God and gatekeepers preventing them from entering the place where that secret is. Sweet foods, silk garments, and the beautiful girls of China keep people from worship. They waylay aspirants and travellers on the path. Only some of these people get away from these bandits on the path, by moaning day and night, mentioning God and reciting "There is no fear nor power save in God." They bring the burdens of their worship as far as God's way-station of good-pleasure and acceptance. But God Himself stands guard and protects his friends so that no one should have contact with them, or know them, or find a way to them.

With "There is no strength nor power.." and mention of God it is possible to drive away the creatures like devils and fairies who keep people from worship. But if the obstacle is God, what recited formula can make Him go away? In this sense it is harder to find and know friends of God than it is to know God. Surely a person who knows a friend of God knows God. But the reverse is impossible. To know God does not mean that one knows a friend of God. There are many people who do not know God's friends even though they know God and serve Him. When they see the friends they even take offense and repudiate them.[209]

- Although if humans throw off the burden of soul in them and become pure spirit, their level can be superior to that of the angels, the number of them who are able to dedicate themselves to God and become free of worldly filth is always small compared with those who do not and cannot. And most of those who are able to do it keep their

---

209. Sultan Veled, trans. Meliha Anbarcıoğlu, *Maarif* (Konya: Altunarı Ofset 2002), pp. 6-8.

15th Verse

shedding of their own creatureliness secret from the crowd. Divine love cannot be known to all or told to every ignorant person. One must keep great secrets from those not intimate with them.[210]

They suppose themselves the equal of prophets
They imagine that they resemble God's friends

"Behold," they say, "they are creatures as are we
We are both enslaved to hunger and to sleep."

What they do not know in their blindness is this:
There is between them infinite difference

Two species of insect feed on the same things
But one makes honey and the other just stings

Two deer species graze on grass and drink water
One produces dung, the other musk so pure

Two reeds drink from the same bank by a river
One is empty, the other full of sugar

Ponder hundreds of thousands such likenesses
Ponder their seventy years' road differences

This one eats and from him feces is discharged
That one eats and becomes all the light of God

This one eats, envy and greed are his offspring
That one eats, love of the One is his offspring

There the earth's brackish and bad, here it is pure
That angel's a beast, a devil, this one's pure[211]

- **Commanding soul:** Dominated by undesirable evil states and actions. Its practice and works are all forbidden things. It does not know forbidden from permitted, but will knowingly commit the for-

---

210. Ken'an Rifâî, *Şerhli Mesnevî-i Şerif* (Istanbul: Kubbealtı Neşriyatı 2000), p.502.

211. Şefik Can, *Konularına göre açıklamalı Mesnevî Tercümesi*, vols. 1-2 (Istanbul: ÖtükenNeşriyat 1997), p. 30.

bidden. It says, "God is All-Concealing (*Ghaffār*) and Compassionate. I am still young, I have time, I have many years of life before me to live. I will repent when I am old. Even if I do die without regretting, without repenting, torment is not fitting for God's glory. We are servants of Hazret God the Truth and so it is not appropriate for Him to torment us." It supposes that it has been accorded the good news and will go to the Garden if it gives alms or does a good deed once in forty years. It says, "I am not one of those left on the path, I have reached my God," and because it is sure of God's grace, finds consolation and distraction for itself.

Lordliness is the name of the level necessitating the Names, which seek the existents. It includes the names Knowing, Hearing, Seeing, Everstanding, Desiring, King and other similar ones. For all of these names and attributes seek a being to belong to, to be connected to.

The names under "Lord" and those shared by God and the creation are, from the point of view of effect, special to creation. Those shared names that are special to God and have a face (*veche*) toward the creation are the names like "Knowing."

The name "Knowing" is a name that belongs to the soul. That is why those who knows their own souls know the creation. Those who hear their souls, hear others.

What we mean by names shared between God and the creation is that those names have two faces, and one face is special to the Divine (Cenâb-ı İlâhî) and the other special to the existents. The names belonging to action are under the name "King." Because there can be no king without a country. The names special to the creation and the names belonging to action are the names like "Powerful."

For example, you can say of "the creation," which is a noun belonging to action, "God created the existents." But you can't say: "They created themselves." You can say: "He gave sustenance to the existents." But you can't say: "They gave sustenance to themselves." The name "Lord" is the name of the level that includes those shared names both faces of which are special to the creation.

"Merciful" is the name of the level comprising all the divine, sublime qualities. The divine essence wishes to be single with those qualities:whether special to the creatures, like "Creator" and "All-Provider,"as with "Tremendous" and "Solitary," they are coequal. "Allah"

15TH VERSE

is the name of a level of the essence that comprehends the realities of the existents in their sublimities and contemptibilities. In this respect the name "Merciful" is subsumed under the name "Allah." As for the name "Lord," it is subsumed under the name "Merciful."

Lordliness is the throne of the Merciful. In other words, it is a site of manifestation for the Merciful, from which He faces the existents.[212]

- There are three reasons to resist believing in messengers:

  Jealousy.
  Fear of a reckoning.
  Pride.[213]

- "Merciful" is a name and it belongs to the essence. "Merciful" is the station of gathering-together and that is the station of not-knowing. The most estimable station to be achieved on the path of God is the station of not knowing Him and knowing that one cannot know. Because that is the reality of servanthood.[214]

- To accept the Lord: To swear fealty to what He has said and try to live according to its moral precepts. The order created by the Merciful is protected by the name "Lord."

  Before the city of Medina accepted Hazret Muhammad (s.a.s.), it was called Yathrib. It took the name Medina, meaning "civilization," when it accepted the name "Lord."

  The author of *Vâridat* says:

  "What is the reason why all messengers and friends of God were met with hatred and enmity in their time and followed by very few people, but after death their names became famous and lived forever and most of humankind believed in them and loved them?

  "I say: First of all, many were jealous of the messengers and friends in their lifetimes. These jealous people kept saying things to make the people around them run away, to cloud their hearts, and

---

212. Abdü'l-kerîm b. İbrahim el-Cîlî, trans. Seyyid Hüseyin Fevzîpaşa, *İnsan-ı Kâmil*, vol 1 (Istanbul: Kitsan Yayınları n.d.), pp.153-155.
213. Haluk Nurbaki, *Yâ-Sîn Sûresi Yorumu* (Istanbul: Damla Yayınevi 1999), p.30.
214. Muhyiddîn İbnü'l-Arabî, trans. Ekrem Demirli, *Fütuhât-i Mekkiyye*, vol. 2 (Istanbul: Litera Yayıncılık 2006), p.304.

shake their faith. But when the messengers or friends died, the envy died away too, and all that was left was the record of what they did. Thus most people then began to believe in them and love them.

"Secondly: To be among people, socialize with them, live with them, brings over-familiarity. And this reduces love and the belief in the special position of a messenger or friend of God.

"Thirdly: The truth of a messenger or friend only emerges gradually."[215]

• When I was child I spake as a child, I understood as a child, I thought as a child: but when I became a man I put away childish things. For now we see through a glass, darkly; but then face to face: now I know in part; but then shall I know even as also I am known.[216]

• God made the prophets a means so that the envy hidden in the breasts of human beings should be plain to see. For one does not envy God.

Mortal creatures are envious, and they look at the Messenger and say, burning furiously with the torment of envy, "He is a mortal like me." But those who see the greatness of the Messenger through the support of the Glorified and the proofs of God the Truth say, "In form he bears resemblance to a mortal creature. But with regard to his messengerhood, and the face he has toward God the Truth, he does not resemble a human being," and they attain to presence.

Those of evil temperament envy the Human Being. They are in no way able to escape the denial and opposition born of envy and have become companions of the fire.

Those of beautiful temperament have escaped enmity toward the Human Being and reached eternal felicity.[217]

• *God the Truth fashioned the prophets as a means*
So that envy in disquietude be seen

---

215. Niyazî-i Muhammed Mısrî, trans. Prof. Dr. Süleyman Ateş, *İrfan Sofraları* (Istanbul: Yeni Ufuklar Neşriyatn.d.), pp.71-72.

216. The Holy Bible, King James Version, Corinthians 1:13.

217. Şemseddin Yeşil, *Kitab'üt-Tasavvuf; Mesnevi'den Hikmetler* (Istanbul: Ş. Yeşil Kitabevi 1986), p. 291.

15th Verse

Since no one can be ashamed by God the Truth
Neither is there place to envy God the Truth

He who thinks they can be compared with himself
Feels envy toward them for that reason itself

Since the Prophet's greatness cannot be denied
No one envies him that it is recognized

Every age has a vicegerent friend of God
Till the Resurrection his proof carries on[218]

- *On the outside he is old, and young within*
So what kind of thing is that prophet and friend?

If they're not manifest to both good and bad
What is this envy for them base persons have?

If they have no certain knowledge of the friends
Why this hatred, trickery and resentment?[219]

- What perverts a person's soul and sets in motion the devil within him is that abominable envy. It was because Satan was jealous of Adam that he did not bow down to him. That is why he was driven away from God the Truth and the realm of light. Do not you then regard with envious eye those who are superior to you, especially the perfect human beings.

It is that envious gaze which makes the universe appear black as black can be. As long as you avoid envy, as long as you do not fall into the trap of the devil of envy, you will see that great light.

Think of the body as a home in which intellect, comprehension and emotions take shelter. The function and safety of each of them is shaken when envy intervenes. Envy blackens the pure white of their faces. Just as God makes the hearts of his prophets and friends totally

---

218. Mevlânâ Celâleddin Rûmî, trans. Veled İzbudak, ed. Abdülbaki Gölpınarlı, *Mesnevî* (Istanbul: Milli Eğitim Basımevi 1991), vol. 2, vs. 811-815.

219. Mevlânâ Celâleddin Rûmî, trans. Veled İzbudak, ed. Abdülbaki Gölpınarlı, *Mesnevî* (Istanbul: Milli Eğitim Basımevi 1991), vol. 2, vs. 3101-3104.

purified of envy, he purifies by means of knowledge and gnosis the hearts of all those who tread the path of His love.[220]

- *Counselors compound, to bring on God's mercy,*
Medicines of rose water or ambergris

But the impure are not worthy of the sweet
Trusted friends, it is not suitable or meet

Revelation's scent made them lost and confused
So they cried out, "We auger evil from you!

"This discourse is pain and malady for us
It does not indicate good fortune for us

"If you start to give us counsel once again
At that very instant we will stone you dead

"We are fat on empty talk and idle play
We are not accustomed to the things you say

"Our food is lies, amorous sport and self-praise
This message you bring us gives us stomachache

"Hundredfold and more you increase our defect
You use opium to treat the intellect"[221]

- Those who do not believe are unfortunates who cannot see the universe with the eye that takes lessons from things, who cannot hear with the ear of the heart the sounds rising up from creation, who cannot understand its language of inner states nor smell the divine fragrance wafting from it. They are like the *câl* beetle which is disgusted by rose scent and cannot bear its color or its fragrance, and so turns away and faints whenever it smells rose scent.[222]

---

220. Ken'an Rifâî, *Şerhli Mesnevî-i Şerif* (Istanbul: Kubbealtı Neşriyatı 2000), pp.66-67.

221. Şefik Can, *Konularına göre açıklamalı Mesnevi Tercümesi* (Istanbul: Ötüken Neşriyat 1997), vol. 3-4, p. 400 [Nicholson vol. 4, vs. 282-288].

222. Ken'an Rifâî, *Şerhli Mesnevî-i Şerif* (Istanbul: Kubbealtı Neşriyatı 2000), pp.289-290.

16. They said, "Our Lord knows, truly we have been sent as messengers to you.

Qalū rabbunā yaʿlamu ʾinnā ʾilaykum la mursalūn.

17. And our duty is only clear deliverance of the message."

Wa mā ʿalaynā ʾllā'l-balāghu'l-mubīn.

- His messenger is Him. In other words, He Himself. His messengerhood is Him. In other words, He is His messenger. In other words, He Himself. Because He is His word. That is to say, He Himself. He sent a messenger from Himself, with Himself, to Himself. There is neither cause nor means, none of that. Remove these from your mind. The one who sends the messenger, what the messenger brings, the messenger himself and the one from whom the messenger comes are all the same being; they are one thing. There is no difference, no distinction and no separation between them. But neither should you forget that you are neither a mortal nor an existent... You are He, and He is you. When you know that you neither possess an existence, nor are you one who will reach a mortal state, that is when you are counted to have truly understood God the Exalted.[223]

- Those who give their hearts to the world are unaware of love of the Lord. In fact, since every particular is part of the universal, it is in a state tending toward and attracted to the universal. For this reason, the moment the particular grasps the particular, it has lost it. But because it has a fondness for it, because it has given its heart

---

223. Muhyiddin İbnül'l-Arabî, trans. Abdülkâdir Akçiçek, *Mir'atü'l İrfan—İrfan Aynası* (Istanbul: Bahar Yayınları 2000), pp. 22-27.

to it, it suffers from being deprived of it. That is why those who have a fondness for and feel affection for the particulars of the world and the transient delights born of them are disappointed.

If you put aside the real and bind yourself to appearances instead of God's beautiful names and the sublime essence that finds expression with those names, you will either make your path longer or lose it entirely.

If the connection of the part with the whole, that is, the part's being the whole, were perfect in every respect, there would have been no reason for the Lord to send messengers into the world. The job of the messengers is to tie parts to the whole in every respect that they should be tied to the whole. For example, which events are merciful, and which satanic? Which bonds bring a person to God, and which leave him lost in heedlessness? Who are the friends, and how and in what manner do they guide the parts?

So, the problem is the struggle to reach a level where one can comprehend how the part is connected in every respect, in every single respect, with the whole.

What need is there of messengers whose job is to bring bondsmen to reach God? Whom will the messenger take hold of, and to whom will he bring him?

The messenger's job is to awaken not those who have become one being with God but those who have not. The messenger's job is to bring back to that great road not the masters of heart, but those who slip and fall in this darkness of night and lose the path.[224]

A murshid is the officer (*memur*) of God the Truth. But not everyone can see them that way. Or people see them according to their own comprehension, their own understanding.[225] But it is the officers and educators charged by God with the duty of guiding to the straight path who bring the aspirant (*sâlik*) to truth and perfection.[226]

- O brother! O sister!

Don't say that if you had listened to my counsel you would have followed me, "If you had wished, you could have made me follow you."

---

224. Ken'an Rifâî, *Şerhli Mesnevî-i Şerif* (Istanbul: Kubbealtı Neşriyatı 2000), pp.411-412.

225. Ken'an Rifâî, *Sohbetler* (Istanbul: Kubbealtı Neşriyatı 2000), p. 551.

226. Ken'an Rifâî, *Sohbetler* (Istanbul: Kubbealtı Neşriyatı 2000), p. 361.

16TH-17TH VERSE

For my duty is merely counsel. It falls to you to listen always and conform. Continue to obey God! Show acceptance of the decree He has decreed. Bring forth intimacy with remembrance of God so that you may be one of God's chosen servants. One who attains gnosis of God is saved from the sorrow of the measuring out. For the true gnostic is the one who migrates (*hicret*) to God the Truth by disengaging the spirit from its attachment to the body.[227]

• Hazret Moses called Pharaoh back to religion again and again and worked hard, but seeing that he nonetheless did not come to faith, Moses implored God the Truth and said: "O my Lord, such as these do not come to religion and do not try to be good. You have stamped them with the seal of evil, You know that they will not come to faith because you know the state of Your servants, but what is Your wisdom in sending me to call him?" God the Truth said: "O Moses, conform to Noah, you are charged with the office of invitation, look no further. Such as these conform to Satan, they draw away from prophets and friends of God, in truth they have no choice because this pertains to their beginningless states (*ezelleri*). Their paths were drawn for error in eternity without beginning.[228]

• Once the eye is blind it cannot see the truth. Why is it that although the Messenger of God brought a proof like the Quran and so many miracles, not everyone affirmed his messengerhood? In fact his greatest miracle was his immaculate countenance. Did Abu Bakr require any other miracle for faith?[229]

Hazret Messenger's Farewell Speech:
   In the name of God, the Merciful, the Compassionate
   O people!
   Listen well to what I say! I do not know, it may be that after this year I will not be able to meet with you here.

---

227. Ahmed er-Rifâî, ed. Dr. H. Kâmil Yılmaz, *Marifet Yolu* (Istanbul: Erkam Yayıncılık 1995), p. 44.
228. Ken'an Rifâî, ed. Kâzım Büyükaksoy, *Mesnevî Hatıraları* (Istanbul: İnkilap Kitapevi 1968), pp. 66-67.
229. Ken'an Rifâî, *Sohbetler* (Istanbul: Kubbealtı Neşriyatı 2000), p.544.

People!

Just as these days of yours are sacred, just as these months of yours are sacred, just as this city of yours (Mecca) is a blessed city, your souls, your property, and your honor are sanctified in the same way, protected from any and all violation.

My companions!

You will surely meet your Lord. And He will call you to account for what you have done. Beware, when I am gone do not return to your former erring ways and do not cut off each other's heads! May those here transmit this legacy of mine to those not here. It may be that someone here will transmit it to someone who better understands.

My companions!

Whoever has possession of a trust, let them give it to its owner immediately. Know that usury of all kinds has been abolished. God has commanded it so. The first usury I abolished was that of Abdülmuttalib's son Abbas. Because your principal belongs to you.

My companions!

Beware, all the customs of the time of ignorance have been abolished, they are under my feet. The blood feuds carried on during the age of ignorance too have been abolished. The first blood feud I abolished was that of Abdulmuttalib's granddaughter Rabia.

O people!

Surely Satan has given up all hope of being worshipped in this land of yours. But if you otherwise conform to him in small matters, that will please him also.

In order to protect your religion beware of these things also.

O people!

I recommend that you observe the rights of women and fear God in this respect. You have taken women as a trust from God, and by God's command you have made their honor lawful for yourselves. You have a right over women, and women have rights over you. Your right over women is that they not violate family honor and your nobility. The rights of women over you are that you procure their food and clothing according to lawful custom and rule.

O believers!

16th-17th Verse

I am leaving you two trusts. If you embrace them and conform to them, you will not go astray. Those trusts are God's book, the Gracious Quran, and the practice of His messenger.

Believers!

Listen well to what I say and remember it well! Muslim is brother/sister to Muslim and thus all Muslims are siblings. It is not lawful to stretch out one's hand toward what is someone else's right as long as that someone does not give it with the heart's pleasure.

My companions!

Do not oppress your souls. Your souls have a right over you also.

O people!

Your Lord is one. Your father is also one. You are all the children of Adam, and Adam is of earth.

Just as the Arab is not superior to the non-Arab, and the non-Arab not superior to the Arab, the red-skinned is not superior to the black-skinned, and the black-skinned not superior to the red-skinned.

Superiority is solely in godwariness (*takva*), in fear of God. The one most valuable to God is the one who most fears God.

Even should a black slave with a limb cut off be appointed as emir over you, if he rules over you by God's book, listen to him and obey him.

A person who is guilty may not accuse anyone else of their crime. A father may not be accused of his son's crime nor a son of his father's.

Beware!

You must never do any of these four things:

You will not stipulate any thing as partner to God.

You will not unlawfully slay any soul that God has made forbidden and immune to prosecution.

You will not commit adultery.

You will not commit theft.

People!

Tomorrow they will ask you about me, what will you say?

The noble Companions have all said:

"We bear witness that you practiced the messengerhood of God, you performed your duty as it should rightly be performed, you gave us legacy and counsel!"

Then our Efendi, the Most Gracious Messenger (s.a.s.) raised his index finger and said:

Bear witness, O Lord!
Bear witness, O Lord!
Bear witness, O Lord![230]

---

230. Taken from the *sahih* hadith texts, based on the speeches at Arafat and Mina.

18. "Truly we find in you an evil omen, and if you do not desist, we will certainly stone you, and grievous harm will surely be inflicted on you by us.

Qālū 'innā taṭayyarnā bi kum la 'in lam tantahū lanarjumannakum wa layamassannakum minnā 'adhābun 'alīm.

19. They said, Your evil omens are with yourselves, although you have been admonished. On the contrary, you are a people transgressing all bounds."

Qālū ṭā'irukum ma'akum 'a 'in dhukkirtum bal 'antum qawmun musrifūn.

- The reason it is said that there is a thing in the soul of a human being that does not exist in animals and predators is not because human beings are worse than they. Perhaps it is because the bad humors, souls and infelicities found in human beings are there due to a divine substance hidden within them. But these humors, infelicities and evils become the veil covering that divine substance. However better, more beautiful, greater and more honorable the substance may be, its covering is like that too. In this respect infelicities, evils and bad humors were the means of that covering and it is not possible for that veil to be raised. Only with much struggle is it possible. Those who struggle are of various kinds. The greatest associate with the friends whose faces are turned toward God and away from this world. Struggle is no more difficult than to sit with a good and honest friend. Because to see them is the melting and annihilation of that soul. It is for this reason they say that if a snake does not see a human being for forty years, it will become a dragon, in other words, because the snake has not seen anyone who will melt and eliminate its evil and inauspiciousness. Wherever they hang a great lock, it is an indication of the existence of something fine and valuable there. And wherever the covering is great, the substance there is finer. For example, snakes are found on top of treasures. But don't you look at its ugliness, look at the fine things in the treasure.[231]

- *But the impure are not worthy of the sweet*
Trusted friends, it is not suitable or meet

Revelation's scent made them lost and confused
So they cried out, "We auger evil from you!

"This discourse is pain and malady for us
It does not indicate good fortune for us

"If you start to give us counsel once again
At that very instant we will stone you dead

"We are fat on empty talk and idle play
We are not accustomed to the things you say

"Our food is lies, amorous sport and self-praise
This message you bring us gives us stomachache

"Hundredfold and more you increase our defect
You use opium to treat the intellect"[232]

- If you do not want to lose the water of your life in the sand of such shiny words, give ear not to the shininess of words, but to the one who speaks of God the Truth and the truth!

But there is speech which is a spring of knowledge and gnosis, even in the form of one word; speech which is spoken while stringing pearls of knowledge and gnosis on the string of words; know that such words are beneficial and mighty like waters bubbling up from

---

231. Mevlânâ Celâleddîn Rumî, trans. Meliha Ülker Anbarcıoğlu, *Fîhi Mâ Fîh* (Istanbul: Milli Eğitim Basımevi 1990), pp. 355-356.

232. Şefik Can, *Konularına göre açıklamalı Mesnevi Tercümesi* (Istanbul: Ötüken Neşriyat 1997), vol. 3-4, p. 400 [vol. 4, vs. 282-288].

18TH-19TH VERSE

sand and scattering blessings everywhere, and enrich your pouch of knowledge and gnosis with such words.[233]

- *"Auspiciousness is good character. Inauspiciousness consists in bad character"* (noble hadith).

"Everthing has its own repentence. Only those of bad character have no repentence. For they will repent of no sin that they may not do another that is worse" (noble hadith).[234]

- The Quran says: *"When kings enter a country they despoil it and make the noblest of its people the meanest"* (27:34).

Thus when sultans of love have entered the land of love, they too either kill the great of the soul—self, pride, boasting, arrogance and lust—who are the prominent ones of that land, or make subjects of them. That is to say, they break those who rule in the heart just as our Master the Messenger of God broke the idols.[235]

- Each person is the architect of the building of their life. People find expansiveness, sorrow, Paradise or Hell, good or evil according to whether they have built the building of their life well or badly. The responsibility for the end we arrive at is not others' but our own.[236]

- To say humanity is to say intellect. Not the subsistence intellect, that understands eating, drinking, clothing and walking, but the intellect that finds the meaning of being human and of coming into the world and leaving it. You will remember that Socrates asked his circle if they wanted an intelligent spirit or a spirit without intellect. They answered that they wanted an intelligent spirit. "Then why do you not search for it?" he asked. "Because we already have it," they replied. Their answer brought Socrates to make this reproach: "Well then, what are these disagreements and conflicts that you have between you?"

---

233. Ken'an Rifâî, *Şerhli Mesnevî-i Şerif* (Istanbul: Kubbealtı Neşriyatı 2000), p. 146.
234. Ken'an Rifâî, *Sohbetler* (Istanbul: Kubbealtı Neşriyatı 2000), p. 392.
235. Ken'an Rifâî, *Sohbetler* (Istanbul: Kubbealtı Neşriyatı 2000), p. 511.
236. Ken'an Rifâî, *Sohbetler* (Istanbul: Kubbealtı Neşriyatı 2000), p. 426.

O Humankind

And so it is, behold the way of the world! The intellect finds ways to annihilate in a second a person raised with the toil of so many years! Is this humanity? Even were it not the twentieth, but the fortieth century, there would still be this perfecting, or even one more savage! The civilization that leads the world to ruin![237]

- It is excessive love of the world and wild pleasures the ends of which is bitterness and regret, while those who are rational take example from the events passing before their eyes and do not get swept up in them.[238]

- Profligacy is the wasteful spending of a divine boon that is not appreciated, the destruction of a divine boon by conformance only to the soul and its desires, and it is haram. Thus:

Our health is a divine boon. We can appreciate it by performing the ritual ablution, by prayer, by avoiding bad things, in other words by not committing profligacy.

Time is a divine boon. If you waste it for the sake of wild desires, will you later see your failure and inauspiciousness, see the realities in the religion taught to you?

Another important discussion here concerns those who count religion an opiate. They waste all national revenue in the production of weapons and then come to a dead end and try to blame the sin on society's concept of religion.

The Muhammaden character forbids profligacy for the sake of the ugly and wild desires of the soul and increases national revenue to the maximum. Profligacy is the most important cause of our contemporary economic dilemma in particular and thus of the inauspicious disasters in society.[239]

- It is acceptable to disburse endowments and expenditures when they are appropriate to the situation. Excessive and inappropriate generosity is profligacy. You should spend the boons of God in the place and measure God the Truth commands. Considering that every

---

237. Ken'an Rifâî, *Sohbetler* (Istanbul: Kubbealtı Neşriyatı 2000), p. 410.
238. Ken'an Rifâî, *Sohbetler* (Istanbul: Kubbealtı Neşriyatı 2000), p. 444.
239. Haluk Nurbaki, *Yâ-Sîn Sûresi Yorumu* (Istanbul: Damla Yayınevi 1999), p. 35.

boon and all wealth is given by God and belongs to God, we must know where we should expend it. Expenditure for unworthy persons and things is waste. This is so much the case that you must give not only wealth and boons to the worthy, but also knowledge and gnosis. Learn the commands of God the Truth from those who have reached God the Truth. If you will spend, spend in their way and according to their wishes. Ask them, and spend in the ways they show you and earn their hearts. For not every heart knows and understands the command of God the Truth.[240]

---

240. Ken'an Rifâî, *Şerhli Mesnevî-i Şerif* (Istanbul: Kubbealtı Neşriyatı 2000) p. 323.

20. And a man came running from the outskirts of the city, saying, "O my People, follow the messengers.

Wa jāʾa min ʾaqṣāʾl-madīnati rajulun yasʿā qāla yā qawmi ʾttabiʿūʾl-mursalīn.

• "From the outskirts of the city" also makes one think of a person prominent among that country's leaders. This person came running when he heard that the messengers were about to be assassinated. That he came running means that he was struggling to set an example for the believers and guide them.[241]

• The way of God was filled with fear, closed off and covered with snow. He was the first to put his life at risk, riding his horse and making his way down the road: It is thanks to his showing the way and his kindness that everyone can go down this road. Because he was the first to find this path and place signs everywhere saying, "Do not go that way; if you do, you will die. You will be destroyed like the people of Ad and Samud. But if you go this way, you will be saved like the believers," the entire Quran is explication of this, as in the verse, *"In it are signs manifest"* (3:97). That is to say, we have put signs along the roads, and if someone tries to cut down one of these posts, they will want to kill him, saying, "You are destroying our path, you are trying to destroy us; are you a highwayman?" Know that because of this, Hazret Muhammad (s.a.s.) is the leader. Nothing can reach us without reaching Hazret Muhammad (s.a.s.) first.[242]

---

241. Elmalılı M. Hamdi Yazır, *Hak Dini Kur'ân Dili* (Istanbul: Feza Gazetecilik 1992), vol. 6.

242. Mevlânâ Celâleddin Rûmî, trans. Meliha Ülker Anbarcıoğlu, *Fîhi Mâ Fîh* (Istanbul: Milli Eğitim Basımevi 1985), pp. 342-343.

- The spirit is God's messenger in the body, his trustee. It is the spirit that commands, and the angels that carry out commands.[243]

- The spirit that is God the Truth's deputy in the human body, the heart that is the Messenger's trustee.[244]

- The heart is the shah of the land of body. Actions that manifest from the heart are certainly worthy of a shah. An action worthy of a shah must be magnificently shah-like.[245]

- If you are uncertain whether you are one of the rejected or one of the accepted, turn within yourself and listen to your own spirit. If there is in your heart a profound love and inclination toward them, be glad for your good fortune and share.[246]

- God's friends are the substitutes of God's messengers. They are the persons who stand in the place of the messengers. Thus you should accept what they tell you. Perform what they command. For there is no doubt that they command you only with the commands of God and the Messenger, prohibit you with their prohibitions. They speak as God causes them to speak. They take what is given by God. They engage in not even one single action of themselves. In the religion of God they are not partners to him with actions inspired by the soul. Whether in their words or their actions and movements, they follow the Messenger of God. For they have given ear to the speech of God who is the Exalted and Glorious. God whose dignity is sublime says: *"Embrace what the Messenger commands and avoid what he has forbidden"* (59:7) [247]

- Shaykh Mansur Rabbani says: for you to take refuge in God Most High and trust in Him is for you to be cleansed in your mind from all

---

243. Ken'an Rifâî, *Sohbetler* (Istanbul: Kubbealtı Neşriyatı 2000), p. 470.
244. Ken'an Rifâî, *Sohbetler* (Istanbul: Kubbealtı Neşriyatı 2000), p. 419.
245. Ken'an Rifâî, *Sohbetler* (Istanbul: Kubbealtı Neşriyatı 2000), p. 644.
246. Ken'an Rifâî, *Şerhli Mesnevî-i Şerif* (Istanbul: Kubbealtı Neşriyatı 2000), p. 361.
247. Hacı Ahmed Kayhan, *Abdülkadir-i Geylânî* (Ankara: Özben Marbaacılık 1998), pp. 94-95.

beings other than Him. The community of Sufis has guided us, they have shown us the way. They have opened for us the curtain covering the treasures of pearls in the Quran and sunna. They taught us the wisdom of the courtesy to be observed with God and His Messenger. The Sufis are such a community that those who sit with them never go astray. Let those who have faith in God, who comprehend the greatness of the Messenger, love that community and follow them...[248]

- The perfect murshid is the person who has attained divine attraction and, trained (*sülûk etmiş*) in the presence of a perfect murshid according to shariat law and tarikat custom, seen the invisible realm from beginning to end. They are the site of manifestation of the pure spirit of the Noble Messenger (s.a.s.) and his spiritual inheritor. Such persons have completely effaced their being in the ocean of annihilation in God (*fenâfillah*) and become colorless in the sea of unity. They have donned the kaftan of true subsistence (*bekâ*) and subsist with God the Truth, and then returned to where they began in order to complete the levels of perfection and guide those who seek them out to the way of God the Truth.[249]

- Hazret Mevlana says: "There is a divine preacher in the heart of every Muslim. People could not benefit from preaching or advice if not for the advice they give themselves."

Your heart tells you what path you are on and what condition you are in more correctly than anyone outside of you. A person will not be mistaken if they take a fatwa from the mufti within. If this mufti says: "You are following the desire of your soul, you are becoming more degraded as time goes on!" or "You are inclining toward God the Truth, your heart is filling with God the Truth's light, you are progressing!" this fatwa is truly effective for you. But if this fatwa will not affect you, the words of external advisors will not affect you at all.

Thus this mufti within your heart is a divine preacher. External preachers and advisors only show you the good and bad path and

---

248. Ahmed er-Rifâî, *Kurtarıcı Öğütler* (Istanbul: Bedir Yayınları), p. 80.
249. Mûsâ b. Şeyh Tahir Tokadî, İsmâil Hakkı Bursevî, Hacı Bektaş-ı Velî, Muhammed Nûru'l-Arabî, *Gayb Bahçelerinden Seslenişler*, ed. Tahir Hafızalioğlu (Istanbul: İnsan Yayınları 2003), p. 41.

advise you to avoid the bad and the evil and prefer the good. But they do not know which of these you favor and attend to, and whether it is the path of goodness or evil that pleases you.[250]

• Our souls are a piece of Hell. Just as Hell has seven gates, the soul has seven attributes. They are arrogance, greed, violence, lust, envy, malice and resentment. If the light of God the Truth's encouragement and right guidance enlighten a heart, and the fire of the Merciful's attraction conquers the soul, that person will find felicity.[251]

• Higher knowledge is not found in books. People must derive it from the treasury of their own hearts by means of profound reflection and seek the sacred fire in their own essential source. There is no school for this; this knowledge is bestowed upon a person by God the Truth.

The first result of the heart-knowledge that aims to know God is that the soul becomes wholesome. How is the soul made wholesome, how can this be done?

As long as bad characteristics such as lust, greed, selfishness, arrogance, resentment, rancour, envy and the like are present in people, it is not possible for their souls to become wholesome and use their bodies to rule their countries in prosperity and justice.

But one should know also that it is no easy thing to get free of these characteristics I have mentioned. To remove one of them is like moving the Himalayan Mountains.

Just as there are different teachers for each science and art, there is a teacher for this science of the soul. If candidates for a science or art forget their own knowledge, open their eyes and ears to what their teacher teaches and submit to their master's science without objecting, they can gain their teacher's knowledge.[252]

• Hazret Mevlana Rumi says: Bravo to that absolute physician who divided his soul in two.

---

250. Ken'an Rifâî, *Sohbetler* (Istanbul: Kubbealtı Neşriyatı 2000), p. 243.
251. Ken'an Rifâî, ed. Kâzım Büyükaksoy, *Mesnevî Hatıraları* (Istanbul: İnkilap Kitapevi 1968), p. 259.
252. Ken'an Rifâî, *Sohbetler* (Istanbul: Kubbealtı Neşriyatı 2000), pp. 447-448.

One of these souls is the Animal spirit and the other is the spirit called relative or sultan-like or divine, that distinguishes the good from the bad.[253]

- In sum what is meant by Noah's Ark is this attraction that the Perfect Man breathes, this relative spirit. If that is not produced, it is not possible for a person to set out upon the ocean of spirit and the realm of truth with his partial intellect.[254]

---

253. Ken'an Rifâî, *Sohbetler* (Istanbul: Kubbealtı Neşriyatı 2000), p. 257.
254. Ken'an Rifâî, *Sohbetler* (Istanbul: Kubbealtı Neşriyatı 2000), p. 144.

21. "Follow those who ask no reward of you, and who have been guided.

'Ittabi'ū man lā yas'alukum 'ajran wahum muhtadūn.

• Hazret Mevlana Rumi, in the blessed noble hadith language of our Master the Messenger, says: The price of my inviting my people to God the Truth is God's countenance (*dīdār*), His beauty (*jamāl*). It is true that Abu Bakr Siddiq donated forty thousand pieces of gold for my sake, and because there was nothing left for his family, even refrained from leaving his house for three days. But this money was not the price of my mission, because God the Truth had paid my fee. My fee is the countenance of the friend. Thus those unable to get free of greed and avarice do not attain the divine vision. Those who have no assigned portion of God the Truth's invitation and feast, their way is that of the beggar even should they be padishahs, that is to say, they can not get free of greed and avarice or poverty and need."[255]

• The messengers, who are God the Truth's vicegerents, bring news from God and show you the right and the wrong. It is vain to seek in their bringing news any thought of gaining the people's favor or self-interest.

Those heirs to the messengers are Perfect Men, for the trustee is the match of the owner of the trust and his secret heart flows within them.[256]

• The prophet said, "Give me something, I have need; give me your cloak or clothes or property." What should he do with clothes or cloak? He wants your clothes so that the heat of the sun may reach

---

255. Ken'an Rifâî, ed. Kâzım Büyükaksoy, *Mesnevî Hatıraları* (Istanbul: İnkilap Kitapevi 1968), p. 167.
256. Ken'an Rifâî, *Sohbetler* (Istanbul: Kubbealtı Neşriyatı 2000), p. 528.

you. As it is said in the Quran, *"And loan to God a beautiful loan"* (73:20), he wants to lighten your load. He does not only want property and cloak, for he has given you many things other than these, like knowledge, thought and vision.

What he means to say is: Spend your vision, your intellect, your thought for me! Did you not obtain this property, this wealth, with those tools I gave? Thus he asks for alms from both his birds and his traps.

You may strip under the sun, it will be better; for that sun does not tan a man, it even makes him white; at least lighten your clothes so that you may feel the pleasure of it. You have for a while been accustomed to the sour; try the sweet for once.[257]

- Because those who are truthful (*sıddık*) have in their hearts no desire for fee or reward for their good works, God has released them from the expectation of recompense and reward.

Thus the truthful continuously witness their own servanthood. As for servanthood, it is realized in them by their acceptance that the actions issuing from them are not by their own power and capacity. For this reason, that they ask no fee or reward for the good works they perform.

Since God the Truth is both the doer and the giver, can there be any more beautiful recompense than to seek God the Truth?

The truthful see themselves as "Servant" (*Abd*) in reality and "Proprietor" (*Mâlik*) by analogy. That is to say, they accept that everything they perform in the world is a trust and that they are trustees.

"Those who have faith in God and his messengers, they are the truthful" (57:19). God has not mentioned a "thing given in exchange" (*'iwaḍ*) for their good works. For since they witness no power or capacity of their own in the good works they perform, there exists in their hearts no thought whatsoever of recompense for those good works.

The truthful are free from the claim "we did this" in the things that they do. They witness that all their actions and rest come about through the power of God the Truth.[258]

---

257. Mevlânâ Celâleddîn Rumî, trans. Meliha Ülker Anbarcıoğlu, *Fîhi Mâ Fîh* (Istanbul: Milli Eğitim Basımevi 1990), p. 346.

258. Muhyiddîn İbnü'l-Arabî, trans. Abdullah Tâhâ Feraizoğlu, *Yıldızların Mevki* (Istanbul: Kitsan Yayım 1999), pp. 88-89.

- **Guide (Hâdî):** This concept is produced from the root guidance (*hidayet*) and its dictionary meanings are "to show the way, to show the true path and to guide." One of God's sublime names, "Guide" is explicated as "the One who shows His servants the way to know Him and causes them to attest to His sublimity and lordliness; who encourages each creature to do the things necessary to be able continue its existence."

Ragib al-Isfahani indicates that the concept of guidance has four different meanings in the Quran and explicates them thusly:

The granting to all beings for whom the sacred law is prescribed of intellect, understanding and required knowledge in a way appropriate to their capacity and preparedness. To this type of guidance must be added all the means granted to all creatures other than those for whom the sacred law is prescribed that make it possible for them to continue their existence. The Quran indicates this type of guidance with the following verses: "Glorify (*and attest*) the sublime name of your Lord who creates and arranges, measures out and shows the way, who brings the green plant out (*from the ground*) and then transforms it into the remainder of a darkest flood." "And he said: 'Our Lord is the one who gives each thing its nature and then shows it the right way.'"

The guidance to which God invites human beings by means of His messengers: "We made them the leaders who show the right path according to Our command and inspired them to do good works, perform the prayer, and give alms. They were those who continually worship us" [no citation].

The guidance of encouragement (*tevfik*) portioned out to those who accept "the right path shown" by means of the messengers: "Human beings were one community. Then God sent messengers as bearers of good news and warners. With them he also sent books showing the path of truth so that they might judge the matters in which people fell into disagreement. But after clear proof came to them, due to the jealousy between them, those who were given books fell into disagreement over religion. Then God showed to those who have faith the truth of what they disagreed upon. God guides aright whom He wishes."

The guidance those in Paradise speak of in the Hereafter, saying, "Praise be to God who with His guidance brought us to these boons with His guidance": "While rivers flow beneath them (*in Paradise*), We remove whatever there is in their hearts of rancor. And they say: 'Praise be to God who with His guidance brought us (*to this boon*)! If God had not conducted us to the right path, we would not have found the right path by ourselves. Truly our Lord's messengers brought the truth.' It is said to them: For you, Paradise; you were made heirs to it in recompense for the good works you performed."[259]

- The Guide is the one who brings people to the straight path.

If in compulsory progress, for example according to the necessities of the soul under the influence of the name Guide, death should come and take one away from oneself, one will not be able to see the truth. But here whatever of good or evil a soul has done, that is what it finds, that is what it reaches, it cannot find its source. The human body has the rank of capacity to reach its source but because the soul's posture is unworthy of this humanity, compulsory death comes and it cannot reach its source when it dies.

They who seek may find their Lord or their damnation. Self-disclosing to His seeking servants in the form of a murshid, God the Truth conveys them through the levels of matter, vegetable and animal. He purifies their interior and cleanses it. In this way they come to know their source while in this world. They find what they will find, see what they will see, that is to say, die by their own wish, escaping the slavery of the soul, and they become the intimates, the friends of God's mystery and find their source directly.[260]

- Knowledge is: There is no god but God. Good works are justice and straightness (*istikamet*). There is no one who gives guidance but God.[261]

- Hazret Muhammed (s.a.s.) is a light of guidance.[262]

---

259. Yrd. Doç. Niyazi Beki, *Abdülkadir Geylânî ve Esmâ-i Hüsnâ Kasidesi* (Istanbul: Sultan Yayınevi 2001), p. 222.
260. Ken'an Rifâî, *Sohbetler* (Istanbul: Kubbealtı Neşriyatı 2000), p. 308.
261. Ken'an Rifâî, *Sohbetler* (Istanbul: Kubbealtı Neşriyatı 2000), pp. 538-539.
262. Yaşar Nuri Öztürk, *Kur'an-ı Kerîm Ansiklopedisi* (Istanbul: Hürriyet Marbacılık 1990), p. 134.

21th Verse

- One who has found the light of guidance, cleansed their heart of the dirt of creatures, escaped all that is other than God and worldly things, is called the owner of straightness.[263]

- When God the Truth wishes guidance for a servant of His, that is to say, wishes to raise a servant of His from knowing at the level of knowledge to knowing at the level of the eye of certainty (*ayn el-yakin*), that is to say, of seeing, He self-discloses the light of guidance in that servant's heart. That is the time when the servant's spirit becomes Jesus, and this is the reason why it is said that Jesus came down from the sky, that the Messiah (*Mehdi*) has come into manifestation...

  When this guidance, this attraction of the Merciful comes, spirit becomes the attributed spirit (*ruh-i izâfî*) and whatever amount of good-for-nothing character traits there may be—and these are Dajjal—it kills them. And when they die and are gone there is manifest the secret heart of:

Plurality gone, unity come, we're alone with the friend
All the world is God the Truth, nor city nor bazaar remains

Thus spirit becomes soul, and soul becomes spirit.[264]

---

263. Ken'an Rifâî, *Sohbetler* (Istanbul: Kubbealtı Neşriyatı 2000), pp. 581-582.
264. Ken'an Rifâî, *Sohbetler* (Istanbul: Kubbealtı Neşriyatı 2000), p. 328.

22. "What do I have that I should not worship the one who created me, and to whom you will be returned?

Wa māliya lā 'a'budu'lladhi faṭaranī wa 'ilayhi turja'ūn.

- O my tribe, follow the messengers, follow those who do not ask for wages from you and who have found guidance. Why should I not worship the Essence (*Zāt*) who created me and all of you will return to that Essence.[265]

- **Abdullah:** The servant whose station and honor are such that none among God's servants is of higher station or more honorable.
  God's self-disclosures in that servant are the most perfect, the most general, the most perfect and the most valuable of self-disclosures. Just as there is no unveiling more perfect than such a person's unveiling, there is no self-disclosure higher than the self-disclosure in that servant; There is no name or attribute or any way of being known whatsoever that He has not opened to the servant He has named Abdullah.[266]

- **Absolute servant (*mutlak kul*):** The servant who makes no claim to lordliness over any creature whatsoever. A person in this condition is absolute servant.
  Those who protect their souls from there being any Lordly characteristic found in them are absolute servants.

---

265. Kemâlüddin Abdürrezzak Kâşâniyyüs Semerkandî, trans. Ali Rıza Doksanyedi, ed. M. Vehbi Güloğlu, *Te'vilât-ı Kâşâniyye* (Ankara Kadıoğlu Matbaası 1988), vol. 3, p. 12.

266. Abdürrezzâk Kâşânî, trans. Dr. Ekrem Demirli, *Tasavvuf Sözlüğü* (Istanbul: İz Yayıncılık 2004), p. 366.

The absolute servant is the servant in whom there is no characteristic of masterly behavior toward any creature whatsoever. Such people see themselves as in need of every thing in the world. This neediness toward the world is due to the world's being the mirror, behind a name-veil, of God the Truth.

True servanthood is such an attribute that its right is for its master to be cut off from everything else. Servanthood is to abandon everything total and partial, less and more. Servanthood is to not seek merit. Servanthood is to preserve the limitation in the structure of Adam-hood. Servanthood is humility and awe in the course of divine measuring out. As long as the servants do not reach the level of freedom, they cannot become perfect servants. True freedom is to be completely liberated from the slavery of worldly things.[267]

- The aim of servanthood is to surrender to God and request all things from Him. But this cannot occur without acquisition of true knowledge (*yakîn*).[268]

- Those who come from outside the gate absolutely must enter the sultan's palace through the gate. But a Padishah has certain special servants who are always inside anyway. This is a formidably hard subject. There is great danger here. Hazret Muhammed (s.a.s.) is among these special servants. He performed his office of servanthood perfectly. Even when Hazret Messenger gained full capacity and power in servanthood, the meaning of servanthood never lessened in him and always became more powerful. He was tasting the highest station of servanthood. When he was at the gate he would see himself inside, and when inside found himself inside too.[269]

- Hazret İbrahim Adham asked some poor fellow: "Do you want a friend of God from the People of God?" and received the answer, "I do!" "In that case," he said, "Sever your desire and demand for the

---

267. Suad el-Hakîm, trans. Ekrem Demirli, *İbnü'l-Arabî Sözlüğü* (Istanbul: Kabalcı Yayınevi 2005), p. 481.
268. Ken'an Rifâî, *Sohbetler* (Istanbul: Kubbealtı Neşriyatı 2000), p. 385.
269. Şems-i Tebrîzî, trans. Nuri Gençosman, *Makalat* (Istanbul: Hürriyet Yayınları 1975), p. 237.

22TH VERSE

world. For to have desire for the world and the Hereafter is to part from God. Prepare yourself for friendship (*muhabbet*). That is, remove all friendship in your heart for the sake of God's friendship. Leave room only God's friendship and love, and turn toward God the Truth, for that is the true niche of prayer. Servanthood is exclusively for the beautiful countenance (*cemal*) of God."[270]

• Our Master the Messenger says: "God gave the intellect to be used in service to Him. Not for the comprehension of the mysteries of lordliness..."

So, if you have intellect, do not say you have need of nothing; purify your self from worldly filth and wipe away the ignorance and heedlessness from your spirit, and look to bring forth its original cleanliness.[271]

• The names and attributes of God the Truth exist in every place and in every thing. But His Essence is only in the heart of the gnostic. That is why our Master the Messenger said: "Whoever sees me, sees God. Whoever betrays God's friend betrays God." That is why servanthood is servanthood to God. That is why a Perfect [Human] never accepts someone that a friend of God has driven away, because they are persons who have become sites of manifestation for the secret heart of "Truly those who swear fealty to you, swear fealty to God" (48:10).[272]

• The illustrious name (*ism-i celîl*) "the Lord" makes a person a servant who does not accept manumission. In the past, people were servants of servants, servants of the soul, servants to gods. With this word "Lord" a person feels his or her true servanthood. Only with the word Lord do those who were slaves of the wealthy in the time of ignorance, those who are slaves to beauty, those who forget their Lords, confess that they are servants of God.[273]

---

270. Ken'an Rifâî, *Sohbetler* (Istanbul: Kubbealtı Neşriyatı 2000), p. 346.
271. Ken'an Rifâî, *Sohbetler* (Istanbul: Kubbealtı Neşriyatı 2000), p. 474.
272. Ken'an Rifâî, *Sohbetler* (Istanbul: Kubbealtı Neşriyatı 2000), p. 405.
273. M. Kemal Pilavoğlu, *Muhyiddin-i Arabi* (Ankara: Pilavoğlu Kitabevi ve Yayınları n.d.), pp. 170-171.

- The return is that act by which a person goes back to the place from whence he came. Here "return" has no other meaning but to go back to one's origin. So death is the return to the true homeland of we who have broken away from God and been in exile so many years.

    I feel happy thinking that death is the servant's going to God. I have faith that this is a beginning not an end; that it is immortality, not death.[274]

---

274. Ken'an Rifâî, *Şerhli Mesnevî-i Şerif* (Istanbul: Kubbealtı Neşriyatı 2000), p. 582-583.

23. "Shall I take gods other than He? If the Merciful should intend adversity, their intercession will be of no use to me at all, nor would they save me.

'A 'attakhidhu min dūnihi 'alihatan 'in yuridni'r-rahmānu biḍurrin lā tughni 'annī shafa'attuhum shay'an wa lā yunqidhūn.

24. "I would then truly be in manifest error.

'Innī 'idhan lafī ḍalalin mubīn.

- What is it you think you are
You rely on mortal beings
One fine day you will awake
Come to union, to union[275]

- Human Beings are of three groups:

    1. Those who do not know why they came to this world; they have taken eating, drinking, sleeping and lovemaking as their idols. They are qualified with the animal attributes.
    2. Those who know the goal is to gain perfection, but have inclined their souls toward the idols of lovemaking, progeny, property and position. They have not been able to reach the goal.
    3. Those who have broken the idol of the soul and become Perfect Human Beings.[276]

---

275. Kemaleddin Şenocak, *Kutbu'l-ârifîn Seyyid Azîz Mahmud Hüdâyî (q.s.): Hayatı, Menâkıbı ve Eserleri* (Istanbul: İslam Neşriyat Evi 1970).

276. Ken'an Rifâî, *Sohbetler* (Istanbul: Kubbealtı Neşriyatı 2000), p. 436.

- Hazret Ali says: "People have excessive greed for the pleasures of the world. But worldly pleasure is mixed with sorrow."[277]

- You will call this world, where beings are on the one hand created and on the other decline and degenerate, the realm of generation and corruption. If you are taken by the eye and heart-distracting images of this world of generation and corruption, and suppose that is all there is, you will be wasting time on the path that leads to being able to see the reality of them. Being the sultan of a world is not an accomplishment [*marifet*]; accomplishment is to be a padishah with the Padishah of the two worlds.[278]

- Consider the fool who hunts the shadow of a bird on the ground while the real bird is flying in the air. He exhausts his strength and power and is left out of breath for nothing. The poor thing! He doesn't know that there is a bird in the air. He can't imagine it. He chases the shadow of it on the ground.

    That blockhead hunter shoots arrows at the shadow of the bird running on the ground. He uses up all the arrows in his quiver in this vain pursuit, but he can't hit the fleeting shadow. Many are they who exhaust in vain the arrows of time, valuable as gold, in the quiver of their span of life. The fool sunk in worldly heedlessness does not know that the shadow he chases is the reflection of God the Truth's names and attributes. To put aside the real and run after the image is to waste one's life and end up empty-handed and broken-hearted.

    Again it is God's arrived who save people from being so mistaken and from running after seductive images. In reality, God's arrived are the reflections, the shadows of God on earth. If you are going to seize anything, seize their skirts, so that they may protect you from spending your life in pursuit of seductive images.Consider what your spirit has been through in order to be enveloped in your body and become human in your heart:

    It fell from the sublime heavens. It passed through the realms of meaning and likeness. It became air, it became fire, it became water, it became earth, vegetable and animal. Thereby it reached you. Stay-

---

277. Ken'an Rifâî, *Şerhli Mesnevî-i Şerif* (Istanbul: Kubbealtı Neşriyatı 2000), p. 132.
278. Ken'an Rifâî, *Şerhli Mesnevî-i Şerif* (Istanbul: Kubbealtı Neşriyatı 2000), p. 78.

23th-24th Verse

ing in you is not its goal. Perhaps its goal is to stay in you without you and return to the heavens to mingle with that divine being.

In Messenger Abraham's statement, *"I do not love those that set"* (6:75-79), "to set" means to be extinguished and become invisible, like the setting of the moon, stars, and sun.

One night Messenger Abraham went to look for God, acting on a feeling he had within him, and when he saw the planet Jupiter, he said: "This is my Lord." But when it set and became invisible, he realized he had been mistaken. "I do not love those that set," he said. The next evening he saw the moon rise, and until it set, he thought it was God. Afterwards, when he saw the sun rise, he no longer had any doubt. The sun, larger and more dazzling than the others he'd seen, was God Himself.

It was when the sun set like the others that Abraham understood God was the one who had created heaven and earth, the starts and the sun.

The sun in the sky may bring an understanding person to know God, but if you find a sun like Shams of Tabriz, you will learn the realities from closer up. Bind yourself tightly to his commands and warnings. Shams of Tabriz brings one to union with God the Truth, but if you cannot find him, ask the ray of God Husameddin.

But beware of envy! What perverts a person's soul and sets in motion the devil within him is that abominable envy. It was because Satan was jealous of Adam that he did not bow down to him. That is why he was driven away from God the Truth and the realm of light. Do not you then regard with envious eye those who are superior to you, especially the Perfect Human Beings. It is that envious gaze which makes the universe appear black as black can be. As long as you avoid envy, as long as you do not fall into the trap of the devil of envy, you will see that great light.

The heart is darkened especially by envy felt toward those whose hearts are pure. Hazret Mevlana says: "Learn from my example. Before I met Shams of Tabriz, I thought I knew so many things. My eye and heart were lit with the light of knowledge. But when I met him and, without feeling the slightest envy, bound myself to his gnosis, his grace, my gnosis was increased many hundredfold. My heart filled with the light of the greatest knowledge."[279]

---

279. Ken'an Rifâî, *Şerhli Mesnevî-i Şerif* (Istanbul: Kubbealtı Neşriyatı 2000), pp. 65-67 [vol. 5, vs. 300-304].

- Even with the help of Solomon, the result of fleeing the contentment and virtue of dervishood for the pleasures and ambitions of the world is the same. In fleeing from yourself, and worse, from God, you arrive at the most dead-end of roads, the most perilous of errors.

   Compare yourself in Azrael's eyes with the man who fled to India! Consider that you yourself are that man.[280]

- *What a fine table there is spread in the world*
But from the eyes of the vile it is concealed

   If the world became an orchard full of fruit
Still the portion of mouse and snake would be dirt

   Whether winter or spring, its portion is dust
You're creation's lord; why like a snake eat dust?

   Inside a piece of wood, the termite recites
"Who is there who has such halva sweet delight?"

   The dung beetle with its head thrust in offal
Knows no other sweet dessert in all the world[281]

- The greatest and most magnificent pleasures in the world are the pleasures pertaining to the body's base parts. People give even their lives for these kinds of passions. Is there any more evident weakness and slavery for humanity than this? Then consider the greatness of spiritual pleasures. True pleasure is awe, astonishment, spirit.

   You have bound yourself in the wrong direction. Because a sublime and supernumerary being has been proven to exist in bodies, such denial as yours will no longer be possible. If after seeing the truth, the eye of your heart grows blind, and swept away by selfhood falls into denial, if you meet mysteries with loss, turning away and practicing scorn out of grandiosity, you will finally have lost your right to make excuses. Your bill has been made out with warnings and threats. It is feared you will be of the people of Hell. Still, when

---

280. Ken'an Rifâî, *Şerhli Mesnevî-i Şerif* (Istanbul: Kubbealtı Neşriyatı 2000), p. 132.

281. Şefîk Can, *Konularına göre açıklamalı Mesnevi Tercümesi* (Istanbul: Öteken Neşriyat 1997), vol. 5-6, p. 39.

the light of your spirit withdraws and rises up from your exterior body, when death prevents your spirit from taking precautions and ruling, the interpretation of the thing you have denied will come to you and the truth will be evident to you. When you witness that your imitating the heedless and following the ignorant has done you no good and you see the truth to which you could not submit, then you will say: *"Indeed the messengers of our Lord brought truth"* (7:53). Just as God the Sublime describes you and those like you thus: "Were they expecting a result different from that of which the book informed them?" On the day when the result arrives at last, first those who have forgotten it will say, *"Indeed the messengers of our Lord brought truth. Have we now no intercessors to intercede for us? Or could we be sent back, that we might do differently from what we have done?"* (7:53). Unfortunately you will only realize the truth when you awake from sleep.

How much I do fear that you will be disappointed. Unfortunately you will only realize the truth when you awake from sleep.[282]

- When Satan said to God the Truth, "O my Lord, you have charged me with leading astray. But with what shall I deceive your servants? Give me an instrument, I am powerless!" God the Truth said, "I gave you alcoholic drink." When Satan objected, "O my Lord, there are those who do not enjoy it," he heard the reply, "I gave you money, pomp and magnificence!" Still Satan did not accept this: "There are those who will not be fooled by these." Then he was given woman, and in his joy Satan could not be still.

Of course, what is meant by woman is the animalistic aspect of womanhood, and by means of women Satan can overthrow those he wishes to drive into error. How helpless we men are. Into what heedlessness have we sunk.[283]

- One day our Master the Messenger met Satan: "Where are you going?" he asked. "To lead people astray," he said. Then our Master the Messenger said: *"I have been sent to make beautiful character known.*

---

282. Ahmed er-Rifâî, ed. Dr. H. Kâmil Yılmaz, *Marifet Yolu* (Istanbul: Erkam Yayıncılık 1995), p. 174-175.

283. Ken'an Rifâî, *Sohbetler* (Istanbul: Kubbealtı Neşriyatı 2000), p. 268.

But I have nothing of guidance. Satan was sent to cause sin to be performed. But he has nothing of corruption."[284]

The divine decree (*kaza*) is the general judgment summarized completely on the Preserved Tablet.

The measuring out is for this judgment to come to exist according to a human being's preparedness and constitution (*yapı*). The result is the manifestation of that decree.

God gives to his creatures only what their preparedness requires, what they desire. He measures out whatever name's manifestation is appropriate to them in their measuring out. If, knowing that God is Majestic, we ask why He does not punish them, the Judge and the All-Knowing does not judge them beyond what their preparedness and capacity require. This is the subject of the fixed entities. It is related to the Essence and there can be no change or becoming other in the Essence.

If someone questions God's knowledge and says, "What you have taught me is beyond my capacity," God replies, "I know you only as you are; if the situation changes, I know the new situation also. You do not have the right to accuse me." God does not oppress them, they oppress themselves. Thus divine decree is applied in the measuring out and it is possible for it to come into manifestation again through people's understanding the knowledge in their selves. Or for the purpose of this knowledge (the straight path) being understood.[285]

- Adam saw the flaw in his soul and said, "O my Lord, I have oppressed my soul." God the Truth said, "O Adam, you know that this was required by My decree and measuring out, so why do you blame yourself? Adam answered, "I know, O my Lord… But my courtesy did not allow me to say it was from You." It was Adam's seeing himself as base and vile, knowing his own helplessness, that raised him again to himself, to his sublime station.

As for Satan, he was driven out of the court of God the Truth by saying, "It was You who gave me corruption!"[286]

---

284. Ken'an Rifâî, *Sohbetler* (Istanbul: Kubbealtı Neşriyatı 2000), p. 303.
285. Ken'an Rifâî, *Sohbetler* (Istanbul: Kubbealtı Neşriyatı 2000), p. 303.
286. Ken'an Rifâî, *Sohbetler* (Istanbul: Kubbealtı Neşriyatı 2000), p. 321.

23th-24th Verse

- Know that no one has anything. If some harm is to come to you, no one has the power to avert it. If some good is to come to you, no one has the power to change that either. So do not curse anyone. Know that everything is from God the Truth. Whatever occurs, it is by God's command. For judgment is His: *The Judgment belongs to God, the sublime, the great.* The keys to the heavens and earth are in the hand of His power.

  The aim of servanthood is to submit to God and refer all matters to Him. Ah but this too cannot occur without acquisition of true knowledge (*yakîn*).[287]

- It is those in love with particulars who become servants of others and their buffoons. If a person who falls into the rolling waves of events reaches out not for those who know how to swim but those who are drowning, if he hopes for help from them, of course his end will be drowning.

  The person he expects to help him does not have the power to protect and save himself let along be of use to someone weaker than himself.

  If you are going to hold on to something, hold on to the skirt of a perfect friend! If you will love, love a beauty created with care by divine art that will lead you to God, so that all this may be of use to you, so your heart beating with good and superior emotions will not be used in vain.[288]

- Those who have closed their eyes to all truth, taking only the path to imitation, while they could have been freed from their souls, they became donkeys instead. God sent them a prophet to guide and illuminate them. So that the spirits worthy of Hell and their hellish ways should be evident, and those heading for Hell should see the path to Paradise.

  But alas, between the two is a veil which although not apparent to the eye keeps the deniers separate from God's pure servants, like the barzakh which keeps the two seas apart, one salt, one sweet.[289]

---

287. Ken'an Rifâî, *Sohbetler* (Istanbul: Kubbealtı Neşriyatı 2000), p. 385.
288. Ken'an Rifâî, *Şerhli Mesnevî-i Şerif* (Istanbul: Kubbealtı Neşriyatı 2000), p. 411.
289. Ken'an Rifâî, *Şerhli Mesnevî-i Şerif* (Istanbul: Kubbealtı Neşriyatı 2000), p. 371.

- Guidance of Muslims and believers and corruption of those who deny God the Exalted both occur completely by the action and art of God the Exalted. He has no partner in His own kingdom.[290]

---

290. Abdülkadir Geylânî, trans. Abdülkadir Akçiçek, *Gunyetü't-Tâlibîn* (Istanbul: Sağlam Yayınevi 1991), p. 201.

25. "Truly I have faith in your Lord, so listen to me."
'Innī 'amantu birabbikum fa'sma'ūn.

- **Lord:** Meaning "to make something wholesome" and "to guard something," the Lord is King, Creator and Owner. The Lord is the one who makes something wholesome. God is the Lord because He makes the deeds of His creatures wholesome.

  The name someone has is their trainer, their commander. But if we go higher than the Fixed Entities, it manifests unity.[291]

- Pharoah asked Moses, "Who is your Lord, O Moses?" Moses replied, *"Our Lord is the one who gave to every thing the requirement of its created nature; then the doing of this task became the straight path for it, and He guided and referred this person to that thing to perform this task"* (20:49-50).[292]

  To say that every thing became the site of manifestation for a name means for that name to perform the duty of its site of manifestation. Once we know that everyone does their own duty, can any contention remain? Whom then will you blame, whom will you criticize?[293]

- Sitting here I look at those passing by in the street: People in various dress pass by, soldiers, citizens, police, janitors, garbage men. If you ask them, "Where are you going, Sir?" they will all mention the centers and destinations to which they are tied. For example, I am a

---

[291]. Ken'an Rifâî, *Sohbetler* (Istanbul: Kubbealtı Neşriyatı 2000), p. 183.

[292]. [The Turkish translation of this Quranic verse given in the text is a considerably expanded explication of the Arabic.]

[293]. Ken'an Rifâî, *Sohbetler* (Istanbul: Kubbealtı Neşriyatı 2000), p. 136.

teacher, I am tied to education. The doctor to health, the engineer to public works, etc. But there is a government that collects all of these centers into a total, a main center that governs them all at once. Let us take one of these centers tied to the main center, for example the municipality: from the smallest official tied to this office, the garbage man, the corporal, the secretary, the accountant, all the way up to the mayor, they are all occupied within the bounds of their own duties, necessities and responsibilities. They all serve the same center, but among them there are differences of rank. For example, is the proximity of the mayor to the center of the municipality the same as that of the garbage man? Thus we can compare this tableau with the fixed entities.[294]

• As stated in the gracious verse, *"For those who say, 'God is our Lord,'" and remain firm, there is no fear and they do not grieve"* (46:13), since we say there is no agent but God, it is He who acts and causes to act.[295]

• The spirits replied "Yes," to the address, *"Am I not your Lord?"* Those who knew Him there know Him here as well. There the truth is manifest, there is nothing hidden. It was natural that they would say yes. The real purpose is to confess that yes here. On the day of Alast every spirit was able to say yes according to its own preparedness.[296]

• To meet tolerantly the reproaches and cruelties one is subject to in the world is to say yes to the pact made in Alast. Every breath is an Alast transaction.

To remain true to the pact when God says, "Is it not I who gave you these things?"[297]

• Because when the spirits in eternity without beginning were asked, "Am I not your Lord?" they said, "Yes, You are my Lord!" it was said to them that they should go and prove this claim in the court of the world with the witnesses of knowledge and action.

---
294. Ken'an Rifâî, *Sohbetler* (Istanbul: Kubbealtı Neşriyatı 2000), p. 183.
295. Ken'an Rifâî, *Sohbetler* (Istanbul: Kubbealtı Neşriyatı 2000), p. 302.
296. Ken'an Rifâî, *Sohbetler* (Istanbul: Kubbealtı Neşriyatı 2000), p. 541.
297. Ken'an Rifâî, *Sohbetler* (Istanbul: Kubbealtı Neşriyatı 2000), p. 478.

25th Verse

Knowledge means to know and find one's owner. What is intended is not external knowledge, that is, transmitted knowledge.

As for action, it is to work to do that in body and heart, to try to make ones actions conform to that.

Thus what happiness it is for you if you bring these two witnesses before your murshid and verify the pact here! In that case when you go to the afterworld you will be in comfort.[298]

- The perfect human being is Lord in relation to the world. That is, from the point of view of meaning and spirituality, Lord and King compared with every thing in creation. Because God made them His vicegerents (*halife*). Thus perfect humans give to the people what they want, taking it from God in its inward aspect (*batini yönüyle*) and giving it to them in its bodily aspect (*cismani yönüyle*). Thus those who gather these two aspects in themselves were deemed worthy of vicegerency. That is why God the Exalted appointed prophets and friends mediating between Himself and His creatures so that they might bring strength to reach gnosis and sublime mysteries.[299]

- The Lord is the one who turns the earth and the stars, who adds the night to the day, moves ships on the sea, makes those who fly in the air to fly, and manages, distinguishes, gathers the varied creatures under the sea and grants them instruments.[300]

- Gnosis (*marifet*) is to comprehend the lordliness of God the Truth, that is to say His being Lord, and to know the self with the actions and qualities worthy of the glory of servanthood, and know there is nothing outside of God the Truth's command and it is He who provides livelihood. Only such a person possesses gnosis and remembrance.[301]

---

298. Ken'an Rifâî, *Sohbetler* (Istanbul: Kubbealtı Neşriyatı 2000), p. 297.
299. İsmâil Rusûhî Ankaravî, ed. İlhan Kutluer, *Nakşel-Füsusşerhi* (Istanbul: Ribat Yayınları n.d.), p. 297.
300. M. Kemal Pilavoğlu, *Büyük Velî Muhyiddin-i Arabi*, p. 171.
301. Ken'an Rifâî, *Sohbetler* (Istanbul: Kubbealtı Neşriyatı 2000), p. 377.

26. It was said to him, "Enter the garden." He said, "Alas! If only my people knew...

Qīla 'dkhuli 'l-jannata qāla yā layta qawmī ya'lamūn.

- What came to Habib the Carpenter is the self-disclosure of unity. That is to say, let no one be offended by you, nor you be offended by anyone. Wish for others the goodness that you wish for yourself.[302]

- Habib the Carpenter prayed for those who wanted to kill him: If only my tribe had known that my Lord forgave me and made me one of those to whom He is generous.

This is what you must say to everyone: If they knew what they did was evil, would they have done it?

Although people may be truly far from these words, they should not be condemned, for there is a place in this world for error also.

If there is nothing in a person's body that is without benefit, evil or unnecessary, still there is a reason for every thing that exists in the world. But just as alongside the sublime organs, such as the eyebrow, the eye, the mouth and the nose, there are also base organs such as the intestines, etc., the bodies of such people is not devoid of benefit either. Thus one must tolerate them and regard them with compassion.[303]

This is the essence commanded to be included in the paradise of essence. In other words, If only my tribe, who are veiled from my station and state, knew that my Lord had forgiven me and covered the sins of my carving idols and serving them. And if they knew that because of my nearness to the presence of unity my Lord has made

---

302. Ken'an Rifâî, *Sohbetler* (Istanbul: Kubbealtı Neşriyatı 2000), p. 78.
303. Ken'an Rifâî, *Sohbetler* (Istanbul: Kubbealtı Neşriyatı 2000), pp. 371-372.

me among those to whom He is generous. It is said in the hadith of the Prophet, *"Every thing has a heart. The heart of the Quran is Ya-Sin."*

It is hoped that Ya-Sin's being the heart of the Quran is because Habib, who is known as the owner of Ya-Sin, had faith in Hazret Prophet and comprehended the secret of his prophethood six hundred years before he was sent. For the Prophet (a.s.) said, "There are three persons prior to the communities that never cursed God even for the blink of an eye. One is Abu Talib, one is the owner of Ya-Sin, and one is great pharaoh's believer."[304]

- Knowledge was made obligatory in the Quranic verse, *"Truly that is life itself, if they only knew"* (29:64), by the phrase *"if they only knew."* If they had known, the Hereafter would have been the home of life for them too. But their being without knowledge veiled them and left them deprived, thrust them into the darkness of forms, and imprisoned them in the prison limited by three dimensions where they will be thrust again and tortured.[305]

Knowledge is to know knowledge
Knowledge is to know oneself
If you do not know yourself
What good is learning to you?

What might be learning's intent?
One has to know God the Truth
If you've learned and you don't know
It's just a dry piece of bread

Don't say I've read and I know
Don't say my good deeds are much
If you don't know God the Truth
All of that has been in vain

---

304. Kemâlüddin Abdürrezzâk Kâşânîyyü's-Semerkandî, trans. AliRıza Doksanyedi, ed. M. Vehbi Güloğlu, *Te'vilât-ı-Kâşâniyye* (Ankara: Kadıoğlu Matbaası 1988), p. 13.

305. Ahmed er-Rifâî, *El-Burhânü'l-Müeyyed* (Istanbul: Erkam Yayınları 1995), p. 223.

26th Verse

The meaning of the four books
Is clear in just one alif
You don't even know alif
What kind of learning is that?

You can read from start to end
Twenty and nine syllables
Still you ask the master what
Is the meaning of alif

Yunus Emre, master says
Thousands perform pilgrimage
Far better than all of that
Is to enter just one heart.[306]

- The highest level of knowing is to know that you know nothing.[307]

- Someone who does not know God's judgment cannot be a servant to God in the full sense, cannot fully worship God. Without doubt, God does not accept an ignorant person as one of His friends. All of these are sections and chapters of gnosis. A person who can fully learn and take possession of this knowledge is called "Gnostic" (*Arif*). Gnostics have a continuous intimacy with God. Their hearts are a mirror of the Exalted God the Truth. They are gentle and wholesome. They stand apart from the world and the Hereafter in possession of fear and awe. Their tasks and actions are taken from God and they apply to God for them. Hungry or naked, they never grieve because their eyes see nothing but God.[308]

---

306. Mehmet Açıkgöz, *Yunus Divanı* (Önsöz Basım ve Yayım n.d.), p. 429.
307. Ken'an Rifâî, *Sohbetler* (Istanbul: Kubbealtı Neşriyatı 2000), p. 92.
308. Muhyiddîn İbnü'l-Arabî, trans. Mahmut Kanık, *Marifet ve Hikmet* (Istanbul: İz Yayıncılık 1995), pp. 153-155.

27. "How my Lord forgave me and placed me among those to whom He is generous!"

Bimā ghafara lī rabbi wa jaʻalnī mina'l-mukramīn.

• Read the book of your own being, find God the Truth's Trust (*emanet*) hidden in your heart. The human being is a discriminating book in which the world and the Hereafter have taken refuge. So take crowbar in hand and start digging for the ethics of annihilation (*fena ahlakları*). There is new progress at every level. First there is earth, then clay, and then you see water. Thus the goal of reading your own book is gnosis. In other words, the goal is to know yourself.[309]

• Those who polish their hearts with the love of God see a different kind of beauty shining there each instant; each instant they are witness to another of God's infinite beauties. For them the colors and scent whose beauty we embrace do not exist; they have risen beyond color and scent. For they are the ones who know God. They have abandoned the images in the rind of worldly sciences and raised the flag of the eye of certainty, and as a result they have reached the level of the reality of certainty and see the divine beauty.

This is the reality Hacı Bayram Veli described as knowing, finding, and becoming:

Bayram came to know himself
And he found the knower there
He became the finder too
Know yourself, know your own self[310]

---

309. Ken'an Rifâî, *Sohbetler* (Istanbul: Kubbealtı Neşriyatı 2000), p. 622.
310. Ken'an Rifâî, *Şerhli Mesnevî-i Şerif* (Istanbul: Kubbealtı Neşriyatı 2000), p. 513.

- Our Master the Messenger relates from his Lord by way of a story: "God the Exalted said, 'He who knows Me seeks Me, he who seeks Me finds Me, He who finds Me loves Me, and I slay whoever loves Me. When I slay someone his blood price falls to Me. When someone's blood price falls to Me, I pay it in person.'

"Gnosis requires seeking. And seeking makes finding necessary. Finding requires love, and love, death. Death makes a blood price necessary. The blood price of the slain can only be the slayer. If someone takes the right path to God and His Messenger, and then dies, the compensation for that is left to God." That is to say, He gives that person immortality with His Essence (beka).[311]

The hearts of those who possess gnosis are God's treasury on earth. God the Exalted has put into their hearts the trusts of His secret heart, the subtleties of His wisdom, the truths of His affection, the lights of His knowledge, and the verses/signs (ayetleri) of His gnosis known without His permission neither to intimate angel nor prophet sent nor anyone but God.[312]

- Plato says: "To know is to remember things formerly known."[313]

- The most superior knowledge is that which brings the person who wants to learn closer to God. This knowledge is of many kinds. It is best for seekers to take enough of the most beneficial knowledge to provision themselves on the path. They learn this by reading and listening. Then the seeker should through practice, through struggle with the soul and with desire, turn toward the highest goal, which is inherited knowledge. For the Messenger (s.a.s.) said: "If a person acts with what he knows, God will make him inheritor of the knowledge he does not know" and "Fountains of wisdom spurt from the hearts to the tongues of those who worship sincerely for forty mornings." This knowledge is the knowledge that belongs to the messengers and the friends. For prophets and friends attain to prophethood or friendhood not with knowledge acquired by study but with inherit-

---

311. Sadreddin Konevî, *Kırk Hadis* (Istanbul: Bahar Yayınları 2000), pp. 97-98.
312. Ken'an Rifâî, *Sohbetler* (Istanbul: Kubbealtı Neşriyatı 2000), p. 569.
313. Ahmed er-Rifâî, , trans. Dr. Ali Can Tatlı, *Sohbet Meclisleri* (Istanbul: Erkam Yayın 1996), p. 147.

ed knowledge, that is, knowledge acquired as the result of practice and struggle (*with the soul*). This knowledge put the fear of God in the servant's heart. Thanks to this knowledge the servant hears, sees, speaks and walks with the light of God. God the Exalted has said: "My servant comes near to Me with supererogatory acts of worship until I love him. When I love him, I become his ears, his eyes…"

Exterior knowledge is beautiful, it is the seed of actions. But the beauty of exterior knowledge comes with Adam's knowledge, the knowledge of the names, which is interior knowledge. For in itself exterior knowledge makes those who possess it hard-hearted and coarse, though they be angels.

But interior knowledge makes those who possess it gentle and wholesome, tolerant, humble and sincere, not boorish.[314]

- "All-Concealing" is one of God the Truth's names. If human beings had been created to not commit sin, the meaning of the Forgiving would never have emerged. The servant cannot be without fault. From the servant, flaws; from God, gifts.[315]

- If God the Truth commands kindness, grace, mercy and compassion for human beings, He puts tears in their eyes, cries and moans and supplication and entreaty in their hearts, and they cry and moan to God with their tears. When that happens, it should be known that there is an exchange occurring between them and God's kindness and grace (*lutuf ve inayet*). It means that their tears have been accepted by God the Truth. But if you ask where should we find these tears, you will find them by showing compassion and kindness for those who weep, that is to say, the poor, the orphaned and oppressed, and good behavior toward all creatures. One attains to God's mercy and forgiveness through pity and compassion for the helpless, for eccentrics, and the powerless who have no recourse.[316]

- God says:

---

314. Niyâzî Mısrî, trans. Süleyman Ateş, *İrfan Sofraları* (Istanbul: Yeni Ufuklar Neşriyatı n.d.), pp. 117-119.

315. Ken'an Rifâî, *Sohbetler* (Istanbul: Kubbealtı Neşriyatı 2000), p. 602.

316. Ken'an Rifâî, *Sohbetler* (Istanbul: Kubbealtı Neşriyatı 2000), p. 91.

O David, tell sinners that I am the Forgiving. And tell the righteous that I am the Jealous.

O David, I do not torment those who come to Me in fear. I do not plunge into the sorrow of separation those who come to me in love; and on the Day of Judgment I do not shame those who return to Me in shame.

O David, My Paradise is for those who have not given up hope of My mercy. I am offended by those who think the fault they have committed is greater than my forgiveness.

If I wish to punish someone right away, I first punish those who give up hope of My mercy. But haste does not suit My glory.

I know the hearts of those I love. When night comes, I disclose Myself to their hearts. They talk with me, they speak with Me with peace of mind.

O David, I have a group of servants who are the people of goodness. It is their share to be My traveling companions. May they prosper in happiness. How beautiful is their station.[317]

---

317. Ahmed er-Rifâî, *Onların Alemi* (Istanbul: Beyda Yayınevi 1996), pp. 344-345.

28. We did not send down upon his people after him any army from the skies, nor were We going to.

Wa mā 'anzalnā 'alā qawmihi min ba'dihi min jundin mina's-samā'i wa mā kunnā munzilīn.

29. It was no more than a single cry, and then they were extinguished.

'In kānat 'illā ṣayḥatan wāḥidatan fa 'idhā hum khāmidūn.

30. Alas for the servants! There comes to them no messenger but they mock him.

Yā ḥasratan 'alā'l-'ibādi mā ya'tīhim min rasūlin 'illā kānū bihi yastahzi'ūn.

- After the spirit went to Hazret God the Truth, We did not send Angels from the heavens to reform its soul and attributes. Their reform was in their destruction; they were destroyed in an all-subjugating self-disclosure disclosed by God the Truth.[318]

- The souls' wishes and desires were for the Tribe of Ad a sandstorm, for the Tribe of Noah a flood, and for such-and such, for individuals and societies, various kinds of winds. The wishes and desires of that tribe's, that society's, that individual's own souls were the cause of their destruction and burned them up and ruined them.

  Thus those who wish to have pleasure and comfort must abandon the appetites and desires of their souls. The punishments that

---

318. Şemseddin Yeşil, *Füyûzat* (Istanbul: Ş. Yeşil Yayınları 1984), vol. 6, p. 243.

occur in the world, the prisons and murderers, are all things caused by the soul's caprice and desire. It is the passions of the soul that have caused disasters and brought so many to prison and execution. That is why they say: "Whatever comes to me is from me"—and it is a true saying. The fault is in the person, not in anyone else.[319]

• You have been deceived by your apparent freedom in the world. Here you are free in every case. You have set aside all fatigue; you do not work. You have been certain of the loss of goodness and grace, superiority and beauty, and the benefits that actually belong to others than yourself. Consider for once that these benefits came to you from others. They were left to you by those who passed on. They belonged to Pharaoh, Haman, Qarun, Shaddad, Ad, Caesar and Khusraw. They were left to you. And they belonged to even more kings and communities who passed on. The world made playthings of them. They were deceived by the deceits of various communities. God's command arrived in the end. Deceiving Satan beguiled and deceived them. He deceived them by saying, "God will forgive you, do as you like." But in time a curtain was drawn between them and what they desired. All that they amassed was scattered and gone. They were cut off from what they had been free to do as well. In the end they could do nothing at all. They slipped off those feather beds they prepared for themselves. They were thrown out of the strong mansions they had built. Their names were erased from what they supposed were their victories and the superiority they assumed for them. They lost too the properties they were so proud to own.

And then they were asked for the things left with them in trust. They were asked for the things that were given to them for a certain period of time. Not only will they be asked to give them back, they will be called to account for them. In the end, the thing they never took into account will come to them from God. In fact it has come already.

The evils they have done will be described to them. The things they have done will be examined in all their detail. Just as they imprisoned others while they lived in the world, they will be thrown into a place more confined. They will meet with hardness more vi-

---

319. Ken'an Rifâî, *Sohbetler* (Istanbul: Kubbealtı Neşriyatı 2000), p. 265.

28TH-29TH-30TH VERSE

olent than the hardness they showed themselves. They will face a punishment more comprehensive than punishments they meted out while they were in the world. There will be fetters on their hands and feet. They will eat the seeds of the oleander, which will tear up their insides. They will drink red hot water.

Among them there was a community that drowned. Another community sank under the earth. One tribe was stoned. Another was slain. The faces of the members of another tribe turned into the faces of pigs and monkeys. In the case of another community, their hearts were transformed. Their hearts became as hard as stone. The oppression of misbelief came over them; they were branded with *shirk*; oppressed by unrelieved and unending oppression and darkness. Into such hearts neither faith nor Islam can enter.[320]

• Whatever catastrophe befalls humans, whether it descends from heaven or rises up from earth, it comes from not knowing one's limits and being so far from human humility as to try to violate God's frontier (*Allah'ın hududu*).

If a society has little faith and its spirituality has been exhausted, if people no longer love one another or help one another, it is natural that catastrophes should occur. For there is a profound connection between the spiritual realms and this realm of bodies which appears to us in material form. Moreover, several screens can intervene between the realm of bodies and the spiritual realms and leave our world in darkness, as if the light of the sun were cut off. Heaven's mercy may not be seen. Greed, self-interest, lust and fornication become more and more common on the earth. Moral distortions spread across the world, envy, lust, and disaster. However many people may be killed by plague in a city, these ferocious perversions destroy the love of God in the habitations of the heart, they destroy gratitude and contentment, in sum, all the virtues which make a person human.[321]

• Life, with its sorrow and grief, its happiness and joy, is always the fruit of things earned in the past.

---

320. Abdülkadir Geylânî, trans. Abdülkadir Akçiçek, *Gunyetü't-Tâlibîn* (Istanbul: Sağlam Yayınevi 1991), vol. 1-2, pp. 379-381.

321. Ken'an Rifâî, *Şerhli Mesnevî-i Şerif* (Istanbul: Kubbealtı Neşriyatı 2000), p. 21.

Socrates says, "Just as people prepare their own disasters, they prepare their own prosperity as well."

God the Truth says in the Gracious Quran, "He who has done an atom of good will find good, and he who has done an atom of evil will find evil," and "When you do good, you do it for yourself, and when you do evil, you do it for yourself." People see and hear all of these and so many similar phrases yet those whose heads are like empty skulls take no warning from them. It is true not only for those things we do randomly out in the open. Yes, but the end is very painful! In sum, the events we see hear and there and in ourselves, disaster or felicity, are nothing but the performance and execution of the decisions made in the divine court where events are tied to judgment.

It is very difficult to transform the judgment given in the divine court to the good even for the honor of God the Truth's beloveds. Fire burns the place where it falls. The fireman's duty is to prevent the spread of fire. The purpose of the spiritual support of the People of God is to prevent the burning up of faith by the fires of sin and rebellion. Otherwise the arrow let fly will strike flesh. The spiritual support of God's friends prevents it from passing through to the soul.[322]

- The Messenger of God's light will bring you to the moment of lights (*nurlar demine*), it will attract you. If you have not reaped that light, you will remain in darkness, see before you only your corpse, and after moaning pitifully under that darkness for many a year, proceed to the rank of the goodness and worship you performed in the world.

You will roll like a barrel, like a ball from the heights through many trials, and afterwards a certain level of light will appear, that is, those who love you will begin to appear.

Those who cannot reap that light will remain in darkness, as in a nightmare they will have voices but be unable to speak, they will have hands but be unable to grasp.[323]

- *"That cry overtook the oppressors and they fell to their knees in their homes"* (11:67).

---

322. Ken'an Rifâî, *Sohbetler* (Istanbul: Kubbealtı Neşriyatı 2000), p. 357.
323. Ken'an Rifâî, *Sohbetler* (Istanbul: Kubbealtı Neşriyatı 2000), pp. 170-171.

28th-29th-30th Verse

The subjective meaning of "cry" is the moment of death. It represents the separation of the body from the spirit and from the soul. In the moment of death, also called the lesser resurrection, every denier will suddenly be extinguished with a violent explosion like that. "Cry" and "sudden extinguishing" are defined in the spiritual world as the cutting off of the Merciful's current. When the current of the Merciful is suddenly cut off, the soul living in the delusion of its own existence will feel a violent blast and, realizing it has no power of its own left, will be suddenly extinguished.[324]

- There was nothing left for the Thamud tribe to do. They waited in profound fear for the signs of the first day and indeed on that day they saw each other's faces turn yellow like saffron. On the second day the color was red. On the third day the faces of the people of the Thamud tribe were now black. They no longer appeared human and their behavior was not human. Then they came to their knees.

And as it says in the seventh chapter of the Quran, Gabriel the Trusted brought this verse to Hazret Muhammed: "*So the earthquake took them unawares, and in the morning they crouched kneeling in their houses.*"

But for the Thamud tribe there was nothing left to be done. They waited for God's wrath and final self-disclosure. This punishment came right on time and an earthquake brought the underside of the earth to the surface. Black-faced, on their knees, all creatures were buried under the earth in an instant. Wails were heard coming from their broken bodies, or from the parts of their bodies. Their bones wailed, the eyes of their souls shed tears onto the black earth.[325]

- Thus while the camel of mystery bearing the trusts of gnosis grazed in the holy gardens of God, eating the fruits of God the Truth's mysteries and drinking the water of the spring of self-disclosure, it gave the milk of the mysteries of the Unseen to the senses and faculties. But the Thamud soul gathered the powers of nature and resisted the sheriat, objected to the tarikat, and killed that camel of mystery.

---

324. Haluk Nurbaki, *Yâ-Sîn Sûresi Yorumu* (Istanbul: Damla Yayınevi, 1999), p. 44.
325. Ken'an Rifâî, *Şerhli Mesnevî-i Şerif* (Istanbul: Kubbealtı Neşriyatı 2000), pp. 369-370.

In this way they remained ignorant and heedless, and yellowness, redness and blackness were manifested as Messenger Salih said they would be. In other words, the tribe was occupied by darkness, ignorance, heedlessness and abandonment of humanity, and thus were they destroyed.[326]

- On the first of the three days mentioned the faces of Messenger Salih's tribe turned bright yellow, on the second, bright red, and on the third day, blackest black. When the three days passed in this way their preparedness for death was realized, the existence of corruption was manifested, and this manifestation was called destruction. The yellowing of the faces of the wretched is the counterpart to the brightness of the faces of the felicitous indicated by God's verse, "*On that day there are faces that are bright.*" For brightness is the sign of manifestation. Just as yellowness was the manifestation of the traces of evil in Salih's tribe on the first day. Then as the counterpart of the redness seen in them on the second day, God used the expression "smiling" for the felicitous. For smiling is one of the reasons for a face to redden. Thus for the felicitous, smiling is the reddening of cheeks. Then afterwards, as a counterpart to the darkening of the skin of the wretched, God said of the felicitous that they were "joyful." Joy and happy news appeared in the effect of cheerfulness on the faces of the felicitous, just as blackness affected the color of the wretched. That is why God gave good news about the two groups. That is, He spoke a word that affected the color of their faces. And just so, He said of the felicitous, "Their Lord have them good news with Mercy and Paradise." And of the wretched He said, "O My beloved Messenger, give them good news of sorrowful torment." In this way the thing manifested with these words showed its effect in the faces, in the souls, of each group. Thus only from the concepts in their interiors did the property of the thing inhabiting their souls became evident upon them. This means that they too affected nothing but what their preparedness required. Thus whoever understands this wisdom and sees in themselves the mystery of applying this to their own soul and creation will find relief in themselves from being concerned with others and know that the good and evil that comes to the soul is from

---
326. Ken'an Rifâî, *Sohbetler* (Istanbul: Kubbealtı Neşriyatı 2000), p. 190.

themselves. What I mean by "good" here is the things appropriate to the servants' nature and temperament and wishes, and what I mean by "evil" is the thing that they do not like, the thing contrary to their temperament. Those who attain this view appreciate the excuses made by all beings, and however much no apology is made by them, understand, and they know that whatever manifests in their own souls is from themselves.[327]

- When people are placed in the grave they hear a cry. O heedless one, you abandoned the world, and the world abandoned you. You tried to collect the world, and the world collected you.

If we liken the grave to the body, those who waste time letting the world sweep them away and being slave to their desires will feel those torments while their bodies are in the grave. For example, while the means of subsistence were well available, they will be afflicted by distress and meet with varied trials and deprivations.[328]

- Hazret Noah said to his tribe: "O people without understanding, do not think I am like one of you and try to abuse me. I am not I. I have become free of the animal spirit, alive with the Beloved and eternal with Him. And so God has become my hearing ear and my seeing eye: The breath filling and emptying my chest is His breath. The voice I am instrumental in bringing to your ears is His voice. Although I appear like you to be in human form, in reality, what has taken on this form and showed you the way to reach Him is not me, it is Him. Those who do not believe this, who do not understand the truth in these words and actions, are deniers, disbelievers."

The form which appears to you may be a fox or a sheep. But within that fox's fox appearance and hidden under that sheep's coat there is a lion. One can't pretend to bravery before that image of a fox or that sheep's coat.

God's messengers and God's arrived may in form and appearance be small, weak and unpretentious. But in the mirror of their hearts there is the lion of being and unity. With this light which shines in

---

[327]. Muhyiddîn İbnü'l-Arabî, trans. Nuri Gençosman, *Fusûs'l-Hikem* (Istanbul: Kırkambar Kitaplığı n.d.), pp. 147-148.

[328]. Ken'an Rifâî, *Sohbetler* (Istanbul: Kubbealtı Neşriyatı 2000), pp. 191-192.

their hearts they are more powerful than the most magnificent of beings.

If Messenger Noah had not had in him the hand of God' power, how could he have re-established creation in the world? When he cursed them, all the faithless on the face of the earth died. With one lion's roar he set the world and the creatures of the world against one another. He was like a fire, and the world and all the creatures in it like a haystack. When the haystack did not give him even his rightful share of one tenth, he knew that the haystack was good for nothing but burning and he let loose such a fire into the world that everything burned to ashes.

All those who before a hidden lion sent into the world are like wolves with their mouths hanging open and do not know their limits will sooner or later be punished. For only fools pretend to bravery in the presence of a lion.

But if only it were just the human body torn and broken in the paws of lions and panthers. If only disbelievers and hypocrites attacked like wild animals, to break the human body merely, and not the heart, one's faith and heart, with perversion. If only there were not such an end people came to, when faced with the friends and prophets who are God's lions, as going astray into the ways of stubbornness, denial, and infidelity, and being broken off and separated from Islam and faith.[329]

- Why is that these ignorant people in every place and time never listen to the righteous who are intimate with God?

Do they not know that one should not offend the spirits of God's friends? For their spirits are in a continuous state of union with God.

God says in a sacred hadith, *"Whoever treats ill a friend of Mine has in truth declared war upon Me."* And a hadith of the Prophet says, *"He who offends me offends God."*[330]

So, you with unwashed face, what are you about?
Whom is it you envy, whom you hope to rout?

---

329. Ken'an Rifâî, *Şerhli Mesnevî-i Şerif* (Istanbul: Kubbealtı Neşriyatı 2000), pp. 456-457.

330. Ken'an Rifâî, *Şerhli Mesnevî-i Şerif* (Istanbul: Kubbealtı Neşriyatı 2000), p. 368.

28th-29th-30th Verse

It's the lion's tail that you are playing with
It's the angels you charge out to battle with

Why is it that you will speak ill of pure good?
Don't think that abasement is a higher good

What is evil? That base copper so in need
Who is the shaykh? The unbounded alchemy

Although copper may not receive alchemy
Copper never made copper of alchemy

What is evil? A rebel who sets fire free
And the shaykh? The sea of pre-eternity

They can always use water to frighten fire
When was water afraid to be set afire?

You find flaws in the moon's face up in the skies
You are hunting for thorns in a paradise

If you go to Paradise, seeker of thorns
You will find that there you are the only thorn[331]

The world is for us a great kindness. The self-disclosure of the Lord manifests while in the world. Those who see His beauty conform to it, know it, find it and are colored with its color. The fundamental thing is that the love that is Habib Najjar annihilates the powers of the soul in the human being and makes its spirit dominant in the body. For this there is need of a teacher, that is to say, Lordly self-disclosure. Prostration to the Lord and servanthood is the cause of the self-disclosure of the Lord.[332]

---

331. Mevlânâ Celâleddin Rûmî, trans. Veled İzbudak, ed. Abdülbaki Gölpınarlı, *Mesnevî* (Istanbul: Milli Eğitim Basımevi 1991), vol. 2, vs. 3340-3348.

332. Compiler's note.

31. Do they not see how many generations We destroyed before them, that will not return to them?

'Alam yaraw kam 'ahlakunā qablahum mina'l-qurūni 'annahum 'ilayhim lā yarji'ūn.

• Human beings who have in their bodies a window opening onto Hell are the contrary of the believers, who have a window opening onto Paradise. They always see within themselves fear, grief, sorrow, death, bad luck and darkness, all of which are the effects of Hell visible to them. Their condition means for them: "This is what you deserve; this is the place you will go in the end." In order to escape this sorrow, this darkness and this disappointment within, they emerge from their own realm and go out into the realm of the world. They plunge into the skies, the earth, gardens, meadows, beautiful women, friends, music and so on, distracting themselves with these in order to forget the ugliness within them. They do not see their end. They distract themselves with such fantasy and foreign things in order to take greater advantage of the delights and benefits of the world. It was the same for Pharaoh. He saw himself in a dream falling headlong from heights, suffering in poverty and facing several evils. When he awoke he comforted himself that it was only a dream and paid it no mind. But in the end he saw that it was completely real. When Moses appeared, he lost his throne and sultanate. He suffered poverty and an evil end exactly as in his dream. He drowned in the Nile and the truth of *"Women impure are for men impure, and men impure for women impure"* (24:26) emerged, and he returned to the hell that was his origin.[333]

---

[333]. Sultan Veled, trans. Meliha Anbarcıoğlu, *Maarif* (Konya: Altunarı Ofset 2002), pp.6-8.

O Humankind

- And if they did not know they will be raised up
How would they throw themselves upon swords sharp?

He is smiling at you, don't see him that way
Hid in the Pir are a hundred Judgment Days

Hell and Paradise are all the parts of him
He is far above all you may think of him

Whatever you think of, it can become naught
That which comes not into thinking—that is God

Why such arrogance at the door of this house
When they know well who it is inside the house?

The interior of God's friends is a mosque
The house of worship for all, that place is God

God has never put any people to shame
If the heart of a man of God was not pained[334]

- Like the disbelievers who in the Messenger's time
Had intent to do him evil by design

Due to their plans and designs, the Messenger
Took refuge inside a cave with Abu Bakr

Jesus too, when the Jews pressed him cruelly
Rose to the dome of the sky mysteriously

And Pharaoh, when he threatened Moses's life
Had no help from God and died, drowned in the Nile

Nimrod had designs upon Abraham's life
Planning to throw him into the smoke and fire

But for him fire was transformed into a rose
Godless Nimrod was killed by a mosquito

---

334. Mevlânâ Celâleddin Rûmî, trans. Veled İzbudak, ed. Abdülbaki Gölpınarlı, *Mesnevî* (Istanbul: Milli Eğitim Basımevi 1991), vol. 2, vs. 3104-3108, 3111-3112.

31TH VERSE

The peoples of generous Noah and Hud
Were destroyed when punishment arrived from God

They were wiped out either by water or wind
To be struck down under ground was meet for them

Those devious, miserable communities
Intended to do evil iniquities

That is why disaster came to afflict them
Because they deserved that rage and violence

That is why they struck themselves with their own swords
And their blood poured down as through a raging gorge

Else why would they cause their own selves to be crushed?
For what reason would they bleed rivers of blood?

Who has seen the fool who murders his own self?
Who enraged, cuts his throat with a sword himself?

The fool thinks that he is wounding someone else
In the end he's wounded his liver himself[335]

- Perfect human beings have collected all of the names within themselves. Everyone has a name in the fixed entities (*the fixed, determined forms of existents in God's knowledge prior to their acquiring being*), and that is their lord, in other words, their teacher in courtesy. Each person is under the rule of that name's courtesy. That name says to them, "Wander for a few days where you wish, in the end I am the place where you will arrive!"

When compulsory death comes after the life of this world, those who were not able to establish intimacy with their source and maintain knowing with certainty, those who could not find their source, they will not find it there either.[336]

---

335. Sultan Veled, trans. Abdülbaki Gölpınarlı, *İbtidâ-name* (Konya: Konya ve Mülhakatı Eski Eserleri Sevenler Derneği 2001), p. 42.

336. Ken'an Rifâî, *Sohbetler* (Istanbul: Kubbealtı Neşriyatı 2000), p. 275.

O Humankind

- "Come and sit in your father's ark," Noah said
"Shameless boy, so you will not drown in the flood."

"No," he said, "For I have learned how to swim now
I have lit a candle other than yours now."

"These are the waves of the flood of trial, do not
Hand and foot and swimming—today all are naught.

This wind is subjugation's wind, candle's trial
Do not speak, none but God's candle will survive."

He said, "No, I will climb to that mountaintop
It will protect me from all sort of mishap."

"Now the mountain is but straw, do not go there
He will save none but the one He loves, beware!"

"When," he said, "have I ever listened to you
"That you should have hope that I am one of you

"I have never found your words pleasing to me
In both worlds I'm quit of you, you're far from me."

"It is not the day for feigned pride, don't do it
Unto God there is no kin or partnership

"You've done what you've done, this is a crucial time
Who in this conqueror's court is allowed pride?

"He does not beget nor is He begotten
He has neither father nor uncle nor son

"How should He put up with a son's feigned disdain?
How should He listen to fathers' feigned disdain?

"'I am not begotten—be not proud, old man
I do not beget—less entreaty, young man

"'I'm no husband, lust has no hold over Me
Put aside disdain here, O modest lady.'

31th Verse

*"Here in this presence there is no dignity
But constraint, servanthood and humility."*

*He said, "Father, you've for years been saying this
You say it again, deranged with foolishness*

*"You've been saying it for years to everyone
And received a cold response from everyone."*

*"These cold words of yours never entered my ear
I am wise and grown up now, how should I hear."*

*He said, "Son, what harm will it do if just once
You allow yourself to hear father's advice?"*

*Thus he spoke, giving his son kindly counsel
Thus the son continued his harsh refusal*

*Neither did he tire of counseling Canaan
Nor did his words enter the ear of that cad*

*While they were engaged in this talk a fierce wave
Dashed against Canaan's head sweeping him away*

*"O long-suffering Padishah," Noah said
"Your flood has carried him off, my ass is dead*

*"Time and time again You have promised to me
That the flood would surely spare my family*

*"I fixed my hopes on You, simple that I am
Why then has the flood carried away Canaan?"*

*He said, "He was not your or kin or family
You are white and he is blue, did you not see?"*[337]

---

337. Şefik Can, *Konularına gore açıklamalı Mesnevi Tercümesi* (Istanbul: Ötüken Neşriyat 1997), vol. 3-4, pp. 95-96 [vol. 3, vs. 1309-1334].

32. But each of them—all—will be brought before Us.
Wa 'in kullun lammā jamī'un ladaynā muḥḍarūn.

- "Presence" (*huzur*) means a special kind of attention to what enters into the servant's heart, in such a way that the servant is "present" with that thing (*conscious of it*). In that state one must be unaware (*gaybet*) of everything other than the object of attention (*huzur is the opposite of the state of gaybet*).

People cannot know at what moment they will die. A person may die in a state of heedlessness, which is not equivalent to dying in the state of presence.

My child! Hearing is only possible in a state of presence, that is, with the consciousness of the heart.

When presence remains unaware of creation, it is for the heart to be present with God the Truth (*huzur bi'l-Hak*)

As one can see, presence consists in an attention realized in the heart and visible in the limbs, and manifests in creatures in varied levels: In this context presence may manifest perfectly, deficiently or comprehensively or narrowly.

No one has mentioned God without being aware of him. Thus there is either perfect presence, with a person turning away from everything, or presence with attention continuing to be connected to other things.

Mary took refuge in God with all her strength in order to protect herself from the thing she saw (*Gabriel*). Thus for Mary presence was manifest perfectly with respect to God.[338]

---

338. Suad el-Hakîm, trans. Ekrem Demirli, *İbü'l-Arabî Sözlüğü* (Istanbul: Kabalcı Yayınevi 2005), pp. 305-306.

- The state of presence (*el-Muhadara*) is the heart's finding presence with the certainty of proof. According to Kashani, *muhadara* is neighborliness with the divine names and all the realities they possess.[339]

- Resurrection is of three parts. One is the lesser resurrection, meaning the resurrection at the time a person dies.

  The second resurrection is the scattering of all existents when the trumpet is played.

  The third resurrection is when all are raised up in their own corpses and gathered together at the second blast of the trumpet in order to be called to account; what happens there and what we find is the result of our own actions.[340]

- On the Day of Resurrection the trumpet will be blown. The "trumpet" here is a creature in the shape of a horn with holes as many as the number of the souls of all creatures. Because the trumpet has a hole for every being, those beings that have formerly fallen without dying go into a trance at the effect of its sound.

  It is Israfil (a.s.) who blows the trumpet. The spirits form one line and the angels another. Divine command and the angels will come within shadows from the clouds.

  After the trumpet is blown so that the creatures faint and fall down, it will be blown again so that they come to life and rise up, and after that people will look and wait for what God the Truth wants of them.[341]

- And so, on the Day of Resurrection God will say: O My servants! What beautiful, good deeds have you brought Me as a gift? For what and to what end have you spent your lifetimes? I gave you bounties, what did you do? I gave you powers, to what end did you expend them? I gave you intellect, in what way did you use it?"

  The terror that will meet a faithless spirit who comes empty-handed on Resurrection Day, without the gifts of faith, deeds and

---

339. Abdürrezzâk Kâşânî, trans. Dr. Ekrem Demirli, *Tasavvuf Sözlüğü* (Istanbul: İz Yayıncılık 2004), p. 496.

340. Ken'an Rifâî, *Sohbetler* (Istanbul: Kubbealtı Neşriyatı 2000), p. 194.

341. Ahmed er-Rifâî, ed. Dr. H. Kâmil Yılmaz, *Marifet Yolu* (Istanbul: Erkam Yayıncılık 1995), p. 176.

32th Verse

love that should be conveyed to God, is great. To be sure, God, who creates countless bounties and kingdoms for both worlds, has no need of a gift from His servant. But the spirit's need for wealth in worship and faith when it ascends to God's presence is great.

In order to repay the debt and give thanks for having been created as a human, one's pouch must not be empty on the Day of account. We cannot return to God's presence as we were first created, naked and empty-handed. Those who do not believe they will be God's guests one day can only get fire, ashes and earth from His eternal kitchen. What can a person who has not avoided sleep and gluttony to store up spiritual provisions, who has taken no delight in worship and had no share of the abandonment and expectation of fasting present as a gift to the afterworld?[342]

- *"When the earth quakes mightily and throws forth her burdens, and man cries out, 'What is wrong with her?' on that day she will declare her tidings: for that your Lord will have inspired her. Then whoever has done an atom' weight of good will see it, and whoever has done an atom's weight of evil will see it"* (99:1-8).

The dust, thorns, plants, trees and everything on earth will conform to that divine inspirations and speak, and tell every word, every secret, every piece of information with profound openness.[343]

- *Resurrection's the great presentation day*
They want to present who have splendor and grace

For those who are like double-dealing Hindus
That day is the day that they will be accused

Since their faces are not shining like the sun
They want the veil of night to cover them up

Since their thorns possess not one single rose leaf
Spring becomes for them their secret's enemy

And if they're roses and lilies end to end
Spring is like a pair of shining eyes for them

---

342. Ken'an Rifâî, *Şerhli Mesnevî-i Şerif* (Istanbul: Kubbealtı Neşriyatı 2000), p. 464.
343. Ken'an Rifâî, *Şerhli Mesnevî-i Şerif* (Istanbul: Kubbealtı Neşriyatı 2000), p. 480.

O Humankind

Thorns without spirit long for autumn to come
So they may kneel down and sit beside the rose

To hide the beauty of that and shame of this
So you won't compare colors of that and this

For them autumn is their spring season and life
The pure ruby and the stone appear alike

Even then gardeners can put them to the test
But there is one who sees better than the rest

Truly the world is that one person, the fool
Every star in the sky is part of the moon

Thus they cry out, every beautiful, fair form
"Good news! Good news! Look, the spring season has come!"

While blossoms are shining like coats of mail there
How should those fruits make their bulk manifest there?

When the blossom falls the fruit comes to a head
When the body breaks the spirit shows its head

33. A sign for them is the dead earth; We give it life and produce seed from it that they may eat of it.

Wa 'āyatun lahumu'l-'arḍu'l-maytatu 'aḥyaynāhā wa 'akhrajnā minhā ḥabban faminhu ya'kulūn.

- The root ḥ, ba, of the word *ḥubb* (*affection, love*) means "attachment and need" or "seed and flower. "Need" means "love and affection." Seed is the self-disclosure of God's love in the dead earth of our bodies. The plural of the word "seed" (*ḥabba*) is *ḥab*, which is God's will being manifested from creaturely acts.[344]

- Vitality is a mathematical program loaded onto a great chemical molecule. First He created nitrogen bacteria in soil. In the terms of chemistry, these are synthetic laboratories. That is, they take nitrogen from the air and make negatively charged compounds. These bacteria reduce nitrogen in a way we have not yet been able to understand, and make it capable of combining with hydrogen. For this water, rain, is necessary.

  That is the reason why we see dead soil come alive with rain. A second group of bacteria in earth is the analysis group necessary to the program. It breaks down everything that falls onto the earth and prepares synthesizing microorganisms. In this way soil virtually resembles a vast city of alchemy.

  The part of one gram of soil that is not water is mostly living microorganisms.

  In botany soil is considered to be a structure that is completely alive. That is to say that soil has been a living being since life began on earth.

---

344. Suad el-Hakîm, trans. Ekrem Demirli, *İbü'l-Arabî Sözlüğü* (Istanbul: Kabalcı Yayınevi 2005), p. 300.

The second part of the gracious verse we are trying to interpret gives the principle of the continuation of life. It says that after readying vitality first in soil, We created plants bearing the substances of skeletal structure for living creatures.

As we know, the seed mentioned in the verse is on the one hand the seeds of plants and on the other, the substances of all living cells. This seed represents all the basic substances of life as a whole.

Thus it is stressed that the building blocks of plant cells and animal cells are the same. The difference lies especially in their measuring out programs.

One of the most important pieces of wisdom in the gracious verse is that the soil that gains vitality by God's command also provides support for the creatures. The second part of the verse declares this secret especially.

The fertilized egg develops in three ways:

Under the soil (*all plants*),
Development within the egg (*the great majority of animals*),
In the womb.

Actually, from the point of view of science, for living things to find life in the three ways has the same aim. In order for the fertilized egg to bring forth a new living creature, it needs a period of waiting and development. Biologically this process is the process of the seeds and thus the fertilized egg's gradually replicating to take on the shape of a new living creature. In this period the seed needs protection and must take on certain chemical substances and ions varied in electrical charge that we do not yet understand. In the process life is born as programmed.

In this verse God the Truth emphasizes that he has given this special property to soil. If we take this quality of soil as an example, the coming to life of seed is demonstrated.

Actually this property in soil is an important piece of wisdom regarding Judgment Day also.

On Judgment Day when the command for the dead to rise up comes—which is a mathematical program—that is when the secret of the verse will be open to view once more, and the dead will be raised in an instant.

33TH VERSE

This verse is also counted as an indication in two ways of the wisdom of Hazret Adam's physical creation from earth. As we know, it is the Quran that declares Hazret Adam was created from earth in the consistency of wet clay.

What is important here is that God gave of the secret of the name "the Alive" to earth. God both gave life and vitality to earth and made it an instrument of vitality. In other words, earth, like the mother's womb, conveys a fertilized creature into life.[345]

- *"Truly We created the human being from a quintessence of clay. Then We brought him into the state of seminal fluid in a safe and secure place of rest. The We created that seminal fluid as a clot of blood, then created that blood clot as a lump of flesh, then that lump as bones, then clothed those bones in flesh, and then formed it as another creature. So blessed be God, the best of creators"* (23:12-14).

"O human beings! If you are in doubt about the Resurrection, truly We created you from earth, then out of sperm, then out of a blood clot and then out of a bit of flesh partly formed and partly unformed, in order to make evident to you what you are. We make whom We will rest in the wombs for an appointed term. Then We bring you out as a babe. Then We leave you to mature to full strength, and of you some We kill and some we bring to the worst stage of life, so that after their former knowledge they know nothing. And you see that the earth is dried up, but when We pour down upon it rain it stirs, swells, and grows every beautiful growth in pairs" (22:5).

In commentaries on the Quran the bringing forth of the living and the dead out of one another is generally explained in four ways:

Human beings and animals from sperm, and sperm from human beings and animals;
Disbelievers from believers and believers from disbelievers;
Green plants from a dry seed, and seed from plants;
Animals from eggs, and eggs from animals.[346]

---

345. Haluk Nurbaki, *Kur'â-ı Kerîm'den Âyetler ve İlmi Gerçekler* (Ankara: Diyanet Vakfı Yayınları 2001), pp. 71-76.

346. Hüseyin Güllüce, *Kur'ân Tefsîri Açısından Mesnevî* (Istanbul: Ötüken Neşriyat1999), p. 255.

- The earth is the realm we live upon with our bodies that are created out of it. It is the space where daily nourishment manifests. Although the earth is the realm we live upon, Ibn Arabi never forgets that we were created from the earth of that realm, that we came from it and are in it and thus we are it. The bodies of human beings, or their material aspect, is an earth where they live and thus the human body and the earth become one enclosed meaning (*mazmun*). This meaning is understood from Ibn Arabi's phrase regarding the earth's being the place where daily nourishment manifests. The place where daily nourishment manifests is none other than the world and the human body.[347]

- Hazret Abraham's father was a disbeliever and fashioned idols. For a believer to come out of a disbeliever is for the living to be brought out of the dead. Causes are only an occasion; the one who does a thing and creates is God. In order for people to know this, joy and happiness are manifest from grief and sorrow.[348]

- *Since He draws the living thing out from the dead*
The living soul moves toward a state of death

  Be dead so the living God who needs nothing
  May draw out from this dead one a living thing

  If you are winter, you will see spring brought forth
  If you become night, you will see day come forth[349]

- When branches and leaves come out of the prison of earth, they raise their heads and become the mates and companions of the wind. For living things to be imprisoned in water and earth means that they are bound to matter and sensuality. Freed of this fetter, their hearts become joyful, dancing in the air of God the Truth's

---

347. Suad el-Hakîm, trans. Ekrem Demirli, *İbnü'l-Arabî Sözlüğü* (Istanbul: Kabalcı Yayınevi 2005), p. 79.

348. Sultan Veled, trans. Meliha Anbarcıoğlu, *Maarif* (Konya: Altunarı Ofset 2002), p. 203.

349. Mevlânâ Celâleddin Rûmî, trans. Veled İzbudak, ed. Abdülbaki Gölpınarlı, *Mesnevî* (Istanbul: Milli Eğitim Basımevi 1991), vol. 5, vs. 549-551.

love and affection, and become free of imperfection like the full moon.[350]

- *Although the soul may be sagacious and quick*
Know it to be dead, the world is its prayer niche

When the water of God's inspiration comes
From the earth of one dead springs a living one[351]

On this long road you will not find what you need
On one made of earth We've bestowed mysteries

Go to him, if you are not a reprobate
Though you may be reed, he'll make you sugarcane[352]

- The heart of the earth is watered by the tears that come of awe of God, and if the seed of worship that is the nourishment of the spirit is planted, the spring of wisdom will boil up from that heart, produce fruits of ardor and love, and unveilings and witnessings will self-disclose.[353]

- O seeker! You must continually repent and weep and keep yourself in a state of abasement and poverty. If you are a child of Adam, observe courtesy, do not be stubborn like Iblis, that is to say Satan, and weep and wail from the depths of your heart, weep tears from the fire of your heart, and roar with sighs like the sky and weep like the clouds, water the earth of creaturehood, and in this way let the sun of affection adorn the garden of your heart with the fruits of wisdom and when it rises on the field of preparedness let roses of gnosis and hyacinths of reality become manifest and bloom, and let the nightingale of your heart be happy and gay and sing to the rose-garden of the beauty of the beloved.[354]

---

350. Ken'an Rifâî, *Şerhli Mesnevî-i Şerif* (Istanbul: Kubbealtı Neşriyatı 2000), pp. 184-185.

351. Mevlânâ Celâleddin Rûmî, trans. Veled İzbudak, ed. Abdülbaki Gölpınarlı, *Mesnevî* (Istanbul: Milli Eğitim Basımevi 1991), vol. 4, vs. 1656-1657.

352. Mevlânâ Celâleddin Rûmî, trans. Veled İzbudak, ed. Abdülbaki Gölpınarlı, *Mesnevî* (Istanbul: Milli Eğitim Basımevi 1991), vol. 4, vs. 3329-3330.

353. Şemseddin Yeşil, *Füyûzat* (Istanbul: Ş. Yeşil Yayınları 1984), vol. 6, p. 245.

354. Ken'an Rifâî, ed. Kâzım Büyükaksoy, *Mesnevî Hatıraları* (Istanbul: İnkilap Kitapevi 1968), p. 190.

O Humankind

- *You are less than earth, for when earth finds a friend*
It reaps a hundred thousand blooms from one spring

The tree that finds for itself a loving mate
From the sweet air blooms flowers from head to foot[355]

- *"See how I have planted a seed in the earth*
I have raised it up and you are dust of earth

Take on the practice of earthiness once more
That I may make you of emirs the emir

Water travels from above and goes below
Then it travels up on high from down below

Wheat went underneath the ground from high above
Then it became ear of corn quickly sprung up

The seed of each fruit has gone into the ground
Then from burial it raised heads from the ground[356]

- *The Sadr-i Cihan, said, "Breath has left this man;*
When I give him breath, he'll live," and took his hand

"His body is dead, and when he lives through me
It will be my spirit that turns to face me

"I'll make him through this spirit magnificent
The spirit I give will see that I give it"

He began to hear the call of union then
Slowly the dead man began to stir again

He's not less than earth who feels the morning breeze
And lifts up his head from death, all dressed in green[357]

---

355. Mevlânâ Celâleddin Rûmî, trans. Veled İzbudak, ed. Abdülbaki Gölpınarlı, *Mesnevî* (Istanbul: Milli Eğitim Basımevi 1991), vol. 2, vs. 33-34.
356. Mevlânâ Celâleddin Rûmî, trans. Veled İzbudak, ed. Abdülbaki Gölpınarlı, *Mesnevî* (Istanbul: Milli Eğitim Basımevi 1991), vol. 3, vs. 455-459.
357. Mevlânâ Celâleddin Rûmî, trans. Veled İzbudak, ed. Abdülbaki Gölpınarlı, *Mesnevî* (Istanbul: Milli Eğitim Basımevi 1991), vol. 3, vs. 4677-4679, 4687-4688.

33TH VERSE

- *O brother, how comes being in nothingness?*
How is opposite concealed in opposite?

Know this: He brings forth the living from the dead
The worshipper's hope is in non-existence

Non-existence is the storehouse of God's craft
There He constantly fashions gift after gift

God originates; the originator
Produces without root or support luster[358]

- *If this is Bayazid, what then is spirit?*
And what is this image if he's that spirit?

He is both, but grain is origin of growth
While the green broad leaf above is its top growth

Spirit cannot do its work without a form
And without spirit form is frozen and cold

Your form is visible and your spirit hid
The world's business is arranged by both of them[359]

- *"The wisdom in making the world manifest*
Is for God's knowledge to be seen," the Shah said

Where do these accidents spring from? From forms
And these forms, where do they spring from? From thoughts

This world is Universal Intellect's thought
Forms are envoys and the intellect, a shah

Fruits first in the heart's thought come to existence
At the last they are manifest in actions

---

358. Mevlânâ Celâleddin Rûmî, trans. Veled İzbudak, ed. Abdülbaki Gölpınarlı, *Mesnevî* (Istanbul: Milli Eğitim Basımevi 1991), vol. 5, vs. 1018-1019, 1024-1025.

359. Mevlânâ Celâleddin Rûmî, trans. Veled İzbudak, ed. Abdülbaki Gölpınarlı, *Mesnevî* (Istanbul: Milli Eğitim Basımevi 1991), vol. 5, vs. 3421, 3423-3424.

O Humankind

Though its boughs and leaves appear first, and its roots
All of them are sent for the sake of the fruit[360]

That's why the Messenger explained that point thus:
All who know their own selves have come to know God

He has given it so that you will seek more
Don't you say He has only this much, no more

The gardener shows you a few pieces of fruit
So you'll know the orchard's saplings and produce

He gives the customer a handful of wheat
So he may know that granary's special wheat[361]

---

360. Mevlânâ Celâleddin Rûmî, trans. Veled İzbudak, ed. Abdülbaki Gölpınarlı, *Mesnevî* (Istanbul: Milli Eğitim Basımevi 1991), vol. 2, vs. 994, 977-978, 971, 973.

361. Mevlânâ Celâleddin Rûmî, trans. Veled İzbudak, ed. Abdülbaki Gölpınarlı, *Mesnevî* (Istanbul: Milli Eğitim Basımevi 1991), vol. 5, vs. 2114, 2116-2118.

34. And we put there gardens of date palm trees and grapevines, and made springs gush forth in them.

Wa ja'alnā fīhā jannātin min nakhīlin wa 'a'nābin wa fajjarnā fīhā mina'l-'uyūn.

- The date palm tree is in reality the fruit-laden tree of Islam.[362]

- The date palm branch said to Hazret Muhammad (s.a.s.), "Destroy me, so that I may be annihilated (*fani*) in you and your God, and become eternal in that unique light." A date palm can be the site of manifestation of the Prophet's intercession because it does not want this transient world but wishes to reach the level of the perfect human being.[363]

- The date palm in the end attained a level of gnosis and truth that many a traveler on the path of God the Truth has not been able to reach.[364]

- Pain always shows a person the way. Whatever work there is in the world, if a person does not feel love, desire, and longing for it, that person will not do that work and that work will not give him or her success in a painless, carefree way. This is true for this-worldly or otherworldly work, whether it be business, the work of a Padishah, the religious or material sciences, or anything else.

Mary, for example, would not have gone to that tree of good fortune if not for the pains of childbirth. As it is said in the Quran, "*The pains of childbirth drove her to the trunk of a date palm tree*" (19:23); that

---

362. Ken'an Rifâî, *Şerhli Mesnevî-i Şerif* (Istanbul: Kubbealtı Neşriyatı 2000), p. 193.
363. Ken'an Rifâî, *Şerhli Mesnevî-i Şerif* (Istanbul: Kubbealtı Neşriyatı 2000), p. 307.
364. Ken'an Rifâî, *Şerhli Mesnevî-i Şerif* (Istanbul: Kubbealtı Neşriyatı 2000), p. 310.

pain brought her to the tree and the dried-up dead tree came into a fruit-bearing state.[365]

- The grape and the date declare the secret of God the Alive. In tasavvuf the date represents patience, and the grape, courage.[366]

- The grape is the most honorable of fruit species. It is beneficial from its first emerging shoots to its final state. Very fine green threads emerge at its first stage, which have a delicious astringent taste, and it is possible to prepare delicacies from them. Then the unripe grapes appear, which are a pleasant food, whether for those who are ill or for making the drink şalgam. Syrups of refined taste can be made that are beneficial for those who are bilious. They are boiled as a sour to be added to foods, and are the most delicious of boiled sours. When the grapes are ripe, they are the sweetest of fruits, the most appetizing. Ripe grapes are hung up to dry, and may be gathered and stored for a year or more. And they really are the sweetest of fruits gathered and stored. Four things are made from grapes: Raisins, *pekmez*, vinegar and wine. The best part of a grape is its seed. Doctors make many compounds from them that have great benefits for weak and humid stomachs (although the doctors of our time are unanimous in saying that the benefits of chewing and swallowing grape seeds are great). In sum the grape is a fruit worthy of the name "sultan of fruits."

The other verses of the Quran mentioning fruits are the following:

"It is He who raises up gardens with trellises and without, and dates and crops with varied products, olives, and pomegranates alike and unalike. Eat each fruit when they bear fruit and give its due on harvest day, and do not waste in vain, for He does not love those who waste" (6:141).

"From the fruit of the date palm and vine you obtain wholesome drink and food" (16:67).

"Or until you have a garden of date palms and vines..." (17:91).

---

365. Mevlânâ Celâleddin Rûmî, trans. Meliha Ülker Anbarcıoğlu, *Fîhi mâ Fîh* (Istanbul: Milli Eğitim Basımevi 1985), p. 33.

366. Halûk Nurbaki, *Yâ-Sîn Sûresi Yorumu* (Istanbul: Damla Yayınevi 1999), pp. 50-51.

34TH VERSE

"With it He grows for you crops, olives, date palms, grapes, and every kind of fruit" (16:11).

"With it we grow for you garden of date palms and vines, in them abundant fruits" (23:19).

The Latin name for grape is *vitis vinifera*. It is the fruit of grapevine, rich in glucose and grown in the south of North America, southern Europe, Spain, France, Italy, Turkey and North African countries. In our country the grapes grown in the Aegean region are especially renowned.

The most important substance contained in the grape is the great amount of glucose. There are also apple and lemon acids, tannin, sodium, potassium, magnesium and sulfur. It is a food with very powerful medical benefits. It also has diuretic, sedative and purgative effects. According to one source, 100 grams of raisins contains 340 calories, 3 grams protein, 1 gram fat, and 77 grams carbohydrate.

Grapes are a great source of energy. What gas is to a car, energy is to human beings. Grapes are a food with high calories. In this regard grapes give people vitality and vigor. They increase physical and mental strength.

They are hematinic. They ensure the evacuation of harmful substances that accumulate in the body. They lower blood pressure. They are beneficial for stomach ulcers, gastritis, diseases of the liver and spleen, rheumatism and arthritis. They relieve constipation, strengthen the heart and clean the blood. They prevent morning sickness in pregnancy. They clean the skin. They help to overcome periods of remission.

An important vitamin in grapes is vitamin C. The chemical name of vitamin C is ascorbic acid. It is a vitamin that prevents scurvy, an illness that manifests with bleeding gums, inflammation, loss of teeth and hemorrhage. While it has extreme forms, its milder forms are quite common. The agglutinant substance that binds cells together begins to waste away in the absence of vitamin C. In this regard vitamin C has been likened to the mortar spread between the bricks of a building. In vitamin C deficiencies tiny hemorrhages occur in the joints. Grapes are good for fatigue both because of their calories and their vitamin C. Another substance in grapes that imparts vigor is its vitamin A. The B1, B6, calcium and phosphorus, as well as the vitamin

C grapes contain plays an important role in their nervine effect. The first effect of eating grapes is the prevention of pallor (*due to their vitamins*). The second is the prevention of hemorrhage sites thanks to vitamin C, and the third, thanks to their A and C vitamins, is the prevention of microbial diseases and the negative presentations they bring about in the body.

The vitamin A in grapes resembles substances used in the development of photographic plates. Vitamin A aids in the continual renewal of the substance in the retinal layer of the eye called rhodopsin.

Vitamin A is necessary for the health of the skin and mucous membranes. It is necessary to the protection of these organs from germs and thus the harm caused by them. Thus vitamin A protects the respiratory tract and empty spaces of the body from certain internal microbial infections. We can also say that vitamin A is beneficial for the vitality of the eye.

Because calcium and phosphorus have a role in nerve and muscle function, they also have a role in the desired vitality mentioned above.

B1 and B2 vitamins are also found in grapes. When these are lacking, infections occur on the tongue, lips, and in the mouth, and diseases of the skin and eye may result.[367]

- When grapes are yet unripe there is a bitterness in their juice. But when they ripen and mature, the same juice becomes sweet, tasty and fragrant. Yet if the same juice is poured into a jar and ferments and turns into wine, it becomes bitter again and unlawful. In order for it to become lawful again, it must turn into vinegar.

This means that the purest of God's bounties may lose their purity and taste in the jar of the interiors of those nourished on them. The same grape juice that becomes in immature people lust and madness sheds its sinfulness like vinegar in a mature person. It becomes nourishment and power for the love of God and attraction felt by that person. While it once was matter, it now becomes spirit, love, and faith.[368]

---

367. Prof. Dr. Davud Aydüz, *Kur'an-ı Kerîm'de Besinler ve Şifa* (Istanbul: Timaş 1997).
368. Ken'an Rifâî, *Şerhli Mesnevî-i Şerif* (Istanbul: Kubbealtı Neşriyatı 2000), p. 377.

34th Verse

- Let them be solved by fellowship of the pure
Even a grape grows through fellowship from earth

In the dark ground a seed's substance is through grace
With seclusion and with fellowship effaced

Of all selfhood in the earth till naught is left
Of color and scent, or of yellow and red

That annihilation leaves then no constraint
The seed expands, takes wing and speeds on its way

Since it stands before its source now without self
Form is gone, its meaning discloses itself[369]

- If you're human, dig in this body of clay
Like a well digger to reach water someday

If craving for God arrives, the flow will come
Though no well be dug, bubbling up from the ground[370]

- What is absorption? Loosing the spring to flow
When spirit leaves the body, they say it flows

That Hakim whose spirit struggled to get free
Of the body's fetter and wandered the field

Gave to life and spirit these two names, so that
They be told apart. Hail the soul who knows that![371]

- Intellect is the dish, not roast meat and bread
On intellect's light, son, is the spirit fed

There is no food but light for a human being
But in that spirit one finds no fostering

---

369. Mevlânâ Celâleddin Rûmî, trans. Veled İzbudak, ed. Abdülbaki Gölpınarlı, *Mesnevî* (Istanbul: Milli Eğitim Basımevi 1991), vol. 3, vs. 2066-2070.

370. Mevlânâ Celâleddin Rûmî, trans. Veled İzbudak, ed. Abdülbaki Gölpınarlı, *Mesnevî* (Istanbul: Milli Eğitim Basımevi 1991), vol. 5, vs. 2044-2045.

371. Mevlânâ Celâleddin Rûmî, trans. Veled İzbudak, ed. Abdülbaki Gölpınarlı, *Mesnevî* (Istanbul: Milli Eğitim Basımevi 1991), vol. 6, vs. 2187-2189.

O Humankind

What makes this bread bread is that light's reflection
Spirit's spirit by that spirit's effusion

If the stream of knowledge rises from the breast
It does not stink, turn yellow, or become less[372]

- *He said, "O vain man, it's the heart is God's sign*
Those external things are the signs of God's sign

Plants and gardens are inside the spirit there
Their reflection, as on a flowing stream here

Fruits and gardens are in the heart, it's their grace
Reflected on earth and water of this place[373]

- *One must set one's foot on the heart's open plain*
For there is no opening on plain of clay

Friends, the heart is the abode of surety
Of rose gardens upon rose gardens and springs

Turn toward the heart and travel, Wanderer
There are trees inside it and flowing water[374]

- *Each and every tree was crying out to say*
"O people of bitter fortune, come this way!"

Toward the trees there came from rivalry the cry
"No, there's no refuge, We have bound up their eyes

If someone had said, "Come in this direction
And you'll find in these trees gratification"

---

372. Mevlânâ Celâleddin Rûmî, trans. Veled İzbudak, ed. Abdülbaki Gölpınarlı, *Mesnevî* (Istanbul: Milli Eğitim Basımevi 1991), vol. 4, vs. 1954-1955, 1958, 1965.
373. Mevlânâ Celâleddin Rûmî, trans. Veled İzbudak, ed. Abdülbaki Gölpınarlı, *Mesnevî* (Istanbul: Milli Eğitim Basımevi 1991), vol. 4, vs. 1362-1363, 1365.
374. Mevlânâ Celâleddin Rûmî, trans. Veled İzbudak, ed. Abdülbaki Gölpınarlı, *Mesnevî* (Istanbul: Milli Eğitim Basımevi 1991), vol. 3, vs. 514-516.

34th Verse

They would all have said, "This poor drunk in misery
Has been driven mad by the divine decree."[375]

- *The Shaykh laughed and then, "O simpleton," he said*
"That is the tree of knowledge within a sage

Very high and very grand and very wide
It's water of life from the all-circling sea

It is sometimes named 'tree,' and sometimes named 'sun'
Sometimes its name has been 'cloud,' sometimes 'ocean'

That one thing from which thousandfold works arise
The least of its works is everlasting life

It is single, but has a thousand effects
The names that one thing deserves are numberless[376]

- God the Exalted has said: "*The likeness of the garden promised to the righteous is that in it are rivers of incorruptible water, rivers of milk whose flavor does not change, rives of wine delicious for those who drink, and rivers of purified honey. And there are all kinds of fruits for them and forgiveness from their Lord. Are they like those who abide in the fire and are made to drink boiling water that tears their bowels?*" (47:15).

The likeness of water, milk, wine and honey in the world of humanity is thus: Know that the person seeking knowledge must be like water seeking the ocean, just as water day and night overcomes everything to reach the sea without bothering whether it is a mountain, a valley, rocks, a forest, or spaces beautiful or ugly. The seeker of knowledge must not stop, must not begrudge humility to anyone—even if they do not possess honor and virtue—who has found what they seek, until reaching the sea of knowledge. The knowledge must be beneficial for nourishing their own spirit and the spirits of others, just as milk nourishes bodies. With their knowledge and action they must run to a perfect murshid, so that they may reach a gnosis that like wine intoxicates

---

375. Mevlânâ Celâleddin Rûmî, trans. Veled İzbudak, ed. Abdülbaki Gölpınarlı, *Mesnevî* (Istanbul: Milli Eğitim Basımevi 1991), vol. 3, vs. 2016-2020.

376. Mevlânâ Celâleddin Rûmî, trans. Veled İzbudak, ed. Abdülbaki Gölpınarlı, *Mesnevî* (Istanbul: Milli Eğitim Basımevi 1991), vol. 2, vs. 3668-3669, 3671-3673.

both the saki and those who drink it. The murshid's character must give wellbeing to hearts as purified honey does. The company (*meclis*) of a person who internalizes these—that is to say their knowledge, action, gnosis and beautiful character—will be Paradise.

Know that just as these four rivers are found in Paradise, these four things, the likeness of the four rivers in Paradise, should be found in the leader of remembrance and shaykh. If one of them is lacking, the shaykh's company will not be Paradise. For Paradise lacks none of them. If the relationship between them is not perfect, the shaykh's company will not be pleasing. It will not be company that people seek out. In other words, if a shaykh's conduct, desire for knowledge and humility before the people of knowledge is not perfect, his knowledge will lack something and not be sought out. For example, if shaykhs gather knowledge but do not act in accord with it, that knowledge has had no benefit for them, and cannot be expected to be beneficial to others. No benefit can be hoped for from such shaykhs, and people will not seek them out. If they are both knowledgeable and act with knowledge, but do not have authorization from a perfect and perfecting murshid and are only pious (*zahid*) for themselves, there will be no flavor in them, neither for themselves or anyone else, for how should moths gather around a lamp of the whole if love has not been made to burn in it? If the great grace of gnosis has not made them soft, their words will not bestow wellbeing. People will not establish intimacy with them. In order for people to come from every direction, they must gather all four within themselves. Just as Paradise is the desire of all peoples but not everyone can enter it. Only those who bear suffering can enter. For Paradise is encircled by things that are not haram but are abominable. The four merits are not easily gathered in one person. They can be obtained only through much exhausting effort, suffering of difficulties, bearing of trials, and by showing humility to those who have mastered them. For God the Truth has said: "*Did you think you would enter Paradise without God testing those of you who fought hard and remained steadfast?*" (3:142).

"*Whence will delight and comfort be in the life of love?*
For Paradise has been adorned with abominable things."[377]

---

377. Niyâzî Mısrî, trans. Süleyman Ateş, *İrfan Sofraları* (Istanbul: Yeni Ufuklar Neşriyatı n.d.), pp. 55-56.

34th Verse

- Love and affection are found in a person who has a relationship with the river of honey among the four rivers that exist in Paradise. One who has a relationship with the river of milk there will posses knowledge, skill and gnosis, and those with a connection to the river of wine there will be occupied with God's command and obedience here, and perform that command and worship with taste and intoxication; those with a connection to the river of water there will have vitality of heart, wholesome deeds and perform good works with vigor; these things will sprout in their hearts.[378]

- *When your hand performs good works and offers alms*
In that world your hand is herbage and date palms

The stream of your patience, water in Heaven
Your love is the river of milk in Heaven

Your joy in devotion is the honey stream
See your drunken elation in the wine stream

That effect there does not resemble this cause
How He puts it in place of that, no one knows

Since these causes here were under your command
Those four rivers too were under your command

In this world that attribute obeyed your rule
And those spirit streams also obey you too

Those heavenly trees are obedient to you
Because they bear fruit due to your attributes[379]

- Thus the heart's presence makes its temperament paradisical. The paradise of intellect is the paradise of gnosis; each meaning it comprehends by intellect is its attainment to God. The spirit's presence is its bringing about a life like a paradisical garden bearing much fruit. The emergence of secrets is the paradise of rising to the

---

378. Ken'an Rifâî, *Sohbetler* (Istanbul: Kubbealtı Neşriyatı 2000), p. 420.
379. Mevlânâ Celâleddin Rûmî, trans. Veled İzbudak, ed. Abdülbaki Gölpınarlı, *Mesnevî* (Istanbul: Milli Eğitim Basımevi 1991), vol. 3, vs. 3460-3464, 3468-3469.

station of witness. The rivers flowing in the paradise of the heart are nourished by the water of unity and never become sorrowful with personal sorrow, for because the light of certainty has brought the heart to life, it can never be ignorant and dead. The trees of the paradise of heart are faith, its flowers conscience, and its fruits the light of creation. The river of the paradise of intellect is the milk of power that God the Truth has brought into manifestation with the light of His own power. Its trees are wisdom (comprehension of the meaning of creation), its flowers are thought, its fruits are natural intelligence (*fitnat*), clarity of mind and awareness.

The river of the spirit paradise is the unveiling of Beauty that comes from the sea of Majesty, that is, the unveiling of God's beauty with the grace of creation. In other words, spirit dons body and wants to see God's Beauty. God the Truth waters that garden with the delight of seeing His beauty and the comprehension of creation. The trees of this garden are affection, its flowers are ardor, and its fruits are love.

The river of the paradise of secrets is the unveiling of Essence. The witnessing of the secrets garden is watered with the wine of comprehending God's Essence. Its trees are unification (*believing in God's unity*), its fruits are sincerity (*sincere devotion*), and its flowers are asceticism (*tefrid; to be bound to God in every state and detach the heart from every thing*).

These all are the people of not-being and nothingness. It is for this that the people of witness are in contemplation (*murâkabededir; submerged in the inner world, contemplating one's essence, God*). The people of unveiling (*who see incomprehensible matters with the eye of the heart*) possess station. The people of drunkenness and being possess state. The people of not-being (*knowing themselves naught before God's being and will*) possess uprightness (*istikamet*) and intimacy.

Just as clear water shows the stones, bricks and shards on the bottom and everything above it, the human spirit also shows all the knowledge and invisible things kneaded together with human nature. This revealing of everything beneath it and above it, without adding or instructing anything, is the temperament of water; but if that water is mixed with earth or other colors, this quality and knowledge is lost, separated and forgotten.

34th Verse

God the Exalted has sent friends (*servants who have earned the level of intimacy*) and prophets (*messengers*). They are like great and pure waters. God's aim in doing this is for every cloudy and small body of water to be liberated from accidental color and cloudiness, and after that, for it to remember when it sees itself pure: "Surely I was once pure like this!"; for it to know that the colors and cloudiness were accidental, and from these accidental things to bring to mind its previous state. It is said in the Quran, "After soundness, they degrade it. They separate what God has commanded to be joined." Thus the friends and prophets remind them of their previous states. They add no new thing to its substance. Now recognizing that great body of water, every cloudy body of water that says, "I was from it, I was it," has united with that water. That cloudy water, not recognizing this water, seeing itself as separate and of a different kind, mixed with such colors and cloudiness in order not to mix with the ocean, in order to remain distant from mixing with the ocean.[380]

---

380. Mevlânâ Celâleddîn Rumî, trans. Meliha Ülker Anbarcıoğlu, *Fîhi Mâ Fîh* (Istanbul: Milli Eğitim Basımevi 1990), p. 52.

35. That they may eat of its fruits and of what their hands produce from it. Will they not then give thanks?

Liyā'kulū min thamrihi wa mā 'amilathu 'aydīhim 'afalā yashkurūn.

- For he knows that this world of sowing today
Exists for gathering of fruits on Judgment Day[381]

- Here that image is hid, while its work is seen
From that image He brings forms there to be seen

The geometer has the thought of a house
Is his heart like a seed deep within the ground

From inside him that image comes into view
As the earth gives birth from seed within it too[382]

- Thanks; praise: for those who seek God the Truth the first part of ethics (*ahlâk*) we have described is in the nature of the ritual prayer requirement.

The first of conditions is patience, and then gratitude. Because in patience there is steadfastness in obedience and renunciation of sin, while in gratitude there is confession of boons granted by the giver of boons. Gratitude means to praise the giver of boons. In that praise one praises in a way showing that one acknowledges the boon one has received, and confesses, with heartfelt respect, that the boons belong to Him and that one finds them valuable.

---

381. Mevlânâ Celâleddin Rûmî, trans. Veled İzbudak, ed. Abdülbaki Gölpınarlı, *Mesnevî* (Istanbul: Milli Eğitim Basımevi 1991), vol. 4, vs. 2989.

382. Mevlânâ Celâleddin Rûmî, trans. Veled İzbudak, ed. Abdülbaki Gölpınarlı, *Mesnevî* (Istanbul: Milli Eğitim Basımevi 1991), vol. 5, vs. 1790-1793.

In that view, gratitude means for a person to think as one should about the boons God has given and the unpleasant things He has kept away from one; the giving or keeping away can be related to the soul or the body or to this world or the other.

Abu Ismail al-Ansari has said: "Gratitude is the name for acknowledgment of boons. Because that knowledge is the way to knowing the giver of boons. In the Gracious Quran guidance to Islam and faith is named 'gratitude.'"

In this context righteousness, humility, modesty, moral character, preferring others, generosity and chivalry also enter into gratitude. Because these qualities are aspects of temperament qualifying the characteristics we have mentioned for confessing a boon and being grateful for it.[383]

- One night our Messenger of God Efendi (s.a.s.) got settled in bed and said to me: "O daughter of Abu Bakr, permit me to worship my Lord." I said, "I like being next to you," and I gave him permission. The Messenger of God got up and did his ablutions with running water. Then he stood for prayer. His eyes wept so that they emptied water onto his chest. Then he reached the position of bowing halfway, and wept again. He came into full prostration, still continuing to weep. He continued in this way until Bilal-i Habashi performed the morning call to prayer. I said, "Why are you weeping? God the Exalted has forgiven your past and future sins." He said, *"Shall I not be a grateful servant, O Aisha?"*[384]

- Gratitude is of three kinds. One is gratitude of the heart, which is the heart's knowing that a boon is from the giver of boons. That is, it is the gratitude of the heart knowing that material or spiritual, boons are from God. Another is gratitude of the tongue, which is to praise the giver of boons with language. As for the third, it is gratitude with the limbs, and that is to obey and worship God. But the basis of all these is gratitude of the heart.

---

383. Abdürrezzâk Kâşânî, trans. Dr. Ekrem Demirli, *Tasavvuf Sözlüğü* (Istanbul: İz Yayıncılık 2004), p. 315-316.

384. Ahmed er-Rifâî, ed. Dr. H. Kâmil Yılmaz, *Marifet Yolu* (Istanbul: Erkam Yayıncılık 1995), p. 36.

35TH VERSE

Just as gratitude is of three parts, it is also of three levels. The first level is to be grateful for things you desire, things you like. Both the common run of humanity (*avam*) and the select servants of God (*havas*) are included in this level. It is to give thanks for such things as having children, for one's work to go well, to get a raise in salary, things that are pleasing. The second is to hold the things one likes and does not like as one and be content with whatever comes from god the Truth. But this is not work for everyone. The third is to be so drowned in the boon-giving God of Majesty as to not even have the time to see the boon, and this is the essential meaning of gratitude.[385]

- Gratitude is to work. It is to view the tremendousness of God, taking warning in every place God the Truth is pleased. It is to serve the family of gratitude. To not hear with your ear anything related to what is bad or haram; not to hold with your hand anything outside of God's consent (*rızâ*); not to incline with your feet toward any place where that consent is not; in sum, gratitude means to use your entire being in God the Truth's consent.

For example, you see a drunkard. Do not say, "Drunk, degenerate... Look at the state of that man... His head is never in prostration." In other words, do not blame him! Beg God, saying, "O my Lord, guide that servant of yours, protect me from that condition... I know that if You wish, you can in an instant make his condition my condition, and mine, his. O my Lord, I take refuge in You. Protect me, and grant him your guidance!"

If you do not do that, and blame that person, you will have both spoken ill of him behind his back and, satisfied with yourself, clothed yourself in the satanic attribute. In sum, gratitude is to not fall into self-satisfaction, to view tolerantly the grace and subjugation that comes from God, to greet sweetly both the delight and torment that God gives.[386]

- Gratitude is to hunt and bind boons. When you hear the voice of thanks, you are present to the increase of grace. Gratitude is to suck

---

385. Ken'an Rifâî, *Sohbetler* (Istanbul: Kubbealtı Neşriyatı 2000), pp. 315-316.
386. Ken'an Rifâî, *Sohbetler* (Istanbul: Kubbealtı Neşriyatı 2000), p. 398.

the teat of boons. However full of milk the teat may be, it does not come out; in other words, one must suck it.[387]

- *Gratitude for boons is sweeter than the boon*
How should one drunken with thanks go for the boon?

Thanks is the soul of the boon, the boon is skin
For gratitude brings you to where the friend is

The boon makes you heedless, and thanks wakes you up
Hunt the boon with the snare of thanking the Shah

The boon of thanks makes you satisfied, a prince
So that you give the poor a hundred benefits[388]

- "*Truly if your give thanks, I will give you increase*" (14:7). "One day while Hazret Abul Hasan Shadhili was sitting in a cave, he said, 'O my Lord, how shall I give thank to You?' It was said, 'When you know that I have given you more boons than to anyone else, you will have thanked Me.' He said, "Mercy, O my Lord, how shall that be? It is evident that You have given more boons to the prophets, the learned and the rulers than You have to me.' The answer came, 'If I had not given those boons to the prophets, how would you have found the path of God the Truth? If I had not given those boons to the learned, how would you have been able to conform to them? If I had not given those boons to the rulers, how could you have been secure in your property and life? Therefore I have given those boons to you also."[389]

- God bestowed gnosis upon David as favor. As it is said in the Quranic verse, "*We compounded his sovereignty, and gave him wisdom and sound judgment in speech and decision*" (38:20), He gave knowledge to Solomon and David. And what is intended in the verse, "*They said: 'Praise be to God, who has made us more virtuous than many of his believing*

---

387. Mevlânâ Celâleddin Rûmî, trans. Melika Ülker Anbarcioğlu, *Fîhi mâ Fîh* (Istanbul: Milli Eğitim Basımevi 1985), pp. 164-165.

388. Mevlânâ Celâleddin Rûmî, trans. Veled İzbudak, ed. Abdülbaki Gölpınarlı, *Mesnevî* (Istanbul: Milli Eğitim Basımevi 1991), vol. 3, vs. 2895-2898.

389. Ken'an Rifâî, *Sohbetler* (Istanbul: Kubbealtı Neşriyatı 2000), p. 342.

servants'" (27:15), is that the knowledge they were given of knowing God is a favor, not a repayment for their deeds. If that gnosis had been a repayment for their deeds, it would not have been favor but recompense. The gnosis of the messengers with regard to God, His names and stations (*mertebe*) is a grant of the Merciful and a gift God makes special to them. Earning and acquiring does not enter into it at all. And so He granted Solomon to David. That is to say, the manifestation of Solomon did not occur due to deeds issuing forth from David himself. On the contrary, it was pure boon and granting of superiority. Above all, the hand of power given to David was due to God's name of Giver (*Vehhâb*) and was not in the nature of recompense in repayment for deeds. Thus God's saying, "We gave David a superiority from Ourselves," remained everlasting for him. If one pays attention, the word "boon" (*bağış*) is not mentioned openly in that Quranic verse. So now, is this gift a repayment and recompense, or is it pure boon? It is perfectly clear that if it had been given as repayment for something, the Giver would not have given it as a superiority. In any case the meaning can clearly be understood from the phrase, "from Ourselves."

In the same way, God did not seek repayment from David for what He gave him. Although He asked gratitude for the boon, He asked it from David's family, not from David himself. By asking gratitude from David's family in repayment for the boon, the gift became for David a superiority and boon but for his family a recompense. So because gratitude was incumbent upon his family, He asked them to give thanks. And He said: "*Family of David, give thanks. Few of My servants give much thanks*" (34:13).

With this statement God the Exalted made incumbent both the boon that was a grant and the gratitude for the boon He gave as recompense. This means that He will increase a boon manyfold in repayment for gratitude.

Voluntary, non-incumbent gratitude is that mentioned in the Messenger's (s.a.s.) hadith, "*Shall I not be a servant who gives many thanks?*" This gratitude is done not with God the Truth's demand, but perhaps rather as a gift from his soul. As for the gratitude about which there is a command, it is gratitude made compulsory. While God the Exalted says, "Thank God," in one place, He says in another, "Give thanks for God's boon." Now, for those who use their intellect because of God, the difference between those who give thanks in these two Quranic verses is as much as the difference between the two things for which one is giving thanks. The servants for whom giving thanks for boons is incumbent are "lovers" (*muhibbîn*), that is to say at the station of those who love God, and what they give thanks for is boons. On the other hand, those who voluntarily thank God beyond what is incumbent are at the station of beloveds (*mahbubîn*), that is to say beloved of God, and what they give thanks for is directly God the Truth.[390]

---

390. İsmail Rusûhî Ankaravi, ed. İlhan Kutluer, *Nakşel Fusus Şerhi* (Istanbul: Ribat Yayınları n.d.), pp. 117-120.

36. Glory to the One who created all things in pairs from what the earth produces, and from their souls, and from things they do not know.

Subḥāna'lladhī khalaqa'l-'azwāja kullahā mimmā tunbitu'l-'arḍu wa min 'anfusihim wa mimmā lā ya'lamūn.

- The Glorified (*Sübhan*) means God who is pure and exempt from any lack and flaw, and especially creaturely qualities. Know that God is the Glorified. So that you may not fall into a state to be ashamed of before Him and in His sight. God the Glorified knows all your secrets and all your thoughts. Every dark feeling, thought and action is known to Him, like a black hair in white milk. For God is All-knowing, All-aware.[391]

- He is the Glorified, beyond everything conceivable. He has ninety-nine names in the Quran, the Torah, the Gospel and the Psalms. His greatest name is the Glorified. When you say "the Glorified," you have said all of the names, but even if you say all the other names and do not say "the Glorified," you will have said nothing. Everything depends on that name. When you pronounce it, everything opens up and sins are erased. The likeness of that is the rosary with a thousand beads that elderly women have. One of the beads is bigger than the others, and they call it the *imâme*, the one who calls to prayer. If that one bead breaks, all the others will break also. In the same way, when you say, "Glory to God," you have found (and said) all the names. Thus one must strive to say "Glory to God" much.

All creatures say "Glory to God," but due to your heedlessness you cannot hear them reciting their rosaries. The word Glorified is

---

[391]. Ken'an Rifâî, *Şerhli Mesnevî-i Şerif* (Istanbul: Kubbealtı Neşriyatı 2000), p. 458.

repeated in thousands of songs, with a thousand kinds of melodies, but you cannot hear those tunes. God the Exalted says, "*There is no thing that does not recite His praise with gratitude. But you do not understand their recitations*" (17:44).[392]

• The Messenger of God (s.a.s.) said, "*Whoever spends a pair in the way of God, the gardens of Paradise turn swiftly toward him*" (hadith). It was said, "What is a pair?" The Messenger of God said, "Two horses, two slaves, two camels." Ragib al-Isfahani mentions these meanings and says, "'mate' and its plural, 'mates,' are incorrect terms," and he adds, "Every thing has come into being from a substance, an accident, a material and a form. There is nothing having the accident of being compound that you cannot demonstrate to be made. And everything made has a maker. But God is single. Everything found in the world has an opposite, something like it, or a compound. All things that have an opposite and a like are compounded of substance and accident. Substance and accident are two mates. In the Quran the word 'mate' is used in all these senses. 'Glory to the One who created all things in pairs from what the earth produces, and from their souls, and from things they do not know." (36:36). Just as the pairs in these Quranic verses may be taken in the sense of male and female, so they may also mean genus, class, like or opposite. The concept of His creating in pairs gains greater breadth in these verses.

Many Quranic verses about types of plants can be mentioned. "*We send down water from the sky and produce on the earth every gracious pair*" (31:10). "*Of every fruit He made two in pairs*" (13:3). "*The One who made the earth a cradle for you and opened pathways in it, and sent down water from the sky. With it We produced diverse kinds of plants in pairs*" (20:53). It is stated that there are pairs of fruits in Paradise as well: "*In both of them are fruits of every kind in pairs*" (55:52).

"*He created you from a single soul, then made from it its mate, and sent down for you of herds eight pairs*" (39:6).

God also created human beings male and female, and they reproduce by way of generation. "*And We created you in pairs*" (78:8). "*And of it He made two mates, male and female*" (75:39). "*And that it is He who created*

---

392. Muhammed Ibn Münevver, *Tevhidin Sırları* (Istanbul: Kabalcı Yayınevi 2003), p. 234.

36TH VERSE

pairs, male and female" (53:45). *"It is He who created you from a single soul and made from it its mate that he might rest in her"* (7:189).[393]

- *"And of every thing we created pairs, that you may remember"* (51:49).
  "It is He who created pairs, all of them, and made for you ships and animals upon which you ride" (43:12).

All the world's parts, due to that predestinate
Are in pairs and are in love with their own mate

In the world each particle desires its pair
Like a blade of straw attracted by amber

The heavens declaring to the earth, "Well met!
With you I am as iron is with magnet"

God the Truth made man and woman thus incline
So the world ever in that concord abide

He made each particle seek another one
So from their union arise generation[394]

- The mightiest and most perfect vehicle for the affinity between man and woman, and God the truth and the human being, is form, because form paired being, which is single. In other words, form was the cause that dualized God the Truth's being. Just as women, by being created, dualized the male and made him her mate. Thus there came about a trinity of God the Truth, man and woman. And the male, as something like the longing of the woman for her own origin, also longed for his own origin, his Lord. Thus while God loved the person who was upon His own form, He made woman also love him. Thus a man's love became directed both toward woman who is a part of his own self, and toward God the Truth who created him. That is why Hazret Muhammed (s.a.s.) said, *"I was caused to love woman."*[395]

---

393. Veli Ulutürk, *Kur'an-ı Kerîm'de Yaratma Kavramı* (Istanbul: İnsan Yayınları 1995), p.127.

394. Mevlânâ Celâleddin Rûmî, trans. Veled İzbudak, ed. Abdülbaki Gölpınarlı, *Mesnevî* (Istanbul: Milli Eğitim Basımevi 1991), vol. 3, vs. 4401-4404, 4415-4416.

395. Muhyiddîn İbnü'l-Arabî, trans. Nuri Gençosman, *Fusûs'l-Hikem* (Istanbul: Kırkambar Kitaplığı 1981), p. 327.

- The murshid's guidance of a disciple begins by impregnating the disciple's ear. If that seed of the murshid's unites in the disciple's womb of the heart with the disciple's egg of affection, a heart-child is produced thereby. If that heart-child is born and is male, he will be competent to guide others. If it is a girl, she will be her own murshid. If that heart-child is not nourished by prayer, it will die.[396]

- There before my eyes was not a telegraph, but the head of a lily-white pale-faced new mother bending over her child. But I wanted to lift up that head and see that little newborn head. The more I begged to see my child, the fresh face of my child, the head of the new mother leaned over further and completely obscured it. I approached; I came near to those two beautiful heads welded together and I too leaned over the little one as she did, so much so that my head touched hers. It was understood. In order for me to see my child, my head must first unite with the head of my wife.

  It was only in that moment of unity that I was able to see my child, little traveller of great and mysterious worlds.[397]

- *Many are the wondrous children it has had*
But all of them have been surpassed by Ahmed

  Earth and sky are laughing, happy and joyous
Saying, "Such a shah came from the two of us!"[398]

- *From these two souls' union with one another*
There will arrive from the Unseen another

  Wherever two people in love or hate join
A third one will certainly come to be born

  But those forms come to be born in the Unseen
When you journey to that quarter, you will see

---

396. Ömür Tuğrul İnançer, *Sohbetler* (Istanbul: Keşkül Yayınevi 2006), p. 235.
397. Sâmiha Ayverdi, *Ateş Ağacı* (Istanbul: Kubbealtı Neşriyatı 2005), pp. 61-62.
398. Mevlânâ Celâleddin Rûmî, trans. Veled İzbudak, ed. Abdülbaki Gölpınarlı, *Mesnevî* (Istanbul: Milli Eğitim Basımevi 1991), vol. 4, vs. 1017-1018.

36th Verse

Those progeny were born of your conjunction
Do not take joy in just any companion

Wait in readiness for the appointed time
Know that progeny join their parents in time

For they are born of causes and of actions
There is form and speech and body for each one[399]

- *He has said, "If you revert, I will revert*
We have wedded each action to its desert

When I make one of a pair to come to Me
The other comes running inevitably

We have made that action the effect's partner
When one of them arrives so does the other"[400]

- *Because God created pairs of every kind*
Consequences issue forth when they combine[401]

- *Since angel and intellect are spun as one*
There's a reason why they have taken two forms

Like a bird that angel took pinions and wings
While intelligence took luster and left wings

Since each has the same meaning as the other
Each beauty is a support for the other

Both the angel and the intellect find God
Both prostrate to Adam and come to his aid

---

399. Mevlânâ Celâleddin Rûmî, trans. Veled İzbudak, ed. Abdülbaki Gölpınarlı, *Mesnevî* (Istanbul: Milli Eğitim Basımevi 1991), vol. 5, vs. 3892, 3894-3898.
400. Mevlânâ Celâleddin Rûmî, trans. Veled İzbudak, ed. Abdülbaki Gölpınarlı, *Mesnevî* (Istanbul: Milli Eğitim Basımevi 1991), vol. 3, vs. 2872-2874.
401. Mevlânâ Celâleddin Rûmî, trans. Veled İzbudak, ed. Abdülbaki Gölpınarlı, *Mesnevî* (Istanbul: Milli Eğitim Basımevi 1991), vol. 6, vs. 523.

O Humankind

Self and Satan have since long ago been one
Enemies and enviers both of Adam[402]

- However much poisons work poisoning effects
  Antidotes work soon to root out their effects
  One dust-mote is always flying to the left
  While the other heads off right on its own quest[403]

  > Intellect gives direction to soul and eases its perfecting; if together they go forward within the meaning of God, from the union of such an intellect and soul, an intellect that comprehends the secret and a soul that has reached the station of the heart, there is produced the heart-child; it is with that new meaning come to life that there emerges the self-disclosure of God in the human being.[404]

- For in this one person both actions exist
  One minute he's the hook and next he's the fish

  Half of him is disbeliever, half believes
  Half of him patience and the other half greed

  Your God said, "of you believers," and again
  "Of you unbelievers," fire-worshipping old man

  Like an ox that's colored black on its left side
  And is white as the moon on the other side[405]

- Human beings carry within themselves both Lordliness (*God's pedagogic attribute*) and servanthood. That is why none but human beings have made claim to Lordliness because of the power in themselves. No creature in the universe has ever claimed it was Lord or possessed the attribute of Lordliness. Only human beings, due to the

---

402. Mevlânâ Celâleddin Rûmî, trans. Veled İzbudak, ed. Abdülbaki Gölpınarlı, *Mesnevî* (Istanbul: Milli Eğitim Basımevi 1991), vol. 3, vs. 3193-3197.

403. Mevlânâ Celâleddin Rûmî, trans. Veled İzbudak, ed. Abdülbaki Gölpınarlı, *Mesnevî* (Istanbul: Milli Eğitim Basımevi 1991), vol. 6, vs. 35, 37.

404. Compiler's note.

405. Mevlânâ Celâleddin Rûmî, trans. Veled İzbudak, ed. Abdülbaki Gölpınarlı, *Mesnevî* (Istanbul: Milli Eğitim Basımevi 1991), vol. 2, vs. 604-607

Lordly capacity and divine power (*God's beginningless power*) found within them, have made that claim. Those who saw those qualities related to Lordliness in themselves without the eye of the heart having opened supposed that they originated purely in themselves, and made the claim, "I am the greatest Lord." Pharaoh and Nimrod were among them.

Others, feeling the power of Lordliness to the extent that unbounded reality was reflected in them, said, "I am God the Truth." They are like Abu Yazid and Mansur Hallaj. But there is a great difference between that "I" and the other "I"s.

No other creature in the universe but the human being has in their own essence taken a strong stand in the station of servanthood. In other words, no other being but the human being has borne, soundly and deeply, the characteristic of servanthood in that station. And because of the characteristic, seeing the aforementioned Lordliness and divine qualities in other things, they may suppose those qualities in fact originate purely in that being. And in the end, they may decide to be servant to that being, as in the worship of idols. Thus they may practice servanthood toward the most low-level, inanimate things and stones.

Just as there is no creature made more exalted than the human being with regard to rank in bearing the qualities of Lordliness, so with regard to qualities of servanthood there is no creature made lowlier. Just as Lordliness is the highest of all levels, its opposite, servanthood, is the lowest. The human being is a double-faced mirror, one face showing the qualities of Lordliness and the other the deficiencies of servanthood.[406]

- One end of the soul rises to "the most beautiful stature" (*ahsen-i takvim*) and the other descends to "the lowest of the low" (*esfel-i sâfilîn*). One end to the heights of Paradise, and the other to the lowest levels of Hell!

The human being is a creature who comes and goes between these two opposites! Both conditions depend on the soul, the person's self.

---

406. İsmail Rusûhî Ankaravi, ed. İlhan Kutluer, *Nakşel Fusus Şerhi*, (Istanbul: Ribat Yayınları n.d.), p. 20.

The soul is a nuclear power station that God, who is the Creator and King of all power and exaltedness, has established within the human being. It can be used for good, and it can be used for evil...

Muallim Nâci says in his *Lügat-i Nâci*:

Speech
Moderate and positive: wisdom
Excessive: effusiveness
Excessive in reverse: credulity, irrationality

Anger
Moderate and positive: courage, boldness
Excessive: rage
Excessive in reverse: cowardice

Lust
Moderate and positive: chastity
Excessive: perversity, whoredom
Excessive in reverse: impotence

The faculties between excessiveness and deficiency are known as superiority and virtue; the faculties near to excessiveness and excessiveness in reverse, vileness and infamy. For the human being, all human beings, society, the great family of humanity, whose one end is infamy and the other superiority, to turn toward virtue depends on that nuclear energy power station being used for the common good and benefit.[407]

- While transforming each thing from one state into another, God brings it forth by means of its opposite and keeps you changing from state to state.

In this way you continually fear becoming one of the Companions of the Left (those listed on the left in the book of deeds, who will go to Hell), and hope, like manly men, for the delight of the Companions of the Right. When you fear on the one hand, and hope on the other, you will have two wings. A bird with one wing never can fly, it is helpless.[408]

---

407. Mustafa Özdamar, *Niyâzî-yi Mısrî* (Istanbul: Kırk Kandil Yayınları 2000), p. 75.

408. Mevlânâ Celâleddin Rûmî, trans. Veled İzbudak, ed. Abdülbaki Gölpınarlı, *Mesnevî* (Istanbul: Milli Eğitim Basımevi 1991), vol. 2, vs. 1552-1554.

36th Verse

- Each thing is better known by its contrary. If not for plurality, the value and significance of oneness would not be known, and the same is true of color and colorlessness, evil and goodness, ugliness and beauty and especially death—which is to say nothingness, and existence. And that is also the reason why there are disbelievers and people who are unrighteous, lustful, without character and without faith, along with prophets, friends, believers and people with pure hearts and spirits loyal to the Creator.[409]

- God the Truth has names that are opposites of one another. For example, just as there is the One Who Gives, there is the One Who Destroys. Just as there is the One Who Guides, there is the One Who Leads Astray. Just as there is the One Who Forgives, there is the One Who Avenges.[410]

- God created our Messenger of God Efendi from two opposite things. From delicacy and grossness. From spirit and matter. In other words, he is both material and spiritual. God created his materiality and creaturely condition for the sake of the converse he would have with human beings and for the comparison of forms. So that with his creaturely body he would give them strength, be with them, be a helper to them, be for them an example of what should be done, and a goal. So that thus he would be intimate with them, saying, "*I am a creature like you.*" So that he should declare that he took on their forms. As for the reason God gave him a spiritual capacity, He granted that to him so that those in the spiritual realms should witness him also. And those in the sublime realm of Sovereignty also. So that there should thus be for the spiritual beings also a complete blessing and mercy and they too should witness his blessed body.[411]

- In order to bring health to the sick liver, I have in my compound not only honey but vinegar as well. Just as oxymel is made by mixing

---

409. Ken'an Rifâî, *Şerhli Mesnevî-i Şerif* (Istanbul: Kubbealtı Neşriyatı 2000), p. 357-358

410. Ken'an Rifâî, *Sohbetler* (Istanbul: Kubbealtı Neşriyatı 2000), p. 135.

411. Muhyiddîn İbnül-Arabî, trans. Abdülkâdir Akçiçek, *Şeceretü'l-Kevn-Üstün İnsan* (Istanbul: Bahar Yayınları 2000), pp. 113-114.

honey and vinegar, and is given to the patient and heals his liver, in order for me to be of use to humans made of dark earth I must not be simply light. That is why I was made of a mixture of dark and light.

For the power that will cure men is such a mixture. Nor the eye nor the heart nor the nature of mankind can tolerate a spiritual light that is not darkened with even a little of the dross of matter.[412]

- Every single atom in the universe carries its opposite inside it. For there are God's attributes of Beauty and Majesty. God self-discloses in every atom. There is in every atom the trace of the manifestation of all His attributes.[413]

- "Allah," the Name of Majesty, is composed of five letters:

The first letter of the word "Allah" is *alif*. It consists of oneness in which plurality is destroyed. In other words, for there to be plurality, eternal subsistence must not in any way remain; *"Everything but His Essence is doomed to perish"* (28:88) [sic].

Oneness is the first of the self-disclosures of Essence that is for itself, in itself and with itself.

The second letter of the word "Allah" is its first *lam*. It too consists of majesty. For majesty is the most sublime of the self-disclosures of Essence, and in Essence is prior to Beauty. *"Exaltedness is my shirt, and Greatness my dress"* (hadith). The Beauty attributes concern two attributes. One is exaltedness, and the other is power.

The third letter in the word "Allah" is the second *lam*. It consists of the unbounded beauty included in the sites of manifestation of God the Exalted. All His attributes of beauty concern two attributes. The first is knowledge and the second is grace.

The fourth letter in the word "Allah" is the *alif* omitted in writing but remaining in pronunciation. This is the perfect *alif* that gathers within itself the perfections without limit or end. Furthermore, the fact that it is omitted in writing indicates its having no end or limit. For neither the similitude nor the effect of a thing that does not exist can be comprehended. The fact that it remains in pronunciation

---

412. Ken'an Rifâî, *Şerhli Mesnevî-i Şerif* (Istanbul: Kubbealtı Neşriyatı 2000), p. 538.
413. Niyâzî Mısrî, trans. Süleyman Ateş, *İrfan Sofraları* (Istanbul: Yeni Ufuklar Neşriyatı n.d.), p. 140.

indicates the reality of the being of the soul of perfection that exists with regard to the Essence of God the Truth.

The fifth letter in the word "Allah" is *h*. The letter *h* here indicates the He-ness [Essence] of God the Truth, and this He-ness of God is the same as the human being. The *he* here expresses the spiritual meaning of the human being. What is meant by "He" is the perfect human being who gathers and contains within his essence the attributes of lack and perfection and shines on the earth of all creatures with the light of his sublime sun.[414]

- God who is the Glorified is single within the secret of incomparability. What He created is dual; that is, opposing similar twins.

According to the classification in the Quranic verse these opposing twins are in three groups:

a. Opposite twins of what the earth grows
b. Opposite twins of the soul
c. Opposite twins we do not know

"Pair" means that which is the same but opposite in character, like male and female, minus and plus.

Maurice Dirac says in his renowned parity theory that no quantum in the universe comes to be as a single material particle; it must be born with its pair. When a proton is created, its opposite mate (*antiproton*) is always created with it.

The pairs that are produced from the earth are:

Opposing similar pairs in terms of character: Metal and non-metal.

Opposing pairs in terms of biology: Male and female plants and animals.

Physically opposite pairs: Positively and negatively charged ions. Thus electrical structural opposites. The opposing magnetic mates are the magnetic effect extremes known as north and south.

Synthetic and analytic events that nest and transform death and life into one another in the earth: Opposites such as the creative and

---

414. Abdü'l-kerîm b. İbrahim el-Cîlî, trans. Seyyid Hüseyin FevzîPaşa, *İnsan-ı Kâmil* (Istanbul: Kitsan Yayınları), pp. 94-103.

destructive (*nitrogen processing bacteria*) syntheses that give life to plants, and the deadly and dissipating effects of bacteria known as putrefacients, which perform analysis.

As for the opposing twins of the soul, every temper in the soul has been created in pairs.

These paired characteristics of the soul are of two kinds.

> Similar pairs: hypocrisy-dissembling, pride-dignity, poverty-trust in God.
> Opposing pairs: cowardice-courage, compassion-cruelty, humility-pride...[415]

- So that both of them should be evident, God the Exalted brought humanity and animality together. Things are evident by their opposites. It is impossible to describe a thing that has no opposite. Just as God the Exalted has said, "*I was a hidden treasure and I wanted to be known*" (hadith), because He has no opposite, so did He create this dark world as darkness in order that light might be evident. That is why He brought prophets and friends of God into being, saying, "Go out with My attributes and be seen by the people." They are the sites of manifestation of God's light. By means of them friend is distinguished from foe, and beloved from stranger. Because that spiritual meaning as meaning has no opposite and can only be shown by way of form. Satan, for example, is evident by comparison with Adam, Pharaoh by Moses, Nimrod by Abraham and Abu Jahl by Mustafa; endless examples can be given. Thus although it has no opposite with regard to meaning, the opposite of God comes into view by means of the friends of God. For example, as it is said in the Quranic verse, "*They want to extinguish God's light with their mouths. But God will complete His light, even though the unbelievers oppose it*" (61:8), no matter how much enmity and opposition they show, the work of the friends of God will proceed and they will become known to that extent.[416]

> *All hidden capacities and hidden boons become evident by their opposites. Only God has no opposite. There are opposites for His sub-*

---

415. Halûk Nurbaki, *Yâ-Sîn Sûresi Yorumu* (Istanbul: Damla Yayınevi 1999), pp. 52-54.

416. Mevlâna, trans. M. Ülker Târıkâhya, *Fîhi Mâfih* (Istanbul: Milli Eğitim Basımevi), pp. 126-127.

36th Verse

lime attributes of being, beauty and goodness. They are not-being, ugliness and evil. But no opposite exists for God the Truth himself. That is why He, God the Exalted who has no partner in being and Allah-ness, will always remain hidden.[417]

• Form is from the point of view of relatedness the greatest, mightiest and most perfect vehicle. Because form paired being, which is single. In other words, form became the cause of the dualization of God the Truth's being. Just as woman by being created dualized man and made him her mate. Thus there came to be a trinity of God, man, and woman.[418]

• God the Exalted is the one who wills good and evil. But He will accept nothing but the good. Because He has said, "*I was a hidden treasure and I wanted to be known*" (hadith). There is no doubt that God has the will to command and forbid. A command will not be right unless the agent does not naturally desire the thing commanded. For example, "O hungry one, eat sweets and sugar," cannot be commanded; this is not called command, it is counted a kindness. And prohibition cannot be about something a person likes. For example, one does not prohibit, saying, "Don't eat stones, don't eat thorns." That cannot be called prohibition. In order to give a command for a good to be performed and to prohibit evil, there must be a soul inclined to evil. To desire the being of such a soul is to desire evil. But He will not accept evil; if He did, He would not command the good. For example, if a teacher desires to teach a lesson, this is also to desire the student's ignorance. For there can be no teaching without the student's ignorance. To desire a thing is also to desire what that thing requires. But the teacher does not desire the student's ignorance; if that were the case, the teacher would not teach. Doctors wish people to be ill so that they can practice medicine, for that skill can only exist if people are ill. But a doctor will not assent to people being ill; if that were the case, the doctor would not cure them. Bakers wish people to be hungry so that they can earn money. But the baker's heart will not

---

417. Compiler's note.
418. Muhyiddîn İbnü'l-Arabî, trans. Nuri Gençosman, *Fusûs'l-Hikem* (Istanbul: Kırkambar Kitaplığı 1981), p. 327.

assent to their being hungry; if that were the case, the baker would not sell bread. Commanders want their Sultan to have enemies and opponents, for without them the commanders' bravery and love for their ruler would not be shown. If the Sultan had no need, he would not muster them. But they do not accept opposition; if they did, they would not fight enemies. It is the same with human beings; God wants there to be evil in their souls, because He loves those who are grateful, who worship, and fear Him, which can only happen if there is evil in the souls of human beings. To desire a thing is also to desire what that thing requires. But He will not assent to that.[419]

- *"But she in whose house he was called him to her. She locked the doors and said, 'Come, you.' He said, 'God forbid! Your husband is my lord, and he has made my stay wholesome. Truly no good comes to those who do wrong'"* (12:23).

"Indeed she desired him, and he would have desired her had he not seen the proof of his Lord. Thus We warded off from him evil and indecency. Truly he was among our sincere servants" (12:24).

Do not pluck your feathers, root them from your heart
For the foe is necessary to this war

When there is no enemy, war makes no sense
Without lust there can be no obedience

If you are not partial, there's no self-restraint
When there's no opponent, what need for your strength?

Don't castrate yourself, do not become a monk
For chastity is redeemed in trade for lust

If there's no desire, it cannot be forbid
One can't show heroism against the dead

Since the Shah gave the command, "Show self-restraint!"
There must be something from which you turn away

When there is no predicate in the sentence
The subject of the statement cannot exist

---

419. Mevlânâ Celâleddin Rûmî, trans. Meliha Ülker Anbarcıoğlu, *Fîhi mâ Fîh* (Istanbul: Milli Eğitim Basımevi 1985), pp. 273-274.

36th Verse

When you do not suffer the pain of patience
There is no condition for the consequence

For a test there must be freedom of the will
With no power to act you cannot have free will

Free will is a good for one who is possessed
Hearing, "Fear God," of mastery of the self

Those who have patience esteem their feathers naught
So their feathers don't tempt them to evil thought[420]

- God can with that struggle remove these things from the soul. From this we understand that human beings desire evil on the one hand and good on the other. But those who oppose this say, "Human beings never desire evil." But that is impossible. It is not possible to desire a thing but not desire what that thing requires. To incline toward evil by one's nature, a headstrong soul that hates the good, are necessities for command and prohibition. The evils in the whole world are the necessities of that soul. He who did not will those evils and that soul would neither desire the command and prohibition that are the requirements of that soul. If human beings assented to goodness and evil, He would not have commanded and prohibited them. In sum, evil is desired for another. If it is said that human beings desire every good, to ward off their evils is to be counted a good. And warding off evil can only happen if evil exists. Or one who desires faith says, "Faith is only possible after unbelief." That is why unbelief is a requirement of faith. To directly desire evil is ugly, but if it is desired for a good, it is not ugly. God says for you in the Quran that there is good in retaliation (*for a person who commits a crime to be punished in the same way*). There is no doubt that retaliation is an evil. It is an attack on God's house. But it is a small evil. To rid the people of a murderer is a complete good. To desire a partial evil for the sake of a complete good is not ugly. For example, to abandon God's partial will and assent to complete evil is ugly. A mother does not want her

---

420. Mevlânâ Celâleddin Rûmî, trans. Veled İzbudak, ed. Abdülbaki Gölpınarlı, *Mesnevî* (Istanbul: Milli Eğitim Basımevi 1991), vol. 5, vs. 574-578, 581, 583-584, 625, 649, 652.

child to be scolded because she is thinking of the partial evil. But a father wants the child to be scolded, because he is thinking of the complete evil. God is very forgiving and His punishment is severe. He can be forgiving due to the existence of sins. To will a thing is to will what that thing requires. For example, He commands us to forgive, to make peace, and to ameliorate. There would be no benefit in such command if enmity did not exist. The Sadr al-Islam says, "That is similar to what the Sadr al-Islam said. He says, 'God says, "*Spend in the way of God.*"' With this He commands us to gain wealth, for gaining wealth happens with wealth. This can be considered a command to earn. If someone is told, 'Get up and pray,' it means that person is commanded to perform ablutions, find water and obtain the requisites of prayer."[421]

- If a police officer has in the past committed theft, pickpocketing and banditry, that former state of trickery and thievery is transformed into justice and wholesomeness when he takes up police work and the Muslims attain more security and welfare through his administration. For the officer knows more about the tricks and intrigues, the character and temper of thieves. The officer can easily capture them, and will not find it hard to discipline and intimidate them. A shaykh is like that too. If a shaykh has formerly lived in the worlds of depravity, perversion and pleasure, and later repented and become a shaykh, the people will benefit more from their being a shaykh.[422]

- There comes a time when servant certainly becomes Lord. At another time servants descend without stain to the lowest level of servanthood; if so, they expand with God the Truth. If servants become Lords, their living narrows. By being servants, they see the source of their souls and their wishes certainly expand from God the Truth. By being Lords they also see all the creatures in the Realm of Kingdom and the Realm of Sovereignty asking them for things. But they by es-

---

421. Mevlânâ Celâleddin Rûmî, trans. Meliha Ülker Anbarcıoğlu, *Fîhi mâ Fîh* (Istanbul: Milli Eğitim Basımevi 1985), pp. 265-266.

422. Sultan Veled, trans. Meliha Anbarcıoğlu, *Maarif* (Konya: Altunarı Ofset 2002), p. 147.

sence lack the power to satisfy those requests, and that is why some gnostics weep.

So be servant of the Lord, do not try to be Lord of His servant; because of that you will later be condemned to fire and melting.[423]

- God the Truth gave a heart to me
That's awestruck at any moment
Happy, joyful at one moment
Weeping at another moment
Now you would think winter had come
Darkest coldest winter had come
And then it's reborn of glad news
Like a garden with fruits and blooms
The time comes it speaks not a word
Cannot explain a single word
Then it pours pearls from off its tongue
Healing salve for suffering ones
Now a fairy now a demon
Making its home in a ruin
Now it's flying with Sheba's Queen
As Sultan of human and jinn
Now it rises up to God's throne
Now it descends under the ground
Now you'd think it one drop alone
Then it swells into an ocean
It travels to the mosques around
Humbly rubs its face on the ground
It goes to the monastery
Recites the Gospel like a priest
Now it turns to Gabriel there
Scatters compassion everywhere
Comes a time it loses its way
Wretched Yunus is all amazed[424]

---

423. Muhyiddîn İbnü'l-Arabî, trans. Nuri Gençosman, *Fusûs'l-Hikem* (Istanbul: İstanbul Kitabevi Yayınları 1981), p. 57.

424. Mehmet Açıkgöz, *Yunus Divanı* (Önsöz Basım ve Yayın n.d.), p. 449.

37. And a sign for them is the night; We draw from it the day, and then they are in darkness.

Wa 'āyatun lahumu'l-laylu naslakhu minhu'n-nahara fa 'idhāhum muẓlimūn.

- "Truly in the creation of the heavens and the earth and the alternation of night and day there are signs for those who understand" (3:190).

In truth, day is the secret heart of the saints
Next to their moons like to shadows is the day

Again, "By the night" is Muhammad's substance
Earthen, rusty-colored and the veil of faults[425]

- *Thus in mutual embrace the night and day*
Differing in form but joined in harmony

Day and night appear at odds and contrary
But they both spin around one reality

Like kinsfolk each one desires the other one
For to perfect the work each wants to see done

For without night, man's nature would have no gain
So what would there be to expend in the day?[426]

- **Body and spirit in the sense of night and day:**

---

425. Mevlânâ Celâleddin Rûmî, trans. Veled İzbudak, ed. Abdülbaki Gölpınarlı, *Mesnevî* (Istanbul: Milli Eğitim Basımevi 1991), vol. 2, vs. 293, 299.

426. Mevlânâ Celâleddin Rûmî, trans. Veled İzbudak, ed. Abdülbaki Gölpınarlı, *Mesnevî* (Istanbul: Milli Eğitim Basımevi 1991), vol. 3, vs. 4417-4420.

This is the night of creation, its natural body; and day is the spirit blown into it.

Moses gave me knowledge of unveiling, interpretation and the changing of day and night. When this knowledge appeared in me, night had gone and day remained the whole day. Now for me the sun neither rose nor set. This unveiling was God's informing me that in the Hereafter I would have no share of misfortune.

Night and day in the sense of sense and intellect, form and spirit, and the Unseen and witnessing:

Noah called upon his people *"by night"* (71:5) from the point of view of intellect and spirituality—these are invisible—and *"by day"* (71:5) from the point of view of form and external sense. Noah did not combine these two in his invitation. Whereas Muhammed did not call upon his people by night and by day; indeed he called upon them by night within day and by day within night.[427]

- "I have 3 pairs of eyeglasses. One shows things that are near, and I use another to see distances; with the third I see both near and far. In other words, the third has lenses that function for both. If I look in the distance with the near eyeglasses, my head starts to spin, and if I use the distance glasses to look at something close up, the same thing happens, but the third is not like that. From this one can reach the conclusion that those who want to see only the world, form, and matter cannot see the Hereafter, meaning and spirit, and those who want to see only the Hereafter cannot see the world. But people need glasses on their eyes such that to see the world, that is, to see external form, does not prevent them from seeing spiritual meaning, and to see meaning does not prevent them from seeing form."[428]

- Night gives itself to those who look. Night comprehends, it does not ensure comprehension. Invisibility and darkness perceive, they do not ensure perception.

---

427. Suad el-Hakîm, trans. Ekrem Demirli, *İbnü'l-Arabî Sözlüğü* (Istanbul: Kabalcı Yayınevi 2005), pp. 207-208.

428. Sâmiha Ayverdi, Nezihe Araz, Safiye Erol and Sofi Huri, *Ken'an Rifâî ve 20. Asrın Işığında Müslümanlık* (Istanbul: Hülbe Yayınevi 1983), p. 179.

37th Verse

Night means descent, and thus takes the following form: Either its opposite emerges with the descent of night; or the descent of night, regardless of darkness, preserves the meaning of incomprehensibility. The first interpretation:

After that there were periods (*the first century and the second century*) of interruption, events occurred, passions were aroused, blood was shed, there was disorder in the cities, the sense of defeat spread, wrongdoing increased, and the daylight of justice turned to night and changed places with wrongdoing.

The second interpretation:

A bright light hates the darkness of night; indeed that is hatred itself, and with it night remains as night. The condition for the existence of night is not darkness. The meaning of night is for the sun to have set until the time of dawn, whether or not darkness or a light other than local sunlight has spread. Thus a confusion has emerged about the nature (*inner face*) of darkness. God says, "*By the night when it is still*" (153:2). If the nature of night were darkness, God would not have characterized it as "when it is still." Certainly it can be night without any darkness.

There are two expressions Ibn al-Arabi uses frequently: The night of the human being and the last third of that night or the remaining third part or the last third part of the night: What is the nature of that night? According to Ibn al-Arabi the human constitution is entirely night. In this regard Ibn al-Arabi divided it into three: The first third part is the earthen form, that is, the body; the second is the animal spirit, that is, the soul; and the last third part is the blown spirit, that is, spirit.

The human constitution is entirely night. Divine self-disclosure arrives to bestow the greatest prize upon the last third of that constitution. The last third part consists of the spirit blown upon it; the blown spirit possesses constancy, depth and superiority upon the remaining third. The first third is the body that comes from earth; the second third is the animal spirit; and the human being came to be thanks to the third third.

In the last third of the human night God the Truth descends and distributes gifts to those of His servants who repent, pray and ask to be forgiven.[429]

---

429. Suad el-Hakîm, trans. Ekrem Demirli, *İbnü'l-Arabî Sözlüğü* (Istanbul: Kabalcı Yayınevi 2005), pp. 208-209.

- Our Messenger of God Efendi's noble hadith:

"*God the Truth descends to the worldly paradise in the last third of every night and asks, "Is there no one who asks for something?"*" indicates God the Truth's manifestation in all the particles of being. What is intended by "night" in this hadith is the darkness of the creatures' createdness. What is intended by "the worldly paradise" is manifest externality of the being of created creatures. And by "the last third," the reality of the being of created creatures.

Because every thing of being (*every being*) is divided into three parts:

One part is the Manifest. The name "Kingdom" is given to that part.

One part is the Non-Manifest. The name "Sovereignty" is given to that part.

The third part is incomparable (*münezzeh*); it cannot be divided into Kingdom and Sovereignty parts. It pertains to the Divine Realm of Domination...

Thus that part named (*last third*) with the language of indication in the noble hadith is the part pertaining to Divine Domination. The reason for saying that the Domination part is incomparable is that just as a thing's Manifest consisting of form and its Non-Manifest consisting of soul must be understood in order for it to be accepted as capable of division into parts, there must also be a reality found in being that would be cause for its eternal subsistence.

The descent of God the Truth means for His likeness pertaining to the creatures to be manifest in Himself through incomparability...

The "first third" means that it consists of the divine attribute self-disclosing to the servant. The manifestation of the reality of Essence is only at the end of that self-disclosing attribute. In other words, the manifestation of Essence is at the ends of the self-disclosing attributes. But there is no end for any thing pertaining to the attributes. The end mentioned is due to the properties of Essence. Thus the manifestation of Essence is manifest (*in the last third*) pertaining to the night of attributes.

The expression "*to the worldly paradise*" in the noble hadith means the descent of God the Truth to the attributes that are cause (*vehicle*) of knowing the created creatures through divine names.

For in relation to Essence and attributes the divine names mean the world, because just as God has sublime attributes, the creatures have servanthood toward Him. Servanthood is (the world) that comes to be from "baseness," which is the precise opposite of sublimity. As for the divine names, they are the worldly paradise that is cause of the continuance of the servanthood of creatures. God the Truth becomes manifest to His servants in the attributes they know. And this manifestation comes about when the manifestation of those attributes ends. In other words, divine worship is with the attributes prior to the perfection of the manifestation of the aforementioned attributes. They are not together with God. When the divine attributes begin to come to an end in manifestation, divine worship is not with attributes but with Essence. The noble hadith signals something else as well, in a mysterious way. The sign emerges concerning the perfect of God's friends. That is, what is intended by "night" is the divine Essence. By "the last third" is intended the perfection of knowledge appropriate in relation to the Essence. For gnosis of God the Truth occurs in two forms; the first is the gnosis appropriate to comprehension of His perfection. The other is the gnosis that is not appropriate. Thus what is intended by "the last third" is that perfection of knowledge appropriate in relation to God the Truth, because the gnosis of a friend's knowing God the Truth has three forms:

The first gnosis signals the meaning of the hadith, "*He who knows his self knows his Lord.*"

The second gnosis is the gnosis of sublimity. And that is to know the attributes of God the Truth's Essence through His Beauty. This second form emerges after the gnosis of the Lord delimited by the soul's gnosis.

The third gnosis is a divine pleasure that pervades the servant's being; the servant with that gnosis becomes the site of manifestation of witness from the Unseen concerning their Lord. In other words, works of Lordliness appear in their being. To that extent the power appears in the hand, creativity in the tongue, steps in the foot, development in the eye so nothing remains hidden, and in the ear the power to hear every word spoken in existence. Hazret Messenger indicated this meaning with the sacred hadith, "*I become the ear with which he hears and the eye with which he sees."* And to that extent God the Truth is manifest and the servant non-manifest. What is intended in the hadith by the descent of the Lord is the manifestation of the divine attributes and the works that are the necessities of Lordliness. By the worldly paradise is intended the manifest body of the Friend. What is intended by the last third is the gnosis of the divine pleasure that pervades the servant's being.[430]

- *I went to sleep and saw in a dream one night*
A naked body aloft on a high bed
My beloved was whirling upon my breast
Begging and refusing, that body of light,
Said, "I am become my beloved's mirror
The love of the lover, the Glorified's light
I collect and disperse, I am free and slave
For love's breast I am become the heart alight[431]

- The dark night of the soul is a sign for them also. We, imbued by ecstasy, steal from it the sun of day and spirit. Then they are suddenly left in darkness.[432]

- The learned who are heedless have made the world the prayer-niche of their hearts, preferred the easy side of the sheriat, taken control of worship of sultans, made padishahs their site of circumambulation, transformed winning the esteem of the people into their prayer-niche, become deluded by the tricks of their own cleverness, busied their hearts with the subtlety of their own words, let lose their denigrating tongues on the learned and masters who do research, and busied themselves cursing the great figures of religion with their too numerous statements. They would not be satisfied even if they

---

430. Abdü'l-kerîm b. İbrahim el-Cîlî, trans. Seyyid Hüseyin FevzîPaşa, *İnsan-ı Kâmil* (Istanbul: Kitsan Yayınları), pp. 409-413.

431. Ken'an Rifâî, *İlâhiyat-ı Ken'an*, ed. Yusuf Ömürlü and Dinçer Dalkılıç (Istanbul: Kubbealtı Neşriyatı 1988), p. 98.

432. Kemâlüddin Abdürrezzâk Kâşânîyyü's-Semerkandî, trans. AliRıza Doksanyedi, ed. M. Vehbi Güloğlu, *Te'vilât-ı-Kâşâniyye* (Ankara: Kadıoğlu Matbaası 1988), vol. 3, p. 13.

put the two worlds in the scales of their balance. Thus have they made rancor and envy their chosen way of life.[433]

• All the world has taken up residence in the parade grounds of heedlessness and put their trust in disastrous conjecture. They believe that their works have been rightfully accepted and their words are the mysteries of communion with God. With these words the Shaykh has brought attention to the delusions of nature and the simplemindedness of the soul. For even if people are ignorant, in their ignorance they believe (they are perfect). This is the case especially for the Sufis. Just as the learned of the Sufis are the greatest and most precious of God's creatures, the ignorant among them are the lowest of beings created by God. For the things that are true and not fantasy for the learned of the Sufis, are for the ignorant among them fantasy and not true. They stroll the parade grounds of heedlessness but think they are on the field of divine friendship. They trust in conjecture but they suppose it is certainty. The take action according to form, imagining it is reality. They speak based on caprice (*the soul's harmful and sinful desires*) and passion (*of the soul*), but suppose it is insight. For conjecture will not leave the mind of human beings until they see the Majesty and Beauty of God the Truth (*when God is witnessed conjecture disappears*). For in His manifesting of His Majesty they see every thing as Him, and thus their conjectures pass away. In discovering His Majesty they cannot see themselves and thus their conjectures cannot rise up, they are dispersed and disappear. It is God who knows best.[434]

• God created in one day this time consisting of night and day. Thus time is the sun, and night and day exist in time. God made these two father and mother of the things they bring about within themselves. And so God says, "*The night covers the day.*" This statement resembles His statement that "Eve became pregnant when Adam embraced her." Thus when night covers day, night is father and day is mother.

---

433. Hucvirî, *Keşfu'l-mahcûb Hakikat Bilgisi*, ed. Süleyman Uludağ (Istanbul: Dergâh Yayınları n.d.), p. 97.

434. Hucvirî, *Keşfu'l-mahcûb Hakikat Bilgisi*, ed. Süleyman Uludağ (Istanbul: Dergâh Yayınları n.d.), p. 251.

Every thing God brings about in the night is in the position of a child to whom a woman gives birth.

God says, *"He adds night to day, and day to night."* Thereby He explained more about the marital relationship between night and day. And with the verse, *"Night is a sign for them. We bring the day out of it,"* He explained that night is the mother of day, and that it came about as the child is born from its mother or as a snake sheds its skin. Thus day was born in another realm that includes night. *"Every day He is upon a task"* (55:29). The father is the day of which we speak. Thus this night and day are in one sense father and in another sense mother. The species God brings about with their influence in the realm of elements are called the sons of night and day.[435]

- *Happy are they who see in their early days*
Rich opportunity for their debt to pay

In those days when they posses the strength and power
When they have health, strength of heart and have vigor

Before that time when the days of old age come
Haltering your neck with fibers of the palm

When the ground is dusty, feeble, brackish soil
Healthy crop has never grown from brackish soil

Splendor of strength and lust cut off at the root
Nor to others nor to themselves any use

The eyebrows drooping down like a crupper band
The eyes full of water, grown dim, dark and dank

Face convulsing, twitching like a lizard's skin
Speech, appetite, teeth no longer what they'd been

The day late, the carcass lame and the way long
The shop in ruin, tools and craft all gone wrong

---

435. Muhyiddîn İbnü'l-Arabî, trans. Ekrem Demirli, *Fütuhât-ı Mekkiyye* (Istanbul: Litera Yayıncılık 2006), vol. 1, p. 407.

37th Verse

The roots of bad habit grown strong, firmly bound
With no power left to tear them from the ground

You who say, "tomorrow is another day,"
Be well aware that the time is on its way

That tree of evil is growing younger still
While the one to dig it up grows old and ill

It is growing younger while you're growing old
Hurry now, and do not let your chance grow cold[436]

- *Beware O traveller, beware, it is late*
The sun of life is now headed toward the pit

While you have strength, be quick in these two brief days
Do your utmost to be youthful in old age

Plant this small amount of seed you have left now
So that from these two moments long life may grow

While this lustrous lamp has not died out, take care
Trim its wick and freshen its oil quick, beware

Don't say tomorrow, tomorrows have all passed
So that all the days of sowing not be past[437]

- *What do you have now, what is the yield you've gained?*
From the ocean's bottom what pearls have you claimed?

Your senses will be void on the day of death
Do you have light of the soul for your heart's friend?

Dirt will fill these eyes of yours when in the tomb
Do you have what will illuminate the tomb?

---

436. Mevlânâ Celâleddin Rûmî, trans. Veled İzbudak, ed. Abdülbaki Gölpınarlı, *Mesnevî* (Istanbul: Milli Eğitim Basımevi 1991), vol. 2, vs. 1215-1216, 1220-1226, 1235-1236, 1239.

437. Mevlânâ Celâleddin Rûmî, trans. Veled İzbudak, ed. Abdülbaki Gölpınarlı, *Mesnevî* (Istanbul: Milli Eğitim Basımevi 1991), vol. 2, vs. 1265-1269.

*When this sense-perceiving soul no more remains
You must have immortal spirit in its place*[438]

- The lover, while a lover, is sultan. But be the source of that, be love itself, so sultanate may last forever.

  The burning of love is the requirement of the self-disclosures of love given to the lover. In other words, it does not belong to you, it belongs to the giver. Whereas what I want is for it to be yours, for you to be love. So that one day if that flame of self-disclosure leaves you, the state of love will be your state.

  The robe of love is a temporary privilege and given to you so that you will destroy qualities of the soul and animal spirit. When the time for it is complete, of course it is taken away.

  It is shameful, even a loss, not to know the value of those to whom love has been bestowed.

  What was the point of this gift? To see nothing but the beloved, and see the same thing after the robe is in time removed, that is, to know every act and action is from God.

  While you are possessed by the pleasure and madness of the state of love (*the phase of excitement on the spiritual path*) you think neither of money nor position nor even children. There is nothing left of arrogance or resentment or lies or tricks. That is how you must be also when the robe is taken away. Why is it that you then change, that you are not able to preserve that same state when you are left face to face with the human condition? When what is desired is that the gnosis bestowed by love should be seen in you.[439]

- The truths of the potential kind are like things hidden in the darkness of night. Just as the light of the sun is what makes them visible, what makes the nature and truths in the darkness of not-being manifest is the light of [divine] self-disclosure.

  Despite this visibility and manifestation, things and truths are still covered and secret.

  To indicate this meaning, the Gracious Quran says, *"The day we bring out of night is a sign for them..."*

---

438. Mevlânâ Celâleddin Rûmî, trans. Veled İzbudak, ed. Abdülbaki Gölpınarlı, *Mesnevî* (Istanbul: Milli Eğitim Basımevi 1991), vol. 2, vs. 939-941, 943.

439. Ken'an Rifâî, *Sohbetler* (Istanbul: Kubbealtı Neşriyatı 2000), p. 155-156.

37th Verse

Thus day is still night. When night is stripped from it the real night comes into view without covering. Just as the flesh of sheep comes into view when its skin is stripped off. In this way the light of day returns to its source, which is a part of day.

Thus although the light of day liberates things from darkness, in truth they are still hidden. In the same way what brings out the thing you imagine in your mind is your tongue, or your pen. Still, that imagined thing is hidden in your mind. Comprehend the divine self-disclosure thus.

Never give existence to yourself. For your manifestation is by the light of God the Truth, and you are the prior not-being, that is, you do not exist.

Never turn toward your own desire. And annihilate the mortal in the immortal. If not, you will be forced to turn. And then it will be difficult for you.

In sum, a person must be illuminated with that light so that they are never darkness again. And they call that light "Light upon light, the light of lights." For other lights are its shadow. And such things as rising and setting cannot be imagined of God's essence.[440]

- Just as the colors and forms of beings cannot be seen in dark of night, the spiritual beings in the heart are condemned to remain colorless and hidden as long as the light of God the Truth does not self-disclose.

The light of a person's eye is in reality the light of his heart. Because in reality the light of the eye comes into being out of the light of the heart.

God the Exalted has brought into being pains and sorrows so that the heart should taste that suffering and see the light of pleasure and joy.

Without illness a person cannot know the value of health; without hunger, of satiation; without trouble, of ease; without evil, or good; without ugliness, of beauty; and finally, without not-being, of being.

The limitlessness of God's concealment lies in the perfection of the attributes which self-disclose Him to us. For in contrast to His in-

---

440. İsmail Hakkı Bursevî, trans. Abdülkâdir Akçiçek, *Kenz-i Mahfi-Gizli Hazine* (Istanbul: Bahar Yayınları 2000), pp. 180-181.

finite concealment, every color and every light and every form in this realm of the created is, for the eye that sees and the heart that loves, nothing but the self-disclosure of divine being in a limitless mirror.

And so we know light by darkness, the opposite of brightness. In other words, everything becomes known by its own opposite. But it is in this world of the created that things are known by their opposites. That is why no opposite can be conceived of for God the Truth's being. Because there is in created existence no opposite to God the Truth's light. That is why it is not possible to know God, who has no partner and no likeness, by means of His opposites.[441]

- Among people there are some for whom God increases their knowledge, faith and certainty and annihilates the sign of the night of ignorance, and they pass their lives upon light. And there are some for whom God, toward the end of their lives, annihilates the illuminating sign, special to night, of the night that comes of the darkening of their hearts by the darkness of sins, and they pass their lives thus in darkness. From that we take refuge in God. And there are some whose hearts are darkened by the darkness of rebellion and just when God is about to completely seal their hearts, by repentance from sin the light of faith, works and sincerity dawns; that light and certainty increases as much as God wishes, and they are liberated from darkness.[442]

- For the people of heedlessness the greatest and most humiliating sin is to not know their own flaws. Those who do not know their own shame and fault while in the world remain ignorant of them in the Hereafter; those who are ignorant here are ignorant there as well. For God the Exalted has said, *"Those who are blind in this world are blind in the Hereafter"* (17:72).

- In truth, if God the Exalted does not purify peoples' hearts from willing lust, He will not protect the eyes in their heads from aspects

---

441. Ken'an Rifâî, *Şerhli Mesnev'i-i Şerif* (Istanbul: Kubbealtı Neşriyatı 2000), pp. 156-157.

442. Niyâzî Mısrî, trans. Süleyman Ateş, *İrfan Sofraları* (Istanbul: Yeni Ufuklar Neşriyatı n.d.), pp. 24-25.

37th Verse

difficult to understand. If He does make His will abide in their hearts, He will not protect their vision from what is other than God.[443]

- Because it makes gold grow, you worship the sun
Turn your face to the one who creates the sun

You worship the sun up in the whirling sky
Contemning the splendid spirit of high price

The sun is our cook by the command of God
It is foolishness to say that it is God

What will you do if the sun should be eclipsed?
How will you remove the blackness covering it?

Won't you place on God's doorstep your aching brow
Begging, "Take the black, give back the sun's rays now!"

If they kill you in the night what good will come
When you wail and beg for mercy from the sun?

Most calamities occur when it is night
At the time when your idol is out of sight

If you bow humbly at the threshold of God
You'll be freed of stars, an intimate of God

I'll open my lips to share secrets with you
So that you will see a sun at midnight too

The East where it rises is the pure spirit
Whether day or night, there's no difference in it

What they call the day is that on which it shines
Night can be night no longer once that sun shines

As a dust mote is visible in the sun
So is this sun in the pure mind of that sun

---

443. Hucvirî, *Keşfu'l-mahcûb Hakikat Bilgisi*, ed. Süleyman Uludağ (Istanbul: Dergâh Yayınları n.d.), pp. 259-260.

O Humankind

You will see a sun that shines with brilliant light
So the eye is blinded, awed before its light

As a mote of dust in the light of God's throne
The limitless, abounding light of God's throne

You will see it as base, impermanent, poor
With the eye empowered by the Creator

The alchemist whose one glorious chemistry
Fell upon vapor and a star came to be

Rare elixir from which half a lustrous ray
Struck the dark and it became the sun of day

The wondrous alchemist who by one action
Bound these manifold properties to Saturn

Other planets and spiritual substances
Know them, seeker, by analogy with this[444]

- *Be my fool and let me violate your trust*
Renounce the sun and become a mote of dust

Leave home and let your residence be my door
Be a moth and claim to be a lamp no more

So that you may taste the savor of life's food
And see the sultanate hid in servitude

You'll see horseshoes nailed upside-down in this world
You'll see the title of shahs on slaves conferred

Many with ropes on their necks the scaffolds crown
While the crowd cries out, "To him belongs the crown!"[445]

- *Plot to become a slave lowly as can be*
Go in lowliness and you will be lordly

---

444. Mevlânâ Celâleddin Rûmî, trans. Veled İzbudak, ed. Abdülbaki Gölpınarlı, *Mesnevî* (Istanbul: Milli Eğitim Basımevi 1991), vol. 4, vs. 576-594.

445. Mevlânâ Celâleddin Rûmî, trans. Veled İzbudak, ed. Abdülbaki Gölpınarlı, *Mesnevî* (Istanbul: Milli Eğitim Basımevi 1991), vol. 5, vs. 412-416.

37th Verse

Be like a moth and rush straight into the fire
Do not stich up a purse with that, play fair

Renounce force, O dervish, and take up wailing
Mercy goes in the direction of wailing[446]

- *To the double-colored peacock we come now*
That displays itself for the sake of renown

It hunts people's admiration, without sense
Of good or evil or gain or consequence

This has been your work ever since you were born
With the trap of love to hunt the people down

All this hunt and striving, being and has been
Let it go—in this have you found anything?

Most of life is gone and now the day is late
While you are still busy trying to catch your prey

The night falls and in your trap there is no prey
The trap is naught but a shackle and headache

So you have caught none but yourself in this trap
You're deprived of what you seek, jailed in a trap

Is there anyone with a trap in this day
Such a fool as we who become our own prey?

There is one thing worth the hunt, and that is love
But how should anyone's trap hold it captive?

You, however, may come and renounce your trap
You can be its prey and be inside its trap[447]

---

446. Mevlânâ Celâleddin Rûmî, trans. Veled İzbudak, ed. Abdülbaki Gölpınarlı, *Mesnevî* (Istanbul: Milli Eğitim Basımevi 1991), vol. 5, vs. 471, 473-474.

447. Mevlânâ Celâleddin Rûmî, trans. Veled İzbudak, ed. Abdülbaki Gölpınarlı, *Mesnevî* (Istanbul: Milli Eğitim Basımevi 1991), vol. 5, vs. 395-396, 400-402, 405-407, 409-410.

38. And the sun runs in the place appointed for her; that is the measuring out of the Exalted, the All-Knowing.

Wa'sh-shamsu tajrī limustaqarrin lahā dhālika taqdīru'l-ʿazīzi'l-ʿalīm.

- *"And that is not difficult for God"* (35:17).

The Sun is moving at a speed greater than 700,000 kilometers per hour toward the Vega Star along a trajectory named the Solar Apex. One should not forget that while the World turns both on its own axis and around the Sun, it is also moving along with the Solar system.

The sun rises every morning and sets every evening. But each rising and setting occurs at a different point in the Universe. The World is traveling around a sun that moves without ever passing again through the same point in the Universe.[448]

- **The Fourth Heaven** is a substance most worthy of praise; it is the color of flowers, the heaven of the luminous sun. It is the axis of the heavens. God the Exalted created that heaven from light bound to the heart. There He created the sun in the mansion of the heart for the existent. The faith of the existent comes of that sun. The beauty of the existent comes from it. The stars derive their lights from it. Their lights rise with it in levels. God the Exalted made that star regarded as the sun the site of manifestation of exaltedness in that heaven likened to the heart. He made it the site of manifestation of various qualities that are pure, incomparable, and holy. The sun is a source for the other creatures bound to the elements, in the same way that God, His name of majesty, is a source for the other exalted stations. Because Enoch (a.s.) knew the heart reality, he was placed in this station of soul. And he was distinguished from others by the station of lordliness.

---

448. Kur'an Araştırmaları Grubu, *Kur'an Hiç Tükenmeyen Mucize* (Istanbul: İstanbul Yayınevi 2002), p. 84.

O Humankind

God the Exalted the Truth the Exalted made that heaven the mine of secrets and the place where lights triumph. The glorious angel named Israfil is the ruler of the angels in that heaven, for he is the spirituality of the sun possessed of superiority. The ascendance in being of a lowly thing, the events of constriction and expansion, occur only by the disposal of that angel whom God the Exalted made the source of that heaven. And in his aspect of grandeur he is the most exalted. In his aspect of breadth he is the largest. In his aspect of aspiration he is the most powerful. From the Farthest Lote Tree to the trigonometrical point of earth, all has been given to him; in other words, he disposes of all. His power of disposal is such that he disposes of all from the lowest to the highest. His pulpit is by the Throne. He is even the source of this heaven bound to the sun. His realm is the heavens, the earth. Whatever is known in them by way of intellect or sense, he is all. God the Exalted made the circumference of the heaven related to the sun a journey of 17,029 years and sixty days. That distance is covered in twenty-four equal hours. As for the greatest heaven, it takes 365 1/4 days, three minutes. That is the station where Enoch (a.s.) is. That place is a station of the stations of Muhammed (s.a.s.). Do you not see that when he reached the fourth heaven on the night of the Miraj, he also left that behind; he rose higher. That our Messenger (s.a.s.) Efendi reached this station related to Enoch, with his rank of servanthood, is witness to his having reached reality in that sublime station. Most of the messengers who are the people of self-possession (*temkin*) are included in the circle of this worldly heaven. For example, Jesus, Solomon, David, Enoch, George and many more prophets of great aspiration all alighted at that stopping-place of manifestation; they are the residents of that sublime station.[449]

- The sun of the spirit shines with a constancy special to itself, so that the final abode (*mustaqarr*) of the spirit's journey is the station of God the Truth. This state of affairs is measured out by (the All-Knowing) who forbids everything from reaching Hazret Oneness, vanquishes everything by subjugation and annihilation, the Essence

---

449. Abdü'l-kerîm b. İbrahim el-Cîlî, trans. Seyyid Hüseyin FevzîPaşa, *İnsan-ı Kâmil* (Istanbul: Kitsan Yayınları), vol. 2, p. 332.

38th Verse

who knows the perfection of the limit of the observer of everything and the end of the journey.[450]

- **All-Knowing (Alîm)** means one who knows all that is known. It self-discloses in the forms alîm, âlim, allâm. As for the learned (ulemâ), they are of three kinds. The knowledge of the first, alîm, is essential. The knowledge of the second, âlim, is granted [by God]. The knowledge of the third is acquired.

  Only God is âlim by essential knowledge. Granted knowledge is the knowledge taught by God the Truth (*as in the knowledge of Hizir, a.s.*). Human beings gain acquired knowledge with difficulty through work and effort.

  If God the Truth self-discloses in existents, He teaches them knowledge they do not have. That is why one of the people of God is superior to another. He self-discloses to some people of God in the aspect of essential knowledge. To some, He self-discloses through awareness of the reality of the divine names. He self-discloses in the quality of spirituality of some with awareness of thousands of sciences.

  The Learned (el-Âlim) are those God the Truth has caused to witness His sublimity and Essence; states do not manifest in that them, rather their state is knowledge.[451]

- **Illumination (tenvir):** Human beings are distinguished among other creatures by knowledge. If the knowledge is related to spiritual heights it is sublime, and if related to ordinary worldly things it is lowly. The knowledge of the people of God is through unveiling (keşfî). If self-disclosures manifest in a person with various lights according to place and time and intention, that person becomes aware of knowledge.

  The knowledge belonging to the Realm of Witnessing manifests with the light of external vision. The knowledge belonging to the Realm of Sovereignty manifests with inner vision. External vision never knows the knowledge proper to inner vision.

---

450. Kemâlüddin Abdürrezzâk Kâşânîyyü's-Semerkandî, trans. AliRıza Doksanyedi, ed. M. Vehbi Güloğlu, *Te'vilât-ı-Kâşâniyye* (Ankara: Kadıoğlu Matbaası 1988), vol. 3, p. 13.

451. Abdürrezzâk Kâşânî, trans. Dr. Ekrem Demirli, *Tasavvuf Sözlüğü* (Istanbul: İz Yayıncılık 2004), p. 363.

The knowledge belonging to the Realm of Domination manifests with a light special to itself. While the knowledge learned in medrese colleges manifests through study, grammar, transmission and reading, the knowledge of the people of gnosis manifests by the light of witnessing. This knowledge is a kind of granted knowledge, which is also called "divine knowledge" (*ilm-i ledün*). Because this knowledge is acquired with presence, it is also called "presence knowledge."

Because medrese knowledge is acquired through study, reading and transmission, it is also called "specialized knowledge."

The knowledge of the people of God (the friends) is the knowledge of presence. God the Truth teaches a friend what he does not know to such an extent that this knowledge is the greatest of miracles. Being the knowledge of truth, every boon earned in this way is superior among others. Thus it was ended with Muhyiddin Arabî, because of his knowledge.[452]

- **Exalted (*Aziz*):** The one who spares what he has protected. When God gives the name "Exalted" to one of His servants, the person named "Truth" and "Exalter" (*Muizz*), in other words, He who exalts, is also recalled by the name "Exalted." Thus He spares the person He protects from the revenge and torment intended by the names Avenger and Tormentor.[453]

- **The Final Abode (*müsteqarr*)** was measured out and settled and is constant for the sun, thus a fixed decision occurring according to an orderly law, not random, aimless, mere coincidence.

It is for the sake of constancy, in other words coming about with the wisdom and aim of a decision and measure in its own realm, or in order to arrive and remain at rest in the end.

Because it is a noun of time, it is for a time of stability special to itself, in other words the time it will stop until a specific time.

Because it is a noun of place, it is special to a place of stability proper to itself, in other words fixed in its place. It revolves on its own axis, or occurs for the sake of the realm that is its own quarter. In this

---

452. M. Kemâl Pilavoğlu, *Büyük Velî Muhyiddîn Arabî Hazretleri*, p. 176.
453. Muhyiddîn İbnü'l-Arabî, trans. Nuri Gençosman, *Fusûs'l-Hikem* (Istanbul: İstanbul Kitabevi Yayınları 1981), p. 134.

sense it has an incentive to serve its homeland. It is moving toward a point of rest for itself.[454]

- *Does a painter paint for the sake of painting*
Without hope of benefit from that painting?

Does a potter make a pitcher double quick
For the pitcher's sake and not water to drink?

Does a calligrapher write beautifully
Just to write, and not to make something to read?

The manifest form is for sake of one unseen
That takes shape for yet another one unseen[455]

- Although the word *mustaqarr* is a noun of place meaning final stopping place, movement around an axis is also intended. In this way the Glorious Quran was the first to put forth the basis of the sun's movement.[456]

- God created the Throne and made it a place of orientation for the hearts of servants and made it a location toward which hands stretch forth, but it is neither a location of the Essence nor a similitude of its quality. A judgment may perhaps be made on the basis of the Quranic verse, *"The Merciful is seated upon the Throne"* [20:5], but one must be careful. Merciful God the Exalted is a name. "Seated" is His adjective and attribute. But His adjective and attribute stand with His Essence. As for the Throne, it is one of His created things. It is not adjacent to Him. It does not even touch Him. It cannot be added to Him, and He has no need of such a thing.

The heart is also in the high rank of the Throne. His throne is in the heavens; its place is clear. But the other has made a dwelling. The throne of hearts is far more virtuous than thrones in the heavens be-

---

454. Elmalı M. Hamdi Yazır, *Hak Dini Kur'an Dili* (Istanbul: Feza Gazetecilik 1991, vol. 6, p. 416.

455. Mevlânâ Celâleddin Rûmî, trans. Veled İzbudak, ed. Abdülbaki Gölpınarlı, *Mesnevî* (Istanbul: Milli Eğitim Basımevi 1991), vol. 4, vs. 2881, 2884, 2887.

456. M. Kemâl Pilavoğlu, *Büyük Velî Muhyiddîn Arabî Hazretleri*, p. 61.

cause the throne in the heavens cannot take everything into it. And it is not the bearer of anything either; it does not possess comprehension. But the throne that is the heart is something that God the Truth is always watching. He self-discloses there. He brings his benevolence down upon it from the heavens. This sacred hadith expresses this meaning well: *My heavens and My earth embrace Me not, but the heart of my believing servant embraces Me.*[457]

• Just as the light of the moon is invisible once the sun has risen, or no longer has sufficient brightness to illuminate, if the light of truth rises and the heart is illuminated by love of God, the moon called intellect becomes invisible. The eye can no longer see the things it has tried to comprehend by means of intellect up to that point. Even if it does see them, these things now make a person lethargic, like bedtime stories heard before sleep, and they fade away and are erased as his heavy eyelids close.

A stranger is in reality someone who has broken off from God's being and fallen far away. Like strangers separated from their homelands who wander miserably in foreign lands, spirits have fallen far from the one true homeland, the land of God, and they sense their alienation, whether slightly or keenly.

The sun is such a stranger too. It wanders in the unlimited vastness of space. The only sun that subsists without setting is the sun of spirit. The sun of spirit is the attributes of God the Truth; it is His self-disclosure; it is "the arrived human" in whom God the Truth has disclosed Himself.

However unique the sun may be in appearance, painters have succeeded in making pictures of it. But the sun of spirit cannot be pictured. Although it was born in the created universe, it is not possible to see it or draw it, perhaps because its light is so dazzling. The sun of spirit is God, His self-disclosure, it is the mystery or reality called "the reality of Muhammed."[458]

---

457. Muhyiddîn İbnül-Arabî, trans. Abdülkâdir Akçiçek, *Şeceretü'l-Kevn-Üstün İnsan* (Istanbul: Bahar Yayınları 2000), pp. 66-67.

458. Ken'an Rifâî, *Şerhli Mesnevî-i Şerif* (Istanbul: Kubbealtı Neşriyatı 2000), pp. 28-29.

38TH VERSE

- The Muhammeden Reality is a sun of spiritual meaning existing from eternity without beginning to eternity without end that, dawning in the east of Messenger Adam's body, finally found perfection in our Messenger of God Efendi's subtle body and came to the station that embraces all. Then it dawned in the body of every friend of God, and each friend of God became Hazret Messenger's inheritor in their own age. If gnostics in their own age see the perfect human being who is precisely of the inheritor rank, they immediately know that this sun and this spiritual meaning and this special quality is that same spiritual meaning, that same quality, but self-disclosing in another covering and appearing in another body.

The perfect human being who is the inheritor of the Messenger appears to the world with the Reality of Muhammed as a ray of light that reflects the light of that sun of spirit and spreads its light by degrees until it sets.

Is not the system of the sun and the planets around it the symbol of the realm of spirit? When the spirit heaven of a person whose heart is truly alive is illuminated, there is seen what many a world observes with awe. For it is easily seen that the arrived person who is the site of manifestation of God's names and attributes and Essence is possessed of what God possesses.[459]

- The exterior likeness of the sublime realm is the realm of the heavens. God has put there a sun that brings the people of earth illumination.

As He put the sun in the heavens, he put in this body the spirit that this body may with it find its way. If it is lost in the end with death, the body is buried in utter darkness.[460]

This messenger says, "Give me something, I am in need; either give me your own robe or clothes or your property." What should he do with those clothes, with that robe? He wants your clothes so that the heat of the sun may reach you. Just as when it is commanded in the Quran, *"Give a loan to God in contentment of heart,"* He wants to lighten your load. It is not merely property and robe that He wants,

---

459. Meşkûre Sargut, *Gönülden Gönüle* (Istanbul: Kubbealtı Neşriyat 1994), p. 164.
460. Muhyiddîn İbnül-Arabî, trans. Abdülkâdir Akçiçek, *Şecretü'l-Kevn-Üstün İnsan* (Istanbul: Bahar Yayınları 2000), p. 66.

for He has given you many other things besides these, for example knowledge, thought and views.

He means to say: Expend your views, your intellect and thought for Me! Have not you acquired this property, this wealth, by means of the instruments I have given you? Thus He wants charity both from the bird and the snare.

You may strip under the sun, and that is better, for that sun does not darken a person, it even whitens him or her; at least lighten your clothes that you may feel the pleasure of that. For a while you have got used to the sour, so now give the sweet a try.[461]

- "We did not create the heavens and earth and what is between them in vain" (38:27).

---

461. Mevlânâ Celâleddin Rûmî, trans. Meliha Ülker Anbarcıoğlu, *Fîhi mâ Fîh* (Istanbul: Milli Eğitim Basımevi 1985), p. 334.

39. And for the moon We have measured out mansions until he returns like the curved date-stalk.

Wa'l-qamara qaddarnāhu manāzila ḥattā 'āda ka'l-'urjūni'l-qadīm.

• And We determined for the local journey in the journey of the moon of the heart mansions, such as fear, hope, patience, gratitude, trust in God and the other stations, so that at the time of its annihilation in the station of the secret heart and spirit it returned like an old date-stalk, withered and curved like a bow. Before the complete annihilation in spirit of the moon of the heart, because of the covering of the soul and its faculties due to the illumination of its face turned toward spirit and the intimacy and illumination of being inside the secret heart, it became old like a withered date-stalk. The moon of the heart becomes full only facing the station of the secret heart, the position of the breast.[462]

• The moon does not flow along in a steady manner like the sun. We have appointed for it several mansions and a measure according to each mansion.

It travels, every day it comes to a mansion and appears in a shape according to each mansion. According to the Arabs its mansions are:

Al Sharatain, Al Butain, Al Thurayya, Al Dabaran, Al Hak'ah, Al Han'ah, Al Dhira, Al Nathra, Al Tarf, Al Jabhah, Al Zubrah, Al Sarfah, Al Awwa, Al Simak, Al Ghafr, Al Jubana, Iklil al Jabhah, Al Kalb, Al Shaula, Al Na'am, Al Baldah, Al Sa'd al Dhabih, Al Sa'd al Bula, Al Saad al Su'ud, Al Saad al Ahbiyah, Al Fargh al Muqdim, Al Muakhar, Alrescha...

---

[462]. Kemâlüddin Abdürrezzâk Kâşânîyyü's-Semerkandî, trans. AliRıza Doksanyedi, ed. M. Vehbi Güloğlu, *Te'vilât-ı-Kâşâniyye* (Ankara: Kadıoğlu Matbaası 1988), vol. 3, p. 13.

It stops every night at one of these mansions and its light increases and then decreases little by little according to how far it has come, and at the last mansion—which is before conjunction—it becomes very thin, a crescent. Finally it turns until it becomes like an old date-stalk.

Date-stalk: The bottom husk of the date vine in particular, which is old, in other words, the previous year's husk, in thinner, more curved, and more colorful. This simile is of very surprising beauty. It does not, as has been supposed, merely show the first and last form of the crescent, but also one line of the orbit around the earth that the moon completes in one month as it moves through the mansions.[463]

- The Moon moves in an orbit that curves around and embraces the Earth. While the Earth completes its journey around the sun, the Moon also follows a spiraling path around the Earth, at times in front of it and at times behind it. Thus the Moon has an orbit that travels turning in a curling motion along the Earth's orbit, like a branch that curls and twists.

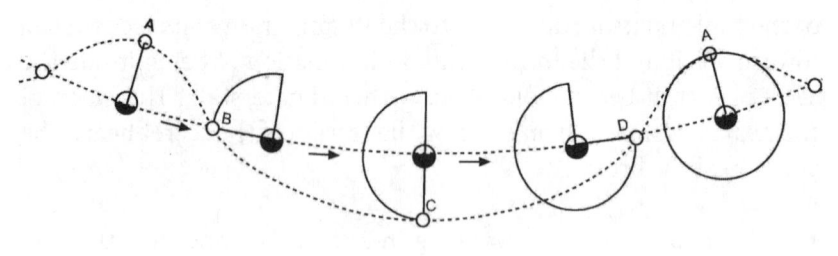

Figure 2 (p. 255)

With its regulated distance and rather large mass for a satellite, the Moon fixes the axis of our Earth. This ensures our planet's climactic conditions, appropriate for life, for millions of years. Some scientists say that the liquid state of the core of our Earth is preserved by the Moon's gravitational force. It preserves the magnetic field of our planet. By attracting the oceans to itself, the Moon slowed the Earth's rotational speed and gave it the form it has today.

With the term "measuring out" God brought attention to the mathematics He used in the Universe. In Arabic the term *qadar* ex-

---

463. Elmalı M. Hamdi Yazır, *Hak Dini Kur'an Dili* (Istanbul: Feza Gazetecilik 1992), vol. 8, p. 417.

presses measure and the giving of measure, in other words mathematical distribution. Everything, down to the distance between the Earth and the Moon, its mass, its rotational speed, its mutual gravitational pull with the Earth, and its position and gravitational force relative to the Sun has been calculated mathematically in a precise manner.[464]

• The mansions God named, saying, "We appointed mansions for the moon," are twenty-eight mansions. In other words, the moon stops in a mansion every night in its journey until it reaches the last, and then begins a new rotation. *"For you to learn,"* that is, for you to learn the number and calculation of years from the movement of the moon and the sun in the mansions. God has detailed every thing for us. Then He placed those angels in those mansions. They are the heralds of the governors (the angels governing the twelve zodiacal signs) of the faraway heavens.[465]

• God the Exalted made the moon the site of manifestation for His name "Alive." Then He put its heaven into operation in the heaven of the zodiacal signs, for the life of being is there. In the same way it is the orbit of things imagined and things witnessed.

Then He made the star bound to the moon responsible for directing the earth. Just as he made the spirit director of the body... If sublime God the Truth the Exalted had not created the heaven of earth from the reality of spirit, wisdom would not have made necessary the existence of any living thing on earth... It would have been the location of inanimate things. And when that work was done, God placed Adam in this firmament of earth. For Adam is the spirit of the realm bound to earth; God the Truth's gaze upon the world is through Adam, and His mercy upon the world... And then He gave to those beings He created a life bound to the life of Adam... The world continues as long as the human species lives there. When it is transferred and leaves, the world will also be destroyed... Every thing will

---

464. Kur'an Araştırmaları Grubu, *Kur'an Hiç Tükenmeyen Mucize* (Istanbul: İstanbul Yayınevi 2002), pp. 88-91.
465. Muhyiddîn İbnü'l-Arabî, trans. Ekrem Demirli, *Fütuhât-ı Mekkiyye* (Istanbul: Litera Yayıncılık 2006), vol. 2, p. 394.

be jumbled together... Just as when Spirit leaves, the body will be destroyed and everything will be jumbled together...[466]

- I know where I will place the burden I carry. It was the greatest of prophets who loaded me with that burden. My burden is the light of guidance and the human trust of divine vicegerency. I can deposit these two great values only with a friend of God who like me is able to be a perfect mirror to divine light. In sum, I am like the moon in the sky and my guide is the sun.[467]

- God's friends take their light from God. Divine mysteries fill their hearts as light which dazzles the eye and heart. And like the moon in the sky, they remain silent, preferring to relate with the language of state the wisdom they have attained. But if the moon also spoke and showed the way to those lost, as it does with its light, what great bounty that would be for those who have lost their way. This means that if the friends would speak, if they would make people aware of mysteries and truths, surely there would be fewer lost in the world.

In chapter thirty-three of the Gracious Quran groups that opposed Hazret Muhammed are mentioned, the disbelievers and Hypocrites: *"O Prophet! Fear God and do not hearken to the disbelievers and Hypocrites! Follow that which comes to you by inspiration from your Lord! O Prophet! Verily We have sent you as a witness, a bearer of good tidings and a warner, and as one who invites to God's grace by His leave, and as a lamp spreading light."*

O God's gate of mercy! Remain open! By means of the path of shariat, you show the people of knowledge the way. In the path of tarikat you are guide to the people of gnosis. Your light is a window opening onto God's realm of oneness. If you will not be the means, if you wil not help, if you conceal your light, neither gate nor view nor window can be opened from the spiritual realm onto our spirits.[468]

---

466. Abdü'l-kerîm b. İbrahim el-Cîlî, trans. Seyyid Hüseyin FevzîPaşa, *İnsan-ı Kâmil* (Istanbul: Kitsan Yayınları), vol. 2, pp. 317-318.

467. Ken'an Rifâî, *Şerhli Mesnevî-i Şerif* (Istanbul: Kubbealtı Neşriyatı 2000), pp. 564-565.

468. Ken'an Rifâî, *Şerhli Mesnevî-i Şerif* (Istanbul: Kubbealtı Neşriyatı 2000), pp. 555-566.

39th Verse

- The divine spirit moon does not shine from anywhere but the night of the body, and no one can become familiar with it anywhere but in this realm of body. If you want to know it, you can find that opportunity in the seclusion of the night of the body. It is said that the Water of Life is such that whoever drinks it does not die. That there is eternal life for a person when the Water of Life is found means that eternal life is death. It is natural that those who die from self attain eternal life. That the body is composed of earth means that it is grossness and darkness. But spirit is light. It is by God's command, from His spirit. If you want to have a connection with that spirit, you will find it in this darkness of body. And the seclusion of this bodily darkness is the heart. That is why the heart is the place of seclusion of God the Truth.[469]

- When Shaykh Hazret Awhaddeddin said, "I see the moon in the basin," Shams of Tabriz said, "If you do not have a boil on your neck, you would lift your head and see it in the sky."

    The purpose in Shaykh Awhaddedin saying, "I see the moon in the basin," is that it means "I see God the Truth in beautiful people." And the purpose in Hazret Shams saying he would see the moon in the sky is that it means he would see it not only is formal beauties but everywhere. Beauty is loved because the light of God the Truth has manifested there. But just as you observe that self-disclosure in a beautiful person, you must see the same self-disclosure in, for example, the eye of a camel.[470]

- God gives the straight and the crooked according to your preparedness and demand.

    The mental imaginings, pictures in the mind, intellectual lights and spiritual gleams that appear in the hearts of human beings are all the lights of the moon of reality in that treasury of unity or dawning and self-disclosed in the interiors of the people of God, reflected according to the preparedness of every person.[471]

---

469. Ken'an Rifâî, *Sohbetler* (Istanbul: Kubbealtı Neşriyatı 2000), pp. 651-652.
470. Ken'an Rifâî, *Sohbetler* (Istanbul: Kubbealtı Neşriyatı 2000), p. 242.
471. Ken'an Rifâî, *Sohbetler* (Istanbul: Kubbealtı Neşriyatı 2000), pp. 285-286.

- Know that the moon has a face toward the Sun. That face is always complete. It does not increase or decrease. And it has a face turned toward the people that, due to its rotation, it shows to human beings in part. But the fact that this face appears in part does not harm the completeness of its face that follows the Sun. Thus let the face of your heart, which is the site of viewing God the Truth, and that is turned toward God the Truth, be complete through being nurtured by faith, certainty and good supposition about Him. The partialness of its external face, which is turned toward the people, does not harm the completeness of its hidden face. Appropriate here is the story of how when Umar and Ali (*may God be pleased with both of them*) found Uways al-Karani in Yemen and surrendered to him the cloak bequeathed by the Most Generous Messenger (*s.a.s.*), they said to him:

"Give us counsel," they said. He said, "Do you know your Lord?" "Yes."

"In that case, having known Him, there will be no harm to you in not knowing any other than He." "Say more."

"Did your Lord teach you?" "Yes." "In that case, if no other teaches you, there will be no harm to you."

Look at the moon and take warning from it, directing your soul to nurture good suppositions about the people. In other words, whenever you see a fault or lack in the exterior of people, say to yourself, "Perhaps their behavior with God is perfect, and the fault is relative to me."

It is related that one day in Baghdad, Hasan Basri (*may God be pleased with him*) encountered a black man at the side of the Tigris River. The man was drinking wine with a woman next to him. It came to his mind, "If that black man did not drink, he would be more virtuous than I." It was Hasan Basri's custom to see himself as lower than every thing. Then he looked and saw two men drowning in the Tigris. Immediately that black man walked across the water and saved the men. He turned to Hasan Basri and said, "O Hasan, you are more virtuous than I in the sight of God; walk over the water like me and save someone who is drowning," and he added, "The woman with me is my mother. What we are drinking is the water of Zamzam. We sat here in order to find out if your eye of inner vision is open or not." Hasan fell at his feet and said, "You saved them from drowning, and me from nurturing ill supposition about a believer. The man prayed for Hasan, saying, "O my Lord, rescue Hasan from the state he is in. For in your eyes Hasan is a hundred degrees more virtuous than I."

Most people want their faces the people see to be full moons, but do not care about the faces of their hearts. That is why in some there are moons like disbelievers, invisible at the end of the month, in some contraries like degenerates, and in some full moons like believers.[472]

- The eyes of those who comprehend the secrets of the Unseen realm see the beauty in unity. But not every servant is favored with this felicity.

O Ali, think of three people, one of whom sees the moon in the sky shine as brightly as it does. For the second, even the world seems dark. There is infirmity and calamity in his eye, and that is why he is deprived of the gift of sight. As for the third, his gaze is so sharp that he has the power to see three moons at the same time.

The eyes of all three men appear to be open. Their ears hear. O Ali, you know their secrets while I do not. However much each of these three kinds of people believes they are on the path of God, what is their relationship of nearness to you? How will they return to God? O Ali! God gave you the secret of knowledge of divinity, He has shown you the external and internal states of every kind of servant. For you there is nothing hidden or mysterious about them. So, O Ali, you know these three types as well. What path are they on, what way-station have they reached?

The soldier bowing to the feet of Hazret Ali's spirituality saw those levels on the path of God but did not know the secrets of them. In reality, those of the three groups who saw the world as dark were at the station of dispersion and difference. Their comprehension knew only their own selves. Those who saw one moon shining in the sky were at the station of coincidence (*cem*). There is nothing but God in their consciousness.

Those who saw three moons in the sky were at the station called coincidence of coincidence (*cemü'l-cem*). They have achieved the se-

---

472. Niyâzî Mısrî, trans. Süleyman Ateş, *İrfan Sofraları* (Istanbul: Yeni Ufuklar Neşriyatı n.d.), pp. 69-71.

cret of seeing God in three states at once. The three states of God are the states of essence, creator (*halik*) and creature (*mahluk*).[473]

• The intellect in the body is like the moon in the sky. Sometimes it increases, and sometimes it decreases. At first it is small and its name is crescent. It is like the intellect of a child in the time of childhood. Later it increases, as on nights when the moon becomes complete and takes on the state of the full moon.[474]

• Among the messengers there is no difference with regard to light. If we look at the moon, the new moon is like Adam, and when it rises a bit higher, Noah, then Abraham, Jesus, and finally the full moon is like the manifestation of Muhammed. From the point of view of their light, in other words with regard to their being moons, their source is one. There is no difference between them. But is the spare, wan light spread by the newly risen moon the same as the shining of the full moon?[475]

• *That new moon and full moon are in unity*
Far from lack, corruption and duality

That new moon is free of all fault inwardly
What appears to be lack fills in by degrees[476]

• There are different kinds of angels. Some are slim as a crescent moon, some appear like a three-day's moon, and some are at the final line of light like a full moon. These angels, some more mature, brighter than others, bear witness to the divine light. Just as people on earth have different levels of intellect, thought, understanding, beauty and maturity, the angels on earth and the friends and prophets on earth are ranked in levels also.[477]

---

473. Ken'an Rifâî, *Şerhli Mesnevî-i Şerif* (Istanbul: Kubbealtı Neşriyatı 2000), p. 554.
474. Muhyiddîn İbnül-Arabî, trans. Abdülkâdir Akçiçek, *Şeceretü'l-Kevn-Üstün İnsan* (Istanbul: Bahar Yayınları 2000), p. 67.
475. Ken'an Rifâî, *Sohbetler* (Istanbul: Kubbealtı Neşriyatı 2000), pp. 10-11.
476. Mevlânâ Celâleddin Rûmî, trans. Veled İzbudak, ed. Abdülbaki Gölpınarlı, *Mesnevî* (Istanbul: Milli Eğitim Basımevi 1991), vol. 6, vs. 1208-1209.
477. Ken'an Rifâî, *Şerhli Mesnevî-i Şerif* (Istanbul: Kubbealtı Neşriyatı 2000), p. 536.

- Messengers, not as gnostic friends of God but as messengers, have the state and level of the communities where they are. In this regard messengers have only the share of the knowledge belonging to messengerhood that their communities absolutely need, no more, no less. And communities are at different levels, some superior to others. According to the level of their community, some messengers are superior to others in messengerhood knowledge. This difference of level is fixed by God's verse, "*We made some of those messengers superior to others.*" Messengers are also different in knowledge and wisdom about things related to their souls, according to their preparedness. It is the difference stated in God's verse translated as "*Certainly we have made some prophets superior to other prophets.*"[478]

- A traveller cannot reach the way station of his journey before leaving the first. Nor can one enter the Kaaba of witness before passing through all the way stations.[479]

- When the time of our Messenger of God Efendi's physical manifestation drew near, the branch of being began to grow straight. As required by the verse, "*Go straight, as you have been commanded*" (11:112), the attribute of our Messenger of God Efendi became straightness (*righteousness, being just in all things*). His station became the heaven of servanthood called Dār ul-Muqāma.

In time he found perfect straightness; he passed through this world and the next, and the duty entrusted him was performed and complete. Then he went on from one beautiful station to another. When he stopped in that place he had passed to his true abode. The first of these stations is being in the world, which is called "The Station of Being." This station is indicated by the verse, "*O you who are covered, arise and enter the station of warning*" (74:1-2).

The expression "Station of the Praised" is also used. This is indicated by the verse, "*It may be that your Lord will raise you to a praised station*" (17:79). The Station of the Praised is a station special to the realm

---

478. Muhyiddîn İbnü'l-Arabî, trans. Nuri Gençosman, *Fusûs'l-Hikem* (Istanbul: İstanbul Kitabevi Yayınları 1981), p. 114.

479. Niyâzî Mısrî, trans. Süleyman Ateş, *İrfan Sofraları* (Istanbul: Yeni Ufuklar Neşriyatı n.d.), p. 30.

of form, and is a land in the world. The people see it and trust in its blessed existence. It is the necessity of that station that it should enjoy the blessing of his messengerhood and prophethood. The verse, *"We did not send you but as a mercy to the worlds"* (21:107), was revealed in order to explain the Station of the Praised. In that station the Messenger of God was seated upon the pulpit of the command, *"O Messenger, proclaim that which was sent down to you"* (5:67).

Thus in this station he is the one who accedes to the people's existing call. In counsel he is their speaker. He is their physician in any spiritual upset. In love he is their share. This much is the first part of the Station of the Praised, the part specific to the people of the world. The second part will be established in the Hereafter, and is the share of the Highest Assembly (*malā-'l'alā*).[480] Because of the blessing of this station they attain to many attainments, and they witness its beauty there and hear its speech. The verse, *"The day that the spirit and the angels stand in ranks"* (78:38), describes their standing before that station. In that station the speaker rises to his feet. The angles stand to the right side with hands folded in front of them. The speaker in that station is our Messenger of God Efendi himself. He makes the opening speech of his address to intercede for his community and says, "My community, my community..." In answer to this comes the good news, "My mercy, My mercy..." As for the third form of the Station of the Praised, we can take it up as the "station of witness." It is the station of eternity, of continuance, which will be in Heaven. And the people of Heaven will take their share of it. The houris will witness it and take their share of it. The pavilions of Heaven gain nobility with the establishment of that station. Then the light of Heaven increases, the curtains open. Evil things cease to exist. Joy comes with his entrance there. We understand that station from the verse, *"Who has, out of His bounty, placed us in the Abode of Everlasting Life* (the heaven of servanthood)*"* (35:35). The fourth station is the station of witness; the station of the "vision" of the beloved God the Exalted. In other words, seeing the sublime, exalted Lord, the beloved. This is the station fixed by the "Two Bows" verse, *"The union of two bows... or even nearer"* (53:9). This nearness, seeing, witnessing and sublimity has been estab-

---

480. [38:69].

lished only for our Messenger of God Efendi. There is in that station no share for strangers.[481]

- Those who remove from their hearts the bad emotions in their breasts, such as deceit, transgression, hatred, envy, arrogance, conceit and hypocrisy, command and invite us to do such things as slay the commanding soul's desire with various ascetic practices for uniting the attributes, not do what the soul tells us to do, and renounce bad habits. In this way the soul attains tranquility. If the soul attains tranquility, it enters the house of safety of the attributes of beautiful tempers. It is saved from the flames of evil that leap into hearts in the prison of bad character. And it is ever at ease from the torment of those bad tempers.[482]

---

481. Muhyiddîn İbnül-Arabî, trans. Abdülkâdir Akçiçek, *Şeceretü'l-Kevn-Üstün İnsan* (Istanbul: Bahar Yayınları 2000), pp. 103-116.

482. Niyâzî Mısrî, trans. Süleyman Ateş, *İrfan Sofraları* (Istanbul: Yeni Ufuklar Neşriyatı n.d.), p. 31.

40. It does not befit the sun to catch up with the moon, nor the night to outstrip the day; each swims round a sphere of the sky.

Lā'sh-shamsu yanbaghī lahā 'an tudrika'l-qamara wa lā 'l-laylu sābiqu'n-nahāri wa kullun fī falakin yasbaḥūn.

- "It is He who created the night and the day and the sun and the moon. Each of them swims round a sphere of the sky" (21:33).

It is not fit or favored by God for the sun of spirit to take in the states of the two worlds, comprehending the moon on its journey, and have with its character and attributes the emergence of the self-disclosure of perfections. The night does not outstrip the day by comprehending the moon and the sun. And the darkness of the soul does not change the daytime of the light of the heart. For when the moon of the heart rises to the station of spirit, spirit reaches hazret unity. In the same way the moon cannot catch up with the sun. Thus the soul is illuminated in the station of the heart and no darkness remains in it. That is why the darkness of the soul cannot outstrip the light of the heart. Perhaps the darkness of the soul no longer exists. Because the heart and the heart's light are in the station of spirit, if the darkness of soul continues, that darkness would not be able to outstrip the light of the heart, and *"Each of them swims round a sphere of the sky."* Both the sun and moon travel in an orbit and a place with a specific beginning and end, and they cannot transgress their boundaries until God the Exalted gathers up the spaces between them at a boundary. And they will travel in this way until the moon is eclipsed by the sun and the Resurrection that makes the sun rise in the West.[483]

---

483. Kemâlüddin Abdürrezzâk Kâşânîyyü's-Semerkandî, trans. AliRıza Doksanyedi, ed. M. Vehbi Güloğlu, *Te'vilât-ı-Kâşâniyye* (Ankara: Kadıoğlu Matbaası 1988), vol. 3, p. 13.

- Sin-ba-ḥa [Arabic root letters of the verb "to swim"]: To change place by a motion special to itself. God said, *"Each person has a direction"* (2:148).

  Glorification (*tesbih*): To remember God the Glorious. Only remembrance of this kind with continuous turning in an orbit is called *tesbih*.

  Yasbaḥūn are those who repeat the same motion of continually turning in an orbit. In its other meaning, they remember God, performing *tesbih*. In fact both meanings are valid for every being in the universe.

  Electrons continually perform an orbiting motion around atoms. At the same time they vibrate before the nucleus and perform a magnetic satellite motion that is precisely a *"yasbaḥūn"* motion. The nucleus is the prayer-niche of the atom. It demonstrates its servanthood both by its gyroscopic motion and its condition of magnetic satellite. All planets, solar systems and galaxies are representatives of the same type of motion. In order to remain in a given place, a being is required and condemned to perform this gyroscopic turning motion, this *yasbaḥūn* action.[484]

- *"It does not befit the sun to catch up with the moon, nor the night to outstrip the day; each swims round a sphere of the sky"* (36:40). In other words, they turn in a circular thing.[485]

- The Manifest is God, and the non-Manifest is God... The First is God, and the Last is God... The gracious verse says, *"There is nothing that does not glorify Him in praise"* (17:44)

- We suppose that this table here is inanimate. But no. Its interior is full of life. Like the stars around the sun, these atoms are moving around their centers. What is in motion is life. And life exists by God the Truth. Without doubt, God manifests from whatever is alive.[486]

---

484. Halûk Nurbaki, *Yâ-Sîn Sûresi Yorumu* (Istanbul: Damla Yayınevi 1999), p. 60.
485. Muhyiddîn İbnü'l-Arabî, trans. Ekrem Demirli, *Fütuhât-ı Mekkiyye* (Istanbul: Litera Yayıncılık 2006), vol. 1, p. 408.
486. Ken'an Rifâî, *Sohbetler* (Istanbul: Kubbealtı Neşriyatı 2000), p. 351.

40th Verse

- Every religious community, every individual, every member of the body, every faculty of the soul and the spirit, has an aim, a goal, and a specific prayer niche. That prayer niche and aim is one of God's names, and that person goes toward it. A person apparently takes a direction but in reality the attraction of the goal toward which s/he turns is drawing him or her toward it. Action draws a person to God. Understand at last, no one turns away from his or her prayer niche, his or her goal.[487]

- Every science and act in the sheriat is also found in reality. But still there is an isthmus (*a line that separates and connects two things*) between them required by God's wisdom and power. Because of this obstacle, one cannot outstrip the other. This obstacle is the groundless fears of those on either side. In fact the two sciences are one science, but regarded as two. For that reason there is always contention between the masters of each. A difference of path.

  Because of wisdom hidden from the people of both sides, one cannot bear the judgment of the other. That is why they cannot mix. Except for those who attain complete perfection.[488]

- O you who have come from a father to a mother and from a mother's womb into the world, going either from joy to joy or sorrow to sorrow, or from joy to sorrow! You are a mote in the universe. You are an itsy-bitsy part subject to the great whole. Now, many are the tiny beings like you subject to that law. When all of the parts, having passed through state after state, subject to that law, are gathered together, they form the great whole.

  A totality each of whose parts passes from one state to another. This means that not only the parts, which pass from one state to another and keep going in order to reach the final state, but also the totality they form when they all come together, is subject to the same law.

  If a person has a wound in his smallest member, his entire body feels pain because of it. A small affliction burns the entire body with

---

487. Niyâzî Mısrî, trans. Süleyman Ateş, *İrfan Sofraları* (Istanbul: Yeni Ufuklar Neşriyatı n.d.), pp. 35-36.

488. Niyâzî Mısrî, trans. Süleyman Ateş, *İrfan Sofraları* (Istanbul: Yeni Ufuklar Neşriyatı n.d.), p. 19.

fever. If on the contrary the entire body suffers a general affliction, a person's every member, every cell of his body, takes it on and under its influence becomes jaundiced, pale and listless.

It is the same with the totality of this world, made of such opposing elements as fire, air, water and earth. Since this world is compounded of four elements which challenge one another as much as possible, of course just as these opposing beings are parts in the whole of the world there will be deterioration and change.[489]

- Because all exterior causes are under the command of interior causes, every force becomes effective according to its nature if God wishes it so. If God does not so wish, even fire whose nature it is to burn loses that effect it has. Once the great fire into which Abraham was thrown by mangonel became a rose garden for him. From that day to this, no fire has ever burned a person with the created nature of Abraham.[490]

- That God's judgment in and about things depends on them themselves is called the secret of the measuring out. Divine decree is God's judgment in things according to the information known things give about themselves in the state they are in; and the measuring out, without adding anything, organizes the things according to the state they are in. Therefore decree has passed judgment in things only by means of things. That is the secret of measuring out, according to the verses, *"Who listens and witnesses"* (50:37), and *"To God belongs the conclusive argument"* (6:149). Thus judgment is truly bound to the reality of the thing under question; whatever that thing's essence requires, judgment is given according to that. The thing that is subject to judgment determines the judgment given about it by the one who judges. God has said, *"We do not send it down but in specific measure"* (15:21). That measure is the rights creatures demand, because God has given every thing its nature and sent down what it demands in specific measure. What God the Truth wishes, knows and judges about it is what He gives. What God knows is what the known thing has given to itself.[491]

---

489. Ken'an Rifâî, *Şerhli Mesnevî-i Şerif* (Istanbul: Kubbealtı Neşriyatı 2000), p. 178.
490. Ken'an Rifâî, *Şerhli Mesnevî-i Şerif* (Istanbul: Kubbealtı Neşriyatı 2000), p. 117.
491. Abdürrezzâk Kâşânî, trans. Dr. Ekrem Demirli, *Tasavvuf Sözlüğü* (Istanbul: İz Yayıncılık 2004), pp. 296-297.

40TH VERSE

- Hazret Umar asked our Messenger of God Efendi, "You see that we have done something. Is that thing written and done with? Or is it something newly created and begun?" Our Messenger of God Efendi said, "That thing is over and done with. Hazret Umar asked again, "In that case should we not trust this situation?" Our Messenger of God Efendi said, "O Son of Khattab, look to action. Everyone finds the way to the work they were created for. If someone is of the people of felicity, they will do the work of the people of felicity. If someone is of the people of wretchedness... That person will do the work of the people of wretchedness.[492]

---

492. Abdülkadir Geylânî, trans. Abdülkadir Akçiçek, *Gunyetü't-Tâlibîn* (Istanbul: Sağlam Yayınevi 1991), p. 207.

41. And a sign for them is that We carried their progeny in a loaded ship.

Wa 'āyatun lahum 'annā ḥamalnā dhurriyyatahum fī'l-fulki'l-mashḥūn.

- Here the loaded ship is a figure of speech for the wombs of pregnant women, a clear metaphor. The generations of the father's lineage tossed out by a storm find in the wombs of mothers a ship of salvation like Noah's ark.[493]

- And it is also a sign for them that we have loaded their progeny onto Noah's laden ark. In this verse there is a secret from the secrets of fine rhetoric and that is that is to not mention their fathers on the ship and perhaps mention the progeny of the lineages of those on the ship. Therefore the progeny must exist.[494]

- That the progeny are carried on a "loaded ship" sheds light on two important scientific facts:

- In once sense progeny means genetic cards. Thus genetic cards really do launch upon an incredible journey within the fluid of sperm and complete their assigned task. In multicellular creatures it is out of the question for a single cell to move on its own. Even blood cells move within the flow of the blood. But sperm cells have a capacity for independent movement inside such a special fluid that the length

---

[493]. Elmalı M. Hamdi Yazır, *Hak Dini Kur'an Dili* (Istanbul: Feza Gazetecilik 1992), vol. 6, p. 418.

[494]. Kemâlüddin Abdürrezzâk Kâşânîyyü's-Semerkandî, trans. AliRıza Doksanyedi, ed. M. Vehbi Güloğlu, *Te'vilât-ı-Kâşâniyye* (Ankara: Kadıoğlu Matbaası 1988), vol. 3, Yâ-Sîin Sûresi, p. 14.

of this journey is nearly 20 meters. This journey is two million times the size of a sperm cell; in other words, it is like a twenty thousand kilometer-long journey made by a human being.

The adventure of the female cell is more interesting. The female cell falls into a barely perceptible liquid in the abdominal cavity. Then at the tips of two fallopian tubes like extensions of the womb with vacuum cleaners on their tips suck it up and take it into the canal, again in a fine liquid. Thus our progeny, our genetic cards, are an incredible journey in such liquid.

- A second type of interpretation of "a loaded ship" is the growth of the baby in the liquid inside the mother's womb.

    a. This system ensures that the child is nurtured appropriately for its forty-week life in the mother's womb. Whatever nutrient is needed for the embryo on whatever day, it is transferred to the baby from the system to the list. In other words, at every moment a new chemical substance is prepared in that loaded ship. The substances are transferred to the baby filtered through the blood. If this incredible computer makes the slightest chemical or biological mistake, it will cause us to be defective our whole lives long. Since this system is calibrated not according to what the mother eats but to what the baby needs, it develops the new generation in the best way.

    b. The second important function of this system is to protect the baby from any chemical or biological dangers that may come from the mother. It filters out all the harmful germs and chemical substances in the mother's abdomen by means of an incredible blocking system. The third function of this "loaded ship" is to manufacture hormones. The system prepares all hormones for the production and development of the baby in every phase of its 280-day life in the mother's womb. The hormones of this system are so effective that all the growth and sexual hormones in particular are manufactured from this system, in other words from the placenta and its fluid.[495]

---

495. Halûk Nurbaki, *Yâ-Sîn Sûresi Yorumu* (Istanbul: Damla Yayınevi 1999), pp. 64-66.

41th Verse

- What is meant by Noah's ark is the attraction that the perfect human being breathes, the relative spirit. Without that, it is not possible for a person to travel by means of his or her own partial intellect to the sea of spirit and the realm of reality. Safety and mercy on this road, in other words, salvation, consists in taking refuge in that ship of love and attraction.[496]

- Happy is the one who in this deluge of the world trusts not in his or own ability to swim but throws him or herself into Noah's ark![497]

- Our Messenger of God Efendi says, "*The sheriat is the ship, the dervish path is the sea, and reality is the pearls in that sea.*" Heedless are the adepts who tread the path without the sheriat and the sheriat without the path.[498]

- For Us to load their progeny, in other words their roots and branches, their families, on a laden ship, for Us to house them on the water, to will the continuance, education and care of generations, is one of Our proofs, Our clear signs declaring to them Our great power, the tremendousness of Our glory.

  Just as this meaning is produced by the Gracious Verse, the loaded ship indicates the mother's womb where is the site of engendering. Yes, the mother is the site of engendering and has intimacy with the Creator. That is why after people die they are attributed to their mothers and funeral rites are done in the name of the mother; by this is intended a plea for the descent of divine mercy. The share the child derives from its mother is the area of the breast, and from its father, the area of the back. The area of the breast is the site of mercy. Thus Our loading the human substance into the mother's womb and making them come to be there, giving it life, is a clear sign of Our glorious power.

  Common folk are in the sea of the world, and the elect are in the sea of reality. What a great sign it is that those who board the ship of salvation in order to attain the vision of God's beauty reach

---

496. Ken'an Rifâî, *Sohbetler* (Istanbul: Kubbealtı Neşriyatı 2000), p. 144.
497. Ken'an Rifâî, *Sohbetler* (Istanbul: Kubbealtı Neşriyatı 2000), p. 304.
498. Ken'an Rifâî, *Sohbetler* (Istanbul: Kubbealtı Neşriyatı 2000), p. 605.

the shore of oneness without drowning in waves of doubt, pleasure and lust.[499]

- "And truly We created the human being from a quintessence of clay. Then We placed him as a drop in a secure place of rest. Then of the drop We created a clot of congealed blood. Then of the clot We created a lump of flesh, and of the lump created bones and clothed the bones with flesh. Then We made him as another creation. Blessed is God, best of creators" (23:12-14).

"Did We not create you from a despised fluid? We placed it in a secure place of rest for a specific measure. Thus We measure out, best of measurers" (77:20-23).

"O Humankind! If you are in doubt concerning the Resurrection, indeed We created you from dust, then from a drop, then from a clot, then from a lump of flesh formed and unformed, that We may clarify for you. And We cause whom We will to rest in the wombs for an appointed term, then We bring you forth as an infant..." (22:5).

- Then are there a hundredfold hopes, O brave youth!
Step up and put talk aside like lovers do

While you think you're only closing your eyelids
You are crossing the sea asleep on the ship

Interpretation of the hadith, "The likeness of my community is the likeness of Noah's Ark; whoever clings to it is saved, and whoever holds back from it is drowned."

The Messenger has said with regard to this
"In the flood of the age, I am like a ship

"I and my companions are like Noah's ark
Whoever takes hold of it will reach the mark"

You are far from filthiness when with the shakyh
You are on the ship and travelling night and day

Protected by spirit that bestows spirit
You are travelling asleep upon the ship

---

499. Şemseddin Yeşil, *Füyûzat* (Istanbul: Ş. Yeşil Yayınları 1984), vol. 6.

41th Verse

Set foot on the ship and keep on at a run
Like the spirit runs to its beloved one[500]

Know each of God's friends is Noah and captain
Know the flood to be companionship with them[501]

- In order for the progress of the ship to beneficial of course it has need of water, in other words, the ocean. As long as the water of the ocean is outside the ship, it is beneficial to it, it becomes a path. But when the same water comes into the ship, it sinks the ship. A container that is closed tightly floats on water. If the water of the world does not get into a person's heart, and that heart is full of love for God, it flows into the sea like a ship with open sails.[502]

- If a spirit whose goal is perfection gets swept up in the passions and desires of the body given to it as an envelope and, forgetting the reality that is the purpose of its coming into the world, plunges into lowly things, it is natural that it should become wretched. But if the body of a spirit that knows its true function and makes efforts in that way becomes lofty like that spirit, body becomes spirit and spirit becomes body.[503]

---

500. Mevlânâ Celâleddin Rûmî, trans. Veled İzbudak, ed. Abdülbaki Gölpınarlı, *Mesnevî* (Istanbul: Milli Eğitim Basımevi 1991), vol. 4, vs. 536-541, 557.
501. Mevlânâ Celâleddin Rûmî, trans. Veled İzbudak, ed. Abdülbaki Gölpınarlı, *Mesnevî* (Istanbul: Milli Eğitim Basımevi 1991), vol. 6, vs. 2225.
502. Ken'an Rifâî, *Şerhli Mesnevî-i Şerif* (Istanbul: Kubbealtı Neşriyatı 2000), p. 134.
503. Ken'an Rifâî, *Sohbetler* (Istanbul: Kubbealtı Neşriyatı 2000), p. 612.

42. And We created for them its like upon which they ride.

Wa khalaqnā lahum min mithlihi mā yarkabūn.

- And for them to ride We created a ship like Noah's ark, art, which is the Muhammeden ship.[504]

- Warring against the world is a war in vain. Such struggles by the world's people resemble the battles of neighborhood children or their games of war. Children who play pretend wars with wooden swords and horses made from trees are left sweating in vain. They run in the delusion that they are directing their horses, and even that they are riding on horses. Although they carry loads on their back they think their horses are carrying them.

Now, you who remain children all your lives! You whose eyes are enchanted by the show of this world! Wait until you see the horsemen God has mounted. It is they who will gallop their horses beyond the nine heavens.

On that Day spirits purified of worldly filth will like angels *"ascend unto Him in a day the measure of which is fifty thousand years"* (70:4). On that Day they will rise to God the Truth. But while even the angels cannot approach God beyond a certain level, beyond the **Sidre** tree, the ascension of the spirits will pass beyond that level as Hazret Muhammed (s.a.s.) did. This ascension of God's friends will arouse a profound trembling in the heavens.

But you who do not consider these things, you ride on a wooden horse thinking you hold the reins are like children holding up the

---

[504]. Kemâlüddin Abdürrezzâk Kâşânîyyü's-Semerkandî, trans. AliRıza Doksanyedi, ed. M. Vehbi Güloğlu, *Te'vilât-ı-Kâşâniyye* (Ankara: Kadıoğlu Matbaası 1988), vol. 3, p. 14.

edges of their own skirts. Your little intellect is like the edge of a skirt, your conjectures and fantasies are like a wooden horse.

When the life of this world comes to an end and eyes are opened to the truth you will see in amazement and terror how we have supposed our own feet to be a pure Arab steed and have been riding nothing but the horse of our own body. You will understand that your conjectures and vain thoughts, your false sense and understanding are all like that wooden horse, and it will be put before you with convincing clarity how childish you have been all your life.

Why do those people of the heart, those travelers in God, fly as if winged beyond the delights of this world? Because it is not feet that carry their bodies but the knowledge of truth. It is they who fly upon the pure Arab steed of knowledge. It is the people of body and soul who are crushed under the burdens they suppose to be knowledge.

Only if you know how to bear the burden of divine knowledge, understand the value of carrying it, will God teach you what you do not know. *"Whoever acts upon what he knows, God the Exalted will teach him what he does not know"* (sacred hadith). It is such peace of heart that it will relieve you of the burden of all knowledge, transform all the evils of your life and the ugliness around you to goodness and beauty, and you will be one of the saved and attain to the truth. The day you mount that ambling horse of gnosis you will see that the burdens of what is other than God have been removed from your back and you are left to consist of spirit and light so that you can fly.[505]

- The signs seen on mounts are each of them signs of God. That is because of the differences between schools of law.

Some of the riders on those mounts cleave to those signs by right, and some take the road through deserts. Those among them who remain in place are people of vision (*seeing with the eye of the heart*) and witness (seeing God the Truth with God the Truth). Those who fall to the deserts have grown distant from reality.[506]

---

505. Ken'an Rifâî, *Şerhli Mesnevî-i Şerif* (Istanbul: Kubbealtı Neşriyatı 2000), pp. 505-507.

506. Muhyiddîn İbnü'l-Arabî, trans. Nuri Gençosman, *Fusûs'l-Hikem* (Istanbul: İstanbul Kitabevi Yayınları 1981), p. 91.

42th Verse

- *These companions rob each other on the way*
Spirit riding on the body goes astray

Far from God's Throne in exile the spirit yearns
Body's like the she-camel, in love with thorns

Spirit spreads its wings to take flight high aloft
Body deep into the earth has stuck its claws

"Long as you who long for home with me remain
Then my spirit far from Leyla will remain

My lifetime has been spent in this kind of state
Like Moses's tribe and years in desert waste

It was just two steps to union on this road
Your snare has kept me sixty years on the road

The way is short and I've so long been held up
I'm fed up with this riding, fed up, fed up!"

He threw himself down from the camel headlong
He said, "Grief has consumed me, how long, how long?"

The desert expanse seemed narrow to him now
He flung himself down onto the rocky ground

He threw himself down thus so violently
That the body of that brave man became weak

When he threw himself on the ground violently
His leg broke that instant by divine decree

He bound up his leg and said, "I'll be a ball
In the curve of His bat I will roll along"

The sweet-talking sage curses on this account
Riders who will not from the body dismount

Should love of the Lord be less than for Leyla?
It is worthy for His sake to be a ball

O Humankind

From now on this journey is for God's service
And that journey on the camel was for us

This journey is unlike any other one
Surpassing the struggles of humans and jinn

It exerts attraction not of common stuff
Ahmed gave to it preeminence—enough![507]

- Seeing that it has been said, "*I pass the night with my Lord. He gives me to eat and drink,*" there is nourishment for you other than food and sleep. You have forgotten that nourishment, busy with this world. You feed your body night and day with material nourishment. At most, this body is your horse and this world is that horse's stable. The horse's feed cannot be food for the rider. The rider has his or her own sleeping habits, diet and daily bread. But because animal feeling has overpowered you, and you are in the horse stable and next to the horses, you have no place in the rank of the emirs and shahs of the realm of immortality (*baqā*). Your heart is here, but because your body has conquered you, you are under its dominion and have become its captive. It is just as when Majnun wanted to go to Leyla's country, he drove his camel there while he was in his right mind, but when he dreamed of Leyla, he would forget himself and his camel. In that interval the camel remembered its foal back in the village and began to go backwards. When it reached its village, Majnun came to himself and realized he had gone backwards for two days. He had a journey of three months before him. "This camel is the ruin of me," he said to himself and leapt off it and began walking.[508]

- Spirit is a divine light that is neither inside the body nor outside it, neither attached to it nor separate. But in the human body there is a vitality called the animal spirit that is produced by a biological compound. That spirit is the mount and container of the divine spirit. The animal spirit spreads into every corner of the body.

---

507. Mevlânâ, trans. Şefik Can, *Mesnevî Tercümesi* (Istanbul: Öteken Neşriyat 1999), vol. 3-4, pp. 497-498 [vol. 4, vs. 1544-1561].

508. Mevlânâ Celâleddin Rûmî, trans. Meliha Ülker Anbarcıoğlu, *Fîhi mâ Fîh* (Istanbul: Milli Eğitim Basımevi 1985), pp. 26-27.

42th Verse

Behold the work and self-disclosure of God the Truth, so that because the divine spirit is in love with the animal spirit, it accepts the animal spirit as its mount. Thus the divine spirit manifests all beauty, knowledge and perfection through the body by means of that spirit.[509]

- *Spiritual mounts carry a person to the Miraj, while material mounts convey him or her to the lowest of the low.*[510]

Our Messenger of God Efendi's first mount was Buraq. It took him as far as the al-Aqsa Mosque. With the His second mount he went as far as the earthly heaven. The name of this journey was the Miraj. The third mount was the Angels' Wing. With it he went as far as the second heaven. After that his journey through the heavens continued all on angels' wings, until he reached the seventh heaven. After the seventh heaven the fourth mount's mission began. This was Gabriel (*the angel of revelation*). He flew with Gabriel's wings as far as the Lote Tree of the final limit (the final limit of creaturely knowledge). Here it was the Gabriel's mission ended, he remained there, saying, "O Messenger of God, if I step the distance of an ant's length further, I will burn up."

Gabriel slowly departed; he left that place. And at the instant seventy thousand veils opened to our Messenger of God Efendi, all of them of light. Then the fifth mount arrived. That was Rafraf (*the mat upon which the Messenger ascended beyond the Lote Tree of the final limit.*) And it was made of green light. It was of a size to fill the east and the west. With it he went as far as the Throne. Our Messenger Efendi ascended to the Throne with the mat of kindness, and there the Realm of Sovereignty and its secrets became clear to our Messenger Efendi. Entrusted with the Throne, our Messenger of God Efendi did not even glance at it. He did not read even one letter of the lines that came to him revealed through it. For he conformed to the divine command, *"The vision did not swerve, nor did it go wrong"* (53:17). After that the sixth mount was presented to our Messenger of God Efendi. Its name was Support (*ta'yīd*). There came to him the call, "Approach, O Muhammed!" "Then he drew near... he held on." When this nearness became like the meeting of two bows, time and space no longer

---

509. Ken'an Rifâî, *Sohbetler* (Istanbul: Kubbealtı Neşriyatı 2000), p. 277.
510. Compiler's note.

remained. There came the call, "Step forward, O Muhammed!" Our Messenger Efendi made this plea: "O my Lord, space has disappeared. The concept of space is erased. Where should I put my foot?"

Thereupon he received this address: "Put one foot on top of the other." Then came the call, "Behold, O Muhammed!" When he looked he saw a very bright light. Then it was said, "This is not a light. It is the heaven of Firdows (*the garden of the sixth heaven*). And as you ascend, it will be left under your feet. And what is under your feet is a sacrifice for you."

At that point, came the call, "O Muhammed, the place you have stepped is the place where the imaginings of *mebde-i halk* (*created folk*) end." In other words, they cannot even imagine what is beyond.

Later came the address, "O Muhammed, while you traversed time and space, Gabriel was your witness, and Buraq your mount. But space has been erased... Now I am your witness. I am opening the door for you, raising the veil for you, because even while in the realm of the Unseen, you with true faith recognized My unity. Recognize it now also... In other words, arrive at My unity also in the realm of witness and clarity. *'We have sent you as a witness, a bearer of good news and a warner.'*"

Thus he would see God the Truth and bear witness. A witness is someone asked only what he or she has seen. There can be no witness to the invisible and unknown. Paradise and Hell were shown to him. In the end the sublime ascension was realized and our Messenger of God Efendi arrived at that sublime Hazret. And He communicated with him orally, He spoke. He revealed to His servant what He revealed (53:10). But that was secret, between God and His Messenger![511]

- *He who made the body manifest spirit*
He who made Noah's Buraq to be the ship

Know all friends of God are Noah and captain
Know the flood to be companionship with them[512]

---

511. Muhyiddîn İbnül-Arabî, trans. Abdülkâdir Akçiçek, *Şeceretü'l-Kevn-Üstün İnsan* (Istanbul: Bahar Yayınları 2000), p. 136.

512. Mevlânâ Celâleddin Rûmî, trans. Veled İzbudak, ed. Abdülbaki Gölpınarlı, *Mesnevî* (Istanbul: Milli Eğitim Basımevi 1991), vol. 6, vs. 2208, 2225.

42th Verse

To transcend the limit of intellect is to go beyond the point where Gabriel stopped (*the Lote Tree of the final limit*).

When one reaches the point where intellect must be transcended, intellect speaks with the heart as Gabriel did and says, "O Sultan of Spirit! You too, abandon me at this place! This is my limit. Mount now on the Rafraf of love! O great rider, drive your mount on to the heights of the path of reaching God!"

If you are going to be, be like the one who tires out his feet on the path of worship, so that Buraq may come to your aid on the path of God the Truth; let it be a reality for you to mount that Buraq of faith and spirituality and roam the realms of the heart.[513]

---

513. Ken'an Rifâî, *Şerhli Mesnevî-i Şerif* (Istanbul: Kubbealtı Neşriyatı 2000), pp. 146-147.

43. And if We will it, We drown them; then there would be none to help them, nor would they be saved.

Wa 'in nasha' nughriqhum falā ṣarīkha lahum wa lā hum yunqadhūn.

- People who have concocted plots and designs to raise mountains from their foundations to escape the decree and measuring out have also had to bend their necks to the writing on their brows. To work against that writing on the brow has never been more than a vain fancy. In the end, whatever God has willed, that is what has happened.[514]

- Resurrection Day is the day of understanding one has been fooled, the day of terror, the disastrous day when permission will not be given for excuses and no one will be able to speak, the day of weeping and wailing, the day children will grow old from terror, the day of quaking, the ill-omened day, the day when mountains will be uprooted from the earth. *"The day when no soul will avail another soul. The command that Day will belong to God"* (82:19).[515]

- Know that God the Exalted is in a different state every day. He changes things, moves them, lowers and raises them. He brings some up to the highest heaven, and thrusts some down to the lowest of the low. The fear of those in the highest heaven is to fall to the lowest of the low. Their hopes are to preserve that sublime station and remain there. The fear of those in the lowest hell is to remain there for eternity. Their hopes are to rise to the highest heaven.[516]

---

514. Ken'an Rifâî, *Şerhli Mesnevî-i Şerif* (Istanbul: Kubbealtı Neşriyatı 2000), p. 130.

515. Ahmed er-Rifâî, ed. Dr. H. Kâmil Yılmaz, *Marifet Yolu* (Istanbul: Erkam Yayıncılık 1995), p. 102.

516. Abdülkâdir Geylânî, trans. Docent Dr. Abdülvehhab Öztürk, *Tasavvuf Yolu* (Istanbul: Sultan Yayınevi 2002), p. 59.

- Efendis!

If you seek help from God the Exalted's servants the friends, beware, do not suppose that they give the help you receive. Such opinion is to associate others with God. However, because the friends of God are the sites of manifestation of God the Truth's love, everything there is to desire is asked of God the Truth for their sake. The one who will give is He, none other...

Hadith: *"Many are those in rags, driven from dusty doors, whose prayers are answered. God makes them successful in the oaths they take."* Thus because God loves them, he accepts their requests for their sake.

Despite all of that, it is possible for them to make certain dispositions with God's permission. They can make certain dispositions in creation, with God's permission; being the site of manifestation of God's secret (*"Be! And it is"*), if they say (*"Be!"*), it can occur with divine permission.

Do you not see that with God's permission Jesus (a.s.) created a bird out of clay, and raised the dead. Even date palm trunks wept for our Messenger Efendi, unable to bear being separated from him... Many inanimate things greeted him. God the Truth brought together in our Messenger miracles performed separately by several messengers. The secrets of his miracle occurred even in the friends of God in his community. While these miracles are temporary for the friends of God, they are continuous for the messengers!

My son! When you say, *"O my Lord! I take recourse to your mercy,"* it is as if you have said you ask of God through the trusteeship of His servant Shaykh Mansur! And thus for the other gracious friends of God. For trusteeship is a special devotion, and God gives what he or she asks...

So beware of attributing the power of the merciful (*God*) to the one who receives mercy (*the servant*)! For action, ability and power are special to God alone. Recourse is a mercy He has made special to His friend servant. Thus when it is necessary, try to approach Him thought the mercy and love He has bestowed upon his intimate servants! Witness his unity with every action! Make His divine unity your refrain! If not, one must fear His glorious rivalry.[517]

---

517. Ahmed Rifâî, simplified by H. Naim Erdoğan, *Vaazlar* (Istanbul: Pamuk Yayınları n.d.), pp. 124-126.

43th Verse

- As we know, our situation in the world is hardly something to laugh about. Our end consists in dying and being taken to the grave. If there were immortality in the world, building would not fall! Thus one must turn to the Lord and renounce all that is other than God.[518]

- Whatever a man of God—one who has passed away from self with God—does is worthy. There is no fault in what is done for God. Thus whatever he does is right.

  If God the Exalted wishes, he makes to live, and if He wishes, he kills. He kills the just and makes the unjust live to old age.

  He brings about comfort and security in the lands of disbelievers; he brings about discomfort, danger and famine in the lands of Muslims. He makes disbelievers victorious over Muslims; he enslaves Muslims, the pious and the wholesome to them. He conveys misbelievers and thieves over the sea in ships, and sinks the ships of the devout and those who worship God. The wealthy, the padishahs, due to the excess of property and wealth they possess, have made all people members of their households and feed them. They wish for a son with thousands of prayers and for that reason take many wives, but still what they wish for does not happen, while He gives a poor man who is sick of life and cannot feed his own self fifteen girl or boy children instead of one. If it were not God but human beings who did these things, they would be captured and torn to pieces. Thus *"they kill the prophets without right"* (3:21).

  In the same way all things are from God. Anyone who makes distinctions among them and objects to them is a disbeliever.[519]

- *People of body and soul are enemies of the messengers and the arrived; for they are not of the same kind; "opposites do not unite."*

  Like the disbelievers in the time of the Messenger; they conspired against him with tricks and evils.

  Because of their thoughts Ahmed Muhtar and Abu Bakr hid in the cave.

  The Messiah rose to the sky mysteriously because of tricksters' trouble.

---

518. Ahmed Rifâî, simplified by H. Naim Erdoğan, *Vaazlar* (Istanbul: Pamuk Yayınları n.d.), p. 127.

519. Sultan Veled, trans. Meliha Anbarcıoğlu, *Maarif* (Konya: Konya ve Mülhakatı Eski Eserleri Sevenler Derneği yayını 2002), p. 47.

Pharaoh, too, conspired against Moses, and drowned without help from God.

Nimrod planned to throw Abraham too into fire and smoke.

But the fire had turned into roses; and disbeliever Nimrod was destroyed by a mosquito.

The people of Hud and gracious Noah were destroyed when God's age of torment struck.

They all were destroyed by wind and water; for they deserved to be struck and sunk in the ground.

The intentions of those devious, wretched people were evil.

That is why disaster turned and struck them; because those societies deserved that wrath.

That is why they put themselves to the sword and their blood flowed in a flood.

Otherwise why would they have destroyed themselves; why should their blood have flowed like a river?

Who has seen the fool who kills himself, who cuts his own throat with a sword?

The fool thinks he is wounding another; in the end he sees that he has wounded his own liver.[520]

- Earth, water, fire and air appear spirit-less and dead to you and me. But they have an ear that hears only the command of God the Truth. In the same way, fire is under God's command and constantly at the ready. You know how God's lovers are constantly waiting at the Beloved's door full of longing, wondering how and when divine beauty will appear, in the same way fire waits for God's will, wondering when He will give the command, "Burn!" That is why not every fire can burn everyone, but when it does burn, does not stop until it reduces what it burns to ashes. You know that when iron strikes stone it produces sparks. Beware that you do not strike the stone of the soul against the iron of the soul. For just as rebellious children are born of the union of many a woman and man, from those two come sparks of disbelief, mayhem and corruption that set everything on fire. In fact

---

520. Sultan Veled, trans. Abdülbaki Gölpınarlı, *İbtidâ-nâme* (Konya: Konya ve Mülhakatı Eski Eserleri Sevenler Derneği yayını 2001), p. 42. [I have translated Gölpınarlı's prose.]

43th Verse

stone and fire are only the apparent causes of the birth of such fires. Pay them no mind and consider God the Creator, who is the sole cause of all goodness and evil. Because all exterior causes are under the command of interior causes, every force becomes effective according to its nature if God wishes it so. If God does not so wish, even fire, whose nature it is to burn, loses that effect it has.[521]

- *Into mercy's ocean God has carried me*
To fill me up with what art, and dispatch me?

He fills one person with light of Majesty
And another with baseless fear and fancy

Had I in myself any judgment or skill
My thought and plan would be subject to my will

Since my hand has not His power to loose and bind
Whence, I wonder, comes this self-conceit of mine?[522]

- *Like Noah's son Canaan, who when shamed by him*
Went and climbed up to the top of that mountain

However much it was deliverance he sought
Going toward the mountain he was further off[523]

- *In the seas of spirit roll riotous waves*
Hundredfold more than the ones Noah's flood made

But a strand of hair appeared in Canaan's eye
He left Noah and ark for the mountain high

Then Canaan and mountain, by just half a wave
Were swept down below into the depths of waste[524]

---

521. Ken'an Rifâî, *Şerhli Mesnevî-i Şerif* (Istanbul: Kubbealtı Neşriyatı 2000), p. 117.
522. Mevlânâ Celâleddin Rûmî, trans. Veled İzbudak, ed. Abdülbaki Gölpınarlı, *Mesnevî* (Istanbul: Milli Eğitim Basımevi 1991), vol. 6, vs. 2322-2324, 2337.
523. Mevlânâ Celâleddin Rûmî, trans. Veled İzbudak, ed. Abdülbaki Gölpınarlı, *Mesnevî* (Istanbul: Milli Eğitim Basımevi 1991), vol. 6, vs. 2359-2360.
524. Mevlânâ Celâleddin Rûmî, trans. Veled İzbudak, ed. Abdülbaki Gölpınarlı, *Mesnevî* (Istanbul: Milli Eğitim Basımevi 1991), vol. 6, 2084-2086.

O Humankind

- So many people asleep to the illumination of their gaze by love of God are powerless to see the arrived of God, even though they are right next to them and in front of them, even touching them hand-to-hand. So many are unaware of the intimacy the arrived enjoy with the true Beloved, and catch no scent of it from their company and conversation.[525]

- When God asked Iblis, "What is preventing you from bowing down to the human I created with my own hand?", Satan said, "Certainly fire is superior to earth. I was created of fire. Since Adam was created of earth, I compared fire with earth and reached the conclusion that I am superior to Adam and cannot bow down to black earth. For what is original is light. What is subsidiary, that is, secondary to the original, is darkness. Since earth is dark, how can it be that light should be subject to earth?"

  God's response was: "Relations and ancestry are not considered; those who abstain from what God has forbidden and worship God with perfect sincerity of heart are the prayer-niche of virtue."

  If one ascended to such spiritual heights by means of ancestry, the son of Messenger Noah would not have been among the deniers and lost his way. If it were simply a matter of relations, the son of that rebel of rebels Abu Jahl would not have been a believing Muslim in every sense of the word.[526]

- *Wither efforts spent in vain, wither this struggling and action*
  Certainly the hour of death will come to each and every one

  In this world no one can grasp in hand the bird of happiness
  Day and night you struggle, but can that phantom ever be grasped?

  "There is no comfort in the world," said the Beloved of God
  Since this is so, is speech not all in vain, is it not absurd?

  All who come here pass away, and still they go on one by one
  Some of them the world lets go wondrous free from this direction

---

525. Ken'an Rifâî, *Şerhli Mesnevî-i Şerif* (Istanbul: Kubbealtı Neşriyatı 2000), p. 62.
526. Ken'an Rifâî, *Şerhli Mesnevî-i Şerif* (Istanbul: Kubbealtı Neşriyatı 2000), pp. 499-500.

43th Verse

Do not say you have been suffering from the day you came here
There will come a day when you will long for the time you were here

Regard the past, look at the messengers, what all has gone on
What all have the reprobates done to the Beloved of God

Consider what happened to the children of the Messenger
God have mercy! What trial, what heart-burning events did occur

How many innocents were drowned all in red blood on that day
Crying, "One drop of water!" with burning sighs they passed away

See the value of just one soul when you take a look at them
When compared with their struggles ponder what your efforts have been

The pain and suffering you have endured, sighing and crying out
When compared with theirs, is it all not merely a single drop?

Look inside your soul, Ken'an, sorrow, regret and suffering
This is what they call the world, it will go on as it has been.[527]

---

527. Ken'an Rifâî, eds. Yusuf Ömürlü and Dinçer Dalkılıç, *İlâhiyat-ı Ken'an*, (Istanbul: Kubbealtı Neşriyatı 1988), p. 10.

44. Except by a mercy from Us and provision for a time.
'Illā raḥmatan minnā wa matāʿan 'ilā ḥīnin.

• Only by a mercy of Ours did We not drown them, We gave them salvation, rescued them to live for a time so that they might recognize that time as booty and opportunity, take pleasure in the gnosis that is the goal of their creation, taste unification and faith, and attain perfection in this world and reunion in that world. And self-disclosing with Our mercy, We sent to them from Our name of Glory heralds bringing good news, warners, prophets and messengers who have been taught those realities and explain them.[528]

• Remaining behind the covering of the Unseen, God the Truth wants His servants to pursue hope and dreams and worship Him with hope. The hopes and dreams of those who seek the spiritual pleasures and tastes of the Hereafter and those who pursue worldly pleasure and desires mean a bond between God the Truth and them.

God wants not only the believer but the wretched and even the disbeliever to have hope of Him. And who knows, maybe if one day while still in the realm of body and the world one of those walking toward the cliff as a captive to his or her soul awakens from heedlessness even if just for a moment and prays for help and goodness from God, have no doubt that God is so great that He will forgive them and not hesitate for even a moment to take them among His good servants.

People are as close to God as their expectation of mercy from the heavens and greenery from the earth and their faith that the Unseen will one day satisfy their wishes.[529]

---

528. Şemseddin Yeşil, *Füyûzat* (Istanbul: Ş. Yeşil Yayınları 1984), vol. 6, p. 251.
529. Ken'an Rifâî, *Şerhli Mesnevî-i Şerif* (Istanbul: Kubbealtı Neşriyatı 2000), pp. 532-533.

- In order for the spirit to be freed from the fetters of soul and body on the path to God, one must ask for intercession only from the friends of God the Truth, the fellow-traveler of eternity without beginning and eternity without end.

It was no coincidence that fire did not burn Abraham, that the flood did not harm Noah, and the boulders sliding down the mountain spared only John. Those who escaped these disasters were in fact spirits who had attained the secret of escaping their own souls.

Thus when you have escaped the filth of the world and taken refuge in God's kindness you will not bow before disaster, disaster will bow before you.[530]

- *Since "If not for you..."[531] is on his signet ring*
His boon and disposal include everything

Means of sustenance consume means he bestows
Fruits are dry-lipped for the rain that he bestows

A disgrace like you, that worthy spirit's mate
Are like Noah's disbelieving wedded mate

Were it not for your relation to this house
I would have torn you into pieces right now

I would have delivered that Noah from you
Honored when my life was taken for it too

But it's not for me to commit such outrage
In the house of the shahinshah of the age

Go and thank God you are the dog of this house
Otherwise I will do what should be done now[532]

- The Messenger (s.a.s) said, "*Invoke blessings upon me, because invoking blessings upon me is purification for you. Ask God to make me an*

---

530. Ken'an Rifâî, *Şerhli Mesnevî-i Şerif* (Istanbul: Kubbealtı Neşriyatı 2000), p. 260.
531. [Sacred hadith: "*If not for you, I would not have created the heavens.*"]
532. Mevlânâ Celâleddin Rûmî, trans. Veled İzbudak, ed. Abdülbaki Gölpınarlı, *Mesnevî* (Istanbul: Milli Eğitim Basımevi 1991), vol. 6, vs. 2103, 2107, 2110-2114.

intermediary, because 'intermediary' is the highest level in Paradise. Only one man can occupy that rank, and I want to be that man." This hadith signifies that just as a scholar cannot be a teacher without students, a father can only be a father if he has a child, and a murshid can only be a murshid if he has a disciple, the Messenger of God (s.a.s) can only be an intermediary if others accept him as an intermediary. People accept him as an intermediary by following his path and acquiring his character traits. He cannot be an intermediary for someone who does not follow his way. The Messenger's (s.a.s) saying, *"Ask God to make me an intermediary,"* is a command for obedience to him. So that Hazret Muhammed may realize his being an intermediary with regard to that person. God the Exalted's saying, *"Truly God and His angels invoke blessings upon the Prophet. O you who believe, invoke blessings upon him and greetings of peace"* (33:56), is also like that. They said that God's intention in invoking blessings is mercy. The invocation of blessings by the angels is repentance. The invocation of blessings by believers is prayer. What is meant by prayer is to ask for him to be an intermediary. Prayer is absolute in the Quranic verse. The hadith has proven it. What is meant by asking for him to be an intermediary is to pray for the community's increase, the exaltation of the word Truth and increase of the amelioration of the states of the people of faith and to pray for the amelioration of the soul. So that the Gracious Messenger's mediation may include all creation and uncountable spiritual recompense may be produced. For he has said, *"If someone establishes a good habit, for him or her nothing of the recompense for the habit or recompense for those practicing it will be reduced."* From this is understood that God's mercy descends upon Hazret Messenger both with and without intermediary. Just as the thing descending without intermediary has descended totally, he wanted that the thing descending with intermediary should descend in summary, so that the summary should be capable of explication in detail. Now, you too understand.[533]

- *Joseph is in the well, it is the wolf's turn*
  Pharaoh is shah, it is the Egyptians' turn

---

533. Niyâzî Mısrî, trans. Süleyman Ateş, *İrfan Sofraları* (Istanbul: Yeni Ufuklar Neşriyatı n.d.), pp. 110-111.

*So those dogs for a few days may have a share
Of sustenance without stint and laughing there*

*Deep within the jungle lions lie in wait
For the order, "Come on forth!" to propagate*

*Then those lions emerge from the pasture grass
And God shows seizing and wasting unabashed*[534]

- Although all doors shut in your face, yet wait for a door to be opened by God the Opener. In fact whenever servants close a path, God will definitely open it. He does this singly, as a requisite of His lordliness. He does it as the exaltation of sublimity. That God is single in His lordliness and exalted in His sublimity requires the path closed by servants to be opened. *"So do not give up hope of His mercy. Do not despair of His aid. What you must do is turn to God. God is enough for a true friend and protector"* (4:45) [sic].[535]

---

534. Mevlânâ Celâleddin Rûmî, trans. Veled İzbudak, ed. Abdülbaki Gölpınarlı, *Mesnevî* (Istanbul: Milli Eğitim Basımevi 1991), vol. 6, vs. 1871-1874.

535. Ahmed Er-Rifâî, trans. Yaman Arıkan, *Hak Yolcusunun Düsturları* (Istanbul: Erkam Yayınları 1985), p. 96.

45. When they are told, "Fear what is before you and what is behind you, that you may receive mercy."

Wa 'idhā qīla lahum'uttaqū mā bayna 'aydikum wa mā khalfakum la'allakum turḥamūn.

- **The Bursevi Commentary:** As a warning to "them," the Meccan deniers [of Muhammed's mission], "Beware of your past and your future!" In other words, beware of the torment that descended upon communities of the past who considered their messengers to be liars; beware of the similar torment you will suffer if you do not believe, and of the torment prepared for you in the Hereafter after you are destroyed.

Or it has the following meaning: "Beware of the conditions in the Hereafter that lie before you and act accordingly; beware of the world you have left behind you and do not be fooled by it." Thus God the Exalted has frightened the deniers with two things; firstly the disasters that befell communities of the past, and secondly the torment of the Hereafter.

"That you many receive mercy." Do thus hoping that you will receive mercy, or that by receiving mercy you may be delivered from that evil condition, for such deliverance is only possible thanks to God's mercy—"when they are told..." they turn away their faces, imagine something greater and resist. The following gracious verse emphasizes the situation.[536]

- **The Kashani Commentary:** Like you, your ancestors before you turned away from God the Truth and from accepting God the Truth when it was said, "Beware of the greatest Resurrection before you

---

536. İsmâil Hakkı Bursevî, *Rûh'l-Beyan Tefsîri* (Istanbul: Damla Yayınevi 2004), vol. 7, pp. 65-66.

and the littlest Resurrection behind you, so that you may receive mercy." Because the first is with regard to annihilation and God, and the second is with regard to liberation and avoiding the life of the body and the self, (*what is before you*) has been interpreted anagogically as the greatest Resurrection (*and what is behind you*) as the littlest Resurrection. The first of the two cries mentioned in these verses, because of the occurrence of the beginning and the sudden expulsion of all faculties from their local resting place, produces the awakening by the first blast of the trumpet. The second produces the second blast of the trumpet with the occurrence of the cry and the sudden awakening of faculties and their spreading from their localities. The corpses are the bodies that are their graves.[537]

- Avoidance is the result of fear. The person who avoids a thing and takes precautions against it will not be harmed by that thing. Most of the disasters that befall people come from things they are sure of. People generally meet disaster from a thing they believe to be safe for them. Thus a person possessed of intellect must not be sure of things other than those made safe for them. For God's word, which is not in vain from before or behind, is true and God speaks the truth. Thus this is a warning. Even if the measuring out is favorable, the precaution taken is beneficial. For it has been said, "much avoidance will not save one from the measuring out." But for that avoidance to be part of the measuring out is another matter. In that case precaution and avoidance saves one from disaster.

The ultimate degree of avoidance is within the avoidance of avoidance, making of it a support. One sign of God's mercy toward us is that He makes us beware of Him. There can be no clearer or more emphasized avoidance than this. God the Exalted says, *"God warns you to beware of Himself, and God is kind to His servants"* (3:30).

The journey of avoidance takes people from the material to the intellectual, from boons to torments, from secrecy to clarity, from mortality to continuance in becoming and life that is the result of our knowledge about the world. This gives birth to knowing human

---

537. Kemâlüddin Abdürrezzâk Kâşânîyyü's-Semerkandî, trans. AliRıza Doksanyedi, ed. M. Vehbi Güloğlu, *Te'vilât-ı-Kâşâniyye* (Ankara: Kadıoğlu Matbaası 1988), vol. 3, p. 14.

becoming, it teaches from whence the human being issues with regard to physicality. If one knows both, it is without doubt with regard to nature. In addition, one knows also all stations requiring its increase and refinement towards others. One becomes possessed of vision in everything one sees and encounters.[538]

- If God did not exist, station would not be known. Nor would there be any before or behind. For we came to be with God. We were called to Him and returned to Him. "*Behold, all affairs return to God* (42:53)." When God placed me in the station of fear, I became afraid to look at my shadow, I worry that it will become a veil separating me from God. What is true for the shadow is true for everything, for even if a person be given the good news of happiness, the world is not a secure place.[539]

- **Imperative Mercy (*rahmetü'l-vücûbiyye*):** The mercy special to those possessed of piety and goodness.
  God has made it obligatory not because He is forced to but because He will be merciful to them by His generosity and goodness/beauty. The verse, "*My mercy encompasses all things,*" indicates the mercy of broad security. "*I shall prescribe it for those who practice piety,*" (7:156) indicates imperative mercy, as does the verse, "*My mercy is near to those possessed of goodness*" (7:56) [sic].[540]

- When in the language of our messenger it was said to those resisting in the desert of error, "Do not throw off the collar of servanthood, do not leave the high road of safety leading to the summit of unification for a dead end, beware of the catastrophes before you and behind you, consider God the Truth that you may receive mercy," they ridiculed him and turned away.[541]

---

538. Muhyiddîn İbnü'l-Arabî, trans. Vahdettin İnce, *Risâleler* (Istanbul: Kitsan Yayınları n.d.), vol. 3, pp. 315-317.
539. Muhyiddîn İbnü'l-Arabî, trans. Vahdettin İnce, *Risâleler* (Istanbul: Kitsan Yayınları n.d.), vol. 3, p. 313.
540. Kemâlüddin Abdürrezzâk Kâşânîyyü's-Semerkandî, trans. AliRıza Doksanyedi, ed. M. Vehbi Güloğlu, *Te'vilât-ı-Kâşâniyye* (Ankara: Kadıoğlu Matbaası 1988), vol. 3, p. 264.
541. Şemseddin Yeşil, *Füyûzat* (Istanbul: Ş. Yeşil Yayınları 1984), vol. 6, p. 251.

- With your interior you must be on the side of bringing together (*cem'*), and with your exterior on the side of separation. Unity should not be veiled from plurality nor plurality from unity, you must reconcile servanthood and gnosis so that you may escape danger.

- In the language of the Sufis, the meanings of *cem'* (*to view God without creation*), *tefrika* (*separation*), and *cem'ul'l-cem* (*for travellers to see neither their selves nor creation, to see only the sultan of truth*) are the following: *Tefrika* (*separation, to be in the state of distinguishing creation and God the Truth*) is what is attributed in relation to you; *Cem'* is what is divested and taken from you. This means that the actions performed by servants according to their duties of servanthood, their creaturely requirements, are *tefrika*. The meanings, graces and boons that come to them from God are *cem'*. Both are necessary for the servant, because a person without *tefrika* cannot have servanthood. For the servants to say, "We worship only you," is proof of *tefrika* insofar as it demonstrates their servanthood. For them to say, "We seek aid only from you," is to request *cem'*. *Tefrika* is the beginning of will, and *cem'* is its end. *Cem'ul'l-cem* is a more perfect and higher station. *Cem'* is to see the things together with God and to know that capacity and power belong to God. *Cem'ul'l-cem* is to be completely destroyed and find that everything other than God passes away, which is the level oneness. You must work and struggle. Where and at whatever time, eating, drinking, speaking, remaining silent, coming and going, in action and stillness, every moment you must not be empty of Him. That is why it has been said, "The Sufi must be the son of the moment." In other words, you must not waste time, you must not lose the present moment feeling sorry about the past or worrying for the future. For to worry about the future is greed. You must spend your time in turning toward what is necessary for you at the time, in purifying the heart and in reflection.[542]

- If people think constantly of their past mistakes and feel crushed under the weight of their former sins, it means that they have not yet got free of being (*vücût*).

---

542. Niyâzî Mısrî, trans. Süleyman Ateş, *İrfan Sofraları* (Istanbul: Yeni Ufuklar Neşriyatı n.d.), pp. 122-123.

45th Verse

To mourn over the past, or think on future material or spiritual accounts, is to lose time on the path leading to God. Travelers on the path of unity are those who have dedicated themselves to God without any doubt whatsoever. They have risen so far above taking account of past and future that they repent even of repentance.

That is why Hazret Umar felt it necessary to give the old minstrel advice. He said: "This weeping of yours shows that you are still awake to anxieties of the world and the body (*vücût*) and that you are not freed from its calculations and anxieties. For those who attain the spiritual level of annihilation there is no longer any past or future, fear or mourning." Umar continued: "The path you have taken is not the infallible path to annihilation. On that path one must be free of worldly and bodily attractions and even concern for sin. As our Prophet said, 'The body is such a sin that no other sin can be compared with it.' In short, it takes awareness to remember the past. Past and future are a veil separating the servant from God. In fact the arrived couldn't care less about the past and future, they care only for God.

"Set both past and future afire, let them burn to ashes. What use is there in being knotted with the past and future like a reed? If the flute made of reed has knots stopping it up, it can't share a lip's secrets. It won't produce a sound when it is blown. These knots are veils inside the reed. If you think of the human body as a flute, the veils inside it are anxieties about the past and future and the ties binding it to time and space, in short worldly desires and connections. As long as the body is veiled like a reed, the spirit cannot find the way to get free of these veils and take wing to divine mysteries.

"If you continually think about your own body, virtually circumambulating it, how will you circumambulate God? The person struggling on the path of seeking God will abandon everything but that goal, especially his own self. For a spirit that has earned the human level, that is the one condition for being annihilated in God.

"As long as a person is bound by the limitations of the soul, as long as he thinks constantly of his own being, his own works, his pleasures and even good deeds, and does not get free of selfhood (*benlik*) and duality, he is like a person preoccupied with thinking about the insufficiencies of his own house while circumambulating the Kaaba.

"Those who circumambulate the Kaaba remove their usual clothes and put on the plain white ihram. In the same way, lovers must remove the clothes of body and soul and wear the ihram of annihilation in God so that their circumambulation of divine beauty and divine being may be acceptable."[543]

• When the heart abandons the love of worldly passions it becomes like crystal and sees before and behind itself.[544]

• If the heart becomes wholesome it becomes the site of the descent of revelation and secrets and lights and angels. If it is corrupt, it is the site of the descent of wrongdoing and devils. If the heart becomes wholesome, it tells you what is before and behind you and, teaching you important things, puts you on your guard; and if it is corrupt, it tells you useless things and causes your right judgment and happiness to disappear.[545]

• The people of Hell are divided into four groups. One of these is the group that like Pharaoh claim to be lord and, rejecting God's Lordliness, see themselves as great compared with God. Pharaoh said, *"O community! I know of no other god of yours but me."* And another time he said, *"I am your lord most high"* (79:24). Here he meant to say that there was no other god in the heavens but himself. Nimrod and the others were that way also.

The second group is those who set up others as partners to God. They accept other gods together with God and say, *"We worship them only so that they will bring us close to God."* And once they said, *" (The Messenger) makes the gods into one god. This is a strange thing to do."*

The third group is the atheists. They are those who reject god entirely. Thus they do not accept the existence of a god for the world or from the world.

The fourth group is the hypocrites. They are those among the aforementioned three groups who pretended to be Muslims because of the pressure upon them. Because of that pressure they feared for

---

543. Ken'an Rifâî, *Şerhli Mesnevî-i Şerif* (Istanbul: Kubbealtı Neşriyatı 2000), p. 319.
544. From Ken'an Rifâî's notes on Ahmet er-Rifâî, p. 58
545. From Ken'an Rifâî's notes on Ahmet er-Rifâî, p. 51.

their lives, their property and their descendants. They shared the beliefs of one of the three groups.

These four groups are the communities of jinn and humans who go to Hell and will not leave there. The reason their number is four is that the verse states that Satan will come to us from before us, behind us, from our right side and left. Satan comes to those who set up partners with God from in front of them. He comes to atheists from behind, to the arrogant from their right side, and to the hypocrites from their left. The left is the weakest side. For the hypocrites are the weakest of these groups. He comes to the arrogant from their right. The right is the place of strength. For the arrogant see themselves as great due to the strength they find in themselves. To those who set up partners to God he comes from the front, because the front is the direction of sight. Thus those who see accept the existence of God and do not reject Him. Satan ensures that they set up partners to God. He comes to atheists from behind them, because the rear is not the direction of looking. He says to them, *"There is nothing."* In other words, there is no such thing as god.[546]

---

546. Muhyiddîn İbnül'l-Arabî, trans. Ekrem Demirli, *Fütuhât-ı Mekkiyye* (Istanbul: Litera Yayıncılık 2006), vol. 2, pp. 412-413.

46. No sign came to them from the signs of their Lord but they turned away from it.

Wa mā ta'tīhim min 'āyatin min 'āyātin rabbihim 'illā kānū 'anhā mu'riḍīn.

• Never is a sign of the signs of their Lord revealed to those who declare Our wisdom and justice, and announce Our power and might belongs to them, but they turn away, denying and ridiculing it. Whatever of our signs has been revealed to them, surely they have turned away.[547]

• *Because speaking is in order to accept*
Idolatry's spirit of God's faith is quit

Partitioned among the stuff of the heavens
A spirit is shared among sixty passions

Thus silence is best, it gives it constancy
Thus silence the answer given fools will be[548]

• If you tell believing Muslims that God says thus, the Messenger of God says thus, they immediately accept. But you cannot oppose with Quranic verses or hadiths those who in their own opinion suppose themselves to be knowledgeable, scholars and familiar with truth and who pursue fantasies.[549]

---

547. Şemseddin Yeşil, *Füyûzat* (Istanbul: Ş. Yeşil Yayınları 1984), vol. 6, p. 251.
548. Mevlânâ Celâleddin Rûmî, trans. Veled İzbudak, ed. Abdülbaki Gölpınarlı, *Mesnevî* (Istanbul: Milli Eğitim Basımevi 1991), vol. 4, vs. 3295-3297.
549. Ken'an Rifâî, *Sohbetler* (Istanbul: Kubbealtı Neşriyatı 2000), p. 522.

- Do you not know Jesus (a.s.)? The Jews at first believed in him because they thought he certainly would not add anything to the sacred law of Moses, but when Jesus (a.s.), as a messenger, began to add certain judgments to the sacred law of Moses or changed some judgments, they could not bear with him. Because it seemed contrary to their belief. That is why they wanted to kill Jesus.

  There are judgments brought by the prophets who came prior to Hazret Muhammed (s.a.s.) that continue today. By keeping those judgments in place, we conform not to the sacred laws of messengers who came prior to our Messenger but only because our Messenger accepted them, we conformed to our Messenger's sacred law.[550]

- When you are asked of your belief, who will protect you from His torment, who will rescue you from the flames of His fire? For with that belief of yours you have, by abrogating and denying the divine sovereignty, attributed powerlessness to divine power. Not knowing divine wisdom, you have not considered the Lordly signs. You have even tried to ridicule them. Just as you do not believe in the Unseen, you have tried to deny what your knowledge cannot comprehend. With your faulty knowledge and skewed thinking you have tried to be aware of the truth of things.

  "They deny things knowledge of which they cannot comprehend, even before their interpretation has reached them. So did those before them deny" (10:39).

  Your eyes are veiled by material things and you are heedless of the creator of material things. Likewise there are those who try to deny, when they see material things, that there is being added to them. Such people deny the invisible true being that appears thanks to the colors and forms of material things apparent through His being, because they know nothing of the "Light" that is the cause of being. They cannot comprehend that it is hidden from the eyes of those looking because of the violence of manifestation of invisibility among material things, because of the excess of light.

  Do they not see that the difference between bodies, which appears through the manifestation of Light, becomes invisible when

---

550. Muhyiddîn İbnü'l-Arabî, trans. Nuri Gençosman, *Fusûs'l-Hikem* (Istanbul: İstanbul Kitabevi Yayınları 1981), pp. 154-155.

light is no longer present to the eye and darkness falls, and forms and colors are invisible? Just as their denials would not be possible if they could see that, their refutations too would not be possible.[551]

- If those possessed of the book believe in all the [holy] books, they will never go wrong. But those who believe in some books and reject others, they are true disbelievers.[552]

- If you want the intellect of your soul not to remain in uncertainty, do not stuff up your soul's ear with cotton wool of ignorance and heedlessness. So that you may understand the riddles of God the Truth, His hidden and open secrets! What is revelation? Words the five senses will not be able to attain![553]

- The signs and works on the horizon (*the world of existence outside of the human soul seen with the eye*) are for the purpose of knowing and showing what is inside a person. However many signs and works there are self-disclosed by God the Truth in the world, they are all gathered within the human soul.[554]

- Whatever is visible is all the mirror of signs. They must all be viewed every moment with purity and sincerity, in other words, with the gaze of God the Truth.[555]

- Those who turn away from God the Truth and busy themselves with other than Him have turned toward the concerns of the world. Some kinds of darkness are more oppressive than others. The face turned toward worldly concerns has turned away from God and is as distorted as the degree to which it has turned away. If the turning away of the face is just as much as the blink of an eye, the eye will be

---

551. Ahmed er-Rifâî, ed. Dr. H. Kâmil Yılmaz, *Marifet Yolu* (Istanbul: Erkam Yayıncılık 1995), pp. 171-172.
552. Muhyiddîn İbnü'l-Arabî, trans. Vahdettin İnce, *Risâleler* (Istanbul: Kitsan Yayınları n.d.), vol. 1, p. 45.
553. Ken'an Rifâî, *Şerhli Mesnevî-i Şerif* (Istanbul: Kubbealtı Neşriyatı 2000), p. 198.
554. Ken'an Rifâî, *Sohbetler* (Istanbul: Kubbealtı Neşriyatı 2000), p. 82.
555. Ken'an Rifâî, *Sohbetler* (Istanbul: Kubbealtı Neşriyatı 2000), p. 651.

light brown. If it is longer, the person will be cross-eyed. If it is done as a favor to someone, the chin will be twisted. If a person turns their face away and it takes longer for them to turn back, their chin will turn as if they are running backwards and their book of deeds will be of things given from behind. They are those who forget God. God forgets them also, and makes them forget themselves.

In the time of Hazret Moses a man came to him and said, "O Moses, I do nothing of the things you say and yet my property increases day by day, my children are healthy and I am a person respected and influential person in the city. Tell me what your God will say to that?"

Hazret Moses refrained from saying these sentences to God out of good manners. God said to Hazret Moses, "O Moses! Tell that servant of mine that I am God Allmighty, and I have taken from his mouth the authority to repeat my name. Can there be any greater punishment than this?"

Although there appear to be many houses, in fact there are only two: One is the house of knowledge, in other words, the soul, and one is the house of secrets. Whoever has neither, his or her house is ruined.

...

A person is obliged to use the remembrance belonging to God, in other words, the Quran. Look to the language in which a person reads the Quran. For peace of mind and stability come down with the Quran, but according to the language. (...)

People must look to their spirit; how did it turn toward the city of the body? Let them observe how it entered in order to help with such things as the wisdom and beautiful order God placed in the city of the body. For the human being possesses the most beautiful creation. When you begin to examine this event, go deeply into it, leaving out no single corner that has not entered into human beings, no single secret that they do not know. For the human being is God's treasury. You stand upon a great knowledge: *"We will show them Our signs on the horizons and within their souls until it becomes clear to them that it is the truth"* (41:53). *"And within your own souls. Do you not see? (51:21).*

"He who knows his self, knows his Lord." Those who know themselves best know their Lord best. (...)

The character of property is action; it is in a state of constant change. Do you want proof of this? Bring your ear near to a locked

46th Verse

chest; you will hear the things moving inside the chest. For you may feel the need to accumulate and store any kind of property. The key is your tongue; understand.

Those who are stingy are stingy only with their own selves. Thus it has been said, *"If you turn away from Him, he will substitute a people other than you in your stead. Then they will not be like you"* (47:38).[556]

---

556. Muhyiddîn İbnü'l-Arabî, trans. Vahdettin İnce, *Risâleler* (Istanbul: Kitsan Yayınları n.d.), vol. 2, pp. 236-238.

47. And when they are told, "Spend of that which God has provided for you," those who disbelieve say to those who have faith: "Shall we feed those whom God would have fed if He wished? You are in manifest error, nothing more."

Wa 'idha qīla lahum 'anfiqū mimmā razaqakumu'llahu qāla'lladhīna kafarū lilladhīna 'āmanū 'anuṭ'imu man law yashā'u'llahu 'aṭ'amahu 'in 'antum 'illā fī ḍalālin mubīn.

• When it was said to those who deny the divine verses, "Maintain others with the things that God has provided for you, spend in good works, use the divine boons as the should be used," (help the poor), aid them, so that you will prepare a good station for yourselves in the Hereafter, those disbelievers ridiculed the Muslims and said, "The God you believe in, have faith in, will make them poor and we will look after them, is that so? Shall we feed the people He will feed? If He had wished, he would have provided food for them. You stand in opposition to God's desire and will; thus if you are not in manifest error, what are you?"[557]

• It is incumbent upon those who have more property than they need to give to wholesome poor people, in the amount required by the sheriat. Thus the zakat of the rich is to give to the poor, give of their possessin, and the zakat of the poor is to erase from their hearts hope and trust of the rich, in other words, to not expect them to give. The zakat of lovers is to expend their lives for the sake of the beloved, to spend freely of their spirits for the love of God, to give, always to give. The zakat of gnostics is to give of their states and their knowledge, their gnosis, to those who deserve it, those who ask for it, who

---

557. Şemseddin Yeşil, *Füyûzat* (Istanbul: Ş. Yeşil Yayınları 1984), vol. 6, p. 252.

seek it, to practice friendship and provide sustenance from their own states to lovers. The zakat of knowledge is to teach those who seek teaching. The zakat of offspring is to give to orphans, the zakat of homes is to entertain and honor guests, the zakat of conversation is to avoid gossip; the zakat of the strong is to help the weak, the zakat of the soul is to get rid of bad characteristics. God the Truth says, "*Successful are those who give the zakat*" (23:1-4) [sic].

Hazret Mevlana says, "What is worthy of those who are generous is to give money and property. For lovers it is to give one's life." In sum, what is necessary is to spend freely, to expend, in the way of God the thing most fitting for the person—knowledge, property, or being.[558]

- God is the author of every act. However, God has given us the power to distinguish between the good and evil of what we do and will do. The great proof of this truth is that we are able to entreat God, sometimes blushing in shame, "O my God! Show us the right way!" and ask for the good, the right, and the beautiful from the One who created us.

For if we had no power and no free will, how could we entreat God to bestow upon us the best of acts and actions, how would it even occur to us to do such a thing?

Considering that animals, who have spirits as we do, do not think to be shamed of their actions either before God the Truth or before the creatures, since they do not even know of doing so, how can we be heedless of the partial free will given to us, the power by which we distinguish between good and evil?

To suppose that there is no free will is to think that humans are lifeless matter and to misunderstand divine domination (*cebir*) to such a degree as to pervert understanding.

A human is human to the extent that he is able to be the gnostic of such power coming to him from God the Truth.

First of all you will know the level of God's greatness and power. Then, you will understand the worth of the value He has given you by bringing you to the human level.

---

558. Ken'an Rifâî, *Sohbetler* (Istanbul: Kubbealtı Neşriyatı 2000), pp. 472-473.

47th Verse

You are not a captive in the prison of God the Truth's will. You must realize that you have divine freedom, given to you so that you may enjoy peace of heart and mind as free people do.[559]

• Fatalism[560] (*to deny the partial intellect*) is to fall asleep among thieves and abandon work and combat and conform to the soul, bending one's neck to its voice. But like the flight of a chick whose wings have not yet grown, that will end in a painful fall.

Do not forget that a head is a head to the extent that it has an intellect and can use that intellect. When a head has lost the ability to use its intellect, how is it different from a tail?

Know that you are charged with the duty of expressing gratitude toward God! So work, struggle, and trust in God! Don't forget that in this way you will have such a protector and forgiver as God![561]

• Wherever you look with the gaze of truth, you will not be able to see anything but oneness. The entire realm of plurality consists of signs, each one created in order to perform its task. Power, force, acts, capacities, every thing is from God. (*Nor power nor strength but in God, the Sublime, the Tremendous*).

But here one must try not to abandon a moderate fatalism. If we go to pure fatalism the order of the world will be upset and people of that opinion will fall into error and lose their way.

A man by chance went into a garden, climbed a date palm and began to eat dates. The owner of the garden noticed this and, coming under the tree, asked him what he was doing there. The man, unperturbed, said, "I am eating God's dates from God's date palm from God's garden!" The owner said, "Good appetite, go on and eat, my brother," then went to get a rope and a whip, tied the man to the date palm and began beating him. When the man began to shout and scream in pain, the owner said, "I have tied you with God's rope, and I am bringing down the whip He tells me strike wherever it may land on you."

---

559. Ken'an Rifâî, *Şerhli Mesnevî-i Şerif* (Istanbul: Kubbealtı Neşriyatı 2000), pp. 92-94.

560. [Here the term *cebir*, "domination," is used in the sense of "fatalism."]

561. Ken'an Rifâî, *Şerhli Mesnevî-i Şerif* (Istanbul: Kubbealtı Neşriyatı 2000), p. 129.

According to the view of the people of the Messenger's path and community, in moderate fatalism there is partial will, by which the order of the world is possible through being able to apply to life the point of understanding that preserves the delicate relationship between effort and acceptance of fate.[562]

• Gratitude is to suck the teat of divine boons. However full of milk the teat may be, it will not come out; in other words, one must suck it.[563]

• Our Messenger Efendi said, *"Merciful God has mercy on those who suffer. Have mercy on those on the face of the earth. In this way those in the heavens will have mercy on you."* This noble hadtih commands us to have mercy on those on the face of the earth. For that is how God's mercy comes to the servants. The compassion felt by those in the heavens reaches the servants in that way. The sky is the location of divine mercy's descent. And it is the spring of Merciful God's grace and blessing. It is the station of the angels. Those angels convey secrets between God and His servants. God the Exalted has appointed them that way. He does His works by means of them. If God's mercy is placed in the interior of the angel of livelihood, its shares come in plenty to the servants. If the secret of mercy is given to the heart of the angel that travels with a person always, its aid to the servant is much. It is compassionate and spares the servant from all evils. Those possessed of gnosis are their Lords that hearts long for. That is why they are the sites of manifestation for God's mercy. That is how they are among servants. God is the Glorified and His mercy is greater than anyone's. He has mercy on His servants and rains His mercy upon them. The day my son reaches the rank of mercy for servants is the day he attains to God's mercy. The moment he enters the gathering of the people of gnosis let him know he has arrived at salvation. When you ask something of persons possessed of wisdom, believe that you will perfectly receive the answer to your question.[564]

---

562. Ken'an Rifâî, *Sohbetler* (Istanbul: Kubbealtı Neşriyatı 2000), p. 479.

563. Mevlânâ Celâleddîn Rumî, trans. Meliha Ülker Anbarcıoğlu, *Fîhi Mâ Fîh* (Istanbul: Milli Eğitim Basımevi 1985), p. 164.

564. Ahmed er-Rifâî, trans. Abdülkâdir Akçiçek, *Onların Âlemi* (Istanbul: Bahar Yayınları 1996), p. 166.

47th Verse

- "O People of Iraq! I swear by God that this heedlessness has spread to cover you all, universally. Pay attention, be awake. O common folk and elite, warn and call one another to wakefullness. Efendis! Enough of this luxury, comfort, excess and expenditure. Enough of this sleep. Alas for us. For we do not know what all will await us behind this curtain of secrecy and obscurity.[565]

- What brings a person closer to God is God's compassion for His creatures. God and His angels, those on earth and in the sky, the ants in their cells and the fish in the sea all bless and pray for the good of those who teach people goodness. For it is said in the noble hadith, *"All creatures are God's family, His children. The servants considered good by God are those who are of benefit to their families."*[566]

- Charity is certainly not to sacrifice from one's purse. Every goodness done in the name of God is charity. It is also charity to do good with one's tongue, to encourage people to goodness. Just as it is also charity to serve and aid others with one's body.[567]

---

[565]. Ahmed er-Rifâî, trans. Dr. Ali Can Tatlı, *Sohbet Meclisleri* (Istanbul: Erkam Yayınları 1996), p. 186.
[566]. Ken'an Rifâî, *Sohbetler* (Istanbul: Kubbealtı Neşriyatı 2000), p. 312.
[567]. Ken'an Rifâî, *Sohbetler* (Istanbul: Kubbealtı Neşriyatı 2000), p. 596.

48. And they say, "When will this promise come to pass, if you be truthful?"

Wa yaqūlūna matā hādhā'l waʿdu 'in kuntum ṣādiqīn.

- And they were saying, sneering and mocking, "If the promised day and that court of punishment, is true, when will the raising of the dead and that being brought into presence occur?"[568]

- Where are the things you call the Gathering on the Day of Judgment, the great court, the Hereafter and the spiritual realm? Morality and principles of conscience have been announced in all religions as the unavoidable duty of servanthood. And the reality of calling to account against those who do not conform has been explained as the divine rule. Most people have avoided those disciplined moral principles and have wanted to pretend not to see the existence of God. They have always asked for miracles from prophets and messengers and those who tried to tell society of the truth in this way; they have insisted that they show the proof of the event of Resurrection. Yet all throughout the history of religions they have rebelled and rejected the clear, evident miracles prophets have shown. For example, the Jews who clearly saw Moses's staff later worship the Samaritan calf. Hazret Jesus raised the boy from the dead, but those who saw that signed his death warrant (*Marcus of the Roman jury*). Whereas to ask for proof of Resurrection is completely in vain. Resurrection will only be manifest when its hour arrives. As for asking proof of the spiritual, the spiritual is a system intuited and recognized by the heart. It is not possible to make people whose hearts are hardened and void of compassion see.[569]

---

[568]. Şemseddin Yeşil, *Füyûzat* (Istanbul: Ş. Yeşil Yayınları 1984), vol. 6, p. 252.
[569]. Halûk Nurbaki, *Yâ-Sîn Sûresi Yorumu* (Istanbul: Damla Yayınevi 1999), pp. 71-72.

- When Moses first started, all his effort and desire consisted of vision (*of God*). And that is why he spoke of it. Thus God the exalted says that he said, "Show Yourself to me, let me see You!" This phrase is a delerium manifested from not being able to obtain and find what he sought. But our Messenger was the last and he was possessed of stability. When he reached the station of personal effort, his effort was annihilated and he said, "I cannot count your praises." (While Hazret Moses asked God for the vision, Hazret Messenger spoke of how he was powerless to praise God. For that rapture was in this station of stability).[570]

- Your being is like a sack; what resembles your exteriority, however, is not a sack but the wheat inside it. As long as that wheat does not become flour, the benefit expected from it has not been produced, and as long as that flour does not become dough, it is good for nothing. As long as the bread is not eaten, there can be no strength in it for the intellect and spirit. And just as intellect and spirit cannot be saved from danger if the bread is not destroyed in the body, they will not be saved as long as they are not annihilated in God the Truth. Evidently "ascension" occurs by changing thus from state to state. Semen becomes a clot of blood, then aquires a form, and this form accepts the spirit. The same is true for fairies. Plants and animals, all things are pass from state to state. They die in the first state, and come to life in the second. Everything is thus and in this manner. Without death, there is no life; when something lower dies in you, another thing higher will certainly come to be. For example, childhood dies, then in its stead youth comes to be, ignorance dies, and knowledge comes to be. Seed is annihilated in the earth and a tree emerges. Life is in death, being is in not-being. This law encompasses and rules all things. See the ass who objects, "How can there be death before death?" That itself is the very same. Considering that you struggle day and night with the same thing in the same state, when another speaks to you of that, and it seems impossible to you, if this action of yours is not misbelief, what is it? For example, when it is said that of the bridge of the straight path that it is narrower

---

570. Hucviri, ed. Süleyman Uludağ, *Keşfu'l-Mahcûb Hakikat Bilgisi* (Istanbul: Dergah Yayınları 1996), pp. 228-229.

48th Verse

than a hair and everyone crosses it, that seems impossible; but you are crossing a bridge narrower than that, which is your thought. Of Paradise you say, "It is neither on earth nor in the sky; seeing that it is neither on earth nor in the sky, where is it?" Although you feel in your body a definite pleasantness and unpleasantness, you cannot ascertain where; you know that these occur in your body, but you are powerless to ascertain where. Paradise and Hell are exactly like that. Although you cannot see their locations, they exist. A fool is someone who is in a state night and day, and when this is mentioned to him or her, finds it impossible. Thus from that point of view, such a person is the same as an ass and does not know what they are.[571]

- It is said that to seek explication of the obvious is a loss. God the Exalted is more evident, more manifest and more visible than the sun. Whoever seeks proof and a witness of the sun's being is plunged in loss and blind from birth. There is no recourse or cure for that person's affliction and illness. That person is an absolute animal, and perhaps lower that an animal and even than inanimate things. For soil, which is inanimate, accomplishes whatever it has been created to do. Earth was created for plants to grow from it. It will nurture and propagate whatever you plant in it and entrust to it. It returns ten, maybe a hundred seeds for one. If you plant barley it gives barely, if wheat, then wheat, if fruit, then fruit, if grapes, then grapes. In the same way animals were created to carry burdens and human beings, to convey them to their goal and take them from city to city.[572]

---

571. Sultan Veled, trans. Meliha Anbarcıoğlu, *Maarif* (Konya: Altunarı Ofset 2002), p. 202.

572. Sultan Veled, trans. Meliha Anbarcıoğlu, *Maarif* (Konya: Altunarı Ofset 2002), p. 39.

49. They wait for nothing but a single cry; it will take them while they argue amongst themselves.

Mā yanẓurūna 'illā ṣayḥatan wāḥidatan ta'khudhuhum wa hum yakhiṣṣimūn.

• Unfortunates! Poor wretches who have taken no warning from this self-disclosure kneaded by power! The blind who do not every moment see God's power to condemn and create! What they await (*is a command!*). They await a cry, nothing else. (*They await the first blast of the trumpet*). That is such a cry that while they quarrel with one another, while they arrange agreements and transactions, the terror of that cry will suddenly overwhelm and capture them.[573]

• O Humankind, as long as you live what you fear most is to become naught and you tremble with that fear. But know this, even not-being fears God.

Why do you embrace worldly position, station and wealth? Why do you hold onto things you suppose to be secure, like property and wealth? Is it not from that same fear of becoming naught? For you to so embrace the world that you will anyway one day abandon is an agony of which you are not aware.

The lovers of God are the only ones who escape this agony that invisibly encircles all human beings. Because they do not hold onto the world and wish only to be annihilated in God, they happily abandon all that they own.

Everything other than the love of God, be it the boons of both worlds, is nothing but the agony of death.

Those who look with eyes full of fear upon the earth which will one day clasp their fragile bodies to its breast are blind, deprived of

---

[573]. Şemseddin Yeşil, *Füyûzat* (Istanbul: Ş. Yeşil Yayınları 1984), vol. 6, p. 252.

the ability to see the truth. If they could see, they would see the love of God, which is the Water of Eternal Life their spirits have longed for since eternity without beginning.

You who kill time sowing seeds of heedlessness in the earth dark as night, if you do not have enough strength to lift your head from empty things and the sleep of heedlessness, it is because you incline overmuch to earth.[574]

• Messenger Salih said to the Tribe of Thamud: "You have followed your own envy and killed an innocent camel. God will ask you to account for this, and in three days will deliver unto you His great punishment. On the first day signs of the punishment will appear and all of your faces will change color. You will see each other's faces in different colors. First your faces will become yellow like saffron, then on the second day red like the flowers of the argawan tree, and on the third day black as ebony.

But there was nothing left for the Thamud tribe to do. They waited in profound fear for the signs of the first day and indeed on that day they saw each other's faces turn yellow like saffron.

On the second day the color was red.

On the third day the faces of the people of the Thamud tribe were now black. They no longer appeared human and their behavior was not human. Then they came to their knees.

And as it says in the seventh chapter of the Quran, Gabriel the Trusted brought this verse to Hazret Muhammed: "So the earthquake took them unawares, and in the morning they crouched kneeling in their houses."

But for the Thamud tribe there was nothing left to be done. They waited for God's wrath and final self-disclosure. This punishment came right on time and an earthquake brought the underside of the earth to the surface. Black-faced, on their knees, all creatures were buried under the earth in an instant.[575]

• There was going to be a great storm. The wind went into action by God's command to destroy the Âd tribe, which had strayed from

---

574. Ken'an Rifâî, *Şerhli Mesnevî-i Şerif* (Istanbul: Kubbealtı Neşriyatı 2000), p. 544.

575. Ken'an Rifâî, *Şerhli Mesnevî-i Şerif* (Istanbul: Kubbealtı Neşriyatı 2000), pp. 369-370.

49th Verse

the path of God and run riot. Messenger Hûd gathered those from the tribe who believed in him and in the religion of God the Truth which he had shown them. He drew a circle around them with his staff. The terrifying wind tore to pieces whomever it found outside that circle, but inside the circle blew cool and soft as an eastern breeze.

The true people of God, like those sheep entrusted to God or the believers protected by the line Hûd drew around them, are safe from the harm caused by wolves of greed and storms of soul. As long as they stay far from worldly filth and worldly ambitions, no wolf's paw can snatch and no storm can blow away the gem of humanity from within them.

Even the wind of death gives them a new life, like the scent of Joseph which reached Jacob.

Even the fire of lust cannot burn them, just as fire could not burn Abraham. But the same lust does not hesitate to produce wolf's paws and terrifying winds and thrust the disbelievers into the depths of the earth.

That is why the same sea let the people of Messenger Moses pass while destroying Pharaoh and his army.

Think of the command that thrust Qarun into the depths of the earth with his throne and his treasure! Just as water and clay were transformed into a bird of paradise when the breath of Jesus touched them, with the breath of God's affection, love and knowledge of reality, the human body made of clay and water escapes its materiality and takes wing to God.[576]

---

[576]. Ken'an Rifâî, *Şerhli Mesnevî-i Şerif* (Istanbul: Kubbealtı Neşriyatı 2000), pp. 119-120.

50. And then they will be able to make no bequest, and they will not return to their people.

Falā yastaṭi'ūna tawṣiyatan wa lā 'ilā 'ahlihim yarji'ūn.

51. And the trumpet will be blown and then, behold, they will rush from the graves to their Lord.

Wa nufikha fī'ṣṣūri fa'idhā hum min al-'ajdāthi 'illā rabbihim yansilūn.

• "They are shown to one another (but concerned with themselves). The guilty will wish to be ransomed from the punishment of that day by his children, his spouse, his brother, his nearest kin who sheltered him and all who are on earth, to save himself. But no, indeed it is the fire of Hell" (70:11-16).

To become erect (*kıyâm*) is the opposite of to sit; it is to get up. The Day of Resurrection (*kıyâmet*) means the day of being revived to life. On that day human beings will stand up before the Alive and Ever-Standing (*God*) (*kayyûm*).

Ibn Arabi distinguishes between two resurrections, the lesser resurrection and the greater resurrection. The greater resurrection is the general resurrection when all human beings will be revived to life again (*yeniden dirilicekleri*). It is the day of the greatest Gathering. Two things are called the lesser resurrection; the first is a person's death, because when a person dies it means that his or her personal resurrection in the life of the grave is realized. The second is what followers of the path see in their visions and the resurrection that gives an example of the life of the Hereafter.

The greater resurrection, the Great Gathering:

God created two resurrections in the universe, the lesser resurrection and the greater resurrection. The Lesser Resurrection is the transfer of the servant in a body in the Realm of Imagination from the life of the world to the Barzakh.[577] The Greater Resurrection is the greatest Gathering and Revival to Life (Diriliş) for which human beings will be gathered. Here is the day when acts will be presented to the servant without any debate.

The lesser resurrection, the servant's death and the example of the life of the Hereafter:

"Worship your Lord until there comes to you certainty" (15:99). The coming of certainty is realized by seeing these things in visions. That is what the lesser resurrection means.[578]

- *When Abraham died, his spirit arrived at God's gate. God the Exalted asked him:*

"O you who are most fortunate of all creatures, what did you find most difficult in the world?"

Abraham said, "It was hard to slay my son; it was hard to see my father in Hell;

Being thrown into the fire, to live a life of trials,

Was very hard, very difficult, but all that was nothing compared to dying."

God the Exalted adressed him thus: "Although it was torment to die, there are a great many difficulties beyond measure after death.

If a person encounters those difficulties, dying will seem like contentment and ease."

Since you have fallen into such a difficulty, why do you spend your days and nights in heedlessness?

Find the recourse for that difficulty, the road is long; first prepare a mansion for yourself.

Abandon the world and prepare for death; the road has been established upon death, look to your provisions.

While long life is the best thing, do not spend it on the world, which is the worst thing; do not drift into the game of the world.

O you who sell spirit for just a barley grain of the world's gold, they sold Joseph too as cheaply.

---

577. [Defined above in this text as the Realm of Sovereignty.]

578. Suad el-Hakîm, trans. Ekrem Demirli, *İbü'l-Arabî Sözlüğü* (Istanbul: Kabalcı Yayınevi 2005), pp. 434-435.

50th-51st Verse

You bought Joseph that cheaply, you chose him and accepted him with all your heart and soul.

He who makes the Joseph of spirit his sultan will give even his life to buy him. The Joseph of spirit is very dear, son. What is there better than Joseph?

The blind cannot know Joseph's value; no heart but the passionate heart can burn and melt.[579]

- Remember these verses of the Gracious Quran: "Then no intercession of intercessors will profit them. So what is the matter with them that they turn away from admonition, as if they were frightened asses fleeing a lion? ...Nay, this is surely an admonition" (74:48-51, 54).

So, it is a sin to kill an ass as long as it works in service of human beings. But if an animate being is both an ass and becomes wild, its blood is lawful.

You may ask what sin it is for an ass to behave that way at first, since it has no intellect, no knowledge or insight to free it from wildness. But God did not make it a sin to kill the ass He did not give insight to, on the contrary, He made it permitted.

So, O sublime beloved! O friend! If a human to whom intellect and insight have been given becomes wild like a mountain ass, a stranger to and uncultivated by the sacred words which blow like breath from the divine breezes of the prophets and friends, why and how should God forgive him?[580]

- The life of the world takes a person away from the life of the Hereafter. It is well known that those who turn away from preparing for true life regret it when they are separated from worldly life, and are deserving of the torments of Hell. They remember the admonitions made to them, but in vain... If only I had done something before for this life of mine, they say. None can torment as God torments on the day. None can bind as He binds. If only they'd known that the Hereafter is the home of life, they would have had the home of eternal life.[581]

---

579. Feridüddin Attar, trans. Yaşar Keçeci, *Mantıku't-Tayr* (Istanbul: Kırkambar Yayınlar 1998), s. 211-212.

580. Ken'an Rifâî, *Şerhli Mesnevî-i Şerif* (Istanbul: Kubbealtı Neşriyatı 2000), pp. 485-486.

581. Ahmed er-Rifâî, ed. Dr. H. Kâmil Yılmaz, *Marifet Yolu* (Istanbul: Erkam Yayıncılık 1995), p. 164.

There are some who think on the end, and some who remain stuck on merely the pleasures of daily life and the desires of the soul.

Thus seeing is a matter of degree. Some understand a bad thing from its smell and immediately give it up. Some understand when they take a thing between their teeth, and drop it... others chew it, but understand before they swallow and spit it out. Other swallow, and when they do, that evil causes various kinds of harm and loss inside them. They understand the nature of that thing they felt such greed for only then, and regretting it, are repentant. Others understand in the grave, in other words, when the torment of the grave arrives.

When people are placed in the grave, they hear a cry, "O heedless one, you have abandoned the world, and the world has abandoned you. You tried to gather up the world, and it gathered you up."[582]

- Gazing at the molten lead-colored evening fog from the window of her house, a beautiful young woman said to herself, "I am beautiful, I am young, but what good is it, I am poor as a beggar."

There were many things the young woman wanted from the world. Even as a young child she would board the carriage of fantasies of adornment and pomp and glide off to distant lands. With the passage of time that longing, that secret bitter yearning, became so unbearable that finally one day the world placed in the palm of that beggar for splendor seeking alms more largesse than she'd hoped for. Thus in the whirl of grandeur she'd suddenly gained, time passed without the young woman noticing the flow of years going by.

Wasn't what she wanted the world? After these years that went by without being felt, the world suddenly appeared before her as a beggar, a bullying, relentless beggar who does not leave without getting what he wants, and from that aquaintance to whom it had once shown generosity, kindness, care and friendship, took away first her youth and then her beauty.

Perhaps that could be counted a settled account. But that desiring, ever desiring merciless beggar would not be satisfied and kept at the ready, kept taking and taking, never leaving with empty hand.

---

582. Ken'an Rifâî, *Sohbetler* (Istanbul: Kubbealtı Neşriyatı 2000), pp. 191-192.

50TH-51ST VERSE

That old woman, finally a spiteful hag, one day again gazed at the molten lead-colored evening fog. That defeated head, her desires unsatisfied, the flame of her greedy passions still burning, wearied by the neverending pleasures of the world, again flitted from one star to another in the skies of fantasy. But the merciless world must have decided to now throw her down utterly, for it sent before her the herald of another realm to receive her last wish.

The next day those who came into the old woman's room found her still in her usual corner. But this time she had placed her spirit in the world's cracked begging-bowl. She was finally a pitiful corpse showing no sign of her insatiable desires.[583]

- The Day of Resurrection will come for them. They will be called to account and suffer torment in the grave.

The energy of the body will then be lost. The years of recourse will be cut off. Emotions will melt. Their family members and neighbors will abandon them. Friends and enemies will perch on the possessions they accumulated. Women, men and children will swarm over their possessions. Nothing they leave behind will save them from the rights of the servant. If only they had given those with rights their due while in the world... If they have nothing to give, they must obtain forgiveness from those they owe, ask God for forgiveness, and regret what they have done.[584]

- Resurrection has three parts. The first is the lesser resurrection. As stated in noble hadith, when a person dies it means their resurrection has come. The second resurrection is the scattering of all existents when the trumpet is blown. The third resurrection is when at the second blast of the trumpet everyone is revived to life in their own body and gathered together for their account to be settled on Judgment Day (*mahşer*); whatever we find there is the result of our own actions.[585]

- O Beloved, when spirit is separated from body, with what quality will it be qualified? Some will be qualified with the form of a pig,

---

583. Sâmiha Ayverdi, *Yusufcuk* (Istanbul: Kubbealtı Neşriyatı 1997), pp. 69-70.
584. Abdülkadir Geylânî, *Gunyetü't-Tâlibîn* (Huzur Yayın Dağıtımı), p. 986.
585. Ken'an Rifâî, *Sohbetler* (Istanbul: Kubbealtı Neşriyatı 2000), p. 194.

some the form of a dog or a monkey or savage beast. The heads of some will be under their feet. Some will not be able to speak or move. There are many hadiths and verses of the Mighty Quran pertaining to this, as in, *"Like an animal, and worse"* (25:44).

O Beloved, struggle to find those qualities in your own self, and before you die find the recourse to expel those qualites from yourself.

And the greatly necessary condition for knowing oneself is to know to what the conclusion of an affair has reached. You must be aware of what the excesses of your own state are, its lacks, passions and insensitivities, its being stationary and progressing. The soul's bestial and rapacious, satanic and angelic qualities exist in you, and you should find them. You should know which ones are dominant and try to eliminate them.

O Beloved, when the aspirant arrives at the state of self-knowledge, visions occur between sleeping and waking. And visions are among the human being's miracles, even the share of messengerhood. Thus the Messenger said, *"The wholesome vision is one piece of the forty-six pieces of messengerhood"* (hadith).

If the quality of greed is dominant, they will see the forms of mice and frogs. If the quality of niggardliness is dominant, dogs and goats. If resentment (*kin*) is dominant, the form of a snake. If the quality of lust is dominant, the form of a donkey. If the quality of harshness is dominant, the form of a fox. O Beloved, if we were to try to enumerate all of them it would take too long. Whatever quality is dominant in you, you will be the same as that quality on the Day of Resurrection. You will come upon the field at the Day of Judgment with that quality.

The wholesome are resurrected with the wholesome, the evil with the evil, the pure with the pure and the corrupt with the corrupt. Whichever is appropriate to you, that is your right.[586]

- In the other world each person's notebook of good deeds and sins is distributed. And again they say, "In the other world there are angels, the Throne, the fire and Paradise. There are the scale, the account and

---

586. Mûsâ b. Şeyh Tahir Tokadî, İsmâil Hakkı Bursevî, Hacı Bektaş-ı Velî, Muhammed Nurü'l-Arabî, ed. Tahir Hafızalioğlu, *Gayb Bahçelerinden Seslenişler* (Istanbul: İnsan Yayınları 2003), p. 251.

the book." But as long as an analogy is not given, although there is no similitude in this world, it is not clear. It can only become clear through analogy. the likeness in this world is, for example, all people, like padishahs, judges, tailors, cobblers and others, sleep at night. When they sleep, their thoughts fly and no thought remains in anyone. But when the morning light like the breath of Israfil blows, and all the atoms in their bodies are brought to life, the thoughts of each one come toward them like flying writings and there is no error. The tailor's thoughts come to the tailor, the jurist's to the jurist, the blacksmith's to the blacksmith, the oppressor's to the oppressor and the just to the just. Does anyone go to sleep a tailor and get up in the morning as a cobbler? For whatever that person's trade is, they are occupied with it, and you should know that it will be the same in that world. This is not impossible; the truth has even occurred in this world. Thus if people serve this likeness and arrive at the end of the thread, they see and witness all the states of the world, take their scent, and these are unveiled for them. See then that all take refuge in God's power.[587]

- On the Day of Resurrection the trumpet will be blown. The trumpet is a creature in the shape of a horn with holes in the number of the souls of creatures. Because the trumpet has a hole for each creature, those existents that had not died before will swoon at its sound.

The one who blows the trumpet is Israfil (a.s.). The spirits are in one row, and the angels in another. The divine command and the angels will comein shadows from the cloud. All of these will be unveiled to you, but it is not permitted for such knowledge to be disclosed and explained to such as you before the intoxication of death comes. But, when death does come, it will be said to you, "This is the truth from which you fled," and the anagogy will be manifest. For that anagogy and unveiling has been promised to you. Because it is not permitted for them to be unveiled to you before the intoxication of death, it will be said that these are the things you wanted not be involved in.

After the trumpet is blown so that the creatures swoon, it will be blown for them to be resurrected and human beings will await what God the Truth wants from them.

---

587. Mevlânâ Celâleddîn Rumî, trans. Meliha Ülker Anbarcıoğlu, *Fîhi Mâ Fîh* (Istanbul: Milli Eğitim Basımevi 1985), pp. 256-257.

That is the day when all things will be gathered and the organs of the creatures will be collected and God will create them again according to the divine promise. All human beings will be resurrected in the form and shape of Adam, father of humankind. In other words, children will be gathered together beside their fathers and mothers.

On that day the angels and spirits will form rows. The jinn, created of smokeless fire, will be in one row, and the devils not counted among jinn or angels will be in one row, and the greatest devil Azazil, Adam's opposite and demon, will be in front of them. Azazil is among the devils in the station of Adam among humankind. When Adam, father of humankind, had a male or female child, Azazil raised a child to be its friend. Thus the number of devils is the same as the number of Adam's descendants. They gave birth as many times as the number of angels writing down the actions of the servants. The angels who write the actions of a servant are two, one on the right and one on the left. What comes after is a profound matter you will see on the day its interpretation is shown to you. Woe to those who remain heedless (*of God the Truth*) until that day. Fortunate are they who awaken before death!

The real awakening is for the soul to abandon concern for form and matter and turn toward God the Exalted, to turn in the direction of Him; all who turn toward Him turn toward His Essence. "This is better for those who seek God's approval. It is they who attain deliverance." To work for children is not cause of deliverance.

And whoever turns toward God turns their face away from their soul. And whoever turns their face away from their soul understands the meaning of death. They know that death is to abandon favoring and seeking after the world of matter and form perceived with the senses, to look to the Realm of Sovereignty and take the path of God. It is to know that one will come into the presence of God and to show fidelity to His convenant, to accept His lordliness and perform the divine law. And that is to shed blameworthy character and be adorned with beautiful character. When people are qualified with those qualities, they become sites of manifestation for divine discourse. They arrive in the divine presence, they pleased with their Lord and the Lord pleased with them. "*O tranquil soul! Return to your Lord, you please with Him and He with you!*"

50th-51st Verse

Whoever binds theirself to God in this world, their return to the Hereafter is a return in accord with acceptance, not one detestable and undesirable.

Thus death is of two kinds.

Natural death: The extraction of the spirit from the body, even if unwillingly, because the spirit loves the body. Without doubt, it means that spirit is withdrawn by means of hooks and cuts off its connection with the human body. This is the natural death.

Voluntary death: For the spirit to abandon its tie to the body and, distancing itself from love for the body, be plunged in seeking God's pleasure and the acts of the Hereafter, which is a voluntary death. Those who die this death no longer die eternally. *For fear and pain of death is as much as a person's love of what is other than God.* When actions such as seeking pleasures that are dominant, and trying to realize worldly desires, increase, so do sorrows. When these cease, many actions too are removed. And where there is no sorrow there is no fear. And where there is no fear, there is security. And where there is security, there is joy and good news. Servants who attain joy and good news wish to be reunited with their Lord. *"For the friends of God there is no fear nor sorrow."*

"Whoever loves to be reunited with God, God too desires to be reunited with them. They are those who see now what will appear before them. Those who are sites of manifestation of such a witnessing have the properties of a martyr. A martyr is not dead. To be martyred in the war with the soul, killing the soul's desires and pleasures, is in terms of rank higher in the sight of God than to be martyred as a result of battling with the sword against disbelievers. Thus it was said, *"We have returned from the lesser jihad to the greater jihad"* (hadith). The jihad against the soul is dangerous. For those able to aquire sound intention are few. Attainment to true spiritual martyrdom is not possible by supposition. Those who attain that level through the jihad of the soul arrive at certain knowledge (*ayne'l-yakîn; the heart's sight of truth by way of witnessing*).

Voluntary death requires good works, and natural death, punishment; good works require suffering. Whoever would attain death voluntarily must awaken prior to natural death. And those who awaken see the truth without interpretation; they are the people of vision.[588]

---

588. Ahmed er-Rifâî, ed. Dr. H. Kâmil Yılmaz, *Marifet Yolu* (Istanbul: Erkam Yayıncılık 1995), pp. 176-180.

- One day Israfil will blow his horn and the sound rising from his divine instrument will be heard by all who have died. Bodies rotting for centuries and centuries will tingle with that voice and come alive with its joy. The horn Israfil will blow will be the most enlivening of such instruments and the one that bestows true life. But Israfil is not alone in making such enlivening sounds. The words of the prophets and friends do too. Understand well these words and the meaning of these words. The prophets are those who bestow eternal life upon those who hear, understand and believe their words, and who rejoice in those words. Only those who believe in them and in God's friends, who take wing with their words and speeches, will attain eternal life and be raised after the real death, and after dying to their souls.

These voices which come out of the hearts of the prophets, whether heard for centuries like the voice of David, or like Jesus raising those who have just died, are in fact more spiritual than material. It is only the ears of the heart prepared for them, which will hear that invaluable voice and attain eternal life. These voices address more the heart and conscience than the external ear. In fact the world is always filled end to end with these hymns and enlivening sounds like the horn of Israfil, the breath of Jesus, and David's voice.

The melodic tones overflowing from the hearts of the friends address the ears of the hearts of those who are not deaf, making a deep impression. They say, "O representatives of not-being on earth! O particles of that which will disperse into not being in the end! Wake up!" and they continue: "Do not keep on saying 'No.' If you will say it, say 'There is *no* god but God,' say 'There is *no* god but God!'"

This means that there is no God but the one and unbounded God. Say that! In order to be able to say it, rid yourself of desires for all that is other than God! For every desire felt for other than God distances a person that much more from God.

O you who live in the world of those who are created and made to live, and who rot away and are destroyed! If you do not hear the voice rising from the hearts of the friend, if you do not see the various self-disclosures of divine being around you, know that there is no eternal and subsisting spirit in your body. That spirit was not born with you. Or the ear of your spirit has not opened, the eyes of your heart have remained unseeing.

50TH-51ST VERSE

In truth if there were anyone in the worldly realm to hear the holy tones in the hearts of those friends, not only the living but even the spirits of those dead for centuries and buried in the ground would raise their heads from their graves.

Hold the ear of the spirit close to those who speak to you with the language of meaning! In every age, every place in the world, unceasingly, there are those who will articulate that beautiful voice for you. But often they are not permitted to transmit that **divine music (ledün musikisi)** in words and meaning to you.

If you bring the ear of the heart near you will hear the voice within them. For the friends of God are the Israfil of the time and place in which they live. Many a dead spirit lying in the grace of the body and the cage of flesh hears the voice of the friends and awakens from the sleep of death, comes to life, tears its shroud and gets up on its feet.

They listen to the voice they hear in a swoon, feel that divine music bringing them to take wing to the heavens, and they say, "The voice of the friends is a music completely different from that of other creatures. These voices point to the voice of God. These are the voices of God the Truth. We were spirits buried and lost in the tomb of the body and the graveyard of not-being. The voices of God the Truth have come to us by means of God's friends. It is because the ear of our spirit has heard that voice that we have been brought to life, we have risen up and found life with that voice."[589]

• Hazret Muhammed said, *"My Friends, expose your bodies to the coolness of spring. (Take broad advantage of the spring air.) For whatever effect spring has on trees, it has that same effect on your bodies, it gives you life and vitality.*

"On the contrary, beware of the damp and cold of autumn. For its effect is the same as that which can be observed in trees. Look at what autumn does to gardens and vines and take care that you do not become like that too."

For those who look at the outward form of this hadith it may appear to be merely about the life of nature. In reality it was an inward meaning and that is the meaning which must in fact be known.

In short, the autumn in that beautiful saying is the soul, the soul's desires and ambitions. Spring represents the intellect and spir-

---

589. Ken'an Rifâî, *Şerhli Mesnevî-i Şerif* (Istanbul: Kubbealtı Neşriyatı 2000), p. 272.

it. It tells of the eternity of the spirit and how in the path of God it finds a new and immortal life each instant.

One should consider that human beings have an intellect, however partial. This intellect works to obtain and ensure what the body needs in order to live. But one cannot know with this intellect the great mysteries that place creation in an order having a beginning and end, this intellect is not enough for the attainment of the great and eternal realities beyond the veils.

The duty that falls to a person here is to seek out an arrived person in the world and act according to the requirements of the intellect perfected in him. The universal intellects (*küllî akılları*) of the arrived cause the partial intellect in you to mature. They bring it to perfection. They do not leave it adrift. They ensure that it not go to waste. That is their duty. The intellects of the arrived certainly perform this great duty, which is to tie human hearts to God and bring their spirits to God, with infinite joy and enthusiasm.

Just as the juice of dates becomes wine and makes the intellect lose its wits, so do people who possess partial intellects drink the wine of divine love that those who possess universal intellects serve with neither cup nor lip, and thus pass away from their souls.

So, like the winds of spring, the pure exhalations of God's friends bring life, and as the winds of spring bring water and leaves to thirsty and naked trees, so do they refresh and beautify the spirit.

The method of God the Truth's arrived is like that of spring. Like spring, whose winds sometimes blow harshly, whose waters sometimes rise up and rush in floods, they sometimes rage as well.

With their sometimes soft and caressing, sometimes harsh and branch-breaking behavior, they show you the horizons of eternity.

You must bear with this. A person who tolerates the thorns of roses will certainly pass over the thorn fences of the rose gardens of eternity and enter in.

Just as the value of spring is not known without autumn, if it were not for the harshness of the arrived, which withers the leaves of soul in a person's body and causes them to fall, the gates of the countries of eternity's spring would remain closed to that person.

Thus the obedience shown to a murshid is righteousness and a surrender far from all manner of doubt, which brings you to attain the goal you long for.

50TH-51ST VERSE

The breezes that blow through the gardens of spirit have the effects of the breath of Jesus. The heart is full of giant pearls of gnosis and spirituality. Guard like your life those magnificent pearls in the treasury of the heart. For every pearl lost from the heart takes away a kind of joy. Hearts that thus lose their pearls are embraced only by a profound sorrow.[590]

- Let them not be vexed with me who suppose themselves among the people of union while they have not found the truth and remain in separation, and compare themselves with the learned while remaining ignorant; for those who aquire have aquired, those who sell have sold, and the season has passed.[591]

- A sign of resurrection is that those whose faces are white will be distinguished from those whose faces are black. Therefore, because the black-faced and white-faced are manifest though the existence of his sun face, the Messenger's existence is resurrection; and that whiteness and blackness is in the sight of the prophets and true believers. Yes, the existence of the Messenger is resurrection; for whatever will happen tomorrow at the Resurrection, they see it all today beforehand. Because they have torn the veil of heedlessness, necessarily there is nothing concealed from their sight. Now, they call that universal Resurrection a resurrection because when the world that is the refuge and station of disbelievers is no more, without doubt their veil of heedlessness will be torn and they will see their black-facedness as it is. Resurrection and the miracles of the Lord Guide (*the efendi who brings one to attain guidance*) are not invisible; they are plain to see and closer than the jugular vein. It is only the veil of heedlessness (*the heart's remaining deprived of remembrance of God*) that prevents their being witnessed. (*In other words, "Whoever dies, their resurrection occurs."*) Whoever dies from the quality of creatureliness and the nature of the disbelieving soul (*the disbelieving, veiled soul*) and is annihilated, their resurrection occurs and becomes manifest. Now, resurrection is to emerge from the veil of heedlessness and selfhood and to witness the

---
590. Ken'an Rifâî, *Şerhli Mesnevî-i Şerif* (Istanbul: Kubbealtı Neşriyatı 2000), pp. 295-296.

591. Ken'an Rifâî, from his notes to *Ahmed er-Rifâî*, p. 118.

sun of perfect beauty (*to see the beauty of the Essence in that manifests in the sun as well*). Therefore the Prophet's existence is resurrection. Whoever awaits resurrection with his existence and knows their resurrection to be other than him, they are squint-eyed, cross-eyed; they see double; they are far from unity, they are strangers. Even that resurrection will be this beauty and form and clarity; it will not be other than this. The first and last will be one. From every form only that one secret will show its face; and the end draws the intimate to itself and expels the stranger. God the Truth gave resurrection the title, "Day." For it shows the beauty that is red and yellow. Therefore the reality of "day" is the friends' secret. Day is like the shadows in the confrontation of their suns. It is in order that the not intimate be distinguished from the intimate and the false coin from true and the alloyed from the pure and they are inside the commotion of the world's existence; and when you look with the eye of secrecy, you see that each one is inside this struggle and commotion of the whole of the world in order to be joined to its own source.[592]

- "O My greatest messenger, that nomad's lamp
What is it before My tempest's freezing draft?

"Rise and blow upon the trumpet full of dread
That there may spring from the dust the thousands dead

"Since you are the time's Israfil, upright one
Bring resurrection before Resurrection

"Beloved, if they say,'What resurrection?'
Show yourself, say, 'I am the Resurrection'"[593]

- *A dervish should not be heedless, safety in the two worlds is this
The good pleasure of Hazret God
The heart's speech in remembering God*

---

592. Mevlânâ Celâleddin Rûmî, trans. Ahmet Avni Konuk, ed. Selçuk Eraydın, *Fîhi Mâ Fîh* (Istanbul: İz Yayıncılık 2002), pp. 227-228.

593. Mevlânâ Celâleddin Rûmî, trans. Veled İzbudak, ed. Abdülbaki Gölpınarlı, *Mesnevî* (Istanbul: Milli Eğitim Basımevi 1991), vol. 4, vs. 1477-1480.

50th-51th Verse

If faithfulness is what you seek, keep promises and act rightly
Do your work for the love of God
The goal of all of it, one God

This dervishood, what a fine path
It sees nothing but God, nothing
Its work is God and only God, it sees everywhere light of God

Body and soul must be thrown off
It has no regard for the world
To be naught in the way of God
Its hope and its desire is God

It's placed in your body as trust
Seek, find there the secret of God
Slough off your being, O Kenan
You'll see the one who is, is God[594]

---

594. Ken'an Rifâî, *İlâhiyat-ı Ken'an*, ed. Yusuf Ömürlü and Dinçer Dalkılıç (Istanbul: Kubbealtı Neşriyatı 1988), p. 28.

52. They will say, "Ah, woe to us, who has raised us from our beds of repose? This is what the Merciful promised, and the messengers spoke the truth."

Qālū yāwaylanā man baʿathanā min marqadinā hādhā mā waʿadaʾrrahmānu wa ṣadaqaʾl-mursalūn.

53. It was but a single cry and then all of them were immediately brought before Us.

ʾIn kānat ʾillā ṣayḥatan wāḥidatan faʾidhā hum jamīʿun ladaynā muḥḍarūn.

- "*If a person dies without seeing the Imam of the time, their death is a death in the time of ignorance*" (noble hadith).[595]

- You will consider and awaken to the reality that so many people asleep to the illumination of their gaze by love of God are powerless to see the arrived of God who are right next to them and in front of them, even touching them hand-to-hand.

For that reason so many are unaware of the intimacy the arrived enjoy with the true Beloved, and catch no scent of it from their company and conversation.

In order to be aware of these people of God, hidden like the Companions of the Cave in the cave of non-existence, the eye must tear apart its veil of heedlessness, awakening to the divine light, and the ear must hear the voice coming to us from the realm of the Unseen.

---

[595]. Mûsâ b. Şeyh Tahir Tokadî, İsmail Hakkı Bursevî, Hacı Bektaş-ı Velî, Muhammed Nûruʾl-Arabî, ed. Tâhir Hafızalioğlu, *Gayb Bahçelerinden Seslenişler* (Istanbul: İnsan Yayınları 2003), p. 108.

As Yunus Emre said, the world is full of God the Truth and God the Truth's friends:

God the Truth fills up the world, but no one knows God the Truth
  Look for Him within yourself, He is not separate from you

But where are those possessed of quick understanding and comprehension that they might be capable of seeing them with the eyes of inner vision. For they are invisible like spirits which are hidden.

Acquire for yourself an eye and a heart worthy of seeing them. See how the divine light shines in the hearts of those who truly love Him and are loved by Him![596]

- According to the gracious verse, "They will be brought before us," in the thirty-sixth chapter of the Gracious Quran, the senses and intellects of people who are invisible in the light of that sun of gnosis, that God-knowledge, dive at the slightest summons into the oceans of eternity and are lost to their own existence. This is a state of attraction, of ardor, of passing away from the body. When that state of attraction and ardor is withdrawn from those annihilated and lost in the light of God's existence according to the level of His summons, the limitation of body begins again. It is like when the stars appear after the sun has gone. The stars of sense and thought shine once more in the dark night of humanity, and worldly burdens and worldly difficulties recommence within humans.

The lover spirits God attracted thus return to consciousness, troop after troop. But rings of gnosis appear in the ears of their spirits and they awaken knowing various sciences and truths.

On the Day of Resurrection the rotted skin and bones will rise up like the dust raised by galloping horses, and hasten to give their accounts.

This is what the state of the arrived of God, who burn with the love of God in this world and pass away from self through an attraction, is like. While they are dead and rotted away, become dust and invisible, God returns them to the world and they find body and life.

---

596. Ken'an Rifâî, *Şerhli Mesnevî-i Şerif* (Istanbul: Kubbealtı Neşriyatı 2000), p. 62.

52TH-53TH VERSE

With one difference, that on the Day of Resurrection all spirits, Muslim or disbeliever, will be clothed in a body.[597]

• If you have obeyed teachers who are veiled by heedlessness, buried in the darkness of matter, bound to the limitations of what is other than God and, imitating their fathers, have not arrived at the light of certainty, you will recognize no other tablet but that made of paper and wood, no pen but that made of reed, no hand or body but that consisting of flesh and nerves, and no scribe but matter. If that is so, do not hunger to understand anything we have indicated! For you do not understand these things. You are among those who remain in the darkness of matter. Such people recognize nothing but body and the material things dependent upon it. They are under the shadow of matter in the three dimensions known as length, height and width. That is why what you know consists of what you perceive with your senses. You try to deny those things that have no quantity or amount, cannot be measured, seen or divided. These are the qualities of existents in the realm called the All-Comprehending Realm (*alem-i vasî*), and in comparison with them, bodies have the property of shadows. That is such a noble realm that command and the measuring out descend from there.

O you who are proud of form and exteriority! You are heedless of God, awake!

The people of exteriority whom you have favored and inclined toward, even the figurativists and anthropomorphists, take refuge from God's wrath in His kindness and boons.[598]

• There was a man who was very thin, feeble and short. Everyone saw him as a contemptible sparrow. He was so despised and ugly that even people with contemptible, ugly faces who complained of their state before they saw him would thank God when they saw how contemptible he was. Despite that, he was very arrogant and boastful when he spoke. He was an officer in the Padishah's court and was

---

597. Ken'an Rifâî, *Şerhli Mesnevî-i Şerif* (Istanbul: Kubbealtı Neşriyatı 2000), pp. 542-543.

598. Ahmed er-Rifâî, ed. Dr. H. Kâmil Yılmaz, *Marifet Yolu* (Istanbul: Erkam Yayıncılık 1995), p. 171.

always annoying the Vizier, who put up with it. At last one day the Vizier had had enough and lost his temper. "O people of the court," he shouted, "this man has become what he is by sharing our table, eating our bread and enjoying our wealth. And now he says such awful things to me." The ugly man sprang up in the Vizier's face and said, "O people of the court and great men of state! Yes, what he says is true, I have become contemptible and ridiculous like this by being nurtured on his and his ancestors' wealth and bread. If I had been raised and nurtured on someone else's bread and wealth, my face, my stature and my value would have been better than this. He raised me from the dirt. As it is said, *'We have warned you of an impending punishment. The day when a man sees what his hands have sent forth and the disbeliever will say, "Woe is me, would that I were dust"'* (78:40), if only someone else had raised me from the dust! Perhaps then I would not have been ridiculous like this."

The spirit of a disciple trained by a man of God will be pure, while the man raised and educated by a talebearer and hypocrite will be contemptible, weak and sorrowful like that feeble man; he will be indecisive, his feelings will be deficient and he will not work well.[599]

---

599. Mevlânâ Celâleddîn Rumî, trans. Meliha Ülker Anbarcioğlu, *Fîhi Mâ Fîh* (Istanbul: Milli Eğitim Basımevi 1985), pp. 50-51.

54. On that day no soul will be wronged in the least, and you will suffer only the requital for what you have done.

Fa'l-yawma lā tuẓlamu nafsun shay'an wa lā tujzawna 'illā mā kuntum ta'malūn.

- *"Those who fear to stand before their Lord and forbid their soul caprice, truly their abode will be Paradise."* (79:40-41).
  Oppression is to put a thing in a place other than and inappropriate to its proper place.[600]

- Oppression is to yield to the desires of the soul.[601]

- To oppress one's soul is to give it everything it wants. Justice is to resist the soul's desires. If you see an existent in yourself, you are an oppressor. Opression is not to put a thing in its own location. When you know these so many kindnesses and boons of God the Truth, you are just.[602]

- The guidance of Quranic verses and hadith such as, "We did not wrong them, but they wronged their own souls" (11:101) and *"Your Lord oppresses no one,"* best express the attribution to servants of oppression and rebellion. Furthermore, Satan was driven away because he lied, attributing oppression to the Exalted Lord by saying, *"Because You have led me astray,"* and Hazret Adam was accepted because he was truthful, attributing oppression to his own soul by saying *"We*

---

600. Hucviri, ed. Süleyman Uludağ, *Keşf'ul-Mahcûb Hakikat Bilgisi* (Istanbul: Dergah Yayınları 1996), p. 537.
601. Ahmed er-Rifâî, ed. Dr. H. Kâmil Yılmaz, *Marifet Yolu* (Istanbul: Erkam Yayıncılık 1995), p. 95.
602. Ken'an Rifâî, *Sohbetler* (Istanbul: Kubbealtı Neşriyatı 2000), p. 213.

oppressed our own souls," and *"O Lord, we oppressed our own souls!"* One must say that good and evil are from God, and that creating and ruling are from God but aquisition and will are from the servant. If that were not so, it would be necessary to deny the partial will and choose the fatalist school (*cebriye mezhebi*). To err in precaution and find excuse in God's measuring out is folly.[603]

• Human beings wander in the gardens of the works and actions they have left behind. However, it is possible that those gardens will not be the garden of Paradise but one of the deepest pits in Hell (*Gayyâ*). If what they have left behind are good works, spirit will be pleased to be connected with them. But if they are evil works, it will feel sorrow and suffer torment.[604]

• The world is God's location of trial. It is a school of gnosis. Those who acquire the diploma of a sound heart here are without doubt fortunate in this world and the Hereafter. Those who do not will have their faces in the dust, be ashamed and reduced. The world is the planting field of the Hereafter. We will reap there whatever we sow here.[605]

• Everyone is the architect of their own house of life. Let us suppose that you build a rotten, badly planned structure using inferior materials; your building will fall down and as a result they will hold you responsible. The expansive states, sorrow, Paradise and Hell, good and evil a person finds are because they have bult their house of life well or badly. The responsibility for the result we achieve belongs to us, not to others.

If we build the building of our being with rotten character traits and evil, it will one day collapse of itself. At last we will be brought into the presence of God the Truth. He will say, "I gave you that being in trust. Why did you build it with rotten, inferior materials?" and we will be judged and condemned as a result.[606]

---

603. Azîz bin Muhammed Nesefî, ed. M. Tarık Yüksel, *Zübdetü'l-Hakaik* (Istanbul: Asya Yay. 2003), pp. 128-129.
604. Ken'an Rifâî, *Sohbetler* (Istanbul: Kubbealtı Neşriyatı 2000), p. 349.
605. Ken'an Rifâî, *Sohbetler* (Istanbul: Kubbealtı Neşriyatı 2000), p. 521.
606. Ken'an Rifâî, *Sohbetler* (Istanbul: Kubbealtı Neşriyatı 2000), p. 426.

54TH VERSE

- In order to acquire fame and honor you have bound your thoughts to things that are inappropriate and vain. They are like shifting sands on a beach that the waves cover with other sands and upon them another layer of sand; each layer covers and erases the previous one.

   You pursue fame and honor, expending your thoughts and your existence on empty values, and like the other layers of sand that cover layers of sand, the waves of events, too, draw a covering, a veil of darkness over that fame and honor.

   So is it not a waste of your efforts? If you are going to expend your power and strength, expend it in the way of truth for once... Use your ardor for the sake of the duty you have been given to seek the truth.

   Not to put a thing in its place, in other words its true location, is oppression. Then: O my Lord, we have oppressed our souls. We did not know the value of the boons You have given. While it was necessary to use these in their proper places, we wasted them on things empty and vain. If you put vinegar in a rosewater container when you should have put rosewater, have you not oppressed both the container and the rosewater?

   If you are not liked when you put vinegar in a rosewater container, then how would you not be punished by God for your inappropriate states? Will you not be reproached if you do not fulfil your covenant with God and expend all your attention on unneccesary things? And then you entreat Him, saying, "Forgive me." I have given you intellect. Why did you waste it? You must forgive yourself and not return to the impertinence you committed. And although I warned you before, still you put vinegar in the rosewater container. If you trip up your own self, you have no right to cry...[607]

- Before my spirit was captive to a form, a hand took my hand and the wonders of the sun and skies. At last it took me to a certain realm and said, "This is where you will stay as a guest. This is the world. As I looked around in confusion, it continued, "Here everyone plants a seed according to thier own preparedness and gathers its yield. Money, women, children, station, rank, fame and honor are the seeds people most often plant. You, too, plant a seed in this world according to your pleasure and gather its yield!"

---

607. Ken'an Rifâî, *Sohbetler* (Istanbul: Kubbealtı Neşriyatı 2000), pp. 457-457.

Thus I too joined this tumultuous world where everyone toils, none seeing another. Like them, I too began planting and cultivating. But if all the fields were mine, if I were the sole owner of the seeds and ploughs, still my heart, preoccupied with the pleasures of the realms to which I came, would somehow not be able to subsist on the seed it planted. How could the eye that saw the sultanate of the day of eternity without beginning, the lip that tasted its ease, worship the idol it set up itself?

I rebelled. I threw off the belt of seeds from my waist, I threw down my plough, and went straight and buried the seed of my own being in a corner of this field.

They shouted after me, "Oh the poor thing, wasting himself..."

But the truthful lip of the time gave them the lie. That sapling from whose branches they now gather the fruits of love is none other but the seed that I once buried in ecstasy and humility.[608]

- God the Truth says in verses 71-72 of the thirty-ninth chapter of the Quran, *"Everyone will be punished tomorrow for for their actions here. Those who have not taken the path of God's commands will be led to Hell and there the demons of Hell will say, "Did not messengers come to you relating the commands of God the Truth and threatening you with the day of Gathering? Why did you not listen to them and rectify your path, but plunged into the false and fleeting pleasures of the world and forgot your God? Now enter into Hell and stay they forever. How ugly a place for the arrogant is this Hell"* [sic].[609]

The reality of the grave is a person's own being. However prosperous and sumptuous were the material lives of those bound for Hell, their hearts are sorrowful in dullness and narrowness, and when they die they will remain in that state until their own resurrection.[610]

- Someone said: "Judge Izzeddin sends you his selams and always praises you, speaking of your goodness and good works." Mevlana said: "Whoever remembers us well, may his memory in the world be good as well! If someone says good things about a person, that goodness is his own and in reality he has praised himself. The likeness of

---

608. Sâmiha Ayverdi, *Yusufcuk* (Istanbul: Kubbealtı Nşriyatı 1997), pp. 41-42.
609. Ken'an Rifâî, *Sohbetler* (Istanbul: Kubbealtı Neşriyatı 2000), p. 455.
610. Ken'an Rifâî, *Sohbetler* (Istanbul: Kubbealtı Neşriyatı 2000), p. 420.

54TH VERSE

this is, for example, when someone plants roses and basil around his own house, everywhere he looks he sees roses and basil and always feels as if he were in Paradise. A person who is accustomed to speak well of others and busies himself with their wellbeing becomes their lover, and when they remember him they remember his love. This is roses and rose beds, spirit and comfort. When a person's wickedness is spoken of, that person seems unlovely. When one remembers him, when his image comes before one's eye, it is as if one sees snakes or scorpions or garbage. So, since you can see day and night roses and rose beds and and the gardens of Iram, why do you walk among thorns and snakes? Love all human beings, so that you will always be among flowers and rose gardens. If you know them all to be enemies, the image of enemies will come before your eye and it will be as if you walk among thorns and snakes day and night. So the friends, who love everyone and see everything as favorable, do so not for others, God forbid! They do it so that ugly, unlovely and disgusting images will not appear to their eyes. Since it is absolutely necessary to imagine and remember the things done in this world, and this cannot be avoided, when remembering people strive for them all to be pleasant and good so that disgusting, ugly images will not enter and block your path. Therefore everything you do about people, and your remembering them well or badly belongs completely to you.

In this regard God says: *"Whoever does good, does it to himself, and whoever does evil, does it to himself."* And that is why *"whoever does an atom's weight of good, will see it, and whoever works and atom's amount of evil, will see it."*[611]

- *Paradise and Hell, sorrow and happiness, darkness and light*
Are your deeds' shadow, did you think them an external thing?
Your knowledge is your richness, whatever you seek, that is you
Did you think being human was just eating and drinking?
Whatever your state may be, you were that state's customer
Did you think the divine justice was what made it lacking?[612]

---

611. Mevlânâ Celâleddin Rûmî, trans. Melika Ülker Anbarcioğlu, *Fîhi mâ Fîh* (Istanbul: Milli Eğitim Basımevi 1985), pp. 306-307.

612. Ken'an Rifâî, *İlâhiyat-ı Ken'an*, ed. Yusuf Ömürlü and Dinçer Dalkılıç (Istanbul: Kubbealtı Neşriyatı 1988), p. 14.

55. Surely the people of Paradise that day have joy in what occupies them.

'Inna 'aṣḥāba'l-jannati'l-yawma fī shughulin fākihūn.

56. They and their spouses are reclining on couches in the shade.

Hum wa 'azwājuhum fī ẓilālin 'alā'l-'arā'iki muttaki'ūn.

57. There is a fruit therein for them, and whatever they ask for.

Lahum fīhā fakihatun wa lahum mā yadda'ūn.

- It is said, "*In the world there is a paradise such that whoever enters it does not long for the paradise of the Hereafter.*" When it was asked, "O Messenger of God, what is that paradise?" he said, "*Gnosis of God...*"

This means that the gnostics and dervishes who have entered the worldly paradise gather in a place on the day of their remembrance ceremony and nourish their spirits with the roses of spirituality and the hyacinths of the secrets of oneness in the gardens of God the Truth's remembrance and thought. Our Messenger of God Efendi says, "*Gatherings of remembrance are the gardens of paradise.*"

Thus these aspirants at the meeting ceremony gather in the shade of the tree of the perfect human being's body, which is in the position of the worldly paradise, and collect the fruits of gnosis and delightfulness that fall from the tree of that body. Our Efendi says, "*When you find a tree from the trees of paradise, sit in its shade and eat of its fruits!"* When they asked, "How can that be, O Messenger of God?" he answered, *"When you find someone possessed of knowledge, it means you have found a tree of paradise."*[613]

- The Paradise of Acts is the paradise of actions and works. The formal paradise that contains the delicious foods, sweet drinks and charming sexual pleasures that will be given as reward to those who do good works, which is called "the soul's paradise."

The Paradise of Attributes is the spiritual paradise consisting of the self-disclosure of divine names and attributes, which is also called "the heart's paradise."

The Paradise of Essence is the viewing of the matchless divine beauties, which is also called "the spirit's paradise."

God the Exalted has self-disclosed to the Form of Muhammed with the name "Munificent" (*Mennân*), after which self-disclosure He created the varieties of paradise.

Later, when He self-disclosed to those paradises with the name "Subtle" (*Latif*), he made that place the location of all worthy of finding honor and gifts there.

Know that the paradises are generally eight layers, in each of which there are many paradises. And each paradise has many levels, whose limit and account cannot be known.

Now let us explicate these eight layers of paradise in order as follows:

The First Layer: In Paradise this layer has taken the name, "The Paradise of Peace." This layer is furthermore spoken of as "The Paradise of Recompense." God the Exalted the Truth created the gate of this paradise from wholesome works. And in that paradise He self-disclosed to the people there with the name "Esteemed" (*Hasîb*). For thus that place became the recompense for purely good works. Our Messenger of God Efendi said in this regard, *"No one can enter Paradise by his works."* In this way he intended the paradise of divine gifts. He did not mean the paradise of recompense. And so God the Exalted said, *"For the human being there is only recompense for his work. The recompense for work will soon be seen. Then a reward complete will be given"* (53:39-41).

---

613. Ken'an Rifâî, *Sohbetler* (Istanbul: Kubbealtı Neşriyatı 2000), pp. 578-579.

55TH-56TH-57TH VERSE

In sum, this paradise is entered only by means of wholesome works; there is no other way, for if a person has no wholesome works, neither will they have entrance here. The name of this paradise is furthermore spoken of as "Ease" (*Yüsrâ*). God the Exalted the Truth has said in this regard in the Gracious Quran, "*Whoever gives charity and guards himself, and verifies the Most Beautiful, We will make easy for him the Ease*" [sic] (92:5-7).

Entrance to the aforementioned paradise for those whose states are as described, in other words, the people of Paradise, is dependent upon very few wholesome works, for God's ease is the share of all for whome He has made it the share.

The Second Layer: This paradise is called "the Paradise of Eternal Duration" or "Paradise of Earnings." If you ask what is the difference between the Paradise of Recompense and the Paradise of Earnings, we will say the following:

The Recompense paradise is as much as the amount of works, in other words, granted as the recompense for works. The Earnings paradise is simply gain, because it is the result of doctrines, the beautiful opinions nurtured toward God. There is no recompense there given in return for works done with this body. God the Exalted self-discloses to the people of this paradise with the name "Originator" (*Bedî*), for as a result of that self-disclosure unimaginable states manifest to those possessed of beautiful doctrines.

They all appear there as divine originations. The gate of Earnings paradise was created of doctrines and opinions and hope regarding God. None can enter Earnings paradise but one having the temperament described. In other words, if there is anything of this temperament missing in a person, they cannot enter that paradise. Know this!

The name of this paradise has been called Earnings. For the opposite of it is frustration, to be duped, and that frustration is the result of opinions of inferior quality nurtured toward God.

God the Exalted said in this regard, "*It is this opinion of yours that you nurtured toward your Lord. That opinion brought you low, and you have come to be among those who remain frustrated*" (41:23).

In sum those having evil opinions burn in the frustration of damage and loss. As for those who have good opinions of God the Truth, their place is the Earnings paradise.

The Third Layer: The name of this paradise is "the Paradise of Gifts." The level of this paradise is higher than that of those mentioned above. For there is no limit or end to God the Exalted's gifts. God the Exalted even so bestows gifts upon the people of this paradise that they have neither works nor doctrines... In other words, the gifts God the Exalted gives to the people of this paradise are more numerous than those He gives to those who have works, doctrines and other goodnesses.

In this paradise I have seen tribes belonging to every nation and some classes of the children of Adam. If the people of doctrine and those who do beautiful works have a gift given to them by God the Exalted, even they can enter here, for when the aforementioned are to enter this paradise He self-discloses to them in the name "Giver" (*Vehhâb*). It could not be otherwise, for one can enter here only by God the Exalted's boon, His gift.

Our Messenger of God Efendi said of this paradise, "*No one can enter there through their works.*" They asked him, "Can you also not enter there, O Messenger of God?" He said, "*I also. Only because God the Exalted has plunged me in his mercy.*"

This layer is the place where paradise is most extensive. It is the broadest. And it is the secret of the meaning expressed by the verse, "*My mercy encompasses all things*" (7:156).

The path given by the realities possible for intellect and delusion is such that there will be no kind of person who does not enter here! But if they have the share, on a day measured out by God the Exalted, they will enter this paradise, for that is the path shown by the realities of fantasized possibility. Our witnessing is other than this.

We witnessed that there was in this paradise a class of persons from every nation and race. More than half of those nations were not there, in other words, not all of them were there; there was only one group from every nation, that is all.

Thus the Recompense paradise is not like that. It is special to those who do good works, and only the people of that paradise can enter there.

If you ask the reason for this, we say that gain is nearer to being recompensed, for in order for there to be gain, there must be wealth.

The wealth of the people of the Earnings paradise at the second layer is their doctrines and beautiful opinions of God.

55TH-56TH-57TH VERSE

But this paradise, I mean the Gifts Paradise, this layer of paradise is broader than the sum of all the paradises. It is even broader than the sum of all the paradises above it. The name of this paradise in the Gracious Quran is "Home" (*Me'vâ*). For mercy is the home of everything. God the Exalted said, *"As for those who believe and do wholesome works, for them is the Paradise of Home, as a resting place for what they did"* (32:19).

The word "resting place" in the gracious verse means "boon," "gift." If one pays attention, here it does not say, "recompense." In other words, it is not said to be in return for works.

If we interpret further, the meaning is that He will place them in the Gifts paradise, not in Recompense or Earnings paradise. Because the Paradise of Gifts is a gift from God the Exalted.

In sum, generosity and gift are not special to those who do good works. Comprehend this meaning well!

The Fourth Layer: This paradise is named "the Paradise of Right," "the Paradise of Bliss," "the Paradise of Innate Disposition." This paradise is the highest of those that have been explicated before. It is neither recompense nor gifts; perhaps it is special to a tribe.

The inhabitants of this paradise are such a tribe that God the Exalted created them according to those rights and some of them will enter this paradise by way of an original granting of rights. Furthermore, they are such people that as they leave the land of the world their spirits remain in their innate disposition.

Some of them pass their worldly lives without their innate disposition changing form. Most of them are cheerful fools drawn to God, madmen and children.

Some of the people of this paradise perform purification of the soul by way of wholesome works, striving, ascetic practices and correct and scrupulous behavior in servanthood toward God the Exalted, and when that is the case, their spirits arise from the pit of creatureliness and return to their innate disposition.

Of the innate disposition for the creature, Exalted God the Truth said, *"We created the human being in the most beautiful stature"* (95:4).

Those in this condition are those purified with this verse: *"Those who beleive and do wholesome works, for them is a reward without obligation"* (95:6)

It is the tribes described above who enter the Paradise of Right. If we would make this clearer, we should say that this paradise is their right, not a gift given with obligation, nor is it a recompense by way of requital in return for works or any other thing.

The class of people who find their innate disposition by way of purification have been remembered with the name, "the Good."

"The Good are in Bliss" (82:13). That those mentioned with the name, "The Good," are in Bliss is based on this secret: Exalted God the Truth self-disclosed to these people of paradise with the name "God the Truth." That being so, He refused to place anyone there but those who had earned the right to be there.[614] The way of nobility and the innate disposition God created require it. Some of those who enter the aforementioned paradise immediately enter there the moment they are separated from their worldly lives. And some enter after experiencing a bit of torment in Hell. In other words, their evilness burns out in Hell and they return to their original created nature. After that, they earn the right to enter Paradise. Here do not forget that they definitely enter Hell first!

Unlike the paradises that have been mentioned before, the ceiling of Bliss paradise is the Throne. Because what is above them is the ceiling of what is below.

Now, for the ceilings of the paradises in order, we must interpret that. They are:

The ceiling of Peace paradise is Eternal Duration paradise.

The ceiling of Eternal Duration paradise is Home paradise.

The ceiling of Home paradise is the Paradise of Right.

Furthermore, this paradise is is also named "Innate Disposition" and "Bliss," and this paradise has no other ceiling than the Throne.

The Fifth Layer: This paradise is named "Firdevs paradise" and "Gnosis paradise." The floor of this paradise is unimaginably broad. As creatures rise there, they witness the ceiling narrowing. The highest ceiling of that paradise is even narrower than the eye of a needle. Yet when they look down from there they see the paradises below and find their infants, houries and kiosks.

---

614. ["Truth" and "right" translate the same term, *hak*.]

55TH-56TH-57TH VERSE

But Gnosis paradise is not the location of such things. Such things are not found there or even above it. This paradise is the gate of the Throne. Its ceiling is the ceiling of the Throne gate.

The people of this paradise are in a continual state of witnessing, for they are the witnesses (martyrs). In other words, they are martyrs to divine beauty, the divine name Beauty.

They have died before death by the sword of annihilation of souls, by love of God. That being so, they witness only their beloved. For that reason the name of this paradise has become "Intimacy with the Sovereign" (*Vesile*). The people of this paradise are fewer than those of the other paradises. For as the levels of the layers of paradise rise, the number of their people decrease.

The Sixth Layer: This paradise is named "the Paradise of Virtue." The people of this paradise are the truthful.

Describing them, Exalted God the Truth praised them with the gracious verse, *"Before an Omnipotent King"* (54:55). This is the paradise of the names.

This layer of paradise is spread over the levels of the Throne. Each class of people from this layer are set up upon a level of the Throne, and the people here are fewer in number than the people of Gnosis paradise.

The Seventh Layer: This paradise is named "the Paradise of the Level of Raising" and "the Paradise of High Level."

It is considered the Attributes paradise by way of name, and the Essence paradise by way of rule.

The floor of this paradise is inside the Throne and its people are called "Those who Realize by the Divine Realities," and its inhabitants are fewer than the number of those in the previously explicated paradises.

The people of this paradise are those allowed near, and they are qualified with divine vicegerency.

Furthermore, through the divine reality they are possessed of tremendousness, people of stability.

In this station, in other words, here, I saw Abraham (a.s.). He was standing at the right of this location, looking toward the center. To his left I saw a group of the friends and messengers, and they too had their eyes fixed on the center of this paradise.

I also saw our Messenger of God Efendi. He was at the exact center of this location and had raised his eye to the Throne. In this way our Efendi (s.a.s.) was requesting the "Station of the Praised" that God the Exalted had promised him.

The Eighth Layer: This paradise is named "Paradise of the Station of the Praised." This is the Essence paradise. The floor of this paradise is the ceiling of the Throne. And no one has a way here. Every single one of the people of Attributes paradise requests to come here. They think he is bound to there only by name, not by any other thing. In fact everyone seeks the right to be there. But that place is special only to our Messenger of God Efendi.

This is understood from this noble hadith: *"The Station of the Praised is the highest station in Paradise. That place is for only one person. I hope that person may be me."* May God the Exalted bless and greet him with peace.

Then, God the Exalted gave him the news he had promised him, and we believe and verify what our Efendi said without doubt.

Because Exalted God the Truth (j.j.) has said of our Efendi (s.a.s.), "He does not speak out of caprice. It is naught but an inspiration inspired" (53:3-4). This has been most beautifully explicated by the gracious verse.[615]

- "God has seventy thousand veils of light and darkness. If He were to open these veils, He would burn the eyes and the skin of the faces of those creatures who comprehend Him." (Hadith) [616]

- Ibn Arabi takes up "paradise" (*cennet*) in the dictionary meaning of the root, that is, "to cover." In that sense the term has the meaning of a concealed boon renewed every moment. Paradise, as the opposite of fire or Hell, is the land of goodness, consisting of generosity and intimacy with God.

---

615. Abdü'l-kerîm Cîlî, trans. Seyyid Hüseyin Fevzî Paşa, *İnsan-ı Kâmil* (Istanbul: Kitsan Yayınları), vol 2, pp. 185-197.

616. Muhyiddîn İbnü'l-Arabî, trans. Vahdettin İnce, *Risaleler* (Istanbul: Kitsan Yayınları), vol. 1, p. 117.

55th-56th-57th Verse

Paradise, due to its subtlety and spirituality, means to be hidden.

In Paradise there are things no eye has seen and no ear has heard that do not come into any person's heart. It is this situation that is the sole reason for Paradise to be named *cennet*, because the term expresses the meaning "to be covered."

The soul (*the contented soul*) enters God the Truth's Paradise, in other words, enters under His covering and curtain.

For the soul, being delighted by something temporary and new is superior to continuance. That is the secret of the boons in Paradise being renewed every moment.

Paradise is the land of intimacy, of seeing God the Truth. It is the place of desires and delights in general.

The land of subtlty and boons is Paradise.

Paradise is the location of beauty, familiarity, and God the Truth's descent (*to His servants*).

There are two way-stations in the Hereafter: Paradise and Hell. There are two way-stations in the world: torment and favor or sorrow and delight.

Fire comes of greatness and Paradise of generosity.

Paradise is to cover; thus everything that has the quality of covering is a paradise. Human beings cover God the Truth by way of being the site of self-disclosure for a specific divine name. Thus by way of the name self-disclosed in them, they are God the Truth's paradise, or put in other terms, the Lord's paradise. Paradise is the Messenger's level.

"Enter My Paradise": I (*God*) am covered by him. My Paradise is nothing other than you, because you cover Me with your own essence.

I am known by means of you, and you are known my means of Me. Thus those who know you, know Me. If I am not known, neither are you known. When you have entered His Paradise, it means you have entered your soul. Thus you know your own soul.[617]

- God the Truth says, "*O soul at peace! Come to Me, to my private paradise, content with Me, and I content with you!*" (89:27-28) [sic].

---

617. Suad el-Hakîm, trans. Ekrem Demirli, *İbü'l-Arabî Sözlüğü* (Istanbul: Kabalcı Yayınevi 2005), pp. 135-136.

What does it mean for the servant to be content with God? It means to accept whatever comes from God. In other words, to meet well whatever comes, whether of Majesty or Beauty, and show acceptance. That is when God, too, is content with His servants, and invites them into His paradise of beauty.

If you continuously receive favor and goodness from Me and for that reason love Me, and avoid Me when I do not show you that favor, then it means your love is not for Me but for that favor, and you do not love Me but love my favors.

As for the people of Beauty, what they want is only Beauty. Otherwise they will not be satisfied to be distracted by favor and pleasure and ease, they will insist on seeking Beauty.

Whereas what the people of Paradise want is houries, male slaves, rivers, kiosks and such boons. God the Truth does not deprive those who want these things either, but grants what they desire.[618]

- **Shugul:** The thing strived for, that occupies one.

"Fruit" indicates the fruit of work rather than simply pleasure. The "couches" are the decorated armchairs that furnish the bride's room.[619]

- To those who listen to God's commands from His officers, and are loyal to God, treading the path that contents God the Truth, His treasurers will say, *"Welcome, God's peace be upon you, come in. Enter the paradises and stay there forever"* (39:73) [sic].[620]

- For God the Exalted has bestowed upon them the honor of self-disclosure in the location of greeting. In their deficient state He has qualified their essences with exaltation. For that reason they are "houries assigned to their masters in pavilions." They are upon an evident proof coming from their Lord, and afterwards a witness from among them has strengthened that proof. Thus He has exalted them

---

618. Ken'an Rifâî, *Sohbetler* (Istanbul: Kubbealtı Neşriyatı 2000), pp. 57-58.
619. Elmalı M. Hamdi Yazır, *Hak Dini Kur'an Dili* (Istanbul: Feza Gazetecilik 1992), vol. 6, p. 421.
620. Ken'an Rifâî, *Sohbetler* (Istanbul: Kubbealtı Neşriyatı 2000), p. 455.

55TH-56TH-57TH VERSE

to the boons of peforming the requisites of faith and Islam, and has supported them with divine power.[621]

• Hazret Messenger has said in a noble hadith, *"While the people of Paradise enjoy boons, a light shines upon them and they lift their heads to see that above them the Lord has honored them with the honor of seeing His face. He says, 'Peace be upon you, O people of Paradise.' This it is that is the divine speech, 'A word of greeting from a Merciful Lord.' Then He gazes upon them, and they gaze upon Him, and while they gaze, they turn toward none of the other boons until He is covered, and then light and blessing remain upon them and their land."*[622]

• On this day the people of Paradise are occupied with the lights of divine self-disclosure and witnessing of divine attributes. Their souls, appropriate to themselves and themselves in love, are in enjoyment.

They rest upon stations and levels in the shade of the lights of the attributes.

For them there are fruits of the lights of comprehension and the classes of what can be understood by the intellect and what is unveiled. For there are the witnessings they sought, and that is *"A word of greeting from a Merciful Lord."*

It is the greeting emanating as speech from the mercifying Lord possessed of mercy with the grace of perfections and perfections and, the desired remedy becoming the cause, what is desired because of their being distanced from the defects of form.[623]

• The gracious verse, *"Your Lord who created you from a single soul and from it created its mate..."* (4:1) expresses that Adam and Eve are, as mother and father, the source of the whole of human beings, and

---

621. Muhyiddîn İbnü'l-Arabî, trans. Vahdettin İnce, *Risâleler* (Istanbul: Kitsan Yayınları), vol. 1, p. 157.

622. Emir Sultan, trans. and commentary Melih Yuluğ, *Yâ-Sîn-i Şerîf'in Meal Tefsiri-Esrar ve Havassı* (Istanbul: Çelik Yayınevi n.d.), p. 364.

623. Kemâlüddin Abdürrezzak Kâşâniyyüs Semerkandî, trans. Ali Rıza Doksanyedi, ed. M. Vehbi Güloğlu, *Te'vilât-ı Kâşâniyye* (Ankara Kadıoğlu Matbaası 1988), vol. 3, p. 15.

its continuation, *"Who in those two brought forth a multitude of men and women,"* that their children are their parts.[624]

• If the intellect is the man, the soul is the woman. In the house of the human body these two are at war, quarreling day and night, asking each other difficult questions of why and wherefore. At the same time, in order to distinguish good from evil a person must know them, and comprehend both the intellect and soul with all their mysteries and reasons.[625]

The beauties described as houries are in one sense our perfected souls, the male slaves our intellects bound to the universal intellect, and the kiosks our bodies adorned with houries and male slaves. Thus when we are perfect, we are Paradise. For perfect human beings are those who continually view God and know their own nothingness.[626]

• Paradise has two parts. One is in this world, and the other in the other world. The body, the grave, of those who attain the good fortune to die before they die will be one of the gardens of Paradise. At that rank the servant enters the paradise of gnosis. And sees God the Truth with the eye of witnessing.[627]

• Know that God has servants whose hearts are full of love of their Lord. They wait for death because of their longing for their Beloved. They consider it despicable to remain long in this world. There is no comfort or peace of mind for them as long as they do not leave this world. They are sorry and sorrowful at have stayed long in this world. Their desire to leave this world is stronger than the desire for water of someone who is dying of thirst. When the hour of death approaches, along with the Angel of Death seventy thousand angels come to them sent by God, who salutes and greets them. This is indicated in the Gracious Quran thus: " (They are) *those whom the angels take in a state of goodness. They will say, 'Peace be upon you, enter the paradise that is the recompense for what you did'"* (16:32).

---

624. Ahmed er-Rifâî, ed. Dr. H. Kâmil Yılmaz, *Marifet Yolu* (Istanbul: Erkam Yayıncılık 1995), p. 177.
625. Ken'an Rifâî, *Şerhli Mesnevî-i Şerif* (Istanbul: Kubbealtı Neşriyatı 2000), p. 381.
626. Compiler's note.
627. Ken'an Rifâî, *Sohbetler* (Istanbul: Kubbealtı Neşriyatı 2000), p. 578.

55TH-56TH-57TH VERSE

A funeral procession passed by the Commander of the Faithful Hazret Ali. He said, "He has attained to repose, or been liberated from." Then it was asked, "Who is it that attains to repose?" Hazret Ali said, "A believing person. For he is liberated from the cares of the world and the torments of the people of the world, and then, reaching the mercy of God, attains to respose. A person to be liberated from is a sinning person. When he dies, servants and lands are liberated from him and attain repose."[628]

- "*Did We not make the earth a couch, and the mountains, pegs?*" (78:6-7). Shaykh Abu Jafar explicated these verses: The couch of the world and the pegs that prevent it from shaking are the believers. The couch of the believers and its pegs (that prevent it from shaking) are the gnostics. The couch of the gnostics and its pegs (that prevent it from shaking) are the prophets. The couch of the prophets and its pegs (that prevent it from shaking) are the messengers.[629]

---

628. Ahmed er-Rifâî, trans. Dr. Ali Can Tatlı, *Sohbet Meclisleri* (Istanbul: Erkam Yayınları 1996), pp. 169-170.

629. Muhyiddin İbnü'l-Arabî, trans. Vahdettin İnce, *Rûhu'l Kuds* (Istanbul: Kitsan), p. 112.

58. A word of greeting from a Merciful Lord.
Salāmun qawlan min rabbin rahīm.

- *Rahîm* is one whose mercy and compassion are limitless; who presents special mercies in a way appropriate to the imperatives of worldly life to those living, and after death.[630]

- One who without taking vengeance, without scolding or shaming, teaches the form of repentance and then forgives.
  The compassionate is one who withholds and bestows, who gives what is asked, and is angered when it is not asked.
  "Muhammed, with his Exalted (Azîz) name, is Messenger; he is troubled by what you suffer. He is very fond of you; he is merciful (Raûf) to the believers, he is Rahîm (protector) " (9:128) [sic]. For the sorrow of punishment is not mixed with his mercy. Thus he is a mercy to the worlds.[631]

- Punishment and torment may be mixed in with the Merciful's mercy, like, for example, drinking a medicine that tastes and smells bad. For just as mercy exists in this for the patient, something inappropriate to created nature exists in it also. But nothing is ever mixed in with the mercy to which the Merciful has guided. That is pure boon. That boon is found only in those possessed of perfection and complete felicity. Compared to the Compassionate (*Rahmân*), the Merciful (*Rahîm*) is like the eye in the human bodily constitution. In other words, the Merciful has a more Exalted state, one glory is more

---

630. Yaşar Nuri Öztürk, trans., *Kuran-ı Kerîm Meâli* (Istanbul: Hürriyet Ofset Matbaacılık 1994), p. 582.

631. Abdü'l-kerîm b. İbrahim el-Cîlî, trans. Seyyid Hüseyin Fevzî Paşa, *İnsan-ı Kâmil* (Istanbul: Kitsan Yayınları), p. 421.

sublime and more particular. Still, the Merciful has an unbounded comprehensiveness over all mercies. That is why it has been said that the mercy in the Merciful appears only in its precise sense in the Hereafter.[632]

• Hazret Muhammed (s.a.s.) returned from the graveyard and when he came to Hazret Aisha, she was amazed. She ran to him and searched him with her hands, looked him in the face, again surprised, and caressed his beard, turban, collar and chest.

Hazret Muhammed (s.a.s.) asked her: "O Aisha, what are you searching me for so anxiously? What are you worried about?" Hazret Aisha answered: "O Muhammed! Today the sky was covered with great clouds and it rained. That is why I am searching your clothes, but how strange, you are not wet." Hazret Muhammed (s.a.s.) then asked: "O Aisha, what were you wearing on your head when you saw clouds and rain in the sky?" Aisha said: "I used your cloak as a veil." Then the Messenger of God said: "O pure-hearted Aisha! What you saw was not the rain of the worldly skies, it was the mercy of the Unseen. (Give thanks for your pure gaze, be glad, give thanks and praise that) God showed you His own essential mercy." That is how it is, many are the eyes that do not see the mercy raining upon the world where they are and where they live. And many a pure gaze illuminated by divine light sees the rain falling in the realms of mystery for the sake of breasts that are burning and thirsty with love of God.[633]

• *Ahad* (*one*) is perfection, and Ahmed is not yet in the station of perfections. When that *mim* (*the letter "m"*) lifts, he will find perfection completely.[634]

• This is the Lord self-disclosure in the Messenger's servanthood.

The "perfect murshid" is what they call persons who have found their perfecittion, become God the Truth with God the Truth, and

---

632. Abdü'l-kerîm b. İbrahim el-Cîlî, trans. Seyyid Hüseyin Fevzî Paşa, *İnsan-ı Kâmil* (Istanbul: Kitsan Yayınları), pp. 151-152.

633. Ken'an Rifâî, *Şerhli Mesnevî-i Şerif* (Istanbul: Kubbealtı Neşriyatı 2000), pp. 290-291.

634. Mevlânâ Celâleddin Rûmî, trans. Melika Ülker Anbarcioğlu, *Fîhi mâ Fîh* (Istanbul: Milli Eğitim Basımevi 1985), p. 333.

who has removed himself and become the messenger of God the Truth; this rank is bestowed only directly by the Lord (*Cenâb-ı Mevlâ*). Those who are messengers of God the Truth certainly show the ocean of the the Muhammeden realities and say to those to whome they show it, "Come, plunge in!"

God's Messenger is distinguished from creatures by the secret of "*I too am a human being, but I receive revelation*" (18:110) [sic]. Murshids also have a human aspect. They mix among people, do what everyone does, they eat, drink, go around, walk. But perfect humans are mirrors of the light of the sun of the Muhammeden realities, and sites of manifestation for God's Essence and attributes. The greatest desire of all creatures is the Muhammeden realities found in the heart of a Perfect Human Being.

Although perfect humans are in form a microcosm, in meaning they are magnificent macrocosms in whom everything has been gathered. Now, traffic with perfect humans is like traffic with God. It is this Perfect Human of whom God the Truth says in the Gracious Quran, "*If the oceans were ink, they could not by writing exhaust the qualities of the perfect arrived person.*" And again, "*If We brought forth that many oceans, even they would dry up and still be unable to write*" (18:109) [sic].[635]

- **The Greatest Murshid:** Look how the Most Gracious Messenger has, with the light of the realities he sent forth, with the ray of God the Truth, turned the night of human beings to day their winter to summer, and with the revolution he wrought in the world changed the shape of the world and put it into an illumined form. Yes, if the illumined beauty of that personage did not look upon creation, creation would appear in universal mourning. All existents would be alien to one another and enemies. Inanimate things would be each display a funereal form. Animals and humans would fade away like orphans and cry out in horror with fear of loss, and creation with its movements, change of color and variations would be regarded as a toy dependent upon coincidence. Human beings especially would be lower than animals, servile and contemptible. Thus if creation were not regarded with the gaze of the faith that personage inculcated, it would have appered in such a horrible dark form. But when it is

---

635. Ken'an Rifâî, *Sohbetler* (Istanbul: Kubbealtı Neşriyatı 2000), p. 518.

regarded with the eye of that perfect murshid and the eye of faith, it will display itself everywhere as an illumined, splendid, animate, living, loved beloved.[636]

- The heart free of defect is brought forth by knowledge and works. This knowledge is the knowledge of unification; it means: *Allahümme yessir lenâ ilme lâ ilâhe illallah*, in other words, "My God, favor me with the knowledge of 'There is no god but God,'" and to ask to have that knowledge.

Unification knowledge is to know everything as being from God, to see God the Truth's self-disclosure in everything you see, to not meddle in God's works, saying that happened in that way and this happened in this way, to know that if you encounter a calamity it comes of your own fault, and if you are the site of manifestation of a kindness, you must accept it thinking, "I am not worthy of this kindness, it is a boon from my God." In sum, one must know one, love one, see one.

Know that the agent and the existent are God
To deny it is calamity

You must not hurt anyone and must not be hurt by anyone. If they do you some wrong, you must take it kindly. You must not lie.

Then comes action. In other words, to not diverge from straightness and justice in your state or in your words, to see and know that before God the Truth you are nothing in your own being.

Justice is to strive to acquire God the Truth's acceptance. For those who behave in that way and go straight, thinking, "God is my Lord," there is no fear or sorrow. That is when He gives them the heart-free-of-defect passport. But if you want to get that passport through your strength, that is very difficult, maybe impossible. Even our Messenger of God Efendi says, "If He had not taught me, I would not have known my Lord." And the Imam-i Azam [Abu Hanife] too, after he became the disciple of Imam Ja'far, expressed gratitude for meeting that sultan,[637] saying, "If not for the past two years, Numan [Abu Hanife] would have perished."

---

636. Abdullah Yeğin, *Yeni Lugat* (Istanbul: Hizmet Vakfı Yay. 2004), p. 493.

637. [The term "sultan" can be used in Turkish for any great and/or beloved person, male or female.]

58th Verse

Thus one must strive to acquire that heart-free-of-defect passport by earning the acceptance of the murshid. The acceptance of murshids is earned by being painted with their paint, by following their path, by seeing and knowing.[638]

- Every messenger who has come and will come into the world, every friend of God, is a trumpet blast of breath from Exalted God the Truth. If people do not arrive at their goal with one breath, and that breath goes to waste, they should not give up hope, they must seek out another breath; for as long as the world exists those blessed ones also exist. And so the Messenger said, "*Truly in the days of our time there are the breaths of your Lord; watch for them.*" Exalted God the Truth conceals some of His friends; everyone in the world increases their truth, their love, their religion and perfect faith because of them, they continue to exist by them, their states increase because of the respect due them but they do not see that and do not know they should be grateful and sacrifice house and home and all they have for them. But they know and see that they (everyone in the world) are alive and have what they have because of them, just as trees and plants grow because of spring but do not know spring. The people of the world benefit from them, but do not know it; they know. Just as infant boys of three or two or one year of age do not know the one who brings them up, but they know that the infants are their children.

Have you not heard what the Messenger, the greatest of the padishahs of religion, said?

There are always breaths of God the Truth, which He commands, blowing from breath to breath in a chain.

Do all of you accept God's breaths sincerely, from the heart, with pure heart.

Thus may darkness be illuminated entirely; may your thorns be rose gardens.

One breath has come and gone, but you are heedless; He has made whomever He wishes mature.

That breath came and went, it was hidden; you all were left soulless and heartless.

Again a breath arrived to bestow purity, knowledge and vision.

---

638. Ken'an Rifâî, *Sohbetler* (Istanbul: Kubbealtı Neşriyatı 2000), p. 215.

Strive and do not remain deprived of it; if not, you will lose that benefit and suffer loss.

For if that breath comes and goes, know that you cannot attain your desire.

Know the value of the breath, strive hard to benefit from it and gain what you wish from the beloved.

There is a gift for us in that breath, by grace of God; those who denied it can only moan.

We acknowledged it and attained the gift; we were purified of the rust of denial.

Breath after breath is on the way, spirit is being bestowed upon us; hundreds of worlds without worlds are being granted.

Is it not so that we have lept from the world of dust and been saved; now we have unfinished business in the world.

We turned our back on ourselves and the world; we turned our faces to the realm of spirit.

We saw the face of the heart without veil; we heard secrets from the friend.

We drank the wine of immortality in God the Truth's hand; we died to our selves and our being, we are alive with Him.

By the grace of that Saki we subsist forever; the wine of God the Truth makes spirit immortal.

In the palace of eternity we have before us wine, tasty dishes, lamp, a young beauty and spirit.

From now on our path and rule is pleasure and ease, love is keen, our mount lightfooted.

Is it not so that he is the saki in both worlds; if you are a lover, open your eyes and

See the drunken; how they have spread through the garden with flute and tambourine.

The wine of spirite is being offered to them all; to the base and the high, to young and old.

And all are cheered with that wine, unware of themselves; all their hearts are joyous and alive with that gaze.

The fresh green branches of spring give flowers rather than fruit, just like him.

58th Verse

Know that those buds, those flowers are so that trees may bear fruit; and once they do, they will all fall.

As the wind blows, they fall and scatter like gold and silver, flying this way and that.

The branch is heavy with fruit but does not know it; it has no knowledge of its worthiness.

The rose blooms from behind the thorn; like a single rider it displays itself on the branches.

But from whom does its beauty come, why is that scent of it so sweet, it doesn't even know.

Plants and animals are unaware of themselves in the same way.

If now in our time a boon is bestowed upon the people by a friend of God,

But the people do not know of his boon, is it any wonder if they do not know how fortunate they are to receive boons from him, both hidden and visible?

That friend serves up a glass for every greeting, and grants a wish at the end of every speech.

Now gold rains down instead of rainwater; now the mine is here, forget the shop.

Grow wealthy from his treasure, all of you; become great and exalted with his rank and sublimity.

You have all become sweet because of him, give thanks; be intoxicated always with his wine.

He gives you gold without demanding anything in return, continually turning stones into jewels.

He has lifted from you your burdens, obligations and toil; being kind, he has raised the flag of generosity.

Troubles and sorrows have read you the spell of love and gone entirely, none remain.

He is hidden in the body of every one like spirit; he flows like blood in your veins and marrow.

Although you may not know him in appearance, know that you are ever pure because of him.

A child slave does not know its master, but ah, he who does know
Knows that his master is his slave; like a fish on his line.

Children gaze awed into the faces of their fathers with every breath, but

They do not know enough to know who he is, although well-being and life come from him.

Thus is the true shaykh in his time; boons come to everyone from him, and aid.

Strength and power, too, come to all from him, and daily bread; all live thanks to him like fish live in the sea.

Although they do not know he is the shadow of God, the two worlds obtain grace from him.

The skies are under his control, and earth as well; the army of the disbelief is under his command, and the army of religion.

Whatever he wishes immediately occurs; those in an evil state acquire good states because of him.

What matter if those donkeys do not know him; for he has no equal nor like.

Whatever there is in the two worlds is near to him; one of these is existence, another is space.

By his decree Hell becomes Heaven; obligation becomes entirely comfort.

He bestows being upon not-being; exaltation manifests from him, as does debasement.[639]

- The human being is like the pupil of an eye gazing from the level of God. And he is the creature known by the quality of seeing. That is why he is called a human. For God looked upon His creatures with man and had mercy upon them. Thus that man of eternity without beginning is (*with his form*) eternal without end and continuous with regard to event, manifestation and origin. He is a distinguishing being who unites two aspects. In other words, his beginningless and eternal aspects are united in his being. The universe became complete with his being. In that respect he is to the world what a gem is to a ring. He is the site of the design on the seal that the Padishah puts on his treasuries. That is why he was given the title of Vicegerent. Just as the seal protects the treasuries, that vicegerent protects God's creatures. As long as the Padishah's seal is on the treasuries, no one dares to open them. They are opened only with his permission. Thus

---

[639]. Sultan Veled, trans. Abdülbaki Gölpınarlı, *İbtidâ-name* (Konya: Konya ve Mülhakatı Eski Eserleri Sevenler Derneği 2001), pp. 320-323.

58th Verse

God made Adam His vicegerent in the matter of protecting the world. Therefore as long as there is the Perfect Human Being in the world, it will always be protected.[640]

• Among all the creatures only those who make their souls safe and sound from lusts and purify their hearts of doubts can reach the holiness of the name "Peace" (*Selâm*). Thus safety (*selâmet*) is from God the Truth to God the Truth.

The safety of the People of God the Truth is for them to be cleansed of the filth of doubt and the darkness of hidden or open şirk.

The sign of those who are qualified with the realities of that name is that they are sober, sedate and patient with those who are stubborn. They do not debate with careless people, or struggle with the ignorant; they are the way God has characterized those who have this characteristic.

Even if those who possess this station wanted to add something to the word "Peace," they would not have the power to. The reason for this is that they have no will, and God protects them, for God is the hearing, the seeing and all the limbs of such people.[641]

• *"No one has ever preceeded God's Messenger in giving greetings of peace"* (hadith). No one has ever given greetings of peace before the Messenger. For he was so extraordinarily humble that he always greeted others first.[642]

• Great God said, "O Messenger, greetings of peace to you!" This means greetings of peace upon you and everyone like you. If that were not Great God's intention, Hazret Mustafa would not have responded and said, "Peace be upon us and many a wholesome servant." If the greeting of peace were specific to him, the Messenger would not have added those wholesome servants. With that he meant to say

---

640. Muhyiddîn İbnü'l-Arabî, trans. Nuri Gençosman, *Fusûs'l-Hikem* (Istanbul: İstanbul Kitabevi Yayınları 1981), pp. 4-5.
641. Sadreddin Konevî, trans. Ekrem Demirli, *Esmâ-i Hüsnâ Şerhi* (Istanbul: İz Yayıncılık 2004), pp. 46-47.
642. Mevlânâ Celâleddin Rûmî, trans. Melika Ülker Anbarcıoğlu, *Fîhi mâ Fîh* (Istanbul: Milli Eğitim Basımevi 1985), p. 164.

that the greeting of Peace God gave him was for him and wholesome servants like him. For example, when performing ablutions, Hazret Mustafa said, *"The prayer is not sound, only this ablution is sound."* The intention in this is not certain. If this had been a specific ablution, no one's prayer would be correct. For what is under discussion here is only the soundness of Hazret Mustafa's ablution and prayer. Thus the intention is that whoever's ablution is not of that kind, his or her prayer will not be correct. For example, they say, "This is just like a pomegranate flower." What does that mean? Does it mean that the pomegranate flower is this same thing? No, it means that this is of the species of pomegranate flower.[643]

- Messages come to one who wails for love of God in this way. Countless states of joy and attraction come to him. He wails in love for You, "O my Lord," and You answer countless times, "I am here!" You give him the good news that You accept his every request.[644]

---

643. Mevlânâ Celâleddin Rûmî, trans. Melika Ülker Anbarcioğlu, *Fîhi mâ Fîh* (Istanbul: Milli Eğitim Basımevi 1985), p. 287.

644. Ken'an Rifâî, *Şerhli Mesnevî-i Şerif* (Istanbul: Kubbealtı Neşriyatı 2000), p. 221.

59. And, O you sinners, depart today!
Wa'mtāzū'l-yawma 'ayyuhā'l-mujrimūn.

- Here by sinners is meant those who construct and maintain Hell and cannot leave it. They are distinguished from those who emerge from Hell through the intercession of interceders and through the precedence of divine boon in those who unify (*birleyenler*).[645]

- The scale of justice and touchstone of virtue did not view it right for true pearl and ordinary bead, true and false coin, gold and copper, crow and falcon to be one and the same and confused with one another in the same row.

God brought forth Moses in order that Pharoah's magicians be distinguished from other magicians and the Jews from the Copts. And so it was with the Messenger of the Last Days, Muhammed. Before the manifestation of Mustafa (*Peace be upon him*), Abu Jahl and Siddiq were one in terms of rank. Indeed, Abu Jahl's name was Abu'l-Hakim. It became Abu Jahl [Father of Ignorance] due to infidelity and denial. This will continue in the same way until the destruction of the world.

The friends of God, inheritors of the messengers, invite the people to God as the messengers do because they have the same breath as them, the same time and the same light. All whose source is tied to God and takes light from Him and are verifiers (*muhakkık*) will incline toward them and accept their invitation. And from that invitation, with the breath of the friends of God, the souls of such people become rooted like a new tree. By means of that spring season, it continually

---

645. Muhyiddîn İbnü'l-Arabî, trans. Ekrem Demirli, *Fütuhât-ı Mekkiyye* (Istanbul: Litera Yayıncılık 2006), vol. 2, p. 402.

brings a freshness and vitality and bears fruit. Those who worship form and are imitators become colder and more lifeless day by day and their faces become blacker. However much progress and acceptance increases in the verifiers, denial increases in the imitators to that degree and they lose value.[646]

- The world is night and the Hereafter, day; the people of the world are the site of manifestation of night, and God's friends, of day. Daylight is a thing seen sometimes in a site of manifestation and sometimes without one. God the Exalted called the Resurrection "The Day of Religion." So the Hereafter is day, for good and evil become evident in bright daylight; that which is of Hell is distinguished from that which is of Heaven. The messengers and the arrived are sites of manifestation for the day, they have the property of daylight. By means of their being, believer is distinguished from disbeliever and denier from avower. By means of Adam's being, Iblis was distinguished from the angels. In the same way by means of Moses's being, Pharaoh and those who followed him, by means of Abraham's being, Nimrod and his followers, by means of Mustafa's being, Abu Jahl, Abu Lahab and their like were distinguished. The world and the people of the world are night; night brings on sleep. That is why people have sunk into the sleep of heedlessess, because the world is night, and to be sure,[647] their sleep will be heavy.[648]

- Hazret Mevlana has put this meaning into verse and explicated the unity of the people of God the Truth:

"That one in the red garment who came like a piece of the moon has come this year in this rust-colored cloak. That Turk I saw plundering that year is the same person coming this year as an Arab. However different the cup, the wine is the same wine. Look, how sweet is what happened to the winemaker! Though the garment has changed,

---

646. Sultan Veled, trans. Meliha Anbarcıoğlu, *Maarif* (Konya: Konya ve Mülhakatı Eski Eserleri Sevenler Derneği Yayınları 2002), p. 18.

647. Sultan Veled, trans. Abdülbaki Gölpınarlı, *İbtidâ-name* (Konya: Konya ve Mülhakatı Eski Eserleri Sevenler Derneği 2001), p. 235.

648. Sultan Veled, trans. Meliha Anbarcıoğlu, *Maarif* (Konya: Konya ve Mülhakatı Eski Eserleri Sevenler Derneği Yayınları 2002), p. 149.

59th Verse

the friend is the same friend. He has changed his garment and come in a different form."

Those who looked at Adam's external appearance and did not see that light shrank away from worshipping him. God created Adam as a test. The arrogance of some, their grandiosity and desire to be equal to him prevented them from worshipping him, from bowing down before him. But some who derive from a powerful source and have much of that original substance in them tear aside that curtain of arrogance and selfhood. That is when they see that original light without this veil of being, and they prostrate themselves. Those in whom the original substance is little and weak do not have the strength to tear aside that veil. They are defeated by the veil. To those who meet with defeat is given the property of nothingness. Although there is a tiny amount of copper mixed into pure silver, they still count it silver. For it has defeated the copper.[649]

- *For he knows this world of planting and sowing*
Exists for sake of the final Gathering

For they took the veil of letter and of breath
So that in moist clay meaning be manifest

Much suffering, trial, and waiting must occur
So that pure spirit be delivered from words

Moses said, "O Lord of the Reckoning Day,
How is it that You destroy the form You made?

"You make form male and female expand spirit
Then you make a ruin of form, why is that?"

God said, "I know that in this your questioning
There's no heedless, denying, capricious thing

"Or I would have disciplined and reproached you
For this question I'd have reprimanded you

---

649. Sultan Veled, trans. Meliha Anbarcıoğlu, *Maarif* (Konya: Konya ve Mülhakatı Eski Eserleri Sevenler Derneği Yayınları 2002), pp. 18-19.

O Humankind

"But you wish to discover within Our acts
The wisdom and secret of continuance

"That you may this to the common folk relate
And bring every raw person to a cooked state

"You are questioning for sake of common folk
To unveil it to them though you yourself know"

Then God said, "O you possessed of intellect
Come and hear the answer, seeing you have asked

"Go, O Moses, sow seed in the earth yourself
That you may know the justice of this yourself"

When Moses had planted and his crop matured
And the fruits were orderly and beautiful

He took up the sickle and set out to reap
When an outcry reached his ear from the Unseen

Saying, "Why is it you plant and tend the seed
Yet you cut it down when perfection is reached?"

He said, "O Lord, I cut it down to the ground
Because there is both grain and chaff to be found

"One cannot store seed inside the barn for straw
And the barn for seed is ruinous for straw

"It is not wise to combine the two of them
Winnowing is needed to separate them"

He said, "In this knowledge who was your mentor
So that you knew to construct a threshing floor?"

He said, "You, O Lord, granted me discernment
Thus how could it be I'd not have discernment?

"Among the creatures there exist pure spirits
And there are also dark and mud-stained spirits

59th Verse

"These shells are not of one and the same degree
One contains a pearl and one a common bead

This evil and good must be made manifest
Just as grain from chaff must be made manifest"

The world's creatures are for manifestation
So that wisdom's treasures not remain hidden

Listen! "I was a hidden treasure," he said
Don't let your substance be lost, be manifest

Your substance of truth is hid within a lie
Like the taste of butter hidden in ayran

For years this ayran of flesh is manifest
Spirit's butter dies within like a carcass

Until God sends a servant as messenger
Who churns the ayran inside the container

Churning it with method craftsmanlike and skilled
So that I may know that I have been concealed

Or a servant's speech, his part, may enter in
The ear of one who seeks for inspiration

True believers' ears keep our inspiration
Ears that match the one who makes invitation[650]

From the world come two cries in opposition
To see which one matches your preparation

One of the cries resurrects those who fear God
While the other tricks the wretched who are lost

"I'm a thorn blossom, O fair one in pursuit
The blossom falls, a thorn branch is left to you"

---

650. Mevlânâ Celâleddin Rûmî, trans. Veled İzbudak, ed. Abdülbaki Gölpınarlı, *Mesnevî* (Istanbul: Milli Eğitim Basımevi 1991), vol. 4, vs. 2989, 2972, 2985, 3001-3007, 3015-3036.

O Humankind

"Here's the flower seller!" is its blossom cry
"Do not hasten towards me," is its thorn cry

You choose one, and you cannot have the other
Lovers are deaf to their beloved's other

Once you're in one of these two sacks you will be
Out of place in the other and contrary

The cry finds the house empty and finds its place
All else seems unnatural or reprobate

In the world each thing draws something to its side
Disbelief infidel, righteousness the guide

There is the magnet and there is the amber
Be you straw or iron, you'll come to the snare

If you are iron, the magnet takes you off
And you will twist to amber if you are straw

Anyone who is not friend to the goodly
Is neighbor to evil necessarily

For the Copts, Moses is quite despicable
For the Jews, Haman is abominable

Haman's spirit was attractive to the Copt
It was the Jews whom Moses's spirit sought

If in darkness you don't recognize a man
Look to whom he has taken as his imam[651]

Mustafa's counselor was truthful Bu Bakr
Abu Jahl was the counselor of Lahab

The root of his nature drew him in so that
The counsels of Mustafa were cold and flat

---

651. Mevlânâ Celâleddin Rûmî, trans. Veled İzbudak, ed. Abdülbaki Gölpınarlı, *Mesnevî* (Istanbul: Milli Eğitim Basımevi 1991), vol. 4, 1622-1626, 1629, 1631, 1633-1638, 1640.

59th Verse

Like kind flies to like upon a hundred wings
Breaking bonds in seeking the image of him[652]

- Although the wretched are wretched in their mothers' wombs, the signs of this invisible wretchedness, which become visible only after the spirit enters the body, are known to those who know. For the body is in a sense the mother's womb within which each spirit matures. Whether the body is white or black, every state that will come forth on the day of death occurs in the spirits while they are in the womb called the body. In other words, when a spirit penetrates a body it gives to the body the form of its own preparedness; it becomes the spirit of that body. In another sense the spirit bows to the judgment of the decree and the measuring out. It travels from the gathering in eternity without beginning to this world as a flawed spirit. But because its shame is hidden under the veil of the body, it is not visible to those whose eyes do not see it.

And all during a lifetime the body is pregnant with the child called spirit. The body carries it in its womb for the space of a lifetime, nourishing it, and death is the pain of the spirit's birth into another realm.

Azrail was created from a unique light called the power of supposition. It seizes each spirit according to the nature of that spirit.

When a spirit enters into a body, it does not leave its station in the realm of spirits. It is joined to the body like a ray of light that is not separated from its source. In fact the connection the spirit makes with bodily form is for the purpose of gaining the character that will please God, in order to reach the meaning of creation. Either it gains this character and ascends with it, or it acquires an animal character and remains in the prison of nature, never reaching the sublime realms.

Azrail approaches such spirits with a terrifying face, not with his own beautiful face. He makes them tremble in terror and seizes them that way. to other spirits he appears in his pure being, and at that moment the spirit binds itself with profound love to the One who wishes to take it; the spirit leaves the body and lovingly throws itself into the arms of the Beloved.

---

652. Mevlânâ Celâleddin Rûmî, trans. Veled İzbudak, ed. Abdülbaki Gölpınarlı, *Mesnevî* (Istanbul: Milli Eğitim Basımevi 1991), vol. 4, 2654-2656.

O Humankind

When a spirit leaves the body in order to be reborn in the realm of spirits there is a struggle between the white faces, that is, the Romans, and the black faces, the Ethiopians. The Ethiopians represent the wretched spirits, who are bad-natured, vicious and envious, in short black spirits. They become excited, thinking that spirit is one of them. The Roman spirits, high-natured, enlightened and white, want the newly arrived spirit to be one of the good ones as they are. And when a spirit which has separated from a body is born at last into the afterworld, the conflict between the black and white spirits is over. Whether the spirit is white or black becomes obvious to the entire spirit realm.

If the spirit is one of those bound to darkness, lust and animal nature, the blacks take it; it is surrounded by angels of torment who take it to the realm of darkness to which it belongs.

If it belongs to light and is one of the good and beautiful spirits, angels of God's mercy and good news take it and bring it to the station of which it is worthy.[653]

---

653. Ken'an Rifâî, *Şerhli Mesnevî-i Şerif* (Istanbul: Kubbealtı Neşriyatı 2000), pp. 516-517.

60. Did I not enjoin you, O children of Adam, that you should not worship Satan? Surely he is an evident enemy to you.

'Alam 'a'had 'ilaykum yābanī 'adama 'an lā ta'budū'sh-shayṭāna 'innahu lakum 'aduwun mubīn.

61. And that you should worship Me. That is the straight path.

Wa 'ani''budūnī hādhā ṣirāṭun mustaqīm.

- *"Surely Satan is an enemy to you, so take him as an enemy. He calls only his party to be companions of the blaze"* (35:6).

   Devils, who are created of fire, are the enemies of humans, who are held to be superior to them even though they are created of earth. For humans are created of water as well as earth. Just as fire is enemy of water, Satan is the enemy of humans, who are created of water. For Satan is the child of fire, and human beings are the children of water. The great advantage water has over fire is that it can extinguish fire.[654]

- Satan was the first creature to pursue the path of analogy by comparing his own nature with that of Hazret Adam in opposition to the speech of God, which as the light of God illuminates spirits and the universe.

   The reason for this was that Satan refrained from bowing down to Hazret Adam, although the one who commanded all the angels and Satan to bow down to Adam was God.

---

654. Ken'an Rifâî, *Şerhli Mesnevî-i Şerif* (Istanbul: Kubbealtı Neşriyatı 2000), p. 544.

When God asked Iblis, "What is preventing you from bowing down to the human I created with my own hand?", Satan said: "Certainly fire is superior to earth. I was created of fire. Since Adam was created of earth, I compared fire with earth and reached the conclusion that I am superior to Adam and cannot bow down to black earth. For what is original is light. What is subsidiary, that is, secondary to the original, is darkness. Since earth is dark, how can it be that light should be subject to earth?"

God's response was: "Relations and ancestry are not considered; those who abstain from what God has forbidden and worship God with perfect sincerity of heart are the prayer-niche of virtue."

In fact if Satan and Adam were to really be compared, relative to the light of the fire from which Satan was created, the light forming Adam's substance is as superior and luminous as the light of the sun relative to night. For the spirit breathed into Adam's body kneaded of earth is a part of the divine light.[655]

- You know that Satan had worshipped God for hundreds of thousands of years. In the end, he abandoned the right road because his thinking was envious and greedy and he did not use his intellect and fell into the greatest of errors.

Because of his pride and arrogance, Satan was deprived of God's greatest bounty and great God presented the knowledge of His own sublime realm to the hearts of Adam and the progeny of Adam.

That is why to think material knowledge enough and remain unaware of the knowledge of truth brought to you by the prophets and friends of God, not learning the knowledge of God, is to be like a calf who cannot drink its mother's milk because its muzzle is bound with a strap.

Neither the spirit mind (*can dimağı*) nor heart's lip of persons who act according to their own intellects in matters of the world and the afterlife, and remain uninformed about the mysteries of the friends and the prophets, are wetted by divine knowledge or the taste of love of God.

---

[655]. Ken'an Rifâî, *Şerhli Mesnevî-i Şerif* (Istanbul: Kubbealtı Neşriyatı 2000), p. 499.

60TH-61TH VERSE

Only those who have been able to turn the faces of their hearts toward the arrived rise up from the pleasures of this material world and reach the secrets of the delights of the heart.[656]

- With the existence of God's vicegerent wrong was distinguished from right, crooked from straight, bad from good, near from far, dregs from pure, false coin from true, friend from stranger. Before that, in the darkness of a night produced by the absence of the shaykh who is like the full moon, everything appeared to be the same and the beautiful and the ugly were one. With the existence of this shaykh like the full moon all things secret and hidden became manifest.[657]

- When a person cannot comprehend the power and sublimity of love, he becomes its enemy. Those who possess the partial intellect sometimes suppose that they possess mysteries and resent this state. They ask, "Does our intellect have no understanding?" One should tell them that although the partial intellect is smart and knowing, it has never experienced becoming naught. Even an angel is no different from a devil as long as it has not become naught. Just as Satan, who was created from fire, claimed to be superior to the human being created of clay and refused to bow down to Adam, nourished a claim to selfhood and for that reason was driven out of God's heaven, even an angel made of light would be the same as Satan if he refused to bow down because he was made of light.[658]

- Every heart in which there is doubt and belief in error instead of perfect faith will tremble like a leaf in autumn on the Day of Resurrection.

Because you suppose yourself to be a good person and think that "superior people are distinguished by their rejection of the invisible," you laugh at devils, devils and jinn. But to suppose that what you do not know and cannot see does not in fact exist is the clearest expression of ignorance and error.

---

656. Ken'an Rifâî, *Şerhli Mesnevî-i Şerif* (Istanbul: Kubbealtı Neşriyatı 2000), p. 139.

657. Sultan Veled, trans. Meliha Anbarcıoğlu, *Maarif* (Konya: Altunarı Ofset 2002), p. 34.

658. Ken'an Rifâî, *Şerhli Mesnevî-i Şerif* (Istanbul: Kubbealtı Neşriyatı 2000), p. 283.

O Humankind

The philosopher rejects the existence of jinn, demons and devils. He thinks these are all fantasies created by supposition, and does not know that he is in the hand of the Satan he rejects even while he rejects him. He has become Satan's toy, his fool.

O believers, there is a philosopher's vein in almost everyone. Almost everyone has moments of doubt. If you abandon the way of the friends and prophets and dip into the branches of philosophy, straying to the paths of the philosophers who each say the contrary of the other, at the end of the road where you have strayed you will meet only disappointment.[659]

- *His servanthood is better than sultanate*
For "I am better than he" is Satan's phrase

O prisoner, see the difference and choose
Over Iblis's pride Adam's servanthood

If you go toward selfhood and forsake this shade
You will soon be insolent and lose the way

Go to the heart, go, for you're part of the heart
Heed, for you're servant of the just padishah[660]

- God's appearance and self-disclosure in the heart, condition of entrance to Paradise, is first to win the love of God's special servants, that is, the love of a perfect human. In this way a person makes his soul-bound being reach the nothingness of bondage to God the Truth. In this way he becomes mature and begins to see and taste the life of Paradise while still in this world.[661]

- The people of the world loved Bal'am ibn Ba'ur to the point of worshipping him. They so believed in his spiritual superiority that they bowed down to no one else. Bal'am's breath did really heal the sick and make them well.

---

659. Ken'an Rifâî, *Şerhli Mesnevî-i Şerif* (Istanbul: Kubbealtı Neşriyatı 2000), p. 481.
660. Mevlânâ Celâleddin Rûmî, trans. Veled İzbudak, ed. Abdülbaki Gölpınarlı, *Mesnevî* (Istanbul: Milli Eğitim Basımevi 1991), vol. 4, vs. 3342-3343, 3347, 3341.
661. Ken'an Rifâî, *Şerhli Mesnevî-i Şerif* (Istanbul: Kubbealtı Neşriyatı 2000), p. 388.

60th-61st Verse

With time Bal'am himself came to believe that he possessed spiritual power and superiority, to the extent that he began to compete against Hazret Moses and tussle with him.

There are there are hundreds of thousands of such Satans and Bal'ams in the world. They too told those who praised them that they possessed spiritual virtues and grew arrogant before those who bowed down to them, coming to believe in their own lies. For that reason they were cursed by God and driven away by God.

God the Truth made Satan and Bal'am renowned so that with their mistakes and the errors they made they might be an example to others and other bondsmen might take lessons from what happened to them.

You may be accepted by God and preciously brought up. But you are still obliged to fear God and not transgress bounds with Him who loves you so. If you err and engage in combat with someone superior to you in God's sight, God will distance you from His light as he did Iblis and Bal'am.[662]

- Beware of envy! What perverts a person's soul and sets in motion the devil within him is that abominable envy. It was because Satan was jealous of Adam that he did not bow down to him. That is why he was driven away from God the Truth and the realm of light. Do not you then regard with envious eye those who are superior to you, especially the Perfect Humans. It is that envious gaze which makes the universe appear black as black can be. As long as you avoid envy, as long as you do not fall into the trap of the devil of envy, you will see that great light.[663]

- The great malady in people is their error in thinking themselves perfect. This is the most harmful of all spiritual diseases, to remain a stranger to divine power and become arrogant and proud in the illusion of one's own power.

Satan's great malady was to see himself as higher than Adam. That is why he refrained from bowing down to Adam. He opposed the divine command and was cursed with the name of Satan. Many,

---

662. Ken'an Rifâî, *Şerhli Mesnevî-i Şerif* (Istanbul: Kubbealtı Neşriyatı 2000), p. 484, 471.

663. Ken'an Rifâî, *Şerhli Mesnevî-i Şerif* (Istanbul: Kubbealtı Neşriyatı 2000), p. 66.

many people have this satanic spirit which is manifested in seeing one's self as superior to everyone and everything. Beware of such thoughts and of such people.

Such people sometimes show false humility, pretending they feel lowly and prostrating themselves. They make a habit of worship and behave as if they are among those who are pure, clean and believing. Know that the humility of such people, who do not submit themselves to a murshid, is arrogance!

If an arrived person, a pir, a murshid, spreads the salve of love, friendship and guidance on that raging wound of yours, the thrill of feeling God, of being in love with God, will free you of your own self and the wounds of your self. You will be filled with a light of God you have not known, and whose limitless delight you could not have known before reaching that state. You will find yourself free of anxiety for this world and the afterlife.

Sometimes it happens that when the salve is applied to the wound, the patient thinks the pus is gone and becomes heedless, suddenly feeling that he is better. But this is only the shining of light on the wound. In order to be healed, to be a spirit exactly as God whishes, the treatment must continue. Do not abandon the murshid! The path he will show you is not just the beginning of the path. One must walk this path to the end.[664]

- Those beset by opinion and doubt cannot understand truth. They seek evidence they can touch with their hands in order to believe. They do not see the evidence that can be seen with the eye of the heart and they do not hear the voices that can be heard with the ear of the heart.

Treacherous Satan puts a doubt in their hearts so icy that they cannot melt it with their own heat. That doubt freezes all their conscience and perspicacity. Although their eyes see forms, they cannot see their meanings. Thus does the devil within them throw them headlong over a foreordained cliff.

In any case, those who do not know God do not know Him because they cannot see Him.[665]

---

664. Ken'an Rifâî, *Şerhli Mesnevî-i Şerif* (Istanbul: Kubbealtı Neşriyatı 2000), p. 469.
665. Ken'an Rifâî, *Şerhli Mesnevî-i Şerif* (Istanbul: Kubbealtı Neşriyatı 2000), pp. 308-309.

60th-61th Verse

- Muaz ibn Jabal relates from Hazret Ibn Abbas: "One day we were with the Messenger of God. We had gathered in the home of one of the Ansar. We were a complete congregation. We were deep in conversation. At that point a voice was heard from outside: 'Master of the house, will you give me leave to enter? I have a request to make of you. There is a matter I wish to discuss.'

"Everyone looked to our Messenger of God Efendi. There as always, he was the greatest of us... Permission would come from him. Our Messenger of God (s.a.s.) Efendi became aware of the situation and said, 'Do you know who it is who has called out?' All together we answered, 'God and His Messenger know best.' Then our Messenger of God Efendi said, 'It is Iblis the accursed.' Immediatly Hazret Umar said, 'O Messenger of God, permit me to kill him.' Our Messenger of God Efendi did not give permission; he said, 'Wait, O Umar, do you not know that he has been given respite until an appointed time... Give up on killing him.' Then he said, 'Open the door and let him come, he has received an order to come here. Try to understand what he will say. Listen well to what he will say to us.'

"Let us hear the rest form him, that is to say, from the Narrator. He said: They opened to the door to him. He came in and appeared to us. We looked and saw that he had the following form: An old man, cross-eyed. And he was beardless. Six or seven hairs swung from his chin. Like horsehairs. His eyes gazed upwards. His head was like a large elephant head. And his lips were like the lips of a buffalo.

"Then he gave the greeting, 'Peace be upon you, O Muhammed; peace be upon you, O community of Muslims.' Our Messenger of God (s.a.s.) Efendi gave to his greeting this response: 'Peace belongs to God, O accursed one.' Then he said to him, 'I hear you have come for a certain matter; what is that matter?'

"Satan explained, 'An angel came to me from your Lord of Exaltation and said: "God the Exalted gives you an order: 'You will go to Muhammed. But in a fallen, servile state. Humbly. You will go to him and relate how you have duped the children of Adam. You will tell him in detail how you have fooled them. Then whatever he asks you, you will tell him the truth.' Then God the Exalted said, 'If you add any falsehood to what you say, if you do not tell the truth, I will turn you to ashes; I will cast you to the winds and disgrace you before your enemies.'"

"'That is how it is, O Muhammed, I came to you by that order. Ask me whatever you wish. If I do not give a true answer to what you ask, my enemies will have their fun with me. This much is certain, that there is nothing so difficult as being the plaything of my enemies.'

"Then Our Messenger of God (s.a.s.) Efendi asked, 'Since you will be truthful in what you say, tell me, who is it among people that you hate most?'

"Satan answered, 'You, O Muhammed. There is none among the creatures that I hate more than you. And who can be like you?'

"Our Messenger of God (s.a.s.) Efendi asked, 'After me, who do you have most enmity for and hate?'

"Satan said, 'A devout youth who has dedicated his being to the path of God.'

"Then the questions and answers continued as follows:

"Our Messenger of God (s.a.s.) Efendi asked, and Satan explained. 'Then whom do you hate?' 'A scholar I know to be patient, who avoids doubtful matters.' 'Then?' 'A person who when washing, washes the part three times.' 'Then?' 'A patient pauper who tells no one of his need. Who does not complain.' 'All right then, how do you know that pauper is patient?' 'O Muhammed, he does not tell anyone like himself of his need. Whoever tells someone like himself of his need for three days in a row, God does not record him as one of the patient. Those who are patient do not behave that way. In sum, I know his patience from his state, his behavior, and his not complaining.' 'Then who?' 'The wealthy who give thanks to God.' 'All right, but how do you know that wealthy person gives thanks to God?' 'If I see that he gets lawfully what he aquires and spends upon his neighborhood, I know that he is a wealthy man who gives thanks to God.'

"Our Messenger of God (s.a.s.) Efendi changed the subject and asked another question:

"'All right then, what is your state when my community stands for prayer?' 'O Muhammed, a fever comes over me and I tremble.' 'Why do you get like that?' 'Because when a servant prostrates himself to God, he is exalted a level.' 'All right, how are you when they fast?' 'I am bound up at that time, until they break the fast.' 'And when they perform the pilgrimage to Mecca?' 'Then I go mad.'

60th-61st Verse

"'And how are you when they recite the Quran?' 'Then I melt. I melt just like lead in fire.' 'And how are you when they give alms?'

"'Ah, then I am in a terrible way. It is as if the one who gives alms takes up a saw and cuts me in two.'

"Our Messenger of God (s.a.s.) Efendi asked why:

"'Why are you cut in two with a saw like that, O Abu Murra?' 'Because alms have four beauties:

"'God the Exalted grants blessing upon the wealth of people who give alms.

"'He makes people love those who give alms.

"'God the Exalted makes the alms that people give a partition between them and Hell.

"'God the Exalted drives trials, unpleasant things and sighs away from them.'

"Then Our Messenger of God (s.a.s.) Efendi asked him several questions about the Companions:

"'What do you have to say about Abu Bakr?' 'Even in the Days of Ignorance he did not obey me... how should he do so after entering Islam?' 'All right then, what do you say about Umar ibn. Khattab?' 'I swear by God that I flee him wherever I see him.' 'All right, what about Osman ibn Affan?' 'I am ashamed before him, very much so... Just as the angels of the Merciful are ashamed before him.' 'All right, about Ali ibn Abu Talib?' 'Ah, if only I could be free of him... If he would keep to himself, and I keep to myself. If He would leave me alone, and I, him... I would leave him alone, but he will never leave me alone.'

"'Praise be to God who grants the boon of felicity to my community, and makes you wretched (*deprived of salvation in eternity without beginning*) until an appointed time.'

"Hearing that sentence from Our Messenger of God (s.a.s.) Efendi, accursed Iblis said:

"'Alas, alas! Where is the felicity of your community? As long as I am alive until that appointed time, how should your community feel as ease? I enter into the channels of their blood. I mix with their flesh. But they do not see that state of mine and they do not know. I swear by God who created me and gives me respite until the Day of Resurrection that I will seduce all of them. The ignorant and the knowledgable, the illiterate and the literate... The sinners and the worshippers... In sum, not one of them can escape me. Except for God's sincere servants. Yes, they I cannot seduce.'

"'Upon that, Our Messenger of God Efendi said:

"'Who, according to you, are the sincere servants?' 'Do you not know, O Muhammed, that those who love their dirhem and dinars... They are not possessed of any sincerity for God. If I see someone who does not love their dirhem and dinar, who is not pleased by being praised and lauded... I know that he or she is possessed of sincerity. Immediatly I leave them and flee. As long as servants love to be praised for their wealth, as long as their hearts are bound to worldly desires, they are the most obedient of those I have described to you. Do you not know that love of wealth is the greatest of great sins. I have seventy thousand children and I have appointed each one of them to a different place. And then there are seventy thousand devils with each of those children of mine. I have sent a group of them to the learned. I have sent agroup to the young, and a group to the shaykhs. I have made a group of them plague old women. As for the young, there is no disagreement between us, we get along very well. As for the children, our followers play with them as they wish. I have made a group of them trouble the worshippers and ascetics. They go among them and bring them from state to state. From one summit to the next... they keep them wandering around. They take on such a state that they begin to curse any cause... That is how I take their sincerity. Thus they perform their worship insincerely and don't even realize it.'

"'The priest Barsisa worshipped God sincerely for a full seventy years. At the end of that worship, such a state was granted to him that by the blessing of his prayer any ill person was made well. I went in pursuit of him and I did not let him escape. He committed adultery. He became a murderer. And in the end, he entered into disbelief.'

"He is the person whom God the Exalted describes in His book thus:

"*Like Satan when he says to a person, 'Disbelieve!' Then when he disbelieves, Satan says, 'Surely I am far from you. Surely I fear God, Lord of the worlds'*" (59:16).

"After that, Iblis spoke of certain evil states, and explained how he takes advantage of them.

"Lying: 'Lies are from me and I am the first to tell a lie. Whoever tells a lie is my friend. Whoever bears false witness is my beloved. Do you not know, O Muhammed, I swore falsely to Adam and Eve in the name of God. *"Surely I am a sincere adviser to you both"* (7:21), I said. I do that, for to bear false witness is my heart's amusement.'

"Slander and gossip: 'They are also my fruits and revelry.'

"To swear upon marriage: 'If a man swears to divorce by repudiation (*talak*), even if only once, or for a good reason, it is suspected that he may be a sinner. Whoever makes verbal repudiation, his wife is forbidden to him until the truth is clear. Any children born to them until the Resurrection are children of adultery. Because of that verbal repudiation, they will all go to Hell.'

"Prayer: 'O Muhammed, as for those who always postpone prayer... Whenever they want to stand for prayer, I hold them back. I whisper to them. I say, "There is still time. You are busy. For now do your work. You'll pray later." In that way they do their prayers in other than the appointed times, and for that reason they prayers they do are thrown in their faces.

"'If they defeat me, then I try to deal with them during the prayer. While they pray I tell them to look to the right and look to the left, and they do so. When they do that, I caress their faces and kiss their brows. Then I say, "You've done something that will never be of use for all eternity," and thus I ruin their peace of mind. You too know, O Muhammed, whoever looks much to the right and left during prayer, God will not accept their prayer. He throws their prayers in their faces.

"'If they defeat me in that also, I go to them when they pray alone, and I command them to pray quickly. And they begin to do their prayers quickly, like a rooster that pecks at things with its beak...

"'And if I cannot succeed in making them do that, then I go to them when they pray in a congregation. I put a bridle on their heads and raise their heads before the imam's in prostration and bending forward. And I make them prostrate themselves and bend forward before the imam does. Because they do that, on Resurrection Day God transforms their heads into the head of a donkey.

"'If they defeat me in that also, then I command them to crack their knuckles during prayer. In that way they become among those who glorify me. But only if I succeed in making them do it during prayer.

"'If I am defeated in that also, then I go to them again and blow into their noses during prayer. When I blow, they begin to yawn. If while yawning they do not cover their mouths with their hands, a tiny devil enters inside them and increases their greed and worldly ties. Then they always obey us. They do what we say.

"'I go to the wretched, to those without recourse and the miserable, and command them to abandon prayer. And I say to them, "Prayer is not for you... It is for those to whom God has granted health and abundance." Then I go to the sick and tell them to abandon prayer. For God the Exalted has said, *"There is no onus upon the sick..."* (24:61). When you are well, you will pray often. And so they abandon prayer. They may even come to disbelief. If they abandon prayer when ill, they will find God angry when they enter His presence.'

"Our Messenger of God (s.a.s.) Efendi asked Iblis certain brief questons, and he answered:

"'O Accused One, who sits with you and keeps you company?' 'Those who benefit from interest.' 'Who are your friends?' 'Those who commit adultery.' 'Who shares your bed?' 'Drunkards.' 'Who are your guests?' 'Thieves.' 'Who are your ambassadors?' 'Magicians.' 'What lights up your eyes?' 'Divorce of a wife.' 'Who is your beloved?' 'Those who abandon the Friday prayer.' 'O Accursed One, what breaks your heart?' 'The neighing of horses running to war for the sake of God.' 'All right then, what melts your body?' 'The repentance of those who repent.' 'What tears and rots your liver?' 'Asking God for forgiveness day and night.' 'All right, what makes your face frown?' 'Anonymous almsgiving.' 'What blinds your eyes?' 'Prayer performed often in congregation.' 'Who are the most fortunate of people in your opinion?' 'Those who knowingly and purposefully abandon prayer.' 'Who are the most wrteched of people in your opinion?' 'The stingy.' 'What distracts you from your work?' 'Gatherings of the learned.' 'How do you eat your food?' 'With my left hand and the tips of my fingers.' 'When the simoom wind blows and it gets very hot, where do you shade your children?' 'Under the fingernails of human beings.' 'What have you requested from your Lord?' 'I have requested ten things:

60th-61st Verse

"'I asked God to make me partner to the wealth and children of human beings... He fulfilled this request of mine for partnership, as the clear verse attests: *"Be their partner in wealth and children, and make them promises.' Satan promises them pride most of all "* [sic] (17:64). I eat all meat slain without the phrase, "In the name of God..." and I eat food tainted by interest and forbidden things. And I am partner to wealth gained without taking refuge in God from Satan. During the act of sex I am with the man who has sex with his wife without taking refuge in God from Satan, and I have sex with his wife together with him. And the child produced by that union obeys us and listens to what we say. Whoever mounts an animal not in the halal manner but instead with desire, I mount with them. I am their companion on the road and their riding comrade. This is established with a gracious verse. God gave me this command: *"Assault them with your cavalry and your infantry"* (17:64).

"'I asked God to give me a house... Upon this request of mine, He gave me baths as a house.

"'I asked Him to give me a mosque, and He made marketplaces a mosque for me.

"'I asked Him to give me a book for reading, and He gave me poetry as a book to read.

"'I asked Him to give me a call to prayer. He gave me musical instruments.

"'I asked Him to give me a friend to share my bed... He gave me drunkards.

"'I asked Him to give me helpers... He gave me fatalists.

"'I asked him to give me siblings. He gave me those who expend their wealth in vain. And those who spend money in the way of sin. These too are established by this gracious verse: "The spendthrifts are the brothers of devils" (17:27).

"'O Muhammed, I asked God that I might see the children of Adam, but they not see me. He also fulfilled this request of mine.

"'I asked that He make the blood channels of the children of Adam a road for me... This was fulfilled also. Thus I flow amidst them and wander around, and do so as I please...

"'Let me add also that those who are with me are more numerous than those who are with you. Thus most of the children of Adam are with me.

"'I have a son whose name is Atama. If a servant goes to sleep before the bedtime prayer, he goes and pees in that servant's ear. If that were not so, it would not be possible for human beings to sleep without performing their prayers.

"'I have another son whose name is Mutakazi. It is his job to try to broadcast actions done in secret. For example, if a servant performs a pious act in secret, and tries to hide what he has done, Mutakasi will nudge him. In the end he will succeed in making that secret action broadcast and known. Thus God will cancel ninety-nine of that servant's one hundred good deeds, leaving one left. Because exactly one hundred good deeds are given for the one secret action a servant does.

"'I have another son whose name is Kuhayl. His job is to apply eyeliner to the eyes of human beings, especially in the gatherings of the learned and while the preacher gives a sermon. Once that eyeliner is applied to people's eyes, they begin to fall asleep. They cannot hear the words of the learned and thus acquire no good deeds.'

"Then Iblis continued:

"'Whoever a woman may be, when she rises from her seat a devil sits in her place. And in the lap of every woman there is definitely a devil that stays there and makes her seem beautiful to those who look at her. And he gives the woman certain commands. For example, he says, "Bring out your hand and arm, show them." She obeys that command. She takes out her hand and arm and shows them. Then he tears that woman's veil of honor with his fingernails.'

"Then Iblis began to tell Our Messenger Efendi about his own situation:

"'O Muhammed, I have no way to lead people astray. I only whisper to them and make something seem beautiful, that is all. If I could have led people astray, I would not have left anyone who says, "There is no god but God and Muhammed is God's messenger," anyone who fasts or prays. I would have led all of them astray. Just as you have nothing in the way of guidance. You are only God's Messenger and your duty is to deliver the message. If you were able to guide, you would have left no disbeliever on the face of the earth. You are a proof of God's creation, and I am for Him a cause for those recorded as wretched in eternity without beginning.

60TH-61TH VERSE

"The felicitous are felicitous in their mothers' wombs. The wretched too are wretched in their mothers' wombs. It is God who makes them one of the felicitous, and God who makes them one of the wretched.'

"Then Our Messenger of God Efendi recited these two gracious verses:

"'*They cease not to differ... Except for those upon whom your Lord has mercy...*' (11:118-119). 'God's command is a measure that is in every case fulfilled'[sic] (33:38).'

"Then Our Messenger of God (s.a.s.) Efendi said to Iblis:

"'Ya Abu Murra, is it not possible that you may repent and return to God? I will be the guarantor for you to enter Paradise, I give my word!'

"'O Messenger of God, it has happened according to the decision given... And the pen that wrote it has gone dry. What will happen until the Resurrection, will happen.

"'It is God who made you the Efendi of the messengers, who made you the preacher of the people of Paradise, chose you among creatures and made you an eye amidst the people, and made me the Efendi of the wretched and the preacher of the people of Hell, and He is beyond all qualities of lack.'"[666]

• God the Exalted created the Muhammeden soul from His Essence. The Essence of Exalted God is the coincidence of two opposites. He created the angels called "Ālūn" [the High] from Muhammed's soul by way of the attributes Beauty, Light, and Lord. Sublime God the Truth created Iblis and his people by way of the attributes Majesty, Darkness and Misguider, and these also like the others from Muhammed's (s.a.s.) soul.

Iblis's prior name was "Azazil." He worshipped God the Exalted for many, many thousands of years before human beings were created. God the Exalted, who is beyond every thing, said one day, "O Azazil, worship no one other than Me!" And at a later time known to God the Truth, when God the Exalted created Adam, He commanded the angels to prostrate themselves to him.

---

666. Muhyiddîn İbnül-Arabî, trans. Abdülkâdir Akçiçek, *Şeceretü'l-Kevn-Üstün İnsan* (Istanbul: Bahar Yayınları 2000), pp. 157-184.

This situation confused Iblis. He thought that if he bowed down to Adam, he would be worshipping other than God. But he could not know that one who prostrates himself at God's command would be bowing down to God. That was the reason why he refused to bow down. That is the subtle meaning of his being given the name Iblis.

God the Exalted asked Iblis, *"What has prevented you from prostrating before what I made with My two hands? Have you become arrogant, or are you one of the ʿĀlūn?"* (38:75).

The angels called "ʿĀlūn" were created of divine light, like the one named "Nun" and other angels. The rest of the angels were created of the four elements and the command to bow down to Adam (a.s.) was given to them.

Iblis answered that question of God's, *"I am better than him. You created me of fire, and You created him of clay"* (38:76). Iblis's answer proves that he was the one who best knew the courtesy of speaking in God's presence, and the gnostic of creatures in comprehending the question and giving an answer. For Sublime God the Exalted did not ask the reason for what prevented him. If He had asked, the form of the question would have been, "What is the reason you have refused to bow down to what I made with My two hands?" Which He did not ask. He asked only the nature of the prohibition. As for Iblis, he spoke about the secret of the matter: *"I am better than him"* (38:76).

The clearer meaning of that phrase is the following: "The reality of fire is natural darkness, and you created me of that... It is better than the reality of clay. You created him of that. That is why I necessarily do not bow down to him."

Fire in its true aspect necessitates sublimity. Earth in its true aspect necessitates lowliness. When you take a candle and turn it upside down, its flame does not turn downwards; it goes upwards... But earth is not like that. When you take a handful of earth and throw it upwards, it swiftly falls down. It does that because of the realities it necessitates. Thus for the reason explained, Iblis said, "*You created me of fire, and You created him of clay*" (38:76), and added nothing to what he said. As for the reason, he knew very well that God the Exalted was aware of the secret. And he knew very well that the station was the station of constriction, not the station of expansion.

If it had been the station of expansion, he would have gone on to say, "I trusted in Your command to not worship other than You!" But he saw that the location was the location of reproach. Thus he assumed an attitude of courtesy. And again he understood that the matter was for him; he lapsed into confusion.

For Sublime God the Truth called him "Iblis" (38:75). This term is a word from the root of the term "ambiguity" (*iltibas*). He had never before been called upon by this name. So the situation realized was this: The matter had surpassed its limit. That is why he was not grieved, and he did not regret what he had done, he did not repent; he did not request forgiveness. He comprehended very well that God the Exalted does only what He wishes. What God wished was the thing the realities required.

Then God the Exalted expelled him from the presence of intimacy to the pit of the distance of nature, and He said, "*Get out of there, you are Outcast!*" (38:77). In clearer words, Sublime God the Truth said, "Separate from the sublime presence and descend to the lowly center!" For an outcast thing is thrown from sublimity to lowliness.

Then Sublime God the Truth said, "*Let My curse be upon you until the Resurrection*" [sic] (38:78). A curse is the instrument of threat and causing to fear. The clearer meaning is: "My curse is upon you alone, not upon anyone else!" His saying, "until the Resurrection," means that there is no curse upon Iblis after the Day of Resurrection. For on the Day of Religion called the "Day of Resurrection," natural darkness is lifted!

For according to this, Iblis is driven out and expelled from the divine presence only until the Day of Resurrection; his original situation makes this a necessary condition. As for what his origin necessitates, it is natural obstacles that prevent the realization of spirit by divine realities. But after that, natural conditions are counted among the sum of perfections. There is no longer any curse upon him, only intimacy! And then Iblis returns to the divine intimacy that is found with God, where he was before. This occurs after Hell has been extinguished. For to be sure, everything God the Exalted creates will return to the state it was in before. Everything returns to its origin.

Iblis was very happy when he was cursed, and was so carried away with joy that he filled up the world with his soul.

When they saw Iblis like this they said, "Why are you like this? You have been driven from the presence!" He answered, "This for me is robe and rank. The Beloved has made me an individual. He has not granted that to any angel or messenger."

Then as soon as God the Exalted's news reached him, he called out to God the Truth, *"My Lord, grant me respite until the day they are resurrected"* (38:79). He knew very well that the natural darkness that was his source would subsist in being until God the Exalted resurrected the people of darkness... Then they would be delivered from natural darkness, and attain the lights of Lordliness...

Strengthening Iblis's desire, God the Exalted answered, *"You are among those granted respite until the day of the time well known"* (38:80-81).

The time well known: The entry of the command of being into the presence of the sublime sultan who is the One Worshipped.

And he swore: *"For the sake of Your exaltedness (I swear that) I will mislead them all"* [sic] (38:82).

For Iblis knew that everything is under the dominion of nature. And he also knew that the requirements of darkness prevent it from reaching the lights and peace of mind. He continued, *"'Except for Your sincere servants among them"* (38:83). They have thrown off the darkness given by nature; they have erased the density that prevents worship. In other words, they have substituted the divine law for it in the human body and been delivered from the darkness of nature. They find salvation by doing good deeds, struggle, resistance, etc.'

In response to Iblis's speech, God the Exalted gave this answer: *"Truly I will fill Hell with you and those who follow you, all of them"* (38:84-85). When Iblis spoke in terms of the prohibition the realities require, as divine wisdom He spoke in terms of Iblis's speech. The natural darkness with which Iblis, as instrument, molests Human beings is the essence of the people Iblis swore to mislead, which draws them to Hell, perhaps even the same thing as fire! The nature that pushes people to darkness is that fire that God the Exalted has placed in the hearts of the depraved. Thus whoever enters that natural darkness will only follow Iblis and will have entered the fire.

The Sites of Manifestation of Iblis, their Varieties, and the Instruments and Ways he Employs to Dupe them: *"Assault them* *with your cavalry and your infantry. Be their partner in wealth and children. Make promises to them. Satan promises them nothing but delusion"* (17:64).

Iblis has ninety-nine sites of manifestation in the human body, which is as much as the number of God's beautiful names. Iblis has seven main sites of manifestation, just as God's Essence names are seven, and these are among the beautiful names. What a wondrous thing! That the sites resemble the number of God's names is because Iblis is created from this existent Soul (*Nefs*) that comes from God's Essence.

The First Site of Manifestation is the world and the things established on the world, which are the stars and the other things, the planets and others. The manifestation of Iblis in one place does not prevent his manifestation in another place. Iblis has different manifestations for every group of human beings and does not remain in one form in his manifestation to any group but takes on various forms. He leaves no guise untried until he has stopped up every path and closed every door for the person in whom he manifests, so that he leaves the person no way of return.

His manifestation to the people of *shirk* is with the world and the things established on the world, which are the elements, the heavens, emptinesses and climes. He appears to disbelievers and practicers of *shirk* in those sites of manifestation. First he attaches their intellects to the ornaments and trappings of the world and blinds their hearts. Then he occupies them with prognostication by the stars. He attracts them to the source material of the elements. He whispers to this group, "These are what are active in existence!"

Thus they begin to worship the heavens. The reason for this is that they see the orderly properties of the stars and witness that the sun rules these bodies of existence by its heat. Then they observe how rain falls from clouds, that it comes from on high, and does not miss its mark. They see that it falls according to a perfect calculation. Once they have seen these things no doubt comes into their minds any longer regarding the lordliness of the stars.

Now they have become like animals. They speak only in order to eat and drink. And after all of that they believe neither in Resurrection nor anything else. Since they have no such faith, they kill one another. They steal each other's property. Now they have drowned in the sea of nature. They can never be delivered from it.

Next come the people of the elements and the materialists. They say, "This existence has been divided between darkness and light. Darkness is a god, and his name is Ahriman. Light also is a god, and his name is Yazdan, and fire is the origin of light." Then they begin to worship fire.

The Second Site of Manifestation is natural things, passions, and material pleasures. His form of manifestation is to the common folk of Muslims. He first misleads them by means of love of things having to do with the passions. First he gives them a desire for animal pleasures. All of this occurs according to the requirements of dark nature. He blinds them with these activities and ruins the feelings of their hearts. He manifests to them in worldly affairs. He says, "All of these things sought are possible only with the world!"

Then they rely upon love of the world. All their effort is in demand for the world. After he has done this much, he abandons them. There is need for no other way, no other medicine in order to ruin them and corrupt them. Thus they become Iblis's people. The do not rebel against any command of his. For ignorance has been combined with love of the world. If he should say at that moment, "Be disbelievers!" they would become disbelievers without a thought. Then he enters their hearts by means of whispering, particularly with regard to the Unseen of which God the Exalted has spoken. Then he thrusts them into atheism, and his work is done!

The Third Site of Manifestation: He appears to the wholesome in the good deed that they do. He makes their deed seem beautiful to them. He makes them admire themselves. When they are in that condition they accept no advice from any of the learned. When they have become like this with Iblis, he says, "It is enough. If others perform one in a thousand of these acts of worship of yours, they will be saved." They then decrease their good deeds. They take their rest. They exalt themselves and take others lightly. They pay no heed to the words of the learned. After they make others acquire their bad habits described, they begin to speak of others with ill intent and drive them to rebellion, one after another.

While making them do this he says to them, "Do what you like, God is Forgiving, Merciful! God is ashamed to torment those whose hair has grown white. God is Generous. The Generous never demands what He is owed! That is when horrendous trials befall them. One must take refuge in God from such states as these.

The Fourth Site of Manifestation: He appears to the people of witness in order to corrupt their deeds, and ruins their intentions. He appears much in intentions and good deeds. Those he haunts do a good deed in order to gain God's acceptance, and immediately a devil pesters them and puts these ideas into their minds:

"Make your deeds even more beautiful. People will see you, and perhaps they will do as you do." These words incite them to hypocrisy and the doing of good deeds so that people will see them.

If he does not succeed in making people arrogant by means of the praise of others, he tries other ways. He pesters them by way of goodness, for example, if they recite the Quran he comes to them and distances them from the Quran by saying, "How would it be if you go to God's house and do the hajj? You can recite the Quran as you wish during the hajj. You can do the hajj and recite the Quran at the same time."

When that person sets out on the hajj, he pesters them, "Be like everyone else! Now you are a guest. You do not need to recite the Quran," and with the accursedness of not reciting the Quran, that person who has now begun to follow Satan abandons the obligatory prayers. He may even prevent that person from rightfully fulfilling the requirements of the hajj.

One way of prevention is to distract that person from all the hajj requirements with the need for food while in the holy lands, encouraging stinginess and similar tendencies. That person acquires bad habits, becoming narrow in heart and unable to enjoy worship.

If he has not led the person sufficiently astray, he will try to fool him or her into neglecting one good deed in order to do a better one, and he keeps on until he succeeds in making the person neglect that one as well.

The Fifth Site of Manifestation is knowledge. Here Satan's work is with the learned. Satan said, "By God, in my opinion it is easier to dupe a thousand of the learned than one illiterate of strong faith." For Iblis has been confused in trying to dupe the ignorant. Satan talks with the learned and pesters them by using proofs they know and tells them that what he says is true, and gains strength thereby.

For example, he approaches a learned person by way of knowledge, and after a while switches to the area of that person's lust, and says, "Marry that woman according to the religion of David!" when in fact that person belongs to the Hanafi or Shafi'i school of Muslim law. Then he says, "Marry her without her guardian's permission!" When he makes the learned man thus marry the woman, she requests a *nafaka* payment for her dowry, clothes and sustenance. Satan suggests to him, "Promise to do it at such and such a time; if you don't there is no harm in that!" For it is lawful for a man to swear to satisfy his wife, even if the oath is a lie.

When he is late in fulfilling the promise and does not do so, Satan says, "Deny that she is your wife! In any case the marriage is corrupt, because it is not lawful according to your school. Since she is not your wife, you were not required to pay the *nafaka*." Thus that learned man becomes one of Satan's special disciples. Very few are those who can escape him in this way. They are more singular than one. Some are Solitaries (*ferdler*).

The Sixth Site of Manifestation is habitual practices and things they do in seeking comfort. He manifests in this way to loyal disciples. When he pesters those disciples he distracts them from habitual practices and attracts them to the darkness of nature through the demand for comfort. In that way he strips their strong efforts in the demand and takes away their inclination to worship. And when the disciples lose these states of theirs they are left alone with their souls. Then he does to those disciples what he did to the others. Those disciples whose inner will is weaker fall prey to Iblis's game especially swiftly, because for the disciples there is nothing as horrible as seeking comfort and reliance upon habitual things!

The Seventh Site of Manifestation is the feelings of divine knowledge (*ilâhî mârifet duyguları*). In this site he pesters the truthful, the friends of God and the gnostics. And of these only those whom God the Exalted protects escape. But there is no way for him to reach the intimates of God. He gets to the others by that means and says, "Is not God the reality of being? Are not you also of the totality of being? In that case God the Truth is your reality." They affirm these words of Iblis's, saying, "Yes, that is right!" Then he continues, "Thus why do you wear yourselves out with the actions performed by those imitators?" Influenced by these words, they abandon their wholesome deeds. When they have abandoned their deeds, he says, "Now do as you wish! For God is your reality. You are Him. What He does is never questioned."

Now that group under the influence of these words of Iblis commits adultery, steals, drinks wine and does similar things. Iblis gets them into such a state that in the end he tears those belonging to that group away from the tie of Islam, strips them of faith and throws them into atheism (zındıklık). Some of them take the path of unity, in other words, they say they have established unity with God. Some of them claim to have reached the station of the Solitary (Ferd). When such people are asked about the evil they do and account is demanded, Satan makes this suggestion: "Deny it! Do not attribute it to yourselves! For you did nothing. In reality the agent is only God. Your being yourselves is not as people believe it to be. It is something else." So they swear in that way. They say they have done nothing.

Iblis tells some of them, "I have made haram things permissible for you! Do as you like, or do such-and-such! Commit those haram actions! For you are the Essence and for you there is no sin!" But God has certain special things, certain secrets, with his servants that are very, very much above Iblis's manifestation. There are signs for the people of states of ecstasy from Sublime God the Truth that there is no way for them to deny. In this regard Iblis's confusion is relative to those who do not have knowledge. Those states are for those who comprehend the basis of the matter.

Otherwise such things cannot in any way be hidden for those possessed of gnosis who are aware of the basis of the matter. Hazret Shaykh Abd al-Qadir Gaylani was in a desert. It was said to him, "O Abd al-Qadir, I am God! I have made haram things permissible for you. Do as you like!" Hazret Gaylani said, "You are lying, you are Satan." When it was asked him how he knew he was Satan, he said, "God the Exalted does not command evil. When that accursed one said that to me I knew that he was Satan. He wants to lead me astray."[667]

- Satan says to God the Truth, "My God, for the sake of the power of the perverted name You have given me, I sit upon the believing serv-

---

667. Abd al-Karīm ibn al-Jīlī, trans. Seyyid Hüseyin Fevzî Paşa, *İnsan-ı Kâmil* (Istanbul: Kitsan Yayınları), pp. 207-230.

ants who desire You and take Your path. I show them lies as truth, sins as good deeds, denial as avowal, disbelief as faith, the bitter as the sweet, poison as antidote and thus I keep them away from Your path of obedience and worship. Just as I have been driven from Your door and expelled with the attribute of misguidance, I deprive them of You and make them grieve for Your beauty. I burn their spirits in the fires of exile. My God, I appear to them in the aspect of soul and the passions, make them trust in their faith and acts of worship and make them feel safe from Your wiles. And in respect of a long life I appear to them in details; I make them say they have much time for obedience and worship, surely one day they will repent; I constrain them from repentence and remorse, make the knowledge they study and acquire seem pretty, and make them trust in their own knowledge. In this way I make those posessed for knowledge and virtue think they are the axis of the world, and I turn them away from perfect humans, and deprive them of being united with You, and attract them to the delights of the world, awaken a thousand of their souls' desires and make them commit rebellion and error. I make them commit acts of hypocrisy and deceit, haram actions, and injustices. And when they perform prayers and give alms and establish charities, I make them do these things so that people should consider them generous, just and virtuous and charitable to the poor, and in this way I corrupt their good deeds and distance them from You. My God! I suggest calumnies to their hearts. In this way I make them ill-intentioned toward the Companions of the Messenger and Your beloveds, make them speak ill of them and against them. I make envy seem pretty; I adorn it with pride, and thus make them experience what happened between Hazret Adam and me. I enter the eyes of merchants as avarice. Thus I make them cheat at the scales and in the promises they make, and I cause many to go bankrupt. I make many of them fail to honor perfect humans, and make them take exception to their states, and distance them from the presence of God the Truth. In this world and the HereafterI make them fill their hearts with the fires of longing. My God, I forbid them from praising You for giving Your servants so many boons and felicity, and make their hearts miserable in so many ways never thought or dreamed of." Then God the Truth said, "And I throw into Hell and burn with

60th-61st Verse

the fire of deprivation you and all the ungrateful and heedless who are swept up by your seductions.[668]

• Satans's greatest fault was to see Hazret Adam as other than God the Truth. And to compare God's love and affection to the soul's love and say may it be only in me and mine alone. This is a subtle point.

The lovers of that Beloved of beloveds say, "If only all the world loved what I love, and all our words were the story of the Beloved." Thus they invite all the people of the world to the love of that Beloved. For their goal is not only to be loved themselves and He love them. They say, "I have become accustomed to this love; you too, all of you, come and be united with that Beloved and love Him."[669]

• Satan is the touchstone of hearts; who is wretched in eternity without beginning? Who is felicitous? Who is the lion? Who is the dog? He has been made the instrument to distinguish between them. He seduces the wretched and the depraved and leads them into error, but he does not have the power to seduce and misguide those who are felicitous in eternity without beginning.[670]

• Satan says, "How do I make the good to be bad? Know that I am only the one who invites them to evil and depravity and encourages them to error, I am not the one who creates error, I do not have the power to give existence to evil and depravity, because I am the mirror of both good and evil, I have nothing of corruption myself. For the felicitous became felicitous in their mothers' wombs, in eternity without beginning. They received the good news of the felicity of the felicitous (in the Mother of the Book). The wretched came black-faced with wretchedness. In this garden of the world I am like a gardener; whenever I cut with the sword of misguidance the bodies of the faithless unjust who are like dried up and useless trees, I do not have the

---

668. Ken'an Rifâî, ed. Kâzım Büyükaksoy, *Mesnevî Hatıraları* (Istanbul: İnkilap Kitapevi 1968), p. 119.

669. Ken'an Rifâî, ed. Kâzım Büyükaksoy, *Mesnevî Hatıraları* (Istanbul: İnkilap Kitapevi 1968), p. 122.

670. Ken'an Rifâî, ed. Kâzım Büyükaksoy, *Mesnevî Hatıraları* (Istanbul: İnkilap Kitapevi 1968), p. 124.

strength for those possessed of faith and gnosis, I only become helper and manifest to them. As long as their beings and selves do not melt in the sea of (the Messenger of God's) love and affection, they cannot attract (God Possesed of Majesty's) love. What can I do? If they had been able to do that, surely a portion would have been given to them in the delightfulness of their own essences..."[671]

- Satan says, "I am the touchstone of false coin. I lead astray those who were measured out as wretched and sinners in eternity without beginning; as for the good, I show them the way. What I cut are not the moist branches but the dried-up ones. I put meat before some animals and before others, hay, so that it should become evident what kind they are. If they go for the bone, I know they have the nature of dogs. If they go to the hay, they have the nature of deer. In fact I do not make vegetarians into meat eaters. I am not the Lord. Even if I take away the food of those who are nourished on spiritual pleasure and offer them a bite of carnality, I cannot make them eat it if the tendency is not in their created nature. I have nothing to misguide them and lead them astray.

  Maybe I am a mirror for both good and evil. If a black-skinned person grieves at the blackness of his skin and breaks the mirror, the broken mirror says, "Is the sin mine? Ask the one who polishes my face and cleans off the rust about this crime. I am only an informer in the way of showing the beautiful as beautiful, and the ugly as ugly. That is all. To be sure, in the chess of this world I have beat thousands of humans, but they should seek the crime in their own selves, not in me. I am a witness. Are witnesses sent to prison for their true words?"[672]

- Worshiping God, loving God, is not for this transient world, that it should be right to connect it with relations and ancestry. Love of God is a virtue which spirits acquired only at the gathering in eternity without beginning at the moment when they were with Him. But

---

671. Ken'an Rifâî, ed. Kâzım Büyükaksoy, *Mesnevî Hatıraları* (Istanbul: İnkilap Kitapevi 1968), p. 126.

672. Sâmiha Ayverdi, *Yolcu Nereye Gidiyorsun?* (Istanbul: Kubbealtı Neşriyatı 1997), pp. 153-154.

60TH-61TH VERSE

this can only be the inheritance of God's messengers. Those who understand His messengers are those who comprehend their superiority of spirit and the spiritual values they have brought to humankind. While they live in the world they take the spiritual food that nourishes a sublime spirit and acquire the comprehension which enables them to turn toward and prepare for the eternal realm.[673]

- If the love of God were merely a thought, there would not be acts of worship in which the body participates, like prayer and fasting.

The gifts people give to those they love do not consist of love and respect alone. Their love and connectedness lead people to give one another material gifts as well. In the same way, leading the human body to prayer, fasting, pilgrimage and charity and working lines of form into worship—all of these are heartfelt gifts.

Form bears witness to meaning. But of these witnesses there are those that lie as well as those that tell the truth. This means that in the world worship pertaining to form can be sincere or false also. Actions done for show, with the appearance of religiosity for the sake of material or spiritual self-interest, may appear in the forms of worship, goodness and charity but yet be no different than false witness.[674]

- There are many people who perform their duties of worship in the expectation of getting something back from God. They expect to be rewarded for it, believing that if they worship God they will be accepted in His sight and He will pay them for that worship.

In reality, they are not afraid to commit all sorts of sins after they perform such worship. They suppose that the worship they do, the ritual prayers they perform, will exonerate them of past and future sins. In reality such worship is no different from sin. It is a hidden kind of sin committed by people who mix trickery with worship.

You cannot perform the ritual prayer not only in the drunkenness that arises from drink but also at times when you are drunk with heedlessness or material or spiritual lusts as well. That is the greatest sin that can arise from not being able to tell in whose pres-

---

673. Ken'an Rifâî, *Şerhli Mesnevî-i Şerif* (Istanbul: Kubbealtı Neşriyatı 2000), pp. 499-500.

674. Ken'an Rifâî, *Şerhli Mesnevî-i Şerif* (Istanbul: Kubbealtı Neşriyatı 2000), p. 382.

ence you are. One only goes into the presence of God pure and with a heart full of the love of God. It is those who can enter His presence completely without body, with a purity and cleanliness that consists simply of spirit, who are in a true state of worship.[675]

- Worship is for God alone and favor only for His people. When there is even the slightest feeling of self-interest and its pleasure in something you do, it is no longer a good deed.

When you give charity and distribute wealth, do not favor those who open their hands to you and not to God. Do not give your wealth to hypocrites who surround you. They are people devoid of purity and cleanliness who will make you sin rather than perform good works.[676]

- There are some people who do not know patience and gratitude. The reason is indolence and agedness. They do not thank God, they have no patience for and cannot bear with God's commands and the worship He has commanded. The aged spirit, like all laggards, finds a reason for this also. It says: "If God wanted me to worship, He would have given me ardor and desire for worship, He would have shown me the way." In saying this, it conforms to the commands not of the spirit but of the soul. It takes not God's path but the path of the world.

Such people are afflicted by fatalism (*cebir*) in the exact sense of the term; they are people without will, bound by the chain of fatalism: A person who exhibits disobedience on the path of obedience and supposes himself to be powerless and too ill to worship, who conforms to his soul out of sloth, using the excuse of a fancied illness, will one day become really ill. He will either die or, tired of life, weary and fed up, be buried in the grave of his baseless fears.

It is their abuse of the power given to them that will one day leave those who suppose themselves crippled on the path of God's commands, and flee from the work that is also God's command, really powerless.

That is why Hazret Muhammed said: "*Illness in jest brings on real illness and extinguishes a person like a candle.*"

---

675. Ken'an Rifâî, *Şerhli Mesnevî-i Şerif* (Istanbul: Kubbealtı Neşriyatı 2000), pp. 496-497.

676. Ken'an Rifâî, *Şerhli Mesnevî-i Şerif* (Istanbul: Kubbealtı Neşriyatı 2000), p. 548.

60TH-61TH VERSE

The dictionary meaning of the word "domination" (*cebir*) is the bandaging and resetting of a broken or dislocated bone. To bind up a broken bone, to attach it to a severed vein, is "domination."

"Domination" is to make healthy, to repair.

If you have not tired yourself out on the path of worship and pious obedience, not broken your foot on that path, why are you now bandaging your foot? You flee your own potentialities, your swiftness, your health, and bind your foot with the bandage of compulsion. You do not obey God's commands and, saying that you are powerless, ill, you stay behind on the path of death while alive.

If you are going to be weary, be like the one who tires out his feet on the path of worship, so that Buraq (*the mount that carried Hazret Messenger on the Miraj*) sent by God the Truth may come to your aid; let your mounting that Buraq of faith and spirituality and roaming the realms of the heart be real.[677]

- It is related that Abdullah ibn Mas'ud (r.a.) said, "The Messenger of God drew a line and said to us, 'This is God's path.' Then he drew several lines to his right and left and said, 'These are also paths. A devil sits on each of these paths and invites people to himself,' and he recited, "*That is My path, straight; so follow it*" [6:153]. "*Surely your efforts are diverse*" [92:4]. *Some of you expend effort with knowledge and action, and enter Paradise. Some of you run toward darkness with ignorance and the soul's desire, and enter Hell.* "*For everyone there is a direction to which he conforms. So vie with one another for the good. Wherever you may be, God will bring you all together*" (2:148).

"Know that people's efforts are diverse because they are in one of four stages. I would like to express these four stages as the realm of animals, the realm of predatory animals, the realm of devils and the realm of angels. The quiddity of each realm pushes a person in the opposite direction of the other realm. Immediately after birth a person's first realm begins, and that is the realm of animals. That realm drives them toward eating, drinking, and permitted or forbidden sexual intercourse. If people do not persevere and turn toward faith and good deeds, love of the world overcomes them and of course they cannot get all they want from the world, and in the end they

---

677. Ken'an Rifâî, *Şerhli Mesnevî-i Şerif* (Istanbul: Kubbealtı Neşriyatı 2000), p. 147.

enter into the realm of predatory animals. They become qualifed by arrogance, hatred, envy, revenge, and if measured out for them, murder, and their form becomes that of predatory animals. If they do not turn from that either, they are overcome by the passion for rank, and attain their goal only by trickery, and in the end they enter the realm of demons and devils. They become qualified by trickey, deceit, lies, backbiting, gossip and calumny, and propensities like inciting rebellion among the people like Iblis. If they remain there, they remain the lowest of the low and the most perverted of human beings. But if they attain felicity and turn to the realm of angels, which is the realm of mentioning God, praising God, declaring that there is no god but God, and repentance, they get on well with all people and acquire beautiful character, which is the perfection of a person. With that they become superior to the others (*the angels*). For such people rise up to that realm through the realms of animals, predatory animals, and demons and devils by means of knowledge and good deeds. They pass over to that realm by means of struggle." "*The good speech rises up to Him, He exalts the wholesome deed*" (35:10).[678]

- God the Exalted said to Moses in secret, "Learn a secret from Iblis!"

When Moses saw Iblis on the road, he wanted to learn a secret, a sign, from him.

Iblis said, "Always keep this saying in mind: do not say I am I, do not be like me!

"*If you have a hair's worth of being, of selfhood, you are a disbeliever; there is no servanthood in you!*

"*The end of the road is at desirelessness; the hero's fame is in the ruin of his reputation.*

"*For on this road, when you reach your desire, right at that moment hundredfold existence and selfhood appears!*"[679]

- A bird said to the Hoopoe, "Iblis is tricking me. Right when I enter the presence, he turns up on my path. I do not have the strength to

---

678. Niyâzî Mısrî, trans. Süleyman Ateş, *İrfan Sofraları* (Istanbul: Yeni Ufuklar Neşriyatı n.d), p. 49.

679. Ferideddin-i Attar, trans. Yaşar Keçeci, *Mantık Al-Tayr* (Kırk Ambar Yayınları 1998), p. 256.

oppose him, my heart has swelled from his deceit and I am in a miserable state. What shall I do to escape him and reach the true life by means of the wine of spirit?"

The Hoopoe made this reply: "As long as this dog soul is in front of you, do not worry, Iblis will cry out and run away from you!"

Iblis's behavior arises from your Iblis-ness. The desires in you, every one, are the desires of your Iblis. When you are completely bound to a desire, hundreds of Iblises arise from it. Is not this the firebox of the world? It is entirely the property of Iblis. Do not stretch out your hand for his country, for his property, so that no one will have any business with you![680]

---

680. Ferideddin-i Attar, trans. Abdülbaki Gölpınarlı, *Mantıku't-Tayr* (Milli Eğitim Bakanlığı 1990), vol. 1, p. 11.

62. And he did lead a great multitude of you astray. Then did you not use intellect?

Wa laqad 'aḍalla minkum jibillan kathīran 'a fa lam takūnū ta'qilūn.

- He says: Our Majesty is Our veil and no eye is worthy of seeing the lights of the vision of Our face as long as it does not discover it.

- What is meant by Majesty? The light that will bring you to [His] Beauty. It is power, awesomeness, subjugation and the exaltedness of divine greatness.[681]

- Majesty means God the Truth's subjugation, the spiritual melting of all forms, existences and being and the self-disclosure and manifestation of God, in other words, the subsistence of His exalted being.[682]

- While a man is wandering in a forest, suddenly lightning begins to strike and rain and hail begins to fall. Afraid for his life, the man throws himself into a cave in fear and terror and waits inside the cave until the weather calms down and the storm and lightning passes.

  But just when he notices that things have calmed down, he becomes aware of a slippery body under his feet and horrified, sees that he is standing on a snake. When the man comes to himself and looks around, he sees that the cave is filled with animals like lions and tigers and lambs and deer, enemies to one another, and begins trembling with fear.

  But just as the same man who a few hours earlier jumped into the cave in fear for his life and, under the influence of subjugation and

---

681. Ken'an Rifâî, *Sohbetler* (Istanbul: Kubbealtı Neşriyatı 2000), p. 111.
682. Ken'an Rifâî, *Sohbetler* (Istanbul: Kubbealtı Neşriyatı 2000), p. 9.

Majesty, did not see any of them, it also did not occur to the animals who are enemies of one another to attack each other.

For being, distinction and otherness had disappeared and they all became one spirit; unity had become manifest. In other words, only fear of God the Truth was manifest; God's subjugation occupied each one of them. For that reason opposition and enmity only appears when they return to the necessities of their created natures and the dominion of the world shows itself.[683]

• The unbounded and whole being of God the Truth self-discloses in various parts. God's manifestation in the form of Majesty means the self-disclosure of divine power and exaltedness. God's All-subjugating power becomes evident in his Majesty.[684]

• If God turns the sheepskin inside-out, that is, if He shows His wrath and Majesty instead of His mercy; if He sees the error of a person's ways and feels it necessary to make the power of His subjugation known; even if that person is apparently in a state of profound faith and worship, the power of God will rip that immovable mountain of faith up from the root and turn it upside-down. He will send the one who ascends the seven heavens like Satan down to the bottom of the seven layers of earth. In an instant He will tear the veil of faith of hundreds of Adams and bring hundreds of devils to a new Muslim's level of faith and purity.[685]

• Although there is guidance and rectitude in your innate disposition, that great enemy, confronted by my Majesty, has ruined the temperament of most of you, led you astray and ruined the character of many a community. Did you have no intellect when you worshipped this evident enemy called Satan? Did you not consider that this would happen to you one day?[686]

• Satan wants to dupe humans and have them fall into deep and dark pits. For this he invites you to sin. He makes sin seem to be a

---
683. Ken'an Rifâî, *Sohbetler* (Istanbul: Kubbealtı Neşriyatı 2000), p. 33.
684. Ken'an Rifâî, *Şerhli Mesnevî-i Şerif* (Istanbul: Kubbealtı Neşriyatı 2000), p. 425.
685. Ken'an Rifâî, *Şerhli Mesnevî-i Şerif* (Istanbul: Kubbealtı Neşriyatı 2000), p. 579.
686. Şemseddin Yeşil, *Füyûzat* (Istanbul: Ş. Yeşil Yayınları 1984), vol. 6, p. 259.

62th Verse

pleasure one cannot do without. You are fooled by this delight and run fast as the wind toward sin.[687]

- For spirit, the body is in reality a cage. Not one but many, many birds enter and exit this cage. The birds that go in are forces of the soul, desires of the body and satanic anxieties. Those that come out are sycophants, people who for sake of their own self-interest flatter others.

All those who enter and exit the body in this way say all sorts of things. One says he is your true friend. Another calls out saying, "No, only I am your companion and friend." Another one flatters you, saying you are beautiful, generous, good and forgiving. Another one flatters you, "Both of the two worlds were created for you, and we are just there to serve you."

Spirits in love with the cage of flesh, those who are unintelligent and immature, are fooled by such things. They think they are something important, they even think they are everything.

The poor things do not know that there is many a devil within them; the devils have planted many such a bomb in their own bodies.[688]

- The intellect is the faculty of intelligence that finds God. If it cannot find Him, it cannot be called intellect. Or if intellect appears to follow Satan, it has momentarily disengaged. For with the command, *"did you not use intellect?"* the Quranic verse is saying that when we follow Satan, the intellect is disengaged.

When the soul cooperates with Satan, first it disengages the intellect and invents a logical deception in its place. And many temperaments have been seduced in this way. Temperament (*cibilliyet*) means character (*karakter*). If you possess an intelligence having sound supports in physics and mathematics, God will be intelligible to you. As long as this intellect of yours is not disengaged, your character will not be compromised.

That is why God gave intellect to Adam alone. But the fine point here does not mean Satan does not seduce the witless and influence

---

687. Ken'an Rifâî, *Şerhli Mesnevî-i Şerif* (Istanbul: Kubbealtı Neşriyatı 2000), p. 568.
688. Ken'an Rifâî, *Şerhli Mesnevî-i Şerif* (Istanbul: Kubbealtı Neşriyatı 2000), p. 263.

the intelligent. The meaning is general. Moreover, it addresses those possesed of intellect in particular.[689]

- *Hero, intellect is contrary of lust*
Do not call intellect what weaves in with lust

That which is beggar to lust, call self-deceit
Of the gold coin of intellect counterfeit

Without touchstone, groudless fear and intellect
Can't be appraised, bring them to the touchstone quick

The Quran and prophets' states are that touchstone
Like the touchstone, they say to false coin, "Come on!"[690]

- An intelligent person is one who understands the wisdom of religion. Hazret Ali said, "Any intellect that has no share of religion is not intellect. And any religion that has no share of intellect is not religion." That religion has come with certain obligatory judgements, brought by the one who communicates it, that we must act in accordance with. The result is either Paradise or Hell. When the intellect is made accustomed to doing what is commanded and avoiding what is prohibited, it arrives at a comprehension that encompasses entirely the secret of Paradise and Hell.[691]

- *Intimate friends who are lucky understand*
Intellect is of Iblis, love, of Adam

Intellect is a swimmer upon the sea
In the end he drowns, he rarely finds release

Stop your swimmming, let go pride and enmity
This is no Jayhun, no river, it's the sea

And a bottomless ocean, without escape
Sweeping the seven seas like mere straw away

---

689. Halûk Nurbaki, *Yâ-Sîn Sûresi Yorumu* (Istanbul: Damla Yayınevi 1999), p. 83.
690. Mevlânâ Celâleddin Rûmî, trans. Veled İzbudak, ed. Abdülbaki Gölpınarlı, *Mesnevî* (Istanbul: Milli Eğitim Basımevi 1991), vol. 4, vs. 2301-2304.
691. Ahmed er-Rifâî, *el-Burhanü'l-Müeyyed* (Bedir Yayınları n.d.), pp. 94-95.

62th Verse

For the elect love is like a sailing ship
Disaster's rare, safety more likely with it

Sell intelligence and instead purchase awe
Wit is supposition, there's vision in awe

Offer up intelligence as sacrifice
In Mustafa's presence say, "God will suffice"

Do not rear back from the ship as did Canaan
It was his cunning soul that deluded him

"I'll go up to that high mountain top," he said
"Why should I suffer to be in Noah's debt?"

O unrighteous man, how should you flee his debt
When the Lord too suffers to be in his debt

How should our souls not bear gratitude to him
When the Lord speaks of thanks and a debt to him?

What do you know, O you sack of resentment!
When it suits Him to bear the burden of debt?

Had he not learned to swim, it would have been best
He would have fixed on Noah and ark his trust

If like a babe he'd been ignorant of guile
So that he'd clung to his mother like a child

Or he'd not been filled with knowledge transmitted
But knowledge from the inspired heart of God's friend

When with such a light you take in hand a book
Your inspirational spirit brings rebuke

Next to the time's Axis, knowledge second-hand
Is like sand ablution when water's at hand

Make yourself a fool and follow in the rear
You'll find release only by this folly here

O Humankind

Father, that's why mankind's Sultan spoke this rule:
"The people of Paradise are mostly fools"

Since wit excites pride and vanity in you
Be a fool so that your heart may remain true

Not a fool who bends double to make a jest
But a fool in awe of Him and astonished

The foolish are those women who cut their hands
Warning of the beauty of Joseph by hands

Sacrifice intellect for love of the friend
Intellects—in any case they come from Him

The intelligent have sent intellects there
Idiots who are not lovers are left here

If your intellect, bewildered, leaves this head
Every tip of hair is head and intellect

There no pain of thought will occupy your brain
Intellect and brain become gardens and plain

From the plain you hear discourse subtle and fine
In the gardens your tree will flourish and thrive

On this path you must abandon pomp and pride
Do not move without the movement of your guide

Anyone who moves without head is a tail
His movement is like that of a scorpion's crawl

Zig-zag, ugly, blind by night and venomous
Piercing bodies that are pure is his business

Crush his head, for his inner secret is this
His fixed nature and temperament is this

Having his head crushed like this will set him free
His weak spirit will flee that ill-starred body

62th Verse

Take the weapon from the hands of crazy men
So you gain the pleasure of just and good men

Since they have weapons but no intelligence
Bind them, or they'll cause a hundred accidents[692]

- When the disbelievers end up in Hell, they will begin to cry out and intellect will say to them, "My dear, did no warner, no messenger come to you?" The spirits of those believers will say, "Yes, a warner came to us and showed us the way, but we rejected him and told him we would not believe in him, and we remained in great error." Thus insofar as the people of the soul are beggars to lust and in love with it, they have no intellect, they have supposition. Pharoah is of the people of supposition, and Moses of the people of intellect.[693]

---

692. Şefik Can, *Konularına gore açıklamalı Mesnevi Tercümesi* (Istanbul: Ötüken Neşriyat 1997), vol. 3-4, pp. 483-485 [vol. 4, vs. 1402-1435].

693. Ken'an Rifâî, ed. Kâzım Büyükaksoy, *Mesnevî Hatıraları* (Istanbul: İnkilap Kitapevi 1968), p. 17.

63. This is the Hell that you were promised.

Hādhihi jahannamu'l-latī kuntum tū'adūn.

64. Burn there today, since you disbelieved.

'Işlawhā'l-yawma bimā kuntum takfurūn.

- O you who trust in your fake self and go against God the Truth and reality! This is the Hell you were always promised and that the book of God (*the Quran*) and the prophets described to you while in the world. You used to deny God and refute and commit misbelief against His book and His prophets. Therefore because of that misbelief of yours, today let us see you rely upon it. You will enter! Your entering here is only the result of your actions that came forth from you while in the world of trial.[694]

- Hell (*Jahannam*) means "deep pit." It has taken this name because it is deep. In the Quran Hell occurs in the meaning of the land of torment in the Hereafter. According to Ibn Arabi, it is named thus because of the ugly appearance of Hell.

"Punish with Hell" those who declare they are gods. In other words, return them to their origin. And that is distance. When the bottom of something is deep, it is called *bi'r-u juhnām*, meaning "deep pit." The punishment for those who make such a claim is Hell, in other words, being really distanced from what they said with their tongues. And this is the best punishment.

The name of Hell comes of its cold and heat. Furthermore it is called Hell by reason of ugliness (*jahāme*); for the appearance of Hell

---

694. Şemseddin Yeşil, *Füyûzat* (Istanbul: Ş. Yeşil Yayınları 1984), vol. 6, p. 260.

is ugly. "*Jahāme*" means a cloud that has emptied its rain, and rain is God's mercy. Thus when God makes the rain of a cloud go away, it is named *jahām* because mercy, which is rain, has separated from it. And God has distanced His mercy from Hell, thus Hell became ugly in appearance and feeling. Another reason why it is named Hell is the depth of its bottom. If the bottom of a pit is very deep, it is called *ruqyat-u juhnām*.[695]

• Those who commit evil are certainly inclined toward the direction of evil, in other words, they wish evil. For the seeds they sow are fullgrown thorns. Do not look in a rosegarden for those who sowed the seeds of thorns while in the world! For the place necessary for them is a bramble patch, is Hell. For those idiots found a friend and became the comrade of the friend but could not benefit from that friendship and strengthen their spirits, and they turned their faces to the side of the soul and while they had attained such felicity they did not recognize it, they did not seek from it spirit, life and salvation! They entered the path of the soul and left their spirit in fire.[696]

• We should know that Paradise, Hell, disbelief and faith, sin and good deeds are all given to servants according to their wish; everyone birngs their own wood and fire to Hell themselves. Thus servants worship the God worthy of them, and do not commit *shirk* in anything and do not give their hearts to any other. What is worthy of God is to not torment His servant who is able to do that. Our Messenger of God Efendi says, "*My sheriat is like the ark of Noah; whoever gets on it is saved, and whoever does not is drowned and destroyed.*"[697]

• They asked Our Messenger of God Efendi, "*What is the world?*" He answered, "*A dream.*" They asked again, "*What is the Hereafter?*" He

---

695. Suad el-Hakîm, trans. Ekrem Demirli, *İbü'l-Arabî Sözlüğü* (Istanbul: Kabalcı Yayınevi 2005), p. 130.

696. Ken'an Rifâî, ed. Kâzım Büyükaksoy, *Mesnevî Hatıraları* (Istanbul: İnkilap Kitapevi 1968), p. 6.

697. Ken'an Rifâî, ed. Kâzım Büyükaksoy, *Mesnevî Hatıraları* (Istanbul: İnkilap Kitapevi 1968), p. 270.

said, "In the Hereafter are Paradise and Hell; Paradise is for those who sell the world, and Hell for those who buy the world."[698]

• O oppressor, do not suppose God's trap and His Hell to be distant from you; if God wishes, He will make you taste those torments of Hell, one by one, while you are in the world; He will give you a headache, and you will not know what to do and bang your head against the walls; you will cry, "Mercy, this is the torment of Hell," and keep on floundering about. But those torments you suffer in this world are a very small examplar of the torments of the Hereafter. And these torments end with death, but the torment of the Hereafter is continuous and subsists for disbelievers. The torments of believers are in the amount of their sins.[699]

• The pain of seperation is much keener than the fire of Hell. Furthermore, if a fire like that falls into the heart of someone while in the world, that person cannot enjoy anything or find ease anywhere, they burn in fire, and may even commit suicide to escape that fire. That state is the result of the fire of separation.

Those who do not interfere in the work of God the Truth, who avoid duplicity and are free of disbelief do not suffer the fire of separation.[700]

• The fire of torment is a spark from the fire of Hell that burns the body and spirit of those who are tormented, reaches into their depths and becomes constant in the depths of Hell, in the fire of Hell. Such people who cannot receive the help of the Lord's grace and the Glorified's guidance, who are captive to the lust of the soul and the pleasure of nature, fall into a pit so dark and deep, a pit that has no bottom. The strange thing is that that bottomless pit is the work of their sins. With their sins and exceeding love of the world, such people make their souls bow to the delights of various lusts and rampage

---

698. Ken'an Rifâî, ed. Kâzım Büyükaksoy, *Mesnevî Hatıraları* (Istanbul: İnkilap Kitapevi 1968), p. 157.

699. Ken'an Rifâî, ed. Kâzım Büyükaksoy, *Mesnevî Hatıraları* (Istanbul: İnkilap Kitapevi 1968), p. 62.

700. Ken'an Rifâî, ed. Kâzım Büyükaksoy, *Mesnevî Hatıraları* (Istanbul: İnkilap Kitapevi 1968), p. 103.

in rebellion while in the world, and the pit has been prepared for them in this way and their place in Hell became the Ghayya Pit of Hell. That Ghayya Pit is like the rivers of fire and lava spurted out by volcanoes. And the the sins and rebellions of such people, and the times they spent thinking in detail and deeply in order to commit sin, became the violence and bottomless depth of the fire of that pit.

But because no trace remains of rage and torment in those who extinguish the fire of anger with the water of gentleness, it is replaced by the water of God the Truth's mercy. And that water of mercy makes of those people's bodies, in other words, their beings, a garden of Paradise.[701]

- The fire of Hell is that thing that is made of the exceeding inclination toward the externally and internally false worldly ornaments and worldly pleasures and bodily delights on the part of a person on the field of this world, in other words, this realm of nature.[702]

- When the number nine manifested in these three letters in the reality of (each of) the three letters of *Kun* (Be!), the nine heavens, from among those countable, were manifested. Through the movements of all of these nine heavens and the courses of their stars, the world and the things in the world came to be. This world and the things in the world will be destroyed through their movements in the same way. Through the movements of the highest heaven of thse nine heavens, Paradise and those inside it came to be. During the movement of this highest heaven, the things inside Paradise emerge. Through movement of the second heaven—which comes after the highest heaven—Hell and those inside it came to be. Furthermore, Resurrection, the rising from the grave and coming to life, the gathering together and scattering, the gathering and scattering on the Day of Resurrection emerged.

For those reasons we have mentioned, the world became mixed, in other words, boons with torments, and torments with boons are

---

701. Ken'an Rifâî, ed. Kâzım Büyükaksoy, *Mesnevî Hatıraları* (Istanbul: İnkilap Kitapevi 1968), p. 68.

702. Ken'an Rifâî, ed. Kâzım Büyükaksoy, *Mesnevî Hatıraları* (Istanbul: İnkilap Kitapevi 1968), p. 33.

in a mixed condition. Also for those reasons we mentioned, Paradise is entirely boon and Hell is entirely torment. That mixing will come to an end for the existents transferring from this world to the other world, for the life of the Hereafter does not accept mixing like the life of the world does. This is the most important difference between the life of the world and the life of the Hereafter. But when divine torment comes to an end in the life of Hell, in other words, in the life of those who are of Hell, when limit and duration reach God's mercy, which surpasses God's torment, the property of Mercy will return for them again; its form will still remain as the same form, it will not change. If the form of that mercy had changed, they would be afflicted with torment. Thus with God's permission and help, the action of the second heaven following upon the highest heaven at first, because of the torment manifested in them, rules against them in every location that accepts torment. Here we said "in every location that accepts torment" because there are those in Hell who do not accept torment (for example, the guards of Hell).

When Hell fulfills its period, which is 45,000 years, Hell is a true torment for those in Hell during this period, such that the people of Hell are first subjected to a continuous and unrelieved torment in Hell and that torment continues for 23,000 years. Then the Merciful sends a sleep upon them; in this sleep they lose all their sense perceptions. In this regard God the Exalted has said, *"Surely whoever comes to his Lord having committed sin, Hell is for him. In it he neither dies nor lives"* (20:74, 87:12). In the same way Hazret Messenger (a.s.) says, "They neither die there nor are they brought to life." That hadith seeks to describe their condition when they lose all of their sense perception. This condition resembles that of people tormented and tortured in this world who faint because of the extremity of their fear and exceeding strength of their pain. The people of Hell thus remain in that state of sleep for 19,000 years.

Then they awake from that faint and *"We shall replace their skins with other skins"* (4:56), and they suffer torment in that condition for 15.000 years. They they are made to faint again. They remain in that state for 11,000 years. Then they again awake from their faint. *"When their skins are consumed, We shall replace them with other skins, that they may taste the torment"* (4:56). In this condition they taste that very sorrowful, very painful torment for 7,000 years. Then they remain in a faint for 3,000 years. In the end they awake. This time God grants them delight, gaiety, happiness and comfort. Just like the condition of a person who has become tired out and slept and awakes rested. This condition is like that because *"God's mercy precedes His wrath"* and *"My mercy embraces all things"* (7:156). Thus at that time God's mercy is for them "All-Embracing," in other words, a property, a ruling produced from the name that means *"embracing all things in Mercy and Knowledge"* (40:7). At that time those existents no longer feel any pain, sorrow, or torment. Now that condition continues in that way for them, and they are pleased by that condition as by a windfall and they say, "We were forgotten, and so because we fear our condition will be remembered, we do not want anything else. But God had said, *'Be despised in there, and do not speak to Me'"* (23:108). Now they do not speak up there, they are silent. They have no fear but the fear of being subject to torment again.

The torment they will suffer forever is fear to that extent. That torment is a spiritual torment, not sensory. They even sometimes forget it. They are happy because they have been delivered from sensory torment and attained comfort. And this happens through the thing God has put into their hearts because "He is One possesed of a mercy embracing all things." Thus God the Exalted says in this regard, *"Today We forget you as you forgot"* (45:34). Thus because of this reality, when they feel no more pain and sorrow, they say, "We are forgotten!" In the same way God says in this regard, *"They forgot God, so He forgot them"* (9:67). *"Thus this day you shall be forgotten"* (20:126), in other words, "You are abandoned in Hell." For "forgetting" is to abandon.

The share of happiness had by the people of Hell is the non-occurance of torment. Their share of punishment is the occurance of torment, because for the people of Hell there is no assurance by way of news coming from God. But they are also sometimes protected from the fear that torment will occur. Thus sometimes, they are protected from that fear for 10,000 years, and sometimes for 2,000 years, sometimes 6,000. And as long as that amount of time has not passed, they are not released from the aforementioned amount. That amount of time must pass for them. When God wishes to give them a boon, a grace from His name, Merciful, they at that moment wait to be released and delivered from the condition they are in and the torment they are suffering. Thus they receive boons in the amount of that waiting. That waiting continues for them sometimes for a thousand years, or 9,000 years; sometimes for 5,000 years. The period may be longer or shorter. Thus the condition in Hell of the people of Hell continues in that way, for they are now the inhabitants of that place.[703]

• The garden of Paradise is the company of the learned. Their fruits are the meanings that arise in your heart. The Jahim pit of Hell is God's removing the contentment from a person's heart and placing therein greed.[704]

• The Muhammeden form is light from which God created Paradise and Hell. It is such a station that therein is found the taste of torment and boons. God created the Muhammeden forms from the light of the names "Originator" (*Badī'*) (*who has no partner or peer, who gives existence to a perfect thing*) and "Powerful" (*Qādir*). With the names "Boon-Giver" (*Mannān*) and "All-Subjugating" (*Qāhir*), He looked at it and then self-disclosed to it with the names "Subtle" (*Laṭīf*) and "Forgiver" (*Ghāfir*),and at the moment of that self-disclosure the Muhammeden Form, as necessitated by that self-disclosure, went into a state of being divided in two.

God the Exalted created Paradise from the half that fell to the right, and that became the place of those possessed of boons. He created Hell from the half that fell to the left, and that became the place of the wreched who are the people of error.

The half that fell to the right, in other words, the part from which He created the paradises, is the part looked after by the term Boon-Giver. That is the secret of the self-disclosure of the Subtle. That is the location of all that is best. The half that fell to the left, in other words, the hells, in other words, the part where He created fire, is looked after with the name "All-Subjugating." It conceals the secret of the self-disclosure of the name "Forgiver."

---

703. Muhyiddîn İbnül'-Arabî, trans. Mahmut Kanık, *Marifet ve Hikmet* (Istanbul: İz Yayıncılık 1995), pp. 221-224.

704. From Ken'an er-Rifâî's notes, Meşkûre Sargut archive.

"When the All-Dominating (Jabbār) sets His foot upon Hell, Hell says, 'Enough, enough!' Then the [green leaves] of the celery plant sprout in Hell (hadith). When God created torment for the people of Hell, He also created for them the power to endure the torment He created. If He had not created the power to endure that torment, they would be destroyed. In other words, they woud cease to be, and thus be delivered from torment. *"When their skins are consumed, We shall replace them with other skins, that they may taste the torment"* (4:56). The power to endure and understand the torment is given to those thrown into Hell, then the torment comes and they are tormented.

The same is true for the people of Paradise; for before the boons come, they receive the good news of the boons.

When the torment suffered by the people of Hell comes to an end, in other words, when another torment arrives, the power to endure the previous torment given to them does not leave them. For that is a grant given to to them by the hand of grace, and God does not go back on His grace.

Torment comes by God the Truth's All-Subjugating hand, and to change the torment and replace it with another is His right.

Until All-Dominating God sets His foot on the fire, the people of Hell gain a new power in every torment. Once the attributes of God the Truth have manifested in someone, no evil comes to that person.

When God sets His foot on the fire it becomes weak and bows the head; it says, "Enough, enough!" When this state emerges, torment leaves those who are of the people of Hell. When fire is no longer a principle existent (*aslî bir varlık*) in the body, it dies out in the end... in other words, the meaning of the phrase, *"My mercy precedes My wrath"* manifests. What is principle is God's Mercy. *"My mercy embraces all things"* (7:156).

God created the things as Mercy from His Essence. Wrath cannot go on until the end of existence because it is not an attribute bound to the Essence. "Wrath" is an attribute that necessitates justice. And justice consists of a ruling given between two acts. The name "Just" is the name of God the Truth's attribute, while "Merciful" is the name of the Essence. The name All-Concealing (*Ghaffār*) is the first site of manifestation belonging to the boons that God's mercy necessitates.

63TH-64TH VERSE

Forgiver (*Ghāfir*) is one who forgives. All-Concealing (*Ghaffār*) is one who forgives the sins of servants. All-Forgiving (*Ghafūr*) is one who continuously forgives.

The name All-Subjugating is the first site of manifestation belonging to punishment; it is necessitated by justice, and in it there are two attributes. There came the attributes All-Subjugating (Qāhir) and Overwhelming (Qahhār), but not the attribute Qahūr. The meaning of this is that mercy precedes wrath.

When the angels of fire depart, the angels of boon arrive. And thus the celery plant sprouts in the place that was the location of fire. The celery plant is green, and the most beautiful color in Paradise is green. In other words, fire turns green, Hell is transformed into Paradise. The most beautiful proof of this meaning is the story of Hazret Abraham. "*O Fire! Be coolness and peace for Abraham!*" (21:69). When this command was given, sweet basil sprouted and it became a garden. When All-Dominating God set down His foot, the torment of the people of Hell was transformed into comfort. The location where they were did not change, fire departed.

If a person is swept away by God's attraction and enters the path of purifying the soul through effort and ascetic practices, for that person the fire of Hell is transformed into the boon of Paradise. Their soul nature ceases to be because the divine light purifies them of faults.

Such difficult works as effort and ascetic practices and opposition to the soul take the place of the violence and torment the people of Hell will meet on Resurrection Day. "*And there is not one of you but will encounter Hell. This is for your Lord an inevitable decree*" [sic] (19:71). The discomforts they suffer through effort and ascetic practices are the price for another torment that would occur in the Hereafter. These difficulties continue until the soul is purified.[705]

- *The believers say at the Gathering there*
"Is Hell not, O Angel, a road that is shared?

"That believer and disbeliever pass by?
On this road we have seen neither smoke nor fire

---

705. Abd al-Karīm ibn al-Jīlī, trans. Seyyid Hüseyin Fevzî Paşa, *İnsan-ı Kâmil* (Istanbul: Kitsan Yayınları), pp. 159-169.

O Humankind

Here is Paradise and the court of safety
So where then will that loathsome stopping-place be?"

"That garden so green," then the angel will say
"That you saw while you passed by such-and-such place

"That was Hell and site of extreme agony
For you it became gardens, orchards and trees

"Since you struggled with the soul's hellish nature
The fiery pagan that seeks strife and error

"It has now become entirely purified
For sake of God you have extinguished the fire

"The fire of lust that sent out flames rising high
Is now leaves of God-Fearing and the Guide's light

"You have made the fire of rage become clement
The darkness of ignorance, become knowledge

"You have made greed's fire become altruism
And thorn-like envy become a rose garden

"Since you've extinguished all these fires of your own
For the sake of God, all of them, on and on

"Since you've made of the fiery soul a garden
And planted the seed of faithfulness therein

"Nightingales of remembrance glorify Him
Singing sweetly on the grass beside the stream

"You have answered the call of God's Messenger
Into the soul's blazing Hell you've brought water

"It is your right that our Hell, too, be transformed
Into greenery, roses, music and song[706]

---

706. Mevlânâ Celâleddin Rûmî, trans. Veled İzbudak, ed. Abdülbaki Gölpınarlı, *Mesnevî* (Istanbul: Milli Eğitim Basımevi 1991), vol. 2, vs. 2554-2568.

- Hell (*Jahannam*) means "deep pit." It has taken this name because it is deep. In the Quran, Hell occurs in the meaning of the land of torment in the Hereafter.

"Is there no place in Hell for disbelievers?"

"There are called to the land of Hell."

Hell is one of the seven gates of the fire into which people enter with their animal souls. Ibn Arabi sometimes uses the word "fire" as the opposite of Paradise.

The names of the seven gates of the fire are the Gate of Jahannam, the Gate of Jahīm, the Gate of Sa'īr, the Gate of Saqar, the Gate of Ladhdhah, the Gate of Khutāma, the Gate of Sijjīn. And there is a gate that is closed, which is the eighth gate that is never opened. It is the veil.

Paradise has been forbidden to those who kill themselves. However, those who commit suicide enter Hell with their animal souls. For Hell is not a place for the rational soul (*nefs-i nâtika*). If the rational soul appeared to Hell, it would certainly put out its fire.

There are two stations in the Hereafter, Paradise and Hell. There are two stations in the world also, torment and boon.

A person's "hell" is his/her nature. But here, Ibn Arabi has used it as a form and simile. He used "hell" as a simile for the structure of the Hereafter with the bridge over it in order to describe our passage on the sheriat bridge over our nature (hell).

The bridge we walk over until it takes us to Paradise, with supports that God has made fixed, is the bridge of guidance. You have built it for yourself of your beneficial inner and outer actions in worldly life. That bridge exists spiritually in this life and has no sensory form. In the Hereafter it stretches over Hell concretely in your name. One foot of the bridge is firmly on the ground and the other is on the gate of Paradise. When you see the bridge, you will realize that it is a thing and a work of your own making. You know that in that world it was a bridge stretching over the hell of nature.

The sheriat is the salvation of a person from the hell of his or her own nature.

As it is in reality, the person who is not My servant is the servant of his or her own nature—meaning hell—and will be contemptible and servile under its dominion.[707]

---

707. Suad el-Hakîm, trans. Ekrem Demirli, *İbü'l-Arabî Sözlüğü* (Istanbul: Kabalcı Yayınevi 2005), pp. 130-131.

- "Fever is the pleasure every believer takes from Hell."[708]

- Struggle with the soul is the greater jihad, and war with the disbelievers, the lessor jihad.

God created the fire from His name, "All-subjugating," and made it the site of manifestation for His name, "Majesty." He furthermore made seven self-disclosures there. Hell has seven gates, and Paradise, eight. The senses of the human being are eight. In other words, a human being's comprehension has eight parts. These are the five senses and imagination, supposition (*doubt, hesitation, baseless fear*) and intellect. Whatever people comprehend or understand, they do so through those five gates. Intellect is not together with those seven, and if those seven work without the command of intellect and conform to the command of nature, they become the gates of Hell. If intellect comes forth and controls those seven, and all seven work with the command of intellect, all eight become the gates of Paradise. Thus all human beings will first pass through Hell. Then they will reach Paradise.

The Hell and Paradise of fools are dissident and concordant, those of the intelligent are need and relinquishment, and those of lovers are veil and unveiling.

Good character is a paradise most spacious and pleasant. Bad character is a hell exceedingly narrow and unpleasant. Compared to the delight of knowledge and gnosis the delight of character is like water drop and ocean. The delight of comprehension is an exceedingly pleasant delight, such that bodily pleasures and physical delights cannot reach the delight of comprehension.

However knowledgeable people may be, they must say or do nothing contrary to courtesy, respect and exaltedness, and they must be secure. They must protect their interiors. However intimate persons may be, their security must be to that extent greater.[709]

- **Hells:**

---

708. Abdü'l-kerîm b. İbrahim el-Cîlî, trans. Seyyid Hüseyin Fevzî Paşa, *İnsan-ı Kâmil* (Istanbul: Kitsan Yayınları), p. 169.

709. Azizüddin Nesefî, trans. Mehmet Kanar, *İnsân-ı Kâmil* (Istanbul: Dergâh Yayınları 1990), p. 130, 133.

The First Self-Disclosure: Muntaqim

"He created this gate of Hell from such darknesses as rebellion and sin. We can count such sins as lying hypocrisy, homosexuality, wine drinking, rejection of obligatory commands, and seeing actions judged haram by God as permitted. The sinner would wish to be ransomed from the torment of that day by his children, his spouse and his brother, his kin who sheltered him and all who are on earth, that it might deliver him. No! For it is a flaming fire, ripping off the scalp, calling all who turned their backs and fled" (70:11-17). The torment of those in this level of Hell is harsh, but despite all its violence, the lightest torment is here.

The Second Self-Disclosure: Jahīm

God self-discloses here with the name "Just." This gate of Hell is created from debauchery, which is oppression, superstition, fanaticism, frenzy and rebelliousness. This is the place of those who wrongly assault God's servants, appropriate their property, spill their blood, bear false witness, curse, speak ill of poeple behind their backs and ridicule the honor of people; those who oppress people and thus owe them their rights.

The Third Self-Disclosure: Shadīd

This gate of Hell is created of things like parsimony and hoarding, resentment, lust and love of the world.

The Fourth Self-Disclosure: Hāwiya

God self-discloses to this hell with the name "Wrath." The gate of this place is created of things like discord, hypocrisy, false pretension, etc.; whoever has these dispositions, this is the dwelling of those who possess them. *"The Hypocrites will be in the lowest pit of the Fire"* (4:145).

The Fifth Self-Disclosure: Saqar

God self-discloses with the name "Abaser." Its gate is arrogance. It brings low people of Phoarah's disposition, in other words, those who wrongfully appear superor and take the way of oppression. Whoever wrongfully claims to posses one of God's attributes or names, God torments him or her with the contrary of the name they claim.

"The he turned his back and was arrogant" (74:23). *"'This is nothing but the speech of a human being.' I will cast him into Saqar"* (74:25-26).

The Sixth Self-Disclosure: Saʿīr

God self-discloses here with the name "Violent." This gate of Hell is created of satanic qualities; it is a fire. It comes to be from the spark of nature and the smoke of the soul. From this fire come sedition, rage, and lust. Trickery and apostasy are produced from it. *"There We made them missiles against the devils and We have prepared for them the punishment of saʿīr"* (67:5).

The Seventh Self-Disclosure: Jahannam

God self-discloses to this hell with the name "Grievous Punishment." It is the hell of those who set boundaries. The world is the place of wisdom and the Hereafter is the place of power. Intellect is bound by the bonds of wisdom. Unveiling is bound to power. Only those who unveil understand what is described. The gate of this level is created of disbelief and shirk.

The sinners who are the people of Hell cannot exit that level of the levels of Hell until they plunge into each and every one of the pits belonging to that level.

Setting foot upon the hell of the All-Dominating is different for each person. Everything that God the Truth works upon the people of Hell bears the meaning of violence. For the King there is sultanate at all levels of Hell. That is the reason why Hell has a treasurer, custodian and guardian. The angels of torment came to be out of the refinements of the possessor of Violence.

The people of Hell are transferred from a lower level of Hell to another of its levels; they are brought one level up so that their torment may lessen. And those at a higher level are brought one level down so that their torment may be greater. In other words, the increase or decrease of their suffering is as much as Sublime God the Truth wills. It depends on His divine measuring.

"Beware of a trial that will befall not only those among you who do wrong!" (8:25).

"That Day We shall say to Hell, 'Are you filled?' And it will say, 'Is there more?'" (50:30).

63TH-64TH VERSE

The soul has a precisely analogous relationship to Hell. That is why you cannot satiate it. The more you give it, the more it wants; it is never satisfied.

There is a delight there for the people of Hell. So many people delight in war and fighting, although they know they also feel sorrow. But the Lordliness that has settled into their essence pushes them to plunge into it and they delight in it.

Aside from this delight there is another delight the people of Hell will feel, which is like the delight felt in scabies. Those who have scabies scratch themselves although they know their skin will come off because of the scabies, and they derive delight form this itching even though they are harmed by it... such people experience both delight and torment at once.

Another delight for the people of Hell comes when those who are ignorant but believe themselves to be intelligent and knowledgable see others they think are more ignorant themselves make errors in something they supposedly know...

They are caught up in the intellect's leadership; they conduct themselves according to the judgment of their intellects and thoughts, and take delight in the state of their souls. Since they abhor the condition of the ignorant, they keep deriving delight from their own harsh condition.

"The inhabitants of the Fire will call out to the inhabitants of Paradise, 'Send to us some of the water or whatever sustenance God provides you.' They say, 'God has forbidden both to the disbelievers'" (7:50).

Some of the people of Hell derive delight from the torment they suffer. Others only suffer, they take no delight in it; they very much hate the torment they suffer.

The reason why some of the people of Hell have been thrown into torment is that in the life of the world they used their intellects in ways quite unnecessary. What pushes others into torment is their ignorance. Vain beliefs have thrust others into torment. Others meet with torment because of things they have done. There is another group that enters into torment because they were praised by people for something they did not possess. Others suffer torment becasue they spoke of their faults as good things, or of evils they did not have. There are those among the people of Hell who are regarded as virtuous by most of the people of Paradise who are near God.[710]

• Everyone is the architect of the building of their life. Let us say that you use bad, rotten materials for a structure you make, and build it without measure; the structure you build will fall down, and in the end, they will hold you responsible. The ease, sorrow, hell and heaven, good and evil people find is because they have built the structure of their life well or badly. The responsibility for the result we achieve is our own, not that of others.

If we make the structure of our being with rotten characteristics and evils, one day it will collapse of itself. At last we will be brought before God the Truth and judged: "I gave you this being as a trust. Why did you build it with rotten and bad materials?" and as a result, we will be condemned.[711]

• *"Tomorrow everyone will be punished for their actions here. Those who disbelieve will be driven to Hell, and there the demons of Hell will say, 'Did not messengers come to you saying the commands of God the Truth and warning you of the day of Gathering? Now enter into Hell and stay there forever. How ugly a place for the arrogant is this Hell'"* [sic] (39:71-72).

To the second group, who are loyal to God and listened to God's commands from his officers, treading the path with which God the Truth is pleased, God's treasurers will say, *"'Welcome, may the peace of God be upon you, come in... Enter the paradises and stay there forever'"* [sic] (39:73).[712]

Humans are the architects of their own being. Pain, sorrow, joy, ease, light, darkness, paradises, hells, elevations and depressions are all the reflections, the shadows of our actions. There is nothing that does not have a cause, period. Whatever we do, whatever we find, it is all what we have sought and found. Thus seekers may find their Lord, or their calamity.[713]

---

710. Abdü'l-kerîm b. İbrahim el-Cîlî, trans. Seyyid Hüseyin Fevzî Paşa, *İnsan-ı Kâmil* (Istanbul: Kitsan Yayınları), pp. 169-185.
711. Ken'an Rifâî, *Sohbetler* (Istanbul: Kubbealtı Neşriyatı 2000), p. 426.
712. Ken'an Rifâî, *Sohbetler* (Istanbul: Kubbealtı Neşriyatı 2000), p. 455.
713. Ken'an Rifâî, *Sohbetler* (Istanbul: Kubbealtı Neşriyatı 2000), p. 438.

63TH-64TH VERSE

- The fire of Hell was not intended for human beings, who are created upon the form of the Merciful. But the creatures carry Hell, in other words heedlessness and separation, in their constitution, and if those veils of soul have not been torn asunder and they have not been cleansed of the soul's qualities, there is burning in Hell for them. For because they have covered the form of the Merciful with animal veils, and are wrapped up in the attribute that is dominant in them, whatever that form may be—fox, wolf, hyena, rooster, pig—they will be deprived of the form of the Merciful and burn with that animal attribute.[714]

- *Jesus's donkey is not begrudged sugar*
But the donkey by nature likes straw better

  If sugar was what made the donkey happy
He'd have poured for it a hundred weights candy[715]

- Beyazid Bistami says: If God the Truth were going to put me in Hell, I would be as happy there too as those who enjoy Paradise. What I need is for my beloved to be with me.

  Because lovers hear and see nothing but the beloved, the suffering and trial they endure is the same as pleasure. Because they their beloved has given it. The beloved's pleasure and reproach are one and the same.[716]

- They drive everyone away from religion and faith with ignorant speech. Religion and wisdom (*the divine purpose in creation and creating*) is humanity and character. Our duty is to bring everyone close to God, not drive them away. Stuff everyone into Hell... So who will be left in Paradise? Why should I go to Hell?

  Do they not read the verse, "*Say: 'O My servants who have transgressed against themselves*"? "*Do not despair of God's mercy*" (39:53). In order to bring a person to love something, should one say that thing is

---

714. From Sâmiha Ayverdi's notes.
715. Mevlânâ Celâleddin Rûmî, trans. Veled İzbudak, ed. Abdülbaki Gölpınarlı, *Mesnevî* (Istanbul: Milli Eğitim Basımevi 1991), vol. 6, vs. 161-162.
716. Ken'an Rifâî, *Sohbetler* (Istanbul: Kubbealtı Neşriyatı 2000), p. 552.

fearful? Or should one make its beauties known? They try to burden Islam with many made-up and imputed tales and judgments, and in this way terrify everyone.[717]

- God the Truth says, *"My mercy has covered My wrath."* For in God's wrath there is mercy itself. There is nothing that divine mercy has not covered.[718]

In explication of the hadith, *"We have returned from the lesser jihad to the greater jihad":*

God created Hell in the form of the soul, and the soul with the character of Hell. Each gate of Hell is one of the seven attributes of the soul. These are the gates of pride, greed, lust, envy, rage, miserliness, and hatred.

So that is the Hell of which the human soul is a piece. Pieces always conform to the whole. That is why we, having the nature of Hell, take more pleasure in the ways of Hell.

In short, we enter this world called Hell, which holds a person back from every kind of humanity, making him really Hellbound, on the path of hatred, through the gate of lust, through greed for position, addiction to reputation, and the gates of envy, rage and pride.

If we know that our soul is a part of Hell, and try to rescue it from the ways of Hell, there will be salvation in the end. If we do the opposite, and drive our souls on to Hell, there will be no way out.

Only the foot of God can kill the dragon soul. Only the hand of God the Truth can draw the bow of the soul. If the arrow set on this bow is a straight arrow, it will hit its mark. Try to be straight as an arrow on the bow of God! If you are an arrow that has not been bent or shot astray, then the training and support of a perfect murshid will be beneficial to you. If you are an arrow that will not agree to rectitude, what can a murshid do with you?

To defeat the soul is harder than to overcome the enemy in battle. It s more difficult than to break a boulder off Mount Qaf with a needle. To be victorious over the soul and rule this difficult country is possible only with the help of God the Truth and by following the

---

717. Ken'an Rifâî, *Sohbetler* (Istanbul: Kubbealtı Neşriyatı 2000), p. 486.
718. Ken'an Rifâî, *Sohbetler* (Istanbul: Kubbealtı Neşriyatı 2000), p. 487.

path shown by the friends of God the Truth. Defeating the soul does not require steel weapons and long lances. It is made possible by the illumination and filling of the human heart with the light of divine love.

Remember the saying of Hazret Ali on this same subject: "To abandon one single attribute of the soul is truly more difficult than to conquer the fortress of Khaybar.

The lion who scatters the ranks of the opposing army is not important. The true lion is he who wins the war he wages on his own soul. He defeats his own soul in battle and annihilates it.[719]

- What is Hell, do you know?
  Hell is the soul. It is torment. Sorrow and grief.
  Rather than pray, "O my Lord, do not throw me into Hell," pray, "Tear Hell from inside me"![720]

- Explaining That Those Who Know the Power of God the Truth Do Not Ask, "Where are Paradise and Hell?"

Wherever He wills, God makes Hell to be there
He makes the zenith for birds a trap and snare

And there may arise from your teeth pangs of pain
So that you will say, "It's Hell and a dragon."

He makes sugar grow from the roots of your teeth
So you know the strength of the judgment's decree

Do not then bite with your teeth those who are pure
Consider the blow of which one can't beware

For the Egyptians God makes blood of the Nile
And He keeps the Israelites safe from trial[721]

---

719. Ken'an Rifâî, *Şerhli Mesnevî-i Şerif* (Istanbul: Kubbealtı Neşriyatı 2000), pp. 190-191.
720. Sâmiha Ayverdi, *Dile Gelen Taş* (Istanbul: Kubbealtı Neşriyatı 2000), p. 129.
721. Mevlânâ Celâleddin Rûmî, trans. Veled İzbudak, ed. Abdülbaki Gölpınarlı, *Mesnevî* (Istanbul: Milli Eğitim Basımevi 1991), vol. 4, vs. 2811-2812, 2814-2816.

- The fire that wishes to pull the human soul to the paths of the left hand, to drag it along and burn it, is the fire of lust. It is the fire of profound attachment to and seduction by worldly passions. Beware of lust, which is the wish awoken in the human soul for any kind of sin or transient desire. For beginning with the denial of the One who created you, to cheat others, to embrace position and wealth, in short to burn with an insatiable feeling of hunger for anything material and for materiality—all are manifestations of the same lust.

  The nature of Hell is dominant in the fire of lust and passion. Water is not effective against it. On the contrary, it rages all the more water touches it. Such fires must be put out not with water but with light. For fire too has light, but divine light extinguishes satanic fire. People whose spirits have become mirrors of God's light and self-disclosure no longer have any fear of fire.[722]

- The greatest torment, the greatest hell, is heedlessness of God. It is to those who censure and slander murshids that God gives that torment.[723]

- *And thus is the world, the dream of those who sleep*
  The sleeper believes it to be enduring

  Suddenly comes the appointed dawn of death
  When they are freed from supposition's darkness

  They begin to laugh at their own sorrows then
  When they see their everlasting abode then

  Everything, evil and good, that you have dreamed
  Will manifest on Judgment Day and be seen

  In this slumber of the world all that you did
  When you wake up there will become evident

  So do not suppose that what you did in sleep
  Is over and done, and has no more meaning

---

722. Ken'an Rifâî, *Şerhli Mesnevî-i Şerif* (Istanbul: Kubbealtı Neşriyatı 2000), p. 545.
723. Ken'an Rifâî, *Sohbetler* (Istanbul: Kubbealtı Neşriyatı 2000), p. 543.

63TH-64TH VERSE

All of you who tore the coat of a Joseph
Will awake from that heavy sleep as a wolf

All your tempers, becoming wolves, one by one
Will tear you apart in a rage, limb from limb

Their rebellious insolence kept you perplexed
So their punishment will be to taste regret

So that Our justice may step forth into view
To give each ugly deed the recompense due

For your body is observed by intellect
Though your vision falls short of perceiving it[724]

- **The Wisdom of Creating The Hell of That World And The Dungeon of This World So That They May be Houses of Worship For The Arrogant Who "Come Willingly Or Unwillingly"**

For the vile are purified by cruelty
They are cruel when they are treated sincerely

Hell is the mosque where they perform their worship
The fetter that binds the wild bird is the trap

For villian and thief the dungeon is cloister
That they may constantly remember God there

Since the purpose of human beings was worship
For the haughty fire is the house of worship

Human beings are able to do every thing
But this service is the purpose of their being

Your being kind is where the gracious worship
Your infecting them is where the vile worship

---

724. Mevlânâ Celâleddin Rûmî, trans. Veled İzbudak, ed. Abdülbaki Gölpınarlı, *Mesnevî* (Istanbul: Milli Eğitim Basımevi 1991), vol. 4, vs. 3654-3659, 3662-3663, 3675-3678.

O Humankind

That they may place their heads down, strike the vicious
That they may be fruitful, give to the gracious

Of necessity God made a mosque for each
Hell is for those and for these, there is increase

In Jerusalem Moses built the Low Door
So the moaning tribe would bring their heads down low

Because they were high-handed and insolent
Hell is that Low Door, gate of the supplicant[725]

- *No, I misspoke, Fire was God's subjugation*
Why should there be need to adduce a cause then?

Love is your friend, nut-like body, know it well
Your soul seeks the kernal and beats on the shell

Those of Hell who take the skin to be their friend
God's "We exchange their skins," bestows skins on them

The human spirit is ruler of the Fire
Is the Ruler of Hell ever destroyed there?

Thus increase not body, but spirit within
So that like the Ruler you'll be the Fire's king

You have been multiplying skin upon skin
Necessarily you are like sooty skin

Since the Fire has no provender but the skin
Skin is ripped off pride by God's subjugation

This arrogance comes as result of the skin
Thus status and wealth are arrogance's friend

What is arrogance? To forget the essence
To be frozen, heedless of sun as ice is

---

725. Mevlânâ Celâleddin Rûmî, trans. Veled İzbudak, ed. Abdülbaki Gölpınarlı, *Mesnevî* (Istanbul: Milli Eğitim Basımevi 1991), vol. 3, vs. 2983-2987, 2993-2997.

63TH-64TH VERSE

When aware of the sun, ice does not remain
It becomes soft, warm, and quickly goes away

They have not raised their eyes to what is within
Thus they supposed the kernal to be the skin

It is Iblis who was leader of this way
For he fell to the net of status as prey[726]

- He (*someone*) said, "The Tatars also believe in the Resurrection and say, "Surely there will be a Day of Judgment." He (Mevlana) said, "They lie; they want to show themselves as united with the Muslims. They want to say, 'We, too, know, and we believe.' They asked the camel, 'Where are you coming from?' and it answered, 'I am coming from the hamam.' They said, 'It is obvious from your heels!' In other words, if they believe in Resurrection Day, where is the proof? These sins, these tyrannies and evils have fallen layer upon layer and piled up like snow. Just as the sun melts snow and ice, the sun of abandoning sin and turning toward God the Truth and feeling regret melts all the snow of that rebellion when the fear of God emerges and the states of that world become real. If snow or ice, while in that state said, 'I have seen the sun; the sun of July has cast its lights upon me," and still remained in the state of snow or ice, would any intelligent person believe it? Let the July sun shine and leave snow and ice on the ground! That is impossible. However much Sublime God promises to punish the parts of good and evil at the Resurrection, we see the likenesses of that in this world every moment, every instant. For example, if someone's heart expands, that is the recompense for their having made someone else happy. In the same way, if a person feels sorry it is because they have made someone else unhappy. These things are the gifts of that world, examples of the Day of Judgment. The purpose is for people to understand the majority of things from these few. As for example when they take a handful of grain and show it in order to show what kind of thing a storehouse of grain is... Although Mustafa (s.a.s.) was so great and mighty, one night his

---

726. Mevlânâ Celâleddin Rûmî, trans. Veled İzbudak, ed. Abdülbaki Gölpınarlı, *Mesnevî* (Istanbul: Milli Eğitim Basımevi 1991), vol. 5, vs. 1928, 1933-1934, 1936-1941, 1943, 1949-1950.

hand hurt. A revelation came to him, saying, 'This comes of the pain in Abbas's hand.' Because Hazret Mustafa had taken Abbas prisoner and bound his hands along with those of all the prisoners. Although that was God's command, still Muhammed suffered the punishment for it. All of these constraints, sorrows and illnesses that manifest in you, even if you do not now remember them, come of the effects of bad things you did and sins you committed. You have done very bad things; but because you were unaware or did not know, you do not know that they were bad, or an unbeliever friend of yours told you they were unimportant. You may even have been unaware that they were sins. Now let us look at the recompense for these—how much do you suffer, how much expensiveness will you feel? Suffering is definitely the punishment for a sin, and expansiveness the recompense for worship. That is why when Mustafa (s.a.s.) turned the ring on his finger, he was rebuked, 'We did not create you in vain and for play!' As it says in the Quranic verse, *'Do you suppose We created you in vain?'* compare how you expend your strength, in worshipping God and doing good, or in sinning?"[727]

---

727. Mevlânâ Celâleddin Rûmî, trans. Melika Ülker Anbarcioğlu, *Fîhi mâ Fîh* (Istanbul: Milli Eğitim Basımevi 1985), pp. 102-104.

65. That day We will set a seal upon their mouths, but their hands will speak to Us, and their feet bear witness to what they have earned.

'Al-yawma nakhtimu 'alā 'afwāhihim wa tukallimunā 'aydīhim wa tashhadu 'arjuluhum bimā kānū yaksibūn.

• God the Truth says, "*That day We will set a seal upon their mouths.*" It is the group oblivious and uncomprehending of this truth whose eyes have gone blind and their mouths have been sealed before waiting for the Gathering, who do will never experience God's acceptance, bits have been set in their mouths and they cannot eat the sugar of meaning. Does a donkey understand sugar? If you put before it a thousand weights, it will not even turn to look. But if you were to give it a bit of hay, it would go at it with appetite.

They are those who cannot eat of the sugar of meaning, but immediately open their mouths for gossip and meaningless nonsense, and listen greedily and set about talking.[728]

• They are those who make excuses when faced with the might of the Exalted, who begin to beg and say, "O my Lord! We did not set up partners to You, we did not deny Your book and messenger." Today We seal their mouths and prevent them from speaking lies. We silence their mouths and they set to indicating with their hands the evils and tyranies, the evil gains they have dishonestly perpetrated, and their feet bear witness.

O seeker!

Just as God the Truth makes the tongue speak, He makes all the limbs of substance speak also, makes the iniquities dishonestly per-

---
[728]. Ken'an Rifâî, *Sohbetler* (Istanbul: Kubbealtı Neşriyatı 2000), pp. 426-427.

petrated to speak, burning furiously. So do not turn toward other than God the Truth before the curtain of heedlessness opens. The result will be disappointment. Be with God the Truth each instant, go with God wherever you go, wit with God wherever you sit. Let Him be your most trusted, your mightiest friend.[729]

• You say you do not recognize the existence of God. What is it that you cannot recognize? Is not that being the witness of this being of yours? God says, *"That day We will set a seal upon their mouths, their hands and feet will bear witness about them."*

There's nothing evident but God
He's secreted from the eyeless

That being appears with complete clarity in every thing. But because their eyes are blind, they do not see that reality.[730]

• And moreover, "I do not look," God has said
"At the outside, but what is within instead"

The praise on your tongue, with repugnance within
Is the tongue's deceit, or degeneration

Then they said to him, "This wretched state of yours
Is bearing witness to those falsehoods of yours

"Where are the signs of thanks and praise due your prince
On your head and feet so lacking in respect?

"Though you weave praises of that shah on your tongue
Your seven limbs are making complaint of him"

"Where the signs of a pure mind, O sour face?
The stink of bent speech comes off of you, silence!"

You plant in the earth of God the Truth, and then
The pure seeds produce no sign of an income?

---

729. Şemseddin Yeşil, *Füyûzat* (Istanbul: Ş. Yeşil Yayınları 1984), vol. 6, p. 260.
730. Ken'an Rifâî, *Sohbetler* (Istanbul: Kubbealtı Neşriyatı 2000), pp. 330-331.

65TH VERSE

You speak praise, but where the signs of those who praise?
Outwardly or inwardly, there is no trace

The gnostic's praise of God is righteous and true
For his feet and hands bear witness it is true

The silk of piety, intimacy's light
He wears the sign of praise on his shoulder plate

Your evil interior reeks on your breath
Your pain, braggart, shines out from your face and head

It's a smell that skilled warriors recognize
You should boast less with your hasty shouts and cries

Do not brag of musk, for bean and onion scent
Upon your breath makes the secret evident

Do not spin fraud amidst those who know true coin
Do not boast to the touchstone, O you false coin

Don't harrow your soul, have shame, don't boast idly
For many spies keep watch over the body[731]

- *All that's hid will be manifest on the Day*
Sinners will all by their own selves be disgraced

Hand and foot will give evidence and explain
Their offence before Him from whom all seek aid

The hand will say, "I have commited theft thus"
The lip will say, "I have asked questions like this"

The foot says, "I rushed to sensuality"
Genitals, "I committed aldultery"

The eye will say, "I winked at forbidden things"
The ear says, "I chose to hear malicious things"

---

731. Mevlânâ Celâleddin Rûmî, trans. Veled İzbudak, ed. Abdülbaki Gölpınarlı, *Mesnevî* (Istanbul: Milli Eğitim Basımevi 1991), vol. 4, vs. 1738, 1737, 1743, 1745-1746, 1756, 1759, 1763-1764, 1766, 1773, 1775, 1782, 1793.

O HUMANKIND

Then from head to foot, they will be all a lie
For their own members will all give them the lie

So act in such wise that your act, without tongue
Will be witness and a clear declaration

So that all your body, limb by limb, O son
Will say, "I testify," in both loss and gain[732]

- If there is reverence in people's hearts, it will also be in their limbs. For example, wind is not visible to the eye but its existence is understood from the movement of leaves and the rising of dust. In the same way the movement of people's hearts will be understood by the movements of the limbs of their corpse. Just as whether the wind blows from the north or south is understood by whether leaves lean and move to the left or right, the movement of that body's limbs indicates the state of its heart. It indicates whether that person's inclination is toward the world or toward the Hereafter.[733]

- Those who wish to reach divine realities by way of philosophy diverge into denial because of their fear of those who believe. For faith defeats their sophistry.

   It is as if there were only the animal soul in their bodies. If that soul says, "Walk!" they walk, and if it says, "Stop!" they stop. The same soul makes their tongues, which are pieces of meat, speak many misbeliefs (*küfür*). But when that same soul departs from their bodies one day and goes away, their hands will not grasp, their feet will not walk, and their tongues will not speak.

   Because they are deprived of the divine spirit, or do not know the value of such a spirit, they will not be able to speak even as trees do; they will not be able to glorify the name of God even as tree branches do.

   While they are alive they do not believe inanimates can speak, they deny this. But their own hands and feet make their lies evident.

---

732. Mevlânâ Celâleddin Rûmî, trans. Veled İzbudak, ed. Abdülbaki Gölpınarlı, *Mesnevî* (Istanbul: Milli Eğitim Basımevi 1991), vol. 5, vs. 2211-2216, 2218-2219.

733. Ken'an Rifâî, ed. Kâzım Büyükaksoy, *Mesnevî Hatıraları* (Istanbul: İnkilap Kitapevi 1968), p. 108.

65th Verse

They say, "O mindless one, even though we are inanimate beings, the divine power has given us motion and skill. It has made us perform actions no other animate beings can. While your mouth and tongue were inanimate bodies, did not God make them speak all kinds of speech? In that case, O you who lack swift understanding, why should the Lord not, when He wishes, make a date palm tree recite a poem of longing, loss and passion?"[734]

- "The time has arrived, O friends," then David said
When his hidden secret is made manifest

"Until now hid by the clemency of God
At last that pimp, never giving thanks to God

"Has by himself lifted the veil from his sin
If he had not, God would have kept his crime hid"

In this round of woe, infidels, profligates
By themseves rip aside their own concealments

Wrong is concealed within the soul's mystery
The wrongdoer brings it out for all to see

Saying, "I have horns, come now and look at me!
Here behold the cow of Hell for all to see!"

Your hands and your feet thus even here in loss
Bear witness to what is in your inmost thoughts

Since your inmost heart is your authority
Saying, "Don't hold back, declare what you believe"

Especially in anger and argument
It reveals, to the slightest hair, your secret

Since your guardian is wrong and iniquity
Saying, "Make me manifest, O hands and feet"

Since your secret's witness takes hold of the reins
Especially in enmity, revenge and rage

---

734. Ken'an Rifâî, *Şerhli Mesnevî-i Şerif* (Istanbul: Kubbealtı Neşriyatı 2000), p. 311.

Thus the person who makes this your guardian
To unfurl your secret's banner on the plain

Can then also on the Day of Gathering
Create other guardians of scattering

With ten hands you wreak injustice and malice
There is no need, your substance is obvious

Your soul shoots off a hundred sparks constantly
Saying, "I am of the Fire, come, look at me!

"I'm the Fire's particle, moving toward my whole
I'm not light, that I should head toward the Lord"

When he approaches near to a friend of God
That hundred-ell tongue he has will become short

A hundred tongues, each a hundred languages
His deceit and guile defy analysis

He fools the whole city, except for the shah
He cannot strike on the path of the wise shah[735]

- At the Resurrection all a person's organs, hands and feet will speak one by one. Philosophers interpret this, asking how a hand can speak; a hand may only make a sign or gesture that takes the place of speech. For example, if there is a wound or boil on a hand, it may communicate through its state to express that it ate something that heats the body and thus became that way. Of if a hand turns black or is wounded, that expresses how it was stabbed with a knife or touched a black pot. They say the speech of hands or other organs must be like that.

The Sunnis say, "God forbid! Never! Especially these hands and feet you see will speak like the tongue and on Resurrection Day when people deny, saying, 'I did not steal,' their hands will say in clear lan-

---

735. Mevlânâ Celâleddin Rûmî, trans. Veled İzbudak, ed. Abdülbaki Gölpınarlı, *Mesnevî* (Istanbul: Milli Eğitim Basımevi 1991), vol. 3, vs. 2442, 2447, 2451-2462, 2464-2465, 2468, 2550-2551, 2553.

65TH VERSE

guage, 'Yes, you stole, and I siezed it.' They will look at their feet and say, 'You never used to speak, how is it that you speak now?' Their feet will say, *'God who makes all things speak, made us speak'* (41:21). He also makes doors and walls and stones and clods and earth speak. The Creator who gave everyone the power of speech made me speak as well. How did He make your tongue speak? Your tongue is a piece of flesh, and so is my hand. It seems to you rational that your tongue which consists of a piece of fleshtalks, and because you have seen it do so all the time it does not seem impossible to you; but for God the tongue is a pretext. It speaks because He commanded it, 'Speak!' In the same way whatever thing He commands to speak, that thing will speak also."[736]

• On Resurrection Day the hand of a wayward person bears witness against him, saying, "Did you not grasp the wine glass with me and pour the wine carafe? Did you not reach for possessions that were not yours, did you not grasp the hand of women unlawful for you, and did you not betray them, did you not strike the oppressed and slap the orphan? Did you not draw your swrod against the innocent?" The tongue says, "Did you not speak thus with me? Did you not speak against so and so many Muslims? Did you not speak falsely so and so many times in the world that robs Islam and religion?" The foot will also bear witness and say, "Did you not go to the tavern with me? And did you not hasten to corruption and things not approved?" And so it will finally be known to him that these kinds of voices consisting of water, earth, fire, hands, feet and heads were united here, that plurality became one. Friend, the parts that appear to be in rapport with one another will become like snakes; they will even compete in hurting him.[737]

---

736. Mevlânâ Celâleddin Rûmî, trans. Melika Ülker Anbarcıoğlu, *Fîhi mâ Fîh* (Istanbul: Milli Eğitim Basımevi 1985), pp. 168-169.

737. Sultan Veled, trans. Meliha Anbarcıoğlu, *Maarif* (Konya: Altunarı Ofset 2002), p. 98.

66. And if We wished, we would have obliterated their eyes. They would race toward the path, but how would they see?

Wa law nashā'u laṭamasnā ʿalā 'aʿyunihim fa'stabaqū'ṣ-ṣirāṭa fa'annā yubṣirūn.

- If We wished, we would have erased the disbelievers' eyes and made them blind. They would have raced to find the path. Because if all who misbelieve had been made blind, that would have made them seek refuge, they would all have believed. But how should those disbelievers see, those visionless disbelievers whose eyes of the heart are blind, that is, unable to see the divine proofs, cannot comprehend that We can do this that way.[738]

- They are those who, preoccupied in the opacity of human nature, do not lift up their heads from their worldly affairs and whose spirits are deprived of the windows opening out onto the realm of meaning. That is why they pay no heed to the advice and the calls of those who wish to refresh them and invite them to God the Truth, to reality and the realms of meaning, and stuff up their ears to their music and close their eyes to their light.

They are the ones described in the seventh chapter of the Gracious Quran. In the gracious verse 179 of that chapter, God says: "Many are the jinn and human beings We have made for Hell. They have hearts with which they do not understand, and ears with which they do not see. They are like cattle—no, more misguided, for they

---

738. Elmalılı M. Hamdi Yazır, *Hak Dini Kur'ân Dili* (Istanbul: Feza Gazetecilik 1992), Elmalılı M. Hamdi Yazır, *Hak Dini Kur'ân Dili* (Istanbul: Feza Gazetecilik 1992), vol. 6, p. 422.

pay no heed." That is how it is, many are the eyes that do not see the mercy raining upon the world where they are and where they live.[739]

• If the thorns of soul-mouthfuls stick in the eye of one's spirit, one is probably deprived of the capacity to see and the light of the eye. How will such people see God's rosebeds of gnosis; how can they stroll those gardens?[740]

• Those beset by opinion and doubt cannot understand that truth. The eye to see spiritual realities and such training have not been given to them. They seek evidence they can touch with their hands in order to believe. They do not see the evidence that can be seen with the eye of the heart and they do not hear the voices that can be heard with the ear of the heart.

It is those whose heart's eyes cannot see who are forced to use the path of disputation as a blind man uses a cane. Although that cane may prevent them from running into boulders and falling down, their condition cannot be compared with the security, certainty and clearness of goal of people who are able to see where they are going.

You know the blind. They cannot sow, nor can they reap, they cannot thresh nor harvest. It is possible neither for them to cultivate the world nor advance their people with understanding of trade and economics.

You understand that here when I say "the blind" I mean those whose heart's eyes are closed. They are the ones who take the path of disputation and seek material evidence in order to see God the Truth.

And the blind, who wander miserably among us seeing where they are going not with their eyes but with a cane, are for us likenesses of a divine wisdom.

It is the Perfect Humans, meaning the pupil of the eye of divine being—as when a person sees another image of himself in the image of the pupil of his eye when he looks in the mirror—and created in that value, who show the way to God to the masses of people who are no different from a caravan of the blind.[741]

---

739. Ken'an Rifâî, *Şerhli Mesnevî-i Şerif* (Istanbul: Kubbealtı Neşriyatı 2000), p. 290.
740. Ken'an Rifâî, *Şerhli Mesnevî-i Şerif* (Istanbul: Kubbealtı Neşriyatı 2000), p. 282.
741. Ken'an Rifâî, *Şerhli Mesnevî-i Şerif* (Istanbul: Kubbealtı Neşriyatı 2000), pp. 308-309.

66TH VERSE

- As long as you see those dear to God as men
Know that view is a legacy from Satan[742]

- Because those who imitate cannot see with the eye of truth, they come to harm verifying and believing by a partial surmise, and do not believe that the glorifications of inanimates and vegetation are real, they fall into doubt and, trying to interpret gracious verses and noble hadiths with their own insufficient intellects, leave the near path and diverge into the path of opinion and fall into the pit of Hell. Such are those whose hearts are blind. The eyes of their hearts are blind. And they can walk with canes, but because their canes consist of opinion and doubt in the path of God the Truth and they trust in them and rely on them, they fall headlong upon the stones of error and hypocrisy, but if they rely on a perfect human whose heart is illumined, that perfect human's seeing eye will be as an eye for that blind-hearted person. If it were not for the prophets with illumined spirit-eyes and their inheritors the friends of God, in other words, the perfect humans in this world that is the planting field of the Hereafter, the ignorant and blind-hearted who remain at exteriority unaware of interiority would remain in the pit of error and disbelief and be destroyed at the hands of the soul-devils. And they could have no power to make their interiority thrive and practice the commerce of the Hereafter. The commerce and felicity of the Hereafter is the appointed share of those who believe in the prophets and freinds and have faith and embrace their advice. But the blind-hearted who rely on intellect and surmise and suppose themselves to be the men of their time pass their lives in disappointment and are destroyed in the well of their soul-nature. And after death they find themselves in the fire of longing and separation, and the greatest torment is this fire of separation and exile. God the Truth had mercy and compassion on these eyeless who are blind-hearted and gave them the cane of reason. But in accordance with *"Say: All is from God"* [4:78], that everlasting Padishah did not give that cane for war and fighting. Perhaps He who gave that cane gave it for finding and seeing the Gracious. He did not give it so that we would torment and vex the friends and the sincere and the perfect humans with our rebelliousness and stubbor-

---
742. Ken'an Rifâî, *Şerhli Mesnevî-i Şerif* (Istanbul: Kubbealtı Neşriyatı 2000), p. 586.

ness. Let us know this also that to torment and vex the friends is like tormenting and vexing the Messenger and God.[743]

- Treacherous Satan puts a doubt in their hearts so icy that they cannot melt it with their own heat. That doubt freezes their conscience and perspicacity. Although their eyes see forms, they cannot see their meanings. Thus does the devil within them throw them headlong over a foreordained cliff.

Such people have legs of wood. Tree-footed people cannot feel the pulse of the stones and earth they step upon. No heat or current of comprehension flows from their own world of feeling and warmth to those stones and earth either. In short, matter that does not conduct current cuts off the pathways between the spirit and the body, even between the spirit and the universe and the spirit and God, and drives a person into a state of severe incomprehension.[744]

---

743. Ken'an Rifâî, ed. Kâzım Büyükaksoy, *Mesnevî Hatıraları* (Istanbul: İnkilap Kitapevi 1968), pp. 225-226.
744. Ken'an Rifâî, *Şerhli Mesnevî-i Şerif* (Istanbul: Kubbealtı Neşriyatı 2000), p. 308.

67. And if We wished, we would have transformed them where they stood, and they would not have been able to move forward or go back.

Wa law nashā'u lamasakhnāhum ʿalā makānatihim famā'staṭāʿū muḍiyyān wa lā yarjiʿūn.

- **Mesh:** Those who commit crimes are metamorphosed into animals according to their beliefs. A group of the Jews became monkeys and pigs. None among the community of Muhammed were transfomed in this way, but the hearts of Muslims were instead made inhuman.[745]

- **Mesh:** To have one's form changed into an ugly state. Noah's flood was an example of a spiritual flood. The eclipsed and transformed were examples of eclipse and transformation in the spiritual realm. For a hundred thousand shameless, arrogant people opposed the command of God the Truth. They were lazy in worship and obedience. That was why their spirits were transformed. But not everyone can see that transformation. Transformation of form was put forth for those with narrow vision who look only at form. Whatever of good or evil has acquired form, it was all because of this meaning, and meaning is in the Realm of the Unseen. A tiny part of it reaches the people of form. Trees, gardens, and flowing water are parts of the spiritual garden. Beautiful beings, which are children and women, are each a part of those angels. He said, *"Little is the enjoyment of this world"* (4:77). He sent a small part of the infinite realms and rich treasuries to those acquainted with form, because

---

745. Ferîdeddîn-i Attar, trans. Abdülbaki Gölpınarlı, *İlâhinâme* (Istanbul: Millî Eğitim Basımevi 1985).

it would not all have fit into form, just as the ocean cannot be fit into a jug.[746]

• And if We had wished, We would have stripped them of the rank of humanity and, just as they are in character at the station of animals, We would have changed their forms and instantly reduced them to inanimate things. In other words, We would have transformed them into the form We wished, and they would have had no power to go forward or backward or to turn or pass by. And they would not have had the strength to shed those qualities and go back into their forms. We would have done all of that, but because We delayed their true punishment until the Hereafter, We did not wish to, We gave respite because Our mercy is prior, and we said they would awaken, gather their wits and understand the value of the vicegerency we bestowed upon them.[747]

• If you would reach for what God the Truth has forbidden, that error will be a black spot on the heart that gradually spreads until the heart becomes completely black.[748]

• When Our Messenger of God Efendi was interpreting the eighteenth verse of the 47th chapter, he said: "Tomorrow in the Hereafter whatever individuals have been conquered by and whatever has most occupied them, in other words, whatever temperament is dominant in them, they will be resurrected with whatever that termperament requires."[749]

• All humans are called Adam. But not all of them are human, some are talking animals. They call a creature human that has reached humanity, that is, reached the truth. If you open the interiority of those in human form, some have the form of pigs, some of wolves and some of monkeys. Those who do not achieve humanity are inferior to animals as well.[750]

---

746. Sultan Veled, trans. Meliha Anbarcıoğlu, *Maarif* (Konya: Altunarı Ofset 2002), p. 65.
747. Şemseddin Yeşil, *Füyûzat* (Istanbul: Ş. Yeşil Yayınları 1984), vol. 6, p. 261.
748. Ken'an Rifâî, *Sohbetler* (Istanbul: Kubbealtı Neşriyatı 2000), p. 589.
749. Ken'an Rifâî, *Sohbetler* (Istanbul: Kubbealtı Neşriyatı 2000), p. 569.
750. Ken'an Rifâî, *Sohbetler* (Istanbul: Kubbealtı Neşriyatı 2000), p. 587.

67th Verse

- The spirit in Hell does not burn in the human form, because God the Truth does not burn His own signs in His own form. The human being was created in the form of the Merciful. The seven verses of the first chapter of the Quran are in the face of the human being. But in whatever animal attribute humans die in the world, they burn in Hell in that form. For example, if they do what is forbidden and are lustful, they are resurrected in the form of pigs; if mockers and imitators, in the form of monkeys, and in that form are punished and burn.[751]

- Messenger Salih's spirit was offended by his tribe, the Thamud, and he said to them: "You have conformed to the envy within you and killed an innocent camel. God will ask you to account for this, and in three days will smite you with a great punishment. On the first day signs of the punishment will appear and all of your faces will change color. You will see each other's faces in different colors. First your faces will become yellow like saffron, then on the second day red like the flowers of the argawan tree, and on the third day black as ebony.

  There was nothing left for the Thamud tribe to do. They waited in profound fear for the signs of the first day and indeed on that day they saw each other's faces turn yellow like saffron. On the second day the color was red. On the third day the faces of the people of the Thamud tribe were now black. They no longer appeared human and their behavior was not human. Then they came to their knees.

  They waited for God's wrath and final self-disclosure. This punishment came right on time and an earthquake brought the underside of the earth to the surface. Black-faced, on their knees, all creatures were buried under the earth in an instant. The Lord covered with the mighty earth their ugly faces, their ugly actions, the black darkness of their hearts, their tongues spewing poison, their dog-like teeth and their glances like scorpions' nests, hiding all their filth, all their ugliness and evil with veils of earth.

  Once the fate God has assigned becomes destiny, no power can overcome it. To have offended to the very heart a person whose nearness to God is evident can sometimes make all efforts to mollify him

---

751. Ken'an Rifâî, *Sohbetler* (Istanbul: Kubbealtı Neşriyatı 2000), p. 237.

ineffective. The art is never to offend such hearts in the first place and so not be left without recourse in the end. For this one must transcend the veils of ignorance, and in order to reach the lights of truth, one must be wakeful. Repentance consisting of fear alone is of no use, one must be sincere.

O you who only fear when disaster has become manifest and only then see the power of God's wrath and kneel, and only at such times pray God and take refuge in Him!

Kneel on the ground before it is too late! See in time the friends of God giving counsel and showing the way; hear their beautiful voices in time, so that when the moment of fear and destiny descends, your knees will not strike upon hard stone.[752]

- On the first of the three days mentioned the faces of Messenger Salih's tribe became bright yellow; on the second, bright red and on the third, blackest black. When three days had passed this way their preparedness for death was realized, the existence of depravity became evident and that evidentness was called destruction. The yellowing of those wretched ones' faces in that way was the counterpart to the brightness of the faces of the felicitous, as God said in his verse, *"Faces that day will be radiant"* [80:38]. Because radiance is the sign of being evident, just as the yellowness on the first day was evidence of wretchedness in Salih's (a.s.) tribe. As counterpart to the redness that then became evident in them, God used the expression "smiling" for the felicitous, because smiling is among the causes that make a face blush. Thus smiling is for the felicitous the blushing of their cheeks. Later God said "joyful" of the felicitous, in counterpart to the reddening of the wretched ones' skin. Joy and good news appeared on the faces of the felicitous as the effect of cheerfulness. Thus God gave good news about both groups. In other words, He said things that affected the color of their faces. Thus of the felicitous He said, "Their Lord gave them good news of Mercy and Paradise." And of the wretched He said, "O my beloved Messenger, give them good news of sorrow and torment." Thus in the faces of each group was displayed the effect of the thing made evident

---

752. Ken'an Rifâî, *Şerhli Mesnevî-i Şerif* (Istanbul: Kubbealtı Neşriyatı 2000), pp. 369-371.

in their souls by those words. This being so, only the property in their souls of the thing among the concepts in their interiority became evident in them. This means that in them nothing other than the state required by their preparedness had effect. Engendering (*tekvin*), too, came from them. Thus was sufficient evidence fixed for human beings. So whoever understands this wisdom and sees the secret of applying and engendering it in their own soul will find repose in their soul from being involved with others and know that the good and evil that comes to the soul comes from themselves. What I mean by "good" here is the things that are appropriate for the servant's nature and temperament and desire, and by "evil" I mean judgments the servants do not like and which are contrary to their temperament. Whoever attains that view evaluates the excuses of all beings, and however much they have not declared an excuse, understands it and knows that everything manifest in their souls came from themselves.[753]

- *The slave replied, "Wisdom has kept it secret,*
So this world of good and evil might be hid

"If the forms of thought were manifest then all
Disbeliever, believer would but praise God

"So if this were evident, not hid, O Shah
If faith and disbelief were stamped on the brow

"How would there be idol and idolatry?
How would any have the bile for mockery?

"This world of ours would then be Resurrection
Who sins and does wrong at the Resurrection?"

On the day of death these senses will be naught
Do you have spirit's light to befriend your heart?

When earth fills these eyes of yours inside the tomb
Do you have the light to illumine the tomb?

---

753. İbnü'l-Arabî, trans. Nuri Gencosman, *Fusûs'l-Hikem* (Istanbul: Kırkambar Kitaplığı n.d.), pp. 147-148.

O Humankind

When your hands and feet are in shreds, at that time
Will you have wings so that your spirit may fly?[754]

- O my God! This visible body of ours struggles to hinder us from reaching our true being, which is invisible like You. Our bodily garment wishes to destroy our spiritual garb and leave us naked without Your robe of honor.

If when our foot wants to go toward the good and true, our own hand prevents it, if our own souls do us the greatest wrong, how should we save our spirits from that devil of error without Your liberating aid?

If You close the way to reach You, if You do not raze the wall of duality between the spirit and the spirit of spirits, if You do not show the way to the spirit separated from You and submit it to a murshid, its state is no longer separation, it is death. The spirit thus separated from You is eternally dead, even though it appears to be alive!

When there was nothing at all, it was You who created all beings. And You are the Powerful who can destroy what He creates and make them naught. To destroy is the right only of Him who can rip the cloth and sew it up, who can make something more perfect.

Each autumn You set the garden ablaze with hues of red, yellowing and withering. Then when the day comes, You send Your mercy to the same garden and make pink roses bloom within greenery, leaving the world You withered in a sultanate of color and harmony.

We have been made slave to a soul. We all cry in error, "My soul! My soul!" We think only of our own souls and cannot see beyond our own noses, and if You do not call us to You with Your beautiful voice, we will all remain at the nadir of the black earth like red devils.

Your grace has rescued us from blindness and the misfortune of not being able to see beyond the veil. With the eyes You Have opened for us, we have seen that there are satans on earth. And again, it is Your grace which has saved us from the satans.

You are the sole guide of spirits that have taken on bodies so as to know You and come to You. For it is You who have said: "O My bonds-

---

754. Mevlânâ Celâleddin Rûmî, trans. Veled İzbudak, ed. Abdülbaki Gölpınarlı, *Mesnevî* (Istanbul: Milli Eğitim Basımevi 1991), vol. 2, vs. 984-988, 940-942.

67th Verse

men, you tread a path other than the path I have shown you, and you are all in error; seek the right path from Me, I will grant it."

For that is what Your Messenger told us. And so we ask you for the path. We request a staff and aid. Would you leave us with no staff, without aid and without eyes?[755]

---

755. Ken'an Rifâî, *Şerhli Mesnevî-i Şerif* (Istanbul: Kubbealtı Neşriyatı 2000), pp. 579-581.

68. He whose life We extend, We reverse him in creation. Then will they not think?

Wa man nuʿammirhu nunakkishu fī'l-khalqi ʾa fa lā yaʿqilūn.

- At the same time, whoever to whom We give long life, whose life We do not take in the time of youth but extend it, We reverse them in creation, We make them weak, cause them to grow old, bending their backs and throwing them head over heels, and in the end make them earth. Is not God who does these these things able to transform them into animals and obliterate them? Why do they not consider the works of Our power? Will they not use their intellects? It is the Righteous Newsgiver (*Hazret Muhammed*) who brings to you these things, and the Book sent is not poetry. It is for remembrance. And they call remembrance the contrary of heedlessness. They call it perceiving, with knowledge and wisdom, God's disposal of His unity and power in His Kingdom and Sovereignty without partner, without peer, independently. Will you still not consider these truths? You listen to these truths as if they were poetry.[756]

- "They ask if there can be games after eighty, and I ask if there can be games before eighty."
God the Truth the Exalted has bestowed of His virtue on the aged desire and inclinations of which children are unaware. For inclination and desire bring freshness because of that virtue. And He makes them leap and laugh and bestows upon them the desire for play. Just as the child sees the world as new and has not become jaded, those aged ones too see the world as new and thus desire the play of that new world and their blood increases.

---

756. Şemseddin Yeşil, *Füyûzat* (Istanbul: Ş. Yeşil Yayınları 1984), vol. 6, p. 261.

O Humankind

"If as each white hair manifests, the old run like playful mounts, the work of old age becomes a tremendous thing. In other words, if occupation with play grows as age increases, that old age becomes a difficult state."

Now, the majesty of old age is more than the majestry of God the Truth. For the springtime of God's majesty becomes manifest and the autumn of old age conquers it; and the temperament belongng to autumn does not leave it. Now, the grace of God is the weakness of springtime, for with the loss of each tooth the laughter of God's springtime grows less; and with the whitening of each hair, the pleasingness of God's grace becomes hidden; and with each raining tear belonging to autumn, the garden of truths becomes sorrowful.[757]

- *Adam was beauty and the angels were bowed*
But even such as Adam was then brought down

"Alas, after being, not-being!" he said
"Your crime is this, that you lived too long," He said

Gabriel dragged him back, pulling on his hair
Saying, "Leave this paradise and group so fair"

"After exaltation, why this fall?" he said
"That is a gift, and this your sentence," he said

"O Gabriel, most sincerely you bowed down
Why do you drive me out of Paradise now?

"In this time of trial my robes fly off of me
As in the fall season do the date palm's leaves"

The cheek that once shown as bright as the moon's rays
Has become like a lizard's back in old age

And that head and parted hair once so comely
In the time of old age is bald and ugly

---

757. Mevlânâ Celâleddin Rûmî, trans. Ahmet Avni Konuk, ed. Selçuk Eraydın, *Fîhi Mâ Fîh* (Istanbul: İz Yayıncılık 2002), p. 123.

68th Verse

And that gay stature like a lance piercing rows
In old age is now bent double like a bow

The tulip color, the color of saffron
His lion's strength, like the courage of women

He that wrestled men with skill down to the ground
They now prop up by his armpits to go on

Truly these are marks of pain and wretchedness
Every one of them a messenger of death

But if his physician be the light of God
Nor from age nor fever is there blow or loss

His langour is like that of a drunken man
For in it he is the envy of Rustam

His bones are drowned in joy tasted if he dies
Every bit of him in light-beams of desire

Those who have it not are gardens without fruit
That the autumn season brings to wrack and ruin

No roses are left, only black thorns remain
Withered like a heap of straw without a brain

O God, what error did that garden commit
That these raiments should have been stripped off of it

It committed self-regard, and such regard
Is deadly poison, beware, you who are tried

The gorgeous youth for whom the world weeps in love
The world drives away, what is he guilty of?

His crime is that he wore borrowed finery
He claimed that those cloaks were his own property

We take them back, so he will know in truth that
Fair ones pick the seeds, but Ours is the haystack

O Humankind

That he may know that those cloaks were transient
One single beam from the sun of existence

That power and virtue and art and beauty
Have made their way here from the sun of beauty

Get used to seeing the light without the glass
So you'll not be blind when they break the lamp's glass

With knowledge that is learned you are satisfied
With someone else's lamp you have lit your eye

He takes that lamp of His back so you may know
That you're not gracious but have only borrowed

If you've striven righteously and rendered thanks
Grieve not, for He'll give a hundred of such back

But if you've not rendered thanks, now bloody tears
For that beauty's long gone from disbelievers[758]

- *He said, "Forbear till the day of punishment"*
But if only he had said, "Lord, we repent!"

Harrowing is a life without repentance
Absence from God is a death in the present

Life and death are both of them sweet when with God
The Water of Life is fire without God

And it was because of God's curse's effect
That he sought more life while in such a presence

To ask of God anything other than God
Seems to be a gain but is entirely loss

To seek more life that he might go further back
Meant to seek more respite to increase in lack

---

758. Mevlânâ Celâleddin Rûmî, trans. Veled İzbudak, ed. Abdülbaki Gölpınarlı, *Mesnevî* (Istanbul: Milli Eğitim Basımevi 1991), vol. 5, vs. 962-985, 991-995.

68th Verse

Until he might become the sign of the curse
Evil is the person who seeks out a curse

Saying, "Give me more life, so I can eat shit
My substance is evil, always give me that"[759]

- Recite, "We reverse him whose life We extend"
Ask for heart, don't set heart on a skeleton

For beauty of heart is beauty that abides
Its good fortune serves up the Water of Life

It is not form that is the object of love
Whether it be this world's love or that world's love

That which you have come to love the form of it
When spirit has left, why do you forsake it?

Its form is here, why are you fed up with it?
O lover, consider who your beloved is

And you who are in love with your intellect
Disdaining worshippers of formal aspect

Comeliness in humankind is like gold leaf
Else how did your love become an old donkey?

Once angelic, at last a satanic thing
Because that elegance was a borrowed thing[760]

- Whomever We give long respite before punishment, their end is more sorrowful and grave.[761]

- Reflection was our Efendi's primary work, so that before all obligatory worship his devotions consisted of reflection upon God's crea-

---

759. Mevlânâ Celâleddin Rûmî, trans. Veled İzbudak, ed. Abdülbaki Gölpınarlı, *Mesnevî* (Istanbul: Milli Eğitim Basımevi 1991), vol. 5, vs. 769-773, 775-776, 778.

760. Mevlânâ Celâleddin Rûmî, trans. Veled İzbudak, ed. Abdülbaki Gölpınarlı, *Mesnevî* (Istanbul: Milli Eğitim Basımevi 1991), vol. 2, vs. 715-716, 703-705, 710, 712-713.

761. Halûk Nurbaki, *Yâ-Sîn Sûresi Yorumu* (Istanbul: Damla Yayınevi 1999), p. 89.

tures and boons. That situation, moreover, continued until the revelation of the commands and forms of worship required by the sheriat. So embrace well reflection upon God's boons and make reflection a means to admonition. For reflection lacking in admonition consists in raw fantasy and satanic whispering. Reflection that is a means to admonition is counsel and wisdom. Construct your actions upon a sound basis after reflection. And after wholesome action, strengthen your character with a beautiful path.

Hazret God the Truth the Exalted says, "*He whose life We extend, We reverse him in creation.*" We reduce his strength. Bind your heart well to the rope of reunion with God the Truth by striving not to see the faults in people, hoping that God will repair them.

Let the final limit of your eyes and your looking not be the viewing of creation. Among human beings all those of mediocre states and the lower levels are equal in helplessness, poverty and pitiableness. God displays the creatures in various forms by means of the veils covering the eye. Thus is the divine decree accomplished. Intelligent people are those who understand this fine distinction and who, passing from the veil to the veiled, become bound to God the Everlasting and Prior to whom sleep and inattention never comes. "*For Him are the creation and the command*" (7:54).[762]

- *What fair thing is there that has not become foul?*
Or what roof that's not been spread out on the ground?

But the voices of God's friends whose echoed breath
Comes from the blast of the trumpet in their breasts[763]

- Reflection (*tefekkür*) is to contemplate one's own not-being and, seeing the divine sultanate everywhere, the endlessness and wisdom of that tremendousness.

Reflection is to take a lesson from the tremendousness of God the Truth and so much wisdom and admonition, and waking up, to open

---

762. Ahmed er-Rifâî, ed. Dr. H. Kâmil Yılmaz, *Marifet Yolu* (Istanbul: Erkam Yayıncılık 1995), pp. 58-59.

763. Mevlânâ Celâleddin Rûmî, trans. Veled İzbudak, ed. Abdülbaki Gölpınarlı, *Mesnevî* (Istanbul: Milli Eğitim Basımevi 1991), vol. 1, vs. 2078-2079.

68th Verse

one's eyes and think upon the time that has passed and thus where your state will take you.

Reflection is to think upon how ridiculous a station people fall into, whether in their present or future states, by supposing that they do everything themselves attributing power and being to themselves.

Reflection is to consider that there is no agent but God, that the command is His and that strength and power are His alone.

In sum, it is to consider that you are naught and helpless, and only God exists.[764]

- Sadi says: They asked the physician Luqman where he learned wisdom. He replied, "From the Cloud!" When they asked, "How is that?" he said, "One feels one's way with a staff so as not to fall upon holes, rocks and obstacles, and thus avoids danger."

Because people do not know the future, they must examine what they do and will do with the staff of reflection. Does not our Messenger Efendi say, *"There can be no worship like reflection"*? Pascal says the same thing: "The humanity of humankind is with reflection, and the basis of morality is reflection also." Our Efendi also says, *"One hour of reflection is superior to a year of worship."*[765]

---

[764]. Ken'an Rifâî, *Sohbetler* (Istanbul: Kubbealtı Neşriyatı 2000), p. 399.
[765]. Ken'an Rifâî, *Sohbetler* (Istanbul: Kubbealtı Neşriyatı 2000), p. 480.

69. We have not taught him poetry, nor would it be suitable for him. This is but a reminder and clear recitation [Quran].

Wa mā 'allamnāhu'sh-shi'ra wa mā yanbaghī lahu 'in huwa 'illā dhikrun wa qur'ānun mubīn.

• Poetry is the location of summary, symbol, allusion and rhyme. In other words, We did not give him anything in figures of speech or teach him by way of metaphor. Just as We did not say one thing to the Messenger while meaning something else, neither did We summarize the address. When We distanced him from himself, brought him near Us and made him present with Us, "What We have taught is only reminding." Thus We became his hearing and his seeing. Then We sent him back to you, "so that by means of him you would find the truth in the darkness of ignorance and becoming." We became the tongue by which he addressed you. Then We brought down someone who reminds you that you saw him.

Thus the Quran is a reminder for the Messenger and the collection (*toplama*) of what he witnessed while with Us. "It is clear," in other words, because the Messenger knows the basis of the thing he saw in the most pure and sacred proximity, this Quran is for him "clear."[766]

• Ibn Arabi takes poetry in the meaning of "summary" (*icmâl*) and sets it in opposition to "explication" (*beyân*), in other words, "detailing." Furthermore, the concept "understanding" (*şuur*), from the same [Arabic] root as "poetry" (*şiir*), is placed in opposition to the concept "knowledge" (*ilim*). Consequently the term "understanding"

---

[766]. Muhyiddîn İbnü'l-Arabî, trans. Ekrem Demirli, *Fütuhât-ı Mekkiyye* (Istanbul: Litera Yayıncılık 2006), vol. 1, p. 151.

has a kind of ambiguous meaning, and so God has said, "*We have not taught him poetry, nor would it be suitable for him*" (36:69). For the Messenger was sent as a detailer and explicator, whereas "poetry," coming from the same root as "understanding," is the location of summary, collected and essential description, narration through symbols. It is not the location of explication, in other words, the conveying of all that language can undertake. Thus poetry is the opposite of explication. Based on this definition, according to Ibn Arabi poetry is thus the art of brevity (*icmâl*), using symbols, riddles and ambiguity.[767]

- "In the Quran there is "they reflect," "they think," "they know." Reflection (tefekkür) occurs by means of the faculty of imagination, which is a human attribute. For angels do not have the capacity for imagination. Understanding is inferior to knowledge. For one understands behind the veil. That is why there are seid to be "poets" who take from imagination. And it was said in the Quran, "*We have not taught him poetry.*" In other words, it is forbidden for the Quran to be a thing like poetry. The Quran descends upon the heart, not upon imagination. The Trusted Spirit [the angel Gabriel] brought it down onto the Messenger's heart. The statement of those who say, 'The Quran is poetry and the Messenger is a poet,' has been rejected. Poetry is not from the truth of knowledge, but from imagination. If it had been knowledge, it too would have been called Quran. Poetry is a divine attribute. God the Truth is the All-Knowing, he is not a poet. Thus it is necessary that the Messenger too not be a poet, for he is of the People of the Heart. The heart is the locaiton of knowledge and God the Truth's essential reality is knowledge."[768]

- We did not teach poetry to that Messenger of God the Truth. And it is not worthy of the glory of his messengerhood. One does not call it poetry (in poetry there is imagination, while in him there is inspiration (*vahiy*). Just as My Noble Messenger is not called poet, nor is My Book called poetry. That Book is only descended speech. It is the sum of all human needs, the guarantor of human happiness, a counsel of God. It brings one to God the Truth and to truth, it announces the

---
767. Mahmut Erol Kılıç, *Sûfî ve Şiir* (Istanbul: İnsan Yayınları), p. 52.
768. İsmail Hakkı Bursevî, *Kitâbu'n Netice*, vol. 1, pp. 363-363.

69th Verse

goal of creation, it instructs one in the basis of the path leading up to the apogee of unification, it is the Clear Quran.[769]

• O you who deny! Sometimes you call Hazret Muhammed (s.a.s.) a sorcerer, sometimes an oracle, sometimes a lunatic and sometimes a poet. Sometimes you call the Gracious Quran sorcery, sometimes poetry, sometimes calumny and sometimes a made-up story. Thus is stated the great truth that you show you are unaware of the path shown by the greatest of Messengers, and you talk nonsense. Thus every spirit must do away with its inner doubts and see that the verses of the Quran rule all creation and the vicissitudes of all beings. The heart's eyes of those who want to see it this way are opened by God. The end of those who stubbornly insist on not seeing will surely be the abyss.[770]

• All causes are like a pen in God's hand. It is God who moves the pen and writes what is written. As long as He does not will it, the pen does not move. Some remain stuck on the pen while some see the hand and due to the pleasure of watching it do not see the pen.[771]

• When a person speaks behind a curtain, some think the curtain is speaking. They do not know that it is nothing but a curtain. Only when the man comes out from behind the curtain do they understand that it was a pretext in between. It is common folk who are stuck on causes. God's friends know the one who is doing the work behind causes.[772]

• There has been many a poet artisan of words who attained the secret of writing poetry in meter and rhyme and genre form, while what he wrote was one thing, and what he wanted to write was another.

---

769. Şemseddin Yeşil, *Füyûzat* (Istanbul: Ş. Yeşil Yayınları 1984), vol. 6, p. 262.
770. Ken'an Rifâî, *Şerhli Mesnevî-i Şerif* (Istanbul: Kubbealtı Neşriyatı 2000), p. 425.
771. Mevlânâ Celâleddin Rûmî, trans. Meliha Ülker Tarıkahya, *Fihi Mâ Fîh* (Istanbul: Millî Eğitim Basımevi 1985), p. 343.
772. Mevlânâ Celâleddin Rûmî, trans. Meliha Ülker Tarıkahya, *Fihi Mâ Fîh* (Istanbul: Millî Eğitim Basımevi 1985), p. 91.

The poet often wanted to put the meaning that arose in his spirit into verses, but either that meaning did not come out precisely as he intended or another meaning resulted. Poetry is in that way like a stone placed in a sling. You take aim at a certain point and draw the sling. The stone flies out and hits a different point.[773]

- There is a miracle in the composition of every word, letter, and calligraphic point in the Quran. When the ignorant read the Quran, they say, "God tells the story of Joseph in this book." But when gnostics read it, they see there the sublime signs of God and discover in its sequence of letters secrets that the rationalist commentators will not be able to understand. But the gnostics, who are aware of this secret, prefer to remain silent.[774]

- *If they should see in the Quran naught but words*
This is no surprise in people who have erred

In luminous sunbeams, for eyes that are blind
Warmth is all that they will be able to find

When the Book of God arrived for them as well
Unbelievers made like reproaches as well

God said, "If this seems an easy thing to you
Pronounce one verse that is easy like this too

Let the skilled among you, humankind and jinn
Bring forth one single verse of this easy thing"

Know that the Quran has an exterior
And an all-subjugating interior

Within that another and a third in that
All intellects become lost inside of that

None has seen the fourth interior at all
But the peerless and incomparable God

---

773. Ken'an Rifâî, *Şerhli Mesnevî-i Şerif* (Istanbul: Kubbealtı Neşriyatı 2000), p. 212.
774. Ahmed er-Rifâî, trans. Dr. Ali Can Tatlı, *Sohbet Meclisleri* (Istanbul: Erkam Yayınları 1996), p. 65.

69th Verse

Do not see the Quran's exterior, son
The Devil saw nothing but clay in Adam

The Quran's exterior is like a man
His form is manifest, his spirit hidden[775]

- *The Quran's meaning from the Quran inquire*
And from those who to idle fancy set fire,

Who are humble sacrifice to the Quran
So their spirit's essence has become Quran

When oil has let the rose take it completely
Sniff either the oil or the rose, as you please[776]

- Considering that the coming into being of the spirit was much prior to the coming into being of the body, the melodies of the spirit's parrot were prior to the manifestation of body, to when the question was asked, "Am I not your Lord?"

Now He is before me in all His beauty, in all his reality. That most beloved friend is conversing with me. I talk with Him. I think one speaks with Him in the language of poetry and the voice of rhyme, and my Beloved tells me to leave off rhyming to think of nothing but the beauty He has promised to display in Paradise. O my rhyme-chasing lover, beware! In my eyes you are the rhyme of felicity and the couplet of good fortune. The harmony of My fortune and felicity is completed by you.

What are words, what use is rhyme, that you should be concerned with them? Forget them, the truth is beyond them.

Do you not know that I in fact speak silently, without letters or words? I speak mysteries, and thus my discourse is mysterious as well. O beloved who is the single mystery of the world and creation! Let me tell you a secret I kept even from Messenger Adam.

---

775. Mevlânâ Celâleddin Rûmî, trans. Veled İzbudak, ed. Abdülbaki Gölpınarlı, *Mesnevî* (Istanbul: Milli Eğitim Basımevi 1991), vol. 3, vs. 4230-4231, 4237, 4242-4248.

776. Mevlânâ Celâleddin Rûmî, trans. Veled İzbudak, ed. Abdülbaki Gölpınarlı, *Mesnevî* (Istanbul: Milli Eğitim Basımevi 1991), vol. 5, vs. 3128-3130.

Now let Me tell you the secret I did not tell My friend Abraham, the state of which I did not inform Gabriel, the truth of which even Jesus did not breath a word.

Know that God the Truth did not self-disclose without the human being. For His self-disclosure is with the human, with the human state of feeling Him in his own self. If you know how to look, if you know how to see, look upon all I have created, and within all that I have created, look at the secret and the cause of creation—the human being! In each human you will find a different self-disclosure of my qualities and states. I gave to a drop a power not possessed by a sea; I gave to a mote a power not seen in a sun.[777]

• Because the People of Pain see themselves become naught in God the Truth's being, only when they say "Allah" is it rembrance (*zikir*) of God the Truth.

• Those who witness the speech, remembrance, thought, etc. that comes from themselves as manifesting from God the Truth, that they themselves are only translators, that the voice manifesting from the other creatures and every thing is from God the Truth and all of them are only translators are sites of manifestation for the self-disclosure of act, attribute and name. And then they arrive at the self-disclosure of Essence.[778]

• Because those who remember God when they thus forget themselves, in other words, abandon intellect, raise the veil of intellect and arrive at love, they attain the secret that all things but God's Beauty are mortal (*fânîdir*). And in that love they are remembrance, rememberer and remembered.[779]

• The poetry of the arrived is entirely Quranic commentary, the secrets of the Quran; for they have passed from their own being to become naught, their being is with God the Truth; their work and

---

777. Ken'an Rifâî, *Şerhli Mesnevî-i Şerif* (Istanbul: Kubbealtı Neşriyatı 2000), pp. 242-243.
778. Ken'an Rifâî, *Sohbetler* (Istanbul: Kubbealtı Neşriyatı 2000), p. 416.
779. Ken'an Rifâî, *Sohbetler* (Istanbul: Kubbealtı Neşriyatı 2000), p. 439.

69th Verse

rest is from God the Truth; as it has been said, "The heart of the believer is between two fingers of the Merciful's fingers of power, and He turns it as He wishes." They are only tools in God's hand of power; a person with intellect does not see the movement of the tool as coming from the tool. Their poetry does not resemble the things poets say woven with their thoughts and imaginations, poetry made up of exaggerated humbug. The intentions of poets are to display their superiority and show off themselves, like the idolators who carve an idol and then make it their object of worship. As it has been said, "Do you worship what you have carved?" The poetry of the arrived comes of abandoning passion and naughting the soul. Other poets think their own poetry is like theirs. That kind of poet does not know that that their work and their words are from the Creator; the creature has nothing to do with it, in that work and that poetry. For their poetry displays God, not themselves. The following is an example of these two kinds of poetry: Wind blows through the rose garden and carries the scent of the rose. But if it blows through the bathhouse furnace, it carries a bad smell. The wind is one and the same but has a different scent depending on where it has been. Whoever has the faculty of smell distinguishes between them. It has been said, "Those who believe are smart." Those who chews garlic may say they chewed musk, but the smell of garlic will reach the noses of those around them; but even if those who chew musk say they have eaten garlic, those with them will smell musk.[780]

- In fact listening to poetry is permitted. The Messenger (a.s.) listened to poetry. His Companions (r.a.) both composed poetry and listened to it. The Prophet (Hazret Muhammed) (a.s.) said, *"Wisdom is the lost property of believers; wherever they find it, it is they who have the most right to take it."* Hazret Messenger (a.s.) says, *"The most correct sentence said by the Arabs is this couplet by Labid: 'Other than God, all things are vain. All boons will surely pass away.'*

- Amr ibn Sharid related this from his father (a.s.): "The Messenger of God wanted me to recite a poem and said, 'Will you relate some poetry of Umayya ibn Abi al-Salt?' I recited one hundred couplets of

---

780. Ken'an Rifâî, *Sohbetler* (Istanbul: Kubbealtı Neşriyatı 2000), p. 464.

poetry to him. When I came to the end of each couplet he said, 'So?" in other words, recite another. The Messenger of God (s.a.s.) said, 'Umayya was almost a Muslim in his poetry'" (*he was a disbeliever but his poetry was muslim*).

When asked about poetry, the Messenger of God (s.a.s) said, "Poetry is words; the beautiful of it is beautiful, and the ugly of it, ugly."[781]

---

781. Sultan Veled, trans. Abdülbaki Gölpınarlı, *İbtidâ-name* (Konya: Konya ve Mülhakatı Eski Eserleri Sevenler Derneği 2001), p. 52.

70. That those who are living should be warned, and the word be proved for those who disbelieve.

Liyundhira man kāna ḥayyan wa yaḥiqqa'l-qawlu ʿalā'l-kāfirūn.

• Our Messenger of God Efendi said, "Those who know God as creator, accept Muhammed as messenger, and choose Islam as religion have tasted faith."

What this noble hadith indicates is a matter of state and taste; it comes of devotion to God. And this devotion is to know God. And the knowledge is gnosis.

This gnosis is a light. God places it in the heart of His beloved servant. There is no thing more sublime, no greater thing than this light. For it is the light of gnosis. The true meaning of gnosis is for the heart to attain life with the creator.

"*Was he not dead? We raised him up*" (6:122).

"*We shall give them new life, a good life*" (16:97).

"*Go to God and His Messenger when he calls you to give you life*" (8:24).[782]

• Know that everything existing in the world has two sides. According to the capacity of those who look at it, it has a good side, and a bad side. When God wants people to do a thing, He shows them its good side, and they do it. If He wants them not to do a thing, He he shows them its bad side and they do not do it. That is why Abu Bakr (r.a.) said to the Messenger, "There is no one more beautiful in the world than you, O Messenger of God!"[783]

---

782. Hucviri, ed. Süleyman Uludağ, *Keşfu'l-Mahcûb Hakikat Bilgisi* (Istanbul: Dergah Yayınları 1996), p. 550.

783. Şemseddin Yeşil, *Füyûzat* (Istanbul: Ş. Yeşil Yayınları 1984), vol. 6, p. 264.

- The Quran is like a bride. It does not open its veil and show you its face. That person (*thing*) you spoke of, that gave you no pleasure and did not cause you to discover anything, did not accept that you should open the veil; it fooled you and showed itself to you as ugly. In other words, I am not that beauty and it has the power to show whatever face it wishes. But if you do not open its veil, and you seek to gain its acceptantance and go to its field, water its crops, serve it from afar and work at the thing it accepts, it will show you its face without you opening its veil.

Seek the people of God so that you may enter among the chosen servants and enter Paradise. Sublime God does not speak to everyone. Worldly padishahs do not speak with just anyone. They appoint a vizier and a regent. They show the Padishah the way. And Sublime God has chosen a servant. Whoever seeks God should go to him. That is why the prophets have come. Only they can show the way.[784]

One of the characteristics of spirit is that it makes whatever it inhabits alive. For spirits are the location where the name "Lord" manifests. God the Sublime educates the things with spirit. As a condition of existence, life is a necessary attribute of those things. And it is the basis of all attributes related to existence. For that reason the name The Alive was made the leader of the seven names. For the existence of knowledge, will and the other divine names can only be conceived after Life. Every thing has a spirit carried to itself from its Lord according to its properties and a life appropriate to itself. Thus that thing becomes manifest with attributes appropriate to life like knowledge, will, power and others like that which require that first there be life. But of course to the extent that its constitution (*mi'zaç*) allows. For example, if it attains the maturity of a temperate constitution like that of the human being, it has the faculty of being manifest with all of the attributes or most of them. If its constitution is distant from temperance, the quality of being alive, along with its requirements, will in it remain hidden. As is the case with things called inanimate and plants.[785]

---

784. Mevlânâ Celâleddin Rûmî, trans. Melika Ülker Anbarcıoğlu, *Fîhi mâ Fîh* (Istanbul: Milli Eğitim Basımevi 1985), p. 349.

785. İsmâil Rusûhî Ankaravî, ed. İlhan Kutluer, *Nakşel-FüsusŞerhi* (Istanbul: Ribat Yayınları n.d.), p. 107.

70th Verse

What is spirit? Aware of evil and good
Weeping at harm and rejoicing in the good

Awareness is spirit's secret and nature
So more spiritual is he who's more aware

Awareness is the effect of the spirit
He is divine who possesses more of it

Since there's knowledge beyond what is put down here
These spirits become inanimate things there

The first spirit's the site of the court of God
Spirit's spirit is truly the site of God

The angels were all intellect and spirit
They became the body for a new spirit

When they were elevated to that spirit
Like the body they came to serve that spirit

Iblis reared his head away from that spirit
A dead limb, he did not become one with it

He did not give himself to what was not his
A broken hand, he did not obey spirit

Spirit lacks naught for having a broken hand
It can make it live, for that is in its hand[786]

- *Homonymy will always lead one astray*
Kafir and believer share body the same

Bodies are like pitchers that are tightly closed
Look and see what it is that a pitcher holds

The Water of Life fills that body's pitcher
The poison of death fills this body's pitcher

---

786. Mevlânâ Celâleddin Rûmî, trans. Veled İzbudak, ed. Abdülbaki Gölpınarlı, *Mesnevî* (Istanbul: Milli Eğitim Basımevi 1991), vol. 6, vs. 148-157.

If you look to the contents, you are a shah
If you look to the container, you are lost

Know that words are likenesses of this body
Likeness of spirit inside is their meaning

Body is what the bodily eye can see
The artful spirit is what the spirit sees

Thus the forms of the words of the Masnavi
Guide spiritually and formally mislead

God commanded that the Quran, by the heart
"Leads many astray and guides many aright" (2:26) [787]

- A gazelle and a wolf married and had a child. They asked the jurist, "Shall we consider it a worlf or a gazelle? If we take it as a wolf, its flesh will be haram and unclean; if we call it a gazelle, it will be halal. Which should we consider it to be, and what shall we call it? We cannot decide." The artful jurist gave the following decision. The judgment on this is not absolute, it is detailed. Put before this young one a bunch of herbs and some bones. If it prefers the bones, it is a wolf and its flesh is haram. If it prefers the herbs instead, it is a gazelle and its flesh is halal." In the same way Sublime God mixed and united that world with the world, and the earth with the sky. We are the children of the two. If we prefer knowledge and our strength is in knowledge and wisdom, then we are heavenly and halal. If we prefer eating, sleeping, worldy boons and clothes, then we are animalistic and belong to earth. Our station is not the highest station but the bottom of Hell.[788]

- Our Noble Messenger of God Efendi said, *"For God the Exalted there are seventy thousand veils of light and darkness."* The Vicegerent of God the Truth is veiled with seventy thousand veils of light and darkness. The body of the world is its own veil; it cannot comprehend God the

---

787. Mevlânâ Celâleddin Rûmî, trans. Veled İzbudak, ed. Abdülbaki Gölpınarlı, *Mesnevî* (Istanbul: Milli Eğitim Basımevi 1991), vol. 6, vs. 649-656.

788. Sultan Veled, trans. Meliha Anbarcıoğlu, *Maarif* (Konya: Altunarı Ofset 2002), pp. 104-105.

70th Verse

Truth. Because the Angel too is a part of the world, it is veiled by its own self and could not witness the all-comprehensiveness of Adam. In sum, the world cannot comprehend God the Truth, just as God the Turh comprehends His own self... Why? Because the world's self is the veil of its own self... Adam was honored with the Divine all-comprehensiveness and created with the two blessed hands. It was kneaded by God's attributes "Beauty" and "Majesty."

He brought together Divine form and created form. As for Iblis, he is a part of the world; thus God the Truth said to Iblis who is a part of that world, "What has prevented you from prostrating yourself to the thing I created with My two hands?"

The sources of Adam and Iblis are contraries of one another. For the greatest part of the source of humanity is water and earth. In terms of their faculties and qualities, these give birth to attributes such as: Acceptance, piety, obedience, faith, endurance, gravity, calm, reverence, humility, and gentleness.

The greatest part of the source of Iblis is fire, and that requires attributes such as grandiosity, pride, arrogance and cheating, molestation, domination, misbelief and denial, malice and envy. Thus that is why Iblis did not prostrate himself, because prostration is the attribute of the Earth. Yes, the assignment of prostration for Iblis was a test. The test was carried out, and his wretchedness became clear. In sum, it is not approved for any part of the parts of the world to be "the Vicegerent of God the Truth." Only to Hazret Human Being was given by God the Truth the right to be "the Vicegerent of God the Truth, because he or she collects together the form of God the Truth and the form of the world. Yes, the interior of the Perfect Human Being is upon the form of God the Truth. "God the Truth said, 'I will be the servant's hearing and seeing, the servant's eye and ear. For God the Exalted is Hearing and Seeing, and eye and ear are the servant's manifest part." How beautifully does that sacred hadith distinguish between the manifest form and the non-manifest form.[789]

---

789. Şemsettin Yeşil, *Şeyh-i Ekber Muhyiddin-I Arabî Hakikati Nasıl Anlatıyor* (Istanbul: Yaylacık Matbaacılık 1997). pp. 59-60.

71. Do they not see that among what Our hands have fashioned We created for them gentle animals that are under their dominion?

'Awalam yaraw 'annā khalaqnā lahum mimmā 'amilat 'aydīnā 'an'āman fahum lahā mālikūn.

72. And that We have subjected them to their use, so that some they ride and some they eat?

Wa dhallalnāhā lahum faminhā rakūbuhum wa minhā ya'kulūn.

73. And in them they have benefits, and drink. Will they not then give thanks?

Wa lahum fīhā manāfi'u wa mashāribu 'a fa lā yashkurūn.

- *'An'ām* (animals) has been translated to mean gentle, tame animals. The word *'an'ām* means "gentle."

Sheep mostly live in warm climates. Thus they are definitely not in need of the hirsute hides that are special to animals living near the poles. Animals living in those zones all have hairy hides (cows, etc.). But sheep have rich fleece even if they live in Africa, and this fleece has been put on these animals only for the sake of human beings.

It has never been possible to produce imitation sheep wool. While the electrons of wool fibers grow outwards from the body, synthetic fabrics gather their electrons and store them. While all natural fibers have been imitated, wool cannot be imitated.

The flesh of sheep has fat and protein beyond the animal's needs. Sheep also produce more milk than they need.

The true secret of the sheep is in its property of fruitfulness. Sheep give birth once a year, eat continuously, and yet they increase in numbers.

All the world's nutrition scholars state that eating meat increases the tendency to violence in people. While that is so, the exception is the flesh of sheep, called 'an'ām. It is not possible to analyse the wisdom of the sheep's flesh not increasing the tendency to violence. For that is a spiritual moment and in tasavvuf the sheep is known as the representative of submission.

Count the sheep as our benefit, from its hide, wool, blood, its glands that produce hormones, its likeness in the womb, to the making of surgical thread from its intestines and fertilizer from its feces.

B and T lymphocytes, very important for cancer, are produced by the blood cells of sheep.

To be sure, just as sheep come at the head of the boon of tame 'an'ām class animals, it is not wrong to study horses and cows as part of this group.

The part of the verse concerning "drink" obviously means milk and milk products. It is impossible not to notice the unique composition of a nutriment having the composition of milk and the importance of the boons to the health of human beings that it offers.

Milk, yogurt and cheese have an indispensible place among our daily nutriments. Studies show that as yogurt is being made, the microorganisms in it develop in the following way. First the bacteria begin to produce from the milk the phosphorus, ribose and amino acids necessary to their propogation. This is their natural function. But after a while they begin to make thousands of times more enzymes and vitamins than they need. The liver produces directly many miraculous chemical substances of its own. Like workers in a biological factory, they prepare at the command of God an inestimable nutriment for human beings.

This fundamental operation is so contrary to their own needs that after a while production ceases. In other words, yogurt bacteria continue to serve human beings although it is against the needs of their own posterity.[790]

---

790. Halûk Nurbaki, *Yâ-Sîn Sûresi Yorumu* (Istanbul: Damla Yayınevi 1999), pp. 91-95.

71th-72th-73th Verse

- The body is soul (*vücut, nefistir*). The soul is the body, source of the malady of duality.[791]

- In the tale's inner meaning, the animals represent the faculties of the soul and satanic thoughts.[792]

- The insignia seen on mounts are signs. Some of the riders on those mounts have a right to cleave to those insignia, and some travel the desert. In other words, some of them are people of vision and witness, and some are people of analogy and inference.[793]

- And just so, the subjective meaning of this tale is given in Ismail Ankaravi's commentary thus: "Each person is the padishah of the country of his own body. And so it is with Solomon. That is, in reality Solomon represents the spirit. When the spirit takes the throne of the heart in order to govern the exterior and interior faculties, it is as if these material and spiritual faculties are ranged before it. They offer to serve it. Each one tries to display its own art, skill and knowledge."[794]

- **Messenger Solomon** commanded the birds, the wolves, the jinn and the ants by virtue of his seal. That seal was actually the seal of knowledge, the charm of knowing the truth. The power that makes human beings able to rule those in the mountains, seas and skies resides in their knowledge and gnosis (*the power to know, by divine grace, the secrets of creation*). Knowledge is also the virtue that makes the human human.[795]

- The things that are other than God the Truth all have the property of being animals. For they are animate. And there is nothing that moves by its own soul. It moves only by an effect other than its

---

791. Ken'an Rifâî, *Şerhli Mesnevî-i Şerif* (Istanbul: Kubbealtı Neşriyatı 2000), p. 52.
792. Ken'an Rifâî, *Şerhli Mesnevî-i Şerif* (Istanbul: Kubbealtı Neşriyatı 2000), p. 136.
793. İbni Arabî, trans. Nuri Gençosman, *Fusûs'l-Hikem* (Istanbul: Kırkambar Kitaplığı n.d.), p. 91.
794. Ken'an Rifâî, *Şerhli Mesnevî-i Şerif* (Istanbul: Kubbealtı Neşriyatı 2000), p. 166.
795. Ken'an Rifâî, *Şerhli Mesnevî-i Şerif* (Istanbul: Kubbealtı Neşriyatı 2000), p. 141.

soul. Thus every creature that moves does so according to the property and requisite of the thing on the right path. For a path takes the name of "path" by being walked upon.[796]

- It is said, "*You are all shepherds and you are responsible for your sheep*" (hadith). This means that if you cannot watch over them and obtain the benefit necessary from them, you are responsible for their goodness and evil.[797]

- Perfection is Found Thanks to the Soul

Why complain of this soul, is it worthy not to know its value?
That weighty boon comes from the Lord Possessed of Majesty to you
It's your companion, do not contemn it, use it most graciously
He who knows his soul knows the taste of unity and God the Truth
Without the soul could one ever arrive at the gate of desire
When the span of life comes to an end, it won't make you pine anew
Know its value, never separate it from eternal knowledge
Serve it in every way possible, let it not complain of you
But these my words will be acceptable after education
He who reforms his soul becomes human, come to Ken'an's aid too[798]

- If you did not take on a form, if you did not suffer separation, how could you know the virtue of the realm of formlessness and the pleasure of the realm of union, how could you conceive of it?

You who say there is no benefit in the spirit's taking on a body! If there is no use in words, don't speak. Understand, leave off objecting and give thanks.

Consider the pleasure and virtue that comes of feeling, thought and meaning being put in a series of letters, in short, in a word. Then set your mind to the incomparably great event of spirit's taking on a body and the virtue in the pleasure, joy, form and meaning gained

---

796. Muhyiddîn İbnü'l-Arabî, trans. Nuri Gençosman, *Fusûs'l-Hikem* (Istanbul: İstanbul Kitabevi Yayınları 1981), p. 128.

797. Ken'an Rifâî, *Sohbetler* (Istanbul: Kubbealtı Neşriyatı 2000), p. 607.

798. Ken'an Rifâî, *İlâhiyat-ı Ken'an*, ed. Yusuf Ömürlü and Dinçer Dalkılıç (Istanbul: Kubbealtı Neşriyatı 1988), p. 68.

71TH-72TH-73TH VERSE

there! Pay attention to the infinite delicacy of spirit's unique self-disclosure in each body, and ask no more! Give yourself over to the pleasure of prostrations of gratitude.

Give thanks to God. Be pleased that he gave you the potential to know Him and love Him! Giving thanks is the greatest worship performed by people of conscience. Gratitude is a duty, a debt of conscience.[799]

• O Master, know that every spirit in the animal stage is dominated by humankind. Those who have attained the level of the friends dominate humankind to the same degree. As much as humans possess and command animals, a friend of God has that much power to dispose of a spirit whose level is still that of humanity.

So pay close attention to the friends of God! With them get free of body and form, become spirit! You will see that in reality one of them leads a hundred thousand spirits. You will see that all spirits are at the disposal and under the command of that mighty spirit who is the Axis of the Age.[800]

• When people become distant from their selves, from their egos, what rules them is God the Truth. It may be for three minutes, an hour, or ten minutes or one moment; during the time that state occurs, God self-discloses, becomes continuous, and the entire world is subject to Him. For the self has withdrawn from in between, self does not remain, only God is left. For example, if people want to walk upon the surface of the ocean during that time, they can do it. If they want to see the people of the Unseen, they will all be evident to them. In sum, the entire world submits to them, just as the birds built nests upon Majnun's head and all the animals of the forest, lions and tigers, gathered around him and became his friends. For the scent of humanity did not remain in him, his existence was erased.[801]

• Do those deniers, those idolators, those who our ungrateful for Our boons, not see this too? Without anyone's action, by the power

---

799. Ken'an Rifâî, *Şerhli Mesnevî-i Şerif* (Istanbul: Kubbealtı Neşriyatı 2000), p. 211.
800. Ken'an Rifâî, *Şerhli Mesnevî-i Şerif* (Istanbul: Kubbealtı Neşriyatı 2000), p. 362.
801. Ken'an Rifâî, *Sohbetler* (Istanbul: Kubbealtı Neşriyatı 2000), pp. 194-195.

and wisdom of Our generosity alone, we Ourself created with Our own hands tame animals of all kinds and made them submissive to them. They became owners of them, disposing of them as they wished. (Do they not wonder how they could have ruled over creatures much stronger than themseves if We had not made them submissive to them? How could they have had disposal over them?) We made those animals helpless before them; we made them submissive despite the perfection of their power and strength. They eat the meat of some of them and ride others. And they have many other uses for these animals. They make use of their wool and their hides, and they drink their milk and do many other things. Although they all work for human beings, will they not be thankful for so many boons?[802]

- It is possible for people to train their speaking souls (*nefs-i natıka*) to analyse the speaking soul's moral character, working its beautiful characteristics and putting its ugly characteristics to one side. For when the speaking soul is trained in the sciences of truth and awakened, it becomes noble and does not condescend to ugly habits; it does not find it becoming to itself to be soiled by ugliness. Thus as a consequence it becomes easier for a person to avoid ugly habits. From what we have expounded so far it is clear that the way to educate the soul, for it to come to possess characteristics worthy of praise agreeable to those around it, to work it so as to make beautiful characteristics a habit, to conform to the beautiful among characteristics, to avoid blameworthy and ugly characteristics, to make the powers of lust and rage submit and to crush them, is to reform the speaking soul and strengthen it, and adorn it with virtue, right conduct and beautiful characteristics. This is the means of politics and the mount of ascetic discipline.[803]

- If the arrow does not see the one who shoots it, if the heart does not see that eternal beloved who gives it the inner secret, in short if it does not sense and comprehend that the one who speaks and under-

---

802. Şemseddin Yeşil, *Füyûzat* (Istanbul: Ş. Yeşil Yayınları 1984), vol. 6, p. 264.
803. Muhyiddîn İbnü'l-Arabî, trans. Vahdettin İnce (Istanbul: Kitsan Yayıncılık n.d.), pp. 99-100.

71TH-72TH-73TH VERSE

stands divine secrets is in itself, that would be like the heedless rider who looks elsewhere for the mount he is riding on.

People are riding such a mount swift as the wind on the road to God the Truth; they have been made to mount it. Heedlessness is to be unaware of the horse one is riding. What is intended here by "horse" is the intellect and spirit of a person who is heedless of God the Truth. To be unaware of both intellect and spirit although one has been mounted upon an intellect and spirit is to ride that horse in vain and look elsewhere for the horse one is riding, moreover to do so with violence and heedlessness. A person may be heedless of that horse of intellect and spirit to such an extent that he is like a rider who runs here and there shouting, "Who stole my horse?" although the horse is underneath him.[804]

- With ascetic practices and training they extricate a rebellious horse from the attribute of animality and make it acquire the attribute of Adamness; they tame it and train it. As a result of this training the horse will take the whip from the ground and give it to its master, push the ball with its foot and do many other things like that. By means of ascetic practices they bring a mindless little boy who is not Arab to speak Arabic. Thus they change his natural style of speech and language. By means of asceticism they bring a wild parrot to such a level that it flies away when they let go of it and comes when they call it. The troubles of being bound become for it a more desirable state than that of being free and let go to roam. With effort they bring a dirty, stray dog to such a level that the animal that dog hunts becomes helal. The prey of a dog that has not undergone asceticism and struggle cannot be halal for a human being. The central point and basis of all external properties is effort.[805]

- In tasavvuf milk means knowledge, gnosis and possessing spiritual knowledge. The river of milk is the science of secrets.[806]

---

804. Ken'an Rifâî, *Şerhli Mesnevî-i Şerif* (Istanbul: Kubbealtı Neşriyatı 2000), p. 155.
805. Hucvirî, ed. Süleyman Uludağ, *Keşf'ul-Mahcûb Hakikat Bilgisi* (Istanbul: Dergah Yayınları 1996), p. 315.
806. Suad el-Hakîm, trans. Ekrem Demirli, *İbü'l-Arabî Sözlüğü* (Istanbul: Kabalcı Yayınevi 2005), p. 578.

- A person having connection to the river of milk acquires knowledge, gnosis and spiritual knowledge.[807]

- The river of milk symbolizes a beneficial knowledge that nourishes both one's own spirit and other spirits.[808]

- Ibn Arabi does not mean by the terms "animal" and "the level of animality" the known characteristic of lust; he refers to the characteristic of life that is the root source of the terms. Ibn Arabi explains that the level of animality and its condition, knowledge, is superior to the level of the human being.

Idris is an absolute animal. Thus all things other than human beings and jinn open up to him. In that way he learns that he has realized his own animality. There are two indications of this. The first is unveiling. Thus Idris sees those who suffer torment in the grave or those experiencing boons. He sees the dead as alive, the silent as speaking, and standing as walking. The second is loss of the faculty of speech. So that if he tries to describe what he sees, he will not be able to. Thus does a person reach the level of animality (*absolute passivity*).

The marriage of one who possesses this station (*the Axis*) is, like the marriages of the people of Paradise, purely with the aim of lust, and takes the place of the marriage of animals that have purely the aim of lust. To be sure, people have remained unaware of this value and thought it to be animalistic lust; they kept their souls distant from it, yet still they named it with the most valuable name. This valuable name is their saying "animalistic," in other words, one of the characteristics of animals. Can there be anything more valuable than life (the word "animal" is generated from the word "life")? Thus the thing people believe to be ugly about them is praise itself.

As for animals, we have some Pirs among them. One of the shaykhs I trust is horses, for a horse's worship is exceeding strange. And there is also the falcon, the dog, the tiger, the ant, etc. I could not manage their worship as they do it. All I have been able to do is

---

807. Ken'an Rifâî, *Sohbetler* (Istanbul: Kubbealtı Neşriyatı 2000), p. 420.
808. Niyâzî Mısrî, trans. Süleyman Ateş, *İrfan Sofraları* (Istanbul: Yeni Ufuklar Neşriyatı n.d), p. 55.

71TH-72TH-73TH VERSE

perform that worship at a specific time. But they believe that I am their master at every moment, and they blame me and criticise me.[809]

---

809. Suad el-Hakîm, trans. Ekrem Demirli, *İbü'l-Arabî Sözlüğü* (Istanbul: Kabalcı Yayınevi 2005), pp. 276-277.

74. Yet they take gods other than God, as if they would be helped.

Wa't-takhadhū min dūni'l-lāhi 'ālihatan la'allahum yunṣarūn.

75. They are not able to help them, though they be an army ready for them.

Lā yastaṭī'ūna naṣrahum wa hum lahum jundun muḥḍarūn.

• Some of those who are firm in faith deny the gods of others and attribute to them curses and misbelief. But there is no helper for them. For no judgment exists for the god that one of them believes about the god the other one believes in. Everyone firm in faith helps the god they believe in by defending the things they believe about it. But the god they believe in does not help them. Thus the god they believe in has no effect on the god they don't believe in. And the god of the ones with the opposing belief does not help them either. This means that God does not allow all having belief to derive help from the god they believe in. For those who are helped are only the gnostics who gather all beliefs within their souls (*in other words, gather all divine powers in one God concept*), and the helper is God who is the sum of all divine self-disclosures. Thus God the Truth is a known that according to the gnostic cannot be denied. The gnostics who are the people of that known are possessed of spiritual knowledge in this world and the next. That is why God said, "For those possessed of heart." Thus because the heart enters form after form, such people understand that God the Truth also enters form upon form among forms.[810]

---

810. Muhyiddîn İbnü'l-Arabî, trans. Nuri Gençosman, *Fusûs'l-Hikem* (Istanbul: İstanbul Kitabevi Yayınları 1981), p. 100.

- Our Blessings and Peace be upon him Efendi said, *"We are returning from the lesser jihad to the greater jihad."* The commander of that jihad is the murshid, and its most powerful instrument (*weapon*) is the Unification given by the shaykh.[811]

- When the Quraysh idolators were asked about the creator, they would say, "God." But although they said "God," their worship of idols was contrary to the spirit of unification. Thus their confession of lordliness was not valid. Because that *shirk* group worshipped idols, they did not found their worship upon God and because of that they were in the condition of rejecting Lordship, in other world, falling into *shirk*. *Shirk* is born of not knowing lordliness, of not comprehending it sufficiently.

  As for the veiled ignorant, because they do not know the levels, they posit a second being and become idolaters. But if only they would consider that being is one but it has varied levels. For the Most Tremendous Sultan is One. But in terms of His trustees, He has many levels. And this meaning is according to the number of the names. The plurality of names indicates the nobility of the One who takes the name.[812]

- *Shirk*, in other words setting up partners to God, is the greatest wrongdoing (*zülüm; to not put a thing in its place*). Here the one to whom wrong is done is the station of divine oneness. For the one who commits *shirk* breaks up this station into parts and attributes plurality to it. But that station is a unique being. (*The one who sets up partners to God*) only sets up its mate. And this is the utmost level of ignorance. The reason for this *shirk* is the confusion of people who do not comprehend gnosis as it is and understand nothing when faced with the varied forms that come from one being. For they do not know that these changes appear from one source. They liken the form they see in this station to the other station. They take only one part of each form appearing from the divine station of matchlessness.[813]

---

811. Niyâzî Mısrî, trans. Süleyman Ateş, *İrfan Sofraları* (Istanbul: Yeni Ufuklar Neşriyatı n.d), p. 133.

812. İsmail Hakkı Bursevî, trans. Abdülkâdir Akçiçek, *Kenz-i Mahfi-Gizli Hazine* (Istanbul: Bahar Yayınları 2000), pp. 62, 64.

813. Muhyiddîn İbnü'l-Arabî, trans. Nuri Gençosman, *Fusûs'l-Hikem* (Istanbul: İstanbul Kitabevi Yayınları 1981), p. 194.

74TH-75TH VERSE

- If those who are among the people of heart and possessed of substance beat a man and break his head, his mouth, his nose, everyone says it is the one who is beaten that is wronged. In reality it is the one who beats him that is wronged. A wrongdoer is someone who does no good and beneficial thing. There is no doubt that the one who is beaten and his head broken is the wrongdoer, and the one who beats him is the wronged. For the one who beats him is possessed of substance and *has become annihilated in God*. Everything that person does is God's doing. They do not call God "wrongdoer." For example, Mustafa (*may the peace and blessings of God be upon him*) killed, shed blood and plundered. Nevertheless, they are wrongdoers and he is wronged.[814]

- God the Truth has a face of self-disclosure at every level. God is veiled by believing in one and denying another. This too is counted as misbelief. For example, someone worships an idol. Because he assigns his worship to that idol and ties his state to it, he rejects another; thus he is counted a disbeliever. And if a Muslim denies one of the beings God manifests, religion does not call him a Muslim. Vain misbelief (*küfr-ü batil*) veiled the unbounded God the Truth; God the Truth misbelief (*küfr-ü Hak*) veiled itself with God the Truth.[815]

- True maturity is this, that when He says so, to be entirely stripped of being and attain obliteration and annihilation. Then not to bind oneself to something by assigning a belief, opinion, limitation. To not turn in any specific direction. Thus it is that after that one adores and worships Unbounded God, the Lord more sublime than all gods. If not, one becomes the servant of the object of worship one has imagined in one's own opinion. One enters under threat of "*Have you seen the one who accepts his own caprice as a god?*"[816]

- The types of all human beings are three:

---

814. Mevlâna, trans. M. Ülker Tarıkâhya, *Fîhi Mâfih* (Istanbul: Milli Eğitim Basımevi), pp. 82-83.

815. Muhyiddîn İbnü'l-Arabî, trans. İsmail Hakkı Bursevî, *Özün Özü* (Istanbul: Rahmet Yayınları n.d.), p. 46.

816. Muhyiddîn İbnü'l-Arabî, trans. İsmail Hakkı Bursevî, *Özün Özü* (Istanbul: Rahmet Yayınları n.d.), p. 52.

The first do not know why they have come to this world and that the purpose of it is to attain perfection, and they make eating, drinking, sleeping and having sex their idols. This class does not return to the true station that is in the sublime worlds.

The second group does know that the purpose of coming to this lowly world is only to attain perfection, but has preferred four idols, such as love of self, children, wealth and station. Although there are those among this group who return to the true station, they are still captives and worship the four idols. Because they have not known themselves and have not attained the sublime station. And they have not performed the purpose of coming to the world.

The third group knows that they have come to this lowly world to attain perfection and consider themselves guests here. By breaking the idol of self, they have become Perfect Human Beings.[817]

- To serve the desires of the soul means to worship one's own self that does not avoid what God has forbidden.[818]

- In the hands of the greed of the lion soul, before his power, a person can be as feeble as a blade of straw. Those looking on would anxiously suppose that the helpless blade of straw would never escape that lion's clutches. But there is God's help, and if intellect goes into action, everything can change with the speed of a miracle. In that case, a blade of straw can obliterate a mountain-like body.

Messenger Moses appeared very small to Pharaoh, his family, and his entire people. But Moses parted the sea with his staff and passed through it easily. Pharaoh, while taking the same way, was drowned as the waters came over him. That's how it is, a mosquito with half a wing can painlessly enter into a great Nimrod's ear and make him dash his head against the ground and crack open his skull. Read these verses of Yunus Emre with that in mind:

A mosquito shook an eagle and made him hit the ground
This is no lie, it's the truth, I too saw the dust he raised[819]

---

817. Ken'an Rifâî, *Sohbetler* (Istanbul: Kubbealtı Neşriyatı 2000), p. 436.
818. Ken'an Rifâî, *Sohbetler* (Istanbul: Kubbealtı Neşriyatı 2000), p. 65.
819. Ken'an Rifâî, *Şerhli Mesnevî-i Şerif* (Istanbul: Kubbealtı Neşriyatı 2000), p. 163.

76. So let what they say not grieve you. Surely We know what they conceal and what they disclose.

Falā yaḥzunka qawluhum 'innā na'lamu mā yusirrūna wa mā yu'linūn.

• The elect of the elect do not grieve. For ordinary people may grieve, but they are in a state of ecstasy and the station indicated by the gracious verse, *"There is no fear for them on that Day, and they do not grieve."* But there is this much that they feel grief due to some accidents and insufficiencies. And they grieve for others. Just as the Messenger of God grieved for his community... Thus God the Exalted said in His gracious verse, *"O Muhammed! So you would destroy yourself with grief that they do not believe in the Quran We have sent down to you, and they turn away"* (10:6) [sic].

Our Messenger of God Efendi (s.a.s.) says, *"On that Day, in terror of Resurrection, everyone will say, 'my self, my self.' But I will say, 'my community, my community.'"*[820]

• Messenger Salih continued to reflect upon the dead of the Thamud tribe: "God told me to bear with cruelty and continue advising them, for their time of death was near. I begged God, saying, 'My Lord! They treat me very cruelly, and I can no longer feel love for them and advise them. You know that one must love in order to advise.' God told me that He would do me a kindness and heal my wounds.

"Thus my Lord made my heart as pure as the heavens. He erased all painful memories from within me and I spoke sweetly to the Thamud tribe, saying, 'I will advise you again.

---

820. İsmail Ankaravî, *Minhâcu'l-Fukarâ-Fakirlerin Yolu* (İnsan Yayınları n.d.), p. 236.

"'But my words still had a poisonous effect on you. For even sugar does no good to beings created of poison.

"'What has died along with you today is my sufferings. But still I am unhappy. Who on earth has shed tears for the death of his sufferings? O wailing man, they have gone beneath the earth, they are not worthy of your tears!'"

In the Quran God spoke in the language of Messenger Shuayb: "*O my people! I vow that I have told you the words of my Lord. I gave you advice. Why should I feel sorry for a denying people?*" (7:93).

This is what Messenger Salih felt at that moment as well. But still the pain in his heart was not lessened. Tears flowed from his eyes. He himself wondered at his tears. God's sea of generosity overflowed and it was as if the vastness of forgiveness was gathered up in his eyes in the form of tears.

He kept asking himself why he was weeping. What was he weeping for? For the ugly faces and ugly actions of the dead? For the black darkness of their hearts? For their tongues spewing poison, for their dog-like teeth, for the scorpion's nest of their eyes and mouths?

Should you not give thanks that your Lord has covered over all of these evils with the mighty earth, hiding all their ugliness and evil with veils of earth?

Why do you regret the loss of such a tribe, whose hands, feet, eyes, hearts and every state is perverse and ugly? What is the mystery hidden in this heartfelt emotion for the loss of those who did nothing all their lives but follow Satan?

They who closed their eyes to all truth, taking only the path to imitation. While they could have been freed from their souls, they were donkeys instead. God sent them a prophet to guide and illuminate them. So that the spirits worthy of Hell and their hellish ways should be evident, and those heading for Hell should see the path to Paradise.

But alas, between the two is a veil which, although not apparent to the eye, keeps the deniers separate from God's pure bondsmen, like the barzakh which keeps the two seas apart, one salt, one sweet.[821]

---

821. Ken'an Rifâî, *Şerhli Mesnevî-i Şerif* (Istanbul: Kubbealtı Neşriyatı 2000), pp. 370-371.

76th Verse

- It is obvious that for the sake of humans God sacrifices the other animate beings He created, that he kills them and has them killed so that humans may live.

  For the good of humans God sacrifices so many animals, and so many humans are sacrificed for the sake of one prophet or friend possessed of the intellect of return.

  The stories of tribes of the past like Ad and Thamud show how preciously favored the messengers are in God's sight. The end of those who cross the messengers is to be destroyed.[822]

- The Glorified (*Sübhan*) means God who is pure and exempt from any lack and flaw, and especially creaturely qualities. Know that God is the Glorified. So that you may not fall into a state to be ashamed of before Him and in His sight. God the Glorified knows all your secrets and all your thoughts. Every dark feeling, thought and action is known to Him, like a black hair in white milk. For God is all-knowing, all-aware.[823]

- When Luqman's wisdom and skill increased, in order to raise it to a level of sufficiency and perfection he said, "God is the Subtle." For a person who is named with this name and has described and limited himself in this way to be in every thing the same as that thing is because of his subtlety and kindness. Then later Luqman qualified and praised God the Truth who is Subtle with the attribute "Aware," in other words, attributed to Him knowledge produced from informing. That knowledge is a relative (*zevkî*) knowledge indicated in the meaning of the Quranic verse, "*We will test you, so that We may know who among you tries hard and is patient.*" Although He knows the thing truly and in its nature, in this verse God shows His own self as if benefitting from knowledge. But it is impossible to deny that knowledge that sublime God communicated for His own self with "human beings" (*nass*). Thus God distinguished between relative knowledge and absolute knowledge. This means that relative knowledge is connected with spiritual and bodily faculties.[824]

---

822. Ken'an Rifâî, *Şerhli Mesnevî-i Şerif* (Istanbul: Kubbealtı Neşriyatı 2000), p. 485.
823. Ken'an Rifâî, *Şerhli Mesnevî-i Şerif* (Istanbul: Kubbealtı Neşriyatı 2000), p. 458.
824. Muhyiddîn İbnü'l-Arabî, trans. Nuri Gençosman, *Fusûs'l-Hikem* (Istanbul: İstanbul Kitabevi Yayınları 1981), pp. 191-192.

- Hearts that are kept far from worldly filth, clean and pure, are hearts that reflect divine mysteries.

If our heart's wealth, our love of God, the divine light self-disclosing in us, strikes the touchstone of that pure-hearted friend, that touchstone will immediately separate truth from doubt. Whether or not our hearts are pure gold is evident in the touchstone of his heart. Only that touchstone which is the mirror of mysteries knows the pure from the corrupt heart's gold.

Thus do the friends know all the faults of those whose hearts are filled with worldly images, worldly colors and worldly filth, like corrupt gold. And in those whose hearts are pure like pure gold, which can be mirrors for divine light, they taste the profound delight of seeing the reflections of that light.[825]

---

825. Ken'an Rifâî, *Şerhli Mesnevî-i Şerif* (Istanbul: Kubbealtı Neşriyatı 2000), p. 458-459.

77. Does man not see that We created him from sperm, yet he has become an open adversary?

'A wa lamyara'l-'insānu 'annā khalaqnāhu min nuṭfatin fa 'idhā huwa khaṣīmun mubīn.

78. He strikes a likeness for Us, and forgetting his own creation, says, "Who gives life to bones that are decomposed?"

Wa ḍaraba lanā mathalan wa nasiya khalqahu qāla man yuḥyi'l-'iẓāma wa hiya ramīmun.

79. Say, "He who made them for the first time will raise them to life, and He knows every kind of creation.

Qul yuḥyīhā'l-ladhi 'ansha'ahā 'awwala marratin wa huwa bikulli khalqin 'alīm.

- God is the continuous creator. The world is in need of God, continuously and a requirement of its essence.

  What is created can never create.

  Creation is renewed with every breath. The moment of perishing is the moment a similar form comes into being. In the view of the Asharites this resembles the renewal of accidents.

  You are recreated all the time; thus you perish and are resurrected.

  God self-discloses with every breath and His self-disclosure is never repeated. The people of unveiling witness each self-disclosure giving a new creation and taking a creation away. The passing of one creation is to be annihilated from the self-disclosure and to abide in the thing given by another self-disclosure.

The creation of human beings is renewed with every breath and they are not aware of it. This is spoken of in the verse, "*We change your likeness and make you in what you do not know*" (56:61). What is intended here is creation with every breath.

Thus God has a new creation in us with every breath. Those who do not know that are those in doubt about renewed creation (18:15).

The renewal of beings with every breath is known by the intellect.[826]

- So that we should taking warning, God puts before our eyes even earth, semen, and clots of blood. He wants to say:

"Malicious man, what thing did I make you of
That you keep finding it worthy of disgust?

You used to be in love with it in its time
You kept denying this virtue at the time

Since this largess rebuts the denial you made
In the beginning when you were merely clay

Your being brought to life disproves your denial
Medicine made this disease of yours more vile

How should clay be able to imagine this?
How should sperm possess denial and animus?

At that moment you had neither head nor heart
So you were denying denial and thought

Your denial rose from being without life
So it confirms that you have been brought to life

Thus you're like the man who rapped upon the door
The master inside said, 'The master's not here'

From this "not," the man knows the master is there
So he keeps knocking with his hand on the door

---

826. Suad el-Hakîm, trans. Ekrem Demirli, *İbü'l-Arabî Sözlüğü* (Istanbul: Kabalcı Yayınevi 2005), pp. 703-704.

77th-78th-79th Verse

Your very denial makes it manifest
He resurrects many arts from the lifeless"[827]

- When you were a drop of semen, God gave a body, health, intellect, and thought. And you, how do you show gratitude for so many boons?

  There was a man named Taha among the professors at The University of Egypt. Although this man was born blind, God gave him enough intellect, cleverness and knowledge to rise to the rank of a university teacher. Then He gave him enough ignorance and idiocy to deny God. Behold this tremendousness.

  Thus although he was deprived of two eyes, what cleverness and intellect did God the Truth give him that he was able to rise to such high stations. Then despite it all he was able to deny God.[828]

- The beginning of everything is pure and simple. The beginning of every thing is one point. Then we cause it to multiply. Suppose that when a war begins, the Master knows how it will end. But in order to reach that result, so many events occur, blood is spilt, cannon and rifles fire, all Hell breaks loose. For God those details have no value... It is we who give them importance.[829]

- *Every sorrow that makes your weary heart pine*
  Is the languor that you've got by drinking wine

  But how should you know which wine it was that made
  Manifest that langour and pain of headache?

  This hangover is the flower of that seed
  They recognise that who are wise and wary

  Bow and flower do not resemble the seed
  When has semen resembled a man's body?

  Semen is from bread, how should it be like bread?
  Man is from semen, how should he be like it?

---

827. Şefik Can, *Konularına göre açıklamalı Mesnevi Tercümesi* (Istanbul: Ötüken Neşriyat 1997), vol. 3-4, p. 447 [vol. 4, vs. 890-899].

828. Ken'an Rifâî, *Sohbetler* (Istanbul: Kubbealtı Neşriyatı 2000), p. 331.

829. Ken'an Rifâî, *Sohbetler* (Istanbul: Kubbealtı Neşriyatı 2000), p. 427.

O HUMANKIND

Jesus appeared from the breath of Gabriel
When was he like him in form or comparable?

Adam is of earth, how should he be like earth?
Never was there grape like the vine gave it birth

No source resembles that which is its effect
Thus you don't know the source of your aching head[830]

- Surely there is Resurrection. The raising of the dead is the return of spirits to bodies. This is the Resurrection according to believers whose faith in God is successful. Just as God has taught His believing servants that coming into the world was not impossible, He bestows the explication of the breast so that it be accepted that being created anew is not impossible. It is well known that it is easier to create anew than to create from nothing. "O Muhammed, say, 'He who made them for the first time will raise them to life, and He knows every kind of creation' (36:79)."[831]

- With this doctrine and denial of yours you have attrbuted weakness to the divine power. Not knowing the divine wisdom, you have not considered the signs of Lordliness. You have even tried to ridicule them. As you do not believe in the Unseen, you have tried to falsify what your knowledge cannot encompass. You have tried to be aware of the realities of things with your insufficient knowledge and crooked thinking.

"*They falsify that whose knowledge they could not encompass and whose interpretation has not yet come to them. Thus did thus before them falsify*" (10:39).

Your eyes are veiled with bodies and you are heedless of the Creator of bodies. Just so there were those who when they saw bodies denied that there was more of an existence to them. Such people deny that there is an Unseen true existence through which colors

---

830. Mevlânâ Celâleddin Rûmî, trans. Veled İzbudak, ed. Abdülbaki Gölpınarlı, *Mesnevî* (Istanbul: Milli Eğitim Basımevi 1991), vol. 5, vs. 3975-3978, 3980, 3982-3983, 3985.

831. Ahmed er-Rifâî, ed. Dr. H. Kâmil Yılmaz, *Marifet Yolu* (Istanbul: Erkam Yayıncılık 1995), p. 165.

77TH-78TH-79TH VERSE

and forms manfest by His being appear. For they know nothing of the knowledge of "Light" that is the cause of being. They cannot comprehend that because of the violence of manifestation of the Unseen between bodies, light is hidden from the eyes due to its excess.[832]

- Time will show you the things you do not know.

"*You were heedless of that. We have lifted the covering from you, so today your sight is sharp*" (50:22).[833]

- Only God has the power to change what He has done. The power to do the exact opposite of what He has done is His. That is why God is evident in invisibility and hidden in manifestation. For if God wishes to change something He has brought about, it is because there is another divine wisdom in it. His will, which dries up the world and turns it to desert with a wind, also uses another wind to turn it into a paradisiacal garden adorned with limitless greenery and giant roses.

God is one in subjugation and kindness. All the wrath and kindness we encounter is His work, in fact both are bounties no different from oneanother. The power to do the exact opposite of what He has done is His. That is why God is evident in invisibility and hidden in manifestation.

He is the sole Sultan in this realm of events and creations. He is the one master and ruler of all continents, all countries and thousands of cities and millions of bondsmen. For what creates, slays, destroys and quickens is only the hand of His power. Truly, God is engaged in perpetual action, bringing the signs of existence He has engraved on the face of the universe which He created from one state to another, from one manifestation to another, turning them from one direction to another, or wiping out completely their original states and substituting for them others which are the complete opposite or similar or far superior and beautiful.

That is why many a lack is transformed into a plenitude, many sins into good works, many infidelities into Islam, many depravities

---

832. Ahmed er-Rifâî, ed. Dr. H. Kâmil Yılmaz, *Marifet Yolu* (Istanbul: Erkam Yayıncılık 1995), p. 172.

833. Ahmed er-Rifâî, ed. Dr. H. Kâmil Yılmaz, *Marifet Yolu* (Istanbul: Erkam Yayıncılık 1995), p. 175.

into the most beautiful morality. And if God wishes, He will transform these again, into other or their opposite states. Even those plunged in the sleep of the grave which has no awakening will on the Day of Resurrection rise again to life and motion as if they have sipped the Water of Life.

The bodies of martyrs and all those who pass away in the path of God die in this world, but this is not death, it is resurrection to eternal life.[834]

• The bodies of human beings consisted of spirits, even Essence. They became gross with the accumulation of forms, descended and these persons came to be. Just as semen is simple when it separates from a human being. Then it descends, gathers form and becomes a person, a speaking animal. Later, when the forms leave, once again it becomes subtle, rises up and becomes simple. Look to your self: The meanings in your soul are produced from abstract spirit. There they are fixed and never depart, just as semen is fixed in the loins. You do not feel it when those meanings are separated from one another, not until they come and fall into the heart (*into memory*), until they settle. When they come into the heart, each one is dressed in an imaginal form. That is when you sense them separating from one another. When they enter into imaginal form, like other visible things they too become visible. Then if they come out, they become completely visible.

If you know what is being indicated here, you understand the difference between fixed knowledge and external being. When external being leaves, meanings rise up to their imaginal forms. Then from there they go up to their first abstraction and fixed entity, and stay there. They began there and there they return. Every thing will return to Him.

If you know this, you understand Who it is that has the use and disposal in bodies. All acts are God the Truth's. Forms are His instruments. "*You did not throw when you threw, but God threw*" (8:17). But because the servants do not know, or have forgotten, that that the only One who has power of disposal in the form of the servant is God, they

---

834. Ken'an Rifâî, *Şerhli Mesnevî-i Şerif* (Istanbul: Kubbealtı Neşriyatı 2000), pp. 573-574.

77th-78th-79th Verse

suppose they have a choice and will and an existence other than God. For example, if artisans, whose being is from God, imagine that they have being in themselves, they heedlessly suppose themselves to be makers. This wrong imagining comes of heedlessness. But if they know themselves to be God the Truth and attribute action and will to themselves, that is not wrong. Because that action has issued from the form. It is God who, in that form and at that level, has performed that act. At last consider and understand. That is why gnostics hit the mark when they say, "I made it, I did it," but when the ignorant say that, they commit a wrong.

In reality, will is for those who act to sense their own actions. In does not mean that people do things when they want to, and not do them when they do not want to. Because actions are with the will of God. God's willing is from the requisites of levels and forms with internal and external causes. God's willing is necessarily born from the union of these causes. When there are causes, actions manifest. People think they have the power to do them or refuse to do them. But they do not. When actions manifest, the person from which they issue can do nothing but sense them. The arising of contrary actions in animals gives them the sense that they have a will and choice. The truth is what you have heard. This is not contrary to partial will. Understand at last. God knows better.[835]

- God says, "*He will blow it once more, they will stand up, and the earth will be illuminated with the light of your Lord*" (39:68-69). "*You will return as We created you*" (7:29). "*Say, He who created them for the first time will create them*'" (36:79). "*They will either be wretched or felicitous*" (11:105) [sic].[836]

---

835. Niyâzî Mısrî, trans. Süleyman Ateş, *İrfan Sofraları* (Istanbul: Yeni Ufuklar Neşriyatı n.d), pp. 142-144.

836. Muhyiddîn İbnü'l-Arabî, trans. Ekrem Demirli, *Fütuhât-ı Mekkiyye* (Istanbul: Litera Yayıncılık 2006), vol. 1, p. 147.

80. He who produces fire out of the green tree for you and you kindle fires with it.

Alladhī ja'ala lakum mina'sh-shajari'l-'akhḍari nāran fa'idhā 'antum minhu tūqidūn.

- Oxygen is the unique thing on earth and only comes out of living trees. The really important aspect of the matter is the Resurrection after death with the making of oxygen by the green tree. Only by means of this scientific reality can a relationship be established between Judgment Day (*mahşer*) and the making of oxygen by living trees.

  It is not that even if you burn a living creature that has become crushed bones, I raise it up at every moment, but you are not aware of that. The secret of this is hidden in the event of the oxygen you burn every day that comes out of the green tree.

  If a living creature is burned up, its basic constitution outside of the ashes becomes steam and carbon dioxide. It is when this mixture comes to the leaf that the two inanimate substances are transformed into sugar and come alive with the divine name Alive's secret that I have given to the leaf. For while the positive charge of carbon is valuable, carbon dioxide was inanimate. But the leaf transforms it into negatively charged carbon and makes sugar; and that is the way of the basic production of the molecule we call DNA. If oxygen emerges in a place (in the green tree), there is a transformation from inanimate to animate in that place.[837]

- The Arabic root *kha-ḍ-r* takes place in two meanings: Green Color. In this meaning the word has been used to express life, the contrary of dryness and death.

---

837. Halûk Nurbaki, *Yâ-Sîn Sûresi Yorumu* (Istanbul: Damla Yayınevi 1999), p. 103.

"Hizir," from the same root, is a proper name. It represents the servant to whom God taught divine knowledge.[838]

- The Green Zumrut is the (universal) soul emerging from the White Pearl.[839]

- In Hizir there are several oddities from the secrets of resurrecting the dead. One of the things God assigned to him is that God creates plenty and plenitude wherever Hizir is. And just so, it is related that Hazret Messenger said that about Hizir. When asked the reason Hizir was given that name, Hazret Messenger answered, "Greenery sprouts under whatever stone he sits upon."[840]

- Moses saw the fire in the tree and a voice said, "*I am your Lord!*" Is God fire? Moses saw the light of the attribute, he did not see the essence. And so he then appealed to Him and said, "O my Lord, show Yourself to me!" Then God the Truth said, "'*You shall not see Me, but look at the mountain; if it remains in place at the moment of self-disclosure, you will see Me*' He said, and when God self-disclosed the mountain crumbled to dust and Moses fell down in a swoon*" (7:143) [sic].

Thus Hazret Moses could not bear even to see that self-disclosure in the mountain. Pay attention to this point: "Show Yourself to me!" means it is duality, in other words, to see the desiring and the desired as separate. Thus how will it be possible for you to see Me as long as you are with yourself? Can God be seen with the eye of this body? He can only be seen by His own light. The one who sees Him is He Himself.[841]

- Why did God the Truth appear to Moses (a.s.) in the form of fire? Because that was what Moses wanted at the moment. In other words, fire. For his wife was about to give birth and he had gone out to find

---

838. Suad el-Hakîm, trans. Ekrem Demirli, *İbü'l-Arabî Sözlüğü* (Istanbul: Kabalcı Yayınevi 2005), p. 286.
839. Suad el-Hakîm, trans. Ekrem Demirli, *İbü'l-Arabî Sözlüğü* (Istanbul: Kabalcı Yayınevi 2005), p. 706.
840. Muhyiddîn İbnü'l-Arabî, trans. Ekrem Demirli, *Fütuhât-ı Mekkiyye* (Istanbul: Litera Yayıncılık 2006), vol. 1, p. 444.
841. Ken'an Rifâî, *Sohbetler* (Istanbul: Kubbealtı Neşriyatı 2000), p. 203.

80th Verse

fire so she should not feel cold. If his wish had not appeared in form, perhaps he would not gone there. Witnessing, in other words, to see, to desire the unbounded, depends on a form, on a body.[842]

- To those who pray continuously, as to Moses, their treesupplication becomes a shade made of fire such that when they approach the fire, the meaning of "You are my Lord" manifests and from the bush they hear the call, "You are in the Holy Valley, take off your shoes of this world and the Hereafter.[843]

- If you ask what is the reason for the manifestation of the light of self-disclosure in the form of fire, it appears that way from outside. It is light, not fire. God the Truth said to Hazret Moses, "*Throw off your shoes*" (20:12), in other words, throw off both the world and the Hereafter, and you will see fire as light.[844]

- The love that is fire for the people of manifestation is light for them. They threw Abraham into fire. But that fire became a rose garden for him. But the same light is fire for someone else.[845]

- With what form will God the Truth self-disclose to His servants in the Hereafter? "He will self-disclose from whatever and whoever they were occupied with in the world."[846]

- Would not God, who self-disclosed to Moses from the tree, self-disclose from the Perfect Human Being? In the Perfect Human Being the world and the Hereafter, Muhammed and God have self-disclosed.[847]

- When God created Hazret Adam He self-disclosed to him with light head to foot, with the Essence. Adam was the site where that self-disclosure was born and shone, where the divine names and attributes manifested.

---

842. Ken'an Rifâî, *Sohbetler* (Istanbul: Kubbealtı Neşriyatı 2000), p. 366.
843. Ken'an Rifâî, *Sohbetler* (Istanbul: Kubbealtı Neşriyatı 2000), p. 405.
844. Ken'an Rifâî, *Sohbetler* (Istanbul: Kubbealtı Neşriyatı 2000), p. 567.
845. Ken'an Rifâî, *Sohbetler* (Istanbul: Kubbealtı Neşriyatı 2000), p. 221.
846. Ken'an Rifâî, *Sohbetler* (Istanbul: Kubbealtı Neşriyatı 2000), p. 620.
847. Ken'an Rifâî, *Sohbetler* (Istanbul: Kubbealtı Neşriyatı 2000), p. 543.

God made a tree manifest in Paradise, gave Eve to Adam for wife and addressed them both, "Do not approach that tree, you would be among the wrongdoers." But what could Adam and Eve do, for beautiful God had made that tree the tree of love and just as He addressed Moses from that tree, saying, "I am your Lord!" He addressed Adam and Eve also. Thus intellect and thought left them and they approached the tree.[848]

• He brings to earth not the fire of lust but the fire of love. He disperses spiritual light and divine fragrance. In his freshness and aliveness there is the wisdom of the sacred Tuba Tree, and this freshness and aliveness is not like that of worldly life.

That arrived person takes those who want to partake of the scent he brings, those who awaken to the eternal life he brings, under his green wings like the giant leaves of the Tuba Tree. With that light he awakens those in the heedlessness of human nature and the darkness of the soul, and shows them the way leading to the eternal world.[849]

• Hizir bears a symbolic meaning in the pairs of contrary concepts that are fundamental to the thought of Ibn Arabi. In this context Ibn Arabi considers Hizir to be the contrary of Elijah and expresses the former as the state of expansion and the latter, constriction. Even if we can shed light on the relationship between Hizir and Elija that led Ibn Arabi to consider them two contrary names, we can only with difficulty make a guess as to the relationship between Hizir and expansion and Elijah and constriction. According to Ibn Arabi, one characteristic unites Hizir and Elijah: life. For God raised Elijah—who is Enoch—to a high level. He is alive in the present. Hizir also is given this continuous life. On the other hand, the Owner of the Time or the Axis aids travellers on the path or believers with several self-disclosures whose result he finds as state of expansion or constriction (the two results are the requisites of the two names Beauty and Majesty) in his self. The Axis conveys that aid in two ways: Elijah and Hizir. The former is connected to the state of constriction and the latter, expansion.[850]

---

848. Ken'an Rifâî, *Sohbetler* (Istanbul: Kubbealtı Neşriyatı 2000), pp. 466-467.
849. Ken'an Rifâî, *Şerhli Mesnevî-i Şerif* (Istanbul: Kubbealtı Neşriyatı 2000), p. 280.
850. Suad el-Hakîm, trans. Ekrem Demirli, *İbü'l-Arabî Sözlüğü* (Istanbul: Kabalcı Yayınevi 2005), pp. 286-287.

80TH VERSE

Constriction destroys and makes annihilated, conveys to annihilation (majesty). The Prophet conveys our heads to prostration with the sheriat. Expansion resurrects and makes be, removes sorrow and conveys to beauty. It conveys to green, in other words to Paradise. The meaning of God manifests in the green tree. The friend of God serves in this meaning. Here the friend is Hizir, and the station of prophethood is Elijah (Enoch).[851]

- "God is the Light of the heavens and the earth. The likeness of His Light is a niche, within which is a lamp. The lamp is in a glass. The glass is as a shining star, lit from a blessed olive tree neither of East nor West. Its oil would as if shine forth even if no fire touched it. He is Light upon Light. God guides to His Light whomever He will, and God sets forth likenesses for human beings. God knows all things truly" (24:35).

The meaning: That niche is the body of the friend of God. The olive oil is his or her pure heart, and God has a relation to that heart. For God has said, *"I who am God did not fit into the heavens and earth, I fit only into the heart of the believer."* From the reflection of the light of that lamp the body of the world is full of light, animate, alive and fresh. That light is not perceived, it is spiritual. It is unique and unqualified. That light shines from souls and intellects. It passes from souls and intellects to animals, and from animals and growing things onto inanimate things in order to bring about life. All of these lights are the effects and reflections of that light. Thus a friend of God who is subsistent with God and God's vicegerent (*halife*) is the owner of true life. All things subsisting in the heavens and earth are alive with the reflection of his or her light. Life has been given to them as a loan.

"Lit from an olive tree" (24:35). The olive oil of that lamp, which is the spirit and heart of the friend, is bright before being the Axis and attaining perfection. When he or she reaches the Beloved and the part is bound to the whole, when the drop returns to the sea, there is light upon light. For if that light had no part or intimate, he or she would not have become bound to that light. The movement of parts is always toward their own wholes. Nothing but light comes upon light.[852]

---

851. Compiler's note.

852. Sultan Veled, trans. Meliha Anbarcıoğlu, *Maarif* (Konya: Altunarı Ofset 2002), pp. 57-60.

- In the Quran (24:35) God the Exalted gives a likeness of the light of His Essence and conveyed the human essence in an imaginative way as Niche, Lamp and Glass. That likeness of the Essence consists of the human form. What is intended by "Niche" is the human breast. What is intended by "Glass" is the human heart. What is intended by "Lamp" is the human secret. What is intended by the blessed tree in the verse is belief in the Unseen. That Unseen is the manifestation of God the Truth as God in the form of creation. This is faith in the Unseen. What is intended by the olive is absolute truth. For it can be said that absolute truth is neither completely God in every aspect, nor is it completely creation in every aspect. The tree of faith is not "Eastern," in other words, its does not require declaration of His absolute incomparability in such a way as to negate similarity. Still, it is not "Western" either. For it does not consist in absolute likness negating incomparability. It is a secret and truth obtained by being pressed between the outer rind of likeness and the essence of incomparability. And for the olive oil, which consists of certain knowledge, to be lit and shine forth light although no fire touches it follows absolutely. Thus the darkness of the olive oil is removed by its own light. For it is light upon light, such that evident light and the similitude light of the eye is the light connected with the one that is the result of the light of incomparability and the light beyond both of them that consists of the light of faith.[853]

- They call out to the spirits circling around them, "I am a spirit burning and illuminated by love! If there are those who wish to burn with the same love, let them come, let them light the caves of their hearts in the hearth of my heart and awake with that fire and run to burn with that fire. Let them not forget that their own hearts too actually have the preparedness to run towards the good and beautiful. Every heart is a cave having the capacity to catch fire. Every heart is a wing in the way of God.[854]

- According to *"I was a hidden treasure and I loved to be known,"* love is an attribute of God the Truth.[855]

---

853. Abdü'l-kerîm b. İbrahim el-Cîlî, trans. Seyyid Hüseyin Fevzî Paşa, *İnsan-ı Kâmil* (Istanbul: Kitsan Yayınları), pp. 174-175.
854. Ken'an Rifâî, *Şerhli Mesnevî-i Şerif* (Istanbul: Kubbealtı Neşriyatı 2000), p. 242.
855. Ken'an Rifâî, *Sohbetler* (Istanbul: Kubbealtı Neşriyatı 2000), p. 511.

80th Verse

- "The tree of the universe" (*kâinat ağacı*) rose up for His love, overflowed and danced. Then those with it went into action. All of them, colors and festivals... they flew... they flew. All of them were one spark of His light.[856]

---

856. Muhyiddîn İbnül-Arabî, trans. Abdülkâdir Akçiçek, *Şeceretü'l-Kevn-Üstün İnsan* (Istanbul: Bahar Yayınları 2000), p. 11.

81. Is not He who created the heavens and earth able to create the like? Yes indeed, He is the Creator, the All-Knowing.

'A wa laysa'l-ladhī khalaqa's-samāwāti wa'l-'arḍa biqādirin 'alā 'an yakhluqa mithlahum balā wa huwa'l-khallāqu'l-'alīm.

- **The Creator** is the one whose creative activity is continuous and who continually brings about new dimensions in what He creates. The one whose intensity and variety in creative activity cannot be tracked.[857]

- The earth is the realm of corruption, of the attributes of creatures in contrast to the attributes of God the Truth's, of lowliness contrary to sublimity, that is the opposite of the orderly realm (*the heavens*).

   God has said, "*God created the heavens, the earth and the things in between of clay.*" The heavens are the sublime realms, and earth is the lowly realms. The heavens are the realm of improvement and the earth is the realm of corruption. The heavens describe loftiness, and the earth, lowliness.[858]

- Creation is not from nothing. The science of creation moves from being toward exterior being. In the thought of Ibn Arabi, to say God is the Creator means God's bringing out or making manifest the fixed entities (*a'yân-ı sâbite*) to exterior-sensible being. Only God can do this; no creature's will can make fixed entities manifest. God has not

---

857. Yaşar Nuri Öztürk, trans., *Kuran-ı Kerîm Meâli* (Istanbul: Hürriyet Ofset Matbaacılık 1994), p. 580.

858. Suad el-Hakîm, trans. Ekrem Demirli, *İbü'l-Arabî Sözlüğü* (Istanbul: Kabalcı Yayınevi 2005), pp. 78-79.

realized in a specific time, on the contrary, that is an action continuous in every breath. God the continuously and eternally Creator; the world is what is continuously and eternally not.

Ibn Arabi regards the term "creative activity" (*halk*) from four vantage points:

> 1. *Halk* = to give existence to (*icat*). For the divine will to intervene in the thing it wants to bring forth.
> 2. *Halk* = to determine (*takdir*). The determining of the time for bringing forth the being of what is possible.
> 3. *Halk* = the act of creating.
> 4. *Halk* = noun. In other words, *halk* is the name of the created thing, and is one of two aspects (*veçh*): *Hak* (God the Truth) and *halk* (created).[859]

- The form of Moses's being thrown into the sea inside a coffin was in appearance death. But for him it was, manifestly and unmanifestly, salvation from death. Thus Moses was raised to life as people are with knowledge raised from the death of ignorance. Just as God said, "*That one who was dead,*" in other words, dead with ignorance, "*We raised to life,*" in other words, We raised to life with knowledge, "*And We bestowed upon him a light such that with it he walks among the people.*" That light is the light of guidance.[860]

- What is intended by "He created" is to say that He manifested from spiritual existence into formal existence.[861]

- If all bodies passed away, there would be for Him neither nothingness nor decrease. If the heavens should fall and the earth collapse, He would suffer no injury. However many living creatures may die, whatever the state of that attributed (*izafî*) spirit, He would be continuous and subsistent in that state.[862]

---

859. Suad el-Hakîm, trans. Ekrem Demirli, *İbü'l-Arabî Sözlüğü* (Istanbul: Kabalcı Yayınevi 2005), p. 254.

860. Muhyiddîn İbnü'l-Arabî, trans. Nuri Gençosman, *Fusûs'l-Hikem* (Istanbul: Kırkambar Kitaplığı n.d.), p. 297.

861. Ken'an Rifâî, *Sohbetler* (Istanbul: Kubbealtı Neşriyatı 2000), p. 252.

862. Muhyiddîn İbnü'l-Arabî, trans. İsmail Hakkı Bursevî, *Özün Özü* (Istanbul: Rahmet Yayınları n.d.), pp. 16-17.

81th Verse

- *"Each day He is upon some task."* Just as there is no end to the Essence and attributes of God, neither is there an end to the realms. For the realms are the sites of manifestation of the names and attributes. Since the One manifesting is infinite, the sites of manifestion too must be infinite.[863]

- God the Truth the Exalted created being, but in Himself (*haddi zatında*) God the Truth created His being. God is the Creator of every thing; there is no other Creator but Him. Even what is manifest in the servants' belief is among the totality of things God the Truth created, so that God the Truth created that too. God the Truth shows face in the mirror of the heart according to the servant's imagination, belief, and understanding.

  He makes being manifest according to the opinion and thought of the thinking servant.

  God the Truth created this world and Adam, and made them the mirror of His own being. He sees and watches His reflection in the mirror of the world and His self in the mirror of Adam.

  He made His essence manifest in the form of a mirror. In that mirror he presented His beauty to His essence. Thus He became the Looking. Seeing His own beauty, He fell in love. He was in awe, and he began to beg. On the other hand, He became beloved, and began witholding and showing Himself. He presented His own beauty to Himself and self-disclosed. Here the one looking, the one looked at, and the mirror are one thing.[864]

- The mirror of all this is the Perfect Human Being, the mirror displaying divine being, the universe. The Perfect Human Being is in the site of self-disclosure of God the Truth in absolute form, such that He is accepted from whatever direction He self-discloses.[865]

---

863. Muhyiddîn İbnü'l-Arabî, trans. İsmail Hakkı Bursevî, *Özün Özü* (Istanbul: Rahmet Yayınları n.d.), p. 21.

864. Muhyiddîn İbnü'l-Arabî, trans. İsmail Hakkı Bursevî, *Özün Özü* (Istanbul: Rahmet Yayınları n.d.), p. 56.

865. Muhyiddîn İbnü'l-Arabî, trans. İsmail Hakkı Bursevî, *Özün Özü* (Istanbul: Rahmet Yayınları n.d.), pp. 30-31.

82. Truly His command when He wills a thing is "Be!" and it is.

'Innamā 'amruhu 'idha 'arāda shay'an yaqūla lahu kun fayakūn.

- When His will is assigned to the creation of a thing, God the Exalted's command is to make the assignation of will incumbent upon only that thing once and the being of that thing without delay.[866]

- Engendering (*tekvin*) is among the attributes of God. When God intends a thing, He simply says to it "Be," and that thing immediately comes to be. According to the Gracious Quran, God the Truth creates with the command *"kun"* [be]. That word is the word expressing God's act of creating. *"The words of God are never exhausted"* (18:109) [sic]. For creating (*hallâkiyet*) is God's most evident quality.

That word occurs also in the Bible. But there it occurs in the form of the third person imperative. Let us read these sentences from Genesis 1: "And God said, 'Let there be light,' and there was light... And God said, 'Let there be a firmament in the midst of the waters, and let it divide the waters from the waters.' ... And God said, 'Let there be lights in the firmament of the heaven to divide the day from the night; and let them be for signs, and for seasons, and for days, and years.'" How worthy it is of God on high, who is dominant over everything, who holds in His hand disposal over the property of everything, whose is the creation and the command (7:54), for those words to be in the imperative. For since God's sheriat commands also occur in the imperative, this mood is certainly the most appropriate for God's creative and commanding action. Hazret

---

[866]. Kemâlüddin Abdürrezzak Kâşâniyyüs Semerkandî, trans. Ali Rıza Doksanyedi, ed. M. Vehbi Güloğlu, *Te'vilât-ı Kâşâniyye* (Ankara Kadıoğlu Matbaası 1988), vol. 3, p. 15.

Jesus is called *"the Word of God"* because he is the self-disclosure of such a command of His. For God is not forced by causes, He is the cause of causes. Just as God is the Creator of all things, He is also the Creator of causes. When He wishes, He makes them ineffective and changes them. No thing can restrict Him, every thing is restricted by His universal will and submitted to Him.

The word occurs in the Quran eight times in the meaning of absolute creation and without a passive form. The first time is in the forty-first (according to the sequence of revelation) chapter, Ya-Sin. *"Truly His command when He wills a thing is 'Be!' and it is"* (82). The second is in the forty-fourth (according to the sequence of revelation) chapter: *"It is not for God to take a child. He is exalted beyond that. When He decrees a matter, He says to it 'Be!' and it is"* (19:35) [sic]. That when God will bring forth a thing He creates it in the shortest time expresses that it is from His glory. Other verses indicate approximately the same meaning (3:47,59) (6:73) (2:117) (16:40) (40:68).[867]

- Whenever God commands a thing, saying "Be!" that thing conforms to the command to make itself be, and brings itself to be. Thus God has attributed creation to the "thing." If that thing were not prepared in itself for creation, it would not be able to attain being when it heard the command "Be!" The ability to be prepared for that creation that is established and hidden in that thing comes about by the Most Sacred Grace (*Feyz-i Akdes*), in other words, the self-disclosure arriving form the realm of Essence.

Divine grace is of two parts. The first is the "Most Sacred Grace," and the other is the "Sacred Grace." With the first come to be all the realities and their fundamental preparedness at the level of knowledge. With the second, the exterior being of those realities in constituted with the things necessary for them to project themselves as beings in the world.

How does it happen that these things, completely naught in their states of not-being prior to the being of a thing, display the ability to conform to the command "Be"? How is it possible for a thing to come to be when its being is dependent upon a thing other than itself? One

---

[867]. Veli Ulutürk, *Kur'an-ı Kerîm'de Yaratma Kavramı* (Istanbul: İnsan Yayınları 1995), pp. 49-51.

82TH VERSE

can answer this question by saying that the being of these things was in the knowledge-being at the level of completely divine knowledge in eternity without beginning and eternity without end. Even though they were not with respect to their being made exterior. Thus they were as knowlege in a form prepared for the command "Be!" and for "becoming."[868]

• God created the world from Himself, His will, and His word. If not for these three things—the Essence, the will that is nothing other than God the Truth's bearing toward a thing's coming to be, and the command "Be!" on the throne of that bearing—nothing would come to be. For the world to be constituted by these three things is not contrary to unification. The Essence is one. What displays variety are relations. And just so, He says, *"When We wish a thing to be, We say to it 'Be'and it is."* Here God is indicating the above three things. These three things exist in everything that has been made to be, of course in correspondence to the three things in what makes itself be. The first of those correspondences is the fixed Essence of that thing at the level of God's knowledge, the second is to listen to the Lord's command, and the third is to conform to His command.[869]

• Thus the ternate oneness of the Creator has met with the ternate oneness of the created. In the coming to be of the created thing from not-being its fixed Essence conforms to the the Essence that gives existence to it, its hearing that address conforms to the Creator's will, and because its acceptance of being, conforming to the Creator's command for it to be, corresponds to God the Truth's command "kun," that thing has come to be. If that thing did not have the faculty of being in its self corresponding to God's command "Be!" it could not have been created. Thus when that thing was not, and heard the command of creation, it created itself. According to this explanation, God the Truth has established that the work falling to Him is only to command the thing He will create. Just as when a commander tells

---

868. İsmâil Rusûhî Ankaravî, ed. İlhan Kutluer, *Nakşel-FüsusŞerhi* (Istanbul: Ribat Yayınları n.d.), pp. 70-71.

869. İsmâil Rusûhî Ankaravî, ed. İlhan Kutluer, *Nakşel-FüsusŞerhi* (Istanbul: Ribat Yayınları n.d.), pp. 88-89.

his slave, who is afraid of him and cannot rebel against him, to get up, the slave conforms to his command and immediately gets up. In the modality of this getting up there is nothing but his master's having commanded him. The getting up is not the action of the master but only the action of the slave.

Thus the foundation of creation is ternate, in other words, dependent upon the three principles that will and command are from God the Truth, and the modality of being from the created.[870]

- Beings are all of them the words of God who has no end. For they have come to be from *Kun*, the command "Be." *Kun* is God's word. Thus with respect to its existing in Him, can the word be attributed to God? Even if it is attributed, its inner face cannot be known. Or did the whatness of God the Truth descend into a form called *"kun"*? If so, because of His descending into that form and appearing there, the word *kun* is realized for that form. In this regard some of the gnostics are on one side and others on another. And some are bewildred and do not know. This is a matter that can only be understood by way of tasting. Just as the moment Bayazid Bistami blew upon an ant he had killed, it came to life. He knew who it was that he blew with and blew in that way. Thus he attained Jesus's tasting and witnessing. As for spiritual resurrection, that is with knowledge. At the same time, life is the life belonging to God's essence, knowledge and light, of which God has said, *"Is that person dead, that We resurrected him and gave him a light, so that he walks among the people with its light."* Thus every gnostic who brings a dead person to life with the knowledge of God and the knowledge of life in a particular aspect, resurrects him with knowledge, and gives him such a torch that he walks with it among the people, in other words, among those who resemble himself in form.[871]

- Resurrection is of two kinds. One is manifest, and the other is spiritual. The dictionary meaning of "resurrection" (*ba's*) is "to detach." In formal resurrection, people enter the grave after natural

---

870. Muhyiddîn İbnü'l-Arabî, trans. Nuri Gençosman, *Fusûs'l-Hikem* (Istanbul: Kırkambar Kitaplığı n.d.), pp. 144-145.

871. Muhyiddîn İbnü'l-Arabî, trans. Nuri Gençosman, *Fusûs'l-Hikem* (Istanbul: İstanbul Kitabevi Yayınları 1981), p. 126.

82th Verse

death and remain buried in the grave for a long while, after which their bodies are resurrected and gathered together for Judgment. Thus the secret and truth of Resurrection comes into manifestation and realities become clear and evident to all on that Day.

And there is also spiritual resurrection in which people die a voluntary death and become annihilated in God the Truth and, freed from the restriction of metaphorical being, remain buried in the lights of Essence for a long while, after which God the Truth, as required by the phrase, "Come forth with My attributes, those who see you, see Me," resurrects and brings them forth, qualified by the attributes of God, from the level of annihilation to subsistence in God, in other words, from not-being to the degree of being with God. And at that level they are subsistent with the subsistence of God and, resurrected with Lordly life, whatever they do, they do with God the Truth. At that level, just as they do not see the things as other than God, they do not see God as other than the things. Perhaps they see creation as subsistent with God, and see God manfiest and self-disclosed in the mirror of all things and creatures.

They see a plurality that is in reality unity itself. They see a unity that is found showing itself in the plurality of things. Just as what appears manifest to them at that level is the non-manifest itself and with respect to the manifestation of the non-manifest, appears the same as the manifest, so does the last appear to be the same as the first and the first the same as the last. At that level they say, "The First is the Last, the Last is the First. The manifest is the non-manifest and the non-manifest is the manifest!"

The saying of the Greatest Shaykh [Ibn Arabi], "Exalted be Him who manifests the things and He is the same as them," and that of Hazret Ali, "Should death raise the covering from my eyes, I will not see more than what I have seen in this world!" confirm the same meaning.

As Hazret Niyazi [Misri] said:

There's nothing clearer than God
He is hidden from the eyeless

In sum, the creatures and this entire world of creation is like a veil covering God the Truth's unbounded beauty. As Hazret Abu Bakr said when that veil was lifted, "I've seen nothing that I would not see in God in it," one only becomes possessed of vision by dying before dying.[872]

• Aspirants do not attain their desire as long as they do not abandon self and habits and all neither commanded nor forbidden passions and the rest. Once that is attained, God the Truth causes aspirants to have disposal in their own beings and the realms of their beings, and then in unbounded creation. After that, their commands are with God's commands and if they say to a thing, "*Kun*," it is.[873]

• I looked upon creation and how it was brought to be, upon what is hidden and how it is registered and I saw that all of creation is a tree. The origin of the light of that tree is the seed of *kun*. Thus from the substance of [the letter] K (*Kaf*) two different meanings have come forth. One is "the k of perfection (*kemal*). *"Today I have perfected your religion for you"* (5:3). The other is the k of misbelief (*küfür*). *"Among them there were some who believed, and among them were some who disbelieved"* (2:253). Next the substance of N (*Nun*) come forth: the N of indeterminacy and the N of determinacy. When God caused them to manifest from not-being according to the judgment of His will, He scattered upon them of His light and fastened His eyes upon the tree of becoming which that light struck and which came forth from the seed of *kun*. Thus in the secret of His K shone the exemplar (*timsal*) of the expression *"You are the best community"* (3:110). And by the explication of N the verse *"Whoever's heart God opens to Islam, he is upon a light from his Lord"* (39:22) [sic] becomes understandable. As for the person that light misses, it is desired that the meaning intended by the letter *kun* be explained, and he errs in the syllables of the letter. Then he looks at the likeness of the word *kun* and supposes that it is the N of indeterminacy with the K of misbelief. Thus he becomes a disbeliever. Each created person's share of the word *Kun* is as much as what is known of its syllables. While one person recognizes the K of perfection and the N of determinacy, another recognizes the K of misbelief and the N of indeterminacy.

---

872. Ken'an Rifâî, *Sohbetler* (Istanbul: Kubbealtı Neşriyatı 2000), pp. 248-249.
873. From Ken'an Rifâî's notes on Ahmet er-Rifâî, p. 49.

82TH VERSE

Kun indicates two hands: according to Ibn Arabi, the two hands under discussion express the attributes of activity and passivity or the levels of necessity and possibility.[874]

- Each person's witnessing is different. In other words, witnessing with regard to the command *Kun*. In other words, witnessing of [the Arabic letters] *Kaf* and *Nun*. One looks and witnesses perfection in the *Kaf* of perfection (*kemaliyet*) and gnosis in the *Nun* of light (*nur*). Another sees the *Kaf* of misbelief (*küfür*) and the *Nun* of strangeness (*nekre*).[875]

- *"His command when He wills a thing is "Be!" and it is."* The first step on the stairway rising to this subtlety is the secret of the sheriat and reality. The second is the red spell lodged in the power of imagination and depiction. It is hidden in God the Truth underneath the covering of vain things and lies. It is the ascension of loss. It is the path of Satan. It takes one as far as the level of abandonment. *"...like a mirage upon a desert plain which a thirsty man thinks is water until when he comes to it, he finds nothing"* (24:39). The water he thinks is "Light" turns out to be fire. The mansion scatters death. But, despite all this, if he turns back from misbelief, God takes him by the hand; if He brings him to the subtlety he has confirmed, in this meaning he ascends to the second ascension and finds God by his side. That is when he knows God's mansion, and in the station of fidelity he understands the state diverging from the path of vanity. In sum, if a person conforms his wayfaring to the path described, if he enters into the command of divine judgment, he will have completed his own account. But if he neglects that situation and... Then the smoke of that fire reaches the nose of the sublime spirit. Thus he kills it too, so that afterwards he will no longer be able to find the path of guidance. Then he cannot understand the meaning of the Mother of the Book (*the Gracious Quran*). After that, all his encounters are from the meanings of [God's] Beauty. Or from works of the perfect type. With these he becomes

---

[874]. Suad el-Hakîm, trans. Ekrem Demirli, *İbü'l-Arabî Sözlüğü* (Istanbul: Kabalcı Yayınevi 2005), pp. 438-439.

[875]. Muhyiddîn İbnül-Arabî, trans. Abdülkâdir Akçiçek, *Şeceretü'l-Kevn-Üstün İnsan* (Istanbul: Bahar Yayınları 2000), pp. 19-20.

lost. However many impossible things may find manifestation in him in that state, still his return to God the Truth is impossible. The condition of such people is described in the gracious verse, *"Those whose effort is lost in the life of this world, while they think they are doing good"* (18:104).[876]

• God the Exalted's command is between (*Kaf* and *Nun*, *Kun*). In some, God self-discloses with the attribute of (*Mercy*). This happens in the following way: when God the Exalted sets up His throne of Lordliness for the servant, the servant occupies it; and the throne of power is set before him. At that time His mercy spreads through the beings and includes them. That is when he becomes bound to the throne of Essence. The attributes find their resurrection. In other words, he too is finally *Sacred of Essence and subsistent of attribute*.[877]

• The Sacred Spirit is exalted beyond being comprised by the command "*Kun*" (6:73)... Furthermore we can never say of it, "It is creature!" For it is a face among the special faces of God the Truth, and subsistent with that face.[878]

• The "fixed entities" are comprised by the word *Kun*.

The "fixed entities" are only comprised by the word (*Kun*) at the time when they are given existence.

But at his sublime summit and in His knowledge of entification the word "engendering" (*tekvin*) does not comprise the "fixed entities." According to this meaning, the fixed entities are God the Truth, not the creation.

For the creation consists in what comes under the word (*Kun*), while the fixed entities are not newly arrived in divine knowledge with that quality. On the contrary, they are included in newly arrived things by the principle of adherence. The reason for that is the need

---

876. Abdü'l-kerîm b. İbrahim el-Cîlî, trans. Seyyid Hüseyin Fevzî Paşa, *İnsan-ı Kâmil* (Istanbul: Kitsan Yayınları), vol. 2, pp. 132-134.

877. Abdü'l-kerîm b. İbrahim el-Cîlî, trans. Seyyid Hüseyin Fevzî Paşa, *İnsan-ı Kâmil* (Istanbul: Kitsan Yayınları), vol. 2, p. 213.

878. Abdü'l-kerîm b. İbrahim el-Cîlî, trans. Seyyid Hüseyin Fevzî Paşa, *İnsan-ı Kâmil* (Istanbul: Kitsan Yayınları), vol. 2, p. 47.

82TH VERSE

for the prior that newly arrived beings in the fixed entities' own essences have.[879]

• Pure friendship (*hullet*) is for the servant to be friend to sublime God and commune with Him, and his communion with Him is so strong that the traces of this communion and friendship are manifest in all the parts of his body.With God's command *"Kun"* the things become constituted for him and drive away his illnesses and infirmities. His hands perform miracles, his feet walk on empty space, and distances become short for him. As a result, each of the forms takes form in its entire stature. What is described here is the meaning of the following hadith: *"My servant approaches me with superogatory works until I love him. When I love him, I become his ear and he hears with it. I beocme his eye and he sees with it. I become his tongue and he speaks with it. I become his foot and he walks with it."* And that servant is finally the part of God the Truth. In other words, His's lights have mixed into his being. In sum he has become for God a friend (*dost*).[880]

• Just as words and phrases manifest by breath and letters being put forth from the mouth, all these visible and existing things are the words of God.

God's friends are sublime, high words and the things are lowly, base words, and all of them have manifested from one command (*kun*). Whatever the origin of a thing, that is its end also. For the beginning is the end, and the end is the beginning.[881]

• None of the existing things came into manifestation from nothing. They all consist in a transformation of essence. What is intended by, "It came from nothing," is to say that while His essence was hidden from His essence it came forth with His wish. For neither can existence become nonexistence nor can nonexistence become existence. The worlds manifested thanks to the transformaiton that came

---

879. Abdü'l-kerîm b. İbrahim el-Cîlî, trans. Seyyid Hüseyin Fevzî Paşa, *İnsan-ı Kâmil* (Istanbul: Kitsan Yayınları), vol. 2, p. 351.
880. Abdü'l-kerîm b. İbrahim el-Cîlî, trans. Seyyid Hüseyin Fevzî Paşa, *İnsan-ı Kâmil* (Istanbul: Kitsan Yayınları), vol. 2, p. 458.
881. Ken'an Rifâî, *Sohbetler* (Istanbul: Kubbealtı Neşriyatı 2000), p. 211.

about from the sea of essence. Let us think of one sea, for example, and another such that one flows into the other, and from that come to be a third, and later a fourth; thus four seas manifest. These things being described are a light. A new form emerges in every transformation. For the gnostics whatever was before is still there now. All of the worlds described are one sea of light; it rolls in waves continuously and new self-disclosures occur one after another. According to the rule, *"Every moment He is at a task,"* that divine wave comes from the Essence, and goes again to the Essence. *"Every thing comes from Him, and returns to Him again." "All things return to Him."* The wave of that sea is called what is other than God (*the world*). The sea and the beginningless and eternal waves are considered to be newly arrived things.

First and last being is God the Truth's. The apparently other than God is considered to be in unbounded being. All existing things come to manifestation from unbounded Essence. If the self-disclosure that is the spirit of that being were cut off for a moment, all would at that moment be buried in not-being.[882]

- Sublime and peerless God desired to see the forms of His countless beautiful names in the realm of fixed entities, and by that seeing to reveal His secret to Himself. God wished to see his own entity (*kendi aynını*) in the world of aggregate being that longs for His command because it is qualified by existence.

Thus the beginning and end of every command is also from Him. Just as all being begins from Him, so does it return to Him. The command made it necessary that the mirror called the world should be silvered. And Adam became the silvering and spirit of that mirror.[883]

- *Over not-beings that have nor eye nor ear*
He recites spells and they start to rise and stir

Because of his spells, quickly those not-beings
Rush head over heels to come into being

---

882. Muhyiddîn İbnü'l-Arabî, trans. İsmail Hakkı Bursevî, *Özün Özü* (Istanbul: Rahmet Yayınları n.d.), p. 25.

883. Muhyiddîn İbnü'l-Arabî, trans. Nuri Gençosman, *Fusûs'l-Hikem* (Istanbul: İstanbul Kitabevi Yayınları 1981), pp. 3-4.

82TH VERSE

Then when He reads a spell over a being
It gallops off right away to not-being

He spoke in the rose's ear and made it gay
He spoke to the stone and made it mined agate

He gave body a sign making it spirit
He spoke to the sun and made it radiant

He puts something frightful in its ear and then
Eclipses fall upon the face of the sun

What did God recite in the ear of the cloud
That like a waterskin its eye poured tears down

What did God recite in the ear of the earth
That it grew watchful and will not say a word

Whoever's confounded in uncertainty
God has spoken in his ear a mystery

So as to imprison him in two fancies
Shall I do what he said, or the contrary?

And the preference for one side is from God too
And from there he makes the choice between the two[884]

- "His command when He wills a thing is 'Be!' and it is." All of His actions are beautiful, wise and beneficial. But He has hidden from His servants what the beneficial things are. What befits those in a state of acceptance and submission is to know that the measuring out is from God, to perform His commands, to avoid what is forbidden and perform worship, to not pretend to Lordliness, to not struggle against and war with fate, and avoid questions such as "Why?" "How?" and "When?"

Those meanings rely upon this noble hadith relatied from Ibn Abbas (r.a.):

"I was riding behind the saddle of God's Messenger (s.a.s.). He turned toward me and said, 'Preserve (the limits of) God, that God should protect

---

884. Şefik Can, *Konularına göre açıklamalı Mesnevi Tercümesi* (Istanbul: Ötüken Neşriyat 1997), vols. 1-2, p. 103 [vol. 1, vs. 1448-1458].

and watch over you. When you wish something, wish for it from your Lord. When you need something, call on your Lord for help. The Pen has written everything that will come to be. Even if all creatures should gather to help you, if God has not determined a thing, they will not be able to help you. And if they all gather and wish to cause harm, if God has not determined it, they will not be able to harm you. Try to act toward you Lord with righteousness and certainty. If you cannot succeed in that, there is great blessing and benefit in being patient. Be patient. Success is obtained with patience. Salvation is reached through trials. Along with difficulty there is ease."[885]

- "*Who created* (the first phase of creation), *then proportioned* (the second phase of creation) " (87:2). "*Who measured out* (the third phase of creation)."

"*And then guided*" (87:3).[886]

- As to the divine command, it is of two parts. The first type is commands through an instrument that are brought by means of prophets and messengers and occur in the imperative, saying, "Do such and such." They are also called "affirmative commands" and "obligatory commands," as in the imperative related to making necessary and incumbent, such as "Perform prayer," "Give alms." The second type is direct commands, in other words, without the intermediary of a prophet. These commands are called creative (*icadî*) or voluntary, because they are related to God's creating and wishing something to be. These are commands in the beginningless Tablet of Decree, and the command *kun*, "be," in this verse indicates that meaning: "*His command when He wills a thing is Be! and it is.*" It is unthinkable to act contrary to this type of command, for God's decree accepts no alteration. But it is possible to think of not conforming to commands brought by means of messengers. If commands brought through intermediaries are not appropriate to voluntary commands, it is possible to act contrary to them. But if the command brought by an intermediary is appropriate to the voluntary command, not to conform to it is unthinkable. Everyone and everything is obliged to submit to that command. Relying upon that we may say that proph-

---

885. Abdülkadir Geylânî, *Fütûhu'l Ğayb* (Istanbul: Sinan Yayınları 1996), p. 121.
886. Halûk Nurbaki, *Yâ-Sîn Sûresi Yorumu* (Istanbul: Damla Yayınevi 1999), p. 105.

82TH VERSE

ets, messengers and their inheritors the scholars are the bearers of commands appropriate to divine commands.

The one charged with performing the command without intermediary, especially the command *kun*, "be," is the one who "is" (*kâin*), not the existent (*mevcut*), in other words, not one whose process of creation is completed. The only things commanded with the creative kind of command are the fixed realities of the things called the fixed entities. For they "are" (*kâin*) and these forms are God's knowledge. Thus the existents, in other words, the things that have come out from God's knowledge onto the plan of being, have been commanded with that command. Briefly, because existent things have already been made to be, have already been given existence, they were commanded not with creative but obligatory and affirmative commands. God is the one who knows best.[887]

- Thus without doubt the world consists of a result. In other words, the result of God the Truth's Essence, will, and command "Be!"[888]

- The body with head does not know the secret of the command "Be!" It is those without heads who know *Kaf* and *Nun*.[889]

- That is the sum of the command "Be!" Prostate toward it that you may hear "God is great" from your own self, your own essence.[890]

---

887. İsmâil Rusûhî Ankaravî, ed. İlhan Kutluer, *Nakşel-FüsusŞerhi* (Istanbul: Ribat Yayınları n.d.), pp. 75-76.
888. İsmâil Rusûhî Ankaravî, ed. İlhan Kutluer, *Nakşel-FüsusŞerhi* (Istanbul: Ribat Yayınları n.d.), p. 90.
889. Mevlânâ Celâleddin Rûmî, ed. Abdülbâkî Gölpınarlı, *Divân-ı Kebîr* (Ankara: T.C. Kültür Bakanlığı 2000), vol. 2, vs. 943.
890. Mevlânâ Celâleddin Rûmî, ed. Abdülbâkî Gölpınarlı, *Divân-ı Kebîr* (Ankara: T.C. Kültür Bakanlığı 2000), vol. 2, vs. 679.

83. So glory be to Him in whose hand is the sovereignty of each thing, and to Him you will be returned.

Fasubḥāna'l-ladhī biyadihi malakūtu kulli shay'in wa 'ilayhi turja'ūn.

The sovereignty (*the spirit or reality appropriate to its own level*) of every single thing is, when it is the time of the self and the acts of the Essence in whose hand is the influence managing that thing and the faculty and power to do so, incomparable with beings and bodies and free of powerlessness, sublime and sacred. And you return to Him only annihilated in Him and with the end in Him. God the Exalted is All-knowing.[891]

- Sovereignty (*melekut*) is the extreme modality of Kingdom (*mülk*). It means the secrets of ruling with perfect authority.[892]

- The Realm of Sovereignty can also be described as the level of the angels. It is also called the Realm of Analogy, the Realm of Imagination, primeness, the Second Entification, the Second Self-Disclosure, the Realm of Command, the Lote Tree Limit (*the point reached at last in the journey, actions and knowledge of all aspirants*), and the Realm of the Lesser Barzakh.[893]

---

891. Kemâlüddin Abdürrezzak Kâşâniyyüs Semerkandî, trans. Ali Rıza Doksanyedi, ed. M. Vehbi Güloğlu, *Te'vilât-ı Kâşâniyye* (Ankara Kadıoğlu Matbaası 1988), vol. 3, p. 15.

892. Elmalılı M. Hamdi Yazır, *Hak Dini Kur'an Dili* (Istanbul: Feza Gazetecilik 1992), vol. 6, p. 426.

893. Muhyiddîn İbnü'l-Arabî, trans. İsmail Hakkı Bursevî, *Özün Özü* (Istanbul: Rahmet Yayınları n.d.), p. 23.

- The distinction between kingdom (*mülk*) and sovreignty (*melekut*) is not a distinction put forth by tasavvuf. It exists in almost all mystical systems. The distinction is found in a precise way in the Gospels. Hazret Jesus said, "*Except a man be born again, he cannot enter the kingdom of heaven.*" The Quran clearly gives place to the term sovereignty. "*We showed Abraham the sovreignty of the heavens and earth so that he might be among those with certain knowledge*" (6:75).

What is sovereignty, what is kingdom? Kingdom and sovereignty are the outside and inside of the same being, its rind and kernal. Kingdom is the manifest aspect of creation, and sovereignty the non-manifest. So when sovereighty and kingdom are mentioned the same being comes to mind. And just so, the Quran clearly states that everything has a sovereignty: "*How sublime is the glory of God who has in His hand the sovereignty of every thing.*" Human beings also have kingdom and sovereignty. Their kingdom is their form, their body, their matter; their sovereignty is their inner faculties, their meaning.

The Realm of Kingdom takes the name "manifest" and means the knowledge not belonging to God's Essence. The non-manifest is its opposite and indicates the true knowledge belonging to God. Hazret Abu Bakr indicated that knowledge by saying, "O the point of perfection of the knowledge belonging to the Essence, God who is not to know!" It is said: "God is Manifest with His signs, and Non-Manifest with His Essence." "God is Manifest, for He encircles the things and rules them; He is Non-Manifest, for He is beyond being encircled." Hazret Ali touches upon this truth: "He self-disclosed so that the servants should not see Him, and showed Himself to them without self-disclosing to them."

So the knowledge belonging to God's Essence is connected with the Realm of Sovereignty. The Realm of Sovereignty is not a realm that can be distinguished by our sense organs. The sense organs can only distinguish the Realm of Kingdom. In order to be able to see the Realm of Sovereignty one must have a heart's eye, in other words, interior vision. A separate training and effort is needed in order to know that realm. According to statements by Hazret Jesus and Shihabuddin Suhravardi, one has to be born again. Suhravardi says that with the first birth one enters the Realm of Kingdom. In order to enter the Realm of Sovereignty we must be born a second time. Thus the connection between entry to the Realm of Sovereignty and wayfaring (*sülük*), in other words, training in tasavvuf, is obvious. In order to bring vision into a working state it may be necessary to rise in wayfaring or even complete wayfaring. That is why the purification acquired at the end of wayfaring and the passage to Sovereignty are events bound up with one another. Muhammed ibn Hasan el-Halveti says, "The first level of annihilation is for the servant to begin to see the Realm of Sovereignty with the heart's eye. The spirit that passes the Realm of Sovereignty transfers to the Realm of Domination and the Realm of Sovereignty becomes his Realm of Witness.[894]

- It is said that those who are not born twice cannot go beyond Sovereignty and the heavens. The first birth is known to all, birth from a mother. The second birth is voluntary death. Those who die a natural death cannot be born of Mother Nature a second time. Those who die a natural death usually remain as the four elements; they cannot go further. It is said in the noble hadith, *"Die with your will, and find life with felicity!"*[895]

- On the Day of Judgment, the disbelievers will say, "O my Lord, you killed us twice. First You brought us into the world with dead hearts, and then the time of death came and killed us with the natural death."

And the lovers will say, "O my Lord, You brought us to life twice. One was when we were separated from our mother's womb, and the other was when You killed us from ourselves and resurrected us with You."

It is Hazret Jesus's saying that, *"Whoever does not die twice cannot pass sovereignty and the heavens."* That is why the life lived by dervishes, intoxicated with divine scents and freed from the ugliness and weight of their selves, is certainly in peace of mind, comfort and happiness.[896]

---

894. Yaşar Nuri Öztürk, *Kur'an ve Sünnete Göre Tasavvuf* (Istanbul: Yeni Boyut 1998), p. 252.
895. Ken'an Rifâî, *Sohbetler* (Istanbul: Kubbealtı Neşriyatı 2000), p. 39.
896. Ken'an Rifâî, *Sohbetler* (Istanbul: Kubbealtı Neşriyatı 2000), p. 231.

- Whatever there is in created things exists in the human being. Mountains, rivers, canals, valleys, plains... And then domination, divinity and sovereignty too exist in the human being.[897]

- Those who stay and remain in the realm of plurality are busy with the world, the divine names, and the details of the world. But those who attain to the uniqueness of God's Essence are with God the Truth not in His formal aspect but his essential aspect, richer than the worlds. Because, God's being richer than the worlds, they attribute that richness of his to His name and attribute, they become the same as being rich. For just as the names belonging to Him indicate Him, they also indicate other things named by those names.

  In chapter 112 of the Quran, "*O Muhammed, say: 'God is unique'*" [sic], means the One who with respect to His entity and Essence has no peer is God. With respect to our dependence upon Him it has been said, "God is our refuge of which we have need. With regard to His own identity and our self He has not given birth and was not born and nothing has ever matched or been equal to Him." This is God's definition. Thus He made His Essence single with the phrase, "Peerless God." As for plurality, it came forth for us with His known names and attributes. So we are born, we give birth, we depend upon God; some of us are equal to some others. But that unique being is beyond those qualities. There is no attribute worthy to describe God other than these words written in the 112th chapter.[898]

- No one can comprehend the attributes of Divinity from the point of view of God the Truth's unique oneness. That is why God's friends have not accepted self-disclosure in oneness (*in other words, the unique realm pure of name and attribute*).

  When you gaze upon God with God (*in other words, when you witness God at the level of annihilation in God*), He has gazed upon Himself. Thus He is continually facing Himself by Himself.

  If you were to look upon Him with your own self, oneness would not remain then either. For if you look upon Him, there is you and He

---

897. Ken'an Rifâî, *Sohbetler* (Istanbul: Kubbealtı Neşriyatı 2000), p. 471.
898. Muhyiddîn İbnü'l-Arabî, trans. Nuri Gençosman, *Fusûs'l-Hikem* (Istanbul: İstanbul Kitabevi Yayınları 1981), p. 77.

in your speech, you are not the same as the thing you look at. Thus there is necessarily a duality between the one looking and the one looked at. Therefore oneness is removed. To be sure, God sees nothing but Himself with Himself, and in this description it is clear that the one looking and the one looked at are both God.[899]

- All beings are in a condition of wayfaring. The wayfaring is between the point of becoming and the point of attaining perfection. "Wayfaring" is a term and an institution expressing the progress of a person under the discipline of tasavvuf. The Quran says clearly that everything is in a condition of wayfaring (16:68-69; 74:40-62; 72:17). *"Your Lord inspired the honeybee... 'Follow the ways that are made easy.'"*

The first point in a person's wayfaring is eternity without beginning, in other words the Covenant [7:172], and the last point is God. Thus a person's wayfaring does not end with death. People are on an endless journey. What we see as its end is the part that takes place on earth. The journey that the people of truth call "progress" (*seyr*) is of four kinds:

Progress toward God is the lifting of the veil of plurality from the face of oneness. This progress is to the end of the degrees belonging to the soul, to the end of station of the heart by doing away with metaphorical loves.

Progress in God is to raise the veil from the face of scientific plurality. This progress is to rise to the highest horizon in God through acquiring traits of character with God's attributes.

To rise to the station of bringing together (*aynü'l-cem*) is to be freed of the restrictions of interior and exterior contradiction. At this point duality has finished and wayfarers have reached the perfection of maturity. They reach *"the space of two bows"* [53.9].

Progress with God from God is the highest station and expresses the return back to creation from God. It is also called subsistence after annihilation, and separation after bringing together. In this station the eye sees plurality in unity and unity in plurality. This station is to see the creation in God, and God in the creation.[900]

---

899. Muhyiddîn İbnü'l-Arabî, trans. Nuri Gençosman, *Fusûs'l-Hikem* (Istanbul: İstanbul Kitabevi Yayınları 1981), pp. 59-60.

900. Yaşar Nuri Öztürk, *Kur'an ve Sünnete Göre Tasavvuf* (Istanbul: Yeni Boyut 1998), p. 88.

- Go past the form of matter and seek the water of meaning, that you may be satisfied. You've seen the carving on the pitcher but you are unaware of meaning.

Due to your idiocy you say, "The body is Solomon, and thought is like an ant."

Why do you not put your ear on the breast of the decree, "*So glory be to Him in whose hand is the sovereignty of each thing, and to Him you will be returned*"? Do you not see the will of the Creator in the one who truly disposes of things?

The world seems to you quite awesome, quite tremendous… You tremble in fear at clouds, the heavens, thunder, lightning, and fortune. You think they alone are agents. You are awed at the grandeur of what is manifest.

You know nothing of the world of thought, you are heedless, you remain in the world of form like inanimate things, you know nothing of the world of meaning. For you are shape and form, you have no share of intellect.

On the Day of Judgment, you will see the tremendousness and glory of that thought and imagination. And you will see that that this cold, hot earth is gone. Other than the One God, Alive and Loving, you will see neither heavens nor stars. You will not be able to see any of the existents.[901]

- *Humans, time, creation is in love with You*
You're one, great, beautiful sublime Glorified
Language is not worthy to qualify You
Essence is hid in the perfect, all is You
Nightingales sing, mountains moan, water cascades
Love is awed, the lover weeping, suffers for You
The beloved laughs, the lover burns and glows
Merciful Sublime, all their states are from You
Human and jinn, all beings are instruments
They are but signs, the one who's working is You
The apparant consists in Your attributes

---

901. Şemseddin Yeşil, *Kitab'üt-Tasavvuf; Mesnevi'den Hikmetler* (Istanbul: Ş. Yeşil Kitabevi 1986), pp. 266-269.

83th Verse

It cannot be denied, all things mirror You
The One who knows, who speaks, who works in all things
You are the One who is seen in all, the Truth
From Ken'an too there's one who always says God
You are God, the one thing without doubt is You[902]

- Exaltedness is of two kinds. The first is the height of space, and the second is the height of rank, in other words of level and station.

Exaltedness of rank is for us. In other words, it is special to the Muhammedans. Sublime God has said, "You are exalted and God is with you in this exaltedness." But He is beyond the need of station. He is sublime, but not beyond rank.

Action wants station, whereas knowledge seeks rank. Thus God united the space between two kinds of exaltedness for us. One of them is the height of station through action, and the other is the exaltedness of rank through knowledge. Then in order to protect us from *şirk*, He said, "Glorify and declare the incomparability of God with those spiritual partnerships." One of the strangest things is that the human being, that is to say the Perfect Human Being, is the highest of beings, whereas height, whether of station or rank which is a matter of level, was made relative only according to him

Exaltedness of station is as indicated in the verse, "*The Merciful is seated upon the throne.*" The throne is the most exalted of stations.

God the High is one of the beautiful names. Over whom is He high, when in the world of bodies there is only He? In that case He is "High," in other words exalted, for His own Essence. Or, what or whom is He higher than, when that whom or what of which we speak is He alone. Thus God is "High" without a relative superiority or exaltedness.

When the manifest says, "I," the non-manifest says, "No." When the non-manifest says, "I," the manifest says, "No." All contraries are like that. There is one speaker, and He is the same as the one listening.

Whoever understands what we have said about numbers and the antilogy in their being on the one hand negative, and on the other positive, knows that however much the creatures appear to be sepa-

---

[902]. Ken'an Rifâî, *İlâhiyat-ı Ken'an*, ed. Yusuf Ömürlü and Dinçer Dalkılıç (Istanbul: Kubbealtı Neşriyatı 1988), p. 62.

rate from the Creator, incomparable God the Truth resembles the creation. The reality is that the Creator is the creature, and it is also the reality that the creature is the Creator. All these are from oneness itself. No, perhaps He is oneness itself; He is plurality itself.

Poem:

Creation is in this sense God the Truth. Take warning; in that sense also it is not creation. Consider well. The inner vision (heart's eye) of those who understand what I have said cannot be deceived. Only those whose vision is sound understand it.

Separate, unite, for the source is one. He is plurality, but when He self-discloses with unity, He leaves no trace of plurality.[903]

The being exalted in itself is He alone, who is a perfection taking within itself all relations of being and not-being; with such an exalted power of gathering that it is not possible for any quality to remain outside Him. Those qualities are coequal (*müsavi*), whether they are approved by intellect and the sheriat or disapproved, while they are special to that perfection and especially the Essence recalled with the name "God."

If someone comes and asks a question like, "How shall we regard all beautiful and ugly things? When we see filth and corpses, shall be call them Sublime God?" we say that God is incomparable with such a thing and exalted. What we say is intended for the person who does not see filth as filth and a corpse as a corpse. Perhaps our address is for those whose eye's heart is open and not blind.

But especially those other than the names recalled with the name "God" are each one a site of manifestation for God, or an appearance from Him. There must be difference between the self-disclosing form and what reflects it.[904]

- While the divine Essence, because it is the hidden of all hiddens, was at the Unseen level, it had no sign at all. One can give this example, for there is no error in simile: Like a seed buried underground... of which there is as yet no sign. That is why no one knows there is a seed there. Only when it opens and comes out of the earth is there a

---

903. [The poem is given in paraphrase in the text.]

904. Muhyiddîn İbnü'l-Arabî, trans. Nuri Gençosman, *Fusûs'l-Hikem* (Istanbul: İstanbul Kitabevi Yayınları 1981), pp. 35-42.

sign, produced from the two parts, one Essence, the other manifest. As it grows and develops, it takes on the form of a tree. It acquires branches and leaves; finally fruits appear, which bear kernals that are the form of the seed. That is the meaning of "All things return to their source." They asked Junayd Bahgdadi, "What is the end?" and he answered, "The return to the beginning." It should not be forgotten that the end's return to the beginning has a form special to itself. After the seed comes out of the earth and the body of a tree manifests, and after the branch and leaves levels until it takes the form of fruit, various forms are seen and those forms, ways and values did not exist while it was underground. The seed of that fruit is in one sense the same as the previous one, and in another sense other. Being the same is as in the case of the prior seed taking on the form of a tree. In that case, if people want to see that seed, they look at the tree. And looking at that tree is like looking at that seed. For the seed is not other than the tree. Being other is as in the case of that seed's fruit coming to be as a result. In relation to the tree it is as father to son. *"The child is the secret of the father."* In other words, semen manifested from the father. A child came to be from him. Just as that child entered into the limit of humanity, that buried seed too manifested as a tree, and fruit was produced from it. With regard to its kernal, the fruit too, is as one with the source and part in the form of the first seed.

That is the likeness of God and the world. In other words, the world and Adam found being through the self-disclosure of the names and attributes of the oneness essence. When? After the manifestations of the name "separating" (*mufassıl*) were complete, according to the gracious verse, *"And you will return to Him,"* gathering together was rejected. And the accidents produced by relations and ties waned and were lost.

However, that return was for some a voluntary death by way of "annihilation" while still in this world, and for some it was an involuntary and natural death. They call those two deaths, "the lesser resurrection."

And they call the disappearance of all the parts of the world the "greater Resurrection." For that resurrection gathers all the mortal parts and there is not resurrection beyond it. In that regard the greater resurrection is called "the greater annihilation."

O Humankind

In the Perfect Human Being all the reality of essence and attribute has been gathered. And, the world is like a tree, the angels like its leaves, and the human being is like the fruit of that tree. Thus the fruit of the Messenger, the most perfect of existents Muhammed, is like the quintessence, *the essence*, of that fruit. Therefore the Muhammedan Form is the Form of God the Truth. Whatever there is in divine knowledge, its unique form is in these souls and on these horizons. And the rarest and most beautiful of these unique, beautiful forms is the Muhammedan Form.[905]

- For God the Truth to destroy the creature called the human being by means of the accident called death does not mean that He destroys what He protects. Death is only a decomposition. Death is God's drawing a person's spiritual self to Himself. For all things return to God. When God takes people to His own world He gives them an arrangement and composition separate from the composition of this elemental world of corruption. Because that new composition, which belongs to the world of subsistence and has elements of the world, will be in equilibrium, it never disintegrates or decomposes.

If humans, when they die or are killed, whoever they may be, were not reunited with God, God would never have ordered anyone's death or made their killing legitimate. Thus all these things are in His hand. Thus no one who dies can be lost. Thus God made the killing of servants legitimate and ordered their deaths because He knows that they will not be separated from Him. In the verse, *"Every thing returns to Him,"* God has indicated that those who die will return, and here God is the same as the existents. In other words, God is both the one who is disposed of and the one who has disposal of. For there is nothing that came to be from God that is not the same as Him. Perhaps God's divinity is the entity of that thing. Thus this is the meaning to be understood by way of unveiling from His words, *"Every thing returns to God."*[906]

---

905. İsmail Hakkı Bursevî, trans. Abdülkâdir Akçiçek, *Kenz-i Mahfi-Gizli Hazine* (Istanbul: Bahar Yayınları 2000), p. 43.

906. İsmâil Rusûhî Ankaravî, ed. İlhan Kutluer, *Nakşel-FüsusŞerhi* (Istanbul: Ribat Yayınları n.d.), p. 163.

83TH VERSE

- All roads end in God. "Every thing returns to its source." For the entities of beings, in other words, their sources, are each one bound to and depend upon one of the divine names. And they continue their flow in the form required by the property of that name. And all of them are walking on His road. Thus the end returns to God's names. And there it brings itself to an end. In the same way the return to God of the sites of manifestation of those names is inevitable. For God is the final aim to which all roads arrive. God the Exalted is the result of all paths. For in order for something to have the meaning of a road, it has to have a beginning and an end. The return, the place to which one arrives, is to Him.[907]

- *How could the light of the moon ever be stained*
Though it falls on all things good and bad the same

  Innocent of all to the moon it returns
  As the mind and spirit's light to God returns

  Viciousness does not accumulate in light
  From pollutions of the road and defilement

  The light of the sun heard the command, "Return"
  And toward its own source made haste to return

  Niether did disgrace from the ash pits remain
  Nor did color from the rose gardens remain

  The eye's light and light-seer came back again
  In passionate love were left desert and plain[908]

- The moon, that seems more beautiful to us than the sun, grows thin like a consumptive with time and becomes a crescent and later only a phantom. So does everything in creation decline and bow to not-being.[909]

---

907. İsmâil Rusûhî Ankaravî, ed. İlhan Kutluer, *Nakşel-FüsusŞerhi* (Istanbul: Ribat Yayınları n.d.), pp. 81-82.
908. Mevlânâ Celâleddin Rûmî, trans. Veled İzbudak, ed. Abdülbaki Gölpınarlı, *Mesnevî* (Istanbul: Milli Eğitim Basımevi 1991), vol. 5, vs. 1258-1264.
909. Ken'an Rifâî, *Şerhli Mesnevî-i Şerif* (Istanbul: Kubbealtı Neşriyatı 2000), p. 177.

O Humankind

- All are waiting in the spiritual world
Now fleeing form, and now taking up abode

When the command, "Enter forms!" comes, they go in
And at His command are disengaged again

Know, "His are the creation and the command"
Creation is form, mounted spirit, command

Rider and mount are under the Shah's mandate
Spirit's in the presence, body at the gate

When he wants water to fill the pitcher up
The Shah says to the troops of spirit, "Mount up!"

Then when He wants the spirits on high again
"Dismount!" is the cry that comes from the Shah's men[910]

---

910. Şefik Can, *Konularına göre açıklamalı Mesnevi Tercümesi* (Istanbul: Ötüken Neşriyat 1997), vol. 5-6, pp. 343-344 [vol. 6, vs. 76-81].

Index

A

Abbas 20, 39, 130, 168, 437, 494, 585
Abd al-Qadir Gaylani 53, 453
abd (servant of God) 45
Abdullah 39, 44, 45, 113, 152, 184, 189, 416, 459
Abdülmelik 153
Abdülmuttalib 168
Abode, final (mustakarr) 246, 294, 296, 309, 310, 393, 490, 600
Abraham 40, 46, 59, 77, 195, 224, 236, 270, 308, 316, 336, 342, 371, 374, 405, 424, 479, 528, 565, 590
absolute 45, 180, 189, 190, 343, 367, 534, 544, 553, 568, 573, 576
Abu Bakr 167, 183, 224, 254, 335, 439, 531, 579, 590
Abu Hanife 416
Abu Jafar, Shaykh 411
Abu Lahab 424
Abu Nasr Sajzi 37
Abu Razin al-Uqayli 57
Abu Said al-Kharrāz 74
Abu Yazid 265

acceptance 65, 109, 158, 167, 184, 362, 381, 408, 416, 417, 424, 451, 495, 535, 577, 585
act 63, 64, 65, 74, 88, 103, 125, 126, 192, 202, 248, 273, 286, 315, 345, 360, 384, 387, 432, 443, 444, 466, 498, 528, 561, 572, 575, 586
action 54, 57, 68, 74, 81, 88, 101, 109, 111, 126, 149, 150, 160, 178, 200, 202, 203, 247, 248, 259, 263, 283, 286, 290, 314, 315, 317, 334, 338, 348, 356, 366, 370, 416, 444, 459, 475, 520, 541, 550, 553, 559, 561, 569, 572, 575, 578, 595
Adam 22, 46, 48, 49, 60, 65, 97, 104, 116, 117, 122, 137, 140, 142, 155, 163, 169, 190, 195, 198, 211, 235, 237, 263, 264, 270, 283, 299, 303, 308, 338, 380, 393, 402, 409, 421, 424, 425, 431, 432, 433, 434, 435, 437, 441, 443, 445, 446, 454, 455, 465, 466, 508, 516, 527, 535, 558, 565, 566, 573, 584, 597
Ad, tribe of 213

adultery 169, 440, 441, 442, 453
affection (muhabbet) 166, 210, 233, 237, 249, 250, 262, 371, 455, 456
Africa 243, 537
agent 125, 202, 271, 416, 453, 521
ahadiyyet (oneness) 53, 56
ahad (one) 43, 85, 414
Ahmed 32, 33, 39, 41, 42, 43, 44, 63, 64, 65, 75, 77, 80, 82, 97, 98, 117, 118, 120, 121, 124, 126, 127, 128, 130, 131, 167, 178, 179, 197, 206, 210, 212, 230, 254, 262, 328, 333, 334, 335, 344, 355, 362, 363, 375, 381, 385, 391, 393, 410, 411, 414, 466, 520, 526, 558, 559
ahsen-i takvim (the most beautiful stature) 265
air 50, 51, 57, 194, 203, 233, 236, 238, 316, 336, 383
Aisha 19, 27, 37, 125, 254, 414
al-Aqsa Mosque 329
Alast, the Feast of or pact of 58, 67, 202
Ali 19, 20, 25, 32, 33, 40, 41, 45, 64, 80, 85, 96, 97, 98, 99, 109, 110, 114, 120, 123, 124, 127, 128, 130, 146, 152, 189, 194, 210, 306, 307, 363, 409, 411, 439, 466, 489, 526, 575, 579, 589, 590
alif (the Arabic letter) 69, 140, 207, 268
Alive 87, 110, 126, 141, 219, 233, 235, 242, 299, 303, 314, 373, 382, 417, 418, 439, 459, 498,
512, 532, 544, 563, 566, 567, 594
All-Comprehending Realm, the 391
All-Concealing 160, 211, 478, 479
All-Dominating (Jabbār) 478, 479, 484
All-Forgiving 479
All-Knowing (Alîm) 72, 87, 126, 198, 259, 293, 294, 295, 524, 571, 589
All-Subjugating (Qāhir) 213, 464, 477, 478, 479, 482, 526
amber 261, 428
America 21, 29, 243
Anas 37, 86
angel 159, 210, 263, 294, 329, 362, 410, 433, 437, 448, 479, 480, 524, 535
animate 121, 375, 416, 499, 539, 553, 563, 567
Ankaravi, Ismail 539
annihilation in God (fena) 179, 350, 592
Antioch 147, 148
Arab 80, 169, 326, 424, 543
arrogance 111, 113, 116, 118, 121, 144, 173, 180, 224, 286, 311, 425, 432, 436, 460, 483, 492, 535
arrow 105, 216, 488, 542
ascension 24, 40, 41, 325, 330, 366, 581
ascent 51, 72, 94
aspect 18, 42, 49, 60, 74, 79, 93, 103, 152, 197, 203, 236, 294, 295, 415, 446, 454, 519, 563, 568, 578, 590, 592

Index

aspirant 166, 378
attributed spirit, the 187
authority 19, 37, 46, 356, 499, 589
autumn 115, 144, 232, 383, 384, 433, 512, 516, 517
awareness 250, 295, 349, 533
awe 114, 130, 132, 135, 190, 196, 207, 237, 299, 467, 468, 573
Awhaddeddin, Shaykh 305
Axis, the (kutup) 139, 152, 541, 544, 566, 567
Azazil 380, 445
Azrail (the angel of death) 429

B

Badr, Battle of 117
Baghdad 306
Bal'am ibn Ba'ur 434
balance 103, 105, 283
barrier 109, 110, 111, 112
basiret 59
batın (non-manifest) 46
Bayhaqi 37
beauty 18, 24, 25, 42, 43, 65, 67, 68, 94, 95, 96, 98, 101, 110, 112, 133, 136, 142, 144, 146, 157, 183, 191, 199, 209, 211, 214, 221, 232, 237, 250, 263, 267, 268, 271, 281, 283, 287, 293, 302, 305, 307, 308, 310, 321, 326, 329, 336, 347, 350, 376, 386, 405, 407, 408, 415, 418, 419, 445, 454, 463, 468, 516, 518, 519, 527, 528, 532, 535, 566, 567, 573, 579, 581
beginningless (ezeli) 49, 60, 75, 80, 94, 102, 119, 128, 143, 167, 265, 420, 586

being 17, 18, 19, 20, 21, 22, 23, 24, 25, 27, 40, 42, 43, 45, 46, 48, 49, 50, 51, 54, 55, 56, 57, 58, 59, 60, 64, 65, 67, 68, 69, 70, 71, 72, 77, 85, 86, 87, 88, 90, 91, 93, 95, 99, 100, 101, 102, 103, 104, 107, 109, 113, 114, 116, 120, 121, 122, 130, 131, 136, 139, 140, 141, 142, 143, 145, 146, 149, 150, 151, 155, 156, 160, 162, 165, 166, 168, 171, 173, 179, 189, 190, 194, 195, 196, 198, 203, 206, 209, 215, 218, 219, 220, 221, 225, 229, 230, 233, 235, 236, 239, 241, 245, 250, 254, 255, 260, 261, 264, 265, 266, 269, 270, 271, 272, 274, 279, 280, 281, 282, 286, 287, 288, 291, 294, 296, 298, 299, 301, 303, 306, 308, 309, 314, 320, 321, 322, 334, 335, 343, 347, 348, 349, 350, 354, 356, 360, 362, 365, 366, 367, 369, 373, 374, 375, 376, 378, 382, 383, 385, 387, 392, 394, 396, 397, 399, 400, 402, 403, 404, 405, 407, 409, 415, 416, 417, 418, 419, 420, 421, 424, 425, 429, 433, 434, 436, 438, 440, 446, 448, 452, 453, 454, 457, 460, 463, 464, 471, 476, 477, 482, 484, 486, 491, 496, 504, 509, 510, 511, 512, 516, 520, 521, 527, 528, 532, 535, 538, 539, 540, 543, 544, 548, 549, 555, 556, 558, 559, 560, 561, 565, 567, 568, 571, 572, 573, 575, 576, 577,

578, 579, 580, 582, 583, 584, 585, 586, 587, 590, 592, 595, 596, 597, 598, 599
believer 42, 67, 89, 130, 132, 150, 206, 236, 307, 341, 424, 479, 482, 511, 529, 533, 567
beloved 17, 18, 25, 38, 42, 43, 67, 80, 83, 94, 96, 104, 111, 112, 135, 136, 145, 149, 156, 218, 219, 237, 258, 270, 282, 286, 310, 323, 336, 338, 339, 359, 375, 377, 378, 386, 389, 405, 410, 416, 418, 428, 429, 441, 442, 448, 455, 487, 510, 519, 527, 531, 542, 567, 573, 594
benefit 19, 71, 126, 132, 179, 205, 248, 266, 274, 297, 363, 366, 417, 418, 442, 472, 538, 540, 586
beşer 155
bezel 49
Bible, the 575
Bilal-i Habashi 254
blind 49, 100, 114, 120, 121, 147, 167, 196, 288, 367, 369, 375, 468, 495, 496, 503, 504, 505, 518, 526, 557, 596
bodily 49, 50, 71, 109, 112, 140, 144, 149, 203, 305, 349, 413, 429, 474, 482, 512, 534, 553
body 23, 29, 43, 46, 48, 52, 64, 70, 71, 72, 88, 100, 103, 109, 110, 112, 113, 114, 133, 144, 145, 148, 149, 150, 157, 163, 167, 178, 186, 194, 196, 197, 203, 205, 217, 219, 220, 221, 232, 236, 238, 243, 244, 245, 250, 251, 254, 263, 267, 277, 278, 279, 282, 299, 303, 304, 305, 308, 315, 316, 323, 326, 327, 328, 329, 330, 335, 341, 342, 346, 349, 350, 356, 363, 366, 367, 371, 374, 377, 381, 382, 383, 384, 387, 390, 391, 399, 401, 410, 419, 429, 430, 432, 442, 448, 449, 457, 458, 463, 465, 468, 473, 478, 491, 492, 497, 498, 500, 506, 512, 527, 533, 534, 537, 539, 540, 541, 550, 557, 564, 565, 567, 583, 585, 587, 590, 594, 597, 600
book 20, 23, 25, 27, 29, 30, 31, 46, 51, 63, 67, 68, 69, 75, 77, 79, 135, 139, 140, 141, 156, 169, 197, 209, 266, 355, 356, 379, 440, 443, 455, 467, 471, 495, 515, 524, 526, 581
boon 41, 174, 175, 186, 253, 254, 255, 256, 257, 296, 342, 402, 403, 406, 413, 416, 419, 423, 439, 475, 477, 479, 481, 538, 540
bows, the two 310, 329, 593
branch 150, 241, 302, 309, 384, 419, 427, 597
bread 17, 76, 206, 245, 246, 272, 328, 366, 392, 420, 557
breath 93, 143, 194, 202, 219, 238, 371, 375, 379, 382, 385, 417, 418, 419, 423, 425, 434, 497, 520, 528, 555, 556, 558, 572, 583
bridge 25, 89, 366, 367, 481
Buraq 157, 329, 330, 331, 459

INDEX

Bursevî 43, 139, 153, 179, 287, 345, 378, 389, 524, 548, 549, 572, 573, 584, 589, 598

C

Caesar 214

caprice 120, 214, 283, 393, 406, 549

cause 50, 104, 165, 174, 198, 213, 221, 225, 249, 261, 271, 280, 281, 320, 322, 337, 354, 380, 384, 409, 440, 444, 454, 469, 486, 492, 515, 528, 532, 557, 559, 576, 586

Ceberut (the Realm of Domination) 41, 53

cebir (domination) 360, 361, 458, 459

cem' (gathering-together) 68, 348

cevher (substance) 50

Christian 105, 106, 135

clay 22, 209, 235, 245, 246, 322, 334, 371, 425, 433, 446, 527, 556, 571

clean 44, 83, 143, 243, 436, 554

clime 52

commentary 19, 22, 25, 27, 29, 31, 39, 75, 141, 345, 409, 528, 539

community 19, 24, 41, 43, 95, 98, 99, 114, 179, 185, 215, 309, 310, 315, 322, 334, 343, 350, 362, 437, 438, 439, 464, 507, 551, 580

compassion 142, 205, 211, 270, 275, 362, 363, 365, 413, 505

comprehension 41, 42, 56, 63, 134, 150, 163, 166, 191, 250, 278, 281, 298, 307, 390, 409, 457, 466, 482, 506

conscience 48, 51, 73, 250, 365, 382, 436, 506, 541

consciousness 128, 229, 307, 390

constancy 279, 294, 296, 353

constitution (mizaç) 113, 156, 198, 279, 413, 487, 532, 563

content 104, 255, 407, 408

contentment 97, 131, 196, 215, 299, 374, 477

copper 116, 221, 423, 425

correct 86, 101, 132, 150, 403, 422, 529

counsel 98, 164, 166, 167, 169, 172, 227, 306, 310, 510, 520, 524

courtesy (terbiye) 143, 179, 198, 225, 237, 446, 447, 482

cover 56, 105, 231, 363, 395, 406, 407, 442

covered 22, 44, 51, 109, 111, 112, 119, 122, 132, 177, 205, 286, 294, 309, 407, 409, 414, 487, 488, 509, 552

covering 55, 105, 110, 171, 172, 179, 287, 289, 299, 301, 341, 395, 407, 520, 559, 579, 581

creation 18, 22, 33, 40, 41, 49, 50, 51, 54, 55, 58, 59, 60, 65, 70, 71, 72, 74, 79, 81, 82, 88, 93, 94, 102, 103, 142, 160, 164, 196, 203, 218, 220, 229, 235, 250, 277, 278, 322, 334, 341, 343, 348, 356, 384, 415, 429, 444, 487, 515, 520, 525, 527, 528, 539, 555, 556, 558, 568, 571, 575, 576, 577, 578, 579,

580, 582, 586, 587, 590, 593, 594, 596, 599, 600
creative 269, 571, 572, 575, 586, 587
Creator, the 571
curse 199, 440, 447, 483, 518, 519
curtain 116, 122, 179, 214, 363, 407, 425, 496, 525

D

dagger 52
dal (the Arabic letter) 41, 69
darkness 81, 113, 115, 116, 124, 136, 149, 166, 206, 215, 216, 218, 223, 270, 277, 278, 279, 280, 282, 286, 287, 288, 299, 305, 313, 338, 355, 391, 395, 397, 406, 417, 421, 428, 430, 432, 433, 445, 446, 447, 448, 450, 452, 459, 480, 486, 490, 509, 523, 534, 552, 566, 568
date 68, 114, 241, 242, 243, 249, 301, 302, 334, 361, 499, 516
date palm 68, 114, 241, 242, 334, 361, 499, 516
David 136, 212, 256, 257, 294, 382, 452, 499
day 36, 37, 41, 46, 47, 48, 52, 82, 86, 89, 100, 104, 105, 114, 115, 116, 120, 121, 124, 131, 133, 134, 144, 148, 150, 157, 158, 193, 197, 202, 203, 212, 217, 218, 226, 230, 231, 234, 236, 242, 247, 253, 256, 277, 278, 282, 283, 284, 285, 286, 287, 289, 290, 291, 301, 306, 308, 310, 313, 314, 316, 320, 322, 325, 326, 328, 333, 338, 339, 341, 356, 362, 365, 366, 367, 369, 370, 373, 374, 375, 376, 377, 378, 379, 380, 382, 386, 390, 391, 392, 393, 394, 396, 397, 399, 402, 409, 410, 415, 424, 425, 429, 433, 437, 439, 441, 442, 445, 447, 448, 454, 458, 464, 474, 476, 479, 483, 484, 486, 490, 493, 495, 496, 497, 498, 500, 501, 509, 510, 511, 512, 518, 551, 560, 563, 573, 575, 579, 591, 594
Day of Account 231
Day of Judgment 89, 104, 120, 212, 365, 378, 493, 591, 594
Day of Resurrection 52, 115, 124, 131, 133, 144, 230, 373, 377, 378, 379, 390, 391, 433, 439, 447, 474, 560
death 29, 51, 105, 114, 134, 144, 148, 161, 186, 192, 197, 210, 217, 218, 223, 225, 236, 238, 267, 269, 285, 299, 305, 338, 365, 366, 369, 371, 373, 374, 379, 380, 381, 382, 383, 389, 405, 410, 413, 429, 459, 473, 490, 505, 510, 511, 512, 517, 518, 533, 551, 552, 560, 563, 572, 579, 581, 591, 593, 597, 598
decree, divine (kaza) 81, 198, 247, 316, 327, 520
denial 81, 113, 115, 162, 196, 220, 418, 423, 424, 454, 490, 498, 535, 556, 557, 558
deputy (naip) 142, 152, 178
dervish 145, 291, 321, 386
descent 48, 50, 51, 57, 70, 71, 72, 91, 94, 96, 100, 279, 280, 282, 321, 350, 362, 407

desire 54, 64, 65, 82, 94, 113, 118, 128, 149, 152, 179, 184, 190, 191, 198, 210, 214, 241, 248, 255, 271, 272, 273, 287, 311, 334, 359, 366, 382, 387, 408, 410, 415, 418, 425, 443, 448, 450, 454, 458, 459, 460, 461, 490, 511, 515, 517, 540, 565, 580

detailed 303, 534

determinate 46

determined 47, 60, 88, 103, 225, 301, 586

devil 52, 119, 127, 130, 159, 163, 195, 380, 433, 435, 436, 442, 444, 451, 459, 465, 506, 512, 527

Dhu'l-Hijja (Islamic lunar month) 47

Dhu'l-Qaʿda (Islamic lunar month) 47

dimension 56

Dirac, Maurice 269

disbeliever (kafir) 111, 112, 117, 122, 133, 219, 224, 235, 236, 264, 267, 304, 307, 335, 336, 341, 355, 359, 371, 381, 385, 391, 424, 449, 450, 469, 473, 479, 482, 503, 511, 518, 549, 591

distinction 23, 29, 165, 464, 520, 590

divine 18, 19, 20, 22, 23, 24, 25, 35, 38, 42, 43, 46, 48, 49, 50, 51, 52, 53, 54, 56, 57, 58, 60, 67, 68, 69, 70, 71, 72, 73, 77, 79, 80, 81, 82, 88, 89, 90, 91, 93, 94, 97, 98, 100, 101, 103, 107, 108, 110, 112, 113, 120, 122, 123, 126, 133, 137, 139, 140, 141, 142, 143, 149, 153, 156, 157, 159, 160, 164, 171, 174, 179, 181, 183, 190, 195, 198, 199, 209, 216, 230, 231, 247, 265, 279, 280, 281, 282, 283, 286, 287, 288, 295, 296, 304, 305, 308, 316, 321, 326, 327, 328, 329, 334, 336, 349, 350, 354, 359, 360, 361, 362, 365, 375, 379, 380, 382, 383, 384, 389, 390, 397, 400, 401, 405, 407, 409, 414, 423, 432, 435, 446, 447, 448, 452, 463, 464, 475, 479, 484, 487, 488, 489, 490, 498, 499, 503, 504, 520, 524, 532, 533, 535, 539, 543, 547, 548, 554, 558, 559, 563, 564, 565, 566, 572, 573, 576, 577, 581, 582, 584, 586, 587, 591, 592, 596, 598, 599

divine love 159, 384, 489

divinity 50, 52, 53, 57, 73, 149, 307, 592, 598

dog 107, 342, 378, 455, 461, 509, 543, 544, 552

domain 22, 52, 136

domination (cebir) 360, 458, 459

Domination, Realm of (ceberut) 41, 53, 140, 280, 296, 591

donkey 76, 378, 441, 487, 495, 519

doubt 21, 35, 48, 50, 60, 66, 72, 87, 89, 115, 125, 133, 178, 195, 207, 235, 271, 273, 314, 322,

341, 347, 349, 381, 384, 385, 394, 406, 421, 433, 434, 436, 449, 482, 504, 505, 506, 549, 554, 556, 587, 595
drunk 106, 247, 255, 457
drunkard 255
drunkenness 250, 457
duality 55, 81, 113, 136, 308, 349, 512, 539, 564, 593
dust 52, 67, 86, 106, 113, 122, 128, 196, 231, 238, 264, 289, 290, 322, 386, 390, 392, 394, 418, 498, 550, 564

E

ear 105, 112, 150, 164, 172, 178, 219, 227, 238, 255, 262, 281, 336, 355, 356, 382, 383, 389, 407, 426, 427, 436, 444, 497, 504, 535, 550, 583, 584, 585, 594
earth 17, 23, 25, 41, 43, 46, 48, 50, 51, 58, 59, 72, 82, 96, 104, 106, 112, 114, 116, 120, 122, 124, 133, 134, 137, 141, 142, 151, 159, 169, 194, 195, 199, 203, 209, 210, 215, 217, 220, 223, 231, 233, 235, 236, 237, 238, 245, 246, 250, 253, 259, 260, 261, 262, 268, 269, 277, 279, 294, 298, 299, 300, 302, 303, 305, 308, 316, 327, 333, 336, 338, 341, 362, 363, 366, 367, 369, 370, 371, 373, 382, 411, 420, 426, 431, 432, 444, 446, 464, 483, 496, 501, 506, 509, 511, 512, 515, 534, 535, 552, 556, 558, 561, 563, 566, 567, 571, 572, 585, 590, 593, 594, 596, 597
education 202, 321, 540
element 49, 58, 69, 88, 284, 293, 316, 446, 449, 450, 591, 598
encouragement 180, 185
enemy 19, 40, 83, 105, 106, 231, 272, 431, 433, 464, 488
engendered 48, 54, 56
Enoch 153, 293, 294, 566, 567
entity (ayn) 56, 584
envy 64, 117, 136, 144, 159, 162, 163, 164, 180, 195, 215, 220, 283, 311, 370, 435, 454, 460, 480, 488, 509, 517, 535
error 113, 115, 130, 133, 167, 193, 197, 205, 347, 359, 361, 379, 433, 435, 454, 455, 464, 469, 477, 480, 505, 508, 512, 513, 517, 596
eşkiya (the wretched) 100, 116, 119, 121, 133, 218, 341, 427, 430, 442, 445, 455, 510
Essence, the (zat) 35, 40, 63, 69, 96, 141, 189, 191, 198, 210, 250, 268, 269, 280, 281, 294, 295, 297, 299, 380, 386, 400, 405, 406, 445, 449, 453, 478, 528, 560, 565, 568, 576, 577, 582, 584, 587, 589, 590, 592, 594, 595, 597
Esteemed 151, 400
eternal 19, 41, 49, 50, 68, 70, 75, 81, 128, 143, 162, 219, 231, 241, 268, 280, 305, 370, 375, 382, 384, 401, 404, 420, 457, 540, 542, 560, 566, 584

INDEX

eternity 40, 41, 45, 48, 60, 67, 85, 93, 100, 101, 110, 119, 120, 121, 122, 128, 135, 143, 146, 157, 167, 202, 221, 299, 310, 333, 342, 370, 384, 390, 396, 418, 420, 429, 439, 441, 444, 455, 456, 577, 593

eternity without beginning (ezel) 40, 41, 45, 60, 67, 85, 93, 100, 101, 119, 120, 121, 128, 135, 143, 146, 167, 202, 299, 342, 370, 396, 420, 429, 439, 444, 455, 456, 577, 593

eternity without end (ebed) 40, 41, 299, 342, 577

ethics 209, 253

Eve 283, 409, 441, 566

evil 37, 95, 99, 102, 106, 110, 129, 144, 148, 149, 150, 151, 159, 162, 164, 167, 171, 172, 173, 180, 186, 205, 216, 218, 219, 221, 223, 224, 225, 231, 266, 267, 271, 272, 273, 274, 285, 287, 291, 310, 311, 336, 337, 345, 360, 376, 378, 394, 397, 401, 410, 420, 424, 427, 428, 440, 453, 455, 456, 472, 478, 486, 490, 493, 495, 497, 507, 509, 511, 519, 533, 540, 552

exaltation (izzet) 31, 90, 117, 135, 142, 344, 408, 420, 437, 516

Exalted (Aziz) 39, 65, 69, 70, 85, 90, 91, 93, 94, 95, 96, 120, 140, 143, 151, 156, 165, 178, 200, 203, 207, 210, 211, 247, 251, 254, 257, 260, 265, 266, 268, 270, 271, 287, 288, 293, 294, 296, 297, 303, 310, 326, 334, 343, 345, 346, 362, 367, 374, 393, 400, 401, 402, 403, 404, 405, 406, 408, 413, 417, 419, 437, 439, 440, 445, 446, 447, 448, 450, 453, 463, 464, 476, 482, 495, 520, 534, 535, 568, 573, 576, 582, 589, 595, 596, 599

existence 17, 23, 46, 50, 51, 56, 60, 69, 70, 72, 74, 90, 93, 102, 115, 122, 125, 127, 139, 143, 165, 172, 185, 217, 218, 239, 267, 274, 279, 281, 287, 288, 303, 310, 350, 351, 355, 365, 385, 386, 389, 390, 395, 420, 433, 434, 449, 450, 455, 460, 477, 478, 496, 498, 510, 518, 532, 541, 558, 559, 561, 572, 577, 582, 583, 584, 587

existent 46, 51, 56, 57, 69, 70, 74, 125, 165, 293, 393, 416, 449, 478, 587

expansion (bast) 136, 294, 446, 447, 566, 567

eye 49, 59, 63, 66, 112, 119, 132, 134, 136, 144, 150, 163, 164, 167, 187, 194, 195, 196, 199, 205, 206, 209, 219, 244, 250, 265, 268, 281, 282, 287, 288, 290, 298, 304, 305, 306, 307, 326, 337, 355, 386, 389, 390, 396, 397, 404, 406, 407, 410, 413, 416, 420, 435, 436, 445, 463, 497, 498, 504, 505, 518, 520, 534, 535, 552, 564, 568,

609

583, 584, 585, 590, 591, 593, 596, 599
eye of the heart 59, 63, 250, 265, 326, 436, 504

F

face 24, 32, 40, 43, 50, 79, 83, 102, 110, 111, 115, 124, 132, 133, 134, 142, 160, 162, 215, 218, 220, 221, 238, 262, 265, 275, 279, 284, 286, 289, 301, 306, 344, 355, 356, 362, 380, 385, 386, 392, 409, 414, 418, 429, 442, 444, 456, 463, 496, 497, 509, 510, 532, 549, 559, 573, 578, 582, 585, 593
father 67, 106, 107, 117, 169, 226, 227, 236, 274, 283, 284, 315, 319, 321, 343, 374, 380, 409, 423, 468, 529, 597
fazilet (virtue) 73
fear of God 109, 134, 135, 169, 211, 464, 493
felicitous, the (said) 100, 119, 121, 218, 445, 455, 510
fellowship 126, 131, 245
fena (annihilation in God) 179, 350, 592
fenâfillah 179
fire 50, 51, 75, 95, 104, 110, 116, 132, 162, 180, 194, 216, 220, 221, 224, 231, 237, 247, 264, 275, 291, 316, 336, 337, 338, 342, 354, 371, 373, 374, 378, 380, 406, 407, 431, 432, 433, 439, 446, 448, 450, 455, 472, 473, 474, 477, 478, 479, 480, 481, 482, 483, 484, 485, 487, 490, 491, 492, 500, 501, 505, 518, 527, 535, 557, 563, 564, 565, 566, 567, 568, 581
flag 43, 209, 419
flood 185, 213, 226, 227, 322, 323, 330, 336, 337, 342, 507
forgiveness 24, 74, 97, 98, 123, 128, 129, 142, 211, 212, 247, 377, 442, 447, 552
form 22, 23, 31, 49, 50, 56, 57, 58, 59, 60, 68, 69, 76, 85, 87, 88, 103, 122, 136, 140, 141, 142, 143, 145, 162, 172, 186, 215, 219, 230, 232, 239, 245, 260, 261, 263, 270, 271, 277, 278, 279, 280, 281, 283, 288, 297, 302, 310, 315, 366, 377, 378, 380, 383, 386, 391, 395, 400, 403, 409, 413, 415, 420, 424, 425, 429, 437, 446, 449, 450, 457, 460, 464, 475, 477, 481, 485, 487, 488, 507, 508, 509, 519, 525, 527, 535, 540, 541, 547, 548, 552, 555, 558, 560, 561, 564, 565, 568, 572, 573, 575, 576, 577, 578, 583, 584, 590, 594, 596, 597, 598, 599, 600
friend 42, 53, 77, 79, 81, 83, 97, 112, 113, 126, 136, 155, 156, 158, 162, 163, 171, 183, 187, 190, 191, 199, 220, 238, 256, 270, 281, 282, 285, 296, 299, 304, 334, 344, 375, 380, 382, 417, 418, 419, 425, 428, 433, 441, 443, 465, 467, 468, 472, 492, 494, 496, 500, 501, 527, 528, 541, 553, 554, 567, 583

INDEX

friend of God 42, 53, 77, 79, 81, 112, 155, 158, 162, 163, 190, 191, 299, 304, 417, 419, 500, 541, 567

G

Gabriel 39, 67, 75, 80, 217, 229, 275, 329, 330, 331, 370, 516, 524, 528, 558

gain 51, 143, 145, 180, 193, 274, 277, 291, 295, 310, 401, 402, 418, 451, 469, 478, 498, 518, 532

Gathering, the (mahşer) 65, 68, 70, 73, 74, 89, 142, 161, 365, 373, 374, 396, 425, 442, 456, 474, 486, 500, 597

gathering-together (cem') 68, 73, 161

Gayyâ 394

gazap (wrath) 73

generosity 71, 128, 174, 254, 347, 376, 403, 406, 407, 419, 542, 552

generous 123, 129, 205, 206, 209, 225, 306, 360, 450, 454, 465

Giver 69, 73, 157, 184, 253, 254, 257, 286, 402, 477

glorification 124, 314

Glorified, the 32, 162, 259, 269, 362, 553

glory 133, 160, 203, 212, 259, 260, 321, 341, 413, 524, 576, 589, 590, 594

gnosis 64, 66, 97, 114, 116, 120, 123, 125, 135, 150, 164, 167, 172, 173, 175, 195, 203, 207, 209, 210, 217, 237, 241, 247, 248, 249, 256, 257, 281, 282, 286, 296, 304, 326, 341, 348, 359, 362, 385, 390, 394, 399, 404, 405, 410, 453, 456, 482, 504, 531, 539, 543, 544, 548, 581

gnostic 55, 65, 67, 167, 191, 207, 309, 360, 446, 497, 547, 578

god 18, 19, 20, 22, 23, 24, 25, 29, 31, 32, 33, 35, 36, 37, 38, 39, 40, 41, 42, 43, 45, 46, 47, 48, 49, 50, 51, 52, 53, 54, 55, 56, 57, 58, 59, 60, 61, 63, 64, 65, 66, 67, 68, 69, 70, 71, 72, 73, 74, 75, 76, 77, 79, 80, 81, 82, 83, 85, 86, 87, 88, 89, 90, 91, 93, 94, 95, 96, 97, 98, 100, 101, 102, 103, 104, 105, 106, 107, 108, 109, 110, 111, 112, 113, 114, 116, 117, 119, 120, 121, 122, 123, 124, 125, 126, 127, 128, 129, 130, 131, 132, 133, 134, 135, 136, 137, 139, 140, 141, 142, 143, 144, 145, 150, 151, 152, 155, 156, 157, 158, 159, 160, 161, 162, 163, 164, 165, 166, 167, 168, 169, 171, 172, 173, 174, 175, 177, 178, 179, 180, 183, 184, 185, 186, 187, 189, 190, 191, 192, 194, 195, 196, 197, 198, 199, 200, 201, 202, 203, 206, 207, 209, 210, 211, 213, 214, 215, 216, 217, 218, 219, 220, 224, 225, 226, 229, 230, 231, 233, 234, 235, 236, 237, 239, 240, 241, 242, 244, 245, 246, 247, 248,

249, 250, 251, 253, 254, 255, 256, 257, 258, 259, 260, 261, 263, 264, 265, 266, 267, 268, 269, 270, 271, 272, 273, 274, 275, 278, 279, 280, 281, 282, 283, 284, 286, 287, 288, 289, 290, 293, 294, 295, 296, 297, 298, 299, 301, 302, 303, 304, 305, 306, 307, 308, 309, 310, 311, 313, 314, 315, 316, 317, 321, 322, 323, 325, 326, 327, 328, 329, 330, 331, 333, 334, 335, 336, 337, 338, 339, 341, 342, 343, 344, 345, 346, 347, 348, 349, 350, 351, 353, 355, 356, 359, 360, 361, 362, 363, 365, 366, 367, 369, 370, 371, 373, 374, 375, 377, 379, 380, 381, 382, 383, 384, 385, 386, 387, 389, 390, 391, 392, 393, 394, 395, 396, 397, 399, 400, 401, 402, 403, 404, 405, 406, 407, 408, 410, 411, 414, 415, 416, 417, 418, 419, 420, 421, 422, 423, 424, 425, 426, 427, 429, 430, 431, 432, 433, 434, 435, 436, 437, 438, 439, 440, 441, 442, 443, 444, 445, 446, 447, 448, 449, 450, 451, 452, 453, 454, 455, 456, 457, 458, 459, 460, 463, 464, 465, 467, 471, 472, 473, 474, 475, 476, 477, 478, 479, 480, 481, 482, 483, 484, 485, 486, 487, 488, 489, 490, 491, 492, 493, 494, 495, 496, 497, 498, 499, 500, 501, 503, 504, 505, 506, 507, 508, 509, 510, 511, 512, 515, 516, 517, 518, 519, 520, 521, 524, 525, 526, 528, 529, 530, 531, 532, 533, 534, 535, 538, 539, 540, 541, 543, 547, 548, 549, 550, 551, 552, 553, 554, 555, 556, 557, 558, 559, 560, 561, 564, 565, 566, 567, 568, 571, 572, 573, 575, 576, 577, 578, 579, 580, 581, 582, 583, 584, 585, 586, 587, 589, 590, 592, 593, 594, 595, 596, 597, 598, 599

God 18, 19, 20, 22, 23, 24, 25, 29, 31, 32, 33, 35, 36, 37, 38, 39, 40, 41, 42, 43, 45, 46, 47, 48, 49, 50, 51, 52, 53, 54, 55, 56, 57, 58, 59, 60, 61, 63, 64, 65, 66, 67, 68, 69, 70, 71, 72, 73, 74, 75, 76, 77, 79, 80, 81, 82, 83, 85, 86, 87, 88, 89, 90, 91, 93, 94, 95, 96, 97, 98, 100, 101, 102, 103, 104, 105, 106, 107, 108, 109, 110, 111, 112, 113, 114, 116, 117, 119, 120, 121, 122, 123, 124, 125, 126, 127, 128, 129, 130, 131, 132, 133, 134, 135, 136, 137, 139, 140, 141, 142, 143, 144, 145, 150, 151, 152, 155, 156, 157, 158, 159, 160, 161, 162, 163, 164, 165, 166, 167, 168, 169, 171, 172, 173, 174, 175, 177, 178, 179, 180, 183, 184, 185, 186, 187, 189, 190, 191, 192, 194, 195, 196, 197, 198, 199, 200, 201, 202, 203, 206, 207, 209,

210, 211, 213, 214, 215, 216,
217, 218, 219, 220, 224, 225,
226, 229, 230, 231, 233, 234,
235, 236, 237, 239, 240, 241,
242, 244, 245, 246, 247, 248,
249, 250, 251, 253, 254, 255,
256, 257, 258, 259, 260, 261,
263, 264, 265, 266, 267, 268,
269, 270, 271, 272, 273, 274,
275, 278, 279, 280, 281, 282,
283, 284, 286, 287, 288, 289,
290, 293, 294, 295, 296, 297,
298, 299, 301, 302, 303, 304,
305, 306, 307, 308, 309, 310,
311, 313, 314, 315, 316, 317,
321, 322, 323, 325, 326, 327,
328, 329, 330, 331, 333, 334,
335, 336, 337, 338, 339, 341,
342, 343, 344, 345, 346, 347,
348, 349, 350, 351, 353, 355,
356, 359, 360, 361, 362, 363,
365, 366, 367, 369, 370, 371,
373, 374, 375, 377, 379, 380,
381, 382, 383, 384, 385, 386,
387, 389, 390, 391, 392, 393,
394, 395, 396, 397, 399, 400,
401, 402, 403, 404, 405, 406,
407, 408, 410, 411, 414, 415,
416, 417, 418, 419, 420, 421,
422, 423, 424, 425, 426, 427,
429, 430, 431, 432, 433, 434,
435, 436, 437, 438, 439, 440,
441, 442, 443, 444, 445, 446,
447, 448, 449, 450, 451, 452,
453, 454, 455, 456, 457, 458,
459, 460, 463, 464, 465, 467,
471, 472, 473, 474, 475, 476,
477, 478, 479, 480, 481, 482,
483, 484, 485, 486, 487, 488,
489, 490, 491, 492, 493, 494,
495, 496, 497, 498, 499, 500,
501, 503, 504, 505, 506, 507,
508, 509, 510, 511, 512, 515,
516, 517, 518, 519, 520, 521,
524, 525, 526, 528, 529, 530,
531, 532, 533, 534, 535, 538,
539, 540, 541, 543, 547, 548,
549, 550, 551, 552, 553, 554,
555, 556, 557, 558, 559, 560,
561, 564, 565, 566, 567, 568,
571, 572, 573, 575, 576, 577,
578, 579, 580, 581, 582, 583,
584, 585, 586, 587, 589, 590,
592, 593, 594, 595, 596, 597,
598, 599

God the Exalted 39, 65, 120, 140,
143, 151, 156, 165, 200, 203,
210, 211, 247, 251, 254, 257,
260, 268, 270, 271, 287, 288,
293, 294, 297, 303, 310, 313,
326, 333, 334, 335, 343, 345,
346, 362, 366, 367, 374, 380,
400, 401, 402, 403, 406, 408,
424, 437, 439, 440, 442, 445,
446, 447, 448, 450, 452, 453,
460, 475, 476, 477, 534, 535,
551, 568, 575, 582, 589, 599

godwariness (takva) 169
gold 106, 116, 149, 183, 194, 289,
374, 419, 423, 466, 519, 554
good deed 160, 450, 451, 458
goodness 52, 95, 96, 99, 102, 129,
133, 143, 148, 157, 180, 205,
212, 214, 216, 267, 271, 273,

326, 337, 341, 347, 363, 396, 406, 408, 410, 451, 457, 540
Gospel, the 59, 152, 259, 275, 590
grace 71, 97, 113, 142, 160, 195, 211, 214, 231, 245, 246, 248, 250, 255, 268, 304, 362, 383, 409, 418, 420, 473, 477, 478, 512, 516, 539, 576
grandeur (heybet) 142, 294, 376, 594
grateful 27, 254, 255, 272, 417
gratitude 27, 215, 253, 254, 255, 256, 257, 260, 301, 361, 362, 416, 458, 467, 541, 557
greed 118, 144, 159, 180, 183, 194, 215, 264, 348, 371, 376, 378, 442, 477, 480, 488, 550
guidance 66, 87, 121, 123, 125, 149, 180, 185, 186, 187, 189, 198, 200, 254, 255, 262, 304, 385, 393, 436, 444, 464, 473, 481, 572, 581
guide 23, 25, 27, 51, 89, 104, 112, 143, 166, 177, 179, 185, 186, 199, 255, 262, 304, 385, 428, 444, 468, 480, 512, 534, 552

H

habib 38, 147, 148, 205, 206, 221
Habib-i Najjar 147, 148
Hacı Bayram Veli 209
hadith 22, 31, 33, 42, 57, 71, 72, 73, 74, 95, 140, 170, 173, 183, 206, 220, 257, 260, 268, 270, 271, 280, 281, 282, 298, 322, 326, 334, 342, 343, 363, 377, 378, 381, 383, 389, 393, 406, 409, 421, 475, 478, 488, 531, 535, 540, 583, 585, 591

hajj 451
halal 443, 534, 543
halife (vicegerent) 203, 567
Hallaj 265
Haman 214, 428
hand 27, 43, 52, 59, 76, 97, 106, 115, 119, 121, 122, 143, 150, 169, 194, 199, 209, 220, 226, 234, 238, 249, 255, 257, 258, 266, 273, 281, 337, 338, 376, 389, 391, 395, 418, 432, 434, 442, 444, 461, 467, 478, 488, 490, 494, 497, 500, 501, 512, 525, 529, 533, 556, 559, 566, 573, 575, 581, 589, 590, 594, 595, 598
haram 119, 174, 248, 255, 453, 454, 483, 534
Hasan Basri 306
Hassan ibn Atiyya 37
haşyet (wariness) 41
hayba (awe) 135
health 95, 132, 174, 202, 244, 267, 284, 287, 442, 459, 538, 557
heart 17, 18, 19, 20, 22, 23, 24, 25, 27, 32, 37, 40, 44, 49, 51, 52, 55, 59, 60, 63, 64, 75, 83, 86, 87, 96, 99, 104, 110, 112, 113, 114, 115, 116, 117, 119, 125, 126, 127, 129, 130, 131, 132, 134, 135, 136, 144, 145, 148, 149, 150, 151, 152, 153, 157, 158, 164, 165, 166, 169, 173, 175, 178, 179, 180, 183, 187, 191, 194, 195, 196, 199, 203, 206, 207, 209, 210, 211, 215,

INDEX

220, 224, 229, 230, 237, 239, 243, 246, 249, 250, 253, 254, 262, 264, 265, 268, 271, 272, 275, 277, 282, 284, 285, 287, 288, 293, 297, 298, 299, 301, 304, 305, 306, 313, 323, 326, 328, 331, 338, 339, 348, 350, 361, 362, 365, 375, 381, 382, 383, 385, 386, 390, 394, 396, 400, 407, 415, 416, 417, 418, 432, 433, 434, 436, 441, 442, 451, 458, 459, 461, 467, 468, 473, 477, 489, 493, 498, 499, 503, 504, 505, 508, 509, 511, 519, 520, 524, 525, 529, 531, 534, 539, 542, 547, 549, 551, 552, 554, 556, 557, 560, 567, 568, 573, 580, 590, 591, 593, 596

heart's eye 144, 590, 591, 596

heaven 17, 23, 39, 50, 106, 134, 136, 195, 215, 249, 293, 294, 299, 303, 309, 310, 329, 330, 333, 420, 424, 433, 474, 475, 486, 575, 590

heedlessness (gaflet) 122, 125, 133, 166, 191, 194, 197, 229, 283, 341, 355, 370, 374, 385, 391, 487, 496, 515, 543, 566

hell 89, 104, 129, 132, 142, 149, 173, 180, 196, 199, 223, 224, 265, 266, 330, 333, 350, 351, 367, 373, 374, 375, 394, 396, 397, 404, 406, 407, 420, 423, 424, 439, 441, 445, 447, 448, 454, 459, 466, 469, 471, 472, 473, 474, 475, 476, 477, 478, 479, 480, 481, 482, 483, 484, 485, 486, 487, 488, 489, 490, 491, 492, 499, 503, 505, 509, 534, 552, 557

Hereafter, the (ahiret) 37, 65, 89, 95, 103, 104, 128, 133, 185, 206, 209, 278, 288, 310, 345, 359, 365, 373, 375, 381, 394, 407, 424, 454, 471, 473, 475, 479, 481, 484, 498, 505, 508

hidden 45, 51, 53, 56, 65, 66, 75, 85, 96, 97, 103, 104, 111, 113, 116, 131, 133, 136, 144, 149, 157, 162, 171, 202, 209, 219, 220, 270, 271, 281, 286, 287, 306, 307, 315, 354, 355, 389, 390, 407, 417, 419, 421, 427, 429, 433, 453, 457, 499, 516, 527, 532, 552, 559, 563, 568, 576, 579, 580, 581, 583, 585, 596

Himalayan Mountains 180

Hizir 66, 295, 564, 566, 567

Hud 47, 225, 336

human 18, 20, 22, 23, 24, 25, 35, 36, 39, 40, 42, 45, 46, 48, 49, 50, 51, 52, 53, 54, 57, 58, 59, 60, 65, 67, 69, 71, 80, 81, 85, 86, 88, 89, 91, 96, 101, 103, 107, 109, 112, 119, 122, 123, 124, 134, 139, 140, 141, 142, 143, 144, 145, 146, 149, 150, 151, 152, 156, 157, 162, 163, 171, 173, 178, 185, 186, 191, 193, 194, 195, 198, 203, 209, 211, 215, 217, 219, 220, 221, 223, 225, 231, 235, 236, 241, 243,

615

245, 250, 260, 261, 264, 265, 266, 267, 269, 272, 273, 275, 279, 283, 286, 295, 298, 299, 303, 304, 305, 306, 320, 321, 322, 328, 335, 338, 346, 347, 349, 355, 356, 360, 367, 369, 370, 371, 373, 374, 375, 378, 379, 380, 381, 384, 394, 397, 399, 400, 403, 407, 409, 410, 413, 415, 420, 421, 431, 432, 433, 434, 442, 443, 444, 445, 448, 449, 457, 460, 482, 484, 487, 488, 489, 490, 491, 492, 503, 505, 508, 509, 511, 520, 524, 528, 532, 535, 537, 538, 539, 540, 542, 543, 544, 549, 550, 553, 556, 560, 565, 566, 567, 568, 573, 590, 592, 594, 595, 598

Human being 22, 23, 24, 40, 42, 45, 46, 48, 49, 50, 51, 54, 59, 60, 65, 69, 71, 86, 91, 101, 103, 107, 122, 139, 140, 141, 142, 143, 145, 146, 149, 150, 151, 156, 162, 171, 198, 203, 209, 221, 235, 241, 245, 261, 264, 265, 266, 269, 279, 299, 320, 321, 322, 347, 356, 378, 399, 400, 403, 415, 420, 421, 433, 482, 484, 509, 528, 532, 535, 543, 544, 560, 565, 573, 592, 595, 598

humanity 17, 18, 23, 50, 60, 66, 87, 119, 134, 173, 174, 186, 196, 218, 247, 255, 266, 270, 371, 390, 487, 488, 508, 521, 535, 541, 597

humankind 21, 36, 39, 40, 51, 89, 104, 134, 157, 161, 322, 369, 380, 457, 519, 521, 526, 541

Husameddin 195

hypocrite 150, 392

I

ibadet 45

Ibāna 37

Ibn Abbas 39, 130, 437, 585

Ibn Arabi 29, 42, 53, 54, 55, 59, 64, 89, 93, 102, 109, 124, 139, 140, 236, 373, 406, 471, 481, 523, 524, 544, 566, 571, 572, 579, 581

icat (giving existence to) 572

ignorant 141, 159, 197, 207, 218, 220, 250, 283, 288, 385, 421, 439, 451, 467, 485, 487, 505, 526, 548, 561

'Ikrima ibn Abdullah al-Barbari 44

illiteracy 41

illiterate 42, 440, 451

illumination (tenvir) 113, 125, 295, 299, 301, 338, 389, 489

imagination 29, 56, 58, 59, 114, 150, 374, 482, 524, 573, 581, 589, 594

Imam Ja'far (al-Sadiq) 416

Imam of the Left 153

Imam of the Right 153

Imam of the time 389

inanimate 51, 121, 265, 303, 314, 334, 367, 415, 499, 508, 532, 533, 563, 567, 594

India 196

influence 186, 284, 316, 453, 463, 465, 589

insect 159
insight 18, 31, 59, 66, 134, 136, 283, 375
instrument 64, 197, 235, 382, 447, 448, 455, 548, 586
intellect (akıl) 29, 39, 49, 53, 54, 60, 64, 65, 66, 74, 107, 124, 140, 149, 150, 151, 163, 164, 173, 174, 239, 249, 257, 263, 278, 308, 321, 331, 355, 361, 366, 375, 383, 384, 390, 395, 402, 410, 433, 465, 466, 468, 469, 482, 484, 485, 491, 515, 526, 543, 594, 596
intelligence 106, 107, 250, 263, 465, 467, 469
intercession 24, 45, 48, 193, 241, 342, 375, 423
interior 23, 42, 70, 103, 186, 211, 224, 314, 316, 337, 348, 362, 497, 526, 535, 539, 590, 593
intimacy 41, 81, 126, 127, 128, 131, 167, 207, 225, 248, 250, 251, 301, 321, 338, 389, 405, 406, 407, 447, 497
intoxicated 36, 419, 591
intoxication 249, 379
invisible 56, 112, 115, 133, 134, 179, 195, 250, 278, 298, 307, 330, 354, 355, 385, 390, 429, 433, 512
inward 23, 42, 64, 72, 74, 89, 93, 124, 203, 383
Iram, gardens of 397
Iraq 363
Israel, children of 43
Israelites 489
Israfil 230, 294, 379, 382, 383, 386

Italy 243
Izzeddin, Judge 396
izzet (exaltation) 31, 90, 117, 135, 142, 343, 344, 408, 420, 437, 516

J

Jabbār (All-Dominating) 478
Jacob 67, 371
jahāme 471, 472
Jahim 477
Jerusalem 492
Jesus 40, 43, 46, 48, 76, 98, 105, 106, 107, 143, 147, 187, 224, 294, 308, 334, 354, 365, 371, 382, 385, 487, 528, 558, 576, 578, 590, 591
Jew 101, 106, 224, 354, 365, 423, 428, 507
jewel 143
jinn 58, 80, 115, 157, 275, 328, 351, 380, 433, 434, 503, 526, 539, 544, 594
Joseph 67, 156, 343, 371, 374, 375, 468, 491, 526
judge 52, 157, 185, 198, 396
judgment 41, 48, 63, 89, 101, 104, 120, 142, 150, 151, 198, 199, 207, 212, 216, 224, 234, 253, 256, 297, 315, 316, 337, 350, 365, 377, 378, 429, 485, 489, 490, 493, 534, 547, 563, 579, 580, 581, 591, 594
Jupiter 195
Jurjani, Abd al-Qahir 53
just 17, 48, 55, 59, 60, 65, 69, 73, 74, 88, 94, 99, 105, 113, 115, 118, 122, 126, 140, 143, 144, 145, 151, 152, 159, 163, 168,

169, 173, 180, 189, 197, 205, 206, 207, 214, 216, 218, 220, 227, 247, 248, 250, 255, 260, 261, 263, 265, 267, 270, 271, 280, 281, 283, 286, 287, 288, 297, 298, 299, 303, 304, 305, 308, 309, 316, 321, 327, 328, 335, 336, 337, 339, 341, 343, 354, 355, 363, 366, 371, 374, 379, 382, 384, 393, 397, 413, 417, 418, 420, 422, 427, 431, 433, 434, 436, 439, 444, 449, 454, 463, 465, 469, 476, 478, 483, 493, 495, 498, 508, 510, 515, 523, 524, 532, 535, 538, 539, 541, 551, 558, 560, 564, 566, 572, 573, 576, 577, 578, 579, 583, 584, 590, 592, 597

justice 103, 152, 180, 186, 274, 279, 353, 393, 397, 416, 423, 426, 478, 479, 491

K

kader (measuring out) 100
kahr (subjugation) 105, 142, 146, 226, 255, 294, 463, 464, 492, 559
kaza (divine decree) 198
keşf (unveiling) 35, 60, 64, 124, 189, 250, 278, 379, 484, 544, 598
Khaybar Fortress 489
king 74, 160, 162, 201, 203, 266, 405, 484, 492
küfür (misbelief) 81, 498, 580, 581
kun ("Be!") 474, 575, 577, 578, 580, 581, 582, 583, 586, 587
Kun fayakūn 35, 575

L

Lahut (the Realm of Divinity) 23, 52
lam-alif (the Arabic letter) 69
lam (the Arabic letter) 69, 268
language 18, 21, 65, 114, 116, 122, 164, 183, 254, 280, 304, 347, 348, 356, 383, 500, 524, 527, 543, 552, 594
La Taayyün 52, 56
latife (subtlety) 35, 74, 105, 282, 407, 553, 581
Latif (the Subtle) 400
law 46, 48, 53, 63, 79, 81, 90, 91, 101, 103, 179, 185, 296, 315, 326, 354, 359, 366, 380, 448, 452, 503, 507
Lawgiver 46
Learned, the (Âlim, ulema) 295
level (mertebe) 59, 257
Leyla 327, 328
lie 118, 155, 344, 345, 396, 416, 427, 441, 452, 457, 493, 498, 550
life 17, 24, 27, 52, 58, 66, 69, 75, 88, 89, 95, 96, 98, 112, 132, 139, 143, 148, 152, 153, 160, 172, 173, 177, 194, 206, 215, 224, 225, 230, 232, 233, 234, 235, 245, 247, 248, 249, 250, 256, 264, 269, 270, 283, 285, 290, 291, 302, 303, 305, 310, 314, 320, 321, 326, 335, 342, 346, 360, 362, 366, 370, 371, 373, 374, 375, 376, 377, 379, 382, 383, 384, 385, 390, 394, 413, 420, 434, 454, 458, 461,

INDEX

463, 472, 474, 475, 481, 485, 486, 515, 518, 519, 520, 531, 532, 533, 540, 544, 555, 556, 558, 560, 563, 566, 567, 572, 578, 579, 582, 591
lifetime (ömür) 51, 230, 327, 429
light 19, 25, 49, 50, 55, 59, 66, 67, 77, 81, 87, 89, 90, 95, 98, 111, 112, 113, 115, 116, 124, 125, 131, 136, 144, 149, 157, 159, 163, 179, 180, 186, 187, 195, 197, 211, 215, 216, 219, 241, 245, 246, 250, 268, 269, 270, 279, 282, 285, 286, 287, 288, 290, 293, 295, 296, 298, 299, 302, 304, 305, 308, 310, 313, 319, 326, 328, 329, 330, 337, 338, 354, 355, 356, 379, 387, 389, 390, 391, 397, 406, 409, 414, 415, 423, 425, 429, 430, 431, 432, 433, 435, 436, 445, 446, 450, 463, 467, 477, 479, 480, 486, 489, 490, 497, 500, 503, 504, 511, 517, 518, 531, 534, 554, 559, 561, 564, 565, 566, 567, 568, 569, 572, 575, 578, 580, 581, 584, 599
lion 98, 219, 220, 221, 375, 455, 489, 517, 550
longing 51, 111, 112, 241, 261, 336, 376, 410, 454, 499, 505
Lord 37, 38, 43, 44, 57, 58, 72, 73, 76, 79, 86, 89, 90, 100, 102, 103, 108, 117, 119, 124, 126, 134, 136, 137, 143, 148, 151, 160, 161, 165, 166, 167, 168, 169, 170, 185, 186, 191, 195, 196, 197, 198, 201, 202, 203, 205, 209, 210, 218, 221, 225, 231, 247, 254, 255, 256, 261, 264, 265, 272, 274, 275, 281, 282, 304, 306, 307, 309, 310, 327, 328, 330, 334, 335, 350, 353, 356, 373, 374, 380, 381, 385, 393, 394, 395, 401, 407, 408, 409, 410, 413, 414, 415, 416, 417, 422, 425, 426, 437, 440, 442, 445, 448, 456, 467, 473, 475, 479, 486, 489, 495, 499, 500, 509, 510, 518, 527, 532, 540, 549, 551, 552, 561, 564, 565, 566, 577, 580, 586, 591, 593
lordliness 57, 73, 81, 82, 90, 160, 161, 185, 189, 191, 203, 264, 265, 281, 282, 293, 344, 350, 380, 448, 449, 485, 548, 558, 582, 585
lordship 548
loss 65, 67, 104, 143, 196, 214, 243, 286, 367, 376, 401, 415, 418, 498, 499, 516, 517, 518, 544, 552, 581
love 17, 18, 24, 36, 40, 43, 51, 53, 55, 60, 64, 75, 77, 81, 82, 83, 94, 96, 104, 107, 109, 112, 114, 127, 128, 132, 134, 135, 136, 144, 145, 149, 152, 156, 159, 162, 164, 165, 173, 174, 178, 179, 191, 195, 199, 209, 210, 211, 212, 215, 216, 221, 231, 233, 237, 241, 242, 244, 248, 249, 250, 258, 261, 262, 272, 282, 286, 291, 298, 310, 321,

619

323, 327, 329, 331, 334, 338, 350, 359, 369, 370, 371, 381, 384, 387, 389, 390, 396, 397, 405, 408, 409, 410, 414, 416, 417, 418, 419, 422, 429, 432, 433, 434, 436, 439, 440, 450, 455, 456, 457, 458, 459, 465, 466, 467, 468, 469, 473, 483, 487, 489, 492, 517, 519, 528, 541, 550, 551, 554, 556, 565, 566, 568, 569, 573, 583, 594, 599

lover 18, 94, 156, 282, 286, 390, 397, 418, 519, 527, 594

Luqman 521, 553

lust 112, 128, 144, 151, 173, 180, 215, 226, 244, 266, 272, 284, 288, 322, 371, 378, 430, 452, 466, 469, 473, 480, 483, 484, 488, 490, 542, 544, 566

M

Mahmud 43, 45, 130, 193

mahşer (the Gathering) 377, 563

Majesty 18, 32, 42, 68, 96, 110, 117, 128, 250, 255, 268, 283, 293, 337, 408, 445, 456, 463, 464, 482, 516, 535, 540, 566, 567

Majnun 328, 541

malice 180, 500, 535

manifest 41, 42, 43, 44, 46, 48, 57, 59, 64, 66, 70, 72, 73, 74, 87, 93, 103, 140, 141, 142, 163, 177, 178, 187, 193, 202, 229, 232, 236, 237, 239, 280, 281, 282, 286, 295, 297, 314, 330, 359, 365, 367, 379, 385, 401, 425, 427, 433, 456, 464, 490, 494, 497, 499, 510, 511, 516, 527, 532, 535, 557, 561, 566, 571, 573, 578, 579, 580, 583, 584, 590, 594, 595, 597

manifestation 23, 41, 42, 43, 45, 48, 49, 50, 51, 53, 54, 56, 57, 58, 59, 60, 67, 71, 72, 85, 86, 88, 91, 96, 100, 102, 110, 113, 161, 179, 187, 191, 198, 201, 218, 241, 250, 257, 268, 270, 280, 281, 282, 286, 287, 293, 294, 299, 303, 308, 309, 334, 354, 362, 380, 381, 415, 416, 420, 423, 424, 427, 448, 449, 450, 451, 452, 453, 463, 464, 478, 479, 482, 527, 528, 559, 565, 568, 573, 579, 582, 583, 584, 596, 599

Mansur Hallaj 265

Mansur Rabbani, Shaykh 178

Mansur, Shaykh 334

Mary 58, 229, 241

material 29, 30, 32, 44, 66, 70, 144, 145, 148, 215, 236, 241, 254, 260, 267, 269, 328, 329, 346, 349, 354, 382, 391, 396, 432, 433, 449, 450, 457, 490, 504, 539

matter 29, 53, 56, 57, 59, 67, 71, 74, 88, 100, 105, 114, 119, 157, 186, 236, 244, 267, 268, 270, 278, 338, 346, 360, 375, 376, 380, 391, 420, 421, 437, 446, 447, 453, 506, 531, 563, 576, 578, 590, 594, 595

meaning 19, 21, 22, 29, 32, 33, 42, 43, 44, 45, 49, 54, 59, 60,

INDEX

65, 68, 70, 71, 72, 75, 76, 79, 81, 85, 88, 89, 94, 95, 96, 99, 100, 101, 117, 124, 129, 141, 144, 145, 161, 173, 190, 192, 194, 201, 203, 207, 211, 217, 230, 236, 245, 249, 250, 255, 257, 263, 264, 269, 270, 278, 279, 281, 286, 297, 298, 299, 314, 321, 345, 380, 382, 383, 402, 403, 406, 407, 415, 424, 425, 429, 446, 447, 457, 459, 466, 471, 478, 479, 481, 484, 490, 495, 503, 504, 507, 523, 524, 526, 527, 531, 534, 539, 540, 548, 553, 563, 565, 566, 567, 576, 578, 579, 580, 581, 582, 583, 586, 590, 594, 597, 598, 599

measuring out, the divine (kader) 100, 190

Medina 161

Melekut (the Realm of Sovereignty) 40, 53, 589, 590

merciful 18, 20, 72, 73, 93, 95, 96, 97, 104, 113, 121, 123, 126, 132, 135, 136, 140, 155, 160, 161, 166, 167, 180, 187, 193, 217, 257, 297, 334, 347, 362, 389, 409, 413, 414, 439, 450, 475, 477, 478, 487, 509, 529, 594, 595

Merciful, the 167

mercy 19, 24, 32, 37, 49, 73, 79, 90, 94, 95, 96, 97, 98, 122, 125, 129, 133, 142, 148, 164, 211, 212, 215, 218, 256, 267, 289, 291, 303, 304, 310, 321, 334, 337, 339, 341, 343, 344, 345, 346, 347, 362, 402, 403, 409, 411, 413, 414, 420, 430, 445, 464, 472, 473, 474, 475, 476, 478, 479, 487, 488, 504, 505, 508, 510, 512, 582

messenger 22, 23, 25, 32, 33, 35, 37, 38, 39, 40, 41, 42, 43, 44, 45, 46, 47, 48, 57, 60, 63, 64, 65, 66, 67, 70, 71, 74, 75, 76, 79, 80, 81, 82, 85, 86, 91, 94, 95, 97, 100, 104, 107, 114, 117, 119, 121, 123, 124, 125, 127, 135, 144, 149, 152, 155, 157, 162, 165, 166, 167, 169, 170, 173, 178, 179, 183, 190, 191, 195, 197, 210, 213, 216, 218, 220, 224, 240, 254, 257, 260, 267, 280, 281, 294, 299, 306, 309, 310, 311, 317, 321, 322, 329, 330, 334, 335, 338, 339, 342, 343, 347, 350, 353, 354, 362, 366, 370, 371, 378, 385, 386, 399, 400, 402, 406, 407, 409, 413, 414, 415, 416, 417, 421, 423, 427, 437, 438, 439, 440, 442, 444, 445, 448, 454, 456, 459, 469, 472, 475, 480, 495, 506, 508, 509, 510, 513, 517, 521, 523, 524, 527, 529, 530, 531, 534, 539, 550, 551, 552, 564, 585, 598

messengerhood 40, 44, 46, 79, 80, 81, 82, 152, 162, 165, 167, 169, 309, 310, 378, 524

Messenger, the 100, 417, 598

Mevlana (Rumi) 30, 31, 106, 119, 148, 180, 183

microcosm 53, 415

milk 217, 247, 249, 250, 256, 259, 362, 432, 537, 538, 542, 543, 544, 553
mim (the Arabic letter) 40, 41, 43, 44, 69, 88, 414
mineral 114
miracle 35, 122, 155, 167, 334, 526, 550
Miraj (Muhammed's ascension to God) 39, 42, 43, 98, 294, 329, 459
mirror 20, 22, 49, 50, 64, 93, 115, 141, 151, 190, 207, 219, 265, 282, 288, 304, 355, 455, 456, 504, 554, 573, 579, 584, 595
misbelief (küfür) 215, 366, 471, 498, 535, 547, 549, 580, 581
moment 35, 42, 57, 125, 133, 134, 165, 216, 217, 229, 262, 275, 320, 341, 348, 355, 362, 369, 404, 406, 407, 429, 450, 456, 460, 477, 493, 510, 538, 541, 545, 552, 555, 556, 563, 564, 578, 584
money 106, 183, 197, 271, 286, 360, 395, 443
moon 43, 77, 195, 221, 232, 237, 264, 298, 301, 302, 303, 304, 305, 306, 307, 308, 313, 314, 424, 433, 516, 599
mortal 20, 50, 117, 129, 155, 162, 165, 193, 287, 528, 597
Moses 40, 43, 46, 48, 66, 76, 95, 98, 100, 117, 124, 167, 201, 223, 224, 270, 278, 327, 336, 354, 356, 365, 366, 371, 423, 424, 425, 426, 428, 435, 460, 469, 492, 550, 564, 565, 566, 572

most beautiful stature, the (ahsen-i takvim) 49, 265, 403
moth 290, 291
mother 27, 67, 68, 100, 107, 119, 135, 140, 235, 262, 273, 283, 284, 306, 315, 320, 321, 409, 429, 432, 455, 467, 581, 591
Muallim Naci 266
Mudāfiʿa-i Kādiya 37
muhadara 230
Muhammed 23, 31, 32, 38, 39, 40, 41, 42, 43, 44, 45, 46, 47, 48, 57, 64, 70, 71, 75, 77, 79, 80, 91, 94, 95, 96, 98, 101, 114, 116, 117, 121, 122, 124, 130, 132, 153, 157, 162, 179, 186, 190, 217, 260, 261, 278, 294, 298, 299, 304, 308, 325, 329, 330, 343, 345, 354, 370, 378, 383, 389, 394, 400, 413, 414, 423, 437, 438, 440, 441, 443, 444, 445, 458, 494, 507, 515, 525, 529, 531, 551, 558, 565, 591, 592, 598
Muhammedan 598
Muharram (Islamic lunar month) 47
mükevvenat 48
Munificent 400
murshid (spiritual guide) 51, 66, 67, 111, 112, 121, 166, 179, 186, 203, 247, 248, 262, 343, 384, 414, 415, 416, 417, 436, 488, 490, 512
Mustafa 32, 39, 40, 82, 266, 270, 421, 422, 423, 424, 428, 467, 493, 494, 549

INDEX

mutlak 52, 189
Mutlak Gayb Alemi 52
Muzzammil 44
Mu'imma 37
mystery 60, 95, 99, 115, 186, 217, 218, 298, 414, 499, 527, 552, 585

N

name 20, 22, 23, 32, 38, 39, 40, 41, 42, 43, 44, 45, 46, 48, 57, 58, 59, 68, 70, 73, 79, 81, 85, 86, 87, 90, 93, 94, 95, 96, 100, 101, 128, 131, 136, 137, 145, 146, 152, 153, 160, 161, 167, 185, 186, 189, 190, 191, 198, 201, 225, 235, 242, 243, 247, 254, 257, 259, 268, 280, 293, 296, 297, 303, 308, 321, 329, 341, 356, 363, 400, 401, 402, 403, 404, 405, 406, 407, 413, 420, 421, 423, 424, 435, 441, 443, 444, 445, 446, 447, 450, 453, 471, 476, 477, 478, 479, 481, 482, 483, 484, 498, 528, 530, 532, 540, 544, 548, 553, 563, 564, 572, 590, 592, 596, 597, 599
names, the divine 50, 57, 58, 60, 88, 90, 137, 142, 143, 153, 230, 281, 295, 565, 599
Naqqash 39
Nasafi, Aziz al-Din 53
Nasut (the Realm of Kingdom) 23, 53
natural death 381, 578, 591, 597
nature 19, 82, 87, 89, 90, 100, 103, 109, 110, 119, 149, 152, 155, 156, 157, 185, 201, 217, 219, 250, 253, 257, 268, 273, 277, 279, 283, 286, 316, 337, 347, 376, 383, 385, 404, 413, 428, 429, 430, 431, 446, 447, 448, 449, 450, 452, 456, 468, 473, 474, 479, 480, 481, 482, 484, 487, 488, 490, 503, 505, 511, 533, 553, 566, 591
nebi (prophet) 79, 81
necessity 310, 492, 581
neck 110, 284, 305, 361
need 45, 53, 66, 69, 70, 79, 88, 98, 123, 127, 136, 166, 183, 190, 191, 221, 231, 233, 237, 272, 278, 297, 299, 309, 323, 357, 359, 438, 450, 451, 482, 487, 492, 500, 537, 538, 555, 582, 586, 592, 595
nefis, nefs (soul) 29, 449, 481, 539, 542
neş'e-i daim 49
newly arrived 49, 68, 70, 102, 158, 430, 582, 583, 584
niche 36, 64, 191, 237, 282, 314, 315, 338, 432, 567, 568
night 20, 39, 42, 55, 98, 115, 116, 134, 158, 166, 195, 203, 212, 231, 236, 247, 254, 277, 278, 279, 280, 281, 282, 283, 284, 286, 287, 288, 289, 291, 294, 302, 303, 305, 313, 314, 322, 328, 338, 366, 367, 370, 379, 390, 397, 410, 415, 424, 432, 433, 442, 468, 493, 575
nightingale 237
Night of Power, the 42
Nile 223, 224, 489
Nimrod 224, 265, 270, 336, 350, 424, 550

623

Niyazi Misri 579
Noah 40, 167, 181, 213, 219, 220, 225, 226, 227, 278, 308, 319, 321, 322, 323, 325, 330, 336, 337, 338, 342, 467, 472, 507
noble hadith 57, 71, 72, 74, 95, 173, 183, 280, 281, 363, 377, 389, 406, 409, 531, 585, 591
non-manifest (batın) 46, 59, 103, 141, 280, 282, 314, 535, 579, 590, 595
not-being (adem, yokluk) 55, 68, 72, 102, 109, 250, 271, 286, 287, 366, 369, 382, 383, 420, 516, 520, 576, 577, 579, 580, 584, 585, 596, 599
Numan (Abu Hanife) 416

O

obedience 107, 249, 253, 272, 343, 384, 454, 458, 459, 507, 535
olive 567, 568
one (ahad) 24, 85
oneness (ahadiyyet) 53
oppress 67, 169, 198, 393, 483
oppression 118, 215, 393, 395, 483
origin 18, 50, 51, 56, 192, 223, 239, 261, 420, 447, 450, 471, 580, 583
Originator 239, 401, 477
outward 47, 57, 58, 59, 63, 74, 87, 89, 93, 145, 383
Overwhelming, the (Qahhār) 479

P

padishah 190, 194, 227, 241, 391, 420, 434, 505, 532, 539

Paradise (cennet) 24, 45, 89, 95, 123, 129, 131, 132, 133, 142, 149, 173, 185, 186, 199, 205, 212, 218, 221, 223, 224, 248, 249, 250, 260, 265, 280, 281, 282, 330, 343, 367, 371, 378, 393, 394, 397, 399, 400, 401, 402, 403, 404, 405, 406, 407, 408, 409, 410, 434, 445, 459, 466, 468, 472, 473, 474, 475, 477, 478, 479, 480, 481, 482, 485, 486, 487, 489, 510, 516, 527, 532, 544, 552, 566, 567
passion 107, 110, 111, 120, 130, 283, 460, 490, 499, 529
path 24, 25, 29, 35, 38, 41, 43, 45, 52, 53, 54, 55, 64, 66, 80, 85, 86, 87, 88, 89, 90, 91, 97, 98, 100, 104, 106, 110, 111, 112, 121, 123, 124, 126, 129, 136, 157, 158, 160, 161, 164, 166, 177, 179, 180, 185, 186, 194, 198, 199, 201, 210, 241, 256, 286, 302, 304, 307, 315, 321, 323, 331, 342, 343, 344, 349, 362, 366, 371, 373, 380, 384, 387, 396, 397, 402, 408, 417, 418, 431, 436, 438, 449, 453, 454, 458, 459, 460, 468, 472, 479, 486, 488, 489, 500, 503, 504, 505, 513, 520, 525, 540, 552, 560, 566, 581
patience 42, 52, 116, 242, 249, 253, 264, 273, 301, 438, 458, 586
peace 23, 24, 32, 45, 75, 82, 85, 96, 113, 126, 134, 135, 212, 274,

INDEX

326, 343, 356, 361, 400, 404, 406, 407, 408, 409, 410, 421, 422, 423, 437, 441, 448, 479, 486, 548, 549, 591

peace of mind (huzur) 113, 212, 356, 410, 441, 448, 591

pearl 385, 423, 427, 564

Pen, the 75, 97, 149, 445, 525, 586

people of God 66, 87, 190, 216, 295, 296, 305, 371, 389, 421, 424, 532

Perfect Human Being, the 573

perfection 40, 45, 49, 55, 58, 68, 69, 70, 79, 85, 95, 96, 98, 117, 120, 135, 136, 156, 166, 179, 193, 269, 281, 287, 295, 299, 315, 323, 329, 341, 384, 413, 414, 426, 460, 540, 542, 550, 553, 567, 580, 581, 590, 593, 596

Pharoah 201, 423, 469

piety 347, 497, 535

pir 109, 224, 436

Plato 151, 210

pleasure 35, 70, 73, 74, 112, 115, 116, 120, 130, 131, 132, 135, 136, 158, 169, 184, 194, 196, 213, 274, 281, 282, 286, 287, 300, 322, 341, 381, 386, 395, 408, 418, 456, 458, 465, 469, 473, 482, 487, 488, 525, 532, 540, 541

poem 499, 529, 596

poet 524, 525, 526, 529

poetry 20, 443, 515, 523, 524, 525, 526, 527, 528, 529, 530

poison 112, 117, 126, 454, 509, 517, 533, 552

power 35, 42, 43, 69, 72, 82, 86, 94, 95, 96, 97, 98, 105, 106, 113, 117, 121, 142, 144, 157, 158, 184, 190, 194, 199, 217, 220, 244, 250, 257, 264, 265, 266, 268, 273, 275, 281, 284, 285, 294, 307, 315, 321, 334, 337, 348, 353, 354, 360, 361, 369, 379, 395, 409, 420, 421, 429, 433, 435, 453, 455, 458, 463, 464, 478, 484, 489, 499, 501, 505, 508, 509, 510, 515, 518, 521, 528, 529, 532, 539, 541, 542, 550, 558, 559, 560, 561, 581, 582, 589, 596

Power, the Night of 42

praise 43, 70, 74, 131, 164, 172, 185, 186, 253, 254, 256, 260, 293, 314, 366, 414, 439, 451, 496, 497, 511, 542, 544

prayer 24, 36, 87, 102, 105, 127, 133, 136, 145, 174, 185, 191, 237, 253, 254, 259, 262, 274, 282, 314, 315, 338, 343, 422, 432, 438, 440, 441, 442, 443, 444, 457, 586

preparedness (of the entities) 45, 57, 58, 85, 98, 99, 100, 123, 135, 142, 149, 185, 198, 202, 218, 237, 305, 309, 395, 429, 510, 511, 568, 576

presence 25, 54, 65, 105, 116, 123, 124, 125, 145, 157, 162, 179, 205, 220, 227, 229, 230, 231, 249, 296, 365, 380, 394, 442, 446, 447, 448, 454, 457, 458, 460, 467, 518, 600

Preserved Tablet, the 37, 100, 101, 119, 140, 141, 145, 198
pride 111, 112, 113, 116, 117, 132, 161, 173, 226, 270, 432, 434, 443, 454, 466, 468, 488, 492, 535
prison 206, 214, 236, 311, 361, 429, 456
prohibited months 47
property 41, 46, 70, 71, 73, 75, 82, 99, 104, 168, 183, 184, 193, 218, 234, 256, 299, 300, 335, 351, 356, 357, 359, 360, 369, 391, 424, 425, 449, 461, 475, 476, 483, 511, 517, 529, 538, 539, 540, 575, 599
prophethood 40, 42, 79, 80, 152, 206, 210, 310, 567
prophet (nebi) 17, 19, 20, 22, 23, 24, 31, 32, 42, 79, 81, 113, 163, 183, 199, 206, 210, 220, 241, 304, 343, 349, 386, 529, 552, 553, 567, 586
prosperity 52, 180, 216
prostrate 109, 263, 425, 441, 445, 535
prostration 36, 221, 254, 255, 441, 535, 567
Protector 45, 50, 85, 106, 344, 361, 413
pupil of the eye 504
pure 54, 106, 110, 116, 123, 129, 132, 143, 145, 158, 159, 163, 179, 195, 199, 221, 232, 245, 251, 257, 259, 267, 289, 293, 326, 361, 378, 384, 386, 392, 413, 414, 417, 419, 425, 426, 429, 433, 436, 458, 468, 489, 496, 523, 551, 552, 553, 554, 557, 567, 583, 592
purity 129, 145, 244, 355, 417, 458, 464

Q

qaf (the Arabic letter) 88, 488
Qahhār (Overwhelming) 479
Qāhir (All-Subjugating) 477, 479
Qahūr 479
Qarun 214, 371
Qatadah 37
Qur'an 17, 18, 19, 20, 21, 23, 24, 25
Quraysh 548
Qutayba 37

R

Rabia 37, 168
Ragib al-Isfahani 185, 260
rain 94, 128, 233, 235, 342, 414, 449, 463, 472
raising 330, 365, 382, 405, 558
Rajab (Islamic lunar month) 47
Ramazan 42
rancour 180
ra (the Arabic letter) 69
reality 19, 21, 25, 37, 42, 43, 48, 53, 54, 55, 56, 57, 59, 60, 63, 64, 70, 71, 72, 80, 81, 82, 91, 95, 96, 100, 101, 102, 103, 105, 114, 120, 133, 135, 142, 144, 145, 161, 184, 194, 209, 219, 237, 241, 265, 269, 277, 280, 283, 287, 293, 294, 295, 298, 299, 303, 305, 307, 315, 316, 321, 323, 326, 331, 365, 371,

383, 386, 389, 396, 405, 446, 452, 453, 457, 465, 471, 474, 476, 481, 496, 503, 524, 527, 539, 541, 549, 561, 563, 579, 581, 589, 596, 598
realm 17, 18, 20, 35, 40, 41, 46, 48, 50, 51, 52, 53, 54, 57, 58, 59, 60, 64, 67, 68, 70, 82, 93, 98, 102, 113, 119, 120, 132, 133, 140, 142, 143, 144, 153, 156, 157, 163, 179, 181, 194, 195, 215, 223, 236, 267, 274, 280, 284, 288, 294, 295, 296, 299, 303, 304, 305, 307, 309, 321, 328, 329, 330, 341, 361, 365, 374, 377, 380, 383, 389, 391, 395, 418, 429, 430, 432, 435, 457, 459, 460, 474, 503, 507, 540, 559, 571, 576, 584, 589, 590, 591, 592
Realm of Divinity, the (Lahut) 52
Realm of Domination, the (Ceberut) 41, 53, 140, 296, 591
Realm of Kingdom, the (Nasut) 40, 53, 59, 153, 274, 590
Realm of Sovereignty (Ceberut) 40, 53, 59, 140, 153, 267, 274, 295, 329, 374, 380, 589, 590, 591
reflection (tefekkür) 63, 126, 180, 194, 246, 348, 519, 520, 521, 524, 567, 573
refuge 37, 52, 53, 74, 96, 107, 126, 128, 132, 178, 209, 224, 229, 246, 255, 288, 321, 342, 379, 385, 391, 443, 451, 503, 510, 592

religion 23, 63, 66, 67, 82, 83, 106, 111, 147, 149, 157, 167, 168, 174, 178, 185, 282, 371, 417, 420, 424, 447, 452, 466, 487, 501, 531, 549, 580
remembrance 114, 123, 124, 125, 126, 127, 128, 129, 130, 131, 136, 167, 203, 248, 314, 356, 385, 399, 480, 515, 528
repentance 95, 104, 111, 128, 131, 288, 343, 349, 413, 442, 460, 510, 518
resentment 163, 180, 286, 378, 467, 483
result 54, 57, 61, 68, 112, 114, 125, 132, 180, 196, 197, 198, 209, 211, 230, 244, 346, 377, 381, 394, 401, 466, 471, 473, 486, 492, 496, 543, 557, 566, 568, 583, 587, 597, 599
Resurrection, the 133, 373, 374, 474
resurrection, the greater 373, 374, 597
resurrection, the lesser 217, 230, 373, 374, 377, 597
revelation 23, 42, 43, 67, 79, 93, 96, 113, 120, 148, 155, 164, 172, 329, 350, 355, 415, 494, 520, 576
reverence 66, 498, 535
right path 106, 185, 186, 210, 513, 540
ring 49, 52, 342, 420, 494
rose 75, 100, 164, 224, 231, 232, 246, 278, 294, 316, 335, 384, 397, 417, 419, 480, 527, 529, 556, 565, 569, 585, 599

rosewater 395
ruh (spirit) 29, 187
Rumi (Mevlana) 17, 18, 20, 30, 31, 75, 106, 119, 148, 180, 183

S

sacred 18, 22, 23, 24, 31, 53, 73, 168, 180, 185, 220, 281, 298, 326, 342, 354, 375, 523, 535, 566, 576, 582, 589
Sacred Spirit 582
Sadreddin 105, 136, 210, 421
safe 45, 85, 235, 346, 371, 421, 454, 489
safety 45, 65, 85, 130, 131, 163, 311, 321, 347, 386, 421, 467, 480
said (felicitous, the) 19, 20, 23, 37, 40, 43, 44, 46, 47, 48, 49, 54, 55, 58, 59, 60, 70, 71, 73, 74, 76, 77, 80, 82, 86, 87, 93, 95, 98, 102, 104, 105, 106, 111, 112, 114, 116, 117, 119, 121, 122, 123, 124, 126, 127, 130, 131, 135, 137, 140, 141, 142, 144, 146, 147, 148, 149, 151, 155, 156, 161, 165, 167, 169, 170, 171, 183, 184, 185, 186, 187, 190, 191, 195, 197, 198, 202, 205, 206, 210, 211, 218, 219, 226, 227, 238, 239, 241, 246, 247, 248, 251, 254, 256, 257, 259, 260, 261, 263, 264, 265, 270, 271, 272, 273, 274, 282, 288, 305, 306, 314, 316, 317, 322, 327, 328, 330, 334, 338, 342, 343, 345, 346, 347, 348, 349, 350, 356, 357, 359, 361, 362, 363, 366, 367, 370, 374, 376, 378, 379, 381, 383, 390, 392, 395, 396, 399, 400, 401, 402, 403, 406, 409, 411, 414, 417, 421, 422, 425, 426, 427, 432, 437, 438, 439, 440, 441, 442, 445, 446, 447, 448, 451, 453, 454, 458, 459, 460, 466, 467, 471, 473, 475, 476, 493, 496, 499, 507, 508, 509, 510, 512, 516, 518, 521, 524, 526, 529, 530, 531, 534, 535, 540, 547, 548, 551, 553, 556, 564, 565, 567, 568, 571, 572, 575, 578, 579, 585, 590, 591, 592, 595, 596
Said ibn Mansur 37
Salih 47, 218, 370, 509, 510, 551, 552
salim 45, 85
salt 52, 199, 529, 552
salvation 132, 319, 321, 341, 362, 439, 448, 472, 481, 488, 572, 586
Samud 177
sanctity (vilayet) 54, 79, 80, 81
Sargut, Cemalnur 17, 27, 29, 30, 32, 36, 51, 120, 143, 299, 477
Satan 37, 52, 106, 115, 116, 120, 122, 130, 163, 167, 168, 195, 197, 198, 214, 237, 264, 270, 338, 351, 393, 431, 432, 433, 434, 435, 436, 437, 438, 440, 443, 449, 451, 452, 453, 455, 456, 464, 465, 505, 506, 552, 581
scale 150, 378, 423
scent 17, 57, 100, 148, 164, 172, 209, 245, 338, 371, 379, 389, 419, 497, 529, 541, 566

Index

Schuon, Frithjof 41, 53
sea 17, 77, 94, 179, 203, 221, 247, 250, 321, 322, 323, 335, 363, 371, 420, 449, 456, 466, 528, 550, 552, 567, 572, 584
seal 42, 49, 105, 119, 134, 167, 288, 420, 495, 496, 539
secret 20, 23, 32, 40, 44, 51, 96, 130, 134, 135, 152, 158, 159, 183, 187, 191, 206, 210, 231, 234, 235, 242, 264, 269, 277, 286, 301, 307, 316, 319, 330, 334, 342, 356, 362, 376, 386, 387, 402, 404, 407, 415, 426, 433, 444, 446, 460, 466, 468, 477, 497, 499, 500, 511, 525, 526, 527, 528, 533, 538, 542, 563, 568, 579, 580, 581, 584, 587, 597
secret heart (sır) 32, 40, 44, 96, 130, 135, 152, 183, 187, 191, 210, 277, 301
security 80, 126, 135, 274, 335, 347, 381, 482, 504
seed 135, 151, 211, 233, 234, 235, 237, 238, 242, 245, 253, 262, 285, 366, 395, 396, 426, 480, 557, 580, 596, 597
self-disclosure (tecelli) 23, 29, 42, 43, 44, 50, 51, 52, 54, 55, 57, 59, 63, 68, 70, 71, 72, 73, 85, 91, 93, 95, 96, 102, 122, 123, 125, 142, 189, 205, 213, 217, 221, 233, 264, 279, 286, 287, 288, 298, 305, 313, 329, 369, 370, 400, 401, 407, 408, 409, 414, 416, 434, 463, 464, 477, 483, 484, 490, 509, 528, 541, 549, 555, 556, 564, 565, 573, 576, 584, 589, 592, 597
selfishness 180
self-possession (temkin) 294
separation 72, 73, 74, 81, 165, 212, 217, 348, 385, 473, 487, 505, 512, 540, 593
servant (abd) 32, 37, 42, 45, 55, 57, 71, 72, 73, 79, 82, 88, 102, 108, 116, 125, 128, 130, 132, 133, 135, 136, 141, 145, 184, 187, 189, 190, 191, 192, 207, 211, 229, 231, 254, 255, 257, 265, 274, 275, 280, 281, 282, 298, 307, 330, 334, 348, 349, 356, 362, 374, 377, 380, 394, 408, 410, 421, 427, 434, 438, 444, 472, 481, 511, 531, 532, 535, 549, 560, 564, 573, 582, 583, 591
servanthood 40, 43, 44, 45, 60, 81, 82, 108, 152, 161, 184, 190, 191, 199, 203, 221, 227, 264, 265, 274, 281, 294, 309, 310, 314, 347, 348, 365, 403, 414, 434, 460
service 104, 191, 328, 375, 491
seyyid 39, 40, 74, 79, 85, 94, 95, 130, 141, 149, 161, 193, 269, 282, 294, 304, 406, 413, 414, 453, 479, 482, 486, 568, 582, 583
shadow 93, 194, 287, 347, 391, 397, 420
shah 49, 134, 178, 239, 256, 262, 272, 343, 496, 500, 511, 534, 600

Shamun 147, 148
shaykh 67, 104, 105, 158, 178, 221, 247, 248, 274, 283, 305, 334, 411, 420, 433, 453, 548, 579
Sheba, Queen of 275
sheriat (Islamic law) 217, 282, 315, 321, 359, 472, 481, 520, 567, 575, 581, 596
shirk (the setting up of partners to God, worshipping other than God) 215, 449, 472, 484, 548
Shuayb 47, 552
Sidre Tree, the 325
signal 43
silver 42, 419, 425
Sinai 41
sincerity 66, 126, 128, 129, 145, 250, 288, 338, 355, 432, 440
sinner 98, 441, 483
sin (the Arabic letter) 21, 23, 45, 69, 85
site 23, 42, 43, 48, 50, 52, 57, 67, 70, 71, 80, 86, 91, 96, 97, 100, 102, 113, 125, 161, 179, 201, 241, 281, 282, 293, 299, 303, 306, 321, 334, 350, 407, 416, 420, 424, 449, 450, 451, 452, 478, 479, 480, 482, 533, 565, 573, 596
site of manifestation 42, 43, 48, 57, 67, 71, 86, 91, 96, 100, 102, 113, 161, 179, 201, 241, 281, 293, 299, 303, 334, 416, 424, 449, 450, 451, 452, 478, 479, 482, 596

sky 42, 43, 53, 72, 77, 94, 121, 133, 142, 148, 187, 195, 224, 232, 237, 260, 262, 289, 304, 305, 307, 308, 313, 314, 335, 362, 363, 367, 414, 534
slave 117, 169, 219, 282, 290, 419, 511, 512, 578
Socrates 173, 216
Solomon 52, 196, 256, 257, 294, 539, 594
soul (nefis, nefs) 24, 29, 37, 44, 52, 79, 96, 104, 107, 110, 112, 114, 118, 120, 124, 127, 129, 135, 144, 149, 152, 158, 159, 160, 163, 169, 171, 173, 174, 178, 179, 180, 186, 187, 191, 193, 195, 198, 210, 211, 213, 214, 216, 217, 218, 221, 236, 237, 245, 254, 256, 257, 260, 261, 264, 265, 266, 269, 270, 271, 273, 279, 280, 281, 282, 283, 285, 286, 293, 301, 306, 311, 313, 315, 326, 333, 335, 336, 339, 341, 342, 343, 349, 350, 355, 356, 360, 361, 371, 375, 376, 378, 380, 381, 383, 384, 385, 387, 393, 400, 403, 407, 409, 410, 434, 435, 445, 447, 449, 454, 455, 458, 459, 461, 465, 467, 469, 472, 473, 479, 480, 481, 482, 484, 485, 487, 488, 489, 490, 492, 497, 498, 499, 500, 504, 505, 511, 512, 529, 539, 540, 542, 550, 560, 564, 566, 593
Spain 243
speech 31, 33, 44, 47, 65, 75, 76, 80, 97, 150, 151, 167, 172, 178,

INDEX

256, 263, 266, 284, 310, 319,
338, 386, 409, 419, 427, 431,
448, 460, 484, 487, 496, 499,
500, 501, 523, 524, 528, 543,
544, 593
spirit (ruh, can) 24, 29, 44, 46,
48, 56, 58, 67, 77, 100, 103, 106,
113, 115, 116, 131, 133, 134,
143, 144, 148, 149, 150, 151,
153, 157, 158, 167, 173, 178,
179, 181, 187, 191, 194, 196,
197, 202, 213, 217, 219, 221,
230, 231, 232, 237, 238, 239,
244, 245, 246, 247, 249, 250,
267, 277, 278, 279, 282, 286,
289, 294, 298, 299, 301, 303,
304, 305, 310, 313, 315, 321,
322, 323, 326, 327, 328, 329,
330, 331, 336, 337, 342, 349,
353, 356, 366, 374, 375, 377,
381, 382, 383, 384, 385, 392,
394, 395, 397, 400, 418, 419,
425, 427, 428, 429, 430, 432,
436, 447, 457, 458, 461, 464,
465, 467, 468, 472, 473, 492,
498, 504, 505, 506, 509, 511,
512, 519, 524, 525, 526, 527,
532, 533, 534, 539, 540, 541,
543, 544, 548, 560, 567, 568,
572, 581, 582, 584, 585, 589,
591, 599, 600
Spirits, Realm of 53, 58, 429, 430
spiritual 17, 18, 30, 31, 35, 40,
41, 42, 51, 53, 54, 66, 67, 70,
77, 80, 89, 96, 98, 101, 112, 123,
126, 129, 131, 132, 133, 140,
144, 145, 148, 179, 196, 215,
216, 217, 231, 254, 267, 268,
269, 270, 278, 286, 287, 290,
295, 299, 304, 305, 310, 329,
338, 341, 343, 349, 365, 381,
382, 400, 434, 435, 456, 457,
463, 476, 504, 507, 512, 533,
538, 539, 543, 544, 547, 553,
566, 567, 572, 578, 579, 595,
598, 600
spring 144, 172, 196, 217, 231,
232, 236, 237, 238, 239, 245,
362, 383, 384, 386, 417, 418,
423
star 157, 232, 290, 293, 303, 377,
567
state 24, 35, 42, 46, 47, 51, 52,
55, 56, 59, 60, 64, 81, 93, 96,
105, 113, 116, 139, 165, 167,
205, 220, 229, 230, 235, 236,
237, 242, 250, 251, 255, 259,
266, 274, 286, 294, 295, 302,
304, 307, 308, 309, 315, 316,
327, 333, 348, 356, 366, 367,
378, 390, 391, 392, 396, 397,
405, 408, 410, 413, 416, 420,
426, 429, 433, 436, 437, 438,
439, 440, 447, 453, 458, 461,
464, 473, 475, 477, 478, 485,
493, 496, 498, 500, 506, 507,
511, 512, 516, 521, 528, 531,
538, 541, 543, 549, 551, 552,
553, 559, 566, 572, 581, 582,
585, 591
station (makam) 39, 40, 41, 42,
43, 45, 53, 54, 65, 126, 135,
140, 143, 149, 158, 161, 189,
190, 198, 205, 212, 250, 258,

264, 265, 266, 293, 294, 299,
301, 307, 309, 310, 311, 313,
333, 347, 348, 359, 362, 366,
369, 380, 385, 395, 405, 406,
414, 421, 429, 430, 446, 447,
453, 477, 508, 521, 534, 544,
548, 550, 551, 567, 581, 593,
595
stature, the most beautiful
(ahsen-i takvim) 49, 265, 403
stone 24, 25, 68, 114, 115, 148,
164, 171, 172, 215, 232, 336,
337, 510, 526, 564, 585
straight 24, 35, 38, 85, 86, 87, 88,
89, 90, 91, 98, 100, 166, 186,
198, 201, 291, 305, 309, 366,
396, 416, 431, 433, 459, 488
straight path, the 24, 35, 38, 85,
86, 87, 88, 89, 90, 166, 186, 198,
201, 366, 431
strength 43, 94, 98, 129, 158,
194, 203, 229, 235, 243, 267,
272, 284, 285, 351, 361, 366,
370, 395, 416, 420, 425, 451,
456, 460, 475, 489, 494, 508,
517, 520, 521, 534, 542
subjugation (kahr) 105, 142, 146,
226, 255, 294, 463, 464, 492,
559
sublime 35, 40, 60, 70, 72, 73,
82, 87, 93, 94, 97, 126, 132, 140,
149, 151, 156, 160, 166, 178,
185, 194, 196, 197, 198, 199,
203, 205, 267, 268, 269, 270,
281, 294, 295, 299, 303, 310,
330, 333, 361, 375, 414, 429,
432, 445, 446, 447, 448, 453,
457, 484, 493, 526, 531, 532,
534, 549, 550, 553, 571, 581,
582, 583, 584, 589, 590, 594,
595, 596
subsistence in God (beka) 579
substance (cevher) 50, 51, 58,
93, 143, 171, 172, 243, 244, 245,
251, 260, 277, 293, 320, 321,
425, 427, 432, 495, 500, 519,
549, 580
Subtle (Latif) 105, 299, 400, 446,
455, 468, 477, 553, 560
subtlety (latife) 35, 74, 105, 282,
407, 553, 581
suffering 148, 223, 227, 248, 275,
287, 339, 381, 425, 477, 484,
487, 494
Sufi 17, 18, 19, 20, 21, 22, 25, 29,
64, 348
Sufyan ibn Waki' 37
Suhravardi, Shihabuddin 590
Sulami 39
sultan 52, 106, 107, 130, 132,
134, 150, 158, 181, 186, 190,
194, 223, 225, 236, 242, 272,
274, 275, 286, 331, 333, 335,
336, 348, 367, 375, 409, 416,
420, 424, 425, 433, 448, 468,
501, 508, 530, 534, 548, 559,
567
sultanate 52, 223, 286, 290, 396,
434, 484, 512, 520
sülük (wayfaring) 179, 591
sun 43, 44, 55, 77, 100, 115, 116,
144, 149, 156, 183, 184, 195,
215, 231, 237, 247, 269, 278,
279, 282, 283, 285, 286, 289,

290, 293, 294, 296, 297, 298,
299, 300, 301, 302, 303, 304,
306, 313, 314, 367, 385, 386,
390, 395, 415, 432, 449, 492,
493, 518, 528, 585, 599
sunna 22, 33, 79, 179
sun of gnosis 390
sweet 70, 158, 164, 172, 184, 196,
199, 238, 244, 300, 327, 400,
419, 424, 454, 479, 518, 552
sword 80, 105, 131, 225, 336, 381,
405, 455

T

Tablet, the (Preserved) 37, 75,
100, 101, 119, 140, 141, 143,
145, 146, 198, 586
Ta-Ha 39, 44, 96
takva (godwariness) 169
talisman 52
Talking Quran, the 40, 124
tarikat (dervish order, path) 53,
88, 130, 179, 217, 304
tasavvuf 39, 48, 61, 97, 162, 189,
230, 242, 254, 295, 316, 333,
538, 543, 590, 591, 593, 594
tasting (zevk) 25, 35, 70, 90, 113,
190, 578
tecelli (self-disclosure) 51
tefekkür (reflection) 63, 520, 524
temperament 162, 219, 249, 250,
254, 401, 464, 465, 468, 508,
511, 516
terror 230, 326, 333, 369, 429,
463, 551
testify 119, 143, 498
tevhid (unification) 35, 45, 54,
55, 85

thanks 21, 27, 35, 42, 177, 211,
231, 244, 253, 255, 256, 257,
258, 279, 345, 354, 414, 419,
420, 438, 467, 496, 499, 518,
537, 540, 541, 552, 583
thievery 274
things, the (eşya) 43, 55, 56, 57,
63, 65, 68, 69, 80, 89, 97, 102,
108, 121, 136, 142, 149, 164,
172, 184, 185, 214, 219, 255,
283, 298, 316, 348, 356, 357,
359, 365, 379, 397, 449, 474,
478, 511, 529, 532, 539, 547,
559, 564, 571, 576, 579, 583,
587, 590
thought 25, 29, 101, 134, 144,
155, 162, 183, 184, 195, 239,
250, 253, 259, 273, 300, 308,
334, 337, 354, 367, 379, 390,
399, 446, 450, 454, 457, 468,
511, 528, 540, 544, 553, 556,
557, 566, 571, 573, 594
Throne, the 149, 378
Tigris River 306
time 18, 20, 29, 35, 46, 47, 48, 52,
53, 58, 69, 76, 82, 93, 99, 103,
104, 110, 125, 140, 143, 144,
147, 153, 155, 157, 158, 160,
161, 168, 174, 179, 187, 191,
194, 214, 217, 219, 220, 224,
226, 227, 230, 242, 255, 263,
274, 275, 279, 283, 284, 285,
286, 289, 295, 296, 298, 301,
307, 308, 309, 314, 329, 330,
335, 339, 341, 348, 349, 350,
356, 370, 376, 377, 383, 386,
389, 396, 410, 417, 419, 420,

423, 435, 437, 438, 439, 441, 445, 448, 451, 452, 454, 467, 476, 499, 501, 505, 509, 510, 512, 515, 516, 521, 541, 545, 551, 555, 556, 558, 559, 561, 566, 572, 576, 578, 582, 589, 591, 594, 599

Tirmidhi 37

tongue 66, 81, 119, 124, 125, 126, 130, 143, 150, 244, 254, 275, 281, 287, 357, 363, 495, 496, 498, 499, 500, 501, 523, 583

Torah 37, 43, 259

torment (azap) 99, 104, 144, 148, 160, 162, 212, 218, 255, 296, 311, 336, 345, 354, 374, 375, 376, 377, 394, 404, 407, 413, 430, 450, 471, 472, 473, 474, 475, 476, 477, 478, 479, 481, 483, 484, 485, 489, 490, 505, 506, 510, 544

training 21, 488, 504, 543, 590, 591

tree 24, 25, 39, 41, 68, 114, 238, 241, 242, 246, 247, 285, 294, 325, 329, 331, 361, 366, 370, 399, 400, 423, 468, 498, 499, 506, 509, 563, 564, 565, 566, 567, 568, 569, 580, 589, 597, 598

tremendousness (azamet) 48, 72, 123, 255, 321, 405, 520, 557, 594

trial 104, 117, 226, 339, 394, 425, 471, 484, 487, 489, 516

tribe 88, 99, 148, 157, 189, 205, 213, 215, 217, 218, 219, 327, 370, 371, 403, 492, 509, 510, 551, 552

trickery 135, 163, 274, 457, 460, 484

trumpet 230, 346, 369, 373, 377, 379, 386, 417, 520

trustee (vekil) 130, 142, 178, 183

truth 31, 39, 41, 42, 43, 45, 49, 50, 54, 55, 58, 60, 65, 68, 69, 70, 71, 72, 73, 74, 77, 79, 80, 81, 82, 83, 85, 86, 89, 90, 91, 93, 94, 95, 97, 99, 100, 101, 102, 103, 105, 110, 112, 113, 114, 117, 119, 120, 123, 124, 125, 127, 128, 130, 131, 133, 134, 135, 137, 139, 140, 141, 142, 143, 144, 145, 151, 152, 157, 160, 162, 163, 166, 167, 172, 174, 175, 178, 179, 180, 181, 183, 184, 185, 186, 187, 190, 191, 194, 195, 196, 197, 198, 199, 202, 203, 206, 207, 209, 211, 213, 216, 217, 219, 220, 223, 229, 230, 234, 236, 241, 248, 250, 253, 255, 256, 257, 258, 261, 265, 267, 269, 271, 274, 275, 277, 279, 280, 281, 282, 283, 287, 288, 294, 295, 296, 298, 303, 305, 306, 314, 316, 325, 326, 329, 330, 331, 334, 336, 341, 342, 343, 345, 346, 347, 348, 353, 354, 355, 356, 360, 361, 365, 366, 370, 371, 379, 380, 381, 383, 384, 385, 386, 389, 390, 393, 394, 395, 396, 399, 400, 401, 403, 404, 405, 406, 407, 408, 410, 414, 415, 416, 417, 418, 421, 424, 427, 432, 434, 435, 436,

437, 441, 445, 447, 448, 452, 453, 454, 455, 457, 459, 463, 464, 471, 473, 474, 478, 484, 486, 487, 488, 489, 493, 495, 496, 503, 504, 505, 507, 508, 509, 510, 515, 516, 517, 520, 523, 524, 525, 527, 528, 529, 534, 535, 539, 540, 541, 542, 543, 547, 549, 550, 552, 553, 554, 560, 561, 564, 565, 568, 571, 572, 573, 575, 577, 578, 579, 580, 581, 582, 583, 584, 587, 590, 592, 593, 595, 596, 598
truthful 40, 97, 184, 365, 393, 396, 405, 428, 438, 452
Turkey 21, 243

U
Ubudiyet 45
Umar 306, 317, 349, 437, 439
Umayya ibn Abi al-Salt 529
unbounded (mutlak) 52, 56, 57, 68, 72, 221, 265, 268, 382, 414, 464, 549, 565, 579, 580, 584
unconsciousness 55
unification (tevhid) 35, 45, 54, 55, 56, 60, 70, 73, 74, 81, 85, 87, 149, 250, 341, 347, 416, 525, 548, 577
unity (vahdet) 23, 48, 53, 54, 55, 56, 57, 70, 71, 72, 73, 90, 113, 122, 123, 124, 139, 140, 149, 179, 187, 201, 205, 219, 250, 262, 305, 307, 308, 313, 330, 334, 348, 349, 386, 424, 453, 464, 515, 540, 579, 593, 596
universal intellect 149, 239, 410

Unseen, the (gayb) 35, 46, 53, 59, 60, 64, 121, 123, 131, 132, 133, 134, 135, 144, 217, 262, 278, 281, 307, 330, 341, 354, 389, 414, 426, 450, 507, 541, 558, 559, 568, 596
unveiling (keşf) 18, 60, 64, 124, 189, 250, 278, 295, 379, 482, 484, 544, 555, 598

V
vahdet-i vücud 55
vahdet (unity) 54, 55, 57
value 40, 52, 60, 118, 130, 150, 155, 267, 286, 287, 326, 339, 360, 375, 384, 392, 395, 418, 424, 498, 504, 508, 540, 544, 557
Vâridat 161
varlık 478
vegetable 50, 51, 114, 186, 194
vegetal 86
vegetarian 456
veil 35, 63, 90, 121, 126, 131, 132, 133, 171, 190, 199, 231, 277, 330, 347, 349, 385, 389, 395, 414, 418, 425, 429, 444, 463, 464, 481, 482, 499, 512, 520, 524, 528, 532, 534, 535, 552, 579, 580, 593
verifier (muhakkik) 423, 424
vicdan 51, 73
vicegerency 60, 203, 304, 405, 508
vicegerent (halife) 137, 142, 152, 163, 420, 421, 433, 534, 535, 567
vilayet (sanctity) 79, 152

violence 142, 180, 225, 354, 474, 479, 483, 484, 538, 543, 559
virtue (fazilet) 73, 74, 103, 134, 151, 152, 196, 247, 266, 338, 405, 423, 432, 454, 456, 515, 518, 539, 540, 542, 556
visible 59, 87, 96, 103, 110, 112, 125, 132, 223, 229, 239, 286, 289, 355, 367, 419, 429, 498, 512, 560, 583
voluntary death 381, 579, 591, 597
vücud 55

W

wariness (haşyet) 41, 127, 132, 135
warning 66, 123, 132, 216, 255, 306, 309, 345, 346, 369, 468, 486, 556, 596
water 22, 24, 46, 50, 51, 98, 106, 114, 149, 159, 164, 172, 194, 209, 215, 217, 221, 225, 233, 236, 237, 238, 245, 246, 247, 249, 250, 251, 254, 260, 274, 284, 297, 305, 306, 316, 321, 323, 336, 339, 370, 371, 384, 410, 431, 467, 474, 480, 482, 485, 490, 501, 507, 518, 519, 532, 533, 535, 560, 581, 594, 600
Water of Life, the 24, 305, 518, 519, 533, 560
Waterskin 585
waw (the Arabic letter) 69, 88
wayfaring (sülük) 581, 591, 593
way-station 143, 158, 307
wheat 238, 240, 366, 367

wholesome 89, 110, 144, 180, 201, 207, 211, 242, 249, 272, 335, 350, 359, 378, 400, 401, 403, 421, 422, 450, 453, 460, 520
will 20, 23, 24, 33, 35, 37, 41, 43, 44, 48, 49, 50, 51, 52, 54, 55, 56, 58, 60, 66, 67, 69, 76, 82, 83, 88, 89, 90, 91, 94, 95, 98, 101, 103, 104, 105, 106, 107, 109, 111, 113, 114, 115, 116, 118, 119, 120, 121, 124, 126, 127, 128, 129, 131, 132, 133, 134, 135, 143, 144, 146, 148, 151, 152, 159, 160, 163, 164, 165, 166, 167, 168, 169, 171, 172, 173, 174, 175, 177, 179, 180, 184, 186, 189, 193, 194, 195, 196, 197, 199, 201, 203, 206, 210, 211, 214, 215, 216, 217, 218, 219, 220, 221, 223, 224, 225, 226, 227, 229, 230, 231, 233, 234, 235, 236, 237, 238, 240, 241, 245, 248, 249, 250, 253, 255, 256, 257, 259, 262, 263, 266, 268, 270, 271, 272, 273, 274, 275, 283, 285, 286, 287, 288, 289, 290, 296, 303, 304, 305, 306, 307, 309, 310, 313, 316, 317, 320, 321, 322, 325, 326, 327, 329, 330, 333, 334, 336, 337, 338, 339, 341, 342, 343, 344, 345, 346, 347, 348, 349, 350, 351, 353, 354, 355, 356, 357, 359, 360, 361, 362, 363, 365, 366, 367, 369, 370, 373, 374, 375, 377,

INDEX

378, 379, 380, 381, 382, 383,
384, 385, 386, 389, 390, 391,
392, 393, 394, 395, 396, 397,
400, 401, 402, 403, 408, 410,
414, 416, 417, 418, 419, 421,
422, 423, 424, 428, 429, 433,
434, 435, 436, 437, 438, 439,
441, 442, 444, 445, 447, 448,
450, 451, 452, 454, 457, 458,
459, 461, 463, 464, 465, 467,
468, 469, 471, 473, 474, 475,
476, 479, 480, 481, 482, 483,
484, 485, 486, 487, 488, 489,
490, 491, 493, 494, 495, 496,
497, 498, 500, 501, 504, 505,
508, 509, 510, 511, 512, 513,
515, 517, 520, 521, 525, 526,
528, 529, 532, 533, 534, 535,
537, 540, 541, 542, 543, 544,
551, 553, 554, 555, 557, 558,
559, 560, 561, 564, 565, 567,
571, 572, 575, 576, 577, 578,
579, 580, 581, 585, 586, 587,
589, 591, 594, 597, 598

winter 196, 236, 275, 415

wisdom 18, 20, 23, 24, 41, 45, 63,
64, 65, 66, 67, 71, 79, 85, 100,
113, 117, 120, 125, 126, 132,
133, 134, 136, 167, 179, 210,
218, 234, 235, 237, 239, 250,
256, 266, 296, 303, 304, 309,
315, 353, 354, 356, 362, 426,
427, 448, 466, 484, 487, 491,
504, 511, 515, 520, 521, 529,
534, 538, 542, 553, 558, 559,
566

witness 46, 48, 55, 59, 68, 74,
121, 145, 169, 170, 184, 197,
209, 250, 267, 281, 294, 295,
304, 308, 309, 310, 326, 330,
334, 367, 379, 385, 404, 405,
408, 441, 449, 451, 456, 457,
483, 495, 496, 497, 498, 499,
501, 528, 535, 539, 555, 591,
592

witnessing 53, 55, 61, 68, 70, 85,
124, 135, 250, 278, 295, 296,
310, 381, 402, 405, 409, 410,
565, 578, 581

world 22, 33, 35, 37, 45, 46, 48,
49, 50, 51, 53, 54, 55, 56, 57,
58, 64, 65, 67, 72, 83, 87, 88,
91, 93, 101, 102, 103, 104, 115,
116, 119, 122, 125, 128, 131,
132, 133, 134, 136, 143, 144,
145, 146, 152, 153, 156, 165,
166, 171, 173, 174, 184, 186,
187, 190, 191, 193, 194, 196,
202, 203, 205, 207, 209, 214,
215, 216, 217, 219, 220, 221,
223, 225, 232, 236, 237, 239,
241, 247, 249, 250, 253, 254,
260, 261, 270, 273, 278, 281,
282, 283, 288, 290, 293, 299,
303, 304, 307, 309, 310, 315,
316, 321, 323, 325, 326, 328,
335, 338, 339, 341, 342, 345,
346, 347, 349, 350, 355, 361,
362, 369, 374, 375, 376, 377,
378, 379, 380, 381, 382, 383,
384, 385, 386, 387, 390, 394,
395, 396, 397, 399, 403, 407,
410, 411, 414, 415, 417, 418,
420, 421, 423, 424, 425, 427,
428, 429, 432, 433, 434, 435,

436, 447, 449, 450, 454, 455,
456, 457, 458, 459, 461, 464,
471, 472, 473, 474, 475, 481,
483, 484, 485, 488, 490, 491,
493, 498, 501, 504, 505, 506,
507, 509, 511, 512, 515, 517,
519, 527, 531, 534, 535, 538,
541, 547, 548, 550, 555, 558,
559, 560, 565, 566, 567, 572,
573, 576, 577, 579, 582, 584,
587, 591, 592, 594, 595, 597,
598, 600
worldly 37, 41, 43, 67, 89, 102,
112, 118, 133, 158, 187, 190,
191, 194, 209, 241, 280, 281,
282, 294, 295, 325, 341, 349,
350, 355, 369, 371, 375, 381,
383, 390, 399, 403, 404, 413,
414, 440, 442, 450, 474, 481,
490, 503, 532, 554, 566
wrath (gazap) 73, 74, 101, 117,
118, 136, 217, 336, 370, 391,
464, 476, 478, 479, 483, 488,
509, 510, 559
wretched, the (şaki, eşkiya) 100,
119, 121, 133, 218, 341, 427,
429, 430, 442, 445, 455, 510
wrongdoing (zülüm) 279, 350,
548

Y

Ya-Sin 23, 24, 25, 27, 29, 35, 36,
37, 39, 40, 52, 206, 576
ya (the Arabic Letter) 45, 85
Yemen 306
Yünüs Emre 207, 390, 550

Z

Zamzam 306
zevk (tasting) 553

zodiac 41, 303
zülüm (wrongdoing) 548